Paul McCartney

'I feel like the sixties is about to happen.
It feels like a period in the future to me,
rather than a period in the past.'
Paul McCartney, 1994

Other books by Barry Miles

Allen Ginsberg: A Biography
William Burroughs: El Hombre Invisible

BARRY MILES

PAUL McCARTNEY

Many Years From Now

Henry Holt and Company
New York

Henry Holt and Company, Inc.
Publishers since 1866
115 West 18th Street
New York, New York 10011

Henry Holt® is a registered trademark of
Henry Holt and Company, Inc.

First published in the United States in 1997 by
Henry Holt and Company, Inc.

Published in Great Britain in 1997 by
Secker & Warburg

Library of Congress Cataloging-in-Publication Data is available.

ISBN 0-8050-5248-8

Henry Holt books are available for special promotions and
premiums. For details contact: Director, Special Markets.

First American Edition 1997

All first editions are printed on acid-free paper. ∞

1 3 5 7 9 10 8 6 4 2

To Theo

Contents

Acknowledgements

The Beatles have become so surrounded by myth, fantasy and speculation that determining anything other than the basic facts of their lives has become virtually impossible. The way the public perceives the really famous is an amalgamation of information of filtered through layers of the media, embellished, stereotyped, politicised according to the position of the writers and editors involved. In the case of rock stars, particularly unreliable since the media – TV shows and the popular music press – are more a part of the entertainment business than serious journalism of record, a situation exacerbated by musicians, who usually only give interviews to promote new product. There was virtually no serious coverage given to pop music by the press until the latter half of the sixties, when the underground press – *East Village Other, Berkely Barb, IT* – started up, and at the end of the decade, when magazines like *Rolling Stone* began publication. As a consequence there are very few reliable interviews with the Beatles at the height of their fame.

Received knowledge is a strange mélange of the Fab Four, the four mop tops, the Lords of Psychedelia, the witty one, the cute one and, in the case of John, the Prince of Peace, combining the wisecracking happy chappies of *A Hard Day's Night* and the tripped-out figures of the '*Strawberry Fields Forever*' promotional film, the chirpy cartoon cut-outs of *Yellow Submarine* and the hallucinatory Richard Avedon portrait posters which adorned so many bedroom walls. The stress was moreover always on the Beatles as a group, not as individuals. They became a part of popular iconography, a convenient signifier of sixties Britain. Just as the Eiffel Tower symbolises Paris, a few frames of Harold Wilson, Christine Keeler and the Beatles now define an entire era.

Fans always chose their favourite Beatle and this bias has continued to colour even the work of modern popular historians. When four people create music together it is difficult to determine which individual is responsible for what and the tendency is to attribute everything you admire to the Beatle you like. Thus, for example, Sinatra regularly introduced George Harrison's 'Something' as a 'Lennon and McCartney' song. Everything remotely experimental or avant-garde is always attributed to John Lennon, including Paul's loop tapes and orchestral experiments on 'A Day in the Life'. In fact John was deeply suspicious of everything avant-garde, saying, 'Avant-garde is French for bullshit.' He only began to revise his opinion when he got together with Yoko Ono in 1969 and then he had to make a conscious effort to overcome his reservations.

This book is an attempt to sort out these attributions, to dispel some of the inaccuracies which are passed on from biography to biography, and to give a close-focus portrait of Paul and his circle in sixties London. Paul was the only Beatle living in town, the only one who was nominally single, and he was to be found at the gallery openings and first nights, the clubs and late-night bars, the Happenings and experimental events that so characterise the mid-sixties. He did his own experiments in the field of loop tapes and film superimpositions, which found their way into the Beatles' work but are usually attributed to John. Because he did not publicise it, this is a little-known side of Paul and one that this book hopes to reveal.

Unfortunately, subsequent to John's murder, any attempt at an objective assessment of John Lennon's role in the Beatles inevitably becomes iconoclastic. He has become St John, a role which would both amuse and horrify him. Though John is no longer here to tell his side of the story, the sheer volume of existing Lennon interviews means that he already covered much of the contentious ground. From 1968 onwards, at the onset of their peace campaign, John and Yoko did as many as ten interviews a day, whereas the other Beatles rarely spoke to the press at all, so we have John's views on most subjects of importance, including, fortunately, his comments on a great many of the Lennon and McCartney compositions.

In the course of writing this book, Paul and I talked about every Lennon and McCartney composition, including those recorded by groups other than the Beatles. Paul purposely did not read John's comments beforehand but in only two cases out of more than eighty songs was there a serious disagreement about whose composition it was. (John had claimed more than 70 per cent of the lyrics to 'Eleanor Rigby' and Paul remembered writing the music to 'In My Life'.)

PAUL: I'd like to say this is just as I remember it, if it hurts anyone or any families of anyone who've got a different memory of it. Let me say first off, before you read this book even, that I loved John. Lest it be seen that I'm trying to do my own kind of revisionism, I'd like to register the fact that John was great, he was absolutely wonderful and I did love him. I was very happy to work with him and I'm still a fan to this day. So this is merely my opinion. I'm not trying to take anything away from him. All I'm saying is that I have my side of the affair as well, hence this book. When George Harrison wrote his life story *I Me Mine*, he hardly mentioned John. In my case I wouldn't want to leave him out. John and I were two of the luckiest people in the twentieth century to have found each other. The partnership, the mix, was incredible. We both had submerged qualities that we each saw and knew. I had to be the bastard as well as the nice melodic one and John had to have a warm and loving side for me to stand him all those years. John and I would never have stood each other for that length of time had we been just one-dimensional.

Paul and John's songwriting partnership elevated the Beatles far above all other rock 'n' roll bands and this book attempts to explore both that relationship and the genesis of those songs. It was a friendship initially disapproved of by both Paul's father and John's Aunt Mimi, and might at first have seemed an unlikely alliance.

PAUL: Whereas my upbringing made me the reasonably secure baby-faced product, John's was the opposite, the very insecure aquiline-nosed product, the angular, angry face, but it was easily explained. His father left home when he was five and never saw him again till John got famous and then was discovered washing dishes at the Bear Inn in Esher by a newspaperman. John had to deal with all that shit. John had massive hangups from his upbringing.

It was a love of rock 'n' roll that first brought together these boys from disparate backgrounds: John middle-class, the product of a broken home, and Paul from a warm working-class family. Their

friendship came first from playing together in a group – the Quarry
Men – and was then strengthened by the formation of the formidable
Lennon–McCartney songwriting partnership. It was a close, protective friendship that would last a dozen years and was renewed once
more before John's tragic death in 1980.

The pressure on the Beatles was at its most acute in the early days of
Beatlemania. Then they were literally followed everywhere by the
press, constantly demanding interviews. It is from these garbled
quotes, lies and utter fabrications that much of the received
knowledge of the Beatles' story is taken.

> PAUL: We often used to say to journalists, 'Look, I haven't got
> time for the interview, just make it up.' So some of it's arrived
> that way ... you know, if it's a good story, it sticks. Or we may
> have felt like joking that day. It's summer and you're in a pub
> having a drink and there's a guy with a little book and he's going
> 'yayayayayaya' so to alleviate that pressure, we started to try and
> plant lies to the press. We used to award each other points for
> the best story printed. One that George got in was that he was
> Tommy Steele's cousin. That was a nice early one. It was
> wonderful because it turned it all around and the press stopped
> being a pressure and became a fun game. They didn't mind.
> Anything to fill a page. I remember John saying to me, 'God, I
> remember walking behind a group of press and you at some
> cocktail reception. I was just hovering near, and you were giving
> them the world's greatest bullshit! Not a word of it was true,' he
> said. 'I loved it, though, it was brilliant.' We did do that, so of
> course one or two of those stories have stuck.

With the exception of Hunter Davies's 1968 biography of the
Beatles, and George Harrison's 1980 autobiography, there has not
been a full-length authorised study of this period; all the existing Paul
McCartney biographies rely heavily on the sort of press sources
described above. In the case of popular music, most of the usual
sources of information – journals, correspondence – are absent.
There are news clips, films, printed sources and the memories of the
participants. Most of the events described in this book took place
more than thirty years ago and memories become coloured or dim. I
have attempted to check facts but this was not always possible.

PAUL: One of my sixties memories is about a fan in the street. I ran up to her and pulled her jacket off and said 'That's my jacket!' because we'd had a burglary and it was like one of mine. But it actually wasn't mine, there were more in the shop and she'd bought one. She said, 'It's the wrong size, it's mine.' So 'Oh, God, I'm sorry, I'm sorry!' Put her down. And I was talking about it to Neil Aspinall years later and I said, 'We jumped out of the taxi and I grabbed her,' and he said 'Yeah,' and I said, 'And it was in front of Savile Row,' and he said, 'No. It was in Piccadilly.' To me, when the complete background of the memory had schisted, you go, 'Oh, fuck, I'd better start talking to somebody.' So I'll give you it as I remember it, but I do admit, my thing does move around, jumps around a lot. But the nice thing is, we don't have to be too faithful, because that's not what we're talking about. We're talking about a sequence of things that did all happen within a period. So, it's my recollection of then ...

The core of this book is based upon a series of thirty-five taped interviews with Paul McCartney conducted over a period of six years, from 1991 to 1996, as well as from information gathered in the course of many other conversations with him at events, rehearsals, concerts and get-togethers.

I first met Paul in the summer of 1965 and saw a great deal of him throughout the latter half of the sixties. Together with John Dunbar and Peter Asher, I started Indica Books and Gallery in Mason's Yard and Paul was very involved in painting the walls and putting up shelves. Paul designed and had printed the wrapping paper for the bookshop and helped design advertising flyers.

Later, when John Hopkins and I started *International Times* (*IT*), Europe's first underground newspaper, Paul was again involved, helping to lay out ads and providing emergency financial aid. When the staff of *IT* ran the UFO club, an all-night underground club featuring the Pink Floyd and Arthur Brown, Paul was often to be found there, sitting on the floor along with the rest of the hippies. We attended lectures and concerts and went to films and plays together. Paul often came to dinner. In 1968 Paul asked me to become the label manager for Zapple, the experimental and spoken-word division of Apple Records, and I recorded a number of albums for the label, some of which I edited at Apple headquarters in Savile Row, which I got to know pretty well.

The descriptions of the Asher household, Beatles recording sessions from *Revolver* onwards, most of the scenes in nightclubs, the Indica Gallery and Bookshop, Paul's experimental recording studio, Marianne Faithfull and John Dunbar's apartment, Robert Fraser's home and gallery, are all based in part upon journal notes I made at the time, though in some cases John Dunbar has jogged my memory. These are my descriptions of places and events and not necessarily how Paul remembers them. Paul's quoted memories are his.

In order to present a more rounded picture I talked with other people who were involved in the London scene at the time and would like to thank the following for allowing me to interview them: William Burroughs, Brian Clarke, David Dalton, Felix Dennis, Donovan, John Dunbar, Marianne Faithfull, Christopher Gibbs, Allen Ginsberg, Linda McCartney, Peter Swales and David Vaughan. I have also drawn upon interviews I conducted prior to this project with George Harrison, Mick Jagger, John Lennon and Yoko Ono.

I have been given enormous assistance by the staff of MPL, in particular Sue Prochnik and Shelagh Jones. I am also grateful to Mary McCartney in the London office and Eddie Klein, Keith Smith, John Hammel, Louise Morris and Jamie Kirkham at the Mill. Thanks also to Zoë and Sylvie at Linda's Pictures.

In a project such as this, many people inevitably contribute ideas and information, often inadvertently in the course of a conversation, at other times by active assistance. I would like to thank Steve Abrams for his considerable help on the section concerning the 'pot ad' in *The Times*; John and Marina Adams; Gillon Aitken at Aitken Stone & Wylie; Anica Alvarez at Secker; Neil Aspinall at Apple; Mike Arnold at Merseytravel for details of Liverpool bus routes; Geoff Baker; Peter Blake; Victor Bockris; Pete Brown; Simon Caulkin; Chris Charlesworth at Omnibus Press; Dave Courts; Andy Davis at *The Beatles Book Monthly*; Paul DuNoyer at *Mojo*; Robin Eggar for sharing his McCartney interviews with me; Mike Evans; Anthony Fawcett; Raymond Foye; Hilary Gerrard; the late Albert Goldman; Jaco and Elizabeth Groot at Die Harmonie in Amsterdam; Michael Henshaw; John Hopkins; Michael Horovitz; Jude at Vibe; Harold Landry for various key magazines; Christopher Logue; Tony Lacey at Penguin; George Lawson at Bertram Rota; Mark Lewisohn for many useful insights as well as for his invaluable chronologies; Gerard Malanga; Gerard Mankowitz; Sue Miles, who was there for much of it; Laury Minard at *Forbes*; Hervé Muller; Jeremy Neech at Apple's photographic archives; Richard Neville; Alan Nichols at NatWest; Pierce and Jackie O'Carroll in Liverpool; the late David Platz; Victor Schonfield for his memories of our visit to AMM; Paul Smith at Blast First; Mat Snow at *Mojo*; Peter Stansill; Martha Stevns; Lionel Tiger; Harriet Vyner for her notes on Robert Fraser; Peter Whitehead; John Wilcock; Peter Wollen; the staff of the London Library and the Liverpool Record Office.

Thanks to Dan Franklin for signing the book and to my editor Max Eilenberg for the laborious task of knocking it into shape. Thanks to Ingrid von Essen for detecting numerous embarrassing errors. Many thanks to my friend and agent Andrew Wylie, who first proposed the idea, and, as ever, to my wife and in-house editor Rosemary Bailey, for her invaluable suggestions and support. And to Paul, whose life it is.

ONE

BEING BORN IN LIVERPOOL BRINGS WITH IT CERTAIN RESPONSIBILITIES

At all seasons, at all states, the River was beautiful. At dead low water, when great sandbanks were laid bare, to draw multitudes of gulls; in calm, when the ships stood still above their shadows; in storm, when the ferries beat by, shipping sprays, and at full flood, when shipping put out and came in, the River was a wonder to me.

John Masefield, *New Chums*, 1944

The Pool

ON 28 AUGUST 1207, KING JOHN GRANTED THE CHARTER THAT MADE the small fishing village of Liverpool a free borough; a second charter, granted by Henry III in 1229, gave the merchants the privilege of buying and selling without paying government dues: thus was the port of Liverpool born. It acquired a castle and a chapel on the quay, both long since gone. But it was not until trade with the New World developed in the latter part of the reign of Queen Elizabeth I that Liverpool's fortunes noticeably improved, when its geographical position established it as the main port to the North American continent. After the Great Plague in 1664 and the Great Fire of 1666, numerous London merchants moved there and the port flourished.

Many ran plantations in the New World, highly profitable enterprises which gave rise to the iniquitous triangle route: British ships laden with manufactured goods sailed for west Africa, where their cargo was bartered in exchange for slaves. The human cargo was then transported across the Atlantic to be sold in the established slave markets in the Caribbean or America. The huge sums of money raised enabled the ship's captains to return to Liverpool, their holds filled with cargoes of sugar, rum, tobacco and cotton. By 1700 there were eighty ships using the port, though not all were engaged in the slave trade, and the population of Liverpool had grown to 5700. The impact of this commerce remains evident to this day: even now Philips's tobacco warehouse is reputed to be the largest in the world, and Liverpool still has its own cotton exchange. Paul McCartney's family was a part of it: his grandfather spent his whole working life as a tobacco cutter and stover at Cope's tobacco warehouse and his father, Jim, worked as a cotton salesman at the exchange.

All through the eighteenth century the docks expanded: Salthouse Dock, George's Dock, the King's Dock and the Queen's Dock. The nineteenth century brought the railways and canals, bigger docks and hundreds more warehouses. In 1817 the Black Ball Line operated four ships between Liverpool and New York, the first regularly scheduled transatlantic packet to Europe, leaving New York on the first of each month. Trade expanded so rapidly that by the next year several other shipping lines sailed between Liverpool and New York, offering a departure every week. Southern planters sent their cotton crops to New York, where it was transhipped to Liverpool for the northern textile mills. In 1830, the world's first railway station opened in Liverpool to transport cotton to Manchester. Wealthy merchants built solid, luxurious town houses along Rodney Street, but the prosperity of the time was overshadowed by mass migration to the New World. The hostels were crowded with tearful families who had often never before left their village or hamlet, preyed upon by a notorious gang of thugs known as the Forty Thieves, as well as by dishonest runners, unscrupulous boarding-house keepers and corrupt officials. The docks were a mass of confusion and emotional departures as families prepared to leave their homeland for ever for an uncertain new life in the Americas. Though emigration to the American colonies began in the seventeenth century, it was not until the nineteenth century, after the USA achieved independence, that Liverpool became the main point of departure.

An estimated nine million people left in search of a new life from Liverpool, mostly heading for the USA, but many going to Canada or even Australia. Most of them suffered primitive conditions in steerage on boats such as the Royal Mail steamers operated by the Allan Line, which crossed from Liverpool to Quebec and Liverpool to Norfolk and Baltimore six times a month. The Black Ball Line built more ships and operated twice a month between Liverpool and New York. Ships left virtually every day: the Red Star Line, the White Star Line, the Castle Line to India, the Cunard Line to the Levant. The emigrants were not just the English and Irish unemployed; they came from all parts of Europe: Scandinavians, Czechs, Poles, Hungarians, Austrians, Greeks and Italians. Even some Chinese used the Asian-European route as a way to emigrate to the USA. Some were robbed and never made the passage, others decided to stay in Liverpool, giving it the heterogeneous mix of people that characterises a great port.

Liverpool became the gateway to the British Empire. A grand neoclassical city centre was built, described by Queen Victoria as 'worthy of ancient Athens'. The docks grew so large that an overhead railway, known locally as 'the dockers' umbrella', was built to connect them. At the turn of the century more than 2000 ships were registered at Liverpool, with a combined tonnage of 2,500,000, a third greater than the Port of London. Liverpool also held the luxury passenger traffic for liners to North America, supported by grand hotels like the Adelphi, described by Charles Dickens as the best hotel in the world and famous for its turtle soup.

The docks remained prosperous during World War I, shipping men and *matériel*, but in 1918 the amount of shipping had dropped to half its pre-war rate. Liverpool was hit badly by the Great Depression and never recovered. Despite this, it remained the primary destination of Irish immigrants arriving in the United Kingdom, as it had been since the 1860s. Among them were the forebears of Paul McCartney, who, like John Lennon, is of Liverpool Irish stock. Paul's parents were both born in Liverpool and, on his father's side, his grandparents were also from Liverpool, but no one is sure whether his great-grandfather James was born in Liverpool or Ireland. James was living in Scotland Road, Liverpool, when he married Paul's great-grandmother Elizabeth Williams in 1864. Paul's maternal grandfather Owen Mohin was born in Tullynamalrow in Ireland in 1880 (as Owen Mohan) but emigrated and married a girl from Toxteth Park, Mary Danher, in Liverpool in 1905.

During World War II Liverpool suffered terribly from the German air raids: from the night of 17 August 1940 until 10 January 1942 there were sixty-eight raids and over five hundred air-raid warnings. Every night thousands of people huddled together in basements and bomb shelters as high-explosive, incendiary and parachute bombs rained down upon the city, killing 2650, seriously injuring over 2000 others and leaving much of the city centre in ruins. The dead were buried in mass graves in Anfield cemetery. Over 10,000 of the homes in Liverpool were completely destroyed and two-thirds of all homes were seriously damaged.

Paul was born on 18 June 1942, five months after the bombing ceased, in Walton Hospital. His mother, Mary, had been the nursing sister in charge of the maternity ward before leaving to have children and was welcomed back with a bed in a private ward. He was named James Paul McCartney after his father, great-grandfather and great-great-grandfather and was later to name his own son James. Eighteen months later, Paul's brother Michael was born on 7 January 1944. The boys were both baptised Catholics, their mother's faith, but religion did not play a part in their upbringing. Their father had been christened in the Church of England but later became agnostic. Paul and Michael were not sent to Catholic schools because Jim thought they concentrated too much upon religion and not enough on education.

Paul's parents were both involved in the war effort. Jim, born in 1902, was too old to be called up for active service and had previously been disqualified on medical grounds: he had fallen from a wall and smashed his left eardrum. When the cotton exchange closed for the duration of hostilities he worked as a lathe-turner at Napiers engineering works, making shell cases to be filled with explosives. At night he was a volunteer fireman, surveying the ruined city from a high rooftop on fire-watch duty when not actually fighting a blaze. No one knew if the air raids would start again. As a district health visitor his mother cared for families in houses that were often without water or electricity because of the Blitz, or for people living in emergency accommodation, frequently in terrible conditions.

Housing was scarce after the war; thousands of people lived in prefabs, single-storey prefabricated buildings assembled on site as temporary housing, intended to last a maximum of ten years, some of which were still in use on the Speke Estate twenty-five years later. Rather than patch up damaged old buildings, the Liverpool Corporation decided to demolish entire neighbourhoods and build anew. Paul spent most of his childhood in the new council estates thrown up around the city on levelled bomb sites or open fields.

In 1947, when Paul's younger brother Michael was three, Mary McCartney became a domiciliary midwife. It was an exhausting, demanding job which entailed being on call at all hours of the day and night, but it enabled the family to move to Sir Thomas White Gardens off St Domingo Road in Everton, a flat which came with the job. Not long afterwards they moved again, this time to one of the new estates on the outskirts of Liverpool.

PAUL: I don't know why that was; maybe she volunteered. Maybe she wanted to get a new house because a house came with the job. The first house I remember was at 72 Western Avenue in Speke, which we moved to when I was four. The road was still being built and roadside grass was being sown and trees were being planted. The city always ran out where we lived, there was always a field next to us. Then the minute they built more houses on that field, we moved to another place where there was another field.

12 Ardwick Road in Speke, where we lived after Western Avenue, was really unfinished, we were slopping through mud for a year or so before that was done, so it was always this pioneering thing, we were always on the edge of the world, like Christopher Columbus, there was this feeling you might drop off.

The McCartneys had money worries. After the war, Jim's job at the armaments factory ended and he returned to the cotton exchange, as a salesman for A. Hannay and company, but the war had changed everything; the cotton market was in chaos, and he was lucky to bring home £6 a week. It meant that Mary also had to work and it was always a cause of slight embarrassment that she earned a higher wage than he.

PAUL: Whilst we weren't a poor family, we weren't rich by any means, so we never had a car, or a television till the coronation in 1953. I was the first one in the family to buy a car with my Beatle earnings. My mum, as a nurse, rode a bike. I have a crystal-clear memory of one snow-laden night when I was young at 72 Western Avenue. The streets were thick with snow, it was about three in the morning, and she got up and went out on her bike with the little brown wicker basket on the front, into the dark, just with her little light, in her navy-blue uniform and hat, cycling off down the estate to deliver a baby somewhere.

The picture of Mary on the sleeve of Michael McCartney's first solo album was taken when she was working at Walton Hospital. She looks more like a nun than a nurse in the royal blue and white uniform and hat, which in those days still showed the religious origins of the profession.

PAUL: If ever you grazed your knee or anything it was amazingly taken care of because she was a nurse. She was very kind, very loving. There was a lot of sitting on laps and cuddling. She was very cuddly. I think I was very close to her. My brother thinks he was a little closer, being littler. I would just be trying to be a bit more butch, being the older one. She liked to joke and had a good sense of humour and she was very warm. There was more warmth than I now realise there was in most families.

I think she was pretty good-looking. To me she's just a mum and you don't look at a mum the same way as you look at film stars or something. She had slightly wavy hair in a bob, I suppose she would have described her hair as mousy. It wasn't jet black or red or blonde or anything, it was kind of an in-between colour. She had gentle eyes and wore rimless spectacles. She was quite striking-looking. She had lovely handwriting and was quite nicely spoken for Liverpool and encouraged us to speak the Queen's English. That's why I never had too thick a Liverpool accent.

They aspired to a better life. That idea that we had to get out of here, we had to do better than this. This was okay for everyone else in the street but we could do better than this. She was always moving to what she saw as a better place to bring her kids up.

Speke was named after the swine fields that surrounded Liverpool; the Anglo-Saxon 'Spic' means bacon. The old village of Speke, together with the hamlet of Oglet, had only thirty-seven houses when construction began in 1936 on a 'new model town'. Over 35,000 houses and flats were built, mainly to house people from the slums of the south end of Liverpool. Despite being well equipped with schools, clinics, parks and playing fields, it was a pretty soulless place. The idea of rehousing people in rural surroundings didn't work. They missed the street life, the local pub, the corner shops and sense of community and felt that the council had taken them and dumped them in a field out of sight. The low, monotonous terraced houses, the lack of nearby shops or entertainment and the great distance from the city centre quickly combined to make it into a rough working-class ghetto, separated from the rest of Liverpool by an industrial estate and the airport. However, there were thick woods nearby, full of bluebells in spring, now engulfed by a Ford motor factory, and it was only a short walk to the River Mersey.

School was only one street away but, as more and more houses were built and occupied, the Stockton Wood Road School rapidly became overcrowded until it eventually had a roll-call of 1500 children, making it the largest junior school in Britain. The problem was solved by taking many of the children, including Paul and Michael, on a school coach each morning to Gateacre, a half-hour drive north through Hunts Cross and Woolton, to the Joseph Williams Primary School in Belle Vale, also newly built, which was then on the edge of the countryside. It was at Belle Vale that Paul made his first appearance on stage.

In 1953, schools were preoccupied with the national celebrations for the coronation of Queen Elizabeth II, and one project was an essay competition on the subject of the monarchy. 'I obviously wrote something reasonable because I won my age group's prize,' Paul remembered. 'I went to Picton Hall, in the city centre, and it was my first ever experience of nerves. When some dignitary in pinstripes called my name – "And for the eleven-year-old age group, from Joseph Williams Primary School in Gateacre, J. P. McCartney" – my knees went rubbery.' His prize was a souvenir book of the coronation plus a book token. 'I used it to buy a book on modern art. It was fabulous. It was just lots and lots of pictures; people like Victor

Pasmore, Salvador Dali, Picasso, and a lot of artists I hadn't heard of. I'd always been attracted to art. I used to draw a lot.'

Jim McCartney took great pleasure in gardening and filled their small front garden with flowers: dahlias, snapdragons and a carefully tended lavender hedge. He would dry and crush the sprigs of lavender to burn in the house like incense, and would sprinkle them in all the ashtrays to kill the smell of burning cigarette stubs. He would always curse the ginger tom from next door for sleeping in the lavender hedge. He kept his eye open for horse manure, and it was the boys' job to collect it. Paul: 'Talk about peer pressure, you would hope your friends didn't catch you shovelling the shit in the bucket. Then you'd have to carry it around to the garden.' Jim's interest in gardening led him to become the secretary of the Speke Horticultural Society and when they were living in Western Avenue he sent Paul and Michael out canvassing for new members.

> PAUL: He had us out aged about nine. I was virtually a door-to-door salesman by the time I was twelve. We used to go, 'Knock knock, would you like to join the gardening club?' 'What's in it for me then? Why should I?' 'Well, there's free manure, and you can get seeds at a discount ...' and I had this spiel! And the people would go, 'Fuck off! Piss off,' so it was a very good way to learn the territory. 'Shit, I'm not going to that house again, he's an old drunk.' I remember a blind couple there and there was only one seeing member of the family, it was quite bizarre really, looking back on it. My brain's full of all that. For some reason I worked like a bastard when I was a kid! I would be out collecting jam jars door to door, doing Bob-a-Job.
>
> I was certainly not shy with people, I think because of all these activities my dad encouraged us into. I think it's probably very good for your confidence with people. It was all right. That was my upbringing.

For Paul and Michael, the best thing about living in Speke was the countryside. In a couple of minutes they could be in Dungeon Lane, which led through the fields to the banks of the Mersey. The river is very wide at this point, with the lights of Ellesmere Port visible on the far side across enormous shifting banks of mud and sand pecked over by gulls. On a clear day you could see beyond the Wirral all the way to Wales. Paul would often cycle the two and a half miles along the shoreline to the lighthouse at Hale Head, where the river makes a 90-degree turn, giving a panoramic view across the mud and navigation channels to the industrial complex of Runcorn on the far side. These are lonely, cold, windy places, the distant factories and docks dwarfed by the size of the mud banks of the river itself.

In the early fifties the McCartneys moved to another new house, surrounded by a muddy building site, at 12 Ardwick Road in the expanding eastern extension of the estate. It was not without danger. Paul was mugged there once while messing about with his brother on the beach near the old lighthouse. His watch was stolen and he had to go to court because they knew the youths that did it. Paul: 'They were a couple of hard kids who said, "Give us that watch," and they got it. The police took them to court and I had to go and be a witness against them. Dear me, my first time in court.'

In 1953, out of the ninety children at Joseph Williams School who took the eleven-plus exam, Paul was one of four who received high enough marks to qualify for a place in the Liverpool Institute, the city's top grammar school. The Institute was one of the best schools in the country and regularly sent more of its students to Oxford and Cambridge universities than any other British state school. It was founded in 1837 and its high academic standards made it a serious rival to Eton, Harrow and the other great public schools. In 1944 it was taken over by the state as a free grammar school but its high standards as well as many of the public-school traditions still remained.

Paul first met George Harrison when they found themselves sharing the same hour-long bus ride each day to Mount Street in the city centre, and identified each other as Institute boys by their school uniforms and caps. George was born in February 1943, which placed him in the year below Paul, but because they shared the ride together Paul put their eight-month age difference to one side and George quickly became one of his best friends. Paul soon made himself at home in the welcoming front room of George's house at 25 Upton Green, a cul-de-sac one block away from Paul's house on Ardwick Road.

The little village of Hale was less than two miles away, with thatched roofs, home of the giant Childe of Hale who, legend has it, was nine foot tall. Paul and Michael would stare at his grave in wonder. The worn gravestone is still there, inscribed 'Hyre lyes ye childe of Hale'. It was a favourite destination for a family walk. On the way back Paul's parents and the two boys would stop at a teashop called the Elizabethan Cottage for a pot of tea, Hovis toast and home-made jam. It was a pleasant, genteel interlude, a touch of quality before they walked back to their very different life among the new grey houses and hard concrete roads of the housing estate.

'This is where my love of the country came from,' Paul said. 'I was always able to take my bike and in five minutes I'd be in quite deep countryside. I remember the Dam woods, which had millions of rhododendron bushes. We used to have dens in the middle of them because they get quite bare in the middle so you could squeeze in. I've never seen that many rhododendrons since.' Sometimes, how-ever, rather than play with his friends, Paul preferred to be alone. He would take his *Observer Book of Birds* and wander down Dungeon Lane to the lighthouse on a nature ramble or climb over the fence and go walking in the fields.

PAUL: This is what I was writing about in 'Mother Nature's Son', it was basically a heart-felt song about my child-of-nature leanings.

I was a Boy Scout and I remembered Baden Powell's saying 'People never look up,' so I would go in the woods and sit in a tree and watch people go by underneath. I'd be like a super spy, the Silent Observer, the Sniper. It became apparent to me that what I was doing was practising to be a soldier. National Service was still going and, like everyone else, I fully expected to have to go in the army for two years' National Service.

George Harrison's elder brother Harry had been to Christmas Island and arrived back with a gorgeous tan in his army uniform and we thought, My God, he's been made a man of. You used to see this quite regularly, people would be *made a man of.*

They'd come back and by then of course they were all used to being soldiers. We hadn't seen the first few months when it had been hell. We saw tanned blokes, fit, happy to be in the army, 'Sure, what's wrong?' So I expected that would happen to me, we all did. But then they ended it. Suddenly they said, 'There will be no more National Service, we're having the regular army, the Territorials. We'll be all right, thanks, we're fixed, lads, we don't need you.' So it was like, Oh, my God! The relief!

However, when I was a kid, living on the outskirts of Liverpool, I didn't know this was going to happen so I had to be prepared. In my mind I would imagine myself with a bayonet, because that was the symbol of it all, and imagine myself running someone through, and I thought, Jesus Christ! That is not going to be easy. Fuck me! What's the look on his face going to be like if I do it? Having quite a vivid imagination, I'd follow all that shit through. So when I went out into the woods, I thought I'd better get some practice in. So I thought, Frogs. That'll do, because all my mates killed frogs anyway. They used to blow them up sticking a straw up their ass. That was the way to kill a frog. I didn't fancy that, I thought that was a little bit pervy. I thought a straightforward killing with a bash, hold the legs and just smash 'em on the head. You feel that you've got to learn to kill, like a farmer's boy who grows up and learns to kill that goose and wring that chicken's neck. But I didn't have the farm, so there was no other way to learn.

I felt very conscious that I was going to shit out completely when this National Service arrived. I was going to be one of the guys who said, 'Sorry, sir, I'm a pacifist, I can't kill,' and I'd have to go to jail. I was in a dilemma in my mind. So I used to kill these frogs. There was a spot in the woods where there was some barbed wire and I used to stick 'em on the barbs of the wire. I had quite a little gallery. I used to call 'em Johnny Rebs, these were the rebels from the Civil War. I had six or seven of them, and I remember taking my brother down there once. He was completely horrified.

Though Paul had a secure home life, growing up in Speke was far from tranquil. It was a tough industrial estate and he had plenty of aggressive and delinquent youths to contend with:.

PAUL: I was looking out for guys on every corner who were going to beat me up. There were fights where George and I used to live in Speke. The next district, about quarter of an hour away, is called Garston and the guys from Garston would sometimes get on a late-night bus and come to Speke. And suddenly the word would go round, because it was like a frontier town in the Wild West: 'The lads from Garston are coming! Fuck off, fuck off!' And you'd have to run! And they would come, forty guys from Garston would come and our bigger guys didn't run. They would go and meet them. It was very very real. It was serious fighting. George and I weren't very involved, but our moment came. There was one fight I remember in Woolton on the day I met John Lennon at the Woolton fête. We went to the pub afterwards, all getting a bit steamed up, then the word went round – God knows who it is who puts that word round, there was always a runner – 'The lads from ...' 'The teds from so and so are coming.' 'Jimmy Ardersly's around. He said he's goin' to get you.'

'What? Jimmy Ardersly? He's fuckin' said he's goin' to 'it me? Oh! My God!' I didn't like all that shit. I was not that type at all. I was much more of a pacifist.

Jim and Mary McCartney were overjoyed when Michael also passed the eleven-plus and got a place at the Liverpool Institute alongside his brother.

PAUL: My parents aspired for us, very much indeed. That is one of the great things you can find in ordinary people. My mum wanted me to be a doctor. 'My son the doctor' – and her being a nurse, too. No problem there. And my dad, who left school at fourteen, would have loved me to be a great scientist, a great university graduate. I always feel grateful for that. I mean, God, I certainly fulfilled their aspirations, talk about overachieving! That was all bred into me, that.

My dad always took the *Express*. He'd have long arguments on Sundays with my cousin Jean's husband, Ted Merry, who was an ardent communist and would come round: 'Look Jim, the workers deserve ... and the management take the lion's share of the profits ...' All the completely true stuff. But my dad would say, 'What can you do about it? What are you going to do about it?' 'Well, if you overthrow –' 'Wait a minute!' So my dad would have long conversations about that.

He was very into crosswords. 'Learn crosswords, they're good for your word power.' At a very early age I was the only kid in class who knew how to spell 'phlegm'.

We had George Newnes Encyclopedias. I can still remember

the smell of them. If you didn't know what a word meant or how it was spelled, my dad would say 'Look it up.' I think that's a great attitude to take with kids. It steers you in the right direction. It was part of a game where he was improving us without having had an awful lot of experience of improvement himself. But I always liked that, and I knew I would outstrip him. By going to grammar school I knew I'd fairly soon have Latin phrases or know about Shakespeare which he wouldn't know about.

This access to new areas of knowledge is one explanation for the great social changes that came about during the sixties. The parents of many of the sixties generation had left school at fourteen and gone straight to work. Their children were far better educated, even those who paid scant attention to what was being taught. They knew more and their horizons stretched beyond that of their families into a world where their parents could no longer guide them; a world unknown to the pre-war generation. It was an area with no rules, an unexplored territory where young people had money; where fashion was for youth, not adults; where music meant rock 'n' roll, not Mantovani; where sex could be practised free from fear of pregnancy; where you could make up the rules as you went along.

In Britain then, the sixties revolution can be attributed largely to a combination of this free education, of open admission to art schools, and of the post-war economic boom. All that was needed to get into art school was a folder of work of sufficient standard to convince the principal that you might benefit from four years of painting and life drawing – and the state would pay the tuition. As Simon Frith and Howard Horne wrote in *Welcome to Bohemia!*: 'The art college was the flaw in the British education system, a space where both middle- and working-class youth could deny the implications of past and future and live out, however briefly, a fantasy of cultural freedom.'

The art schools produced very few fine artists, but turned out brilliant fashion designers and scores of rock 'n' roll artists, who went on to ensure that British rock became the dominant popular music on the planet for more than a decade: Eric Clapton, David Bowie, Pete Townshend, all of the Pink Floyd, Keith Richards, Ron Wood, Ray and Dave Davies of the Kinks, Jeff Beck and Eric Burdon, to name only the most famous. When they arrived in Hamburg in 1960, two members of the Beatles were still technically at Liverpool College of Art.

> PAUL: That was one of the great blessings, we all got a free classical education. None of us wanted to know at the time, of course, but you couldn't help it, they beat it into us. Me and George Harrison didn't do well at school but you had to go and you had to take exams, whether you passed or not. John didn't do at all well at school, and he didn't do an awful lot at art school. He was not a keen painter, but this is where we were coming from and this is why it all happened.

No matter how bad a student John Lennon was, the fact is that he was an art student and not a truck driver like Elvis Presley. British rock 'n' roll had very different roots to its American counterpart, filtering the raw R & B roots through an additional layer of Surrealism and contemporary European art theory.

Paul: 'That's why I'm so keen on my old school. Because it really did turn my head from being a lovely innocent suburban head, somewhat limited, somewhat dour, somewhat picky and provincial, and somewhat blinkered, to being expansive: "Wait a minute, fuckin' hell, there's all these guys wrote those poems ...!" It gave me a feeling that things were allowed.' More than any time before, there were no limits, no restrictions. The Beatles burst out of Liverpool into a world that they made up as they went along.

Forthlin Road

In 1955, Jim and Mary McCartney moved their family for the final time. Through Mary's job as a midwife, they were able to get a council property in Allerton, closer to the city centre and an altogether better neighbourhood than Speke. For Paul it was disruptive because at thirteen he had many friends on the Speke estate, but Allerton is not far from Speke and he was able to keep in touch with some of them.

Allerton – the place of the alder trees – began life as a separate manor and was only incorporated into Liverpool in 1913. Class-consciousness has always been acute in Allerton, and ever since the building of the Springwood housing estate in the 1920s many middle-class Allertonians have preferred to tell people that they live in neighbouring Mossley Hill.

PAUL: My mother was always on the lookout for a better place for us to live. It was a bit of an uproot but we soon settled in there and it was a reasonable area. Her idea was to get us out of a bad area into a slightly posh area so that perhaps some of the posh might rub off on us. It was also a safer area; in fact, it was quite a middle-class area where we were, but they'd built a council estate in the middle of all the posh houses, much to the chagrin of the local residents, I'm sure, though we never heard anything about that.

Mary McCartney's attempts to better herself and her family were the cause of one of Paul's regrets.

PAUL: There's one moment that I've regretted all my life which is a strange little awkwardness for me. There was one time when she said 'ask' and she pronounced it posh. And I made fun of her and it slightly embarrassed her. Years later I've never forgiven myself. It's a terrible little thing. I wish I could go back and say, 'I was only kidding, Mum.' I'm sure she knew. I'm sure she didn't take it too seriously.

Number 20 Forthlin Road, near the corner of Mather Avenue, was a small two-floor brick-built terrace house in a 1950s council housing estate of the type being thrown up quickly all over the country to replace the houses destroyed by German bombs. It had a lavender hedge bordering a pocket-handkerchief lawn and a small mountain ash growing outside the glass-panelled front door. The living room led off to the left from the tiny front hall and a door led through from the living room to the dining room, overlooking the back yard. The dining room was connected to the kitchen, which in turn connected to the hall. Paul: 'It was an all-round plan: if you kept turning right, you would get back into the hall, which is a feature I've used in the house I've designed for myself, because people used to be so amazed to get back to where they started. The architects who helped me design my house have now incorporated that idea in their new houses. It was an amazingly good design for the suburbs in those days.'

Paul had the small bedroom at the front of the house above the front door. His parents had the big bedroom next to it, above the living room, overlooking the street, and Paul's brother Michael had the bedroom at the back, overlooking the back yard. Next to Michael's room was the bathroom. This was a great luxury; their previous council houses, despite being built since the war, all had outside lavatories, as did most working-class housing in Britain at the time. Despite the image of Britain propagated by the British Tourist Board, one of the most widespread British memories of childhood is not of being tucked up in bed by Nanny but of pulling an overcoat over thin pyjamas to brave the cold night air to use the outhouse.

The back of the house overlooked the grounds of the Police Training College, headquarters of the Liverpool Mounted Police. Paul and his brother would watch them training horses, knocking pegs out of the ground with lances just as they had done in the British Raj. 'We used to sit on the concrete shed in the back yard and watch the Police Show every year for free,' Paul remembered. 'One year, Jackie Collins came to open it and we were entranced at the sight of her comely young figure.'

Paul's adolescence in Liverpool seemed staid and old-fashioned compared to the modern, pacy, heroic images of the American television series that dominated the tiny black and white British screen: *77 Sunset Strip, Highway Patrol, Sea Hunt, Dragnet, Whirlybirds*. In 1955 there were still more than 11,000 gas lamps lighting the streets and alleys of Liverpool and the Corporation Cleansing Department still used horse-drawn wagons to collect the garbage: fifty-seven heavy shire horses, direct descendants of the old English war horse, capable of carrying a knight in full armour, pulled the heavy wagons, their iron-shod hoofs striking sparks from the cobbles. Britain's only elevated railway still ran from Seaforth Sands to Dingle Station; a trip on the 'overhead' was a favourite treat for young boys until it was demolished on the last day of 1956. It featured in John Lennon's original lyrics for 'In My Life' and was so well built that the company commissioned to knock it down went bankrupt trying. A gun was fired at 1:00 p.m. each day at Morpeth pier head and Paul would eat lunch in the large basement canteen of the Institute with its scrubbed wooden tables and long benches looking rather like an army mess hall. Life seemed totally predictable and stable.

Each morning Paul would catch the number 86 bus on Mather Avenue to school.

PAUL: I had to do the journey into the centre, half an hour on my own on the bus from the age of eleven. I was pretty independent, and I soon learned how to explore. I know it was something the other Beatles didn't really feel too much. I used to say to George Harrison, 'God, I'd love to go on a bus again.' George would say, 'Why would you want to do that?' His dad had been a bus driver and I think maybe George could not see the romance of travelling on a bus that I would. I always saw it as sitting upstairs, smoking a pipe like a poet. Sitting on the top of a bus composing things.

Liverpool buses were double-deckers with an upstairs compartment where smoking was permitted, a section much favoured by schoolchildren because the conductor couldn't see them up there. It was this removed view of the city that provided a vocabulary of places and characters used in Paul's later songs. Though he often ran into friends on the bus, and his brother accompanied him to school, the long bus rides were an integral part of his childhood and youth; a period of enforced introspection, the detached observer viewing events and places through the frame of the bus window from the godlike height of the upper deck. Such moments was drawn upon in Paul's lyrics to 'A Day in the Life', where he sits upstairs in a bus, smokes a cigarette and goes into a dream. A combination of childhood memories and a high sixties reference to smoking pot.

No matter where he was headed – to school or to see friends – the bus inevitably took him first to Penny Lane.

PAUL: The area was called Penny Lane; we would often use it because a lot of bus routes converge there. It was on the way to Liverpool city centre so I would pass it every day on my bus route or if I was taking the bus to John's, if it was raining or something, I'd take it to there and change and get the bus up to his house. George and I used to to go through there to the cinema and it was also the way to a friend called Arthur Kelly who was a school mate.

Arthur Kelly later achieved success as an actor in the acclaimed television series *The Boys from the Blackstuff* and playing Bert in the West End stage play *John Paul George Ringo ... and Bert.*

The Penny Lane area actually looks much the same as it did thirty-five years ago, but the tourist hoping to explore the Liverpool of the Beatles is in for a unpleasant surprise because much of the city in which they grew up has been demolished: the beautiful Georgian terraces on Upper Parliament Street that Paul saw every day from the 86 bus on the way to school have all gone; Cumberland Terrace, built in 1847, was demolished as late as 1978, and the listed, and therefore supposedly protected, Georgian town houses on the same street were torn down to make way for the ill-advised inner ring road in the 1980s. The Liverpool Corporation has done more to disfigure and destroy Liverpool than the Luftwaffe managed with the blitzkrieg in 1941. The old heart of the city was ripped out: the large Georgian townhouses on St James Road which gave scale to the new Anglican cathedral and the elegant Georgian mansions with their columns and pediments on Upper Huskisson Street are now gone. Fine houses from the 1840s of the type so lovingly restored in Greenwich Village, Dublin or Chelsea were bulldozed into oblivion. The proportions of elegant city squares were destroyed by sixties blocks of flats, so badly built that many are already being replaced. Very few of the Victorian pubs, old warehouses and commercial buildings from the early nineteenth century, with their elaborate façades, ornamental pilasters, finials and patina of age, were retained. Now, at last, the city realises that tourism could be one of Liverpool's main industries, but the sad fact is that there is very little left to see.

There were three BBC radio channels. The Third Programme was for highbrow culture; the few popular records played on the two remaining channels were taken from charts dominated by Rosemary Clooney, Doris Day, Frankie Laine, Vera Lynn and Frank Sinatra. Then in October 1954 a record slipped briefly into the charts called 'Sh-Boom' by the Crew Cuts. It was the first rock 'n' roll-related record to make an impact in Britain. Elvis Presley was yet to have a UK release. Even though the Crew Cuts version was a squeaky-clean white copy of the Chords original, it caused kids all over the country to prick up an ear and when the Crew Cuts played the Liverpool Empire the next year, promoting their cover of the Penguins' 'Earth Angel', Paul was waiting outside the stage door in his short trousers with his autograph book.

PAUL: When I was a kid, I used to get autographs at the stage door at the Empire. It was a fantasy thing, it was amazing to me that you could go to this building and out of this little back door would come these people you'd seen on a record cover. I met the Crew Cuts, who had the cover version of 'Earth Angel', and they were very kind and very nice and I thought, Well, that's possible then, stars can talk to people, and I remembered that later.

The Crew Cuts were followed into the British charts by Bill Haley and his Comets, first with 'Shake, Rattle and Roll', then with 'Rock Around the Clock'. Lonnie Donegan appeared on the scene and introduced skiffle and Paul was there when he came to the Empire. Finally, in May 1956, Elvis entered the British charts with 'Heartbreak Hotel'. The floodgates opened and by the end of the year, half the records in the top 20 were American rock 'n' roll.

If a British home had a record player in 1956, it was most likely to play only 78-rpm records. It also required a needle change every couple of records and probably had to be wound up every three plays. Many R & B records were not released in Britain at all and those that were cost a huge amount at that time since until then records had always been aimed at an adult audience. Liverpudlians, however, had one great advantage over the teenagers of any other British town. Liverpool was the main port for shipping to and from the USA. Everyone knew someone with a brother, a cousin or a father on the boats, and when they returned, they brought with them American cigarettes, comic books (in full colour, not like the feeble black and white British reprints) and rock 'n' roll records.

PAUL: I nearly did very well at grammar school but I started to get interested in art instead of academic subjects. Then I started to see pictures of Elvis, and that started to pull me away from the academic path. 'You should see these great photos ...' Then you'd hear the records – 'But wait a minute, this is very good!' – and then the tingles started going up and down your spine, 'Oh, this is something altogether different.' And so the academic things were forgotten.

The words they used in their end-of-term reports: 'If he would only buckle down ...' and you'd go, 'No! No! Get out of my life! I hate you. You should say I'm great. I've got to take this home, you know.' If I had buckled down, it could have worked out that way, but I'm glad it didn't, of course. There was always the great pull of the other stuff: show business, music, art, the other stuff ...

The happiness and security of Paul's life was brutally shattered when his mother died on 31 October 1956. She had been in pain for several weeks but it is often the case with nurses and doctors that the carers fail to care for themselves. She did not mention the pain or the lump in her breast to the doctors and nurses she worked with every day until it was too late for them to help her. 'I would have liked to have seen the boys growing up' was one of the last things she said. She was given a mastectomy but the cancer was by then too advanced for the doctors to cure her.

> PAUL: I remember one horrible day me and my brother going to the hospital. They must have known she was dying. It turned out to be our last visit and it was terrible because there was blood on the sheets somewhere and seeing that, and your mother, it was like 'Holy cow!' And of course she was very brave, and would cry after we'd gone, though I think she cried on that visit. But we didn't really know what was happening. We were shielded from it all by our aunties and by our dad and everything.

The boys went to stay with Jim's brother Joe and his wife Joan, while friends and relatives tried to calm their distraught father, whose first thought was to join his wife. After his initial anguish, Jim suppressed his own grief in order to make a home for the two bewildered boys. Michael was twelve and Paul just fourteen. The McCartneys were part of a large extended family and aunts and uncles and cousins rallied round, cooking and cleaning, shopping and helping out, but there was a terrible emptiness in the house. There was no one there when they got home from school, just a house filled with memories and regrets. Paul later preserved his mother's memory in the beautiful ballad 'Let It Be', based on a dream he had of her a decade after her death. Paul: 'She was great. She was a really wonderful woman and really did pull the family along, which is probably why in the end she died of a stress-related illness. She was, as so many woman are, the unsung leader of the family.'

Paul dealt with his grief by focusing his attention on his music.

I had a £15 acoustic Zenith guitar, which I still have in my studio. I swapped a trumpet for it at Rushworth and Dreapers. My father had given me the trumpet for my fourteenth birthday, and I used to play it a little bit because that was the hero instrument then, *The Man with the Golden Arm* and everything, but it became clear to me fairly quickly that you couldn't sing with a trumpet stuck in your mouth. If you had aspirations in the singing line it had to be something like a guitar, so I asked me dad if he would mind and he said no. So I went into town, swapped it in, got a guitar, came back home, couldn't figure out at all how to play it. I didn't realise that it was because I was left-handed and it wasn't until I found a picture of Slim Whitman, who was also left-handed, and saw that I had the guitar the wrong way round.

When Paul restrung his guitar upside-down, he found the bridge and the nut which held the strings in tension could not be moved, which meant that the thin top string now passed through the notches intended for the thick bottom string, allowing it to rattle about. Paul carefully shaved down a safety match to make a little block of wood to put under the top string, the one that is most used, to stop it moving around.

PAUL: It was all rather inexact, I never had a really good instrument, but it didn't matter, the whole thing with the Beatles was we never really had great instruments, we never really had great headphones, we never really had great microphones or PAs, we somehow learned to muddle through. In fact I think it was quite good for us, because now all this sophisticated stuff seems such a luxury, it's wonderful. We always made do with whatever we had.

Paul took his guitar everywhere with him, even to the bathroom, and soon wrote his first song, 'I Lost My Little Girl'. Paul: 'I wrote that when I was fourteen just after I'd lost my mother. I don't think the song was about that but of course, any psychiatrist getting hold of those two bits of information would say it was. It's fairly obvious with a title like "I Lost My Little Girl".'

The McCartney family did their best to fill the gap in the boys' lives. 'I had a very nice warm family who I could always talk to about problems,' Paul remembered. 'My old Aunty Jin was like an earth mother: "Sit down and we'll talk about it." There was a lot of security there. She was a central character, she was known as Control within the family.' Paul's work is not often explicitly autobiographical but Aunty Jin is one of the few people to have received a name check in one of his songs; both she and his brother get a listing in 'Let 'Em In' on Paul's 1976 album *Wings at the Speed of Sound*, showing how his childhood continued to be woven into his songs.

Jim now had to face alone the task of guiding his two teenage sons through the difficult period of adolescence. Paul's father had married late. He was born in 1902 and was in his thirties when he met Paul's mother. In the late twenties, he had his own band, Jim Mac's Jazz Band, which played dance halls all around Liverpool. It was very much a McCartney family affair: Jim played piano and trumpet and his brother Jack played trombone and there was also a cousin in the band. They played a repertoire of popular hits of the day: 'Stairway to Paradise', 'Chicago', 'Lullaby of the Leaves', 'After You've Gone'. Music had always been a focus of family life. Jim had an old upright piano at home which he bought from Harry Epstein's North End Music Store in Everton – the McCartneys' first unwitting contact with NEMS and the Epstein family – and one of Paul's early memories is of lying on the floor, listening to him play. It was a great house for family sing-songs with all the aunts and uncles gathered round the piano, children running everywhere.

PAUL: My dad was the original. To us kids he was a pretty good player, he could play a lot of tunes on the piano. I was very influenced by him. I used to ask him to teach me but he said, 'No, you must take lessons,' like all parents do. I ended up teaching myself like he did, by ear.

He thought he wasn't good enough to teach me, that I had to go and learn the real stuff. More aspirations, I suppose, but it would have done me because he was pretty good. I tried a few times to have proper piano lessons. I went to the old lady who smelled a bit, that one we all went to, and didn't like it because she gave homework one week and that blew it. I didn't like that. Then when I was about sixteen I tried again with a young guy, about nineteen, who lived the other side of Mather Avenue. He tried to take me back to the basics but by then I was starting to write some stuff of my own on the piano. Something was making me make it up, whether I knew how to do it or not. I'd already written the tune of 'When I'm sixty-four' when I was sixteen so I couldn't really get on with him taking me back to the beginning.

Not surprisingly there is a strong vaudevillian flavour to 'When I'm Sixty-four'.

PAUL: I grew up steeped in that music-hall tradition. My father once worked at the Liverpool Hippodrome as a spotlight operator. They actually used a piece of burning lime in those days which he had to trim. He was very entertaining about that period and had lots of tales about it. He'd learned his music from listening to it every single night of the week, two shows every night, Sundays off.

He had a lot of music in him, my dad. He taught me and my brother harmony; not the concept, not written down, but he would say, 'This tune is the harmony to that tune,' so I learned very early how to sing harmony, which was one of my big roles in the Beatles. Whenever John sang I automatically sang in harmony with him, and that's due to my dad's teaching. I remember talking to the guys very early on about harmony, in the same way as my dad talked to us, saying, 'This would be the harmony for this.' One of the thrills about being in the music-publishing business now is that I know an awful lot of those old songs through him.

These old songs have become standards, the product of a golden age of show business and songwriting, but not everyone liked the Jim Mac Band's set list. Jim Mac's father, Paul's grandfather, Joe McCartney, called it 'tin-can music'. He came from an older musical tradition. He used to play an E-flat bass, a large brass tuba-like instrument, in the works brass band at Cope's.

PAUL: Even though it was forced on me, it is interesting that I'm a bass player. I certainly didn't pick it because my grandfather had played bass. My dad, presumably because of his dad, would point out the bass on a radio. He'd say, 'Listen to that. You hear that, dum duuum dum dum? That's called the bass.' 'Oh.' My dad would take us to brass band concerts in the band shell in the park, and we would sit and listen, and I would always like that. It was very northern. I did work later with the Black Dyke Mills Band, and made a record called 'Thingumybob' with them which was quite fun. I still have a very soft spot in my heart for brass bands, it's a roots thing for me. And no wonder if my grandfather's semen had a load of bass genes in it, my dad must have passed them on to me.

Though brass band music and show tunes were the musical influences on his childhood, Paul's own choice of music was mainly rock 'n' roll. The BBC did not play rock 'n' roll. Popular music on the radio was played by BBC combos like the NDO, the Northern Dance Orchestra. They just played the tunes, sometimes making a feeble effort to imitate the arrangement of the original record. The Musicians Union saw records as a threat to their livelihood and held the BBC to a strict 'needle time' agreement which allowed them to play only a certain amount of recorded music each week. The main way to hear rock 'n' roll in Britain was to tune in to Radio Luxembourg, broadcast at 208 metres on the medium wave from the tiny European principality.

Luxembourg only broadcast in English in the evenings. Paul usually listened after he went to bed, thanks to a pair of Bakelite headphones which Jim had rigged up for each of the brothers on an extension cord leading from the radio in the living room. After much fiddling, the station's distinctive call sign could be made out for half an hour before programmes began. The signal faded in and out, sometimes swamped by static, but there it was: LaVern Baker's 'Jim Dandy', Fats Domino's 'Blueberry Hill' and 'Blue Monday', the moans and shrieks and wails of Little Richard's 'Tutti Frutti' and 'Long Tall Sally', the grunts and slurs of Elvis, the strange falsetto of Frankie Lyman, great honking saxophones and twanging guitars. Luxembourg played a diet of popular music, richly biased by payola, interspersed by dumb quiz shows like *Shilling a Second*, but it also transmitted syndicated shows such as Alan Freed's *Saturday Night Jamboree*, featuring the latest American R & B and rock 'n' roll by the original black artists; there was no Pat Boone on the Alan Freed show. These were the songs that became the set list for the early Beatles, the benchmark, the classic songs that began rock 'n' roll: Chuck Berry's

'Maybellene' and 'Roll Over Beethoven', Fats Domino's 'Ain't That a Shame', Eddie Cochran's 'Twenty Flight Rock', Gene Vincent's 'Be Bop A-Lula', Ivory Joe Hunter, Jim Lowe, Bill Doggett, the Everly Brothers, the Diamonds, the Coasters, a string of hits from Elvis – the riches seemed never ending, inspiring thousands of British kids to play rock 'n' roll. And each time a song was played, Paul would memorise a few more of the words and perfect the chord changes on his guitar.

Luxembourg also played skiffle, an offshoot of the British traditional jazz revival first popularised by Lonnie Donegan, the banjo player with Ken Barber's Trad Band, who played skiffle on stage between sets. 'Skiffle' was a late-1920s American term for music by people too poor to buy instruments: the line-up consisted of washboard, jug, tea-chest bass and cheap acoustic guitars. In 1956 Donegan had a hit with 'Rock Island Line' and over the next five years had thirty-one further top-30 hits. Other acts joined in and by the spring of 1957 there were three skiffle records in the UK top 20: the Vipers Skiffle Group and Lonnie Donegan, both with 'Cumberland Gap', and Chas McDevitt and Nancy Whiskey's 'Freight Train'. Skiffle had immense appeal to British teenagers who could not afford the electric guitars and saxophones needed for rock 'n' roll. Sales of guitars doubled as hundreds of skiffle groups were formed all over the country – among them the Quarry Men, started by John Lennon.

John Lennon

On 6 July 1957, eight months after his mother died, Paul met John Lennon. Paul's schoolmate Ivan Vaughan lived near John and, knowing they were both obsessed with rock 'n' roll, he thought they should meet. John had a skiffle group called the Quarry Men who were playing at the local village fête in Woolton. It was a typical British summer fête, beginning with a procession through the streets of Woolton led by the twenty-five-piece-band of the Cheshire Yeomanry, followed by floats, Morris dancers, Scouts, Girl Guides, Brownies, Cubs and schoolchildren in fancy dress. The fête itself was held in the field behind St Peter's church, where a first-aid tent, a marquee offering 'refreshments at moderate prices' and a makeshift stage had been erected. It was a very hot day, humid, but with a slight breeze which stirred the bunting and balloons strung between the stalls and sideshows. The Rose Queen, Miss Sally Wright, was crowned to scattered applause.

The Quarry Men were scheduled to begin at 4.15, before the display by the City of Liverpool Police Dogs. When Paul arrived they were already on stage and John Lennon was singing his version of the Dell Vikings' recent hit 'Come Go with Me', but since he had only heard it on the radio, he had the words hopelessly wrong: 'Come go with me, down to the penitentiary ...,' he warbled. No one in Britain knew what a penitentiary was since it is not a word in English usage, though it seemed to occur in a lot of American R & B songs. What Norman Wright actually sang on the record was, 'Come go with me, don't let me pray beyond the sea.' John's line was probably better.

The police dogs showed how clever they were and Paul met up with Ivan Vaughan while the Quarry Men drank beer in the Scouts' hut before playing a second set at 5.45. After a further selection of skiffle and top-20 hits, the Quarry Men left the stage and walked across to the church hall, where they were due to play a set that evening as part of the fête. Ivan and Paul followed five minutes later and Ivan made the introductions.

Paul had just turned fifteen. His head was filled with rock 'n' roll, he had mastered his guitar and was able to demonstrate Eddie Cochran's 'Twenty Flight Rock' with the correct words and chord changes to an astonished sixteen-year-old John Lennon. Paul followed this up with Gene Vincent's 'Be Bop A-Lula' and a medley of Little Richard hits, all of which he had memorised. He and John began talking excitedly; neither of them had met anyone who cared about rock 'n' roll *that much* before. Despite the crucial eighteen-month difference in their ages – John was born on 9 October 1940 – John realised that what the Quarry Men needed if they were going to get anywhere was someone in the group who could play an instrument. After the Quarry Men played their second set they all went down the pub together, though Paul had to lie about his age.

A few days later Paul was out cycling and ran into Pete Shotton, one of the Quarry Men, who told him that John would like him to join the group. Paul said all right but he was going on his holidays first.

Paul's main reason for going to the Woolton fête was not to meet John Lennon but to try to pick up a girl. To this end he wore an outfit loosely modelled on the popular hit 'A White Sports Coat and a Pink Carnation', then regarded as the height of teen fashion. His white sports jacket had metallic threads which made the fabric sparkle. With it he wore very tight black drainpipe trousers. It was a far remove from the school uniform in which, like most teenage boys, Paul was obliged to wear most of the time. That consisted of grey trousers, which he took to a tailor to have narrowed as much as he could get away with without his father's complaining, a school tie and a blazer, which he also had skilfully altered. Paul: 'I took the badge off. I swear to God, I had a removable badge you could pin back on top to go to school. I also had to carry my school cap with me, folded neatly in the pocket, in case I saw a teacher and had to put it on.'

His hair was brushed back from the forehead and set with Brylcreem in a Tony Curtis cut, known as a DA or duck's arse. Other haircuts of the late fifties he could have considered included the crew cut (half an inch all over), a brush cut, the very un-PC 'nigger-wig' (very long and standing on end), and the TV cut (the hair shaped into two bunches meeting in a V on the forehead, a style popular with the teddy boys from Garston, who also affected the variant jelly-roll: hair greased, combed forward and rolled to make a floppy detumescent tube hanging over the forehead, as popularised by Gene Vincent and worn *ensemble* with a long DA); and the flat top (a long crew cut with the top level like the deck of an aircraft carrier).

At the age of fifteen Paul's knowledge of girls came largely from books.

> PAUL: I used to read books, sex manuals. My mum had this big book called *Black's Medical Dictionary*. I'd leaf through that and look up sex things. You'd have to go past graphic pictures of terrible operations and forceps on haemorrhoids, 'Oooo fucking hell!,' and people with terrible boils, 'Ohhhh', to get to the good bit, but to this day I still remember the 'mons veneris'. 'Can I have a peek at yer mons veneris then?' Very nice but quite old-fashioned. I remember being at some place baby-sitting somewhere and they had a book that said, 'the man should take his time' and 'the man should withdraw slowly'. Those were hints I got from that. It's your education.

Paul also had other, vaguely sexual memories of his mother.

PAUL: At night there was one moment when she would pass our
bedroom door in underwear, which was the only time I would
ever see that, and I used to get sexually aroused. Just a funny
little bit. I mean, it never went beyond that but I was quite proud
of it, I thought, 'That's pretty good.' It's not everyone's mum
that's got the power to arouse. I never saw her naked. I saw my
father naked once or twice in the bath, and it was quite a shock.
You just didn't see your parents naked. It's not like me and my
kids. I will be naked around them. I think it's really healthy
because we don't have anything to be ashamed of.

For boys in their mid-teens, most of their sex education came from
their peers: skewed anatomical knowledge, improbable dirty jokes,
stories of dubious authenticity about girls they barely knew, and of
course masturbation circles. John's crowd tended to meet at Nigel
Whalley's house in Vale Road, near Menlove Avenue. Nigel played
tea-chest bass with the Quarry Men until he abandoned his
instrument in the road one day trying to escape from two Woolton
teddy boys. He took on the role of managing the Quarry Men instead.
His father was a chief superintendent, head of Liverpool Police A
Division, whose duties meant that his teenage son was often left alone
in the house at night.

PAUL: We used to have wanking sessions when we were young at
Nigel Whalley's house in Woolton. We'd stay overnight and
we'd all sit in armchairs and we'd put all the lights out and being
teenage pubescent boys we'd all wank. What we used to do,
someone would say, 'Brigitte Bardot.' 'Oooh!' that would keep
everyone on par, then somebody, probably John, would say,
'Winston Churchill.' 'Oh no!' and it would completely ruin
everyone's concentration.

(John later took that experience and used it as the basis for his skit
'Four in Hand' in Kenneth Tynan's 'entertainment' *Oh! Calcutta!*
Tynan copped out and substituted the Lone Ranger for John's
original Winston Churchill; nor did he follow John's suggestion that
they should actually masturbate on stage. Kathleen Tynan said that
Ken's original idea for *Oh! Calcutta!* included Harold Pinter as
director, Peter Blake or Allen Jones to design the décor and Paul to
provide the music; none of which happened.)

Paul was to find that being in a group helped a great deal as far as meeting girls was concerned, and it was not long before he was able to graduate to the real thing. He had missed the first appearance of the Quarry Men at the Cavern because he and his brother Michael were away at Scout camp in Hathersage, in the Peak District. Apart from duetting with Michael in a talent competition at Butlins Holiday Camp in Filey, Yorkshire, in August 1957 – they sang the Everly Brothers' 'Bye Bye Love' as the McCartney Brothers – Paul's first time on stage was on 18 October 1957, when the Quarry Men played the Conservative Club premises at New Clubmoor Hall in Norris Green, Liverpool. Though they didn't exactly take Liverpool by storm, the Quarry Men went on to play enough gigs to get to know the attractions of being in a rock 'n' roll band as the girls in the audience introduced themselves after the set. They were even invited back to the Conservative Club.

Paul's little black book began to fill with names.

PAUL: I remember I had a girlfriend called Layla, which was a strange name for Liverpool. She was slightly older, and buxom, and she used to ask me to help her go and baby-sit, which was a code word. Baby-sit was a very good situation. There were a couple of other early girlfriends; there was Julie Arthur, who was the niece of Ted Ray, the comedian, who's from Liverpool. She was nice. They were nice girls. There they were, suddenly sprouting things to be interested in. The baby-sitting was the big thing, everyone was out and you had the house to yourself so it was the big opportunity, but you always had to be on the lookout for a key turning in the door, 'Ohhhh, sorry!' because if you were caught with your pants down, that would be the ultimate disgrace. That never quite happened but it was a near thing a couple of times.

We always said the only reason to be in a group was to not have a job and to get girls. So when you did a gig, you'd play and you'd try and pick up a girl. And after the show, maybe, it was a knee-trembler, as it's called, in an alleyway or round the back of some shed or garage. In the early days there was no hotel or motel to go to, that was out of the question. You couldn't go back to her house or your house because the parents were nearly always in. I remember meeting some strange girls in those early days. One girl had a girdle on. I'd never met anyone with a girdle before, and that had to be overcome. Fumbling teenage fingers, it was a damn good barrier.

The first thing Paul did was teach John how to tune his guitar; previously John had paid a musically inclined neighbour to do it for him. Once they were both in tune, they began to practise their guitar playing in earnest. John was using two-finger banjo chords taught to him by his mother Julia. She had also taught him to play banjo versions of his two favourite songs, 'Little White Lies' and 'Girl of My Dreams'; Paul was not the only one to grow up with an affection for the old standards.

Paul knew many more guitar chords but, being left-handed, he knew them all in reverse. John had to learn them backwards and then mentally transpose them for a right-handed player. It took a long time but they persevered.

PAUL: We literally once went across town for a chord, B7. We all knew E, A, but the last one of the sequence is B7, and it's a very tricky one. But there was a guy that knew it, so we all got on the bus and went to his house. 'Hear tell there's a soothsayer on the hill who knows this great chord, B7!' We all sat round like little disciples, strum strum. 'How's he doing it?' And we learned it.

Another thing we went across town for was the record 'Searchin'' by the Coasters. Nobody had it. The drummer in the Quarry Men, Colin Hanton, knew some guy that had it, but we had to get on the bus, do two changes of bus routes. Didn't matter. Half an hour away. There was such a passion about that song 'Searchin''. So we got the words, and I think we also stole the record. It was his foolishness for leaving it round. 'Doesn't he know we're hoodlums? Why would he leave it around? Foolish boy!' But I think this dedication is what separated the Beatles from a lot of the other bands.

These memories probably date from the first few months of Paul and John's friendship; the Coasters record, for instance, was released in May 1957, two months before they met, so they probably looked for it shortly after getting together. It was obvious that John and Paul had finally found someone else on exactly the same wavelength, with the kind of deep mutual recognition that can sustain a friendship for many years. With a prescience born of conviction rather than arrogance, they quickly came to see themselves not as rock 'n' rollers but as a future Rodgers and Hammerstein.

Unusually, both Paul and John had written songs before they met, in an era when white performers rarely wrote their own material (artists like Chuck Berry, Little Richard or Fats Domino wrote their own, but Elvis never wrote a song in his life). Paul's knowledge of music, his songwriting and ability to play the piano obviously appealed to John, who must have seen music, and possibly songwriting, as a last chance to express himself creatively. He had failed all his exams at school. He knew he was not an artist and would not pass his intermediate examinations at art college, yet he had a tremendous creative drive that needed to go somewhere. However, it is unlikely that John would have worked for very long with someone he did not like, no matter how many chords they knew. And on Paul's side, here was someone with a quick intelligence. He appreciated John's acerbic wit, and his mother's death gave him the ability to understand John's anger over his abandonment by his parents. John's vulnerability matched his own deep-seated grief.

PAUL: People always assume that John was the hard-edged one and I was the soft-edged one, so much so that over the years I've come to accept that. But Linda said, 'You've got a hard edge, it's just not on the surface. I know, living with you all this time.' It's true, I can bite, I certainly have a hard side, and she said, 'And John had a very soft side too.' I think that's a much better analysis of it than most people have. John, because of his upbringing and his unstable family life, had to be hard, witty, always ready for the cover-up, ready for the riposte, ready with the sharp little witticism. Whereas with my rather comfortable upbringing, a lot of family, lot of people, very northern, 'Cup of tea, love?', my surface grew to be easy-going. Put people at their ease. Chat to people, be nice, it's nice to be nice. Which is the common philosophy for most people. But we wouldn't have put up with each other had we each only had that surface. I often used to boss him round, and he must have appreciated the hard side in me or it wouldn't have worked; conversely, I very much appreciated the soft side in him. It was a four-cornered thing rather than two-cornered, it had diagonals and my hard side could talk to John's hard side when it was necessary, and our soft edges talked to each other.

John was more introverted and much more willing to hurt someone in order to try and save his own neck, but this had never been a requirement for me, except running away from guys who would hit you physically. Mentally, no one could say much to hurt me, whereas with John: his dad wasn't at home, so it was 'Where's yer dad, you bastard?' And his mother lived with somebody and that was called 'living in sin' in those days, so there was another cheap shot against him. John had a lot to guard against, and it formed his personality; he was a very guarded person. I think that was the balance between us: John was caustic and witty out of necessity and, underneath, quite a warm character when you got to know him. I was the opposite, easy-going, friendly, no necessity to be caustic or biting or acerbic but I could be tough if I needed to be.

Not everyone approved of their friendship. John's Aunt Mimi disapproved because she thought Paul was a working-class lad who was encouraging her nephew to devote time to his guitar which should have been spent studying. According to Mike McCartney, Paul's father didn't take kindly to John at all: after one meeting he told Paul, 'He'll get you into trouble, son.' He was right, of course, but mostly it was just playing truant and harmless games. One of their games involved the telephone, a rarity in working-class homes, which had been installed for Mary's work as a midwife.

PAUL: I remember the great excitement at 20 Forthlin Road when we had the phone put in. I still remember the phone number: Garston 6922. George still remembers it. It's ingrained. John and I used to play pranks with our tape recorder: record stuff, then ring up people and play the tape recorder to them and record their answers on another tape. We were supposed to be making demos. We made one for Mr Popjoy, who was one of John's teachers from Quarry Bank. We had a message that said, 'That Mr Popjoy?' then there was a wait for some reaction. 'I'm calling about the bananas.' Then there was another pause. We'd put that to the speaker, call his number, and the minute we heard him answer we'd switch our recorder on and it would talk to him. We had a mike at the hearing end and we would record that, so we didn't know quite what he'd said until it was all finished but we could hear something going on. Then we'd just cut him off and listen back to it. It was great. 'Popjoy here. Yes? Can I help? Bananas? What bananas? I haven't ordered any bananas!'

John could also be a rude and difficult person to be around and Paul often found himself justifying his behaviour.

PAUL: I remember I had a girlfriend called Celia. I must have been sixteen or seventeen, about the same age as her. She was the first art-college girl I'd ever been out with, a bit more sophisticated. And we went out one evening and for some reason John tagged along, I can't remember why it was. I think he'd thought I was going to see him, I thought I'd cancelled it and he showed up at my house. But he was a mate, and he came on a date with this Celia girl, and at the end of the date she said, 'Why did you bring that dreadful guy?' And of course I said, 'Well, he's all right really.' And I think, in many ways, I always found myself doing that. It was always, 'Well, I know he was rude; it was funny, though, wasn't it?'

And George Harrison was another. There was this guy called Ritter who was in our group at school, and George was in the younger group, and I remember we'd been standing around at playground and I'd tried to introduce George to Ritter, introduce him into my peer group. And being a year younger it was kind of difficult. I said, 'Hey, this is George Harrison. He's a mate of mine. We get on the same bus together.' And we'd been sitting around, and George suddenly head-butted this friend of mine. I thought, Fuckin' hell. Now I'm sure he had a very good reason to do it. But afterwards I was going, 'No, he's all right really, you know?' I always had to stick up for these friends of mine. What might have been construed as good old-fashioned rudeness I always had to put down to ballsiness. I had to assume that my mates were a little bit wimpish and that George had done the right thing, for some reason.

From the very beginning Paul took on a particular conciliatory role in the group, one he was almost forced into, explaining away rudeness and bad behaviour, trying to get everyone to like them. Paul: 'I have a reputation now of being a PR man, which has grown over the years, because anything you promote, there's a game that you either play or you don't play. I decided very early on that I was very ambitious and I wanted to play.'

The Lennon and McCartney songwriting partnership began shortly after they met when Paul played 'I Lost My Little Girl' to John. Paul: 'I must have played it to John when we met and we decided to get together and see if we could write as a team.' They began writing and rehearsing during the long summer of 1957, while Paul was still on holiday from school and before John began his studies at art college. The Liverpool Institute and the art college were next door to each other in the same building so they were able to continue their rehearsals uninterrupted when term began, getting together in the canteen or an empty room to play their guitars. Songwriting was a different matter: for this they needed seclusion.

> PAUL: When John and I decided to start to try and write songs, the most convenient location to do this was my house in Forthlin Road. My father went out to work and this left the house empty all day, so I would take off school, sagging off, we called it, and John would take off from art college. Of course, the main requirement was for me to be in school whereas he, being in art college, didn't actually have to be there so it was my risk.

They would take the 86 bus to Forthlin Road. Paul would let them into the house; Paul and his brother had had their own keys to the Yale lock ever since their mother died. He and John would usually work in the living room, where there was a comfortable three-piece suite, a sofa and two armchairs, arranged in front of the fireplace. To the right of the fire was the television with a radio beneath it. The room was south-facing, with a large sash window which filled the room with afternoon light despite the lace curtains and full-length curtains that convention required To the left of the fireplace stood Jim's old upright piano.

There were three different types of wallpaper, ranging from floral through a Chinese willow pattern to imitation stone wall, chosen by Paul and Michael. A clock ticked on the mantelpiece, and there was a sheepskin rug in front of the tiled fireplace.

PAUL: Both my parents smoked and once a cigarette fell on the rug, which introduced me to the world of insurance claims because they asked, 'Did you do it on purpose or did a cigarette genuinely fall on it?' I remember we used to have what they called nickers, which were cigarettes that they'd nicked for later [the end had been pinched to put it out], and if I wanted a naughty smoke I could nick one of those, and that became another meaning of the word 'nick'. But they knew exactly how many cigarettes they'd left around, they were quite amazing that way. The smoking came from Merle Oberon, the gorgeous glamorous image in the movies, the smoke curling up in black and white ... and nobody then knew the connection with cancer.

My dad kept a couple of pipes in the top drawer of the nicely polished chest of drawers in the dining room, the drawer where the Prudential Insurance card and the birth certificates and the pens and the family photographs were kept. We didn't have any ciggies or anything and he always took his tobacco with him, so if we wanted to smoke we used to use Typhoo tea. We'd fill the pipes with Typhoo tea and light them, which made us cough and did nothing else, and we'd think we were right little rebels, doing that.

We would let ourselves in for the afternoon. My dad would probably finish at five and be home by about six. That meant that we had from two till about five, then we had to clean up and get out. That's a good three-hour session. John had a guitar bought from the want ads and its main claim to fame was that it was guaranteed not to split! It was a joke we always used to have. It was guaranteed not to split and by golly, it didn't! So it was not an awfully good guitar; neither was mine, but it didn't matter. I would either plonk a little bit on the piano or most of the time we would sit down opposite each other with our two guitars. And because I was left-handed, when I looked at John I would see almost a mirror image of myself, I'd be playing the guitar as it were upside-down, he'd be reading me, upside-down, so we could clearly see what each other was doing, almost what you were doing yourself, you could see yourself playing the chord D and you could see whether it looked good enough or whether you'd held it too long – 'Time to get off that chord, I think. Do an A.' So it was quite a useful visual aid.

We would sit down with a school notebook which I have to this day, an old tattered copybook, blue lines on white paper, and I would write down anything we came up with, starting at the top of the first page with 'A Lennon–McCartney Original'. On the next page, 'Another Lennon–McCartney Original'; all the pages have got that. We saw ourselves as very much the next great songwriting team. Which funnily enough is what we became! We started off, I think, with a song called 'Too Bad About Sorrows'. They all had very simple chord structures but we learned our craft that way.

There was one called 'Just Fun' we couldn't take any further: 'They said that our love was just fun / The day that our friendship begun / There's no blue moon / That I can see / There's never been / In history ...' 'Ooops! It's horrible, this is horrible.' When we heard that rhyme we just went off that song in a big way. We were never really able to fix it either. But they'd get written down and we'd play 'em. We'd say, 'Wow, we've written some songs, you know, d'you wanna hear them? "Said our love was just fun ..."' We'd do some good rhythm on the guitars, and we probably harmonised a little together, so, you know, for people who'd never seen anyone who could write songs before, we were probably quite a good little sideshow. So we just developed the art, gradually, gaining in confidence.

So we did this every so often through a number of months. We did 'Just Fun', 'In Spite of All the Danger', which I'd written more fully so John didn't have much of a look-in there. I did a very bad song called 'Like Dreamers Do' which the Applejacks did later. 'One After 909' was getting a little bit better, then came 'Love Me Do', which was the culmination of it when we finally got a song we could actually record. 'Love Me Do' was completely co-written. It might have been my original idea but some of them really were 50-50s, and I think that one was. It was just Lennon and McCartney sitting down without either of us having a particularly original idea.

John Lennon remembered differently, telling *Hit Parader*: 'Paul wrote the main structure of this when he was sixteen or even earlier. I think I had something to do with the middle eight.' 'Love Me Do' was written in 1958 when Paul was sixteen. It became the Beatles' first record to be released in Britain and it launched their career.

PAUL: We used to try and persuade people that we had about a hundred songs before 'Love Me Do'. That was a slight exaggeration. It was probably more like four – less than twenty anyway, but if you were writing off to journalists, 'Dear Sir, We have a beat combo you might be interested in writing up …' it sounded better to say, 'We have written over one hundred songs …'

We would write down the words and if we needed to we might write the name of the chords but we wouldn't really bother too much. We had a rule that came in very early out of sheer practicality, which was, if we couldn't remember the song the next day, then it was no good. We assumed if we, who had written it, couldn't remember it, what chance would an ordinary member of the public have of remembering it? And it was a rule we stuck to, right up until the introduction, years later, of Philips cassette recorders. That was a complete revolution in songwriting because you could just record it. It meant you remembered some bad songs. It was a good rule because it meant that we had to write stuff that was memorable and one of us would invariably remember it so the two of us were like each other's tape recorders. The only thing that we would sometimes do to notate was literally write the name of the note over each word, we didn't have any tempo, you'd just have to remember how it scanned and its metre. So over 'She was just seventeen. …' it would be G, A, A …, but that didn't happen very often.

We loved doing it, it was a very interesting thing to try and learn to do, to become songwriters. I think why we eventually got so strong was we wrote so much through our formative period. 'Love Me Do' was our first hit, which ironically is one of the two songs that we control, because when we first signed to EMI they had a publishing company called Ardmore and Beechwood which took the two songs, 'Love Me Do' and 'P.S. I Love You', and in doing a deal somewhere along the way we were able to get them back.

'P.S. I Love You' was the B side of 'Love Me Do' and was also written several years before the Beatles got a recording contract.

PAUL: It's just an idea for a song really, a theme song based on a letter, like the 'Paperback Writer' idea. It was pretty much mine. I don't think John had much of a hand in it. There are certain themes that are easier than others to hang a song on, and a letter is one of them. 'Dear John' is the other version of it. The letter is a popular theme and it's just my attempt at one of those. It's not based in reality, nor did I write it to my girlfriend from Hamburg, which some people think.

I wrote a few instrumentals: 'Cat Call' was one of those, then there was something called 'Cayenne Pepper', but those tended to be me writing tunes by myself. When John and I got together, it was songs. John liked instrumentals; he used to do a mean 'Harry Lime Theme', which we ended up playing in Hamburg. It was his party piece. John was quite a good harmonica player, which showed itself in 'Love Me Do', though not really until then. He had a chromatic harmonica like a lot of kids around that time because of people like Larry Adler and Max Geldray on the radio. It was quite a popular instrument along with the trumpet.

Paul's father allowed the Quarry Men to rehearse at Forthlin Road. He had been in a band himself, so he understood the need. Since rehearsals were held in the evenings when Jim McCartney was at home, they would take place in the dining room, where Paul and John would write if they wanted to work in the evening. Paul: 'The one thing about our songs, they were always quite quickly written, they were never protracted affairs. It would all be over in a matter of hours, thank God. So we never worried, we never had a dry session, which is amazing actually. In all the years, we never walked away from a session saying, "Fuck it, we can't write one."'

There were a number of songs written in this early phase of the Lennon and McCartney partnership that didn't get completed until years later. One of these was 'I'll Follow the Sun' on the *Beatles for Sale* album.

PAUL: I remember writing that in our front living room at Forthlin Road on my own so that's pretty much all mine. On the record we got Ringo to tap his knees. We were thinking in terms of singles and the next one had to always be different. We didn't want to fall into the Supremes trap where they all sounded rather similar, so to that end, we were always keen on having varied instrumentation. Ringo couldn't keep changing his drum kit, but he could change his snare, tap a cardboard box or slap his knees. There were certain songs I had from way back that I didn't really finish up, but they were in the back of my mind. I've still got a couple of them now that I probably won't finish: 'Years Roll Along': 'It might have been winter when you told me …' 'I'll Follow the Sun' was one of those.

Paul and John did not restrict themselves to songs.

PAUL: We once tried to write a play. We sat down with another exercise book, and tried to write a play involving a Christ figure called Pilchard. The whole idea was that he was not going to appear. We only got two pages, but I can remember it quite clearly. There was the mother and the young daughter of the family sitting at home in a kind of John Osborne suburban parlour setting, and they're talking. Suddenly 'knock, knock, knock' comes on the door. 'Who's that?' 'Harold.' 'Oh, my God, it's not him again, is it?' Then he walks in, 'Oh, hello.' Enter left, unwanted Harold. And he's trying to laugh it off because he'd heard them say, 'Oh no, not him again.' He comes in making polite Pinteresque conversation. He says, 'Where's Pilchard?' 'Oh, he's upstairs praying again.' And we were going to have this character: the person upstairs who never comes in, and the play is just people talking about him and his terrible crisis. 'Oh, our Pilchard, you know, he's taken a turn. He's born again, and he really thinks he's the Messiah. He's upstairs praying.' This was the way it was going to go but we couldn't figure out how playwrights did it. The question was, do they work it all out and then work through the chapters or do they just write a stream of consciousness like we were doing? In which case, that was a fairly hard way to do it, because we ran out on the second page.

By the time they met, they had both had a go at writing: John was already composing his Lewis Carroll-inspired verses and stories and at school he had produced his own newspaper, the *Daily Howl*. Paul had also written a few things:

When I was at school I'd written a poem called 'The Worm Chain Drags Slowly'. It was this image of a conveyor belt with people coming out of one hole on a worm chain and disappearing down another. 'The young reappear on the backs of the old,' it was like that. I was looking at a lot of modern art, and I wanted to write a bit of poetry. And that was one of my pretensions. We were both just students doing things together.

The press image of the Mersey groups as rough, cheerful working-class lads in it for the 'crack' – the camaraderie, the good times and the girls – was generally accurate. Few of them saw it as a career or imagined it lasting very long at all. In contrast to most other Liverpool groups, the Beatles – or at least John, Paul and George – were grammar-school boys and though they were famous for enthusiastic partying there was also a level of introspection and seriousness not obvious in the other bands. John and Paul, particularly, were well read and took their songwriting seriously.

PAUL: I had stayed on at school because John had gone to art school and I'd seen a guy there who was twenty-four. He was an old man to us, we were all seventeen or eighteen. But it planted the idea in my mind, 'Ah, you can hang on till you're twenty-four, then you've got to get a job or something. Then the game is up.' So it was art college or any kind of college, after I'd done sixth form. But first I was in remove, because I didn't get enough exams to go into the sixth form. I stayed back a year with all younger kids, which was horrible. The thing I enjoyed most in the sixth form was the feeling of freedom, of being treated slightly more grown up, of being a little more independent.

All the other kids were sending off their applications to Durham University and Oxford and Cambridge but I didn't know you did that three or four months before, so I was way late. Our family had never been to university. It was during that time, A-levels time, I remember thinking, in many ways I wish I was a lorry driver, a Catholic lorry driver. Very very simple life, a firm faith and a place to go in my lorry, in my nice lorry. I realised I was more complex than that and I slightly envied that life. I envied the innocence.

I had the greatest teacher ever of English literature, called Alan Durband, who was a leading light in the Everyman

Theatre, when Willie Russell and everybody were there. He led the fund raising. He'd been taught at Cambridge by F. R. Leavis and used to talk glowingly of him. And he communicated his love of literature to us, which was very difficult because we were Liverpool sixteen-year-olds, 'What d'fuck is dat der?' He'd actually written a ten-minute morning story for the BBC, so I respected this guy. He was nice, a bit authoritarian, but they all had to be in our school because we would have gone had they not held us. We needed holding. He was a good guy.

His big secret, his clever move, was he told us about Chaucer's 'Miller's Tale'. I was wrestling with 'Whan that Aprille with his shoures soote, the droghte of March hath perced to the roote.' It was all done in the old language. He threw us into it without warning. He just said, 'Here's what we're going to do today: "A povre wydwe, somdeel stape in age, was whilom dwellyng in a narwe cotage ..." '

'What the fuck is that? It's German!' But to intrigue me, he told me about Nevill Coghill's translation. I loved having the answers. If you want to get me to learn, give me the answers. I was all right then. He said, 'Look at "The Miller's Tale"' because he knew bawdy young lads would like that:

> Dark was the night as pitch, as black as coal,
> And at the window out she put her hole,
> And Absalon, so fortune framed the farce,
> Put up his mouth and kissed her naked arse,
> Most savorously before he knew of this.
> And back he started. Something was amiss;
> He knew quite well a woman has no beard,
> Yet something rough and hairy had appeared.

'What's this? I *love* this book!' So I totally loved Chaucer after that. Chaucer was my man, and I could get into this strange 'Ful semyly hir wympul pynched was'. I was interested to hear what a wimple was, it was one of those hats, 'They old conical hats, great! Eh!' So he got me fascinated. Then we got into Shakespeare. We did *Hamlet*, which I immediately started to eat up. I became a director in my own mind. I started reading a lot of plays, Oscar Wilde's *Salome*, Tennessee Williams's *Camino*

Real, then a lot of Shaw's stuff, Sheridan, Hardy. We did a lot of great people that year and I got my only A level in English. Art I failed. I didn't realise there was going to be a written paper. I'd put it all into being able to draw or paint. But enjoyed myself when I was there.

When my daughter Mary was doing Shakespeare, I said she should get a translation, like the Coghill, so she went and bought one and what was it called? *Shakespeare Made Easy* by Alan Durband. Amazing! It was a lovely little tie-up of the circle.

Paul did not just read playscripts, he regularly attended the Liverpool Playhouse and the Royal Court, where he would sit up in the shilling seats by himself.

PAUL: I was quite a lone wolf on all of that. I never used to go with anyone. I couldn't find anyone who wanted to go! At the Playhouse you used to have to go out on the stairwell to smoke in the interval and I remember on the stairwell for the first time in my life hearing someone say 'Crikey!' I thought it was just in books! But it was the Liverpool theatre crowd: 'It was very good, wasn't it, but crikey, did you see that fella?'

I'd take a bus to the Pier Head, go on the ferry by myself. I'd take a book of poetry, or a play, or something to read, come back on the ferry, take a bus home. Think of myself as a bit of a poet, observing people, sit on a bench and write a little bit about what I saw. I was very conscious of gathering material. I didn't know then what it would be for. I really fancied myself as an artist. I was preparing. I didn't know how the hell I was ever going to achieve it from my background. People didn't become this. But my mind was full of it, it was an intoxication.

There were millions of characters in Liverpool. I lived about a half-hour from the centre and I remember there was a great guy got on the bus once. All he did was recite comedians' names to himself on the packed bus, 'Tony Hancock! Ha ha ha haaa! Tommy Cooper! Ha ha ha, hmmmph!' He was just talking to himself but by the time he got off, the bus was just heaving. Then there was a guy walking along thinking he had a parrot on his shoulder, 'Hello! Pretty Polly!' and there was no parrot there.

I'd buy books from Philips Son & Nephews: *Under Milk Wood,* a lot of Dylan Thomas; John Steinbeck; a little bit of

Samuel Beckett, *Waiting for Godot*. Or I'd steal them. There was a bookshop you could go in and very easily nick them. Gerald Hoffnung's cartoons was the first book I stole. I'd go to lectures. I went to a lecture on Le Corbusier at the university. I was trying to prepare myself to be a student. I had time, I'd do a little bit of work with the band, but I didn't know if I would actually get to university or get somewhere. What was my next thing gonna be? Teachers' training college?

The idea that the band could be made to develop into something serious had not yet occurred to them.

Menlove Avenue

Sometimes John and Paul would meet at John's house, which was about a mile away from Forthlin Road. They would cycle between each other's houses or take the ten-minute walk across the golf course, where they would occasionally play a round or two.

PAUL: Nine holes. We'd go round for a laugh. We weren't very good but we'd do it. It was there, like Mount Everest, so you do it. I'd also been there a few times to try and caddy but there were always ten kids ahead of me and by the time it came to my turn, the work had gone. You used to get ten shillings for caddying, which was a princely sum. John lived just the other side of the golf course, literally and metaphorically. People don't realise how middle-class he was. It's a very fancy neighbourhood.

The British obsession with class is something that mystifies foreigners and irritates a good many Britons, but at the time the Beatles started there were very clear class divisions drawn in Britain with a variety of subtle levels and subdivisions. Many Liverpudlians, for instance, found it highly amusing that John Lennon could release a song called 'Working Class Hero' when he himself came from a very comfortable middle-class background. He grew up at Mendips, a seven-room semi-detached house owned by his Aunt Mimi and Uncle George, at 251 Menlove Avenue, across the road from the golf course, in the pleasant leafy suburb of Woolton.

PAUL: I suppose John was the nearest to middle-class. The other three of us weren't. We were quite definitely working-class …

upper working-class. We were in a posh area but the council bit of the posh area. John was actually in one of the almost posh houses in the posh area. They had lived there for quite a while; in fact, John once told me that the family had once owned Woolton, the whole village!

John had a relative in the BBC, and somebody who was a dentist. His uncle Cissy Smith taught me handwriting and English at the Liverpool Institute. He was actually quite nice, quite charming, looking back on him, but we thought he was a total berk at the time. John played that down.

John described his background in the 1980 *Playboy* interview:

I lived in the suburbs in a nice semi-detached place with a small garden and doctors and lawyers and that ilk living around, not the poor slummy kind of image that was projected. I was a nice clean-cut suburban boy ... Paul, George and Ringo ... lived in government-subsidized houses. We owned our own house, had our own garden, and they didn't have anything like that. So I was a bit of a fruit compared to them.

The very name of the house, Mendips, betrayed its class aspirations: named not after one of the rugged mountains in the nearby Peak District but after a low range of hills in the prosperous south-west of England between the cathedral towns of Bristol and Wells, home of everything middle-class, comfortable and English.

Paul would go around the left side of the house to the back door, where Aunt Mimi would let him into a small conservatory which opened on to the kitchen and call, 'John, your little friend's here.'

PAUL: She would always refer to me as 'Your little friend'. I'd look at her, she'd smile. I'd know what she'd done. She'd know what she'd done. I would ignore it. It was very patronising, but she secretly quite liked me, she sort of twinkled, but she was very aware that John's friends were lower-class. John mixed with the lower classes, I'm afraid, you see. She was the kind of woman who would put you down with a glint in her eye, with a smile. But she'd put you down all the same. But she'd talk to John later and I remember him telling me, 'She thinks you're a better guitar player than I am,' which slightly miffed John. Did I say slightly?

A lounge led off of the kitchen and there was a front parlour containing Winston Churchill's collected works, bound in blue cloth, which John claimed to have read. John's middle name was Winston, given him by his mother in a fit of wartime patriotism. John and Mimi lived mostly in the lounge and kitchen.

PAUL: John had done a little poem that Mimi had framed in the kitchen. It was nice: 'A house where there is love ...' John had writing aspirations. At first he was writing what turned out later to be *In His Own Write*. He would show me what he'd been typing. I would sometimes help him with it. We would sit around giggling, just saying puns really, that's basically what it was; 'In the early owls of the Morecambe,' I remember, 'a cup o-teeth' was one section that was in the typewriter when I was around there. But I would like all that and I was very impressed.

He was a big Lewis Carroll fan, which I was too. In my view two of John's great songs, 'Strawberry Fields' and 'I Am the Walrus', both come from 'Jabberwocky'. 'I am he as you are he ...' It's thanks to 'Jabberwocky' that he could do that. I had a teacher at school, a swotty guy called Dodd, who could recite 'Jabberwocky' in Latin. One of the less useful things in life ...

I think John saw himself as 'Our correspondent from Alexandria'. It was a romantic dream that I understood and shared. 'I'll write about it as I see it and tell them all what's really happening.' It's a lot of people's dream.

It was a very catty household; John liked cats. They had pedigree Siamese cats, which again is slightly middle-class, if you think about it, rather than a puppy. There was always this slight feeling. His was *Aunt* Mimi, ours were all called *Aunty*: Aunty Edie, Aunty Jin, Aunty Milly, Aunty Flo. John had an Aunt Harriet, and Harriet was not a name we came across, especially when they called her Harrie! We never knew women called Mimi, she would have been called Mary. But Aunt Mary became Mimi, which is very sophisticated, very twenties and thirties, very jazz era. So it was Harriet and Mimi. I can imagine them with long cigarette holders. It was like Richmal Cromp-ton's *Just William* books to me. You read *Just William* books because you like that world. I'm not ashamed of it, I'm attracted by that. I think it's a rich world, the world of Varsity, the Racquet Club sort of thing. So John was a particularly attractive character in that kind of world. And John was the all-important year and a half older than me.

We'd often get in the little glass-panelled porch on the front door looking out on to the front garden and Menlove Avenue. There was a good acoustic there, like a bathroom acoustic, and also it was the only place Mimi would let us make noise. We were relegated to the vestibule. I remember singing 'Blue Moon' in there, the Elvis version, trying to figure out the chords. We spent a lot of time like that. Then we'd go up to John's room and we'd sit on the bed and play records, Fats Domino, Jerry Lee Lewis, Chuck Berry. It's a wonderful memory: I don't often get nostalgic, but the memory of sitting listening to records in John's bedroom is so lovely, a nice nostalgic feeling, because I realise just how close I was to John. It's a lovely thought to think of a friend's bedroom then. A young boy's bedroom is such a comfortable place, like my son's bedroom is now; he's got all his stuff that he needs: a candle, guitar, a book. John's room was very like that. James reminds me very much of John in many ways: he's got beautiful hands. John had beautiful hands.

Sometimes John and Paul would work on a song at Menlove Avenue but it was not as convenient as Forthlin Road. Paul: 'Physically it was always a bad idea for us to sit side by side on the bed in his bedroom. The necks of our guitars were always banging.' One of the early songs written in John's cozy, untidy bedroom above the porch was 'I Call Your Name'.

> PAUL: We worked on it together, but it was John's idea. When I look back at some of these lyrics, I think, Wait a minute. What did he mean? 'I call your name but you're not there.' Is it his mother? His father? I must admit I didn't really see that as we wrote it because we were just a couple of young guys writing. You didn't look behind it at the time, it was only later you started analysing things.

Not long after Paul joined the Quarry Men, he began a campaign to get his friend George Harrison into the group. George not only knew chords, but he could actually play solos. Around the time the Quarry Men played the Wilson Hall, Garston, on 6 February 1958, a sceptical John Lennon accompanied Paul on the bus to nearby Speke to check this out. George nervously performed 'Raunchy' by Bill Justis for them on the empty upperdeck of the bus. John was astonished. There was one big problem: George was only fourteen at the time and no way was John Lennon going to have a fourteen-year-old in his group. (George turned fifteen a few days later, on 23 February.) George, however, was determined; he showed up at every rehearsal, he followed John everywhere, even on dates where he was clearly not wanted. George's persistence paid off and within a month he was in the group.

It has been suggested that one of the reasons John finally relented was because Mimi hated George. If she was suspicious of Paul, with his good manners and easy-going way, then she was appalled by George, who was basically a 'right little teddy boy' with tight drainies and a drape jacket. He also had a thick Scouse accent, something that Mimi was determined that John would not acquire. Paul's mother had done the same, convinced that her sons would never do well with a 'common' accent like that.

Now that the Quarry Men had a soloist, a whole new range of songs could be added to their act. Together they studied the new records as they came out: they were in the middle of the golden age of rock 'n' roll and miniature masterpieces were being released each week: Buddy Holly's 'Peggy Sue', Elvis Presley's 'All Shook Up', Larry Williams's 'Bony Maronie', Little Richard's 'Lucille' … They would note down the words, analyse the chord changes and in many cases added them to their act, particularly songs by Chuck Berry or Little Richard. By 1960 the Quarry Men had a repertoire of over a hundred songs, including some quite obscure cuts, such as the Jodimars' 1956 'Clarabella', which Paul sang, as well as half a dozen of their own compositions.

Though John was brought up by his Aunt Mimi, his mother was a frequent visitor to Mendips, dropping round most days for a cup of tea and a chat with her sister. When John was five years old Julia Lennon had moved in with her boyfriend John 'Bobby' Dykins. He did not want to bring up another man's son so Julia arranged for her sister to care for the boy. John never got over the double trauma of first losing his father, whom Julia threw out when he returned from sea, and then being given away by his mother. Since adolescence John had been visiting his mother at her house in Blomfield Road in Allerton and spent most weekends and holidays with her. 'Twitchy' Dykins, as John called him, gave him weekly pocket money, and John enjoyed being with his younger half-sisters Julia and Jacqui. John and his mother were close and loving, but though he adored her, the relationship was a slightly uneasy one because he felt that she had abandoned him.

> PAUL: His mum lived right near where I lived. I had lost my mum, that's one thing, but for your mum to actually be living somewhere else and for you to be a teenage boy and not living with her is very sad. It's horrible. I remember him not liking it at all. John and I would go and visit her and she'd be very nice but when we left there was always a tinge of sadness about John. On the way back I could always tell that he loved the visit and he loved her but was very sad that he didn't live with her. Being John, he didn't admit to it much unless it was a very quiet or drunken moment when he felt he could let his guard down. He loved his Aunt Mimi, I know he did, but she was always the surrogate. John later tried primal screaming to discover how he felt at being left by his mother.

John was waiting for his mother at her house when she was killed. Julia Lennon died on 15 July 1958, on her way home after visiting her sister at Mendips, knocked down and killed by a policeman on Menlove Avenue. He was late for duty and was speeding, but he was a learner driver not qualified to drive without supervision; when he saw her crossing the road he accidentally stamped on the accelerator instead of the brake. He got off with a reprimand. John was totally devastated. He was seventeen.

> PAUL: It's very sad because he really did dote on his mum. Julia was the light of John's life, he idolised her: 'Julia' was his mother's song. She was a beautiful woman with long red hair. She was fun-loving and musical too; she taught him banjo chords, and any woman in those days who played a banjo was a special, artistic person. It was bohemian to do that. John and I were both in love with his mum. It just knocked him for six

when she died. I always thought it was bad enough my mother dying and what I had to go through, but that was an illness so there was some way you could understand it, but in John's case, the horror of reliving that accident ... Oh, my God! That always stayed with me.

Years later John told *Playboy*:

I lost her twice. Once as a five-year-old when I was moved in with my auntie. And once again at seventeen when she actually physically died ... That was a really hard time for me. It just absolutely made me *very*, very bitter. The underlying chip on my shoulder that I had as a youth got *really* big then. Being a teen-ager and a rock 'n' roller *and* an art student and my mother being killed just when I was reestablishing a relationship with her.

John had never known Paul's mother but now they had a tragic experience in common.

PAUL: Now we were both in this; both losing our mothers. This was a bond for us, something of ours, a special thing. We'd both gone through that trauma and both come out the other side and we could actually laugh about it in the sick humour of the day. Once or twice when someone said, 'Is your mother gonna come?', we'd say, in a sad voice, 'She died.' We actually used to put people through that. We could look at each other and know.

John began drinking heavily; his work at college had never been very good and now he just didn't bother. He began to act the teddy boy. John had a three-quarter-length drape jacket which he wore with skin-tight black drainies and fluorescent green socks, making him look top-heavy. It was quite a convincing guise.

PAUL: The image was a protective measure. You could get hit if you didn't look hard. He wore big long sidies and so we looked up to him as a sort of violent teddy boy, which was attractive at the time. At art college he was considered to be a bit of a hot-head. He got drunk a lot and once he kicked the telephone box in, which got him a reputation. He was a bohemian teddy boy at art school.

John neglected the group and for the next fifteen months the Quarry Men had no commercial bookings. Aside from rehearsals, the only time they played was at private parties. Paul and John still saw a lot of each other, getting together to play records, to rehearse and write. It was a time of dating girls, playing rock 'n' roll, furtive cigarettes, all-night raves, beer, and stealing records at parties.

Though John neglected his studies at art school, he did become involved with art-school life and began seeing a lot of his fellow student Stuart Sutcliffe, a painter whose work was already showing great promise. John began to hang out at art-student flats in Liverpool 8, the run-down area around the massive new Anglican cathedral in the centre of the city. These were bare, bohemian places, with naked bulbs, dirty floorboards and a mattress in the corner, where the curtain was an old blanket tacked over the window and the furniture was sometimes burned to provide warmth. The once grand merchants' houses around Percy Street, Huskisson Street and Canning Street were now the scene of intense all-night talks and as much debauchery as could be managed on a meagre art-school grant.

Stuart lived in Gambier Terrace in a building filled with would-be beatniks. One of his paintings was selected for the biennial John Moores exhibition held at the Walker Gallery in Liverpool from November 1959 until January 1960, and at the end of the show, John Moores bought Stuart's canvas for £75, a huge amount of money at that time. One night at the Casbah Coffee Club, John and Paul used their considerable skills to persuade Stuart to spend the money on a Hofner President bass and join the band. Stuart had little talent for playing, but the bass looked good and Stuart began acting as a booking agent for the group. The Quarry Men used Stuart's flat to practise in and John often stayed over since it was very close to the art college.

PAUL: This was now student-flat time, so this was taking apart a Vic inhaler and putting it in a glass of water and getting the Benzedrine out of it. You're supposed to stay up all night and talk. Well, we did that anyway. I don't remember, probably they didn't give me that much, probably they kept it for themselves. Also I was very frightened of drugs, having a nurse mother and thinking, I'm really hanging out with a slightly older crowd here, so I was always cautious.

Paul had turned seventeen in the summer of 1959 and there had been a slight improvement in the fortunes of the group: through September and October they played a series of seven Saturday-night engagements at the Casbah Coffee Club at 8 Hayman's Green, West Derby, Liverpool, a youth club organised by Mona Best, the mother of Pete Best, who later became the Beatles' drummer during their Hamburg days. The group went through a period of experimenting with names. At the end of 1959, the Quarry Men became Johnny and the Moondogs for one night in order to appear on a Carroll Levis talent show, which, had they won, could have led to an appearance on Carroll Levis's *Discoveries* TV show. Levis did not discover them. In April 1960, in another short-lived incarnation, John and Paul performed together as the Nerk Twins.

This happened at the Fox and Hounds, a pub run by Paul's cousin Elizabeth, known as Bett, and her husband Mike Robbins, in Caversham, near Reading. Mike and Bett were Paul's first link to show business. Mike had worked as a stand-up comedian and been on the radio a few times. He met Bett when they were both working as Redcoats at Butlins Holiday Camp in Pwhelli, the site of Paul's first appearance on stage as a performer with his brother Michael in 1957. Mike and Bett left Butlins and went to run the Fox and Hounds, and Paul and John hitch-hiked down to stay with them during the school and college holidays of 1960.

> PAUL: John and I used to hitch-hike places together, it was something that we did together quite a lot; cementing our friendship, getting to know our feelings, our dreams, our ambitions together. It was a very wonderful period. I look back on it with great fondness. I particularly remember John and I would be squeezed in our little single bed, and Mike Robbins, who was a real nice guy, would come in late at night to say good night to us, switching off the lights as we were all going to bed. And I'd ask, 'Mike, what was it like when you were on with the Jones Boys?' – a group that I knew he'd appeared with because I'd got a cutting. And he'd say, 'Oh, it was really good ...' and he'd tell stories of showbiz. He was the only person we had to give us any information. I think for John and I, our show-business dreams were formed by this guy and his wife. Mike Robbins has an awful lot to answer for!

John and Paul worked in the bar all week and Mike Robbins gave them a fiver each, good money then, and on the Saturday night they performed in the taproom with their acoustic guitars as the Nerk Twins, opening with an instrumental version of the Les Paul and Mary Ford hit 'The World Is Waiting for the Sunrise'. They did a lunchtime session the next day before setting off to hitch back to Liverpool. Not long afterwards, Mike and Bett became the publicans of the Bow Bars, on Union Street in Ryde on the Isle of Wight, and Paul and John hitch-hiked down again to stay with them. (Paul's brother spent the summer of 1961 working there as a short-order cook.) It was a journey which in due course would reappear, punningly, in the Beatles 1965 single 'Ticket to Ride'.

On their return to Liverpool, there was another name change and at Stu and John's suggestion the Quarry Men became the Beatles, later changed for an audition with Larry Parnes to the Silver Beatles. They played as the Silver Beats, the Silver Beetles, Silver Beatles and finally, in August 1960, once again the Beatles.

When Paul, George and Ringo were working on the *Anthology* TV series in 1994, they looked up the origin of the word Beatles. Over the years many theories had evolved, but one thing they knew for sure was that it was inspired by Buddy Holly and the Crickets.

PAUL: I remember talking to John about this. 'Cricket. What a fantastic idea, it's a little grasshopper, and it's a game.' Well, they came over, they had no fucking idea cricket was a game, to them it was just a little chirping grasshopper from Texas, so it was actually quite a boring name. But we were turned on like nobody's business by the idea of a double meaning, so with our wit and wisdom and whatever, we wanted something that would have a double meaning. Beetles were little insects, so that took care of that, but with an 'A' it became something to do with beat. That's the commonly accepted theory given by John in his biblical 'It came in a vision – a man appeared on a flaming pie and said unto them, "From this day on you are Beatles with an A."'

But recently, another theory has emerged. We were into the Marlon Brando film *The Wild One*, particularly John and Stuart, and in that they use the word beetles, and we think that kind of clinched it. It was John and Stuart one night at their art-school flat. I remember being told next day the new idea for the name. It definitely wasn't my idea. I said, 'Oh, great, marvellous.' So in examining this question for the Beatles *Anthology*, we looked at the film:

LEE MARVIN (*to Marlon Brando*): You know I've missed you. Ever since the club split up I've missed you. Did you miss him?
MOTORCYCLE GANG: Yeah!
LEE MARVIN: We all missed you. (*Points to the girls in the gang.*) The beetles missed yuh, *all* the beetles missed yuh. C'mon, Johnny, let's you and I ...

So I got this terrible thought, Fuck me, it's biker's molls. I had to make notes for the *Anthology* and I was watching the video and I wrote in my notes, 'Does "beetles" mean girls or guys?' The director looked it up and found that in forties American slang 'beetles' are girls. It's like 'chicks'. We were actually named after girls, which I think is fabulous. None of us noticed it.

In July 1960, the national Sunday tabloid the *People* ran an exposé headlined, 'The Beatnik Horror, for though they don't know it they are on the road to hell,' illustrated by a carefully posed photograph taken in the flat below Stuart Sutcliffe's. A teenage John Lennon can be seen lying on the floor. The paper commented, 'Most beatniks like dirt. They dress in filthy clothes. Their "homes" are strewn with muck. This, for example, is the flat of a beatnik group in Liverpool. The man on the extreme left, Allan Williams, is a little out of place in these surroundings. He is the only one who is not a beatnik and who dresses in clean clothes.'

Allan Williams was the one who set up the photograph; he had been managing the Silver Beetles, as they were then, since May. Williams owned a small club called the Jacaranda in Slater Street, off Bold Street, where the group frequently hung out. It had the kind of bohemian atmosphere they liked and also did very good sandwiches. Allan Williams already managed or acted as booking agent for a number of other acts, so it was easy for him simply to add the Silver Beetles to his list. The core of the group was now John, Paul, George and Stuart Sutcliffe. They were having problems finding a drummer.

As a result of Allan Williams's involvement, they began to get gigs. In May 1960, he sent them out to back their fellow Liverpudlian

Johnny Gentle, then managed by the London impresario Larry Parnes (known in the trade as 'Larry Parnes, Shillings and Pence'), on a tour of Scotland. It was their first experience of the rigours of being on the road and though it was a financial and musical disaster, they were not deterred. For the tour they assumed stage names; George borrowed the name of his hero Carl Perkins to become Carl Harrison, Stu became Stuart DeStael, after the then fashionable painter, and Paul, for a laugh, chose Paul Ramond. Amusingly the Ramones punk band later used this as the inspiration for their name.

Williams had booked them into a series of Saturday Night, Big Beat Night, gigs at the Grosvenor Ballroom, Liscard, Wallasey, across the Mersey in the Wirral; a venue famous for the violence of its patrons.

PAUL: We were quite used to fights. Funnily enough, it was always when we did a song called '(Baby) Hully Gully' by the Olympics. We'd get to the line 'Hully, hully gully ...' and bam! Rumble! It was basically two sides of a village dance hall: girls and boys or sometimes the Bootle teds and the Garston teds, or somebody would ask the wrong girl to dance. We used to see flying crates and beer bottles and glasses. We always kept out of it, but it would often bubble its way to the front of the stage, then someone would get on the mikes, they all wanted to get on the mikes. I remember we were playing the Grosvenor Ballroom and this ted jumped on stage and grabbed my amp. I think he was going to use it as a weapon. It was only a small one, an Elpico, and I went to get it off him – 'Hey, my amp!' He said, 'One move and you're dead!' You know, in teenage years that was ... effective. 'All right, I don't want it then.' There was a lot of that.

Whenever he couldn't find them a booking, Williams put them into his own club, the Jac, but by the summer he had already found them more than three dozen gigs. The group began to dominate their lives and schoolwork took second place. Paul: 'At first we played little rock 'n' roll clubs, upbeat music really, nobody had done it before so that was enough.' For the Grosvenor Ballroom and the Scottish tour they had with them a drummer called Tommy Moore, but he left them after a couple of months because he could no longer stand John Lennon's ribbing, and his girlfriend thought he was wasting his time when he could be earning real money down at the bottle factory. He was replaced by Norman Chapman, who only played with them for three weeks before being conscripted into the army for his two years of National Service.

The ending of National Service in November 1960 meant that rock 'n' roll groups became a real possibility. Previously, just as a group would begin to get somewhere, its members would have to leave to serve two years in the armed forces. Given their age difference, the Beatles, could never have existed had National Service been maintained.

PAUL: I don't think there would have been the Beatles. I think we would have been a little group in Liverpool and if we'd been very lucky we'd have had some small success in the local clubs. But then just as we were getting somewhere Ringo and John, being the oldest two, would have had to go into National Service, followed shortly by me and then a year later by George and that would have split any chance of being a group.

I always thought it ruined Elvis. We liked Elvis's freedom as a trucker, as a guy in jeans with swivellin' hips, but didn't like him with the short haircut in the army calling everyone 'sir'. It just seemed he'd gone establishment, and his records after that weren't so good. 'Hard Headed Woman' – great title, we thought; Oh, this is going to be great! Then there's a dreadful great big trombone right in the middle of it, and we thought, Good God! What in hell has happened? We were very disappointed about that, and we never really thought he got it back. Then he went into films and we thought he went totally down the pan. And I assume that would have been the end for us too. So that was great luck, the government just stopped that in time, allowing us the parting of the waves, and we went through and we had the freedom and the sixties.

TWO

St PAULI AND
THE CAVERN

Hamburg changed us enormously.

Paul McCartney

Kaiserkeller

BRUNO KOSCHMIDER WAS A CRIPPLED EX-CIRCUS CLOWN AND FIRE EATER who owned a number of strip clubs and porn cinemas in the St Pauli district of Hamburg. He needed live music for his clubs but German bands could only play oompah music or military marches. The cost of bringing rock 'n' roll bands from America would have been prohibitive but news reached him that reasonably authentic groups could be heard playing in London's Soho, so he turned to Britain instead. His first English rocker was Tony Sheridan, a veteran of Marty Wilde's backing group and the *Oh Boy!* TV show. Koschmider met him at the 2-Is coffee bar in Soho and took him to Hamburg. He soon developed a large following and did good business for Koschmider at his club the Kaiserkeller, but one month later Sheridan defected to a rival. Koschmider returned to London to find more British groups. Allan Williams had already visited Koschmider when he travelled to Germany to find one of his acts, the Royal Caribbean Steel Band, who disappeared from Liverpool and then wrote to him from Hamburg telling him to send groups over to play. Now Williams ran into Koschmider again at the 2-Is and within a few days had another of his Liverpool bands, Derry and the Seniors, playing at the Kaiserkeller.

The results were very gratifying and Koschmider asked Williams for a group to revitalise another of his clubs, called the Indra. This time, Williams gave him the renamed Beatles: John Lennon, guitar and vocals; Paul McCartney, guitar and vocals; George Harrison, guitar and vocals; Stuart Sutcliffe, bass and vocals; and Pete Best, a new drummer, hired when the offer of the Hamburg season came up. It was Pete's mother who ran the Casbah, where the Quarry Men had had a residency in August 1959, after which Pete took over with his own group, the Blackjacks. When the offer of playing Hamburg came up, the Beatles were as usual caught short without a drummer. They knew Pete's group was breaking up so they called and asked Pete if he'd like to come to Hamburg with the Beatles. He jumped at the chance. He was to be a member of the Beatles for exactly two years before being unceremoniously dropped in favour of Ringo Starr.

Paul had to do some fancy talking before Jim would allow him to go. None of the group had ever been abroad. Allan Williams was driving them and their equipment out there in his van, but he did not intend to stay. Still, Paul was level-headed and unlikely to get himself into trouble. At the age of 18 Jim himself had already worked for four years and Paul's promised wages were good. The two-month contract was for £2.50 per day per man, out of which Allan Williams would receive ten per cent. This was more than Jim was earning himself so he set aside his misgivings.

For the next two years or so, beginning 17 August 1960, the Beatles were to divide their time between Liverpool and Hamburg. Though their later residency at the Cavern Club in Liverpool would be of vital importance in building a group of loyal fans, it was the 800 hours on stage in Hamburg that transformed them into a world-class act. This was where the early Beatles image evolved: the black leather suits, Paul's distinctive violin-shaped Hofner bass and John's Rickenbacker were both bought there, so were and it was there that they cut their first record. In Hamburg they got their first scattering of intellectuals in their audience and Hamburg also placed them in the front line of what would become the sixties sexual revolution.

The Indra was on the Große Freiheit, a narrow cobbled street of strip clubs and working-class bars in the St Pauli red-light district, separated from the River Elbe by a maze of tiny streets filled with bars, clubs and brothels where young women sat in picture windows. Number 64 was at the quiet end of the street away from the Reeperbahn, the main street leading to the city centre. It was a small, shabby strip club, with only four tables to the right and two on the left before you reached the pocket stage and dance floor. The rest of the room was taken up by five banquettes, each table dimly lit by a small table lamp with a little red lampshade. Heavy curtains concealed the stage and there was thick carpeting. It was doing badly as a strip club so Koschmider decided to try it as a rock 'n' roll club. For a rock band it was an acoustic nightmare because the heavy drapes muffled the sound. Only sixty people could be seated in comfort, but this was not a problem because when the Beatles first arrived there were only two people in the place. It was up to the Beatles to make a go of it.

> PAUL: We were always trying to attract people in. This was one of the great learning experiences for us, to attract people who don't really want to see you. It came in handy later when we were doing something for people who *had* come to see us. The first thing people would look at was the beer price, 'Oh, *ein Mark* ...' Then they'd look around and there would be no one in the club and we'd jump into action, 'Yes! Yes! This is the night! Come on in!' You really have to learn that, and by God we learned it and we really had those clubs jumping.

Derry and the Seniors were playing the Kaiserkeller when the Beatles arrived. Their manager, Howie Casey, remembered how the Beatles looked: 'When they first arrived in Hamburg they had very very pointed shoes in grey crocodile, mauve jackets, black shirts and pants. The length of their hair caused a great stir around the area – it was thick at the back, almost coming over their collars.'

The accommodation was appalling. Bruno owned a run-down cinema called the Bambi Kino, just around the corner at 33 Paul-Roosen Straβe, where the group slept in three airless dressing rooms which had not been cleaned since the long-ago days when the Bambi functioned as a real theatre. They used the cinema toilets to wash. They had a tough schedule: 8.30 p.m. until 9.30, take a half-hour break and back on stage from 10.00 until 11.00; another half-hour off, then play from 11.30 until 12.30, break and a final set from 1.00 until 2.00, seven nights a week. The curtains and carpet may have absorbed much of the excitement of the music, but it did little to dampen the volume and the old woman who lived upstairs was immediately on the telephone to the police. Though Bruno was well connected with the local police, she pestered them with calls until his normally amicable relations with the department became strained. The Beatles logged forty-eight nights on stage before Bruno finally switched the Indra back to a sex club after being told that he would be closed down if the situation did not change.

The old woman was happy to have nice quiet strippers beneath her again and the Beatles were happy because they now got to play at the much larger, and comparatively luxurious, Kaiserkeller, alternating one hour on, one hour off, with Rory Storm and the Hurricanes, who had replaced Derry and the Seniors when their contract expired.

'*Mach Schau! Mach Schau!*' Bruno Koschmider would yell, imitating their manager Allan Williams's exhortations to 'Make a show, lads!', and they did. All traces of English reserve vanished as the Beatles staged mock fights, leaping on each other's backs, feigned arguments and jumped into the audience with the mike. They quickly learned how to pace their act, to include show tunes and ballads to give themselves a breather, to stretch out and keep up the excitement level by picking songs they could improvise upon at length. A recent addition to their act was Ray Charles's 'What'd I Say', which was released in the USA in November 1959.

PAUL: I first heard it played by British disc jockey David Jacobs. And he was so hip because he played the other side as well, it keeps going 'Hey hey hey, c'mon, He-eyy'. I immediately wrote down 'Ray Charles' and went to the record shop the next day and bought the single. This was a huge record for us, we lived off that record in Hamburg, that was our show song. The joke in Hamburg was to see how long anyone could keep it going. One night we did it for over an hour. We used to disappear under tables with the hand mike, 'Woooohhh!' We used to work the hell out of it. It's just such a great number, there's just so many great segments in it, it's like an eight-movement bloody symphony, that thing. You've got the classic riff, then the rising chords! Well, that's enough already. But then it has the verse with the incredible singer and the 'Tell me what I say' chorus. Then comes 'Ohhho Hoho!' And that became our thing. We got very very drunk and kept it going for hours and hours and they loved it. The Germans just ate it up, it was very very popular.

Jerry Lee Lewis's 'Whole Lotta Shakin' Goin' On' was also given the full treatment; stretched to last half the set, with John and Paul leading the audience in a clap-along.

Hamburg changed more than just their music. It was there that the early Beatles image was formed: a dark, slightly *noir*, rebellious look taken from the fashions of German teenagers. German youth in the late fifties and early sixties was divided into two camps: the Rockers and the Exis, each with their own culture and style. The Rockers were into fifties American rock 'n' roll; their heroes were Gene Vincent, Elvis Presley, James Dean, Marlon Brando in *The Wild One*. They combed their hair into greased DAs and wore the black leather jackets of their heroes with perhaps a nod to the black flight jackets of wartime Luftwaffe pilots. It was the style of the rebel, the greaser cowboy, tough, aggressive, visceral, and macho in the extreme. Their territory was the working-class bars and rock 'n' roll clubs of the St Pauli district. Their traditional enemies were the Exis, the student types who hung out in jazz clubs.

The Exis, short for Existentialists, modelled themselves on the habitués of St-Germain-des-Prés, the Paris Left Bank literary crowd which centred on Jean-Paul Sartre, Simone de Beauvoir, Juliette Greco and Albert Camus. The Exis read Beckett, Genet, Artaud and the Marquis de Sade. They were students and artists; anti-establishment in a cerebral, intellectual way. They wore dark clothes, black turtleneck sweaters, tight-fitting corduroy, tight black trousers. Like the Rockers they also wore black leather jackets but in a short boxy style, rather than the oversize flight jackets of the Rockers. The men wore their hair brushed forward in the French fashion. They were cool, disengaged, impassive with no visible show of emotion; they were existentialists, or tried to be.

This was not how they described themselves – both names, Rockers and Exis, were slightly derogatory and were only used by one group to describe the other. The two groups had many things in common. They shared a passion for black leather: a German cultural tradition going back to Horst Buchholz, the German James Dean who wore a black leather jacket and trousers in the 1956 teenage gang movie *Die Halbstarken*, and before that the Red Baron and the flying aces of the Great War, not forgetting to mention the Nazi High Command in their leather greatcoats. They both thought of themselves as cool and unemotional, though the Rockers, fuelled by gallons of beer, often erupted into mindless violence, blowing their image completely. As far as the Rockers were concerned, the Exis were fair game and they beat them up whenever they had the opportunity.

The graphic designer Klaus Voorman was an art student and therefore automatically an Exi. He had argued with his girlfriend and was wandering around the port district of St Pauli, worrying about their relationship. As he strolled along Große Freiheit, he was intrigued by the music coming from the doorway to a basement rock club. Since this was Rocker territory he ventured down the stairs with some caution, but was rewarded by seeing Rory Storm and the Hurricanes, with Ringo Starr on the drum stool, doing their energetic best to entertain a room full of tough-looking Rockers and their girls.

Next on stage were the Beatles. Klaus was even more amazed by what he saw and heard. When the Beatles came off, he introduced himself and enthusiastically praised their music. He returned again the next day, bringing some record sleeves that he had designed. The day after that he brought with him his girlfriend Astrid Kirchherr and a friend, Jürgen Vollmer, who had been fellow students at the Hamburg Master School for Fashion, Textiles, Graphics and Advertising. Vollmer described the experience in his book *Rock 'n' Roll Times*: 'We descended into a strange territory. Everybody looked tough. Black leather jackets and duck-tails dominated. We were strangers in a strange place – and fascinated. We were careful to minimise our presence, exercising extreme discretion.'

Bruno Koschmider's Kaiserkeller was at Große Freiheit 36, on the corner of Schmuck-Straße. The narrow stairs led to the cloakroom and toilets, past the imposing figure of Horst Fascher, the club bouncer, and into a medium-sized, dimly lit room. Since Hamburg is a port, there was a predictable nautical theme: a boat-shaped bar, fishing nets and glass floats on the ceiling and brass portholes on the walls. To the right were three boat-shaped banquettes and a small stage. The dance floor was surrounded by heavy wooden tables and chairs. Jürgen Vollmer described the scene:

> For the rockers the Kaiserkeller was mainly a social place for drinking and dancing and picking up a girl. They were the stars. It was their place, and the rockbands had secondary importance … It wasn't done to glorify the musicians. They merely provided

the music for the atmosphere. Getting drunk and looking for a girl (and if that didn't prove successful, a fight). It was a mixture of bar and dance place. Predominant clothes were black leather jackets, black jeans, pointed shoes. The Beatles looked just like their audience.

Nobody but us sat right at the stage with such fixed attention, utterly absorbed in the music and the players. From then on we went almost every night and always sat at the closest table to the stage. It was also very practical in other aspects; when the frequent fighting among the Rockers became too heavy, we hid behind the piano ... We usually felt relatively safe once at the table, near The Beatles. Getting into the place, crossing it to that table and going to the bathroom, crossing it again, was when we felt most uncomfortable.

The atmosphere was menacing and dangerous; violent fights would erupt at the slightest provocation and the Rockers would hit each other with glass beer bottles and throw the heavy wooden tables at each other.

PAUL: Those clubs were pretty violent; you'd mainly get the violence with visiting servicemen. You could often tell what nationality they were by the smell of their cigarette smoke. You would smell English ciggies, Senior Service, in the club and you knew you might have trouble. The English guys would be very much on our side. 'Ow yes, English! Orrrright, lads, play this! Play this!' The more drunk they got, the more they'd start to think they owned the club, but of course the Germans don't like that. Nobody likes that. And there would come a point when they would get into an altercation with a waiter. The waiters had a system, a little whistle that could be blown and there would be ten waiters where there was once one. And they were all big body-building guys. They weren't chosen for their waiting abilities.

Horst Fascher, the bouncer, was a former featherweight boxer who had represented both Hamburg and West Germany in the ring. He had done time in jail for manslaughter after killing a sailor in a street fight; boxers are not allowed to hit anyone, their fists are classified as lethal weapons. Horst hired friends of his from the Hamburg Boxing

Academy as waiters, a terrifying group of men known as Hoddel's Gang.

PAUL: Horst Fascher was a very good friend of ours and we've kept up the friendship. I think probably the most surprising thing when we really got to know those people, and we got to know them very very well, was that they really loved us. They loved us like brothers. Leaving Hamburg was always terrible, particularly later because we were starting to get a bit good and everyone could sense this might be the last time they'd see us. All of them would be weeping, drunk, 'I love you guys so much, you're like my own brother. Have a drink.' Gangsters are very very sentimental guys. We made some really good friends.

In the event of trouble, Horst's waiters would quickly wade in to restore order; they carried spring-loaded truncheons and wore special heavy boots for kicking the protagonists when they were already down. They all carried tear-gas guns in case things got really out of hand and sometimes used them. Bruno Koschmider himself would occasionally join in, using a particularly lethal-looking black ebony truncheon.

For someone like Astrid Kirchherr it was a scary experience but somehow the Beatles made it all right. In her essay 'Seeing John Lennon Again' she wrote, 'Being the "daughter of a respectable family", I used to spend most of my time in chic, "existentialist" bars, and the idea of going to the run-down Kaiserkeller on Hamburg's notorious Reeperbahn gave me the creeps. But the moment I saw the Beatles on stage, any misgivings I might have had evaporated.'

PAUL: The people that we most liked were Astrid, Klaus and Jürgen. We'd play our set and go down and talk to them. Astrid was a very beautiful blonde Peter Pan girl in a little leather jacket and very tight-fitting tailored leather trousers. There was Klaus, who was kind of her boyfriend, and Jürgen, who was taller and very shy. Real nice people, all of them, and very very sensitive, very understanding, with a great admiration for us. They spoke good English. Perhaps a little faltering, but good.

Astrid: 'When they met Klaus and me, and later on our circle of artist friends, they were completely bowled over. Suddenly they realised that this country also had sensitive, attractive people in it.'

Astrid came from a wealthy family, had her own Volkswagen car and lived with her mother in a large house on the Eimsbüttelerstraße, within walking distance of St Pauli but in a whole different world. The Eimsbütte is an expensive residential area of the city and its very existence came as a surprise to the Beatles. Except to go for a row on the Außen-alster, a large lake in the middle of town, or on shopping trips to the centre, they had remained in the red-light district since they arrived two months earlier. 'That was an eye opener. We didn't realise Hamburg was so posh,' Paul said. 'We'd only seen the Reeperbahn.' In fact, Hamburg shared much with Liverpool: they had both been devastated by bombing during the war, their people were gritty survivors with an unbeatable sense of humour, they were both ports with the tolerance that comes from being a gateway to the world and the new ideas that arrive on each boat. But there the similarities ended: Liverpool was stuck in grinding poverty, not yet rebuilt, whereas Hamburg, a part of the post-war German economic miracle, was a wealthy city.

Astrid's room was painted black, with a black velvet bedspread and black sheets. Silver foil covered the walls and a large tree branch was suspended from the ceiling. Her library included the works of the Marquis de Sade and the existentialists and her large record collection consisted mostly of French chansons, jazz and classical recordings. Paul used to put on Stravinsky but John always took it off again. Some of her photographs were on the walls alongside paintings and sketches by her friends.

Paul: 'Astrid was a photographer and took really nice photos of us. And Jürgen was a photographer, brilliant photos. They were more interested in Stuart and John, they had the more teddy-boy faces. I was a little bit too baby-faced and didn't attract them as much.'

All the Beatles were attracted to Astrid. John called her 'the German Brigitte Bardot' because of her blonde hair and Bardot-like figure and though she and Stuart Sutcliffe quickly fell in love, she was also attracted to both John and George. Unfortunately for Paul, the Exis were not all that interested in him.

> PAUL: They had a particular love for Stu; John was number two, which is understandable. George was number three, which was a little bit miffing, because I had expected at least to get third … Life is very like that. I came fourth, just before Pete Best. Stuart

was entering the good-looking period. Earlier than that he looked a bit pimply and art-studenty. He had never been number one in our pecking order. Pimply and small, but onstage in Hamburg his stature grew. He wore his James Dean glasses, a nice pair of RayBans, and he looked groovy with his tight jeans and his big bass. Suddenly there was this transformation, and with his shades and haircut Stu became a complete dude. It was great.

It was inevitable that there should be a mutual attraction between the Beatles and the Exis. Of all the British rock 'n' roll bands of the time, the Beatles were the most intellectually inclined and appreciative of art. The Exis seemed like an extension of a scene with which they were already familiar.

PAUL: So we were very into them and they were very artsy. They were not the first artsy people we'd seen, but they were the first unique artsy people we'd seen. The rest seemed like students copying each other and just doing paintings.

Astrid fell in love with Stuart. He and I used to have a deadly rivalry. I don't know why. He was older and a strong friend of John's. When I look back on it I think we were probably fighting for John's attention. He was older and John was a year older than me, and that year makes a hell of a lot of difference at the age of eighteen. So I wasn't such a big friend of Stuart's. I was always practical, thinking our band could be great, but with him on bass there was always something holding us back.

Stu Sutcliffe and Astrid became engaged in November 1960, exchanging rings in the traditional German manner. He decided to leave the group, and was to remain in Germany when the others returned to Liverpool the following month. Stuart enrolled in Hamburg College of Art to continue his studies as a painter in the tutorial of the future pop artist Eduardo Paolozzi.

There has been a lot made of the supposed animosity between Paul and Stuart but most of it is rumour, exaggerated and amplified by time.

PAUL: It wasn't just me. Legend so often divides these things neatly down the middle: John was hard, I was soft; John loved Stuart, I didn't. But John was perfectly aware that Stuart couldn't play and it wasn't just me telling Stu to turn his back to the camera, it would often be John saying that. We used to ask him to turn away and do a moody thing looking over his shoulder so no one could see that his fingers weren't in the same key as the rest of us. It wasn't a good thing for a group to have someone who was such an obviously weak link. I think John felt a sense of relief when Stuart stayed in Hamburg. In a way, it was actually very convenient. Nobody wanted to sack him; it would not have got to that because of his personal friendship with John. But nobody was that sad to see him stay in Hamburg. It seemed right that we all had to move on and I quite easily got into bass.

But more than musical ability was needed to keep up. To *mach Schau* for four sets a night, seven days a week, was physically exhausting even for tough, healthy Liverpool teenagers, particularly as their contract had been extended to 31 December, so it was hardly surprising that some of the group began taking speed to stay awake. Pete Best stuck to the booze and Paul was never a great one for pills but John gobbled them down, developing an interest in pharmaceuticals which continued for the rest of his life. Amphetamine was not regarded as a serious drug in Germany. Astrid Kirchherr told Ray Coleman in his biography *John Lennon* that she helped supply the band with Preludin. 'We discovered that when you took them and drank beer, you felt great. You didn't get drunk but you got all speedy and talked away like mad. They were fifty pfennings each and my mummy used to get them for us from the chemist – you had to have a prescription for them, but my mummy knew someone at the chemist.'

PAUL: The speed thing first came from the gangsters. Looking back, they were probably thirty years old but they seemed fifty. I find that one of the interesting aspects of ageing: Brian Epstein never got beyond thirty-two, but I think of him as an older guy even though I'm already twenty years older than he ever got to be. The club owners would come in late at night. They would send a little tray of schnapps up to the band and say, 'You must do this: Bang bang, ya! Proost!' Down in one go. The little ritual. So you'd do that, because these were the owners. They made a bit of fun of us but we played along and let them because we weren't great heroes, we needed their protection and this was life or death country. There were gas guns and murderers amongst us, so you weren't messing around here. They made fun of us because our name, the Beatles, sounded very like the German 'Peedles' which means 'little willies'. 'Oh, zee Peedles! Ha ha ha!' They loved that. It appealed directly to the German sense of humour, that did. So we'd let it be a joke, and we'd drink the schnapps and they'd occasionally send up pills, prellies, Preludin, and say, 'Take one of these.'

I knew that was dodgy. I sensed that you could get a little too wired on stuff like that. I went along with it the first couple of times, but eventually we'd be sitting there rapping and rapping, drinking and drinking, and going faster and faster, and I remember John turning round to me and saying, 'What are you on, man? What are you on?' I said, 'Nothin'! 'S great, though, isn't it!' Because I'd just get buoyed up by their conversation. They'd be on the prellies and I would have decided I didn't really need one, I was so wired anyway. Or I'd maybe have one pill, while the guys, John particularly, would have four or five during the course of an evening and get totally wired. I always felt I could have one and get as wired as they got just on the conversation. So you'd find me up just as late as all of them, but without the aid of the prellies. This was good because it meant I didn't have to get into sleeping tablets. I tried all of that but I didn't like sleeping tablets, it was too heavy a sleep. I'd wake up at night and reach for a glass of water and knock it over. So I suppose I was a little bit more sensible than some of the other guys in rock 'n' roll at that time. Something to do with my Liverpool upbringing made me exercise caution.

Paul's first encounters with drugs proved to be typical of his subsequent rectitude regarding narcotics. It may have been fashionable to be 'elegantly wasted' as Keith Richards put it, but caution was the key to Paul's survival through the temptations of the sixties, particularly temptations of the sort offered to the Beatles. The pressures on them are exemplified by an encounter between Paul and two American models while shooting a scene from *Help!* on Huntington Hartford's estate on Paradise Island in the Bahamas, described by Andrew Yule in his biography of Richard Lester:

There he accidentally overheard two of the most beautiful

women he had ever seen, dressed in identical, stunning black swimsuits, try to coax Paul into taking heroin. The combination of their sexual come-on and the enticement towards hard drugs was one of the most chillingly evil moments Lester has ever encountered ... His sense of relief when Paul rebuffed the twosome was profound.

Club bouncers and Exis were not the only people the Beatles knew in Hamburg. Paul once described Hamburg as 'a sort of blown-up Blackpool but with strip clubs instead of waxworks: thousands of strip clubs, bars and pick-up joints'. Here were five teenage boys – George was only seventeen when they arrived, Paul was just eighteen – away from home for the first time, freed from parental restrictions, living in the sex capital of Europe. But they weren't on a day trip to Blackpool; over their five visits they lived there for almost a year. It was like a teenage party when the parents are away for the weekend, except it went on for months at a time. The young women working in the clubs and sex industry adored these pale English boys and wanted desperately to look after them.

The great change in the attitude of young people towards sex during the sixties in Britain and the USA was caused primarily by the introduction of the pill. But the idea that sex should be enjoyable and guilt-free had been gaining ground throughout the fifties, with most of the role models, precursors of sixties ideas of sexual freedom, coming from a continental Europe which was mercifully free of the icy grip of American puritanism and British hypocrisy. Perhaps its prime example was Brigitte Bardot, who embodied the mythical ideal of sexual freedom for young men of the Beatles' generation and gave it a look: long blonde hair, a youthful gamine body and carefree dress.

Before Bardot, young women wore their hair sprayed and fixed into elaborate waves and perms, wore heavy make-up and fashions designed for middle-aged women. The thick constricting twin-sets of young American suburban women seemed designed to protect them from the communist hordes. Brigitte always looked as if she had just climbed out of bed: no make-up, hair piled on top of her head or hanging loose to her breasts. In photographs she often wore a man's shirt or revealing sexy clothes. 'Dress at my house and I will make you into an elegant woman,' Chanel once promised her. 'Elegance? I couldn't care less,' replied Brigitte. 'It's old-fashioned. Couture is for grannies.' She became the icon of female sexuality for an entire generation: women wanted to look like her, actresses by the score copied her style, and men wanted their girlfriends to be like her.

PAUL: John and I lusted after Brigitte Bardot in our teen years and tried to make our girlfriends look like her. She was it, she was the first, she was one of the first ones you ever saw nude or semi-nude. She was a great looker, and she was French. So Brigitte for us, with the long blonde hair and the great figure and the little pouty lips, was the epitome of female beauty, but if she hadn't whipped them off, she might not have been quite so attractive. It was the fact that she was thought to have loose morals; we could fantasise that she did anyway. She was pretty cool. John once met her. Didn't get on very well. I think he was trying to shag her and I think he was probably drunk and I think he probably misbehaved and was boorish, which was well possible.

I had a girlfriend called Dot, Dorothy Rohne, who was my steady girlfriend for quite a long time in Liverpool. She and John's girlfriend, later wife, Cynthia Powell, came over to Hamburg and I remember buying her a leather skirt and encouraging her to grow her hair long so she'd look like Brigitte. She was a blonde. Cynthia had the same thing, tight skirt, long blonde hair. Cynthia wasn't actually a blonde but John got her to dye it blonde to look a bit more like Brigitte. I remember he and I talking and saying, 'Yeah, well, the more they look like Brigitte, the better off we are, mate!'

Hamburg had none of the draconian censorship laws against sex which, to the amusement of the rest of Europe, Britain still upholds. A major war had been fought in Europe only fifteen years before; in cities like Naples people turned a blind eye as women of all classes sold themselves to the occupying Allies because they were on the verge of starvation. Hamburg had been virtually destroyed during the war: in 1943 the British bombing raid Operation Gomorrah killed 42,000 civilians and destroyed eight square miles of the city in a firestorm. The heat was so intense that the Alster lake boiled. The population had other things to worry about than whether young people were having sex together; any warmth and friendship was to be welcomed. Fifteen years later, they still retained a much more down-to-earth, straightforward acceptance of sex. Just as Astrid's mother saw nothing wrong if her daughter's boyfriend spent the night, so the girls on the Reeperbahn were delighted to find four teenage Liverpool lads looking for a bit of fun and friendship. And a great many of them were natural blondes who modelled themselves after Brigitte. It was a fantasy come true.

PAUL: It was a sexual awakening for us. We didn't have much practical knowledge till we went to Hamburg. We were baptised in Hamburg because there were the girls! Of course it was strip-tease girls and hookers. I remember going out with a shortish dark-haired girl who was quite attractive but I think she was a strip-teaser, she was certainly something professional, and I remember feeling very intimidated in bed with her, spent the whole night not doing an awful lot but trying to work up to it. Those terrible painful years where ... but it was all good practice, I suppose.

You couldn't say any girl coming down to the Reeperbahn was fair game because some of them were quite respectable kids who'd just bunked out on a Sunday afternoon and did observe the *Ausweiskontrolle*, the curfew. We had to announce the curfew at ten o'clock. '*Es ist zweiundzwanzig Uhr*. It is 22 hours. *Wir müssen jetzt Ausweiskontrolle machen*. We must now make a passport control. *Alle Jugendlichen unter achtzehn Jahren*. All youth under eighteen years. *Müssen dieses Lokal verlassen*. Must now leave this club.' We had to make the announcement; then the police used to go through the club, checking everyone. But anyone who stayed after that was fair game.

There were some really nice chicks that we had our eyes on who would have to go home. There was one called Renata, who John fell for quite heavily, and there were a couple of other girls who were quite a bit nicer. And then there was the lot who lived locally in St Pauli, who weren't bussed in on the Sunday afternoon for a bit of dancing but actually lived there, so they were in the clubs and the restaurants later. There were a few chicks there who we went out with who were okay. They were just teenage girlfriends but there was sex, there was sex to be had. St Pauli is certainly the area where all the sailors come looking for it. It's the sex centre of Germany, outside of Berlin. So we learned. We had our real initiations then. Some minor ones in Liverpool, but the major things, when you really get the hang of it, happened there.

You were meeting strip-tease artists: you were a professional musician, and they were professional 'dancers'. So it's just 'members of the entertainment business getting together for social reasons'. Perfectly normal. So we came back from there reasonably initiated. It wasn't so much that we were experts, but that we were more expert than other people who hadn't had that opportunity. Groups in the Beat Boom, as it was called at the time, had freedom before others did, and they certainly made some kind of change.

Astrid had made a leather suit for Stuart to match her own, which the others desired so much that they had a tailor on the Reeperbahn run up copies for themselves.

Unfortunately the seams all split as they were not made to take the wear and tear of hours of on-stage gymnastics, but once they'd been strengthened they looked great: tight leather trousers, hip-length black leather bomber jackets with zips and turned-up collars without lapels worn over black T-shirts. As the writer Mick Farren pointed out, 'The black leather jacket always sets off middle-class alarm bells.'

Their black leathers helped coalesce them as a group. Deprived of the familiar friendships of home and family, thrown together in a non-English-speaking culture, they developed a hermetic Liverpool bubble around them: a secret language of wisecracks and references, gestures and behaviour, an impregnable protective wall which, as portrayed in *A Hard Day's Night*, became the role model for rock 'n' roll group behaviour for years to come.

At the end of October 1960, a new club called the Top Ten opened on the Reeperbahn in direct competition to the Kaiserkeller. Tony Sheridan and his Soho backing group the Jets were the opening act, and the owner, Peter Eckhorn, managed to lure Bruno's chief bouncer Horst Fascher away from the Kaiserkeller to work for him as manager. The Beatles had a high opinion of Tony Sheridan and enjoyed stopping by the Top Ten to see his set, much to the annoyance of Bruno Koschmider, who hated the Beatles to set foot in any club he didn't own. He assigned one of his assistants to keep an eye on them and relations between them and Bruno began to get strained.

The Jets' stint with Tony Sheridan was coming to an end and Peter Eckhorn was looking for a group to back him. The Beatles were getting irritated with Bruno and were attracted to the idea of moving to a new club. They asked for an audition and pulled out all the stops, with Paul doing his Little Richard imitations. Eckhorn was delighted and said they could start the next day.

Their first night was a great success. All the Beatles' regulars deserted the Kaiserkeller and packed out the Top Ten to see them. The members of the departing Jets joined in for a jam session which ended in an hour-long version of 'What'd I Say', but their success was short-lived. Bruno was furious and cut short their engagement because their contract contained a clause forbidding them to play within 40 kilometres of the Kaiserkeller.

Paul: 'One night we played the Top Ten Club and all the customers from the Kaiserkeller came along. Since the Top Ten was a much better club we decided to accept the manager's offer and play there. Naturally the manager of the Kaiserkeller didn't like it.' Bruno soon had his revenge. He informed the police that George was under eighteen and had been working without a permit. The police served him with a deportation order and George stayed up all night trying to teach John all his guitar parts so that the Beatles could stay and play as a quartet, but Bruno soon found another way to foil their plans. John and Stuart had already moved their stuff to a comfortable attic room over the Top Ten. When Paul and Pete Best went to collect their things from the Bambi, it was in darkness. While looking to see if they had left anything behind, they found a condom and as an act of defiance, attached it to a nail on the bare concrete and set fire to it. It didn't burn long but Bruno immediately reported them to the police for attempted arson.

'He'd told them that we'd tried to burn his place down and they said, "Leave, please. Thank you very much but we don't want you to burn our German houses." Funny, really, because we couldn't have burned the place even if we had gallons of petrol – it was made of stone.' Paul and Pete Best spent three hours in the local jail before being deported. They arrived at London airport on 1 December 1960, with just enough money to take a train back to Liverpool.

The Jets had their contract extended for a further two months until Gerry and the Pacemakers could come over from Liverpool to relieve them. John was free to stay, but without work there was no point. He sold some of his clothes to buy a train ticket and arrived back a sad figure carrying a guitar in one hand with his amp strapped to his back in case anyone stole it.

Top Ten

Back in Liverpool the Beatles were so down-hearted that they made no attempt to contact each other for several weeks. Then on 17 December they played the Casbah with a friend of theirs, Chas Newby, replacing Stuart on bass. Posters proclaiming 'The Return of the Fabulous Beatles!' and an almost full house cheered their spirits and they were back in business. Allan Williams quickly got them enough dances and concerts to see them through the winter.

On 27 December 1960, they played Litherland Town Hall, Liverpool, on a bill made up of the Del Renas, the Deltones and the Searchers. This concert is widely regarded as a turning point in the Beatles' career. They had not played in this part of town much before and when the concertgoers saw the posters announcing 'Direct from Hamburg. The Beatles!' they naturally thought they were a German group. From the moment Paul blasted out 'Long Tall Sally', the audience was at first stunned, then ecstatic. They pushed forward and pressed against the stage in a frenzy of excitement. The first signs of Beatlemania had begun. Virtually overnight they became the leaders of the Mersey beat scene as news of the Litherland Town Hall concert spread. From now on they began to build a serious local following of their own with fans who attended every performance.

They were now playing so many gigs, spread out all over Liverpool and its environs, that it became necessary to get a driver. Pete Best had a mate called Neil Aspinall who was studying to become an accountant, but life on the road seemed a much more exciting proposal. He bought a used Commer van for £80 and became the first member of the Beatles' entourage. He was to devote his life to them and is now the chief executive of Apple, still managing the Beatles' affairs.

Despite their local success, they longed to get back to Hamburg. As the result of a lot of haggling and meetings, Peter Eckhorn and Astrid finally straightened everything out with the authorities and, now that George was eighteen and of legal age to perform, the Beatles were issued with new work permits. They returned to Hamburg with a contract with Eckhorn to begin work at the Top Ten on 1 April 1961, playing each night from 7.00 p.m. until 2.00 a.m. with a fifteen-minute break each hour. On the weekends they had to play until 3.00 a.m. For this they received 35DM (£3) each per day plus free lodgings in the attic four floors above the club. Their rooms were next door to Tony Sheridan and his new wife, a German woman called Rosie. It had ex-army bunk beds in two tiers but was luxurious compared with the scruffy, dark rooms at the Bambi. Three washing lines were always heavy with the Beatles' shirts and underwear. The parties went on until dawn as the group unwound from their hours onstage.

The Top Ten was at Reeperbahn 136, about the same size as the Kaiserkeller, with about two dozen small tables surrounding a square dance floor in front of the stage and a cinema-style awning extending out over the wide cobbled pavement. The Beatles still pulled the same Rocker audience they had around the corner on the Große Freiheit, but now they built a small following of Exis as well. Though Stuart was no longer in the band, he sometimes sat in with them and jammed, and most nights he and Astrid, Klaus and Jürgen would be seated by the piano at the left-hand side of the stage just like old times. It was like returning home. One of the first things Paul did on his return to Hamburg was buy a bass, a Hofner with a violin shape which allowed it to be played left-handed without looking strange.

> PAUL: There's a theory that I maliciously worked Stu out of the group in order to get the prize chair of bass. Forget it! Nobody wants to play bass, or nobody did in those days. Bass was the thing that the fat boys got lumbered with and were asked to stand at the back and play. Don't say anything. Don't blow your cool. So I definitely didn't want to do it but Stuart left, and I got lumbered with it. Later I was quite happy, I enjoyed it, but I'd started as a guitarist until my guitar had fallen apart; it was a piece of crap. I then became a pianist, because they had a piano on stage. It was a terrible old piano so to be able to even pick out

anything was an achievement. Then finally I became a bass player. Stuart lent me his bass till I got one, so I was playing it upside down. My God, the conditions I was playing in, no wonder I got pretty good! I never played on anything decent! But it was good for my musical education to have to play all those different instruments.

Since they had obtained the booking at the Top Ten in December before they were deported from Germany, and since they negotiated the new contract with Peter Eckhorn, telephoning him from Pete Best's house, they decided to withhold the 10 per cent a week commission paid to Allan Williams. As Stuart was no longer in the band, and was living permanently in Hamburg, they persuaded him to write the letter. Williams was not pleased, to say the least, and threatened legal action. In his autobiography *The Man Who Gave the Beatles Away*, he described himself as 'seething with wounded heart and indignation', but his retribution was limited to warning Brian Epstein 'not to touch them with a barge pole' when their future manager inquired about his experiences with the group.

One good thing which came from living in close proximity to Tony Sheridan was a recording session. Tony Sheridan was without a band at the time so the Beatles backed him on his solo numbers and he sometimes helped out on their sets. On the sleeve notes for *The Beatles, First*, Sheridan wrote: 'One night Bert Kaempfert came into the Top Ten, introduced himself as an A & R man and record producer, and asked us if we would like to record for Polydor. We said O.K., and the result of the first recording session was "My Bonnie", "The Saints", "Cry For A Shadow" and "Why" ...' Kaempfert was a popular German bandleader who had recently made number one in America with 'Wonderland by Night' so his opinion counted highly with German record companies.

On the morning of 22 June 1961, two taxis arrived to take them all to an infants' school, the Friedrich-Ebert-Halle, where the session was held on stage with the curtain closed. Kaempfert was acting as an independent producer and only after Polydor agreed to release 'My Bonnie' as a single did he bother to sign the Beatles to a recording contract, for one year starting 1 July 1961. Seven tracks were recorded that day, with Sheridan taking the lead vocal on five of them plus a Beatles instrumental, 'Cry for a Shadow', and a rock version of

'Ain't She Sweet' with John taking the vocal. 'My Bonnie' was released as by Tony Sheridan and the Beatles and did reasonably well on the German charts.

Though they now wore their leather suits, the Beatles still combed their hair back in the Elvis Presley teddy-boy quiff favoured by their Rocker audience. Jürgen Vollmer wrote in *Rock 'n' Roll Times*: 'By the time of their Top Ten engagements, our taste in clothes and hairstyle had a certain effect on The Beatles ... Klaus and I had our hair combed slightly forward in the French style, naturally, without grease. Stuart was the first to wear his hair more like us. Astrid had styled it. Occasionally George would comb his hair forward, but always combed it back again. He said the Rockers gave him funny looks.'

The Beatles felt ambivalent: they were attracted to the Exi style but didn't want to alienate either their tough Liverpool audiences or the Hamburg Rockers. They took elements of the style and made it their own. Paul: 'The Exis had this great look to them, dark collarless Pierre Cardin jackets, which is the precursor of all that Beatle look. We took a lot off them, mainly the Beatle haircut.' Both the haircut and the idea for what became the collarless Beatle jacket came, in the end, not from Astrid but from Jürgen when they ran into him in the street in Paris later that year.

On 2 July 1961, the Beatles returned to Liverpool after thirteen exhausting weeks at the Top Ten. On John Lennon's twenty-first birthday, 9 October 1961, his aunt in Edinburgh sent him £100, about two months' wages for the average worker in those days. John decided to use some of the money for a hitch-hiking trip to the Continent intending to go first to Paris then hitch on to Spain; so the day after playing the Village Hall, Knotty Ash, Liverpool, he and Paul got out on the road and stuck out their thumbs. They reached Dover and took the ferry to Calais, but hitching was almost impossible in France so they took the the train to Paris. Paul had picked up quite a bit of German in Hamburg and had taken German and Spanish at school but had not studied French. John had taken a few months of French, but had not paid attention, so between them they barely spoke a word.

PAUL: The only French we knew was '*Avez-vous une hotel pour la nuit?*' and '*Avez-vous un chambre?*' We ended up in Montmartre and by that time it was getting late. Some rather friendly prostitutes kindly took pity on us. They were the only people out. So we say, '*Avez-vous une hotel pour la nuit?*' We thought our luck had really changed, we thought, Wow, this is a prostitute, there may be all sorts of bonuses thrown in here, but in fact it was *un chambre pour la nuit* where the two of us just slept, awaiting great pleasures that didn't come. But we slept, that was the main thing.

I remember we ordered something from a French waitress and she said, '*Merci, m'sieur,*' and we thought, Ohhhh, Jesus Christ, she's so sexy! It was just the French voice, and she had hair under her arms. 'Ohhhh, my God!' That was wild, that was bawdiness in extreme. I'd just never seen anybody with hair under her arms.

They sat in a café on the rue des Anglais drinking banana milkshakes. Paul: 'We got to Paris and decided, "Sod Spain." '

They ran into Jürgen Vollmer, who was living in a cheap hotel in the Latin Quarter, having moved to Paris from Hamburg to pursue a career in photography. He showed them round the city. When he pointed out L'Opéra, they burst into operatic song and laughed and danced together in the street. They were evidently having a good time. He took them to the flea market, where they bought some faded pre-washed jeans and in Mont Martre they saw the short mod jackets which later inspired 'Beatle jackets'.

But Jürgen's greatest contribution to the trip was to get out his scissors. 'John and Paul visited me and decided to have their hair like mine. A lot of French youth wore it that way. I gave both of them their first Beatles haircut in my hotel room on the Left Bank.'

Paul: 'We said "Cut it like yours" but it went different from his. He had a longer bit in front; ours just went "Ping!" so we had a little fringe. People said, "Why'd you do it?" and we said, "Well, you know. Hey!" ' Jürgen's haircut was styled originally by Astrid, who described its origins. 'At the time I was in awe of Jean Cocteau. His favourite actor, Jean Marais, had such a haircut in one of his films, which I am certain was inspired by the ancient Greeks.' Jean Marais played Oedipus in Cocteau's popular *Le Testament d'Orphée* in 1959 with his hair brushed forwards into a proto-Beatle cut. Since John and Paul were not prepared to totally give up their DAs, their hair remained long in the back, combining both Rocker and Exi in one style, the famous Beatles haircut.

There were to be three more residencies in Hamburg, all of them at the Star Club, hired by Horst Fascher, the bouncer, who had moved on from the Top Ten Club to represent Manfred Weissleder, another prominent Hamburg club owner, who was converting his Star Cinema into a rock 'n' roll club. Fascher had been with them at both the Kaiserkeller and the Top Ten and knew the kind of crowds they pulled. He was prepared to outbid Peter Eckhorn from the Top Ten in order to open the club with a star act. So the Beatles found themselves back on the Große Freiheit, this time at number 39. They were there for seven weeks between 13 April and 31 May 1962, fourteen nights between 1 and 14 November 1962 on the same billing as Little Richard, and a final thirteen nights between 18 and 31 December, by which time they already had chart success and would have much preferred to stay in Britain, where they could now command a high fee. By the end of 1962 they had played for more than 800 hours in Hamburg alone and were formidable. Everything they had learned on the Reeperbahn would be consolidated back home.

The Cavern

Even though the Beatles split up more than twenty-five years ago, fans still arrive in Liverpool and ask a cab driver to take them to 10 Mathew Street, the address of the Cavern Club. They are always disappointed because, despite massive opposition, the Liverpool Corporation demolished it, destroying the city's principal tourist site and replacing it with a car park. It has now been reconstructed 'using the original bricks', so it is claimed, but has little of the funky atmosphere of the original. Besides, according to Paul McCartney's brother Michael, they've built it the wrong way round.

At the height of the city's prosperity in the nineteenth century, streets of warehouses were built further and further from the actual docks. Mathew Street lies about four blocks from Canning Dock: a narrow, drab row of late-Victorian warehouses used in the early sixties by fruit and vegetable wholesalers whose rotting produce could often be found underfoot, giving the street a distinctive ambience.

Market-garden lorries filled the street in the early hours of the morning, but as the day progressed traders were replaced by teenagers queuing to get into the Cavern for its lunchtime and evening sessions. The line filled the pavement, sometimes spilling into the road, and stretched almost the full length of Mathew Street, passing a bricked-up bomb site surrounded with an ugly tangle of barbed wire. It was one of the most unprepossessing streets in Liverpool.

Sited in the basement of a produce warehouse, the Cavern was by no means the first venue in Liverpool to present beat music. Indeed it was one of the last to catch the trend: it had opened originally as a jazz club in February 1953 and in those early days, Rory Storm and the Hurricanes had been fined for playing a rock number when they were supposed to be playing skiffle, which was then seen as a type of jazz. Elsewhere, from the late fifties onwards, the Mersey beat was played in the Casbah, the Aintree Institute, Blair Hall, the Litherland Town Hall, the Jive Hive, and many other halls and clubs that held regular dances. The Cavern finally switched to beat music in May 1960 because Ray McFall, the owner, realised that there was money in it.

He could hardly have resisted the tide. By the time the Beatles returned from their first Hamburg season, Liverpool had an astonishingly fertile music scene, with over 300 working groups: many of them – the Merseybeats, the Big Three, Faron's Flamingos, the Undertakers, the Searchers, Howie Casey and the Seniors, Kingsize Taylor and the Dominoes, to name but a few – could be relied upon to pull big crowds. The Swinging Blue Jeans, who began life as the Swinging Bluegenes skiffle group in 1957 – the same year as the Quarry Men – already had their own 'Swinging Blue Jeans Night' at the Cavern when the Beatles first began to play there. Groups like Gerry and the Pacemakers had fans who would trek all over the city to see them. The Beatles had lost ground locally by spending so much time in Hamburg just as they were beginning to take off.

PAUL: There were some guys that were slightly older than us, or had been at it longer or were more successful. Ringo's first group, Rory Storm and the Hurricanes, had been to Butlins for a whole season so they were *seasoned professionals*. In fact, that has to be the meaning of the word 'seasoned'. Ringo had a beard, a suit, and a car! A car, man! A Zephyr Zodiac! They'd

had that extra year. When we'd just been getting out of our
nappies, they were already on the stage, so you'd look to them.

But if the Beatles had lost ground in Liverpool by spending so
much time in Hamburg, they had been playing almost continuously
in the three months since the Litherland Town Hall gig and were well
on their way to establishing themselves as one of Liverpool's premier
beat groups even before they got to Mathew Street. However, it was
the passionate loyalty they inspired in their Cavern Club fans that
helped to push them, over the next two and a half years, to the very
top.

Entrance to the club was by seventeen slippery stone steps which
led down to a space made up of three long barrel-vaulted tunnels,
connected by six-foot archways. The rooms were about ten feet wide,
so narrow that in the central tunnel where the stage was located there
was only space for seven straight-backed wooden chairs in each row.
Many years before, probably when it first opened as a jazz club, the
brick arches had been whitewashed. Since there was no ventilation,
the combined breath and sweat of the hundreds of young people
crammed into the low tunnels formed a film of condensation on the
vaulted ceiling, causing the remaining flakes of whitewash to fall
gently upon the club members. 'Cavern dandruff' they called it. It
was common for young women to faint clear away from the heat and
lack of oxygen. The room reeked of body odour and of disinfectant
from the rudimentary toilets.

The MC, Bob Wooler, played records from a small room to the left
of the stage which doubled as a dressing room for the acts preparing
to go on. The stage backdrop was a crudely painted mural, inspired
by Mondrian, of coloured oblong shapes which became graffitied
with the names of Liverpool bands. It was lit by a couple of fixed
spots; no coloured gels or flashing lights were to be seen at the
Cavern. Wooler screamed the name of the act into the microphone
and the performers ran up the three concrete steps to the wooden
stage; something the Beatles would do 275 times between 9 February
1961 and their final performance there on 3 August 1963.

The Beatles looked terrific in their black leather, the music was
deafening in the confined space and hundreds of hours on stage in
Hamburg made the short lunchtime and evening sessions at the
Cavern seem like a doddle. They were relaxed and at ease on stage,

joking with the audience and taking requests. Any sort of sing-along or show tune gave them a respite because the audience could be made to provide most of the energy. Indeed one of the keys to their success was the introduction of the jam session to rock 'n' roll. Instead of solidly plugging through jerky imitations of the Shadows or whoever was in the charts at the time, their act always featured a long-drawn-out jam on a rock 'n' roll standard such as 'What'd I Say', generating tremendous excitement and leaving their audience drained and exhilarated.

Their act became an eclectic mix of rock 'n' roll, chart hits, standards and old favourites, in part determined by which records they owned.

Because records were so expensive, the only way to build a collection in the late fifties and early sixties was to rummage through junk shops, steal them at parties and accept gifts of records which you would never have bought yourself. Paul's cousin Elizabeth Robbins gave him Peggy Lee's versions of 'Fever' (1958) and 'Til There Was You' (1960), which he sang on the *With the Beatles* album.

PAUL: I had this very diverse little record collection from which I was culling material. I remember I had the Coasters' 'Zing Went the Strings of My Heart' [1958], which was on the B side of 'Yakety Yak'. I can look back on these records and see what it was I liked. With 'Besame Mucho' by the Coasters [1960], it's a minor song and it changes to a major, and where it changes to a major is such a big moment musically. That major change attracted me so much.

This wide variety in their stage act also gave the Beatles access to a greater number of venues. Competition between the groups was acute, and the Beatles had to work hard to stay ahead. It was this competition that drove them to write their own songs, since these were the only numbers that rival groups would not steal.

PAUL: When we got to the Cavern, we realised everybody and his uncle knew all the tunes we knew, so we started to move towards the B sides and the more obscure tunes like Ritchie Barrett's 'Some Other Guy' [1962]. Of course you only had to do 'em once and everyone had 'em. Arthur Alexander's 'Shot of Rhythm and Blues' [1962], Gerry and the Pacemakers did it.

But we always feel we did it better. 'Let them do it, doesn't matter, we'll do it better.' We took James Ray's 'If You're Gonna Make a Fool of Somebody' [1961] to the Oasis Club, Manchester, and Freddie and the Dreamers had it the next week! It was one of our numbers. That was a waltz, a funky soul waltz, and nobody did waltzes. We were looking to be different because we realised the competition out there.

There were groups that did Cliff and the Shadows. There was a group called the Blue Angels that sounded exactly like Roy Orbison; they were immaculate. The Remo Four did a lot of Chet Atkins stuff, with clever guitar picking. So we decided we couldn't keep up, we couldn't better any of them, we had to find our own identity. We looked on Bo Diddley B sides, we looked for obscure rhythm and blues things: 'Searchin'' by the Coasters [1957], 'Anna' by Arthur Alexander [1962].

We did the Shirelles' 'Soldier Boy' [1962], which is a girl's song. It never occurred to us. No wonder all the gays liked John. And Ringo used to sing 'Boys' [1960], another Shirelles number. It was so innocent. We just never even thought, Why is he singing about boys? We loved the song. We loved the records so much that what it said was irrelevant, it was just the spirit, the sound, the feeling. The joy when you did that 'Bab shoo-wap, bab bab shoo wop'. That was the great fun of doing 'Boys'.

So at the Cavern we started to introduce a couple of our own songs along with these obscure B sides. We thought, There's one way they can't do it, they wouldn't dare do one of our songs. The first couple of songs we did of ours were rather laughed off, but a couple of girls in the audience quite liked them and would request them. 'Like Dreamers Do' was one of the very first songs I wrote and tried out at the Cavern. We did a weak arrangement but certain of the kids liked it because it was unique, none of the other groups did it. It was actually a bit of a joke to dare to try your own songs. They didn't go down very well with Gerry and the Pacemakers and other groups. If they told us what they liked it would be 'What'd I Say' or 'Some Other Guy' or Little Richard stuff that I did. It was the more genuine shit, not stuff you wrote yourself. For you to write it yourself was a bit plonky, and the songs obviously weren't that great, but I felt we really had to break through that barrier because if we never tried our own songs we'd just never have the confidence to continue writing.

By the time we got to 'Love Me Do', they started to feel a bit bluesier. When we eventually got down to London, that was the one we insisted on recording rather than 'How Do You Do It', the Gerry and the Pacemakers song, which was more George Formby than anything else. We knew that the peer pressure back in Liverpool would not allow us to do 'How Do You Do It'. We knew we couldn't hold our heads up with that sort of rock-a-pop-a-ballad. We would be spurned and cast away into the wilderness.

Another Lennon and McCartney song that became part of their Cavern repertoire was 'Hold Me Tight', a McCartney number that Paul and John worked on together. It was written in Forthlin Road, but not recorded until the *With the Beatles* album.

PAUL: When we first started it was all singles and we were always trying to write singles. That's why you get lots of these 2 minute 30 seconds songs; they all came out the same length. 'Hold Me Tight' was a failed attempt at a single which then became an acceptable album filler.

The thing about the Beatles is it wasn't vulgar. We were actually very good. It was like being in an art group, it was being in an association with a few artistic friends. That was the kind of underlying feeling we had after having been in Hamburg. I remember we had a joke with the sax player from another band. He knocked on the door and I grabbed a volume of Yevtushenko's poetry and started quoting from it and the guys all sat around, like really into it, like Beat poets. And the sax player crept in, 'Oh, sorry.' He put his sax back in his case and crept back out again. And we howled. But this kind of cheek gave us a feeling of being different from the pack.

We didn't particularly like the girl adoration, although it was marvellous if you wanted a date. The main thing for us, first of all, was just doing our craft. We were genuinely trying to be artists; we'd actually comment on it, 'Hey, there's a guy in the front row who's really clocking all your chords!' If we played a good bit, a new technique or an innovative riff, we saw that they noticed; the guys were watching our guitars and our hands, not our legs and willies. That was what we liked.

There was always an underlying ambition to go in a slightly artistic direction, whereas a lot of our fellow groups didn't have that. This is why we didn't do 'How Do You Do It' when George Martin suggested it. 'It's a number one!' he said, and God knows we needed a number one. We said, 'No, no! No thanks!' And we wouldn't go to America till we had a number-one record either, and again, God knows we wanted exposure, we wanted an American tour. In a strange way we were very conscious of where we were heading whilst having no map whatsoever. We just had a feeling that 'God, this John Lennon guy is pretty special and Paul McCartney's not too bad either. And fucking hell, George is a little bit of a head. And Jesus Christ, Ringo's a dude!' And we all knew, boy, these four qualify for something, there was no dead weight at all. It annoys me when people discount some of us; and obviously the easiest one to discount is Ringo – 'Well, he just hit some skins at the back of it all, didn't he?' George in one book is described 'standing around with his plectrum in his hand waiting for a solo'. Well, you know, 'Too easy, love. Too cheap a shot. You check George out some time and you'll find a little more there than that.'

Brian Epstein

The story of how Brian Epstein visited the Cavern and was so entranced by the leather-clad boys cavorting on stage that he asked if he could manage them is well known. As Brian's autobiography *A Cellarfull of Noise* was ghosted for him by Derek Taylor at the height of Beatlemania and he hardly had time to read it, let alone correct any errors, it cannot be trusted on matters of detail. The account in the book about Brian being intrigued when three people in two days came into his record shop and asked for 'My Bonnie' by the Beatles, causing him to set out to find this elusive record by an unknown German group, is a good story – but it is not true.

Brian knew perfectly well who the Beatles were – they were on the front page of the second issue of *Mersey Beat*, the local music paper. Brian sold twelve dozen copies of this issue, so many that he invited the editor, Bill Harry, into his office for a drink to discuss why it was selling so well and to ask if he could write a record review column for it. He is unlikely to have missed the 'Beatles sign recording contract' banner headline, reporting their session with Tony Sheridan for Bert Kaempfert, nor, with his penchant for rough boys, is it likely that he passed over the photograph of the leather-clad Beatles without giving them a second glance. As for the elusive record, he telephoned Polydor in Hamburg and ordered a box full. There was so much talk about the Beatles and the explosion of beat music in Liverpool that it made good business sense for Brian to go and check out the scene for himself. When he entered the Cavern, Bob Wooler announced over the PA, 'We have someone rather famous in the audience today.' Paul, 'Talk about parochial, the idea that Brian Epstein, a record-shop owner, could be famous, that shows you what Liverpool was like then.'

Brian described his visit to the Cavern in a 1964 BBC Radio interview transcribed by the Beatles buff Mark Lewisohn in his book *The Complete Beatles Chronicle*:

> It was pretty much of an eye-opener, to go down into this darkened, dank, smoky cellar in the middle of the day, and to see crowds and crowds of kids watching these four young men on stage. They were rather scruffily dressed, in the nicest possible way, or, I should say, in the most attractive way: black leather jackets and jeans, long hair of course. And they had a rather untidy stage presentation, not terribly aware, not caring very much what they looked like. I think they cared more even then for what they sounded like. I immediately liked what I heard. They were fresh and they were honest, and they had what I thought was a sort of presence and, this is a terribly vague term, star quality.

For the next three weeks, every time the Beatles played the Cavern, Brian was there in his impeccable pinstripe business suit and tie, watching, listening and, after the set, pushing his way through the crowd for a few words with the band. Then he invited them to a meeting at NEMS and proposed the idea of managing them.

Brian was twenty-seven, the son of Harry and Queenie Epstein, who ran a successful furniture retail business in Walton Road, Liverpool; the shop where Paul's father bought his piano. The Epstein family were affluent; Brian was brought up by a nanny. His family were religious, gave heavily to the synagogue and Jewish charities and were highly respected in the Jewish community. Though he was asked, Harry refused to join the synagogue's executive committee because he felt it would be hypocritical to do so as he was breaking the Sabbath by opening his stores on Saturdays.

Brian grew up very much under the suffocating influence of his mother, who doted upon him and in whose eye he could no wrong. He was educated privately at a series of seven fee-paying schools and did badly at them all before dropping out in 1950, aged sixteen, to join the family firm as a furniture salesman. At eighteen he was called up for National Service and managed to get stationed at the Albany Barracks in Regent's Park, London. He detested the discipline and remained aloof from army life; he was reprimanded because he never bothered to collect his army pay. He hated the 'hideous' uniform and had his tailor run up an elegant officer's outfit which he wore in order to cruise bars in search of young men. Military police picked him up one night at the Army and Navy Club on Piccadilly and arrested him for impersonating an officer. His parents had powerful lawyers who managed to avert a court martial and he was given psychiatric tests instead. He was discharged from the army after ten months' service as 'emotionally and mentally unfit': a euphemism meaning, among other things, that he was gay.

After a failed attempt to become an actor, Brian was made a director of NEMS, North End Music Stores, the sheet-music and musical-instrument side of the family business. In 1957 the family opened a second store on Great Charlotte Street with Brian in charge of the record department and his younger brother Clive looking after the electrical and domestic appliance department. In the fifties, record players were floor-standing affairs with wooden cases and sold mainly by large furniture shops, which also sold the records to go with them. Brian was an enthusiastic manager and the shop turned a profit almost immediately. Harry was delighted and opened another, much larger branch at 12–14 Whitechapel in the city centre. Once again Brian ran the record department, and once again it was a success. By the time Brian met the Beatles, NEMS had nine record shops in Liverpool, stocking over 500,000 records. They were the biggest record retailers in the north-west.

Everyone, even the scruffiest customer, was addressed as 'sir' or 'madam' by impeccably turned-out assistants and it was the house rule that no customer should leave the store dissatisfied. To this end, Brian devised a complex system of stock control involving bits of coloured string to ensure they never ran out of stock of popular items, and if someone ordered a record, he would always order multiple copies. He had an unerring ear for a commercial record and often shocked his staff by ordering hundreds of copies of a record that they would have dismissed, only to see it rise rapidly in the charts.

Brian always looked well scrubbed, as if he had just stepped from the shower. He was a fastidious dresser, his usual attire being a pinstripe suit, with a rolled umbrella and bowler hat; his shirt and tie were always a perfect match and his shoes buffed to a high shine; even as a child he apparently managed to walk off the rugby pitch with brilliantly white bootlaces.

He spoke quietly, with a perfect upper-class accent bearing no trace whatsoever of his Liverpool origin. He was proud, pompous and a bit of a snob; very formal, with immaculate manners. Brian liked to think of himself as a perfect English gentleman. It was a matter of great regret to him that the Beatles received the MBE and he did not. He suffered strong mood swings, from charming and caring to cold and magisterial. He was frequently bad-tempered and temperamental, apologising profusely afterwards. Much of his erratic behaviour stemmed from his homosexuality, the cause of his guilt and insecurity. He spent most of his life concealing his sexual orientation, something that caused him a lot of pain. Homosexuality was illegal in Britain until 1967, the year of his death.

His parents knew; he had been arrested in London for trying to pick up an undercover policeman in a public lavatory, the incident which ended his studies at the Royal Academy of Dramatic Art. There was also another occasion: Brian was attacked by a man dressed as a docker while cottaging at a public toilet one night in west Derby. The man stole his wallet and tried to blackmail him. Brian had no choice but to tell his parents and the police, who then set a trap, with Brian as bait. The man was convicted and jailed for three years. Since it was clearly less dangerous to cruise abroad, Brian took frequent short holidays alone to Amsterdam, Venice or Paris. Though Brian's homosexuality, had it become public knowledge, might have caused great loss of standing among his parents' generation, it was not a cause of concern to the Beatles.

PAUL: The first time we ever heard about gayness was when a poet named Royston Ellis arrived in Liverpool with his book *Jiving With Gyp*. He was a Beat poet. Well, well! Phew! You didn't meet them in Liverpool. And it was all 'Break me in easy, break me in easy ...' It was all shagging sailors, I think. We had a laugh with that line. John became quite friendly with Royston. One thing he told us was that one in every four men is homosexual. So we looked at the group! One in every four! It literally meant one of us is gay. Oh, fucking hell, it's not me, is it? We had a lot of soul-searching to do over that little one.

We'd heard that Brian was queer, as we would have called him, nobody used the word 'gay' then. 'He's a queer.' 'Yes. He's all right, though.' We didn't hold that against him. We didn't really know much about it, there were certain people around but they tended to be the slightly older guys on the scene from what we knew. There wasn't much talk amongst us and our friends about anything like that. Brian was quite a well-known gay, I think. We would go down late-night drinking clubs that we hadn't had access to. They were probably gay clubs, now I think about it, but it actually didn't occur to us at all; there were rather a lot of men there, that's all. But no one ever propositioned me. There was never any bother. Pubs would stay open through Brian's influence, which was fine by us. It meant we could get a drink late at night, fantastic! And the police wouldn't bust us, fantastic! In fact, this is where we started to see the seamier side of society, because the policeman would often come round and have a drink with us. There was a lot of that.

Then we got down to London and Brian had his contacts in the gay scene. People would say, 'How are your boys, Brian?' 'Well, they're doing rather well, they just had a hit.' 'Oh, marvellous, do put them on my show!' So obviously that didn't hurt us.

On 24 January 1962, the Beatles signed a management contract with Brian. He was to get 25 per cent of their gross receipts after a certain threshold was reached, but first he had to get them a recording contract. There were many anxious weeks spent waiting for Brian to come up with the goods. John and Paul would wait in the Punch and Judy café opposite Lime Street station (so called because they used to hold a Punch and Judy puppet show there every Saturday morning) for Brian's train to get in from London. Paul: 'We would rush up to him, "Well? Well? What's the news?" "I'm afraid it's not very good. They don't want you." The devastation! "Oh, God, when? Do you think it will ever happen for us, man?" "Come on, keep your spirits up, it'll be all right." He always said, "Well, I did see someone who might be interested" or "I've got a new idea of who to approach ..." He would always give us hope.'

Along the way there were false starts – most notably with Decca Records. Decca evinced enough enthusiasm to give the Beatles a recording test after their A & R assistant Mike Smith visited Liverpool at Brian's insistence and saw them perform at the Cavern. On 1 January 1962, Neil Aspinall unloaded in the back of Decca's north London studios in Broadhurst Gardens, West Hampstead, and the group helped him to set up. Tony Meehan, the drummer who left the Shadows to go solo, had joined Decca as a producer the year before, and the group were impressed to meet even an ex-member of the Shadows. Since they were not allowed into the control room, they barely saw Meehan after saying hello. Paul found out afterwards that Brian had paid Meehan to produce the session. Paul: 'We gave him some money for doing it. There was a deal struck there, it was the first time we saw that they weren't all doing it just for art. This was commercial realities kicking in. We sat out there in the studio and tried to perform. We'd got a fairly silly repertoire at that time, George doing "Sheik of Araby" and I was still doing "Besame Mucho".' They played both of these on the session, which was one occasion when they allowed Brian to have a say in choosing their material and he thought it best to show all facets of their ability.

Mike Smith cut a number of acetates for his boss Dick Rowe, the head of 'pop' A & R at Decca, to hear when he returned from America. But Rowe turned the group down, telling Brian, 'Groups of guitars are on the way out, Mr Epstein. You really should stick to selling records in Liverpool.' Electric guitars, he told him, were now 'old hat'.

In all fairness, the tapes give a very poor idea of the group's potential. All but three tracks were cover versions of standards, seven of them of fifties material that could have been recorded by anyone. It is possible that the Beatles' covers were too accurate: they moved fairly effortlessly from the breathless teen-idol style of Bobby Vee's

'Take Good Care of My Baby' (1961), which was then number two
in the charts, into a pretty accurate copy of Chuck Berry's 'Memphis,
Tennessee' (1959), without giving much idea of the personality of the
group and hardly any indication of the excitement and energy of their
stage performance. It was fine on stage but the wrong material for a
recording test.

Eventually Brian Epstein's efforts paid off and on 9 May 1962
George Martin, the head of Parlophone Records, a division of EMI,
the world's largest recording organisation, offered them a contract
without ever having seen them play. The paperwork was drawn up so
that, if things went well in the recording studio, Martin could add his
signature right away. On 6 June, the Beatles entered EMI's Abbey
Road studios for the first time for a recording session, which was not
only to record their first single, but to determine whether they were
signed to the label at all. Though none of the tracks was ever issued
commercially, George Martin was pleased by the results and signed
the contract. The Beatles had a deal.

It took two more recording sessions to get something that George
Martin regarded as acceptable, during which time the Beatles made
their final line-up change. Ringo Starr was hired as drummer, and
Pete Best, who had played with them since their first residency in
Hamburg, was out. The story of Pete Best's unceremonious ousting
and the resentment felt by Beatles fans is well known, but it does seem
that it was not so much Pete's drumming that the others objected to –
though George Martin insisted on using a session drummer instead of
Pete – it was more a question of attitude. Pete was moody and just did
not fit in that well with the other three. Ringo was the ideal
replacement. The Beatles knew it would work musically because they
had played with him in Hamburg, and he was already regarded as one
of the top drummers in Liverpool for his work with Rory Storm and
the Hurricanes. Brian Epstein called him up and offered him the
drummer's stool. John Lennon told him, 'The beard will have to go
but you can keep your sidies.'

Their first single, 'Love Me Do', was released on 5 October 1962.
Paul wrote the B side, 'P.S. I Love You', not long before the
recording test. The record reached number 17 in the *Record Mirror*
and *Record Retailer* charts, a good start for a band still virtually
unknown outside the Liverpool area. Normally John took the vocal

lead on 'Love Me Do' when they performed it live even though it was mainly Paul's song, but on the record this was reversed.

PAUL: George Martin said, 'Can anyone play harmonica? It would be rather nice. Couldn't think of some sort of bluesy thing, could you, John?' John played a chromatic harmonica, not a Sonny Boy Williamson blues harmonica, more Max Geldray from *The Goon Show*. I actually had one too but he'd been clever; he'd learned how to play it. He could play 'Oh, Camptown races ...' John expected to be in jail one day and he'd be the guy who played the harmonica. The lyric crossed over the harmonica solo so I suddenly got thrown the big open line, 'Love me do', where everything stopped. Until that session John had always done it, I didn't even know how to sing it. I'd never done it before. George Martin just said, 'You take that line, John take the harmonica, you cross over, we'll do it live.' So, 'Please ...' it had a big harmony, '... love me do.' I can still hear the nervousness in my voice! We were downstairs in number two studio and I remember looking up to the big window afterwards and George Martin was saying, 'Jolly good.'

But when we got up to Liverpool I remember meeting Johnny Gustafson, who was the bass player in the Big Three, and him saying, 'Aw, it was so much better when John sang that "Love Me Do". What's all this?' You had to go, 'Well, it's the blues, hey, man, you know?' At least there was some credibility in the fact it was a bluesy song rather than 'How Do You Do It'. So that was it, we were started and our credibility as songwriters had started then. So we realised, 'Wow, we could get good at this.'

Their second single followed on 11 January 1963: 'Please Please Me' backed with 'Ask Me Why'. This time John was mostly responsible. 'Please Please Me' was written at Menlove Avenue as a Roy Orbison song.

PAUL: If you imagine it much slower, which is how John wrote it, it's got everything, the big high notes, all the hallmarks of an Orbison song. But in the session George Martin suggested we lifted the tempo and suddenly there was that fast Beatles spirit. I did the trick of remaining on the top note while the melody cascaded down from it. A cadence. I remember a music teacher in Liverpool telling us she'd taught it to her kids. That was good. So it began as a Roy Orbison. We used to steal consciously, particularly from American black acts like the Marvelettes and alter it a bit. Something you love, something you're passionate about, is always a great starting point.

'Ask Me Why' had been a part of the Beatles' live act for some time. Written in the spring of 1962, it was one of the numbers they performed at their Parlophone Records audition. Paul: 'It was John's original idea and we both sat down and wrote it together, just did a job on it. It was mostly John's.' This was the first of many Lennon and McCartney compositions to show the influence of Smokey Robinson and the Miracles, one of their favourite Motown groups.

By the time 'Please Please Me' was released, the Beatles had made a number of television and radio appearances, including a key appearance on the television show *Thank Your Lucky Stars* which enabled them to reach millions of viewers and create thousands of new fans. 'Please Please Me' reached number one, the first of a run of fifteen consecutive number ones in the *Melody Maker* charts. Their initial goal, of having a number-one record, had been reached, and they had achieved it without leaving Liverpool and by recording all their own songs.

Because their royalty rate was so low, it would be some time before they made much money from record sales, but having a record at number one meant that they could command top fees for concerts. Brian Epstein worked them hard, mixing concerts with radio and TV appearances to promote the record. They only had one day off throughout the whole of November and December, and that was spent travelling back from Germany. But the hard work paid off. They became known to a wider and wider audience, from Scotland to Kent, as Neil Aspinall's battered Commer van criss-crossed the face of Britain. They would sometimes play a lunch-time session at the Cavern before heading out of town to perform at a town hall in another city, and it was not unusual to play two engagements in one night, often miles apart. Neil could no longer cope with driving, unloading, setting up and acting as personal assistant to all four Beatles so Brian Epstein hired Mal Evans to help him. Mal was a friend of George Harrison, who had recommended him for his job as one of the bouncers at the Cavern. Three months later, he was working for George. His burly six-foot-two-inch frame enabled him to act as a bodyguard to the Beatles, something that they would be needing before very long.

Please Please Me

George Martin thought it was time for an album, and they were even given a day off to get down to London from Sunderland, in order to be fresh on the morning of 11 February when they were due to record ten new songs at Abbey Road. One day was regarded as quite sufficient to record an album in those days. No one had even considered that it might take longer, so the Beatles were booked to play two evening gigs the following day, one in Sheffield, Yorkshire, followed by another in Oldham, Lancashire.

The Beatles' first album, *Please Please Me*, was released on 22 March 1963. Of the fourteen songs, more than half were original McCartney–Lennon compositions (as they were credited on the label). Both sides of their first two singles were included as well as four new original songs.

'I Saw Her Standing There' was written in the living room of Forthlin Road in September 1962.

PAUL: Sometimes we would just start a song from scratch, but one of us would nearly always have a germ of an idea, a title or a rough little thing they were thinking about and we'd do it. 'I Saw Her Standing There' was my original, I'd started it and I had the first verse, which therefore gave me the tune, the tempo and the key. It gave you the subject matter, a lot of the information, and then you had to fill in. I had, 'She was just seventeen, she'd never been a beauty queen.' So we went, 'Ugh, this is one of these.' And by then we'd written a couple in the little book and we'd started to realise that we had to stop at these bad lines or we were only going to write bad songs. So we stopped there and both of us cringed at that and said, 'No, no, no. Beauty queen is out! There's got to be another rhyme for seventeen': so we went through the alphabet: between, clean, lean, mean; 'She wasn't mean; you know what I mean; great! Put that in.' And then the significance of it built as we sang it, 'She's just seventeen, you know what I mean?' and people picked up on the implied significance later. It was a good way out of that problem. So it was co-written, my idea, and we finished it that day.

Paul's brother Michael includes a photograph in his book *Remember* which captures the moment of composition: Paul and John are seen strumming guitars in the front room of Forthlin Road hunched over the working manuscript of 'I Saw Her Standing There' in a Liverpool Institute exercise book on the floor in front of them. Paul later told *Beat Instrumental* that he stole the bass line from Chuck Berry's 'I'm Talking About You' (1961): 'I played exactly the same notes as he did and it fitted our number perfectly. Even now, when I tell people about it, I find few of them believe me. Therefore I maintain that a bass riff doesn't have to be original.'

'Money' was written just before their first nationwide tour, as fifth on the bill to Helen Shapiro, starting 2 February, 1963. Helen was called 'Foghorn' at school in Bethnal Green, London, because of her deep, masculine voice; but this proved to be her claim to fame when at the age of fourteen she had a top-ten hit with 'Please Don't Treat Me Like a Child' in April 1961. This was followed by a couple of number ones: 'You Don't Know' and 'Walking Back to Happiness' and a number two, 'Tell Me What He Said'. They were straightforward Tin Pan Alley pop tunes and Paul and John thought they would try and get her to record one of theirs. They began work on 'Misery' backstage before a gig at the Kings Hall, Stoke-on-Trent, on 26 January and finished it at Forthlin Road.

Paul: 'We wrote it for Helen Shapiro because we were going on tour with her and, being young lads with an eye for an opportunity, we thought, well, even if she does it on a B side, this'll be very good for our songwriting.' It would have suited Helen Shapiro's vocal range perfectly but the song was turned down by Norrie Paramor, head of A & R at Columbia Records, without Helen even hearing it. Kenny Lynch, who was also on the tour, heard the song and liked it. He earned his footnote in history by becoming the first person, other than the Beatles, to record a Lennon–McCartney song. Paul: 'He was another lad with an eye for an opportunity, and he had a minor hit with it. He used to do it on tour with us ... not amazingly well. It was our first stab at a ballad and had a little spoken preface. It was co-written. I don't think either of us dominated on that one, it was just a job, you could have called us hacks, hacking out a song for someone.' Nine days later they recorded it as a filler for their first album.

Each Beatle needed something to perform as a solo spot for his individual fan following. For the most part, the fans at the Cavern actually knew the group but the audiences outside Liverpool were responding to TV appearances, radio shows and press interviews. Many of these were groups of girls who would divide the band up between them to avoid arguments. Beatlemania had not yet properly begun but the way was being paved.

John and Paul naturally sang their own songs; then, in order to give George and Ringo something original to sing, they began to write for them too. It would be some time before George began writing his own material and 'Do You Want to Know a Secret' was written for him. Based on an original idea by John, it was essentially what Paul calls a 'hack song', a 50-50 collaboration written to order. John says that he based the tune on 'Wishing Well' from Walt Disney's 1937 cartoon *Snow White and the Seven Dwarfs*, which his mother used to sing to him when he was two or three years old.

The remaining Lennon and McCartney song was "There's a Place', another product of the front room at Forthlin Road; co-written, co-sung but with a bias towards being Paul's original idea since he was the owner of the soundtrack album of Leonard Bernstein's *West Side Story* with the song 'There's a Place for Us', which is where the title phrase came from.

> PAUL: But in our case the place was in the mind, rather than round the back of the stairs for a kiss and a cuddle. This was the difference with what we were writing, we were getting a bit more cerebral. We both sang it. I took the high harmony, John took the lower harmony or melody. This was a nice thing because we didn't actually have to decide where the melody was till later when they boringly had to write it down for sheet music.

The extra tracks required to make the album took the allotted one day to record. Like the single after which it was named, it went to number one.

The success of *Please Please Me* underlined the transformation that occurred in the Cavern of the Beatles from four leather-clad teddy boys to a highly professional rock 'n' roll band complete with a manager and stage outfits. They were now part of show business; and perhaps Brian Epstein's most significant influence on the group was in refining the stage presence that became part of their image. The theatrical Beatle bow from the waist was one of his many ideas.

PAUL: We actually used to count the bow, one two three, and we'd do this big uniform bow all at once. Brian believed that that would be very good for us, and I was also a great believer in that. Brian was very into the look onstage: 'Maybe you shouldn't do that, maybe you should wait a couple of numbers before announcing ...' His RADA experience came into play a little bit there and I would tend to agree with some of his stagey ideas. I don't think any of us had any problem with that, or else one of us wouldn't have done it. We knew Brian had a good flair, and, when you're on stage, you can't see yourself, so it's often very important to have someone sitting in the stalls to tell you how it looked. Brian's memos to us used to reflect that: 'You're playing Neston tonight. I'm looking for a re-booking here, please wear the shirts and ties.' And we'd do it, it was show business, we were just entering the whole magic realm.

THREE

UP THE SMOKE

Sexual intercourse began
In nineteen sixty-three. . .
Between the end of the *Chatterley* ban
And the Beatles' first LP

Philip Larkin

Swinging London

THE BEATLES ENTERED THE CAVERN CLUB AS FOUR VIRTUALLY UNKNOWN teddy boys and came out with a number-one single and a number-one album. However, in order to keep up the momentum they had to take on London. They were ready to go 'up the Smoke'.

PAUL: I had this strange entrance into London, coming down from Liverpool where everyone had said, 'You'll never make it, coming from Liverpool.' Which had angered us a bit, so we stayed up in Liverpool a lot. We didn't just all move down to London, we tried to prove ourselves from Liverpool. Hamburg, Liverpool, the north – you know, 'Fuck you!' And we had our original success up in the Cavern. But this got us national success and then came the inevitable move to London.

The Beatles arrived just as the sixties were getting into gear. In 1963, the Christine Keeler–John Profumo affair would bring thirteen years of Tory rule to an end, though Sir Alec Douglas-Home, dragged in from the grouse moors in his tweeds, almost won the election after Harold MacMillan resigned. No more 'Mustn't grumble', no more 'Grin and bear it'; the era of the spiv and the wide boy was back. All manner of East End barrow boys and public-school failures emerged with an eye for the main chance. Get-rich-quick schemes bloomed, everything modern was 'in', everything and everyone old was out. The entire city was up for grabs, including the people and buildings.

Paul: 'This working-class explosion was all happening and we were very much a part of it. Making it okay to be common. The East End photographers, the working-class actors. So now we were the wacky chappies from up north. I think we had a lot to do with it.'

London in 1963 was still pitted with overgrown bomb sites, though many of the best sites were under development. The look of the city was undergoing massive changes: the pastoral horizon of Hyde Park was broken first by the London Hilton tower in 1962, then by the Lancaster Gate Hotel, both exceptions made to the London planning regulations 'in order to attract American visitors', who were presumably unable to stay in low buildings. The Post Office Tower rose slowly above the rooftops of Bloomsbury to become the tallest building in London and Richard Seifert's Centre Point, a banal copy of a second-rate original by Marcel Breuer built for Harry Hyams on the site of the medieval village of St Giles, was fitted together like a giant Lego set before standing empty for years.

The atmosphere of excitement that characterised the sixties was already there when the Beatles arrived: the sense of *anything goes*. Businessmen still wore bowler hats and carried rolled umbrellas but any remnants of pre-war ideas of moderation and long-term planning were gone. Spectacular rip-offs and deals were the new order of the day, such as the shameless, though quite legitimate, way that EMI ripped off the Beatles. The smartly dressed man in the pinstripes now fancied himself as Steed from *The Avengers* or James Bond in his Savile Row suit and Turnbull and Asser shirts.

You could get anything you wanted in London in the sixties because the fix was in. Corruption was institutional among Scotland Yard detectives. 'Not so much a rotten apple as a barrel of rotten apples,' as the former Inspector of Constabulary Frank Williamson put it. Endemic police corruption allowed organised crime to flourish. In the sixties the notorious Kray twins extended their gambling and protection empire from the East End to include most of Mayfair and the West End. Graft, kickbacks and nepotism: the birth of Swinging London was fuelled by corruption in high places. It could not have happened otherwise.

The other side of the coin was personal freedom and the party that was sixties London. Experiment became the order of the day. The Pop and Op Art explosion pushed aside the tentative, gloomy canvases of the British art establishment. Bridget Riley's eye-bending Op-Art paintings were shown at Tooth's in 1961. The next year the same gallery showed Allen Jones's colourful Pop Art canvases (his controversial images of women began only in the mid-sixties). That year Bryan Robertson pioneered Pop Art at the huge space of the Whitechapel Art Gallery and the Fluxus Group, including Yoko Ono, were shown at Gallery One. David Hockney received his gold medal from the Royal College of Art dressed in a gold suit with his hair dyed golden. The Robert Fraser, Kasmin and Signals galleries opened their doors and Pop and Op Art were well and truly launched.

In the cinema, the decade opened with a bang when Karel Reisz's *Saturday Night and Sunday Morning* was released in 1960. Lindsay Anderson described it as having 'changed the face of the British cinema overnight ... It opened doors that had been nailed fast for 50 years.' Here was a new writer, Alan Sillitoe, and a new star, Albert Finney, who delighted audiences as the working-class lad who told the authorities where to get off. The film had a new, liberated attitude towards sex, not the hypocritical titillation of Tinseltown but a gritty, down-to-earth, Lawrentian approach in keeping with the changing times. John Schlesinger's 1963 film *Billy Liar*, adapted from Keith Waterhouse's novel and starring Tom Courtney and Julie Christie, continued the theme.

With the ending of National Service and the prospect of two years in the armed forces removed, and with the 'white-heat' of the 'scientific revolution' promised by Harold Wilson's new Labour government, a separate youth culture quickly developed. The country was ripe for it, the atmosphere was different and people wanted change. And all over London, from an East End pub to a débutante's ball in Mayfair, all you could hear was 'She loves you, yeah, yeah, yeah ...'

In 1962 the Beatles had made only a handful of visits to London; the next year they travelled there almost once a week. After signing with EMI, more and more of their business was in London, recording, appearing in concert, on radio and television. Their record company, the recording studios, television stations and the BBC were all in the capital. The motorway network had yet to be built and it took six or seven hours to drive from Liverpool to London through the industrial Midlands. Even at night the ancient highway was crowded with lines of slow-moving lorries, their drivers fortified by the extra-strong tea sold in pint mugs at the 'transport only' all-night caffs. It was impractical to keep returning to Liverpool between each engagement and the group soon developed an intimate knowledge of the cheaper London hotels.

They stayed at the Royal Court Hotel in Sloane Square, Chelsea, or in the cheap hotels around Russell Square in Bloomsbury: the faded grandeur of the Russell and the Imperial on the square itself or, more often, the President round the corner on Guilford Street or the small hotels all down Gower Street, now filled with tourists but then largely used by scholars studying at the nearby British Museum library or visiting the University of London and its campus around Russell Square.

PAUL: It was a group experience, the four of us, that's how we first arrived. We would be staying in Gower Street. It was like 'digs'. It appealed to the artists in us. You could read Lynne Reid Banks's *The L-Shaped Room* and totally associate. 'This is what I'm doing! This is about me.' It was in that kind of spirit we came to Russell Square, and would do photo sessions with Dezo Hoffmann in the square. We'd come out of breakfast at the hotel, have a nice Rothman after breakfast, pop over to the square, do the thing, then we'd have to be off to Birmingham or somewhere.

When we came down to London we were provincial kids coming down to the big city, so it was all magic to us, all the buildings, all the names: 'Kensington, wow! Chelsea, gosh! Soho, wow! Tottenham Court Road, God!' You'd heard about all these places, read about 'em, you'd seen 'em in movies, so we really enjoyed being there. Charing Cross Road, wow! Whenever we came to London we went to Charing Cross Road for the guitar shops. It was like going to Santa's grotto. We just window-shopped and dreamed. 'I'll get one of them!'

We were just young kids experiencing the thrill of this. We'd been to Hamburg but we'd not knocked round London much. We were just in and out in the van trying to find places, though we had quite a lot of fun doing that.

They also got to know some of the London groups. To have five or six different acts on the bill was not unusual in those days so they spent a great deal of time sitting around backstage with the other acts, waiting to go on. They also met fellow rock musicians in the clubs – or, in some cases, actively sought them out, as they did on 21 April 1963, when all four Beatles walked in on a Rolling Stones gig to see what all the fuss was about. Paul: 'We'd heard about this blues band, and we were into American blues so we showed up at the Station Hotel, Richmond. And there they were, the early Stones: Brian, Mick waving his mike in that characteristic way, and of course the little harmonica thing that he'd pull in on that tight microphone. And he saw us all walk in. We all had long suede leather coats and we all had little suede caps.'

The final sartorial embellishment that Hamburg had provided for the Beatles was a set of matching black suede coats and hats from the same shop that had made their leather suits. Paul: 'We knew that when we went back with these suede twat 'ats, as we used to call 'em, cheese cutters; twat hats and long-length full suede coats, then people would notice.' He was right; the Beatles' long coats were one of the reasons that the Rolling Stones abandoned Chicago blues in favour of rock 'n' roll.

> PAUL: Mick says that that is what made him want to get into rock 'n' roll. He saw us come in and he thought, 'Fuckin' hell! I want one of those coats! I want a long coat like that, but to do that, I'll have to earn money.' This is what he said, and that was when he described us as a 'four-headed monster'. Which is true. It was one of our things to go around together because there was a great common bond between us, of having come all this way from Liverpool, through all these experiences in common.

Wimpole Street

On 18 April 1963, the Beatles took part in a BBC concert broadcast live from the Royal Albert Hall. They were at the hall most of the day, for a morning rehearsal and an afternoon run-through of the grand finale when all the acts on the bill assembled on stage to sing 'Mack the Knife'. While they were waiting around, the Beatles did a photo session for the BBC weekly listings magazine *Radio Times*. The photographer posed them with Jane Asher, a seventeen-year-old red-haired actress who had been a guest panellist on the BBC TV show *Juke Box Jury*.

Jane had a wonderful ability to put people at their ease. She had an air of seriousness and a self-assurance rare in someone so young, combined with the energy of a teenager. She was outgoing, but her enthusiastic conversation was informed by a fine education and years of experience as an actress, making her far more sophisticated than the average seventeen-year-old. She was also extremely pretty. Jane had been asked to do a celebrity interview with the Beatles for *Radio Times* so the photographer set up some shots of her screaming at them like a fan. After the concert she joined the group backstage in the green room.

PAUL: We knew her as the rather attractive, nice, well-spoken chick that we'd seen that year on *Juke Box Jury*. We all thought she was blonde because we'd only ever seen her in black and white on television, and we went mad for blondes. Then she came backstage afterwards and so we all immediately tried to pull her. You know, being the order of the day.

Anyway, one thing and another, we ended up back at the Royal Court Hotel where we were staying. We went to a journalist, Chris Hutchins's apartment on the King's Road. It was all very civilised, and we were all there. But at the end of all that, I ended up with Jane. Because I'd maybe made the strongest play or maybe she fancied me, I don't know what. I probably just sort of mentioned, 'Ful semyly hir wympul pynched was.' My only Chaucer line! Probably that did it! She'd be smart enough to know. But I ended up with her. All very innocent and stuff, so from then on I made strenuous efforts to become her boyfriend.

By the summer of 1963, the Beatles had become too famous to stay in regular hotels because of the constant attention of their fans. Hotels objected to mobs of squealing girls rushing through the lobbies and corridors searching for their idols. Since they were spending so much time in London, Brian Epstein rented a flat for them. The 'Beatles flat' was apartment L at 57 Green

Street, Mayfair. The idea was that they would all share the rent and use it when they were in town; a fan-magazine idea of heaven, with the four lovable mop tops all living together. In fact it was the very opposite. To begin with, Paul was late off the mark. By the time he got there, the others had grabbed the best rooms and he was left with a tiny cramped room in the back. They all had beds, but it was an unfurnished flat and the Beatles had no time to buy anything for it so there were no pictures on the walls, no chairs, just bare rooms. Paul: 'We didn't really bother. We'd keep saying, "We must get a table, we must get a kettle." But we were pretty hopeless about all that so it was a very cold place. There was no homeliness about it at all. There was nobody's touch. I hated it.'

By now, the press had found out that John was married with a child. Brian Epstein thought that it would harm the group's image if it became known that John was unavailable and had insisted that Cynthia be kept out of the way. Now there was no longer any need for secrecy and John brought Cynthia and baby Julian down to live in a flat at 13 Emperor's Gate, near the Cromwell Road airport terminal. This freed John's room for Paul, but he only used the Green Street flat a short time before a much better offer came up.

Paul and Jane had hit it off together and every time he was in London he would go and see her. They went to plays and clubs, but spent most of their time together at her parents' house in Wimpole Street, sitting talking late into the night. They were falling in love.

In *A Twist of Lennon* Cynthia Lennon wrote:

Paul fell like a ton of bricks for Jane. The first time I was introduced to her was at her home and she was sitting on Paul's knee. My first impression of Jane was how beautiful and finely featured she was. Her mass of Titian-coloured hair cascaded around her face and shoulders, her pale complexion contrasting strongly with dark clothes and shining hair. Paul was obviously as proud as a peacock with his new lady. For Paul, Jane Asher was a great prize.

Paul soon got to know her family. Jane's mother Margaret managed to combine a full career as a music teacher with running a large household with three children.

> PAUL: She was a very warm person, a very nice mumsy-type woman, great cook, nothing was too much for her, a really nice person. Richard the dad was a wacky medic, very intelligent, very eccentric. But terrific and a great fun person to know. Then there was Jane's older brother Peter, who was an interesting, bright guy, also very interested in music and very musical. There was a lot of connection there. Claire was a very nice younger sister, lot of fun.

Jane's brother Peter was soon to be a part of the successful group Peter and Gordon, and her sister Claire was also in show business, as an actress in the daily radio soap *Mrs Dale's Diary*. The family lived in a large town house in Wimpole Street in the West End of London. It was a Georgian terrace house with six floors, including a rambling basement. On the top floor, in the old servants' quarters, were Peter's bedroom and a little music room. Sometimes, late at night, Paul would be invited to stay over rather than go back to Green Street. Then one day, in the course of conversation, Jane suggested that he could live at Wimpole Street if he hated the Green Street flat so much. Her mother would let him have the attic room.

He did not take long to decide. 'It was everything Green Street was missing; there were people there and food and a homey atmosphere, and Jane being my girlfriend, it was kind of perfect!' In November he moved out of Green Street and took his few belongings to the Asher household. George and Ringo stayed on in the flat until the spring of 1964 when the lease expired, then moved to a better flat below Brian Epstein's in Whaddon House, William Mews, in Knightsbridge.

Jane Asher was educated at Queen's College, a discreet private girls' school on Harley Street, a short walk away from her home in Wimpole Street. In 1951, someone told Margaret Asher that Jane and her older brother Peter were such beautiful children that they should be in films. She decided that it would help their self-confidence and be an amusing hobby for them. Her friend made the arrangements and Margaret took them along to a theatrical agency. Paul: 'Margaret was a bit of a stage mum. She was very ambitious in that particular direction and they were all in films at a very young age. I think

Richard might have wanted to encourage the academic direction but Margaret was very much the artistic and acting side, particularly acting.'

At the age of five Jane appeared in *Mandy*, the story of a little deaf girl, played by Mandy Miller, which also starred Jack Hawkins. Jane and Peter were never in a film together though they worked regularly in films, radio and television throughout their childhoods. At the age of twelve, Jane made her stage début as Alice in Lewis Carroll's *Alice in Wonderland* at the Oxford Playhouse. Her 1958 recording of *Alice in Wonderland* is still selling well on tape cassette.

In 1960, Jane became the youngest actress until then to play Wendy in the West End production of *Peter Pan* and in 1961 appeared in Lewis Gilbert's well-received film *Greengage Summer*. By the time she met Paul she had a decade of stage, screen and radio appearances behind her and was already well known as an actress.

For a time it seemed that Paul's and Jane's careers might have been complementary. She continued to act in plays and appeared in several more films, including Roger Corman's 1964 film of Edgar Allan Poe's *The Masque of the Red Death*, which was made the same year that the Beatles starred in *A Hard Day's Night*. She and Paul began to move in the same film circles: when Jane played a dolly bird in Lewis Gilbert's 1966 period piece *Alfie* starring Michael Caine, Shelley Winters and Eleanor Bron, Paul already knew Eleanor Bron from having worked with her the year before on *Help!* Paul and Jane had become a part of the élite of the London entertainment scene.

The press first caught wind of their romance when a photographer saw them leaving Neil Simon's play *Never Too Late* at the Prince of Wales Theatre. From then on they were sighted all over town, at plays, art galleries and nightclubs. They immediately became the darlings of the media, which loved to find icons of an age: Richard Burton and Liz Taylor, Terence Stamp and Jean Shrimpton, and now Paul and Jane.

'Really, I suppose what solidified London for me was the house that they lived in at 57 Wimpole Street,' said Paul. It was quite an extraordinary household: an eminent doctor, a music professor, an actress in a daily radio soap opera, an accomplished young stage and screen actress and two world-famous pop singers, all sharing a Peter Pan town house in the centre of London and behaving as if this was perfectly normal, which, for them, it was.

The Asher family tended to gather in the long, narrow kitchen at the back of the house; you could usually find one of them or one of Margaret Asher's music students making tea or toast or having a sandwich at any time of day or night. It was a very informal household in that respect, though all proper meals were eaten in the dining room. The kitchen was Margaret Asher's domain. She suffered from terrible migraine headaches which often kept her awake so no matter what time Paul got in, it seemed as if she was always up, asking if he'd like a bite to eat. Paul: 'For a young guy who likes his home comforts, boy, did she spoil me! She's a real great lady, who liked to cook, who liked to fuss over someone. And I'm not averse to a bit of that! If someone says, "D'you want some breakfast?" I'm not going to say, "No, I'm cool, I'll get my own."' Margaret Asher took him in, mothered him and made him very much one of the family. He was to live there for three years.

Paul found himself in what was essentially an English upper-class household, albeit a rather artistic and eccentric one. He was fascinated:

> It was really like culture shock in the way they ran their lives, because the doctor obviously had a quite tight diary, but all of them ran it that way. They would do things that I'd never seen before, like at dinner there would be word games. Now I'm bright enough, but mine is an intuitive brightness. I could just about keep up with that and I could always say, 'I don't know that word.' I was always honest. In fact, I was able to enjoy and take part fully in their thing.

Dinner conversation would veer from a discussion of the date the tomato was introduced to England – a fierce argument between Peter and his father solved by reference to an encyclopedia – to Dr Asher reaching across the table and signing his name on a sheet of paper upside down ('Bet you can't do that!') and explaining that he had taught himself to write upside down in order to save time when nurses presented papers for his signature.

Wimpole Street and Harley Street, which runs parallel, were streets of elegant town houses built in the eighteenth century by the earls of Oxford for gentlemen and their families on what was then the outskirts of London. The essayist Edmund Burke took up residence there in 1757 and it became an area of fashionable portrait painters,

Royal Academicians and military men. Later, in 1891, Sir Arthur Conan Doyle, whose *Adventures of Sherlock Holmes* was set in nearby Baker Street, lived at 2 Upper Wimpole Street, but Wimpole Street is best known for the poet Elizabeth Barrett, who lived at number 50.

During the years she lived there she rarely left the house of her tyrannical father Edward, who was neurotically determined that none of his eleven children should fall in love or marry. However, on 12 September 1846, when Elizabeth was forty, the poet Robert Browning 'pulled her up from her invalid's couch' and they were secretly married at nearby Marylebone church. Elopement to Italy followed a week later and they lived there happily ever after. Elizabeth Barrett Browning's house no longer stands, but most of the 1750s buildings in the street remain, including number 57 where the Ashers lived. Paul: 'I liked the sense of history. My old school had been like that, and I am always fascinated to see that it's still there. Coming from a new estate in Liverpool, old buildings like that are all very impressive … Linda and I were eventually married in Marylebone registry office, which is a strange little twist.'

Margaret Asher gave tuition in recorder, oboe and other instruments. One of her students was Paul, whom she informally taught to play the recorder, a skill he demonstrated later on 'Fool on the Hill'. She received her students in a small, rather stuffy music room in the basement, well away from the main activity of the house. The room had a low ceiling, wooden cupboards with glass fronts along one wall, and was cluttered with metal music stands and old music scores. The small windows opened into the area below the front railings. It was there that Paul and John would get together to write songs, including 'I Want to Hold Your Hand', their first American number one.

Paul: 'The little music room with all the music stands became my base. So instead of John coming to Forthlin Road, that music room was now my equivalent because it was the most get-away-from-it room. We always tried to find a place to get away from it all, plus it had a piano.'

John Lennon told *Playboy* magazine:

We wrote a *lot* of stuff together, one on one, eyeball to eyeball. Like in 'I Want to Hold Your Hand', I remember when we got the chord that made the song. We were in Jane Asher's house, downstairs in the cellar playing on the piano at the same time.

And we had 'oh, you-u-u ... got that something ...' And Paul hits this chord and I turn to him and say, 'That's *it!*' I said 'Do that again!' In those days we really used to absolutely write like that – both playing into each other's noses.

PAUL: 'Eyeball to eyeball' is a very good description of it. That's exactly how it was. 'I Want to Hold Your Hand' was very co-written. It was our big number one; the one that would eventually break us in America.

Among the many songs Paul composed in the little music room were 'And I Love Her', 'Every Little Thing', 'Eleanor Rigby', 'I've Just Seen a Face', 'You Won't See Me', and 'I'm Looking Through You'. It was a work space with no comfortable armchairs or distractions, perfect for getting the job done.

On the ground floor of number 57 was Dr Asher's reception room. Next to his consulting couch was a manual coffee grinder which he turned vigorously as he listened to his patients' woes. An engraved portrait of Alfred, Lord Tennyson, who was a distant relative on Margaret Asher's side of the family, hung in the hall, and in the formal dining room a glass-fronted bookcase contained such prized possessions as the rare 1925 edition of *The Seven Pillars of Wisdom* by T. E. Lawrence (Lawrence of Arabia). It was bound in red buckram and various family certificates and documents were kept inside, commemorating presentations and official occasions as if it were a family Bible. Peter was very proud of the fact that his grandfather had been T. E. Lawrence's solicitor.

The first floor was Dr Asher's parlour where he'd spend most of his spare time playing an out-of-tune grand piano. Paul: 'I sometimes used to borrow it. I remember writing a bit of stuff on that.' In Georgian times, this would have been the main room of the house, with the biggest windows and a balcony overlooking the street. One of Dr Asher's hobbies was to photograph the view using a pin-hole camera: a cardboard shoe box with a hole in one end and a photographic plate at the other. The exposure took two days and though the results were rather fuzzy and blurred, they gave him great pleasure. Since he was a doctor he could write himself a prescription for the film and fill it at the local chemists at no cost.

One of the buildings across the street photographed by Dr Asher was number 35, once the home of the English Surrealist Edward

James. In 1937, James commissioned the Belgian Surrealist René Magritte to paint several pictures for the house and Magritte was his guest in Wimpole Street during February and March of that year. Paul was later to buy a number of Magritte's works and now has a small collection; one of them, *Le Jeu de Mourre*, was the inspiration for the logo of Apple Records.

The family floor came next, and Margaret Asher's sitting room where everyone gathered. It was a small, crowded room containing an overstuffed settee, a large television and items of memorabilia, family photographs and souvenirs. There was no central heating and everyone sat around a little old Victorian fire grate; visitors perched on the arms of chairs and Jane often sat on Paul's lap as tea was passed around. Jane and Claire had their bedrooms on the third floor, with their names on their doors, still there from when they were children. Above Jane and Claire, at the very top of the house, were the attic rooms where Peter and Paul lived.

The house did not appear to have been decorated for some years. A crack ran up the stairwell and across it, at one turn of the stair, Dr Asher had pasted a small piece of paper. On it was written: 'When this paper tears, the house will fall down.' The fissure had probably been there since the wartime bombing. The stairwell was painted in a variety of colours; Dr Asher had acquired a job lot of paint some years before.

PAUL: So I moved in with the Ashers. No lift or anything, so I got pretty fit, walking those stairs. And they were a fascinating family. My family, my dad, my brother and me, after Mum had died, we were really a little suburban family, watching telly in the evenings, getting the bus everywhere, knowing ordinary Liverpool people, aspiring if anything to the local posh houses. Knowing that there was London and all that, but very wide-eyed about it, quite rightly, I think. It was definitely the big place compared to our little suburban life.

And yet there was an element of continuity in the medical connection. Mary, his mother, had also had a certain amount of medical equipment around the house for use in her work as a midwife.

Dr Asher had been the house physician at the London Hospital and was the assistant medical officer at West Middlesex Hospital.

The title of one of his scholarly papers was 'The Physical Basis of Mental Illness', a subject that interested him greatly, and he had written a book called *Nerves Explained*. He could be very entertaining on the subject of his work and said that his method of dealing with violent mental patients was to run into the room and lie on the floor. 'No matter how mad you are, you don't hit an old man who's lying on the floor. Then, once I've got their attention, I can talk to them.' He once quoted a long piece of medical text which, he said, used only the left-hand keys of a typewriter.

Dr Asher loved to shock his family. Once, when Paul had a bad cold, Dr Asher wrote him a prescription for a nasal inhaler and showed him how to use it. 'You take off the top and place it on your little finger, like so.' He demonstrated. 'Then you take a sniff with each nostril as per normal; then, after you've finished with it, you can unscrew the bottom and eat the Benzedrine.' Peter shuffled his feet nervously and Paul grinned, not knowing how much he could confide in the good doctor. Paul: 'We learned about that stuff up in Liverpool but hearing it coming from him was quite strange.'

Margaret Asher often took pains to point out that her side of the family, the Eliots, was the more illustrious, appearing in *Debrett's Peerage*. Her father was the Hon. Edward Granville Eliot, brother of the seventh and eighth earls of St Germans, of Port Eliot, St Germans, in Cornwall, an ancient Cornish lineage with the red hair of the fighting Celt. Margaret Augusta Asher was a good deal taller than her husband; a strong, ambitious woman but also kind and generous. Her immense practicality was shown in many ways; for instance, she had invested money in shares in scaffolding because, as she said, 'People will always want to build things.'

Margaret was an oboist and had played in a number of orchestras before quitting to have a family. After that she taught the oboe at the Guildhall School of Music. One of her students there had been George Martin, who later became the Beatles' producer. Paul wrote 'Yesterday' during the period he was living at Wimpole Street and Margaret used it as a test piece for her students, which Paul found 'very gratifying'. She was in a constant state of activity: her pupils were often in the house for private tuition, yet she seemed to be constantly cooking or mending or making arrangements for her children.

Born on 22 June 1944, Peter was two years older than Jane. Peter took after his father in height but had his mother's red hair, which he brushed forward in a Beatle cut. Margaret's greying hair still had the auburn tint of its past glory. Dr Asher thoroughly approved of Peter's short-lived relationship with Millie Small, who had a hit in 1964 with 'My Boy Lollipop', because she was black and he thought that it would improve the gene pool in the family and get rid of the red hair.

When he was eight, Peter appeared in the film *The Planter's Wife* starring Claudette Colbert and Jack Hawkins and, the same year, in Harold French's *Isn't Life Wonderful?*. He did some stage acting and lots of radio acting, including BBC Radio's *Jennings at School*. He was a day boy at Westminster School, a public school attached to Westminster Abbey and built in the remains of the medieval abbey outbuildings. He found that school interfered with his film career but in any case, he was becoming more interested in music. He sang and took piano lessons, tried the double bass and asked his mother to teach him the oboe but 'I never played anything well.'

In his early teens he listened to bebop and folk music, particularly Woody Guthrie. During the skiffle craze he played guitar in a school skiffle group for a few dates, then his school friend Gordon Waller introduced him to Elvis Presley, Buddy Holly and the Everly Brothers. In 1962, inspired by the Everly Brothers, he and Gordon performed at school events, billing themselves as Gordon and Peter, imitating the Everlys' style of harmonies with Peter taking the high notes. They made the name change to Peter and Gordon early on when they began to do the rounds of Soho folk clubs and coffee bars.

Paul: 'Gordon Waller was an Elvis maniac; he did a very good impression of Elvis. He was a lot of fun, he was slightly less academic than Peter. It was he who encouraged Peter to jump school. Lunchtime sessions were very popular then so they could do daytime gigs.' Peter and Gordon spent two years circulating tapes to record companies, trying to make a name for themselves, but to no avail – until Paul began going out with Jane. Then record companies suddenly became very interested indeed.

Peter met an A & R man at the Pickwick Club who was quickly convinced of their talent and signed them to EMI. Now that Peter had a record label, Paul gave him a song to launch his career. It was called 'World Without Love', something Paul wrote when he was sixteen at Forthlin Road though he changed the words a bit for Peter and Gordon. Paul: 'The funny first line always used to please John.

"Please lock me away –" "Yes, okay." End of song. It was an early song of mine that we didn't use for the Beatles that I thought would be good for Peter and Gordon – and it was.' Paul had previously offered it to Billy J. Kramer, who rejected it. It was released in Britain on 28 February 1964 and reached number one in May, actually pushing the Beatles' 'Can't Buy Me Love' from the top of the charts. In America it reached number one in June. A double US/UK number-one record was not a bad way to start a career. It also showed that even a song that Paul did not regard as good enough for the Beatles could still be commercial.

It did, however, place Peter in a beholden situation with Paul at home. In normal circumstances, a provincial lad from Liverpool would not have a great deal in common with a Westminster public-school boy, but these were not normal times. Peter's interest in music was wide-ranging and genuine, and he was politically to the left, though he did place great store on the fact that he was a member of MENSA, the society for people with high IQs. Peter was an immensely serious young man and they sometimes talked at cross-purposes when Paul made a terrible Liverpool pun or came out with a throwaway line. Paul was only two years older, but he had almost a year of living on the Reeperbahn behind him as well as the rough and tumble of gigging around the Mersey. Peter, on the other hand, was still at school and living at home. Following his mother's family motto, *'Praecedentibus Insta'* (Press close upon those who take the lead), Peter was content to let Paul show him the way.

They got on well. Paul: 'So I got in with Peter and met Gordon. But Peter was part of a crowd and he knew a slightly different group of people from me. I could talk to him about anything. I was slightly older. I was the Beatle. We were both interested in music and I wrote their first hit song.' Paul, in fact, wrote their first three songs. After 'World Without Love' came 'Nobody I Know'. Paul: 'I wrote that, custom built for Peter and Gordon. That little bit of melody always irritated me. It wasn't a very big hit but it was okay.' It was released in May, followed in September by 'I Don't Want to See You Again', which was again written entirely by Paul, specifically for Peter and Gordon. Two years later, in order to test the theory that it was just the Lennon–McCartney tag that was making his compositions into automatic hits, Paul gave Peter and Gordon a song written under the pseudonym of Bernard Webb. 'Woman' was not the best thing Paul had ever written, but it still made the charts.

Peter had an L-shaped attic room overlooking Wimpole Street, done out in sixties modern style with lots of Norwegian pine-wood shelves which would quickly fill with gold records and various trophies and awards from his career with Peter and Gordon. Paul kept his pair of Brenell tape recorders just inside the room on a chest of drawers since there was no space for them in his own room, and there were also a few of Paul's instruments in there alongside Peter's guitars. Peter and Gordon were to tour America and Japan at the height of the British invasion which followed in the wake of the Beatles' success. Peter became in every respect a famous pop star, with groupies and girls jumping off balconies, a house in the country and a £50 a week allowance from his management, Noel Gay Artists. It was everything he could have wanted except for the tempering effect of having a member of the Most Famous Group on Earth living in the next room.

Outside the front door were always a dozen or so Beatles fans, and they were not there for Peter. 'Oh, it's only Peter,' they would mutter as he got out of a cab. It was very galling for him. Peter and Gordon eventually split in 1967, not long after their last big hit, 'Lady Godiva'. Peter: 'We did a few tours and got fed up. We had management problems. Our manager never came on the road with us. We'd get to a place and the tour wasn't what it was supposed to be. Also, Gordon wanted to go out and be a star on his own.' Peter had always been interested in record production, he would always describe a record in terms of its mixing and editing, so when Peter and Gordon folded he had no trouble with moving sideways into production. He became both producer and manager of Linda Ronstadt and James Taylor, recording a series of hugely successful albums with them and finding his true vocation.

Paul's room was next to Peter's, in the back of the house, next to the top bathroom. It was a small, square room with a single window overlooking Browning Mews, where horses and carriages were once kept. The view of rooftops and chimneys gave him a sense of living in an artist's garret. A large brown wardrobe and a single bed occupied most of the room. There was a wall shelf with some bric-à-brac in a jumble – a couple of Jean Cocteau *Opium* drawings, one in a cracked

frame, a stack of first editions – while the space under the bed rapidly
filled with a haphazard pile of gold records and trophies to which was
added his MBE, awarded to the Beatles by the Queen at an
investiture at Buckingham Palace on 6 October 1965. There was little
to show that the room belonged to anyone much richer than the
servants it had been originally designed for, despite Paul's rapidly
accumulating wealth. It was in 1965, during his time at Wimpole
Street, that he received a letter from his accountant, Harry Pinsker,
telling him that he might like to know that he was now officially a
millionaire.

The main object that caught the eye stood in the corner by the
wardrobe: a battered instrument case with white stencilled letters,
B E A T L E S, containing his violin-shaped Hofner bass. His other
instruments were kept in Peter's much larger room. Paul: 'I eventually
got a piano of my own up in the top garret. Very artistic. That was the
piano that I fell out of bed and got the chords to "Yesterday" on. I
dreamed it when I was staying there. I wrote quite a lot of stuff up in
that room actually. "I'm Looking Through You" I seem to remember
after an argument with Jane. There were a few of those moments.'

Paul had no space in his room even for records, which were kept in
a wire rack on a low wooden trunk on the landing outside his door;
the latest American chart entries were sent over each month by
Beatles USA Ltd, one of Brian Epstein's companies. Many of the
singles Paul played were not even released in Britain. Next to the
records was an old black telephone and at the top of the stairs was an
electric bell, its wires trailing off down the stairwell in a very amateur
way, undoubtedly Dr Asher's handiwork. This was to enable whoever
answered the phone to signal to whoever the telephone call was for,
the number of rings indicating whether a call was for Peter, Paul,
Jane, Claire, Dr or Mrs Asher.

PAUL: The whole style of the family influenced me because of
this social diary they kept. The idea that the whole day was
planned was fascinating for me. They were the first people I
knew that would literally have from seven in the morning till late
at night in a diary, laid out. Jane's diary would be: morning, visit
to the agent, lunch with someone about a part, opening a bazaar
or something, doing an article for *Radio Times*. We'd get the day
done, then there would be the theatre or something and a supper

after that. You'd get home and you'd be up at eight the next morning. With Margaret it would be seven in the morning, so-and-so oboe tuition, so Margaret would go over to do that. I think Peter was actually still at school when I moved in, so until later I wouldn't know his diary so much. And Richard of course had his patients and his hospital work, and Claire had a similar diary situation. And it was very very tight too. It could be like nine o'clock so-and-so, five minutes past nine, telephone So-and-so. I've never known people who stuffed so much into a day. I suppose in my case, in the kids' case, it was a lot to do with youth. But the parents did it just as much. I was amazed by the diary. It did actually structure me a lot; I like structure, I liked that kind of thing. It makes things easier, you can think through the problem in hand and not be bothered by every other peripheral thing.

And by the time you got to like six o'clock, a meal and then the theatre! The *evening*, the real big thing, starts then. It seemed great to me. I was very young and energetic and eager to experience all these great thrills that London had to offer. Not in the spend, spend, spend, 'gimme your pills' kind of way but more in a reasonable way about 'let's see what's really good around here'. So, go see if the National Theatre's any good ... And by God they were! With the Jane connection, obviously I did see a lot of theatre and got into it and was interested in it, and still am.

Being a very bright family they could turn their hand to anything. You can still see them on telly: 'I know that face!' and it's a nine-year-old Peter Asher coming in. They got the parts. Margaret would know where the auditions were being held. They took *The Stage*, for instance, the paper. Even the youngest sister Claire Asher had a role in the daytime radio soap *Mrs Dale's Diary*. Looking back on it now I can see why it was fascinating, they were a very interesting family and had lots of points of connection with me. And obviously if you had stage ambitions, at that time to have a Beatle staying with you would not have hurt. Except for the kids outside. We used to have armies of people. Which I felt really embarrassed about, I said, 'God, look! Can't you realise? Look. Cool it! Go and wait round the recording studio. Go and wait where we work.' I was anxious to dissociate myself from that while I was in this atmosphere, which was more me. It was very good for me as well because in their eyes I wasn't just the Beatle. I often felt the other guys were sort of partying whereas I was learning a lot. Learning an awful lot.

In fact, Paul's relationship with the Ashers was ultimately more important than his relationship with Jane

The fans were a terrible nuisance, defacing the street signs and blocking the road. Paul had more of a relationship with the fans than the other Beatles, partly because he lived in town, and partly because he took a genuine interest in them and got to know many of them by name. Jane also went out of her way to be nice to them, even when they were abusive or tried to kick her, which happened more than once. Some fans even managed to break off and steal one of the cast-iron knobs on the railings outside the front door. Always quick to rise to a challenge, Dr Asher put on his boiler suit and scoured the house for iron utensils and cutlery, which he then melted down. He took a cast of the surviving knob and cast a replica of the missing one. Unfortunately Margaret had been rather fond of some of the items he melted down and the incident caused some friction in the household.

When Paul was filming *Help!* in the spring of 1965, the fans gathered outside the front door in such a mob that Dr Asher devised an escape route out of the back of the building from Paul's attic room. After donning his boiler suit, he climbed out of the window and reconnoitred the route himself, tapping on the windows of the startled residents. When the occupants opened their windows to him, he explained, in his impeccable upper-class accent, that he had a chap staying with him who needed a discreet method of ingress and egress to his premises and would it be all right if he occasionally climbed across their roof? Amazingly they all agreed, and Paul was able to slip out and into Browning Mews behind Wimpole Street and away. Dr Asher enjoyed it all enormously.

PAUL: I used to go out of the window of my garret bedroom, on to a little parapet. You had to be pretty careful, it wasn't that wide, it was only like a foot or so wide, so you had to have something of a head for heights. You'd go along to the right, which was to the next house in Wimpole Street, number 56, and there was a colonel living there, an old ex-army gentleman. He had this little top-floor flat, and he was very charming, it was quite amazing going through. 'Uh! Coming through, Colonel!' 'Oh, oh, okay, hush-hush and all that!' and he'd see me into the lift and I'd go right downstairs to the basement of that house. There was a young couple living down there and they'd see me out through their kitchen and into the garage. I remember I bought them a fridge later on to thank them; I'd noticed they hadn't got a fridge during a conversation with them.

The couple lived above the old stable at 10 Browning Mews and Paul would leave through a street door set between the two garage doors on the cobbled mews. 'I'd do a left and then I'd be through the archway into New Cavendish Street. I'd have to watch that the fans hadn't noticed, they were just around the corner, then I'd just run down the road. It's quite funny to think now of some of the people I met doing that.' The Beatles' driver Alf Bicknell lived in a mews cottage in Devonshire Close, just two blocks from Wimpole Street, so Paul would sometimes be picked up by the Beatles' famous big black Austin Princess. Alf could often be found with Paul in the back kitchen, enjoying one of Mrs Asher's breakfasts before driving Paul somewhere.

Paul's London was *Time* magazine's *Swinging London*, a time before drugs and before hippies, a glittering late-night playground of first nights, doormen, red carpets and cocktail parties, Hollywood smiles and wisecracking working-class lads from up north or the East End being wined and dined and bedded by the daughters of aristocrats, while heard above all the gay laughter and the chatter was the high-pitched whine of the motor-driven camera, the soundtrack of the sixties.

Paul and Jane were a stylish couple – 'trendy' was the word then – and everyone wanted to know them. Fashionable London opened its doors to them; invitations to openings, first nights and dinner parties filled the Wimpole Street mailbox. They became icons, more real to people in smudgy news photographs than in the flesh, shocking to see in real life: Paul, taller than most rock stars, standing almost a head above Jane; the richness of Jane's red hair never apparent in the magazine photographs of the time, most of which were in monochrome. Even today, there is a Jane Asher fanzine, *My Sweet Lady Jane*, produced in San Diego and dedicated to preserving the image of Jane as the ethereal English rose of her days with Paul thirty years ago.

In the early sixties, Paul wore the type of modified mod clothes that were requisite wear for rock groups. On stage he appeared in suits bought from Dougie Millings, 'Tailor to the Stars', who also dressed Cliff Richard, Tommy Steele and Billy Fury from his shop at 63 Old Compton Street. It was Millings who made the famous Beatles collarless jackets, based on a steward's uniform, and the dark-blue and dark-grey lightweight wool and mohair stage suits worn on their 1964 American tour. He made a brief appearance as 'A Tailor' in *A Hard Day's Night* and also made the suits worn by the Madam Tussauds waxwork Beatles dummies which were featured on the sleeve of *Sgt. Pepper*.

Paul bought two or three shirts a week from Star Shirt Makers, a family of Hungarian tailors in Wardour Street, Soho, who made shirts to measure for five pounds. He would go upstairs to their workshop and choose the material and the shirts would be ready next time he visited.

He also bought shirts and ties from Turnbull and Asser on Gerrard Street and trousers and jackets from one of the John Stephens mod shops on Carnaby Street – Stephens had nine male boutiques there by 1966, each a little different. In the early sixties men's shirts had high Victorian collars worn with 'slim jims': thin straight ties. Trousers were worn low on the hips, tight round the bottom with narrow straight legs. Cuban-heel boots, 'Beatle boots', from the ballet and theatrical suppliers Anello and Davide on Drury Lane completed the ensemble.

Like the rock 'n' roll bands, Britain's young fashion designers came pouring out of the art schools. Mary Quant met her husband Alexander Plunket Greene at Goldsmith's College of Art and together they started Bazaar on the King's Road, Chelsea, selling quirky women's clothes inspired by the short tight skirts and black stockings worn by their art-student and beatnik friends in Chelsea. Mary Quant became known as 'the mother of the miniskirt' as the hemline of her dresses rose higher and higher. In the early sixties she introduced her Ginger Group line of cheap fashion for young people: pleated dresses ending just above the knee with a variety of bright accessories. All the trendy young women in London flocked to the King's Road to buy. In *Quant by Quant*, published in 1966, she wrote: 'Women had been building to this for a long time, but before the pill there couldn't really be a true emancipation. It's very clear in the look, in the exuberance of the time – a rather child-like exhilaration: "Wow – look at me! – isn't it lovely? At last, at last!"'

Sally Tuffin and Marion Foale came straight from the Royal College of Art and opened their own business without the traditional apprenticeship to learn the trade. From their small showroom on Carnaby Street, with pin-ups of the Beatles on the wall and rock 'n' roll blaring from the speakers, they dressed Jean Shrimpton for *Vogue* and introduced trouser suits to Swinging London. In Joel Lobenthal's *Radical Rags – Fashions of the Sixties*, Sally Tuffin says, 'When we first cut pants, instead of a skirt, with the jacket, we actually fell about laughing.'

Barbara Hulanicki, another art-school graduate, opened Biba in 1964: dark, loud, very young, in a very grand theatrical setting of huge ornate mirrors, polished mahogany tables and Edwardian potted plants, huge bunches of peacock feathers and purple velvet drapes. Furs, beads, feather boas, scarves and jewellery were all jumbled up on the counters. Dresses hung from old wooden hat stands, and the communal changing room was just an area divided from the shop by an antique leather screen. It was like buying clothes from Sarah Bernhardt's boudoir. Biba was staffed by tiny, tough, very young London girls, living away from home, fiercely independent, who seemed to know all the customers by name. On a Saturday afternoon the shop was so full that girls had to push each other through the door.

The Beatles were continually on the road and in 1963 they played a ten-week series of summer residences at seaside resorts: Margate, Weston-super-Mare, the Channel Islands, Llandudno in North Wales, Bournemouth and Southport, as well as recording, filming, and appearing constantly on radio and television. However, in September of that year, Paul and Jane, Ringo and his then girlfriend Maureen, did manage to get away for a holiday to a country that had not yet succumbed to Beatlemania.

PAUL: I remember going with Jane, Ringo and Maureen on a holiday to Greece, and nobody knew who we were. And we were trying to sell ourselves the whole holiday, 'We are in popular singing group back in England,' and they were going, 'Uh, push off, gringo.' 'No, no, really, we are ...' The band at the hotel were actually quite good, they really had a little bit of acoustic stuff down and had obviously been playing there for years. In fact, in the song 'Girl' that John wrote, there's a *Zorba*-like thing at the end that I wrote which came from that holiday. I was very impressed with another culture's approach because it was slightly different from what we did. We just did it on acoustic guitars instead of bouzoukis.

We didn't get pestered at all, but then I remember coming back and hearing, 'Oh, your record's big in Greece now,' and thinking, Well, there goes another little safe haven, and realising we were knocking these little safe havens off one by one. I thought, Oh, shit, either we're all going to get terribly disappointed and it's not going to be what we wanted. Or get hip right now and start looking for things to offset it. I think I realised, before we even got there, that the Beatles would reach a point where there was no turning back, we couldn't be unfamous after it. I never wanted to become a prisoner of my own fame. That always seemed to me the ultimate tragedy.

Those two and a half weeks were probably the only time that Paul and Jane lived as an ordinary young couple on holiday with friends, untroubled by the huge pressure that fame was about to inflict upon them even though they could feel it coming. Paul described how the day before they left on holiday, the Beatles had played the Royal Albert Hall with the Rolling Stones. The two groups had gone to the top of the wide flight of steps behind the hall leading to Prince Consort Road for a photo session and Paul remembers standing there, posing with the others in bright sunshine, 'all in our smart new clothes with the rolled collars, and we looked at each other and we were thinking, This is it! London! The Albert Hall! We felt like gods! We felt like fucking gods!'

Though this was the only actual holiday that they were able to go on without being pestered by the press and fans, Paul and Jane could still get away at weekends.

PAUL: We got off quite often. Jane knew people in the country. This was another rather upper-class thing: going for the weekend to the country, and the people she knew were often very fascinating people. So we'd stay out in the Home Counties for the night. It was the first time I'd seen people leaving a book by your bedside for you to read. I was quite impressed by their choice of books. It was the assumption that you were reasonably intelligent that I liked. They didn't talk down.

Jane had an aunt in the country with a big posh house. We'd drive out there and stay. Or we would go to Scotland, where we'd meet the local vet and the next-door landowner and go and have whiskies late at night and regale each other with great Highland stories. They were all fascinated by the two of us because we came from such a different world from them and we were individually from different worlds.

I remember Jane had an old aunt in Great Smith Street in Westminster and that was intriguing because I'd never seen inside those tiny miniature houses before. She had one of the old freeholds and she had a maid who would appear when she rang the bell. She used to serve us tea on the old silver, and it was really English tea. It was like something you read about in a Hardy novel. That was it for me, it was stuff happening that I'd only ever read of in books. It was an overhang from Britain's genteel past. She was a very old lady and we used to visit her quite often. It was nice because I've never really had a problem with age. I always liked being the young person that the old people found interesting and you could talk to them and ask, 'How was it?' And you could tell 'em all the modern stories and they'd say, 'Oh, really?' It was always a good basis for an afternoon out. So we got around, we could go places, we could visit quite freely. But the big holidays got increasingly difficult.

One of the holidays we went on, again with Ringo and Maureen, was on a yacht in the Bahamas, the *Happy Days*. I remember writing 'Things We Said Today' in one of the cabins below deck one afternoon on my acoustic guitar. I got away from the main party but it was a bit queasy downstairs; you could smell the oil and the boat was rocking a bit and I'm not the best sailor in the world, so I wrote a little bit of it downstairs and then the rest of it on the back deck where you couldn't smell the engine. I don't know why the engine was on, I suppose we were moving.

Written in May 1964 entirely by Paul, the lyrics to this song, in which a boy affirms his love for his girl even though she is far away, reflect the situation in which Paul and Jane found themselves – each with careers that entailed frequent periods of separation. Rather than translate personal experience into a confessional as John Lennon often did, Paul usually preferred to introduce ambiguity, to distance himself and make the song into a universal experience that others could relate to more directly.

PAUL: I wrote 'Things We Said Today' on acoustic. It was a slightly nostalgic thing already, a future nostalgia: we'll remember the things we said today, some time in the future, so the song projects itself into the future and then is nostalgic about the moment we're living in now, which is quite a good trick. It has interesting chords. It goes C, F, which is all normal, then the normal thing might be to go to F minor, but to go to the B flat was quite good. It was a sophisticated little tune.

Then someone like the *Daily Express* got word that we were there so we had the buzzing little boats around. The reporters would say, 'My editor says I've got to stay here till you give us a picture!' So we always had to pose for a picture, smiling hello but thinking, Piss off!

Jane was probably the inspiration for a number of Paul's love songs, one of the most famous being 'And I Love Her', written at Wimpole Street not long after Paul moved in and recorded in February 1964 for the film *A Hard Day's Night*.

PAUL: It was the first ballad I impressed myself with. It's got nice chords in it, 'Bright are the stars that shine, dark is the sky ...' I like the imagery of the stars and the sky. It was a love song really. The 'And' in the title was an important thing, '*And* I Love Her', it came right out of left field, you were right up to speed the minute you heard it. The title comes in the second verse and it doesn't repeat. You would often go to town on the title, but this was almost an aside, 'Oh ... and I love you.' It still holds up and George played really good guitar on it. It worked very well. I'm not sure if John worked on that at all.

John has claimed that the middle eight was his but Paul disputes this:

The middle eight is mine. I would say that John probably helped with the middle eight, but he can't say 'It's mine'. I wrote this on my own. I can actually see Margaret Asher's upstairs drawing room. I remember playing it there, not writing it necessarily.

Despite her forays into the pop business, Jane saw herself primarily as an actress. Most of her friends were in the theatre and she regarded the pop business as rather frivolous in comparison. She was a hard-working actress, prepared to apply herself to most jobs she was offered. In one week in June 1964 she appeared both in ITV's *Play of the Week*, a serious look at the class problem in modern Britain called *A Spanner in the Grassroots*, and on ITV's panel show *The Celebrity Game*. Only the month before, her film *The Masque of the Red Death* had opened in London. It was all work: television, films, pop journalism or the legitimate theatre. They went to all the new plays, and Jane introduced him to her friends. The two of them quickly became a fixture of London's theatreland.

PAUL: It was a very exciting period in the theatre. I used to love to go to the National, just to see such class! I figured this must be the best anyone could see anywhere in the world. I remember seeing Colin Blakely in Sean O'Casey's *Juno and the Paycock* and thinking, This guy is just damn great! It was good fun because it was meeting professional people who were doing something exciting. Jane and I as a couple would start to be invited to things and it was a reciprocal thing. We'd go to dinner with other actors that Jane knew. They'd invite us, we would invite them back. A lot of socialising went on at that time. You'd build up your phone book.

I remember staying up late one night with Maggie Smith and her husband Robert Stephens, the actor. He wrote to me later to see where I got that flying jacket off the *McCartney* cover because he wanted one. So, sitting up late with them, after having dinner. It was great! Great conversation because it wouldn't be just about rock 'n' roll. I didn't think of it as social climbing, I just thought, Boy, these are real interesting people. You get dinner, so you get to see them in their own environment. It's wonderful! So I met many many diverse people.

We went to a party with Harold Pinter, when he was married to Vivien Merchant. It was great sitting around at parties discussing stuff with Harold Pinter with a few drinks inside you. I loved it. We would see Kenneth Williams and Jill Bennett. We used to see quite a lot of Arnold Wesker. You'd meet people like John Mortimer, and Penelope Mortimer when they were married. I remember one or two of Kenneth Tynan's parties; what would now look like very interesting rooms with let's say a Beatle, a playwright, a novelist, an actress, an opera singer, a ballet dancer all just cross-fertilising. It was this that made London *Swinging London*, made London a great place to be.

The theatrical community was delighted by Paul's involvement and he soon received offers to participate more directly.

PAUL: At school from age eleven they said, 'There are opportunities if you're smart enough.' Then London said, 'You're smart enough, here are the opportunities,' and you're getting money and open doors to all these people. I remember going down to the Mermaid Theatre to talk to Sir Bernard Miles, who said, 'Anything you want to do, anything you want to put on, whether it's a musical thing or whatever ...' They all wanted to attract the young people, a young thinking audience. Like the classical world now thinks I'll attract a young audience with the *Oratorio*.

In September 1966 Paul was even asked by Kenneth Tynan to write music for the songs in the National Theatre production of Shakespeare's *As You Like It*, starring Sir Laurence Olivier. Paul wrote back thanking him, saying he had given the matter some thought but he couldn't write music to Shakespeare's words; perhaps he could write the 'Ballad of Larry O' for them.

Paul's involvement was not just with theatrical London. Through *A Hard Day's Night* producer Walter Shenson they met the American writer Larry Geldoff, who later wrote *M.A.S.H.*, as well as the horror-film actor Vincent Price, the actress Coral Browne and many of the American film people who passed through London. Jane had been in movies all her life and already knew numerous producers and directors. Paul visited John Schlesinger, who made *Midnight Cowboy* and *Sunday, Bloody Sunday*, both classic sixties movies. He met the

British director John Dexter and the producer Ned Sherrin, who later made *The Virgin Soldiers* together.

Life then was the fantasy of Swinging London at its best: intimate candle-lit dinners in the little French bistros that were just opening in Soho and Chelsea, followed by drinks at one of the new 'in' clubs: the Ad Lib, the Scotch of St James, Dolly's on Jermyn Street or Sibylla's on Swallow Street, which was 10 per cent owned by George Harrison. For glamour and showbiz he could dress up for a society party and see his picture afterwards in the gossip columns of the glossy magazines. He could go anywhere, do anything he wanted. Paul could not get enough of it. He systematically explored the city's night life, taking in the fashionable hotel bars, the cabaret clubs, the late-night gambling salons and the international nightclubs, some-times with Jane but often alone.

Paul took advantage of his unique situation by calling up people he had always wanted to meet. One of these was the philosopher Bertrand Russell.

PAUL: Somehow I got his number and called him up. I figured him as a good speaker, I'd seen him on television, I'd read various bits and pieces and was very impressed by his dignity and the clarity of his thinking, so when I got a chance I went down and met him. Bertrand Russell lived in Chelsea in one of those little terrace houses, I think it was Flood Street. He had the archetypal American assistant who seemed always to be at everyone's door that you wanted to meet.

Bertrand Russell was then ninety-two years old but was still very active in the peace movement. Four years earlier he had been jailed for two months for inciting the public to civil disobedience at a peace rally in Hyde Park and he now devoted most of his energies to running the Bertrand Russell Peace Foundation and campaigning against the war in Vietnam. His young assistant, Ralph Schoenman, made Paul comfortable until Lord Russell was ready to see him.

PAUL: I sat round waiting, then went in and had a great little talk with him. Nothing earth-shattering. He just clued me in to the fact that Vietnam was a very bad war, it was an imperialist war and American vested interests were really all it was all about. It was a bad war and we should be against it. That was all I needed. It was pretty good from the mouth of the great philosopher. 'Slip it to me, Bert.'

I reported back to John, 'I met this Bertrand Russell guy, John,' and I did all the big rap about the Vietnam and stuff, and John really came in on it all. And he then did *How I Won the War*.

It was rare for someone not to respond to a telephone call from a Beatle. Paul: 'So I'd be ringing people like Len Deighton, having dinner with him. He's a good cook so that was very pleasant.' He was interested to see how everyone lived, not just the rich and famous. The architects John and Marina Adams, who refurbished Paul's London home, were one couple he would visit. Paul: 'It was a pleasure to go round to see people like John and Marina who were young professionals just setting up house. Otherwise it was Dick James and big apartments or Brian Epstein's big house, which was all a bit swish. I'm not sure if the other Beatles used to do it but I got into it.'

Their great fame gave the Beatles access to many of the most famous figures of the time: they were introduced to the royal family and the prime ministers of the day; they met the winning English World Cup football team, Elvis Presley, Cassius Clay and Jayne Mansfield, though John got worried when she put her hand on his thigh. Later they would use their celebrity to meet film-makers, artists and poets but in the early days of their fame, most of the meetings were not requested but arranged, and sometimes not wanted at all.

In one instance the Beatles were staying in the Aldrovandi Palace, a large luxury hotel in Rome overlooking the zoo. Brian Epstein found out that Noël Coward was also staying there.

PAUL: Brian came and said, 'Noël Coward would like you meet you boys.' We all said, 'Oh, fucking hell, no! No, no, no. I'm going to bed.' Nobody was really keen, we were better just casually interacting with people. Once you actually had to meet them, it became a bit official and our black humour would kick in and we'd try and counteract the fact that four of us were going to have to line up to meet the great man, so piss-takes would come fairly readily. No one was going to go, and Brian said, 'You can't, you just can't!' So I went down and met him.

But then he said some not too pleasant things about us after that, so fuck him anyway.

But you don't have an awful lot in common with these people. You would just meet them because they were great people. Sir Malcolm Sergeant would look in at Abbey Road, with his pinstripe suit and his red carnation, or his rose or whatever it was he always wore. George Martin would say, 'Chaps, Sir Malcolm would like to say hello.' 'Hello, boys.' 'Hey, wow, Sir Malcolm. Great, well, fabulous seeing you!' I remember meeting Sir Tyrone Guthrie on the front steps of EMI. To me it seems like he was in a *huge* astrakhan coat but it might just be my memory playing tricks, a big hat, indeed the Great Man of the *Just William* books. And this is what I call the cusp, they were all there. There was a rubbing-up that occurred, and we weren't snobs. They were on the way out, we were on the way in.

Sometimes being a Beatle gave them the edge even over other celebrities. Their favourite restaurant was Parkes on Beauchamp Place. It was very small and very expensive and no matter who you were a table had to be booked weeks in advance because there were only four or five tables. The Beatles, however, knew Tom Benson who ran it and to them it was an outpost of working-class Liverpool where they could always be assured of getting the best table, the one next to the kitchen, whenever they turned up, unannounced.

PAUL: Tom was a very sweet, quiet-spoken Liverpool guy. His mum had a flower stall outside the Liverpool News Theatre which showed cartoons and news all day while you were waiting for a train. He said, 'You know the old lady who sells flowers outside the News Theatre?' 'Yeah?' 'It's me mum!' 'Oh, well, blow me down!' So of course then the flowers on every plate was all explained.

These same flowers made their way into a Beatles song. Tom would bend the petals back on tulips to create a strange organic sculpture for each plate, the stamen and inside colouring of the petals making an almost unrecognisable object. John referred to them in 'Glass Onion': 'Looking through the bent back tulips, to see how the other half live.' The other half being the wealthy Chelsea crowd who patronised the restaurant, as well as, presumably, the parts of a tulip not normally seen. The food at Parkes was excellent and very sixties: there were exciting ways to use an avocado, then virtually unknown in Britain, game with cherries and chicken with grapes. Tom Benson kept cans of bamboo shoots, exotic food in those days, in order to create a vegetarian meal if George Harrison and Patti showed up unannounced. His restaurant was another example of the social fluidity of the sixties which allowed young working-class people to get to the top in previously closed professions.

One of the problems of Paul's fame was that shopping or eating out was made difficult by the continual pestering of autograph seekers and press photographers. The only escape was to shop at the costly boutiques of Mayfair and Knightsbridge where discretion was guaranteed and to eat in the same fashionable and expensive restaurants as other celebrities. Jane was always distressed by what she saw as a waste of money. Once, to Paul's embarrassment, Jane examined the bill at Chi Chi's nightclub and demanded to know how two rounds of drinks for four people could possibly amount to an average week's wages.

West End

The advantages of fame outweighed any inconveniences it might gave. It gave the Beatles the keys to the city. All doors were open to them. In the rock 'n' roll hierarchy they were the top; utterly unassailable. The public adored them; not just the fans but the mums and dads as well. Politicians vied with each other to meet them and the press dutifully reported their every move. It also gave them immunity. As long as the police liked them, they could do anything they wanted. Donovan remembers one occasion in 1966 when Paul dropped by at his flat in Maida Vale. They smoked a few joints, jammed on a few songs together; then the doorbell rang. Donovan wrote:

> I went to see who it was. It was a young bobby asking about a car illegally parked in the Edgware Road. Paul came to the door and the copper stood to attention.
> 'Oh, it's you, Mr McCartney. Is it your car? A sportscar, sir?' Sir, mind you. 'Shall I park it for you?'

Paul gave him the keys to the Aston Martin and the car was parked. The bobby came back with the keys and left with a grin. Now you can see that the Beatles were treated like royalty then, they could do no wrong, yet.

Paul: 'George Harrison was saying there appeared to be nothing else but the Beatles for a couple of years, certainly not in our lives but, he said, even in other people's lives it seemed like there was just nothing else. Everything was to do with the Beatles, the Beatles, the Beatles. There was no other frame of reference.'

In the early sixties, when Paul first began his in-depth studies of London's nightlife, it still consisted mostly of gambling and cabaret clubs. There were no all-night restaurants, except the one at London airport, and that became so crowded with non-flyers, many in party clothes, that they brought in a new rule requiring at least one in the party to have a boarding pass. Until the so-called Beat Boom got fully under way, there were none of the 'in' clubs for rock musicians that were to open later in the decade. In order to get a meal after a late-night recording session or a gig, there was nowhere to go except a nightclub.

> PAUL: I used to go to nightclubs a lot. You know, London, hey! We'd get back from a thing quite late, and my day hadn't ended. I'd have a bit of dough, access to London's nitery. Young guy on my own, what do you want me to do, go to bed? I couldn't go to a play, because they'd all finished by 10.30. Really the only entertainment by then would be a cabaret, a late-night thing.

London's clubland was in Mayfair, around Berkeley Square: Annabel's, the Astor and the Colony were on the square itself, the Blue Angel and the Beachcomber were just off it on Berkeley Street and there were a dozen more within a few blocks. Paul would look at the ads in *What's On* and try them out: Bertie Green's Astor Club where you could dine and dance till 4.00 a.m; the Blue Angel at 14 Berkeley Street. 'Montmartre In Mayfair, where you can shuffle or listen to the Don-Claude Quartet'; the Beachcomber Hawaiian bar at the Mayfair Hotel ('exotic food, swinging music') or L'Hirondelle on Swallow Street with Phil Phillips, 'the continental comedian and the gorgeous L'Hirondelle Lovelies, the dance team all London are [sic] raving about'. The cabaret usually started at 1.00 a.m, there was always a comedian – David Frost was doing his stand-up comedy act at Quaglino's – a singer or two and sometimes several resident combos: 'Dancing to Jack Dorsey's Broadcasting Band'. There were show girls but no strip-tease.

> PAUL: If it was lousy I'd just order a drink and go, and if it was good, I'd maybe order a meal and watch the cabaret. I was very well versed in all of that way of life. I really became a man about London. Every detective story or James Bond novel had all these clubs like the Blue Angel so it was fun for me.
>
> I remember the first of the places I found in *What's On* was the Saddle Room on Hamilton Place, which was owned by a French lady, Hélène Cordet, who had been a TV star, and it was rumoured she had some sort of connection with the Duke of Edinburgh, which was why she'd been set up with the club. But the real point was late-night eating. The restaurants tended to wrap it up around eleven, but there were certain ones started to open later, like Borscht 'n' Tears. There'd often be an acoustic act and it was nearly always pretty good.

One of the biggest dinner clubs was the Talk of the Town, famous for its spectacular shows.

> PAUL: I'd go to Talk of the Town a lot. Part of the thrill for me at the time was the reverential treatment. I would always ring and do it properly but when I arrived I was known by all the maître d's so I could just swan into a place, which I defy anyone to turn down. You'd see dreadful people there but I've got a kind of side of me that's fascinated by dreadful acts, I like to see that kind of thing. I was collecting information, *peep peep peep*, antenna out.
>
> I saw Sophie Tucker, 'A legend', at Talk of the Town. I remember exchanging jokey notes with David Frost because she did this big appeal, 'And I wonder if you'd like to donate to the Sophie Tucker Home for the Injured' or something, so I was sending notes to David Frost, 'I wonder if you'd like to contribute to the Paul McCartney Forest Fund for Young Trees.' To the waiter, 'Could you give this to Mr Frost?' I had a lot of fun with that kind of thing, growing up in London. And I had a bit of money. That was the big thing, of course. I could get

in these clubs with my fame. I could afford them and I could give good tips, what more d'you want, man?

My thing with clubs became later and later and later. Often, after a few drinks, I'd be seriously looking for somewhere to party at four in the morning. By then they would tend to be gambling clubs. There would be the Cromwellian in Kensington which had gambling that went on when the rest of the club was closed. You could go to the casino and do in another hour.

I used to go to the Curzon House, near the Playboy Club, near the Hilton. I'd get thirty pounds in five-shilling chips. It was all very cheap and I'd do lots of roulette and mainly lose. Lots of high speculation, it was so good if I ever got a thirty-six to one. And the idea anyway was to lose this money. The way I figured it was if I'd gone to a theatre and dinner, it would have been about thirty quid, so I thought this is going to be the equivalent. It was just fun.

The Curzon House at 21 Curzon Street was Brian Epstein's favourite club and Paul would sometimes run into him there. Brian would lose thousands at baccarat or chemin de fer. He liked to make an evening of it, eating a superb meal and drinking fine wine, knowing that the club would pick up the tab because he lost so much at the tables.

PAUL: Brian would be, 'Ugghhh, the pills!' The jaw would be grinding away. I remember Brian putting his Dunhill lighter on a bet – 'That's a hundred pounds' – and he'd lose it all. But he didn't mind, some people just like that bumpy ride.

The best fun was if I had to be somewhere and it wasn't that late and I had to get rid of the chips. I remember one evening I didn't want to just change them, so I put them on 36–1, and I kept winning! When you wanted to get away, suddenly your luck changed. 'Oh, oh, oh, good!' That evening I went out with more than I came in with, but generally not. I like characters, I like looking, I like a bit of voyeurism. I would always imagine I was a writer. I would get ideas for songs, ideas for characters, little things, essences of things. I'm a great observer, and a gambling club has a great ambience. I used to really like it. It's like a big game but it's serious. Nobody's laughing. I used to wander round the tables, occasionally throw a five-bob chip on blackjack. It was really a social thing. The kind of people I'd meet there would be Roger Moore looking like James Bond, or Michael Caine, that slightly older film-star kind of guy.

You're talking about some kid from an estate in Liverpool, who'd barely been into the city centre, who then had been thrust into Hamburg, not the city centre but the strip-club district, who now was able to wander freely around London. It just seemed fabulous. You had your own packet of cigarettes. You were growing up and there were all these exciting things happening. Obviously, for me, the great thing was I had an entrée to places like the Curzon House gambling club where even Lord So-and-so had to get nominated and seconded! But it was always, 'Hello, Paul! How are you? Go right in, mate. That'll be all right. Let 'im in.' And you always, 'Oh, thank you. Thanks very much.' Wink wink.

And I could reciprocate occasionally. I remember at the première of *Hard Day's Night*, there was this boxer called Bruce Wells; lightweight, British, quite good. My dad and I liked boxing in Liverpool. We knew all the boxers, we watched a lot of it on telly. We'd arrived in our giant Austin Princess, nudging our way through millions of people in Piccadilly Circus, around Eros and hanging off all the buildings, to the London Pavilion. So we pushed through to the entrance awning, where the crowds of people were held back by ropes, and this guy just pushed out of the crowd and said, 'All right, Paul, all right, Paul,' acting like a bodyguard, and I thought, Who the hell are you? He said, 'All right, Paul, Bruce Wells,' he said, 'I'm with you, right? I'll just stick behind you.' And I caught on very quickly to what he was doing and I said, 'Okay then, go on, just get ...' And he said, 'Make way, please,' and he looked absolutely the part with the dinner suit, and I got him in. And I very nearly got him in the royal line-up! Princess Margaret, I think it was. Because he just stuck with me, and he looked the part.

The Ad Lib

It was not long before the club owners realised the potential of providing a club aimed specifically at the rock 'n' roll crowd. The Ad Lib was the first to play good music, stay open late and tolerate the antics that the groups got up to. It was located above the Prince Charles Theatre at 7 Leicester Place, a pedestrian walkway leading off Leicester Square in Soho, and was reached by a lift. The manager, Brian Morris, used to work at Les Ambassadeurs and knew how to tailor the glamour and elegance of the fifties Mayfair nightclubs to suit the emerging pop aristocracy. He dressed the disc jockey in a dinner jacket and all drinks were served in miniature bottles. The DJ played solid R & B – Otis Redding, James Brown, Wilson Pickett, Bobby 'Blue' Bland and Aretha Franklin – from a pair of turntables housed in a piano case. The same music played in the lift to get you in the mood on the way up.

Once the Beatles had been sighted there, it quickly became home to the Moody Blues, the Hollies and the Rolling Stones as well as the young in-crowd of photographers, boutique owners, dress designers, actors and playwrights, rock 'n' roll managers, hairdressers and fledgling musicians who were busy creating Swinging London.

PAUL: The Ad Lib was the first. We started to get a bit of money and a bit of time, and that was the nightclub where the good music played, mainly Black American. They had a black chef who used to come out about 11.30 and bang a tambourine and everyone would cheer and dance the conga. It was a shouty, lively scene. Lots of silly things happened there. They'd often have to chuck you out of those placcs. I remember arm wrestling with Allan Clarke of the Hollies and he'd been beating everyone. And to my surprise I beat him. I'm really not at all sporty, but I think I vibed him a lot. 'You know, I'm a Beatle after all.'

It was a social scene. You'd sit there and the evening would just build. There was a lot of loud music if conversation got boring. But it was fun, it was the pub, that's really what it was.

Among the regulars at the Ad Lib was the famous sex-change April Ashley.

PAUL: She used to ask me, did I want to go and feed the ducks? She was very nice, she was definitely a sort of woman, but we all knew from the newspapers that she was a man. I'd sit and talk to her, and I guess people could tell that it wasn't worth pulling me. I think you've got to give off scents, and respond correctly to certain things, whereas with me it was just flirting. She used to flirt and I'd be flirted with, quite happily. But when it got to 'Do you want to come and feed the ducks in St James's Park?' I'd say, 'No, I'll give that a miss.'

The main thing was, it was just a great club: great dance, pull birds, chat with unusual people. Then it dwindled, as these things did; their stars rose and waned. Suddenly there's another club that's better, like a watering hole, one has more water, one is drying up. The Lib fell out of favour a bit and the next one was the Scotch of St James. But of course, it was all a family. I used to go to each one and see who was there. Most people had their own favourites, but you would just check out each club and if there wasn't much happening you'd just go on to the other one, like a pub crawl.

I used to also do a few bars. Late night would find me at Trader Vic's or Quaglino's, often, with nobody I knew, hanging, chatting to the barman, never smashed and falling over, always able to get home. I was very controlled about it.

Certainly I've had evenings when I've been out to a club and not been legless but when I've got back I've suddenly realised, Oh, I've had three too many. And now they are beginning to kick in. You're as drunk as three back, and that was more than enough. People would buy you drinks. 'The gentleman over there sent you a drink.' 'Thank you.' So you'd be at one of those speakeasies and another tray would arrive. 'Oh. Really, who is this from?' 'The gentleman over there.' 'Oh, thanks.'

The clubs in those days were very much for drinking; slipping away to the toilets for a line of cocaine was completely unheard of in the mid-sixties. John Dunbar remembers going to the Ad Lib one night with Paul and meeting up with John Lennon: 'I remember John being very shocked when I lit some hash in a little hash pipe I had – "What are you doing, man?" He was very paranoid.' In fact the exclusivity of the club meant they were perfectly safe from the police, but drugs were almost completely unknown in London at the time and tremendous precautions were normally taken before using them. To whip out a hash pipe in a crowded club seemed the height of folly.

Alma

Because they were the first band to really make it big, there was no ready-made rock community for the Beatles to hang out with when they first came to London. The majority of people at the Ad Lib were not in the music business. It was a crossover period and the Beatles found themselves mixing with both the variety stars of the past and the up-and-coming new bands of the future.

PAUL: We'd sometimes get booked on variety bills. I remember a comedian called Derek Roy once introduced us, a poppy-eye English comedian who was now fallen on hard times, and the only way I knew of him was from a comic called *Radio Fun*, when I'd been a little kid. It had a red and white cover and was black and white inside and in it were people like Frank Randle. I had no idea who Frank Randle was but he was in *Radio Fun*. He'd been a star on the radio, he was a famous northern comedian, all stuff that my parents knew about. The radio was equivalent to the big movie stars now so all the people off the radio were in these comics. Now what they would do for a gig would be to introduce us. Well, they'd do anything! They'd MC, tell a few gags, but they used to have a terrible time because the audience only wanted to see us. They did not want to listen to the ramblings of some demented old comedian. But we also had people like Dave Allen, who was just starting off. He was very good. Dave could handle it, he was irreverent, knew how to do this kind of stuff.

So we had associations with these people. For instance, there might be dancers on the bill. Now you get that with Janet Jackson and Madonna, but that's hardly the same kind of thing. Then it was just hoofers. Someone would come on and kick their legs up for a bit. So it was on the cusp of showbiz. We were still in showbiz. It wasn't rock – as it's now offensively named. It wasn't that, it wasn't an industry, it was very small time and we were playing cabarets. It was crossover with the old-time showbiz and one of the people who we'd met doing it was Alma Cogan.

Alma, 'the girl with the giggle in her voice', was famous throughout the fifties and early sixties as much for her huge glittery dresses – she would make as many as eleven dress changes in one show – as for her bouncy novelty records like 'I Can't Tell a Waltz from a Tango'. She had more hits than any other female singer in Britain, though mostly in the early fifties. She was always on television variety shows with her black bouffant hairdo, eyebrows arched high in a moment of frozen surprise, her mouth wide open in a Hollywood smile and yet another new wardrobe to show the viewers. She was a huge star.

The Beatles first met her when they appeared together on *Sunday Night at the London Palladium* on 12 January 1964. They met her in rehearsals and became instant friends, recognising that they shared a similar sense of humour. In Sandra Caron's charming portrait of her sister, *Alma Cogan: A Memoir*, she tells how Alma asked the Beatles back to the family flat at 44 Stafford Court, in Kensington High Street, after the show. Despite her years of fame – she cut her first record in 1952 – at thirty-one Alma still lived at home with her mother and sister. The Beatles were smuggled out of the side door of the Palladium to avoid being mobbed by screaming fans and had left the building before the final curtain even came down, so they arrived at the first-floor flat long before Alma. Alma had not telephoned to say they were coming and Sandra unexpectedly found herself playing hostess to the Fab Four. Fortunately she already knew Paul, who had introduced himself to her in 1962 when Sandra was performing in a satirical revue at Peter Cook's Establishment Club in Greek Street, Soho.

There could be no better representative of the old-fashioned Denmark Street Jewish showbiz side of the London entertainment industry than Alma Cogan, who even had a hit in Iceland with 'Never Do a Tango with an Eskimo', but this unconventional friendship made sense. Alma and her warm and generous family had much in common with the Beatles' old neighbours and friends in Liverpool, like Rory Storm's mother's house where groups could drop by any time for a cup of tea and a chat. Sandra Caron wrote: 'They needed to relax and get away from crowds. Our flat gave them refuge for many months to come, with Mum – Mrs Macogie, as they called her – making pots of tea and sandwiches, and playing charades.'

It is debatable just how much of a refuge the famous Cogan flat was since it was an open house for a very theatrical side of the showbiz crowd: Danny Kaye, Ethel Merman, Sammy Davis Junior,

Cary Grant and Michael Caine were all regulars when they were in town, as were English pop singers of the fifties like Frankie Vaughan, who had many chart hits, including 'Green Door' in 1956, and Tommy Steele, whose 'Singing the Blues' established him as Britain's first rock 'n' roll singer in January 1957. Still, all the Beatles used to visit but, Sandra wrote, 'at first we saw rather more of Paul, who would drop into the flat at all hours. One time, with his niece in tow, a lovely little girl, he brought the three of us a gift. It was the biggest bottle of Hermès perfume I've ever seen. It looked like a gallon.'

PAUL: We'd known Alma as the big singing star. We never interacted musically, she was a little too old for our generation, not much probably, but it seemed like an eternity, so I never took her seriously musically. She was old-school showbiz. She invited us round to her mum's place in Kensington, she and her sister lived with her mum, and her mum was an old Jewish lady. They were very nice, Alma and her sister Sandra. There was a slight romance thing there with Sandra. Sandra was a little younger than Alma. It never sort of took off or anything but I sensed the mum saying when I went to visit, 'That's a nice boy, darling, you could … you know?' Looking back on it now, there was a sense of that. And there were parties and, after all, young people, it was par for the course.

The parties were held in the lounge, a large room filled with Italian leather furniture. Red lampshades cast a rosy hue over the proceedings, wine came in red glasses and the napkins were pink. The only books to be seen were an unopened set of *Encyclopaedia Britannica* but there were hundreds of long-playing records neatly arranged on shelves. Bottles of spirits filled a large silver tray; flamenco-dancer dolls, glass vases and ornaments filled the surfaces. The walls were lined with framed photographs of Alma, put there by her proud mother alongside a rather kitsch portrait of Alma by Fred Wood.

PAUL: I saw a documentary about John Betjeman, who said that when he got out of college there was a country house to which he was invited. And he said, 'There I learned to be a guest,' and that's what was happening to us at Alma's flat. There we learned to play charades, and we started to do it at our own parties. It was just a little learning curve.

Alma's closest circle included the Welsh actor Stanley Baker, whose recent film *Zulu* (1964) had received critical acclaim. Another was Bruce Forsyth, a tall, bouncy, lantern-jawed television comedian and quiz-show host, famous for his appalling catch-phrases.

PAUL: We'd never seen anything like this but we liked a laff so we played charades with Stanley Baker and with Bruce Forsyth; he was always at those things, Bruce was absolutely great ... They were all a little older than us, probably ten, twelve years older than us, but they were great fun, very confident showbiz people who welcomed us into their circle.

It was exciting for us, we would hear all the showbizzy gossip and meet people that we hadn't met before: Lionel Bart would sometimes be there, Tommy Steele, Lionel Blair would nearly always be there. Again we were on this sort of cusp; for instance, if the Beatles did something like *Mike and Bernie Winters' Big Night Out* at Blackpool, Lionel Blair would be the choreographer, he was always the choreographer on those things.

Much as Alma liked the Beatles, her closest friendship was with their manager. Brian was nearer to her in age: she was born in 1932, he was born in 1934; they were both Jewish and they shared a deep attraction for the glittery world of old-fashioned show business. Despite Brian's homosexuality there were those who thought they were destined to marry because they seemed so attached. He always brought her presents from his foreign trips and even took her to Liverpool to meet his parents. Later, John Lennon and Alma became very good friends; he called her Sara Sequin, and they continued to see each other even after Alma began going out with Brian Morris, the manager of the Ad Lib Club.

At the time Alma's circle of friends were so generously welcoming these new members of their profession, they could not have known how profound the changes being ushered in by the Beatles were going to be. The careers of an entire generation of performers were terminated by the rise of the beat groups. The old Tin Pan Alley showbiz schmaltz of Denmark Street music publishers and bookers was replaced with a new breed of independent managers and rock 'n' roll wheeler-dealers who had no respect for the old ways. The choreographers, stage designers, hairdressers and make-up artists, the house combos, comedians and compères who created big variety shows, were all swept away by the revolution started by the Beatles; none of them was needed at a rock 'n' roll concert.

(Only years later, with the advent of the giant touring bands, did some of the traditional jobs reappear. A stadium show requires elaborate lighting, stage costumes, sets, programme sellers and security; an enormous staff of roadies, accountants and assistants accompanies a rock 'n' roll tour, often numbering more than a hundred people in a fleet of trucks and tour buses.)

When the Beatles themselves were first touring, some of the old guard still had a role to play because the transition from show business was not yet complete: they still wore Dougie Millings stage clothes and had comedians and hoofers on the bill. But when the next wave of bands came along, spearheaded by the Rolling Stones, it did not take promoters long to realise that the audience at a rock 'n' roll concert was only interested in seeing rock 'n' roll, and the bands themselves soon dispensed with the wardrobe mistresses, make-up women and hairdressers. Rock 'n' roll was moving on; out from being just another branch of showbiz along with conjurers, clowns and dog acts, into a distinct industry all of its own; one which would earn first millions, then billions of dollars. But though the Beatles are often credited for starting the whole rock 'n' roll juggernaut, this was never John and Paul's intention.

> PAUL: One of the things that it's hard for people to realise is that we were on the cusp of the change-over between showbiz styles. The thing we were doing, rock 'n' roll, was to become an industry. Probably because of us. The Beat Boom. We opened it all up in America and once America gets hold of a thing, it's a thing! We weren't looking to build a huge industry, which is what happened, there was none of that. It was just being in show business, that's how we looked at it. We thought, this is what it's like now so we'd better get ready for it, it'll probably be like this then. But of course it all changed and we were the ones that changed it.

The In-Crowd

The Ad Lib burned down in 1965, but already people were defecting to the Scotch of St James. The Scotch was on two floors at 13

Mason's Yard, an old stable yard hidden off Duke Street, St James's in the heart of Burlington Bertie clubland. Members were auditioned through a sliding panel in the thick wooden door before being granted admission. The doorman must have taken notes when he read the weekly music press because every rising pop star was welcomed by name and ushered in. The club was decorated with panels of Scots tartan but was so dark that the decor was unimportant. Otis Redding, Wilson Pickett, the latest releases from Stax, Motown and Atlantic were played at a volume where even shouting could barely be heard, by a DJ set up in a nineteenth-century coach next to a pocket-handkerchief dance floor. There was also a stage with live music.

The owner, Louis Brown, hired Joe Van Dykes as manager, and he made it into more of a rock 'n' roll place than the Ad Lib. Anyone on that week's edition of *Top of the Pops* was likely to be found there: the Rolling Stones, the Spencer Davis Group, or visiting Americans like Sonny and Cher as well as lots of miniskirted models. Eric Burdon from the Animals lived at Dalmeny Court overlooking Mason's Yard and was a fixture. On Friday nights, Vicki Wickham, the producer of *Ready Steady Go!*, would arrive with the stars of that night's show: the Supremes, James Brown, the Toys or the Ronettes. Rod Stewart, Steve Marriott, Julie Driscoll, Tom Jones and Ronnie Wood were all habitués. Paul: 'The Moody Blues used to hang about there so much that there was a corner called "the Moody Blues Corner". It was a cool little place to go. The Scotch was pretty good.'

The Yardbirds' manager Simon Napier-Bell described it in his autobiography *You Don't Have to Say You Love Me*: 'The Scotch was more than just a club to show off your status and position – it was a positive celebration of being part of what was happening in the world's most "happening" city. It was a nightly indoor festival, a carnival, a theatrical event, and everyone played their parts to the full.'

The next of the watering holes to find favour was the Bag o'Nails, the latest enterprise of the Gunnell brothers, whose previous clubs included the Whiskey A Go Go and the Flamingo All Nighter Club. Witnessing the success of the Ad Lib and the Scotch of St James, Rik and John Gunnell bought the Bag o'Nails at 8 Kingly Street, Soho, a narrow lane parallel to Carnaby Street. The Bag o'Nails had begun life back in Victorian times as a club where gentlemen could meet the better class of prostitute. It was a long basement room with a small stage at the far end, a raised seating area at the other. Tiered alcoves lined each side, with a long, narrow dance floor below taking up the centre of the room. It is still there, its interior unchanged except that for the last two decades it has reverted to its old role and is now a hostess club called the Miranda.

It was said that you didn't want to get on the wrong side of the Gunnells, but they knew how to run a club. They managed Chris Farlowe and the Thunderbirds, John Mayall's Bluesbreakers, Georgie Fame and many lesser-known bands, so there was no shortage of live music. If bookings were short for their bands, they would slot them in one of their clubs.

> PAUL: The Bag o'Nails, the big one. That was my favourite in the end. That was where I met Linda. Bag o'Nails, down the Bag. It was supposed to have been a hookers' hangout before. It probably was then, too. But young, trendy hookers in miniskirts. Now I recall, I might have got asked for money one night after pulling some bird. I wouldn't pay, though, you know ... But yeah, it was basically that, pullin' birds. That was the basis of it.
>
> The thing about the Bag o'Nails was that they had live music. Georgie Fame and the Blue Flames were down there, Alan Price played down there a lot and Jimi Hendrix eventually. I became quite a regular.

The Bag o'Nails was Paul's favourite eating spot after late-night recording sessions. As the other Beatles were chauffeured out to their houses in the country, Mal Evans and Neil Aspinall would often accompany Paul to the Bag, sometimes driving him there in the Beatles' Austin Princess. Steak, chips and mushy peas was the standard fare at the late-night clubs, but Neil would produce a flashlight to inspect everyone's portions and make sure they were exactly as requested, much to Paul's amusement.

> PAUL: The clubs were all more or less the same: birds and occasionally live music. I've been back to clubs since, and I realise it was about pulling birds, because if you're not pulling birds they are very boring places. It's lovely to be looking at some gorgeous bird across the room and giving her the eye all evening; I mean, that's something to do. But if you're sitting there with your wife, it's a completely different matter and I realise that's why I stopped going. There was no need.
>
> There was a lot of that. There was a lot of the power. That

was what a lot of young guys had worked for all that time, that's
why you wanted to be in a group: to avoid having a job and to
pull the birds. And obviously once you got as famous as the
Beatles did ... We were at the peak of our careers, we were
young, we were looking pretty good and we had all this power
and the fame and everything so it was difficult to resist playing
with it.

That was always the argument, 'Look, you don't have to do
this. Nobody's forcing anybody, but if you fancy a bit of fun . . .'
It was the attraction and the spirit of the times. And it would
often end up in going back to somebody's place. And when you
think about it, I was really lucky to have made it through that.

The sexual freedom the Beatles experienced in Hamburg was only
just beginning to develop in Britain when they returned, but as their
career progressed and the sixties moved into gear, the idea of sexual
liberation, as it was then called, rapidly gained common currency.

PAUL: The big clincher was the advent of the pill. Because the
danger had always been pregnancy, and you'd always had to
worry about that. It was dodgy, and you always had to be very
careful. But when the pill started to happen, then all hell broke
loose! Or all heaven broke loose, in our case, because then
people didn't seem to mind. It ushered in a whole new era where
it was kind of expected.

When we went to America I remember being very European
and liberal about sex, and of course with the phenomenal effect
that the Beatles had on America anyway. We felt like trawlers,
trawling for sex, everywhere we went it was on our minds.

We were just guys on the run, guys on the lookout. We were
so pleased that we could finally get girls because in our teenage
years it had been very difficult, and now they were throwing
themselves at you and this was just very pleasing, nothing more
and nothing less. I was pretty free. I got around quite a lot of
girls. I felt that was okay, I was a young bachelor, I didn't feel
ashamed of it in any way, I felt good about it. It felt natural.

My dad used to say to me, 'I had to worry about syphilis,
gonorrhea.' I'd say 'Well, we don't have to worry about that
now.' He'd say, 'I had to worry about getting girls pregnant.' I
said, 'They're on the pill.' It seemed to me that the whole period

when I was there in the hunting game, all the conditions became spectacularly right! For all our generation it became, 'God, there are girls running round in miniskirts, who don't mind sleeping with people'; in fact, at one point it was sort of strange not to. And to me now I always use the image of Moses opening up the waters. The minute we'd done with it, he closed 'em back again. I certainly wouldn't envy anyone out there now. So the attitudes were 'dolly birds, miniskirts, free love, all you need is love'.

Living in the Asher house gave me the base and the freedom and the independence. That, alongside all the other things, because I wasn't married to Jane. I was pretty free. I remember John very much envying me. He said, 'Well, if you go out with another girl, what does Jane think?' and I said, 'Well, I don't care what she thinks, we're not married. We've got a perfectly sensible relationship.' He was well jealous of that, because at this time he couldn't do that, he was married with Cynthia and with a lot of energy bursting to get out. He'd tried to give Cynthia the traditional thing, but you kind of knew he couldn't. There were cracks appearing but he could only paste them over by staying at home and getting very wrecked.

With a lot of those people I met and related to, albeit for a short time, I've mercifully forgotten them and I don't really remember what went on, thank goodness. There may have been a few drinks involved and I was a little merry and, you know, you slip back to someone's flat ...

My main feeling really is one of relief. You do feel like some of it was outrageous. But I'm glad to have had a slightly outrageous period in my life, as long as it didn't hurt anybody, because I'd always felt maybe my character was too careful.

I think the great thing was I never had any deep, dark secrets. That's what the papers wanted. They wanted me to be hiding a little Miss Whiplash somewhere, and for the flat to be in my name. But it was never that. It was always a one-night stand with whoever was around and wanted to party.

FOUR

BEATLES FOR SALE

'And now you know the words,' she added, as she put her head down on Alice's shoulder, 'just sing it through to me.'

Lewis Carroll, *Through the Looking Glass and What Alice Found There*

Northern Songs

JAMES TREVOR ISHERWOOD WAS A CHARTERED ACCOUNTANT AT THE West End firm of Bryce, Hanmer and Isherwood, but before taking over his London practice he had lived in Liverpool, where he once did some work for Harry Epstein's furniture store, a job which ultimately yielded him the responsibility of floating Lennon and McCartney's songs on the Stock Exchange. His involvement with the Beatles began shortly after they began to make serious money. His first job for Brian Epstein was on 12 May 1964, when he set up a company, which he named Lenmac Limited, to collect Paul and John's PRS fees: that is, money collected on their behalf by the Performing Rights Society for their copyrighted songs being played on the radio, television or in concert. During his first visit to Isherwood's office in Albemarle Street, Brian explained the details of his arrangements with the Beatles – how his management company NEMS acted as the Beatles' agents and received 25 per cent of the gross receipts that came in, whether from concerts, records or television appearances. Only after Brian had taken his cut were expenses deducted and the remaining money divided equally between the four of them. James Isherwood was surprised since, in his experience, most agents were working for a 10 per cent cut. He recalled the conversation:

'So,' I said, 'isn't 25 per cent rather a lot? Particularly as all the expenses have to be paid out of their shares as well?'

'Perhaps it is,' he agreed, 'but that's the deal I've made. After all, I've financed the whole thing so far, and they haven't contributed anything.'

'Well, if that's the deal and they're happy, there's nothing more to be said,' I replied.

In the case of Lenmac Ltd, John and Paul did actually own the company outright with no outside percentages, but for the most part Brian's arrangements with the Beatles were very unfair, even by prevailing showbiz standards, and the Beatles had only agreed to them because they did not know any better. They had no legal advice on the matter. The expenses deducted from their share of their income were enormous, not least because Brian himself had very refined tastes in hotels, wine and food, all of which the Beatles paid for, not NEMS. By taking 25 per cent of the gross, Brian made at least twice as much as any individual Beatle, and probably a great deal more than that. This arrangement continued until Brian's death and even though he was an avid gambler, it is surprising that he left so little money when he died. It is known that he had Swiss bank accounts so it is possible that Beatles money is still sitting there, gathering interest.

John and Paul's music publishing was set up in the same way that Brian's management contract was handled. They had no legal advice, trusted him, and were screwed. Brian Epstein gave the publishing rights on their first single, 'Love Me Do'/'P.S. I Love You', to Ardmore and Beechwood, a subsidiary of EMI. Paul was able to get these rights back, years later, as part of a subsequent deal with EMI, and the copyrights now belong to Paul's company MPL Communications Ltd. 'Please Please Me'/'Ask Me Why' were the next songs to be released and were published by Dick James Music because Northern Songs, the company set up specifically to handle the copyrights of John and Paul's songs, had not yet been incorporated. This publishing agreement was the beginning of a business relationship with Dick James which ultimately lost Lennon and McCartney ownership of their songs.

Dick James was born Richard Leon Vapnick in London, the son of

Polish Jewish immigrants. He made his name as a crooner in Henry Hall's dance band. After that he joined Geraldo, who made him change his name to the more commercial-sounding Dick James. He had some success with the Cyril Stapleton Orchestra and in 1955 he had several British hits with the Stargazers: 'Close the Door' and 'Twenty Tiny Fingers'. As a songwriter he was responsible for Max Bygraves's children's hit 'I'm a Pink Toothbrush, I'm a Blue Toothbrush', which the Beatles grew up listening to on BBC's *Children's Favourites*, and in 1956 he was signed to Parlophone by George Martin, who produced his only big hit, 'Robin Hood', the theme tune to a television series. It was the George Martin connection that made his fortune. Brian Epstein was looking for a music publisher and George Martin remembered Dick James, who had founded Dick James Music in 1961 but had met with little success until then. Martin put the two of them together but was too much of a gentleman to ask for a finder's percentage. After publishing the songs on their second single, Dick James proposed that he and Brian Epstein start a separate company to handle John and Paul's songs.

Early on the morning of 22 February 1963, John and Paul were driven to a small mews house in Liverpool before collecting the others and setting out for Manchester to play the Oasis Club.

PAUL: Brian was at the house with a lawyer-type guy, but nobody said to us, 'This is your lawyer and he's representing your interests in this thing.' We just showed up, got out the car, went into this dark little house, and we just signed this thing, not really knowing what it was at all about, that we were signing our rights away for our songs. And that became the deal and that is virtually the contract I'm still under. It's draconian!

John and I didn't know you could own songs. We thought they just existed in the air. We could not see how it was possible to own them. We could see owning a house, a guitar or a car, they were physical objects. But a song, not being a physical object, we couldn't see how it was possible to have a copyright in it. And therefore, with great glee, publishers saw us coming.

We said to them, 'Can we have our own company?' They said, 'Yeah.' We said, 'Our own?' They said, 'Yeah, you can. You're great. This is what we're going to do now.' So we really thought that meant 100 per cent owned. But of course, it turned out to be 49 per cent to me and John and Brian, and 51 per cent to Dick James and Charles Silver.

That company, set up by Brian and James, was Northern Songs. James received 25 per cent of the shares; his accountant and financial partner Charles Silver another 25 per cent. John and Paul got 20 per cent each and Brian Epstein 10 per cent. (It may have seemed as if he was taking less than usual, but 10 per cent was still 25 per cent of John and Paul's total equity so in fact he retained parity.) The share structure appeared fair, but the reality was that matters were so arranged that James and Silver had one more voting share between them than the Beatles camp.

PAUL: There was always this voting share that could beat us. We could only muster 49; they could muster 51. They could always beat us. John and I were highly surprised to find that even though we'd been promised our own company, it actually was a company within Dick James's company that was to be our own company. And we thought that's not fair at all, but this was just the way they pulled the wool over our eyes. And we were on such a roll creatively, you couldn't just take a year off and sort out the business affairs. We had no time. We never met this Charles Silver guy; a character who was always in the background. Jim Isherwood clued us in a little bit as to who he was. He was the Money, that was basically who he was, like the producer on a film. He and Dick James went in together, so Silver always got what was really our share! There were the two of them taking the lion's share, but it was a little while before we found out.

Without realising the financial shenanigans going on behind their backs, John and Paul's main concern was what they were going to call themselves. On the early records it had not yet been settled. The first single credited Lennon–McCartney, but for the next two singles and the first album it was McCartney–Lennon. Paul: 'They said, "You'll be Lennon and McCartney," and I think my main problem was I said, "Why Lennon and McCartney? Why not McCartney and Lennon?" "It sounds better," they said. "Not to me it doesn't," I said.'

For a couple of young Liverpool lads it was a remarkable thing to have a music-publishing company and they took it very seriously, writing whenever they had a spare hour or two, consciously honing their skills. John Lennon told *Beatles Monthly*: 'It's simply a question of waiting for ideas to arrive. Sometimes this will happen in the van or on a train when we're halfway between engagements. Once one of us has come up with a few introductory phrases or a good theme for the lyrics we can bang the whole thing into shape within an hour.' But there were the exceptions. Though the majority of their early songs were co-written, 'All My Loving', for instance, was entirely Paul's, written on tour.

> It was the first song I'd ever written the words first. I never wrote words first, it was always some kind of accompaniment. I've hardly ever done it since either. We were on a tour bus going to a gig and so I started with the words. I had in my mind a little country and western song. We played the Moss Empire circuit a lot, and there were always these nice big empty backstage areas. The places have all become bingo halls now. We arrived at the gig and I remember being in one of these big backstage areas and there was a piano there so I'd got my instrument. I didn't have a guitar, it was probably with our road manager, and I remember working the tune out to it on the piano. It was a good show song, it worked well live.

John described it as 'one of his first biggies'. Another solo effort was John's 'All I've Got to Do', which he described as 'me trying to do a Smokey Robinson', and showed to Paul only in the studio just before recording.

Many of their early songs were composed on the road, including their third single, 'From Me to You', which was written on 28 February 1963 in the tour bus travelling from York to Shrewsbury on the Helen Shapiro tour. Paul regards it as one of the first really good songs they wrote. It had different musical ideas and chords for the middle eight. The lyrics were a play on the words 'From You to Us', the name of the *New Musical Express* letters page.

> PAUL: There was a little trick we developed early on and got bored with later, which was to put I, Me or You in it, so it was very direct and personal: 'Love Me Do'; 'Please Please Me'; 'From Me to You' – we got two of them in there; 'She Loves

You' ... The thing I liked about 'From Me To' was it had a very complete middle. It went to a surprising place. The opening chord of the middle section of that song heralded a new batch for me. That was a pivotal song. Our songwriting lifted a little with that song. It was very much co-written. We were starting to meet other musicians then and we'd start to see other people writing. After that, on another tour bus with Roy Orbison, we saw Roy sitting in the back of the bus, writing 'Pretty Woman'. It was lovely. We could trade off with each other. This was our real start.

Another song composed on the same tour was 'Thank You Girl', the B side of 'From Me to You', written very much with their girl fans in mind. Paul: 'These early songs were wonderful to learn by and were good album fillers. This was pretty much co-written but there might have been a slight leaning towards me with the "thank you, girl" thing, it sounds a bit like me, trying to appease the mob. A bit of a hack song really, but all good practice.'

'She Loves You' was written when the Beatles were in Newcastle-upon-Tyne to play the Majestic Ballroom on 26 June 1963. John and Paul sat facing each other on twin beds in their shared room at the Turk's Hotel.

PAUL: We must have had a few hours before the show so we said, 'Oh, great! Let's have a ciggy and write a song!' So that's how we began 'She Loves You'. I remember for some reason thinking of Bobby Rydell; he must have had a hit that we were interested in. [Bobby Rydell's 'Forget Him' was in the UK charts at the time]. I remember thinking of him and sitting on the bed in this hotel somewhere with John in the afternoon daylight. It was again a she, you, me, I, personal preposition song. I suppose the most interesting thing about it was that it was a message song, it was someone bringing a message. It wasn't us any more, it was moving off the 'I love you, girl' or 'Love me do', it was a third person, which was a shift away. 'I saw *her*, and she said to *me*, to tell *you*, that she loves *you*' so there's a little distance we managed to put in it which was quite interesting.

Years later John told *Playboy*: 'It was written together. I remember it was Paul's idea: Instead of singing 'I love you' again, we'd have a third party.'

Paul: 'It was very co-written as I recall, I don't think it was either of our idea, I think we just sat down and said, "Right!" So who had the inspiration, who came up with what line, in these kind of songs, is very difficult to remember because it was all over in a couple of hours.'

The song was probably finished the next day, which they had off. John came round to Forthlin Road and they retired to the dining room.

> PAUL: We sat in there one evening, just beavering away while my dad was watching TV and smoking his Players cigarettes, and we wrote 'She Loves You'. We actually just finished it there because we'd started it in the hotel room. We went into the living room – 'Dad, listen to this. What do you think?' So we played it to my dad and he said, 'That's very nice, son, but there's enough of these Americanisms around. Couldn't you sing, "She loves you. Yes! Yes! Yes!"' At which point we collapsed in a heap and said, 'No, Dad, you don't quite get it!' That's my classic story about my dad. For a working-class guy that was rather a middle-class thing to say, really. But he was like that.

Because Aunt Mimi disapproved of John's music, John and Paul rarely wrote together at Menlove Avenue. One exception was 'I'll Get You', the B side of 'She Loves You'. This has always been one of Paul's favourite Beatles tracks; it is light-hearted, confident and shows how well he and John had already mastered the tricks of their trade. John later used a variation on the opening line in his song 'Imagine'. 'I'll Get You' was a 50-50 collaboration; what Paul calls 'very co-written'.

> PAUL: To me and John, though I can't really speak for him, words like 'imagine' and 'picture' were from Lewis Carroll. This idea of asking your listener to imagine, 'Come with me if you will ...', 'Enter please into my ...', 'Picture yourself in a boat ...' It drew you in. It was a good little trick that. Both of us loved Lewis Carroll and the Alice books and were fascinated by his surreal world so this was a nice song to write.

It's got an interesting chord in it: 'It's not easy to pre-*tend* ...' That was nicked from a song called 'All My Trials' which is on an album I had by Joan Baez: 'There's only one thing that money can't *buy*'. It's like D, which goes to an A minor, which is unusual, you'd normally go from a D to an A major. It's a change that had always fascinated me, so I put it in. I liked that slightly faggy way we sang. 'Oh yeah, oh yeah,' which was very distinctive, very Beatley.

It is an extraordinary fact that when Paul and John focused their attention on writing a song, they were able to produce something, usually something memorable, within a matter of two or three hours. For some writers, a song can take months. The everyday mechanics of artistic production are often overlooked by critics, who talk only of genius and inspiration rather than the nine-to-five slog. The speed of artistic creation varies enormously from artist to artist – Bob Dylan in his early amphetamine-crazed period could dash off a song in minutes – but all would agree that the printer's boy waiting in the hall, a one-man show in six months' time or a block booking of a recording studio in three weeks' time exert a powerful influence on the creation of art. Though deadlines can focus the mind, many songwriters have found that the task is made a great deal easier, and the results are more satisfactory, if they work with a partner: Rodgers and Hart, Brecht and Weill, Gilbert and Sullivan, Goffin and King, Leiber and Stoller. Sometimes one partner would write the music and the other the lyrics, but not always; in the case of Lennon and McCartney, each of them could write both words and music.

PAUL: Collaborating with another writer makes it twice as easy. It takes half as long with somebody else. With John, I would think of a line, he would think of a line, I would think of a line, he would think of a line, so I wasn't having to think of all the lines. 'It's getting better all the time'; he was just drawing it on, 'Couldn't get much worse', and that sets the tone for the next verse. So it starts to be about painful memories or something by this 'worse'. The ricochet is a great thing.

The thing about John is that it wasn't just a collaboration; John was very special. And I think for him, I must have been special, because he'd have got rid of me. That's the point about John. He didn't suffer fools gladly. Given half a chance he would have elbowed me! And feel right about it! But I was his main collaborator.

With the Beatles

Their first great flush of songwriting, in 1963, produced dozens of early Beatles classics. They had already perfected the basic tenets of composition, but now, with their second album, *With the Beatles*, released in November 1963, they began to introduce little tricks of their own which reappear as signatures in Lennon–McCartney songs. One of these is the play on words. 'It Won't Be Long' is a good example.

PAUL: I was doing literature at school, so I was interested in plays on words and onomatopoeia. John didn't do literature but he was quite well read, so he was interested in that kind of thing. Like the double meaning of 'please' in a line like 'Please, lend a little ear to my pleas' that we used in 'Please Please Me'. We'd spot the double meaning. I think everyone did, by the way, it was not just the genius of us! In 'It won't *be long* till I *belong* to you' it was that same trip. We both liked to try and get a bit of double meaning in, so that was the high spot of writing that particular song. John mainly sang it so I expect that it was his original idea but we both sat down and wrote it together. When I say 'original idea' I mean someone might have the first verse, which then is pretty much the maquette for the whole thing, but the second verse is always difficult because you've got to repeat the first verse but go somewhere new. And your inspiration's gone by that point, so you've got to dig deep to push a new inspiration out to make the second verse as good as the first verse. You don't want to just be rambling. We would often repeat the first verse. The last verse was no problem – 'Two hours is up! C'mon, just put "Repeat 1".' That's how a lot of our songs end, 'Repeat 1'. We'd number the verses, one, two, so we'd write a couple of verses, middle, the chorus, then pretty much repeat verse one. Which was good if it was hooky, it meant that you've heard those lyrics twice, so we'd rammed 'em home, and it saved us having to think of a third verse.

In addition to writing songs for the other members of Brian

Epstein's stable and for their friends, John and Paul tried to provide a song for George and Ringo for each album. On *With the Beatles*, 'Little Child' was for Ringo. 'They had to be fairly simple,' Paul explained, 'he didn't have a large vocal range but he could handle things with good *con brio* and *spirito* if they were nice and simple. It had to be something he could get behind. If he couldn't mentally picture it, you were in trouble. This one was co-written with John.' The original inspiration for the melody was a line in a song by the 1950s English folk balladeer Elton Hayes.

> PAUL: I nicked a bit of melody from one of his tunes, 'I'm so sad and lonely', that little bit came from a line: '*Whistle, my love*, and I will come to thee, *I'll always find you* ...' It's actually not the same tune, but in my mind it was a quote from Elton Hayes. I think it was from a Robin Hood film, it was all 'thee' and 'thou's. 'Little Child' was a work job. Certain songs were inspirational and you just followed that. Certain other songs were 'Right, come on, two hours, song for Ringo for the album.'

Another song originally written for Ringo, 'I Wanna Be Your Man', became the Rolling Stones' second official single and their first top-ten record, reaching number nine in the British charts.

> PAUL: We wrote 'I Wanna Be Your Man' for Ringo because we wanted him to have a song on the album. On the *Please Please Me* album he did a thing called 'Boys', which was very funny because it was a girl group, the Shirelles, that did it; we didn't write it. We didn't use to think what these things meant, we were in love with the sound, the music. We often used to say to people, the words don't really matter, people don't listen to words, it's the sound they listen to. So 'I Wanna Be Your Man' was to try and give Ringo something like 'Boys'; an uptempo song he could sing from the drums. So again it had to be very simple. 'I wanna be your ma-an' – that little bit is nicked from 'Fortune Teller', a Benny Spellman song [which coincidentally was on the B side of the single that the Stones had just withdrawn from sale]. We were quite open about our nicks. 'That's from the Marvelettes, that's from the Shirelles ...' We admired these people so much, we stole quite openly, like two notes, and we were proud of it. Our friends could tell where they

came from. Ringo did a real nice version of it. It became quite popular for him.

Paul remembered how the Rolling Stones came to release 'I Wanna Be Your Man' as a single:

We were in Charing Cross Road, where we often used to go to window-shop at the guitar shops and daydream. It was a great hobby of ours when we first came down to London. Dick James, our song publisher, was on Charing Cross Road. We'd go to his office and window-shop on the way. Coming out of his office one day, John and I were walking along Charing Cross Road when passing in a taxi were Mick and Keith. We were each other's counterparts in many ways because they became the writers in the group and were the twosome, the couple, as it were. So they shouted from the taxi and we yelled, 'Hey, hey, give us a lift, give us a lift,' and we bummed a lift off them. So there were the four of us sitting in a taxi and I think Mick said, 'Hey, we're recording. Got any songs?' And we said, 'Aaaah, yes, sure, we got one. How about Ringo's song? You could do it as a single.' And they went for it and Bo Diddleyed it up a bit. I remember it as a song we had, and in that case it would be a finished song.

John Lennon told *Hit Parader*: 'Both of us wrote it but mainly Paul ... I helped him finish it.' In a more sarcastic mood, he told *Playboy*: '"I Wanna Be Your Man" was a kind of lick Paul had ... it was a throwaway. The only two versions of the song were Ringo and the Rolling Stones. That shows how much importance we put on it. We weren't going to give them anything *great*, right?'

In the normal course of events John and Paul would be given about two weeks' notice that recording time had been booked at EMI. Often they did not even have two clear weeks to prepare material, but Epstein would usually manage to free the daytime for them. Each day they would get together and write songs or work on each other's songs. Paul: 'We would bury songs in albums which other people would listen to and, noting the phenomenal success we were having as performers and as writers, they would say, "I can make a single out of that!" There are quite a number of those.'

A lot of songs were written on the road, whenever and wherever an hour or two of privacy could be snatched. 'This Boy', from *With the Beatles*, shows how they would still try out new things even if they were composing on the run.

PAUL: 'This Boy' was another hotel-bedroom song, twin beds, one afternoon somewhere, we had arrived around one o'clock. We had a couple of hours to kill. So we thought, Well, let's write one. Rather like the hotel where we wrote 'She Loves You'. It's funny, I remember the room and the position of the beds: John and I sitting on twin beds, the G-Plan furniture, the British hotel with olive green and orange everywhere, that marvellous combination, the colours of vomit.

It was very co-written. We wanted to do a close-harmony thing, we liked harmonies and we were quite good at them. We used to do a close-harmony version of the Teddy Bears' 'To Know Her Is to Love Her', which was good for the versatility in the band. We weren't all rock 'n' roll, we could change the pace, which was always nice after you'd played for three hours. So this was our attempt to write one of those. We wrote it in two-part harmony and then put the third part in for George to sing. That was quite a departure for us, the close-harmony thing; we'd never actually tried to write something like that. Nice middle, John sang that great, then we'd go back into the close-harmony thing. It was one of those: *This* boy says that, *that* boy ...

Because they had no knowledge of music theory, they didn't know when they were breaking the rules, or, for that matter, when they were doing something really clever. John's 'Not a Second Time' was reviewed in the London *Times* on 27 December 1963 by the music critic William Mann, who described its harmonic interest as 'typical of their quicker songs too, and one gets the impression that they think simultaneously of harmony and melody, so firmly are the major tonic sevenths and ninths built into their tunes, and the flat-submediant key-switches, so natural is the Aeolian cadence at the end of "Not a Second Time" (the chord progression which ends Mahler's "Song of the Earth") ...'

Aeolian cadences became part of the Beatles' legend, much mentioned by the tabloid press. In 1980 John commented, 'To this day I don't have any idea what they are. They sound like exotic birds.'

With confidence born of their sudden success, the Beatles began flexing their muscles. After *Please Please Me*, which included all four sides of their first two singles, they insisted that their singles not be included on their albums so that fans would not have to buy the same recordings over again. Their next victory came with the sleeve for *With the Beatles*, released on 22 November 1963. Instead of having another jolly colour picture of the four mop tops having fun, they showed the photographer Robert Freeman the high-contrast grainy monochrome photographs of the group members that Astrid Kirchherr took in Hamburg and told him they wanted the sleeve to have the same feel. Freeman had sent Brian Epstein a set of photographs of jazz musicians, including some of John Coltrane. The Beatles liked his work and he was invited to meet the group the next week – in Weston-super-Mare, where they were playing a week at the Odeon Cinema from 22 to 27 July – to take a cover shot for their next album.

PAUL: Robert was much more one of us than the other photographers we'd had. He took some pictures of us and he blew 'em up nice and grainy, he was into graininess, and he did this clever move: he brought us all prints for ourselves, 'I thought you might like this.' Well, we'd never seen big prints; these were 20 by 16s and beautifully grained and we looked so great and we went, 'Woooow! This guy is truly great!' Apparently a lot of photographers are still trying to work out how he did the famous one on the *With the Beatles* sleeve with the half-light on the faces.

It was in a hotel and we had an hour in which he could take our picture. He pulled out four chairs and arranged us in a hotel corridor; it was very un-studio-like. The corridor was rather dark and there was a window at the end, and by using this heavy source of natural light coming from the right, he got that photo. He got this very moody picture which people think he must have worked at for ever and ever in great technical detail. But it was an hour. He sat down, took a couple of rolls and he had it. But Robert was very good. I liked his photography a lot. I thought he took some of the best pictures of the Beatles that way.

Robert Freeman, in his book *Yesterday*, says that the picture was taken at noon in the hotel dining room with the Beatles wearing dark poloneck sweaters sitting in front of dark maroon velvet curtains with large windows letting in bright sunlight. Paul's memory of a single strong source of light seems more likely, so possibly the corridor backed on to the dining room. Freeman also says that though EMI objected to using a black and white photograph for the cover, both George Martin and Brian Epstein felt strongly that the image was right. However, Tony Barrow, who was then the Beatles' publicist, reported in *Beatles Monthly* that Brian Epstein was very disappointed with the photograph and the Beatles had to put tremendous pressure on him to support them and take the picture to EMI. Certainly EMI were strongly opposed to its use. They described the picture as 'shockingly humourless' and one marketing executive said, 'Where is the fun? Why are they looking so grim? We want to project happy Beatles for happy fans.' It apparently took a full-scale battle between NEMS and EMI before the Beatles won, but they did, and the sleeve went on to become another iconic Beatles image, imitated and parodied to this day.

A Hard Day's Night

In the autumn of 1963 United Artists discovered that EMI had neglected to cover film soundtracks in their contract with the Beatles. Though the Beatles had not yet broken in the USA, their popularity in Britain was phenomenal and the idea of a quick exploitation movie, coupled with a soundtrack album, made considerable economic sense to them. As UA expected the Beatles to be a flash in the pan, they wanted the film out on release by July 1964 and made as cheaply as possible; the production budget was £150,000, later rising to £175,000. The producer Walter Shenson's brief from United Artists was simple: 'We need a film for the express purpose of getting a soundtrack album. Just make sure there are enough new songs for a soundtrack album and don't go over budget.' Bud Ornstein, the European head of production for United Artists, tried to get *A Hard Day's Night* made in colour but fortunately UA would not risk spending the extra money so it had to be black and white. Paul: 'It was the only colour it could have been, it would have been crap in colour. They gave us colour for *Help!* and it wasn't anywhere near as good a film.'

Shenson, a Californian producer living in London, had co-produced a hit with *The Mouse That Roared* in 1959 and had been in the business for some time. He was prepared to give the Beatles 25 per cent of the net income from the film so he was overjoyed when Brian Epstein naively opened their business negotiation by saying, 'I must warn you now, I'm not prepared to settle for less than $7\frac{1}{2}$ per cent.' Shenson also very cleverly recognised that the Beatles would be around for a long time, so he got UA and the other parties to agree that all rights to the film would revert to him after fifteen years. When Beatlemania became an international phenomenon, Bud Ornstein pre-empted any complaints by voluntarily increasing Brian Epstein's share of the agreement to 20 per cent, demonstrating what a bad deal it was in the first place.

Walter Shenson says it was Paul who suggested Alun Owen as the scriptwriter for the Beatles' first film. It was an inspired idea: Owen, a Liverpudlian Welshman, was a pioneer of the kitchen-sink school of television drama. He had written plays for Joan Littlewood's company and for the Dublin Theatre Festival. His work was realistic, gritty, full of working-class sympathies; and of all the scriptwriters in Britain he was probably the best able to capture the speech patterns and wit of the Beatles.

> PAUL: The nice thing about *Hard Day's Night* was that there were very good people involved in it: Dick Lester, who made *The Running Jumping Standing Still Film* with Peter Sellers and Spike Milligan, producer Walter Shenson and Alun Owen. They called in Alun Owen, who had written *No Trams to Lime Street* with Billie Whitelaw, which we'd seen on telly and was like an early Bleasdale or Willy Russell. It was a sort of kitchen-sink Liverpool thing. Billie Whitelaw's always in some sort of weird, rather well-thought-of play, she's built a whole thing like that. So Alun was a good choice and Alun was from Wales, and it's often said that Liverpool is the capital of Wales, there are so many Welsh people there.
>
> Alun came and hung around with us for a few days, which was an idea we'd picked up from *Life* magazine, who did it. I remember Brian saying, 'You can get eight pages in *Life* magazine. Think of what that'll do for the American tour!' For some little English group to get eight pages in *Life* magazine; I mean, *Life* magazine was almost like the Bible. But they said we

had to have the journalist and the photographer hang around with us for a few days, and we said, 'Doesn't matter. We're only going to Bournemouth, and then we're going to Coventry, then we're in the bus. We'll play cards with them or we'll have a drink with them, whatever.' It was easy to have people hang with you if you didn't have any particular social scene, no family with you.

For *Life*, the photographer Terence Spencer had travelled with the Beatles over six weeks in the run-up to their first American tour, beginning with the famous Royal Command Performance at the Prince of Wales Theatre in London on 4 November 1963, then on and off till their three-week engagement at the Paris Olympia beginning 16 January 1964. When *Life* heard that the group were booked to appear on *The Ed Sullivan Show*, they made it the lead story and requested Spencer to get a posed cover shot. The Beatles were supposed to show up two hours early for their Christmas show at the Finsbury Park Astoria for the session, but arrived only fifteen minutes before going on stage. Spencer commented in his book *It Was Thirty Years Ago Today*: 'When our story ran in *Life* on 31st January, 1964, the cover picture was of Geraldine Chaplin ... The Beatles must be the only people in showbiz ever to have turned down a *Life* cover.'

PAUL: The journalist Michael Braun wrote a book, *Love Me Do: The Beatles' Progress*, after he'd hung with us, so this became the way to do it. When it came time to do *Hard Day's Night*, we just applied the same idea. They'd hang with you and pick up the feel then they'd go away and write the story and they always wrote something cool because they'd got our sense of humour or they saw we were tongue in cheek. It wasn't just a po-faced group and a handout, it was something more alive, and that was what we were about. Our whole gig was to shake down the temple with our native wit and our blunt remarks. Blunt northern humour!

So, Alun came around with us and picked up all the little things like 'He's very clean, isn't he?' or we would tell him, 'Oh, we met a guy the other day ...' because we did actually meet a guy on a train who said, 'I fought in the war for people like you.' And it eventually found its way into the film. We knew what was going on. This was a writer who'd written something real good for the Beeb. He was a kind of street writer, quite exciting, and so we knew enough to try and pump him full with every good story we could think of. The more we told him, the more of us he'd get in it, which is always a good thing, it would just reflect back. We could play it easier, we could identify with it all easier, and this was our first film.

No rock group had ever successfully made the transition from the stage to the screen so no one was expecting a miracle. Since the Beatles had no acting experience, it was decided early on to have them play themselves in a light-hearted comedy, based fairly closely on their actual life on the road but with surreal touches. Alun Owen was astonished at how little freedom they had on the road. 'At no time could they enjoy their success,' he commented. Confined to hotel rooms and limousines, thrown together with their aides and management, he saw them as prisoners of their own success, trapped by fame, free only when actually performing. He made this the story line, constructing a convincing, though fictional, film portrait. (In fact some of the sequences in it were real: when fans broke a security barrier and the Beatles ran for their lives, Lester filmed the whole thing and used the footage in the actual film.)

The director Richard Lester described the structure of the film:

In the first third or half of the film, all the scenes would be in close confinement and that at a certain point they were going to break out, rip off down the fire escape and escape from their own success. Now whatever we did had to lead to that, whatever scenes took place had to fit that rhythm and that's why there was a careful build-up. The script that Alun Owen wrote produced that movement toward a series of emotional climaxes.

No one, including the Beatles themselves, knew if they would be any good before the cameras so Owen took no chances, relying heavily on action shots and short lines so that they did not have to memorise much dialogue. It is for this reason that the film is often cited as the precursor of MTV and rock videos with its fast cutting and sound bites.

Dick Lester: 'The script was very cleverly written so that there was never a time where any one person had too much to say before someone else said something. They were sound bites. One-line gags or a little speech which could be cut away from.'

PAUL: He put in a few little things that we wouldn't have put in, little Irishisms like 'It's me neb'; Ringo would have never called his nose his 'neb', that was Alun thinking what a Liverpool guy might have said. And 'grotty' was a word none of us used, but that became very big. Grotesque – grotty. I think he made it up for the film. It's a good film. It's very much the period but it's well made, it's well photographed, it's fresh and it was good doing that with good writers and a good team.

Owen himself claimed that 'grotty' was Liverpool slang, but that when he showed the script to the Beatles, none of them had ever heard the term before. The film soon caused it to enter the national vocabulary, regardless.

The music for the soundtrack was recorded before filming began because they would have to lip-synch to it in the film itself. The Beatles flew back to London from Miami Beach on 22 February and two days later were in the studio to begin work. Paul's major contributions were 'And I Love Her', 'Things We Said Today' and 'Can't Buy Me Love'.

Paul: "'Can't Buy Me Love' is my attempt to write a bluesy mode. The idea behind it was that all these material possessions are all very well but they won't buy me what I really want. It was a very hooky song. Ella Fitzgerald later did a version of it which I was very honoured by.' It was Paul's song. John Lennon told *Playboy*: 'That's Paul's completely. Maybe I had something to do with the chorus, but I don't know. I always considered it his song.'

It was written in Paris. The Beatles were playing their season at the Olympia Theatre: two and sometimes three shows a day for eighteen days, from 16 January until 4 February 1964. They were staying at the exclusive George V Hotel on the Avenue George-V, in the expensive residential area between the Champs Elysées and the River Seine. In order to work on songs for their upcoming movie, John and Paul had an upright piano brought to the sitting room of their suite and installed in the corner by a window. Here Paul wrote 'Can't Buy Me Love'. They rehearsed it; George Martin flew over from London;

and on 29 January they recorded it at the Pathé Marconi Studios on rue de Sèvres.

Paul also wrote 'One and One Is Two' in the same hotel room, which was released by the Strangers two months later. Paul: 'Sometimes all you get is the title and then it doesn't really live up to the title. "One and One Is Two" is okay, it's a memorable title, it's not wonderful. The Strangers were mates of ours from Liverpool.'

Although the guide vocals for 'Can't Buy Me Love' were recorded in Paris, Paul did not put the final vocal track on until 25 February, after the Beatles returned from their first American tour. By this time he found that the sentiments of the song were not necessarily correct. For by then the Beatles had spent nine sybaritic days in Miami Beach, Florida, arriving on 13 February, and apart from rehearsals for *The Ed Sullivan Show* at the Deauville Hotel and the show itself, they were able to relax in a private villa and get fit, ready to begin filming *A Hard Day's Night* on their return to England.

> PAUL: Miami was incredible. It was the first time we ever saw police motorbike outriders with guns. I've got photographs I took out of the car window. It was amazing. It was a big time for us, obviously, and there were all the lovely, gorgeous tanned girls. We did a photo session down by the beach and immediately asked them out. And MG Motors were trying to sell their convertibles down there, which was a perfect little Florida car, and lent us one each as a publicity thing. I remember meeting this rather nice girl and taking her out for dinner in this MG in the cool Florida night, palm trees swaying. You kidding? A Liverpool boy with this tanned beauty in my MG going out to dinner. It should have been 'Can Buy Me Love', actually.

Of the other songs used in the film, 'If I Fell', 'I'm Happy Just to Dance with You' and 'I'll Be Back' were all co-written with John.

> PAUL: People forget that John wrote some pretty nice ballads. People tend to think of him as an acerbic wit and aggressive and abrasive, but he did have a very warm side to him really which he didn't like to show too much in case he got rejected. We wrote 'If I Fell' together but with the emphasis on John because he sang it. It was a nice harmony number, very much a ballad.

We wrote 'I'm Happy Just to Dance with You' for George in the film. It was a bit of a formula song. We knew that in E if you went to an A-flat minor, you could always make a song with those chords; that change pretty much always excited you. This is one of these. Certainly 'Do You Want to Know a Secret' was. This one anyway was a straight co-written song for George. We wouldn't have actually wanted to sing it because it was a bit ... The ones that pandered to the fans in truth were our least favourite songs but they were good. They were good for the time. The nice thing about it was to actually pull a song off on a slim little premise like that. A simple little idea. It was song-writing practice.

'I'll Be Back' was co-written but it was largely John's idea. When we knew we were writing for something like an album he would write a few in his spare moments, like this batch here. He'd bring them in, we'd check 'em. I'd write a couple and we'd throw 'em at each other, and then there would be a couple that were more co-written. But you just had a certain amount of time. You knew when the recording date was and so a week or two before then we'd get into it.

It didn't seem like pressure. It was – I suppose you'd have to think it was but I don't remember it being a pressure. It was fun, it was great. I always liken songwriting to a conjurer pulling a rabbit out of a hat. Now you see it, now you don't. If I now pick up a guitar and start to conjure something out of the air, there's a great magic about it. Where there was nothing, now there is something. Where there was a white sheet of paper, there's a page we can read. Where there was no tune and no lyrics, there's now a song we can sing! That aspect of it made it a lot of fun. We'd be amazed to see what kind of rabbit we'd pulled out that day.

It was a very satisfying thing. We knew they were good. People used to say to us, 'Are you conceited?' It's a very difficult question, that, because I'd have to answer yes, because I think we are good, and that actually amounts to conceit, doesn't it? But I'd be stupid to say we weren't because it's so obvious that this is good stuff, and it's number one everywhere so somebody's buying it.

The remaining songs in the film – 'Tell Me Why', 'I Should Have Known Better', 'Any Time at All', 'I'll Cry Instead', 'When I Get Home' and 'You Can't Do That' – were all by John and often sound like John's marriage arguments.

Paul: 'I think a lot of these songs like 'Tell Me Why' may have have been based in real experiences or affairs John was having or arguments with Cynthia or whatever, but it never occurred to us until later to put that slant on it all.'

With the music recorded, the actual shooting of the film began on 2 March 1964 and took a mere six weeks. Thinking that it would inhibit them to see the daily rushes, Dick Lester and Walter Shenson decided to keep quiet about their existence. One day the Beatles followed them and came bursting into the viewing theatre, delighted to find out where they had been sneaking off to each lunchtime. From then on the Beatles watched the dailies with great enthusiasm, showing no signs of inhibition at all. There was only one problem: the movie had no title.

> PAUL: The title was Ringo's. We'd almost finished making the film and this fun bit arrived that we'd not known about before which was naming the film. So we were sitting around at Twickenham studios having a little brain-storming session; director Dick Lester, us, Walter Shenson, Bud Ornstein and some other people were sitting around trying to come up with something and we said, 'Well, there was something Ringo said the other day ...' Ringo would do these little malapropisms, he would say things slightly wrong, like people do, but his were always wonderful, very lyrical, very Lewis Carroll, lovely. They were sort of magic even though he was just getting it wrong. And he said after a concert, 'Phew, it's been a hard day's night.' John and I went, 'What? What did you just say?' He said, 'I'm bloody knackered, man, it's been a hard day's night.' 'Hard day's night! Fucking brilliant! How does he think of 'em? Woehayy!' So that came up in this brain-storming session, something Ringo said, 'It was a hard day's night.'

Acording to Andrew Yule in his biography of Richard Lester, Ornstein declared, 'We just got our title,' and Shenson told UA:

'You're never going to improve on it. It's very provocative. It means nothing and has nothing to do with the film. But it *sounds* like a Beatles title.'

PAUL: There was one objection to it. Somebody said, 'Well, it's a bit like *Long Day's Journey into Night*.' We said, 'Who knows that? Who's ever heard of that, it's a classical play, innit? None of our fans will have gone.' We knew we were pretty safe on that. So that was it, we adopted that as the title and everyone agreed that it was wacky yet it said it. It wasn't too wacky, it wasn't gobbledygook. Of course it got changed around the world. In Italy it became *Tutti per uno* (All for One) and in France it became *Quatre Garçons dans le vent* (Four Boys in the Wind). Very nice that one. We enjoyed seeing how they would retitle it in different countries.

The rest of the music for the film had already been recorded since it was lip-synched in the film itself. Now they had a title, they needed an uptempo title track to run behind the credits. Paul: 'John said, "I'll write it." And he did, he came back the next day with it. I think he might not have had all the words. I might have been in on that middle eight. Something like that would only have taken twenty minutes. That would have been plenty of time to run through it.'

At 8.30 the next morning, Walter Shenson was summoned to the Beatles' dressing room where John and Paul were waiting, guitars in hand, to play it to him. John produced a matchbox cover which he propped open on the dressing-room table; then, reading from John's scribbled lyrics, they gave their first public performance of 'A Hard Day's Night'. The film was probably named on 13 April, and the song played to Shenson on the 14th. The Beatles took time off from shooting to record it at Abbey Road on the 16th, a good example of the speed at which their lives were going. Shortly afterwards, while editing continued, they resumed touring.

A Hard Day's Night was given its world première in London on 6 July 1964, attended by Princess Margaret and Lord Snowdon. The area around Picadilly Circus was closed to traffic because so many fans filled the streets. Four days later, the Beatles flew to Liverpool for the north of England première at the Odeon. A hundred thousand fans lined the route from the airport to welcome them.

The reviews were almost all enthusiastic. In the USA, the *Village*

Voice critic Andrew Sarris described it as 'the *Citizen Kane* of jukebox musicals, a brilliant crystallisation of such diverse cultural particles as the pop movie, rock 'n' roll, cinéma vérité, the nouvelle vague, free cinema, the affectedly hand-held camera, the cult of the sexless subadolescent, the semidocumentary, and studied spontaneity'. UA made a 200 per cent profit over investment on advance record sales before the film itself was even released. *A Hard Day's Night* took $8,000,000 in its first week, making it one of the most profitable films of all time.

The film went a long way towards establishing the individual identities of the Beatles in the mind of the public and, to a certain extent, is responsible for the stereotype characters attributed to each individual Beatle: John the smart, witty one, Paul the cute charmer, et cetera. The film was, after all, fiction and they were speaking lines written by someone else, but the French *nouvelle vague* hand-held camera techniques and lack of conventional 'acting' made audiences think they were seeing a documentary. After *A Hard Day's Night* the public could not only put a name to each Beatle, but was more easily able to typecast them.

Kenwood

Filming was by no means their only occupation that year. Indeed, they continued to work astonishingly hard as a live band – but now on a truly international scale. In February 1964 the Beatles had their first American visit, appearing twice on *The Ed Sullivan Show* and playing concerts at the Coliseum, Washington, DC, and Carnegie Hall in New York. This was followed by a brief tour of Denmark before spending most of June in Hong Kong, Australia and New Zealand. On 19 August they commenced a five-week tour of the USA and Canada, and in October began a lengthy tour of Britain. Touring, combined with massive record sales worldwide, brought in staggering amounts of money and the Beatles now found themselves with a major tax problem. John and Paul, as the songwriters, earned more than the others.

James Isherwood advised Brian Epstein that the only way to minimise the amount of tax that John and Paul would have to pay on their huge income was a stock-market flotation of Northern Songs, the music-publishing company Brian and Dick James had set up to handle John and Paul's songwriting royalties.

JAMES ISHERWOOD:With regard to the houses John and Ringo had bought on St George's Hill, Weybridge, at that time I lived in Ashley Park, Walton-on-Thames, and I'd said to Brian that it would make life easier if they were more accessible while the flotation was in progress. I asked Walter Strach, my taxation assistant, to find houses for them as near as possible to me, which he did. George was around the corner in Esher; only Paul decided to live in London. Their proximity to my own house enabled me to keep in touch with them at frequent intervals, and at short notice. This proved to be of great value.

George and particularly Ringo enjoyed London's nightlife and would have been better suited by living in Chelsea or St John's Wood, where they could have easily afforded a large detached house with a garden and space for a pool close to the restaurants and late-night clubs. But for the sake of the convenience of their financial adviser during the weeks of the stock-market flotation of Northern Songs, three of the Beatles finished up in the sticks.

PAUL: It just happened. You see, we weren't used to wealth. So wealth was dealt with by other people, and we were directed into areas. They did it because Jim Isherwood wanted them living near him. I really don't think they knew that because John was not rebellious enough to say, 'Fuck that!' This is why I was fascinated by the Ashers; because the other guys were being shown Weybridge, and I didn't particularly like the look of it, it was all a bit golf club for me, but Cynthia wanted to settle John down, pipe and slippers. The minute she said that to me I thought, Kiss of death, I know my mate and that is not what he wants. She got a couple of years of that, but he finally had to break loose and because he couldn't tell her he didn't want it, he had to bring Yoko to breakfast.

When Brian Epstein moved his management company to London in March 1964, he took a penthouse in Williams Mews, just around the corner from Harrods in Knightsbridge, and hired a fashionable interior decorator and a black valet. At a party there in August, just before the Beatles' second US tour, Brian introduced John to Ken

Partridge, his interior designer, and recommended that John hire him to renovate his new house. Neither John or Cynthia could remember where the house was exactly but told him it was big. By the next morning Partridge had done colour schemes for eighteen rooms and managed to get them to John before he left for America. John glanced through the sketches and swatches of fabrics and gave Partridge *carte blanche* to redo the house. It took nine months, during which time the Lennons had to live in the staff flat in the attic while the house was literally torn apart. Kenwood had cost £20,000 when John bought it in July 1964, and he was to spend a further £40,000 renovating it, installing a swimming pool and landscaping the grounds.

Kenwood was a twenty-seven-room, mock-Tudor mansion with high gables and ornate tall brick chimneys at the top of St George's Hill, next to the golf course. The St George's Hill estate was thickly wooded, providing seclusion and privacy. Ringo bought a house a little further down the hill called Sunny Heights, and George lived at Kinfauns on a similar private estate in Esher, about four miles away. It was a curious place for John and Ringo to live, considering its history. In 1649, as a protest against the high price of food, Gerrard Winstanley, William Everard and about one hundred of their supporters began to cultivate the common parkland they had appropriated in St George's Hill, Surrey, in order to feed themselves and give the surplus to the poor. The Diggers, as they called themselves, were immediately confronted by the food merchants, who saw their profits threatened, and by local farmers, who eyed the land for themselves. On Oliver Cromwell's orders the Diggers were destroyed and their radical ideas of agrarian reform suppressed for more than three hundred years, until Emmett Grogan and his band of Diggers began to feed and clothe the hippies in San Francisco's Haight-Ashbury. It was on the original site of this suppressed idealism that the St George's Hill estates were built, a development of large, pretentious mansions in London's stockbroker belt, outside the town of Weybridge, Surrey, about an hour's commute from the West End. A symbol of the triumph of greed over compassion.

John and Cynthia had been particularly bothered by fans at their flat in Emperor's Gate, off Cromwell Road; Cynthia had received obscene phone calls and there were sometimes so many fans outside that she could not take baby Julian out for a walk without being jostled and spat at. She and John made a conscious decision to move to the country to get away from the fans. John had little interest in London nightlife anyway; he disliked dancing and the pressures of Beatlemania were so intense that he saw no reason to appear in public more than was necessary.

Ken Partridge designed the house for the way he imagined a trendy young rock 'n' roll star must live, with large reception rooms for parties and an elegant dining room. The enormous living room had a black deep-pile carpet with an oriental rug on top surrounded by three large settees. A colour television filled the fireplace and a valuable Coromandel screen completed the décor. There was a Hollywood Modern kitchen so complicated that someone had to be sent from London to show Cynthia how to use it. A series of watercolour illustrations of vegetables, taken from a broken-up eighteenth-century French botanical encyclopedia and displayed in silver-streaked red lead frames, hung in the dining room on walls of mauve velvet, rather like an upmarket Indian restaurant. John so hated them that when someone asked what they were he gave them to him; even so, the walls contrasted oddly with the scrubbed wood dining table John and Cynthia brought with them.

There was a black study with a bar shaped like a world globe and two rooms in the attic were devoted entirely to John's model racing-car track. A Scalextric electric model racing-car set accompanied the Beatles on their 1964 British tour and was always set up backstage. John was so taken with the little model cars that he is reported to have bought twenty sets. This would have been typical for John, whose first reaction to wealth was not to purchase a Rolls-Royce, but to buy a huge quantity of Jaffa Cakes which he ate untill he was sick.

John retreated to the glassed-in morning room that backed on to the kitchen, which reminded him of the similar room at his Aunt Mimi's. One entire wall was glass, looking out over the swimming pool and the garden, which dropped away from the back of the house in a series of terraces. Another wall was lined with books arranged on built-in library shelving. He lay on a wicker chaise longue surrounded by Pop Art knick-knacks, tour souvenirs, his mother's old upright piano, a colour television and his many cats. In winter a fire burned in the grate. He spent hours there every day, drinking endless cups of tea, watching television and reading all the daily newspapers from cover to cover. His friend the journalist Maureen Cleave called him 'the laziest person in England', but for John television and newspapers were a principal source of inspiration and it was in them that such songs as 'A Day in the Life' and 'Good Morning' had their genesis.

Though John had attempted to personalise the house – a couple of Stu Sutcliffe paintings, a suit of armour wearing a gorilla head with an inverted pipe clenched between its teeth, a 48-play jukebox loaded with mostly fifties rock 'n' roll, a pinball table, books and games, a colour television in every room, usually turned on with the sound off, the flickering image animating the dead spaces – Kenwood remained a stage set; the formal rooms were never used except as corridors to other parts of the house.

John's main hide-away aside from his den was the music room, a small self-contained apartment high in the attic where he could close the door and shut himself off from his family and staff, particularly while the initial building work on the house was going on. Here he kept his tape recorders and instruments. Halfway up to the music room was a Mellotron, beached on the half-landing, possibly because it was too big to get all the way up the stairs. It was in the music room that Paul and John composed dozens of their songs, seated, as usual, facing one another.

> PAUL: To learn a guitar part we would both play exactly the same thing, so it was really like double-tracking a guitar. If we played it to anyone there'd be two guitars pumping out this same thing, two voices often singing the same melody line, so you just got double-strength everything, double-strength Daz. It was a loud demo rather than just one guy wondering enigmatically whether the song was okay or not. The two of us knew it was okay and played it very forcefully, we convinced each other.

Songwriting tended to come in bursts. The songs written individually could appear at any time, but the songwriting meetings for a new single or album were planned in advance. As John told *Beatles Monthly* in March 1966, 'It's too easy to put it off if we just meet without any plan and say, "Shall we write something today?" If you do that you feel as though you're losing a free day. What we're going to do is make dates beforehand and sort of say, "Right, Wednesday and Friday of this week are for songwriting. And Tuesday, Wednesday and Thursday of next week." Then we'll know it's something we've to keep to.'

PAUL: Mostly it was me getting out of London, to John's rather nice, comfortable Weybridge house near the golf course. I would sometimes be driven but normally I'd drive myself out there and would think a bit on the way out. I'd often wake him up so I'd be coming in a little fresher than he was, but after a coffee or a cup of tea he woke up and we nearly always went up to his little music room that he'd had built at the top of the house, Daddy's room, where we would get away from it all. I like to get away from people to songwrite, I don't like to do it in front of people. It's like sex for me, I was never an orgy man. So John and I would sit down and by then it might be one or two o'clock, and by four or five o'clock we'd be done. Three hours is about right, you start to fray at the edges after that. But that's good too because you think, 'We've got to get this done!'

We would normally be rung a couple of weeks before the recording session and they'd say. 'We're recording in a month's time and you've got a week off before the recordings to write some stuff.' You'd say, 'Oh, great, fabulous.' So I'd go out to John's every day for the week, and the rest of the time was just time off. We always wrote a song a day, whatever happened we always wrote a song a day. And after that I'd pack up and drive back home and go out for the evening and that was it.

When I was working on the *Liverpool Oratorio* with Carl Davis there were certain similarities, though obviously Carl's quite a different kettle of fish from John, but he said, 'We never had a dry day, it was marvellous, we never dried,' which surprised Carl greatly. I said, 'Why should we? We just thought up something and you wrote it down. That's how we do it, isn't it?'

At the height of touring and Beatlemania, many of John and Paul's songs were written backstage, on the road in tour buses or in hotel rooms. However, in the case of their next single: 'I Feel Fine'/'She's a Woman', released in November 1964, both sides were partly written in the recording studio itself.

John and Paul were always willing to allow random events to affect their songs: the chance juxtaposition of words, newspaper stories, fragments of popular songs or classical music were all welcomed into their creative flux. It was with a conscious awareness of the Surrealist tradition that they incorporated found objects into their work, and this was what happened with 'I Feel Fine'. It was a co-written song, from an idea of John's, and it opens with a wail of feedback – rare for 1964.

> PAUL: John had a semi-acoustic Gibson guitar. It had a pick-up on it so it could be amplified. John and George both had them; we used to call them Everly Brothers because they were very similar to the ones the Everly Brothers had used and we liked the Everlys a lot. It was mainly an acoustic guitar. They only used a tiny bit of electric, just for colour. If you turned it up too much you don't get any string noise, so the engineers and George Martin used to strike a balance between the colour of the electric thing and the natural acoustic. It's a coloured acoustic.
>
> We were just about to walk away to listen to a take when John leaned his guitar against the amp. I can still see him doing it. He really should have turned the electric off. It was only on a tiny bit, and John just leaned it against the amp when it went, 'Nnnnnnwahhhhh!' And we went, 'What's that? Voodoo!' 'No, it's feedback.' 'Wow, it's a great sound!' George Martin was there so we said, 'Can we have that on the record?' 'Well, I suppose we could, we could edit it on the front.' It was a found object, an accident caused by leaning the guitar against the amp.
>
> The song itself was more John's than mine. We sat down and co-wrote it with John's original idea. John sang it, I'm on harmonies and the drumming is basically what we used to think of as 'What'd I Say' drumming. There was a style of drumming on 'What'd I Say' which is a sort of Latin R & B that Ray Charles's drummer Milt Turner played on the original record and we used to love it. One of the big clinching factors about Ringo as the drummer in the band was that he could really play that so well.

Even in the early days they would compose some of the songs alone, as John did with 'Not a Second Time' or Paul with 'She's a Woman', which was issued as the B side of the new single. It was written on 8 October 1964, walking in the streets of St John's Wood, and recorded at Abbey Road the same day.

PAUL: Like 'Can't Buy Me Love', this was my attempt at a bluesy thing. We always found it very hard to write the more rock 'n' roll things. It seemed easy for Little Richard to knock 'em off, penny a dozen, but for us it wasn't quite so easy, being white boys who'd not been to a gospel church in our lives. So instead of doing a Little Richard song, whom I admire greatly, I would use the style I would have used for that but put it in one of my own songs, so this was about a woman rather than a girl. Bluesy melody is quite hard to write so I was quite pleased to get that.

John did a very good thing: instead of playing through it and putting like a watercolour wash over it all with his guitar he just stabbed on the off-beats. Ringo would play the snare and John did it with the guitar, which was good, it left a lot of space for the rest of the stuff. That was a distinctive sound on that. I have a recollection of walking round St John's Wood with that in my mind so I might have written it at home and finished it up on the way to the studio, finally polished it in the studio, maybe just taken John aside for a second and checked it with him, 'What d'you think?' 'Like it.' 'Good. Let's do it!'

That creative moment when you come up with an idea is the greatest, it's the best. It's like sex. You're filled with a knowledge that you're right, which, when much of your life is filled with guilt and the knowledge that you're probably not right, is a magic moment. You actually are convinced it's right, and it's a very warm feeling that comes all over you, and for some reason it comes from the spine, through the cranium and out the mouth. That was a quicky and it was a nice little R & B thing which I liked.

Beatles for Sale

These were the years when the partnership was at its height. After the success of *A Hard Day's Night* came the *Beatles for Sale* album with eight new Lennon–McCartney compositions. Were it not for the pressure of touring, there would probably have been more originals;

even so, the album contained some classics. One song, 'I'll Follow the Sun', dated back to Forthlin Road (they still had a stock of songs left over from the Forthlin Road song factory to use up) and another, 'Every Little Thing', Paul wrote at Wimpole Street sitting in his garret room alone, strumming his guitar.

> PAUL: 'Every Little Thing', like most of the stuff I did, was my attempt at the next single. I remember playing it for Brian backstage somewhere. He had assembled a few people. It was one of those meetings – 'Oh, we have to do some recordings, who's got what?' and we played a few at Brian. We didn't often check things with Brian, in fact I just remember it in connection with this because I thought it was very catchy. I played it amongst a few songs; it was something I thought was quite good but it became an album filler rather than the great almighty single. It didn't have quite what was required.

Paul and John were much more likely to write songs at Kenwood than for John to come into town to work in the music room at Wimpole Street, which, in any case, wasn't always available. Paul enjoyed the drive out to the country in his Aston Martin, whereas negotiating West End traffic was not a pleasurable experience for John. Paul, Ringo and George were all keen drivers; George in particular developed a taste for fast cars and even bought his own McLaren, whereas John learned to drive much later than the others and had a crash shortly after passing his test, which unnerved him. He normally used a driver. Paul: 'It was always nice to have an excuse to drive out into the country so that generally meant that I got out to John's house.'

Sometimes he would be chauffeured out to Kenwood. On one occasion this provided the impetus for a song. The driver was not one of the regulars that Paul knew, but as they were turning into John's driveway Paul casually asked him if he had been busy. 'Busy?' he said. 'I've been working eight days a week.' Paul went into John's house and told him, 'Well, I've got the title: "Eight Days a Week".' Paul: 'Neither of us had heard that expression before so we had that chauffeur to credit for that. It was like a little blessing from the gods. I didn't have any idea for it other than the title, and we just knocked it off together, just filling in from the title. So that one came quickly.'

December 1961. At the Cavern with Pete Best on drums. [*Apple*]

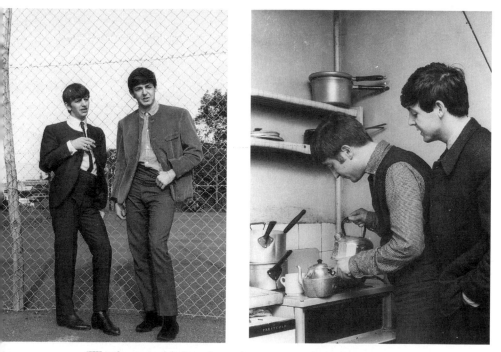

'We always said that the only reason to be in a group
was not to have a job and to get girls.' [*Apple*]
The Forthlin Road hit factory. [*Dezo Hoffmann / Apple*]

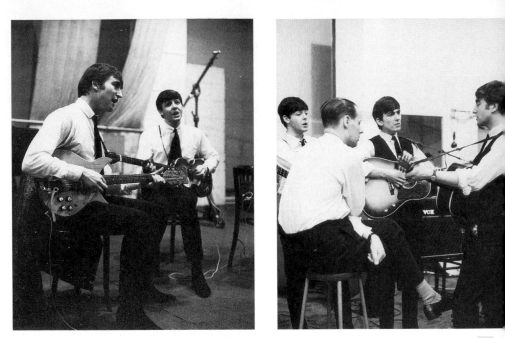

6 June 1962. The Beatles' first visit to Abbey Road Studios to audition for George Martin. [*Dezo Hoffman / Apple*]
11 February 1963. Recording their first album, *Please, Please Me.* With the exception of the singles included on it, it was completed in just one day [*Dezo Hoffman / Apple*]

18 June 1963. *Pop Go the Beatles* on BBC-TV, one of their many BBC shows. An early shot of Paul on drums. [*Dezo Hoffman / Apple*]The star dressing room backstage at the London Palladium with Alma Cogan, January 1964. [*Dezo Hoffman / Apple*]

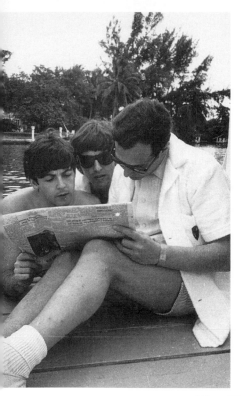

First US Tour:
Relaxing with Brian Epstein, prior to their second live broadcast on *The Ed Sullivan Show*, February 1964. [*Dezo Hoffman / Apple*]
11 February 1964. On the way to Washington, DC from New York in their own coach. [*Apple*]

Lennon and McCartney. [*Apple*]

Backstage:
dressing rooms, rehearsal rooms, hotels, studios; a life spent hiding from fans. [*Apple*

Richard Lester (left) directing a scene with Paul and Victor Spinetti (right) during the filming of *A Hard Day's Night*. [*Robert Freeman / Apple*]
Richard Lester filming a close-up of Paul's bass for the film *Help*. [*Apple*]

The famous Beatle bow, brought to the Beatles by Brian Epstein from his brief stint at RADA. [*Apple*]

Robert Fraser, taken on
14 December 1965, around the
time Paul met him.
[*Graham Keen*]

Brian Epstein with Marianne
Faithfull, November 1965. [*Apple*]

With Peter Asher. Paul's song launched Peter's career in
Peter and Gordon with a double US/UK number one. [*Apple*]

A hint of experiments to come:
shooting the infamous 'Butcher cover'
for the US album *Yesterday and Today*
at Bob Whitaker's Chelsea studio,
25 March 1966.
[*Bob Whitaker/Apple*]

'People always said John was the hard-edged one ...' [*Apple*]

Peter Asher, Barry Miles and John Dunbar outside Indica, 1966. [*Graham Keen*]

Another Kenwood number was 'Baby's in Black'.

PAUL: We wanted to write something a little bit darker, bluesy, the title's dark anyway. It's in 3/4 time, one of the first waltzes we wrote, which was interesting for us because most of our stuff's in 4/4. It was very much co-written and we both sang it. Sometimes the harmony that I was writing in sympathy to John's melody would take over and become a stronger melody. Suddenly a piebald rabbit came out of the hat! When people wrote out the music score they would ask, 'Which one is the melody?' because it was so co-written that you could actually take either. We rather liked this one. It was not so much a work job, there was a bit more cred about this one. It's got a good middle.

For the next three years the Beatles usually performed 'Baby's in Black' as the third number in their set. They would open with 'Rock and Roll Music', followed by 'Long Tall Sally' to get things moving, then announce, 'And now for something different.' Paul: 'And that was "Baby's in Black", we used to put that in there, and think, "Well, they won't know quite what to make of this but it's cool."'

John and Paul wrote 'I Don't Want to Spoil the Party' as a country and western for Ringo. A lot of the boats from Liverpool used to go to New Orleans and Texas, transporting oil from the Gulf of Mexico, and the sailors would bring back blues and C & W records. Ringo loved country and western. He knew the work of all the great early country artists like Jimmie Rodgers and years later, after the Beatles split up, he even recorded his own solo country and western album, *Beaucoups of Blues*.

PAUL: Ringo had a great style and great delivery. He had a lot of fans, so we liked to write something for him on each album. 'I Don't Want to Spoil the Party' is quite a nice little song, co-written by John and I. It sounds more like John than me so 80-20 to him, sitting down doing a job. Certain songs were inspirational and certain songs were work, it didn't mean they were any less fun to write, it was just a craft, and this was a job to order really, which Ringo did a good job on.

'What You're Doing' was a bit of a filler. I think it was a little more mine than John's, but I don't have a very clear recollection so to be on the safe side I'd put it as 50-50. It doesn't sound like an idea that I remember John offering, so it sounds like a way to get a song started, some of them are just that. 'Hey, what'cha doing?' You sometimes start a song and hope the best bit will arrive by the time you get to the chorus ... but sometimes that's all you get, and I suspect this was one of them. Maybe it's a better recording than it is a song, some of them are. Sometimes a good recording would enhance the song.

It was the first song in which the Beatles deliberately distorted the tape by overriding the desk, the beginning of a series of experimental recording techniques which would stretch George Martin's skill and imagination to the utmost and test EMI's archaic equipment at Abbey Road to the limit.

'No Reply', 'I'm a Loser' and 'Yes It Is' were very much John Lennon songs. Paul: 'We wrote "No Reply" together but from a strong original idea of his. I think he pretty much had that one, but as usual, if he didn't have the third verse and the middle eight, then he'd play it to me pretty much formed, then we would shove a bit in the middle or I'd throw in an idea.' John said that the song was his version of 'Silhouettes' by the Rays.

> PAUL: Looking back on it I think songs like 'I'm a Loser' and 'Nowhere Man' were John's cries for help. We used to listen to quite a lot of country and western songs and they are all about sadness and 'I lost my truck' so it was quite acceptable to sing 'I'm a loser'. You didn't really think about it at the time, it's only later you think, God! I think it was pretty brave of John. 'I'm A Loser' was very much John's song and there may have been a dabble or two from me.

The song was recorded on 14 August 1964, shortly before the Beatles embarked on their American tour.

'Yes It Is' was the remaining John Lennon song on *Beatles for Sale*, once again written by Paul and John together at Kenwood.

> PAUL: I was there writing it with John, but it was his inspiration that I helped him finish off. 'Yes It Is' is a very fine song of John's, a ballad, unusual for John. He wrote some beautiful ballads but I'm known generally as the balladeer. The interesting thing is that we actually come out rather equal, the more you analyse it, the more you get to the feeling that both of us always

had, which was one of equality. I don't think John ever felt he was better than me and I don't think I ever felt I was better than John. Certainly when we worked it would have been fatal in a collaboration for either of us to ever think that. It was just that I brought a certain 50 per cent and John brought a certain 50 per cent.

There is a persistent idea that John and Paul only really wrote together in the very early days, but this is not true. They both valued their songwriting partnership highly. It was artistically fulfilling as well as a very valuable commercial asset and it was not something that either of them took lightly. John Dunbar, who was a frequent visitor to Kenwood in 1965–66, remembers that John would often play through Paul's new songs when Paul was not there, running through them, making sure there was nothing more he could do to help. They relied upon each other to finish off a song, even as late as 'The Ballad of John and Yoko', which John brought round for Paul to check before they recorded it in April 1969.

PAUL: John would often have the melody and the lyrics to one verse, and the trickiest thing is making any more of it. The second verse is nearly always the killer because you've often said it all in the first verse, but by pushing yourself you can actually get a second verse better than your first. It's always more difficult because you mustn't repeat yourself, you've got to take the idea somewhere else but it has to have the the same metre and the same melody. That was often where he or I needed help.

Then you have a chorus or a middle. We used to call everything a middle eight, even if it had thirty-two bars or sixteen bars. George Martin used to point out, 'Paul, hasn't this got sixteen bars?' 'Yes, George, it has.' 'But you're calling it a middle eight?' 'Yes, George, we are.' 'I see. Super!' We called them middle eights, we had heard musicians say 'That's a nice middle eight' and we didn't get the significance of the word 'eight'. We just learned the word for it and that was what we called it: there were verses, choruses and middle eights.

There tended to be four verses in our songs: one chorus that repeated endlessly and a middle eight. So if it was John's idea, generally I would come in at the second verse, be there for the middle eight and be there for the third and fourth verses, the resolution. We would often knock out the fourth verse and repeat the first, because it seemed like a nice top and tail and also there was a commercial aspect that we were aware of: if people heard a verse twice they were more likely to remember it. The first verse was always good to finish with, it was like, 'Remember what I told you at the beginning of this song? I'm going to reiterate it now.' That was always a good a little trick.

Their financial adviser James Isherwood's proposal to float Northern Songs on the stock market was a good one. John and Paul's problem was that they were liable for tax at a very high rate on their income. What they needed was some tax-free income and since there was no capital-gains tax in those days, this meant they would not pay any tax on the proceeds when they sold their shares on the exchange. It was, however, an ambitious scheme because no one had ever done anything like this before and Isherwood was not sure that the Stock Exchange would even accept a company whose income consisted solely of music written by two young men with no proven track record: what if they dried up, what if they argued, what if they veered off in a non-commercial direction or, even worse, what if one of them had an accident or died? Every merchant bank that Isherwood approached refused even to consider the idea of supporting an application to the Stock Exchange.

Isherwood went to Lord Goodman, known to *Private Eye* as 'two dinners Goodman', who had risen to power along with the Labour Party hierarchy when Labour won the 1964 election. Goodman acted for Prime Minister Harold Wilson and represented a number of powerful, wealthy Labour supporters, many of them property developers. He had been chairman of the Newspaper Proprietors' Association and, more importantly, he had connections with a large number of stockbrokers. Acting together with a firm of City stockbrokers, Goodman and Isherwood drafted a letter to the Stock Exchange. They estimated their chances of being able to go public at about 10–1, but with Goodman behind them they succeeded.

Brian Epstein took no part in the business. James Isherwood: 'He didn't know enough about the financial side of things to be particularly interested. He left the whole operation entirely in my hands. I'd always felt that Brian was extremely efficient, but it soon became clear to me that while he was adept at arranging tours, he had no financial expertise of any kind.'

Five million five shilling (25p) shares were issued, of which Dick James and Charles Silver took half between them. Paul and John got 1,000,000 each, and Brian 500,000. It was decided to offer 2,000,000 of them to the public at seven shillings and ninepence (38.75p) each, which meant each of the parties was contributing two fifths of their holdings. Brian was so scared that an unsuccessful flotation would destroy Paul and John's reputation as songwriters that he disappeared. He remained incommunicado until several days after the shares entered the market, leaving Isherwood to make all the decisions by himself.

James Isherwood was fearful that adverse press comments might have a disastrous effect on the flotation, and indeed, Frederick Ellis, the chief financial editor of the *Daily Express*, strongly advised his readers not to buy Northern Songs shares. To counter this, Isherwood put together a syndicate using his own money, money under his control and some of Charles Silver's cash. The syndicate had enough to purchase 500,000 shares in case anything went wrong. This turned out to be a very shrewd move. Northern Songs Limited became a public company on the London Stock Exchange on 18 February 1965. Isherwood remembers it well:

> That first morning, I heard from the Brokers just after the Stock Exchange opened at ten o'clock. There were a lot of shares on offer. Accordingly I instructed the brokers to buy every share that came on the market. There didn't appear to be another buyer, and in consequence the price dropped. It continued to fall over the next few days, and I bought every available share until eventually the market reached rock bottom at five shillings and nine-pence, compared with the issue price of seven shillings and nine-pence. I had spent almost all of the syndicate's money.
>
> A few days later Brian re-surfaced and I told him what I'd done. Over the next two or three weeks the public suddenly began to realise that as the music of John and Paul was being so widely played on the radio, perhaps the ownership of shares in Northern Songs was not a bad thing, after all, and buying orders for the shares began to arrive at the brokers. They had none

available! They got in touch with me, and I agreed to release five thousand shares that day, and subsequently about ten thousand each day at gradually increased prices. The last of the syndicate shares I released were at a price of fourteen shillings (70p), nearly double the original issue price. The flotation had been a success and created for both John and Paul, and incidentally, Brian, a substantial capital asset.

At the time James Isherwood was holding substantial sums of money for both George and Ringo so he decided to buy 25,000 shares for each of them at the original issue price of seven shillings and ninepence. This gave them a respectable financial share in the music they were playing.

For John and Paul, when they were sagging off school to write songs in the living room of Forthlin Road, the original dream – even before the fantasy of making it as a rock 'n' roll band – had been to become successful songwriters. They had always seen this as their career and ever since the formation of Northern Songs had given songs to the other members of Brian Epstein's ever-growing management company, and encouraged outsiders to record their material by sending round acetates to likely candidates. Billy J. Kramer and the Dakotas were the recipients of four originals, but it was with a cover of John and Paul's 'Do You Want to Know a Secret' that they had first hit the charts, replacing the Beatles' own 'From Me to You' at number one in June 1963. The B side was a Lennon–McCartney composition, 'I'll Be on My Way', co-written in early Liverpool days. Paul: 'It's a little bit too June-moon for me, but these were very early songs and they worked out quite well.'

Billy J's 'Bad to Me', released in July 1963, written specifically for him by John and Paul, sounded very like the Beatles and also made number one. Since the formula was working so well, Brian Epstein asked for yet another original, and on 1 November Billy J released 'I'll Keep You Satisfied'. Paul: 'That was a good one. Billy J was having a bit of success and because he was out of the same stable as us, it made sense for us, if we weren't having to write a lot of stuff for ourselves, to knock off a couple for friends. It was pretty much co-written: John and I sat down and purposely wrote it for Billy J in a couple of hours. This one is one I still like. I find myself whistling it in the garden.' It was another top-ten hit but this time only reached number four.

The fourth attempt, 'From a Window', was again written purposely for Billy. John and Paul were hot. Brian would come up and say Billy needed a new song and they would write it on the spot. Paul: 'We would just make it up. We would sit down at rehearsal and grab a couple of hours somewhere and just with a pen and a bit of paper, scribble the lyrics down.'

Another signing to Brian Epstein's stable was the Fourmost, who also began their career with two Lennon–McCartney compositions: 'Hello Little Girl' and 'I'm in Love'.

PAUL: Unfortunately the words aren't too wonderful. They're a bit average, but the Fourmost were eager to have a hit and they were very good friends of ours. They were more of a comedy group, a really very funny cabaret act, and when it came to making a record and being serious on a TV show, they always laughed and giggled. They were always having such a laugh, it was very difficult for them. They just weren't the kind of guys who were going to get a major hit. I tried a few times.

Both songs reached the top twenty, which got their name known and enabled them to switch to cabaret later when the hits stopped coming.

Yet another Epstein act who got a start with a Lennon–McCartney song was Cilla Black, the cloakroom girl at the Cavern, who reached number 35 in the British charts with 'Love of the Loved'. Once again, these were purpose-built songs. Paul described 'It's for You', which she released in August 1964:

I wrote it for Cilla. That's not a bad little song. I remember when we first went over to America, plugging it to all these DJs, we used to talk to endlessly, 'Look, there's this girl singer in our stable and you should listen out for this song.' It didn't do very well. I ended up writing a few songs for Cilla, actually. 'Step Inside Love' was a later one. Cilla Black was getting her first TV show with a guy called Michael Hurll and they came to see me backstage somewhere and asked me, would I write the theme tune for it, so I said yes. I did a little demo of it, with myself double-tracked, up at Cavendish, and that was it. I quite like the song, it's very cabaret, it suited her voice. It was just a welcoming song for Cilla.

Not everything that John and Paul wrote was successful, and some of their songs they would have preferred to put away in a drawer and forget about. 'Tip of My Tongue', released by Tommy Quickly in July 1963, is just such a song.

PAUL: Oh, my God! There were always a couple of songs that we didn't want to do because we didn't think they were very good, but other people would say, 'Well, I'll do it, I think it's quite good.' Tommy Quickly was one of our friends out of Brian Epstein's stable. This is pretty much mine, I'm ashamed to say. It sounds like one of these where I tried to work it around the title.

'That Means a Lot', released by P. J. Proby in September 1965, was another example of a song that Paul and John had rejected as not good enough for the Beatles.

PAUL: Normally I'd try and bury these songs and not put them out but there was so much pressure from people, they'd say, 'Have you got *anything*?' I'd say, 'I have, but you really don't want to see them.' They'd say, 'I do! Believe me, I think I can make a good job of it, and your name on it would be a big plus.' So P. J. Proby, a friend of ours that we met during the Jack Good television show that we did, *Round the Beatles*, wanted to do it, so I gave it to him. He had a minor hit with it.

The record went to number thirty.

Paul's earliest work included songs like 'When I'm Sixty-Four', an old-fashioned cabaret song which remained bereft of lyrics until he resurrected it in the mid-sixties. In the days before the Beatles' success, Paul and John were writing with a view to a music career like Rodgers and Hammerstein. In those days, the greatest accolade possible for a songwriter was to write something for Frank Sinatra; as it still is for many people. It was something that they talked about a lot, so much so that one night, when he was still a teenager living at Forthlin Road, Paul wrote a song specifically for Sinatra.

PAUL: I wrote it in bed at that moment when you're just dropping off and all these things are coming to you, but you ought to go to sleep. I used to keep pencil and paper by my bed, and I've got the ability to write in the dark, though some of the lines cross each other. I wrote this song called 'Suicide' which was very cabaret, 'If when she tries to run away and he calls her back she comes ... it's okay, because she's under both his thumbs ...' all that kind of shit. Very Sinatra, I thought. 'She'll limp along to his side ... I call it suicide!' It was murder! Horrible song! But you had to go through all those styles to discover your own. I only had one verse, so I cobbled together another.

And the funny thing was, years and years later, he rang me at Abbey Road studio, and it was a great moment when one of the engineers said, 'Paul, Sinatra's on the phone.' And I was able to go, 'Oh. I'll be there in a minute,' touch a fader and then go off. And everyone would go, 'Oooooo! Sinatra's on the phone!' How many people have that? He was asking for a song, so I found the song, made a demo and sent it to him. Apparently he thought it was an almighty piss-take. 'No way!' he's supposed to have said to one of his people. 'Is this guy having me on?' So my career with Sinatra ended in terrible ignominy. I think he couldn't grasp it was tongue in cheek. It was only supposed to be a play on the word 'suicide', not actual physical suicide. If a girl lets a guy trample all over her, she's committing some sort of suicide. I think he sent the demo back. Looking back on it I'm quite relieved he did, actually, it wasn't a good song, it was just a teenage thought.

FIVE

LENNON & McCARTNEY

The effects of this drug have been frequently and luridly described: disturbance of space-time perception, acute sensitivity to impressions, flight of ideas, laughing jags, silliness. Marijuana is a sensitiser ... it is not habit forming. I have never seen evidence of any ill effects from moderate use.

William S. Burroughs in a letter to Dr Dent at the
British Journal of Addiction, 3 August 1956

I Get High with a Little Help from My Friends

JUST AS MANY OF THE GREAT NOVELS OF THE 'LOST GENERATION' OF THE twenties were largely written in an alcoholic haze, so much of the music of the sixties was made under the influence of drugs. The Doors made their first album on acid; Brian Wilson recorded some of the Beach Boys' greatest tracks lying on the floor of the studio with the microphone adjusted so that he could sing from that position, so stoned on hash that he was unable to stand up; Eric Clapton's most highly acclaimed track, 'Layla', was made on heroin, as were ten years' worth of Keith Richards's contributions to the Rolling Stones.

The Beatles' use of drugs in the mid-sixties caused an enormous change in their music and attitudes. Smoking pot was something at that time largely confined to musicians and students. 'Youth culture' and its attendant drug use did not occur until later in the decade. Pot caused an irreparable shift in perception which coloured the Beatles' music from then on.

PAUL: The awkward thing about it all is you have to talk about drugs. If you don't you're being wildly dishonest. The good thing was that it was the first period of people taking drugs, and the first bloom is always the best really. So it was at a time when, having been to America, we started to expand our horizons. We'd met people like Dylan and we got into pot, like a lot of people from our generation. And I suppose in our way we thought this was a little more grown-up than perhaps the Scotch and Coke we'd been into before then. What makes people smoke cigarettes when they're fourteen? It's peer pressure. It makes them feel older, it makes them feel a bit groovier and that's quite valuable, at that age, to feel a bit groovier. And I suppose it was the same kind of thing in our case. So once pot was established as part of the curriculum you started to get a bit more surreal material coming from us, a bit more abstract stuff. It was just the first time I'd been exposed to all these new influences and had the time and inclination to bother with them all. I always have to give marijuana credit for that.

It was Bob Dylan that turned us all on to pot in America and it opened a different kind of sensibility really; more like jazz musicians. The nearest we'd ever heard of this was like the old joke about the cleaner in the Hammersmith Odeon saying, 'That Ray Charles, he's a tight bastard. You know, he must pay his musicians nothing. There were two of them sharing a cigarette in the toilet last night.' It was somehow plugging into that sensibility. There was a sort of naughtiness about it and yet I knew I'd have to keep my shit very well together because I knew there was a very naughty end to it. Devastation and heroin and the real serious stuff was around the corner. But this was the mild end of it and for quite a number of years there, everyone was at the mild end of it. Instead of Scotch and Coke and ciggies it became pot and wine.

In today's climate I hate to talk about drugs because it's just not the same. You have someone jumping on your head the minute you say anything, so I've taken to not trying to give my point of view unless someone really very much asks for it. Because I think the 'Just say no' mentality is so crazed. I saw a thing in a women's magazine the other day. 'He smokes cannabis, what am I to do? He laughs it off when I try to tell him, he says it's not really harmful ...' Of course you're half hoping the advice will be, 'Well, you know it's not that harmful; if you love him, if you talk to him about it, tell him maybe he should keep it in the garden shed or something,' you know, a reasonable point of view. But of course it was, 'No, no, all drugs are bad. All drugs are bad. Librium's good, Valium's good, ciggies are good, vodka's good. But cannabis, ooooh!' I hate that unreasoned attitude. I really can't believe it's thirty years since the sixties. I find it staggering. It's like the future, the sixties to me, it's like it hasn't happened. I feel the sixties are about to arrive. And we're in some sort of time warp and it's still going to happen.

During their long months on the Reeperbahn, the Beatles had sometimes used amphetamines to keep them going, but had never been into marijuana even though there was undoubtedly plenty of it around in a seaport like Hamburg. They got stoned on pot for the first time courtesy of Bob Dylan and journalist Al Aronowitz after one of their New York concerts during their second visit to the USA. It was 28 August 1964. Beatlemania was at its height and the Beatles had just played the 16,000-seater Forest Hills Tennis Stadium in Queens, New York. An eight-foot-high fence topped with barbed wire separated the Beatles from their zealous fans and the group had to arrive and leave by helicopter from the Wall Street heliport because the police feared that fans would trap them in the Midtown Tunnel. At dawn there had been 3,000 fans outside their hotel, the staid old Delmonico Hotel at 502 Park Avenue at 59th Street. 'We used to be dowdy, but now we swing,' said a hotel spokesman. 'We welcome the Beatles.' Fans stood eight deep behind police barricades, singing Beatles songs and calling out their names. After the concert, they began to reassemble.

Less than an hour after going on stage, the group arrived back at the Delmonico. The Beatles' suite occupied most of the sixth floor of the 500-room hotel and was protected by police in the corridors and lobby as well as the street. In the hospitality suite, their press officer Derek Taylor doled out the drinks and food to the assembled journalists and pacified the celebrity guests – the Kingston Trio, Peter, Paul and Mary and the DJ Murray the K – who were waiting for the party to get going. Meanwhile the Beatles were trying to unwind after the concert and its surrounding madness. Together with

Brian Epstein and their roadies Mal and Neil, they retired to a back room for dinner.

Since it was impossible for them to leave the hotel, they asked the *New York Post* journalist Al Aronowitz if he could arrange for Bob Dylan to visit them. Paul: 'We were great great admirers of Dylan. We loved him and had done since his first album which I'd had in Liverpool. John had listened to his stuff and been very influenced; "You've Got to Hide Your Love Away" is virtually a Dylan impression.'

Dylan was driven down from Woodstock by his roadie in his anonymous blue Ford station wagon, picking up Aronowitz from his home in Berkeley Hills, New Jersey, on the way. Aronowitz, who had been on the fringe of Beat Generation circles since the late fifties, had turned Dylan on to pot the year before. In the hotel lobby, police barred their way until Mal Evans came down and the three were quickly ushered into the main lounge. Brian naturally played the gracious host and asked what they would like to drink.

'Cheap wine,' said Dylan. Unfortunately the Beatles had been drinking good French wine with their meal so Mal was dispatched to buy something suitably nasty for Dylan. In the meantime, Dylan was offered some purple hearts, the little blue Drinamyl pills which kept virtually every British rock group going through the sixties when their bodies told them they should be sleeping. Dylan declined and suggested they smoke some grass instead.

Brian Epstein explained with some embarrassment that they had never smoked pot before.

'But what about your song, the one about getting high?' asked Dylan. '"And when I touch you, I get high, I get high …"'

The Liverpool accent had rendered the words of 'I Want to Hold Your Hand' unintelligible to Dylan. 'It goes, "I can't hide, I can't hide …"' explained John.

Victor Mamudes, Dylan's tall, skinny roadie, was naturally the one carrying the drugs – in those days this was a roadie's most important job – and he passed the bag to Dylan, who began to roll the first joint rather shakily, spilling quite a lot of the grass into the large bowl of fruit on the room-service table. Al Aronowitz wrote: 'Bob hovered unsteadily while he tried to lift the grass from the bag with the fingertips of one hand so he could crush it into the leaf of rolling paper which he held in his other hand. Besides being a sloppy roller, Bob had started drinking whatever expensive stuff was already there.'

With more than a dozen police in the corridor outside and reporters just down the hall, great caution was deemed necessary; Dylan and Ringo retired to the far end of the back room near the front windows, blinds were drawn and rolled towels sealed the locked doors. As snatches of Beatles songs floated up from the fans in the street below, Dylan passed a skinny American joint to Ringo, who smoked the whole thing, not knowing that pot-smoking etiquette requires that the joint be passed around.

PAUL: The first time I took it I got very high indeed. It was quite a breakthrough, it was something different. George Harrison, John and I were sitting in the main room of the suite, the lounge, drinking. We were sitting there with our Scotch and Cokes, and Dylan had just given Ringo a puff of it. Ringo came back in and we said, 'How is it?' He said, 'The ceiling's coming down on me.' And we went, Wow! Leaped up, 'God! Got to do this!' So we ran into the back room – first John, then me and George, then Brian. We all had a puff and for about five minutes we went, 'This isn't doing anything,' so we kept having more. 'Sssshhhh! This isn't doing anything. Are you feeling … ggggzzzzz!' and we started giggling uncontrollably.

And it was very very funny and my, it was. It was! The Beatles were about humour, we had a great humour between us. There was an 'in' side to the track of humour that we would use as a protective thing, so with this on top of it, things were really hilarious. I remember walking round the suite, trying to get away from it all, closing the door behind me without realising George Harrison had walked step by step with me, so I thought I'd lost him, turned around, and he's in the room with me. 'Ohhh! This is hilarious. I can't handle it!' It was like the funniest bloody dream going.

It was me, George and Brian, this little group. Everyone would go in in twos. We were looking at Brian Epstein, who had a little butt, the tiniest little butt, so he looked like a tramp smoking a dog-end,' which we had only ever done when we were poor before … And this, compared to Brian's image … and we were going, 'Awwwww!' Fucking screaming laughing at him. It was hilarious. I remember Brian looking at himself in the mirror and getting the whole joke of all this. We were all in hysterics.

Brian was pointing at himself and going, 'Jew!' And it was hilarious! We couldn't believe this was so funny. I mean, that would be the first time Brian would point at himself and say 'Jew'. It may not seem the least bit significant to anyone else, but in our circle, it was very liberating.

It developed into a bit of a party. We all went back out into the lounge and drank and whatever but I don't think anyone needed much more pot after that. That was it! I spent the whole evening running around trying to find a pencil and paper because when I went back in the bedroom later, I discovered the Meaning of Life. And I suddenly felt like a reporter, on behalf of my local newspaper in Liverpool. I wanted to tell my people what it was. I was the great discoverer, on this sea of pot, in New York. I was sailing this sea and I had discovered it.

So I remember asking Mal, our road manager, for what seemed like years and years, 'Have you got a pencil?' But of course everyone was so stoned they couldn't produce a pencil, let alone a combination of a paper and pencil, so it was I either had the pencil but I didn't have the paper or I had the ... I eventually found it and I wrote it down, and gave it to Mal for safekeeping.

I'd been going through this thing of levels, during the evening. And at each level I'd meet all these people again. 'Hahaha! It's you!' And then I'd metamorphose on to another level. Anyway, Mal gave me this little slip of paper in the morning, and written on it was, 'There are seven levels!' Actually it wasn't bad. Not bad for an amateur. And we pissed ourselves laughing, I mean, 'What the fuck's that? What the fuck are the seven levels?' But looking back, it's actually a pretty succinct comment; it ties in with a lot of major religions but I didn't know that then. We know that now because we've looked into a lot of that since, but that was the first thing. We were kind of proud to have been introduced to pot by Dylan, that was rather a coup. It was like being introduced to meditation and given your mantra by Maharishi. There was a certain status to it.

Pot had a tremendous influence on the music of the Beatles, as it did on virtually every other sixties rock 'n' roll group, and their songs are filled with discreet references to it. After that day in August 1964, any mention of 'high' or 'grass' in their songs was always intentional, from 'With a Little Help from My Friends' to 'A Day in the Life', though some references were more obscure than others. Paul's 'Got to Get You into My Life', which was to be released on the *Revolver* album, for instance, was entirely about pot.

> PAUL: 'Got to Get You into My Life' was one I wrote when I had first been introduced to pot. I'd been a rather straight working-class lad but when we started to get into pot it seemed to me to be quite uplifting. It didn't seem to have too many side effects like alcohol or some of the other stuff, like pills, which I pretty much kept off. I kind of liked marijuana. I didn't have a hard time with it and to me it was mind-expanding, literally mind-expanding.
>
> So 'Got to Get You into My Life' is really a song about that, it's not to a person, it's actually about pot. It's saying, 'I'm going to do this. This is not a bad idea.' So it's actually an ode to pot, like someone else might write an ode to chocolate or a good claret. It wouldn't be the first time in history someone's done it, but in my case it was the first flush of pot. I haven't really changed my opinion too much except, if anyone asks me for real advice, it would be stay straight. That is actually the best way. But in a stressful world I still would say that pot was one of the best of the tranquillising drugs; I have drunk and smoked pot and of the two I think pot is less harmful. People tend to fall asleep on it rather than go and commit murder, so it's always seemed to me a rather benign one. In my own mind, I've always likened it to the peace pipe of the Indians. Westerners used to call it 'native tobacco'. In the sixties we all thought this was what they were smoking.

Help!

The Beatles' use of pot was perhaps most conspicuous in their second film, *Help!*, work on which began in February 1965 with the recording of songs for the soundtrack. Their method of working had changed over the years: in the beginning George Martin was very much in control and they recorded during the appointed day and evening sessions. As years went by and they became EMI's cash cow, they took over more and more of the producer's role and recorded whenever they felt like it. John and Paul always had songs prepared when they entered the studio but as they had free studio time, they did not rehearse beforehand.

PAUL: Normally John and I would go in the studio, sit down with the guys and say, 'Right, what are we going to do?' I'd say to John, 'Do you want to do that one of yours or shall we do this one of mine? Which shall we play 'em first?' 'Oh, this one, right. We'd like to do this song.' We'd show it to the band over the course of twenty minutes, possibly half an hour. It hardly ever took us that long. Ringo would stand around with a pair of drumsticks which he might tap on a seat or a screen or a packing case. John and I would sit with our two guitars. George would bring his guitar and see what chords we were doing and figure out what he could do. George Martin would sit down with us and then we would separate, go to each instrument and come out ready to fight. And we just did it, and within the next hour, we would have done it. We would have decided how we were going to play this song. If for some reason it needed to be mixed quickly we would go upstairs to the control room, but we often left it to them and just went home. But as things went on we might go up to the control room more often.

The rock 'n' roll of the sixties is characterised by tales of excess which often extended into the recording studio. The Beatles, however, had a very workmanlike attitude to the studio and only on one occasion, when John mistook an acid tab for an upper, did they have to abandon a session. They smoked pot, and from *Sgt. Pepper* onwards there were occasions when coke was available in the studio, but they avoided anything that would blur their musical awareness so there was no alcohol to speak of, and no heroin or acid. George Martin turned a conveniently blind eye to any illegal goings-on and they never abused his discretion by openly flaunting their drug use.

PAUL: If you talk to him now about whether he knew we were doing drugs, he would say, 'Well, I suspected it, but they kept it out of my face.' Which we generally did. It wasn't like the scenes of debauchery that followed. The least discreet would be that Mal, our road manager, might be over behind the sound screens rolling a joint. It was fairly good-natured, pleasant stuff. I mean, obviously we had to be in such a state as to be able to record. You don't want to do vocals when you're scared to do vocals. So it had to be controlled, and I think it was, but I think the idea that music can be enhanced by marijuana was definitely being researched at the time, so you would smoke a joint and then sit down at the piano and think, Oh, this might be a great idea! I'm not saying that was the only way to work because before that we worked completely straight, completely clean, no alcohol or anything, and had a bunch of very good ideas under those circumstances.

It was the discipline of EMI. We had a certain attitude towards EMI, that it was a workplace, that was always there underneath it all, although we would often party. There was George Martin himself, who was fairly practical, and the engineers. You didn't want to mess around. Then there was our own controlling factor. We didn't want to be lying around unable to do anything. We knew why we were doing it: it was to enhance the whole thing. I think if we found something wasn't enhancing it, booze for instance, we gave it up. Once or twice we'd try a little wine when people were around, but generally you'd fuck up solos and you couldn't be bothered to think of a little complex musical thing that would have sounded great. You might have wanted to think of a harmony part to something and now it was a bit of a chore and tuning up is a bit of chore when you're stoned.

In the early days we recorded 10.30–1.30, then break for lunch. Nobody paid for your lunch, you just had an hour off to go and buy it for yourself. Very EMI. Then 2.30 till 5.30. And that was generally it, just those two sessions, or then, if you were really going crazy, 7.00 till 10.00, an evening session, which was really working late. By the time you'd done that, you wanted to go home or you wanted to go to the pub or something. Then later we heard rumours that people like Sinatra sometimes worked at three in the morning, so as things got a little wilder and a little more into party frame we did try that, and we had the place and we were able to do it. But I'm not sure how productive it was really. I think most of our best stuff was done under reasonably sane circumstances because it's not easy to think up all that stuff, and you've really just got to get the miracle take if you're stoned. It can be done, just sometimes, but it may be one in a hundred.

The songs for *Help!*, with the exception of the title song, were written before the screenplay was finished. Brian Epstein gave Dick Lester a demo tape of nine songs, from which he chose the six that he thought had cinematic possibilities rather than being the six best songs. Recording began on 15 February 1965 with 'Ticket to Ride', used in the snow scene in the film. As many fans suspected at the time, it was partially about Ryde in the Isle of Wight on the south coast of Britain, where Paul's cousin Bett and her husband Mike Robbins ran a pub. John and Paul had performed as the Nerk Twins in a previous pub they ran, and had visited them in Ryde. The song was written at Kenwood.

> PAUL: We sat down and wrote it together. I remember talking about Ryde but it was John's thing. We wrote the melody together; you can hear on the record, John's taking the melody and I'm singing harmony with it. We'd often work those out as we wrote them. Because John sang it, you might have to give him 60 per cent of it. It was pretty much a work job that turned out quite well. I think the interesting thing was a crazy ending: instead of ending like the previous verse, we changed the tempo. We picked up one of the lines, 'My baby don't care', but completely altered the melody. We almost invented the idea of a new bit of a song on the fade-out with this song; it was something specially written for the fade-out, which was very effective but it was quite cheeky and we did a fast ending. It was quite radical at the time.

When John Lennon was asked about the song, he said, 'Paul's contribution was the way Ringo played the drums.' Paul responds, 'John just didn't take the time to explain that we sat down together and worked on that song for a full three-hour songwriting session, and at the end of it all we had all the words, we had the harmonies, and we had all the little bits.'

The day before recording started on the *Help!* album, Paul flew back from a ten-day holiday in Hammamet, a seaside resort in Tunisia where he had been the guest of the British government, who put him up in a villa owned by the embassy on the coast south of Tunis. It was hard for the Beatles to go anywhere without the press intruding, and this was an ideal set-up, discreet, secure, fully catered and free. The actor Peter Ustinov had stayed there and recommended it. This was the sort of thing that Peter Brown, the Mr Fixit at Brian Epstein's office, excelled at organising.

Hammamet had been an artists' centre since the 1920s when wealthy Europeans had built a number of secluded villas to which they retired with their Siamese cats and long cigarette holders to contemplate their collections of modern art. Paul Klee had stayed there. The light was wonderful; there were two exquisite beaches fronting the bay, colourful gardens and an old medina surrounded by much restored ramparts.

The villa had a small amphitheatre in the garden and was designed as a showcase for British culture. At the furthest end of the house, away from most of the activity, was a magnificent bathroom with a sunken bath and decorated throughout with Islamic tiles. It was isolated and the acoustics were ideal for songwriting. Here Paul wrote 'Another Girl'. The villa was almost perfect but for one thing. Paul: 'You'd be sitting there having a cup of tea when the Russian delegation would be shown through by the government. You didn't have any control over that. "This is one of our cultural guests." "Hello, how are you?"'

'Another Girl' was recorded the day after Paul returned to London while the idea was still fresh, though it was essentially an album filler. Paul: 'It's a bit much to call them fillers because I think they were a bit more than that, and each one of them made it past the Beatles test. We all had to like it. If anyone didn't like one of our songs it was vetoed. It could be vetoed by one person. If Ringo said; "I don't like that one," we wouldn't do it, or we'd have to really persuade him.' In *Help!* Paul mimes the song with the Beatles standing on a coral reef on Balmoral Island, off New Providence Island in the Bahamas, which was the first location for filming. He plays a bikini-clad girl as if she were a guitar.

'The Night Before' was one of Paul's rockers, performed on Salisbury Plain in the film. He wrote it alone, probably at Wimpole

Street, and plays the guitar solo on it as well as bass. Paul: 'I would say that's mainly mine, I don't think John had a lot to do with that.'

'You've Got to Hide Your Love Away' is John's nod to Bob Dylan. This was the first all-acoustic Beatles number, made under the influence of *Another Side of Bob Dylan*, which contains 'Motorpsycho Nitemare' and 'I shall Be Free No. 10'.

> PAUL: Dylan's Woody Guthrie period was very nice and I liked him then, but then he had a second wave of popularity when he became more psychedelic and more associated with drugs and at that time John particularly became very enamoured of him because of his poetry. All those songs were great lyrically. Masses of cluttered lyrics like John had written in his books. So Dylan's gobbledegook and his cluttered poetry was very appealing, it hit a chord in John, it was as if John felt, That should have been me. And to that end, John on this one track did a Dylan impression. I think it was 100 per cent John's song. I might have helped him on it, I have a vague recollection of helping to fill out some verses for him.

'You're Going to Lose That Girl' was written by John and Paul together at John's house in Weybridge and was the last track they recorded for the film before leaving for the Bahamas. It was John's original idea, estimated by Paul as about 60 per cent written by John and 40 per cent by himself.

Whereas they had worked closely with Alun Owen on *A Hard Day's Night*, feeding him lines that could be used in dialogue, there was no such collaboration with Marc Behm, who just gave them a series of off-the-peg wisecracks that could have been said by anyone. The group's resentment at even having to mouth these lines can be seen on screen. Paul later commented, 'It was wrong for us, we were guest stars in our own movie.' John was more succinct: he called it 'crap'.

Marc Behm's original screenplay, then called *Eight Arms to Hold You*, was first submitted to Peter Sellers, who turned it down. Dick Lester had Charles Wood rewrite it as a suitable vehicle for the Beatles, bearing in mind that Brian Epstein still wanted them to play themselves, rather than character parts, but with no smoking, drinking or sex. On the other hand, the Beatles themselves did not want to make a standard rock movie in which the group is discovered playing at a high-school dance. It was almost impossible to write an adequate follow-up to *A Hard Day's Night*; Alun Owen had written the only possible film for the Beatles, which was a thinly disguised version of their own lives. To produce a fictional story with four main leads who have the characters that the fans know and want to see was a very challenging task; but it took Charles Wood just ten days to get the script ready. He opted for a Technicolor romp. 'It was just an assignment,' he told Lester's biographer Andrew Yule, 'I don't think I did a particularly good job.' Bud Ornstein was not that keen on it either but was anxious to get another Beatles film in the cinemas as soon as possible so he gave his grudging approval.

PAUL: They kept offering up scripts. The scripts that were being presented to us weren't that great, nothing was really an inspiration. You do hear actors saying, 'You know, I'd love to get working, love, but I just haven't seen a decent script.' There was a thing called *Talent for Loving*, by Richard Condon, which was the big hot script everyone liked and thought we ought to do, but we hated it. In the end Charles Wood and Marc Behm wrote *Help!*, and it was pretty higgledy-piggledy. We'd have meetings but we weren't that interested.

We just browsed through it, really, rather than taking it very seriously. We didn't bother learning our lines. I'm sure we were reacting against the lousy script. Basically we lost the plot, but I don't think there was much of a plot there to start with. It was this endless, 'The ring must be found! Kali must be appeased.' Maybe that's why we didn't enjoy it. I've always felt we let it down a bit, but we just didn't care and that would fit more readily with a poor script.

To give them their due, we were saying, 'Can't we go somewhere nice for this film?' And they'd say, 'What d'you mean?' and we'd say, 'Well, I've never been in the Caribbean. Could you work that into the plot?' And we said, 'No one's ever been skiing, could you work that in the plot?' I have a friend who says that's the whole thing about writing screenplays. First imagine where you want to be for a year, then: 'The waves were lapping on the Hawaiian beach ...'

The overall impression of *Help!* is that the Beatles have little of substance to say. Their characterisations were so stereotyped that they became wooden cut-out figures: the cute sexy one, the smart sarcastic one, the moody cheapskate and the one with the inferiority complex. The Beatles' lack of real dialogue in *Help!* is very noticeable and the few lines they do get to speak are stilted and unfunny, not helped by the fact that they only looked at their scripts in the car on the way to the set and Dick Lester sometimes had to read them aloud line by line for them to repeat on camera.

It was not surprising that they were consequently overshadowed by the supporting players, all of whom were very accomplished actors able to use the scrappy script to their advantage: Leo McKern, who later became well known for his character role as Rumpole of the Bailey, the comic actor Victor Spinetti, who had been with them on *A Hard Day's Night*, as an incompetent scientist, and Roy Kinnear as his even more incompetent assistant. They used their acting skill to create the funniest scenes in the film. Eleanor Bron was an Indian princess and Viviane Ventura was an aspiring starlet who played a scantily clad girl on a sacrificial altar in the opening scene. But the plot was really just a vehicle for the Beatles to perform a number of songs in exotic settings; a glorified pop video. It was the film people might have expected the Beatles to make had *A Hard Day's Night* not preceded it.

On 23 February 1965, they flew to the Bahamas for two weeks of filming around New Providence Island; then, after a two day stop-over in London, it was straight to Obertauern, Austria, for the skiing and curling-rink sequences. With all the foreign location shots safely printed, Richard Lester now began filming the interior action and London locations.

Most of the interiors were shot at Twickenham film studios but the scenes set in Buckingham Palace and Lambeth Palace were done on location at Cliveden because it has a similar 1850s interior. The house, perched on a 200-foot cliff overlooking the Thames in rural Berkshire, had been the setting the year before for the so-called Profumo affair which toppled the Conservative government. John Profumo, the minister for war, had an affair with the call girl Christine Keeler, whom he first met when she was swimming naked in the pool at Cliveden, where she and her boyfriend rented a cottage from Lord Astor. She was simultaneously having an affair with the Soviet military attaché and scandal erupted when Profumo lied to the House of Commons by denying she was his mistress.

Paul: 'I remember seeing old Lord Astor, who was ill in bed. He would occasionally sniff oxygen that the doctors had given him. "Do you want some?" he said. He was offering it round.' Though Dick Lester obviously tried to organise it so that the Beatles could just arrive and do their stuff, there was still a huge amount of waiting around on set. To pass the time, the crew organised a relay race to be held on the huge lawn at Cliveden one lunch break. It began as five 60-yard dashes between the production staff, electricians and actors, but then the Beatles decided to join in. The crew thought there was no contest; the Beatles all smoked, they took no exercise and were wearing their ordinary street shoes. Mal Evans and their driver Alf Bicknell were recruited to make up the numbers. To everyone's surprise, the Beatles' team won, with Alf just scraping home in bare feet against one of the film crew professionally attired in spiked running shoes. Ringo's speed was particularly commented upon. People had forgotten how adept the Beatles were at escaping from fans and how necessary that extra burst of speed was in potentially life-threatening situations. Lord and Lady Astor presented the winning team with a bottle of vintage champagne and formal photographs were taken.

PAUL: By this time we were starting to smoke a bit of pot and we were getting a little bit more sort of *laissez faire* about the whole thing. We would occasionally get stoned on the way to the film set, which was pretty fatal. My main memory is of being in hysterics, because for all of us, one of the great things about early pot was the sheer hysteria, the laughs. Things could appear very very funny, hilariously so. And nobody quite knew why we were laughing, and of course this made it even funnier. It was like kids giggling at the dinner table, it really was. I remember one of the scenes, it was after lunch and we'd crept off into the bushes and come back a little bit sort of 'Hi there!', pretending we'd had a glass of wine too many or something.

There was a scene where Patrick Cargill, the police inspector, had a gun on us from behind. So we all had our hands up and we were all looking out the window. Then someone would start giggling – 'Stop it, stop it,' – and after a while you could just see the shoulders heaving, and you could feel people going. It was like all those classic out-takes from Peter Sellers movies, and we were just gone! Then there was this added element of this gun behind us. It was loaded with blanks, but he had to keep letting it off and we were hypersensitive – 'Bang!' 'Oh, oh!' And we'd jump a mile when this thing went off! I don't know how Dick ever put up with us but he somehow had to make a movie under those circumstances.

At the beginning of April, the film still had the working title of *Eight Arms to Hold You*, a title that John and Paul were not at all keen on, in part because of the difficulty of composing a title track using those words.

PAUL: I seem to remember Dick Lester, Brian Epstein, Walter Shenson and ourselves sitting around, maybe Victor Spinetti was there, and thinking, What are we going to call this one? Somehow *Help!* came out. I didn't suggest it; John might have suggested it or Dick Lester. It was one of them. John went home and thought about it and got the basis of it, then we had a writing session on it. We sat at his house and wrote it, so he obviously didn't have that much of it. I would have to credit it to John for original inspiration 70–30. My main contribution is the countermelody to John. If you analyse our songs, John's are often on one note, whereas mine are often much more melodic. I enjoy going places with melodies. I like what John did too, but his are more rhythmic. So to take away from the solo note a little bit I wrote a descant to it.

When they finished the song, feeling very pleased with themselves, they took their guitars downstairs to the living room where Cynthia Lennon and the journalist Maureen Cleave were sitting and played it to them.

PAUL: Because it was finished, you see. Once we'd done our writing session there was nothing left to be done except put the instruments on. That's what I was there for; to complete it. Had John just been left on his own he might have taken weeks to do it, but just one visit and we would go right in and complete it. So we came down and played the intro, into the verse, descant coming in on the second verse. It was all crafted, it was all there, the final verses and the end. 'Very nice,' they said. 'Like it.'

Ten thousand fans gathered in Piccadilly Circus outside the London Pavilion on the humid summer evening of 29 July 1965 for the premiere of *Help!* It was a showbiz evening: the Beatles arrived in a black Rolls-Royce and were presented to Princess Margaret and Lord Snowdon. There was a party afterwards at the Orchid Room of the Dorchester Hotel. The film was a financial, though not a critical, success.

The film featured only seven songs; six by John and Paul, and George's 'I Need You', his second song on a Beatles album, the first being 'Don't Bother Me' on *With the Beatles*. For the accompanying soundtrack album, an additional seven tracks were recorded, four of which were Lennon and McCartney compositions.

'It's Only Love' was the product of a writing session out at Weybridge. It was John's original idea and Paul helped him finish it. Paul puts it as 60-40 to John. It was very much an album filler. John later told *Hit Parader*: 'That's the one song I really hate of mine. Terrible lyric.' Paul: 'Sometimes we didn't fight it if the lyric came out rather bland on some of those filler songs like "It's Only Love". If a lyric was really bad we'd edit it, but we weren't that fussy about it, because, it's only a rock 'n' roll song. I mean, this is not literature.'

'Tell Me What You See' was another filler track, this time by Paul: 'I seem to remember it as mine. I would claim it as a 60-40 but it might have been totally me. Not awfully memorable. Not one of the better songs but they did a job, they were very handy for albums or B sides. You need those kind of sides.'

Paul composed 'I've Just Seen a Face' at Wimpole Street and it became one of his favourite Beatles songs, one of the few he was later to play with Wings. Paul: 'I think of this as totally by me. It was slightly country and western from my point of view. It was faster, though, it was a strange uptempo thing. I was quite pleased with it. The lyric works: it keeps dragging you forward, it keeps pulling you to the next line, there's an insistent quality to it that I liked.'

The eponymous title track was released as a single with a B side by Paul: a hard-driving rocker called 'I'm Down' written at Wimpole Street. Paul had always been a big fan of Little Richard; he celebrated his last day of term at the Liverpool Institute by taking in his guitar, climbing on a desk in the classroom and singing his two party pieces, 'Long Tall Sally' and 'Tutti Frutti'.

PAUL: I could do Little Richard's voice, which is a wild, hoarse, screaming thing, it's like an out-of-body experience. You have to leave your current sensibilities and go about a foot above your head to sing it. You have to actually go outside yourself. It's a funny little trick and when you find it, it's very interesting. A lot of people were fans of Little Richard so I used to sing his stuff but there came a point when I wanted one of my own, so I wrote 'I'm Down'.

I'm not sure if John had any input on it, in fact I don't think he did. But not wishing to be churlish, with most of these I'll always credit him with 10 per cent just in case he fixed a word or offered a suggestion. But at least 90 per cent of that would be mine. It's really a blues song. We weren't raised in the American South, so we don't know about Route 66 and the levee and the stuff in all the blues songs. We know about the Cast-Iron Shore and the East Lancs Motorway but they never sounded as good to us, because we were in awe of the Americans. Even their Birmingham, Alabama, sounded better than our Birmingham.

So 'I'm Down' was my rock 'n' roll shouter. I ended up doing it at Shea Stadium. It worked very well for those kind of places, it was a good stage song, and inasmuch as they are hard to write, I'm proud of it. Those kind of songs with hardly any melody, rock 'n' roll songs, are much harder to write than ballads, because there's nothing to them.

Paul had another song on the soundtrack album, one completely unlike anything the Beatles had ever released before. Called 'Yesterday', it was to become the most successful Beatles track of all, even though Paul was the sole composer and no other Beatle played on it.

Yesterday

One morning in May 1965, during the filming of *Help!*, Paul woke up in his little attic room in Wimpole Street with a melody running through his head in all 'the glory and the freshness of a dream'.

PAUL: I woke up with a lovely tune in my head. I thought, That's great, I wonder what that is? There was an upright piano next to me, to the right of the bed by the window. I got out of bed, sat at the piano, found G, found F sharp minor 7th – and that leads you through then to B to E minor, and finally back to E. It all leads forward logically. I liked the melody a lot but because I'd dreamed it I couldn't believe I'd written it. I thought, No, I've never written like this before. But I had the tune, which was the most magic thing. And you have to ask yourself, where did it come from? But you don't ask yourself too much or it might go away.

Very sensibly Paul tried to find out if the tune was already in existence. There have been many instances of hyperamnesic dreams in which the dreamer awakes with an apparently new melody playing in his head which is later identified as something he heard, possibly only once, fleetingly, many years before.

PAUL: So first of all I checked the melody out, and people said to me, 'No, it's lovely, and I'm sure it's yours.' It took me a little while to allow myself to claim it, but then like a prospector I finally staked my claim; stuck a little sign on it and said, 'Okay, it's mine!' It had no words. I used to call it 'Scrambled Eggs'. The lyrics used to go, 'Scrambled eggs, oh, my baby, how I love your legs ...' There was generally a laugh at that point, you didn't need to do any more lyrics.

I was always very keen not to repeat other people's tunes, because it's very easy to do when you write. Ringo's got a funny story of the most brilliant song he ever wrote. He spent three hours writing a very famous Bob Dylan song. We all fell about and laughed. That can happen. You say, 'This is so great,' and someone says, 'Yeah, it's number one at the moment.' 'Ah. That's where I've heard it.'

Given that literally hundreds of millions of people have now heard 'Yesterday', it is certain that someone would have come forward by now to identify it even if it bore only a passing resemblance to an existing work. 'Yesterday' has become the most played song of all time. Paul received an award for 6,000,000 plays on American radio, which was 2,000,000 times more than any other record. It would take twenty-three and a half years to play it that many times non-stop. Paul: 'For something that just appeared in a dream, even I have to acknowledge that it was a phenomenal stroke of luck.' (Incidentally, the record with the second most plays is 'Michelle', also by Paul without the other Beatles.)

Freud suggests that dream formation is determined in part by the previous day's activities and it would be interesting to know what Paul had been listening to the night before. The melody of 'Yesterday' may be a dream-work transformation of something completely unlikely, from a television theme song to a classical piece; or, more probably, a musical idea he had already been playing with but which emerged from the dream state so different that it was unrecognisable. The notes had to be there already in his subconscious, but Paul's musical vocabulary had become so vast, his subconscious so saturated with chord progressions, note combinations and fragments of melody, that in this instance he did not have to even place himself in a receptive songwriting mode; he just put them together in a new way while he was asleep.

> PAUL: I took it round to Alma Cogan at her flat in Kensington and asked, 'What's this song?' because Alma was a bit of a song buff; there are a lot of people around like that and I admire them a lot. Alma was very songy, knew a lot of Jerome Kern and Cole Porter and that kind of thing, and she said, 'I don't know what it is, but it's beautiful.' I later realised, she thought I was trying to give it her, because if you as a composer do that, by implication you're offering her the song, just because she's a singer. The etiquette is almost, 'I'm writing this for you,' so I think there was a little moment of doubt. But I didn't see it as that at all. I was doing it for a very practical reason to see if someone like her who knew all the old classics could recognise it. She covered it, but the thing is to actually give it to someone so it's theirs and you don't even record it yourself.

The melody clearly preoccupied Paul. During the making of *Help!* there was always a piano around on which Paul continually tinkered with the melody, slowly perfecting it, adding a middle eight, working it into shape. Dick Lester finally exclaimed, 'If I hear that once more, I'll have that bloody piano taken away. What's it called anyway?' 'Scrambled Eggs,' Paul told him. When the *Help!* soundtrack album was released, Dick Lester was away on location in Spain. Paul sent him a copy with a note saying, 'I hope you like "Scrambled Eggs".'

On 27 May 1965, Paul flew to Lisbon from London to begin a holiday in the Algarve. Paul had run into his old friend Bruce Welch, the rhythm guitarist with the Shadows, backstage at a Cliff Richard concert at the Talk of the Town and told him he was looking for somewhere to go for a short holiday. Bruce offered his villa in Albufeira, on the southern coast of Portugal near Faro. It sounded ideal and a few days later they met again to fix the dates. It was arranged that Paul and Jane would arrive at the villa the same day that Bruce and his wife were departing so that they could be shown how everything worked.

From Lisbon Paul and Jane took a car and were driven the 180 miles to the south coast. It was a long drive on mountainous roads through Alcácer do Sal, Grândola, and on down the E1 across the River Mira, through São Marcos da Serra Albufeira to the blue Golfo de Cádiz.

> PAUL: It was a long hot, dusty drive. Jane was sleeping but I couldn't, and when I'm sitting that long in a car I either manage to get to sleep or my brain starts going. I remember mulling over the tune 'Yesterday', and suddenly getting these little one-word openings to the verse. I started to develop the idea: Scram-ble-d eggs, da-da da. I knew the syllables had to match the melody, obviously: da-da da, yes-ter-day, sud-den-ly, fun-il-ly, mer-il-ly, and Yes-ter-day, that's good. All my troubles seemed so far away. It's easy to rhyme those 'a's: say, nay, today, away, play, stay, there's a lot of rhymes and those fall in quite easily, so I gradually pieced it together from that journey. Sud-den-ly, and 'b' again, another easy rhyme: e, me, tree, flea, we, and I had the basis of it.

Albufiera was originally a small fishing village, and when Paul was there, before the high-rise hotels and booming Euro-discos, the old town perched on the cliffs still had a Moorish flavour, with cobbled streets and whitewashed cottages. It was a favourite holiday village for British pop stars; both Cliff Richard and Frank Ifield had places there. Bruce Welch owned a large four-bedroom villa with a magnificent sea view, bought from the proceeds of his many hits with the Shadows. Though it is hard to imagine Paul going anywhere without a guitar, his first request on arrival was to ask Bruce if he had one. There was a

1959 Model 0018 Martin in the house which, being left-handed, Paul had to play upside down, but it sufficed.

Paul relaxed and took his time piecing the lyrics of the song together: 'I think I finished the lyrics about two weeks later, which was quite a long time for me. Generally, John and I would sit down and finish within three hours, but this was more organic. I put in the words over the next couple of weeks.' Muriel Young, the presenter of the TV show *Five o'clock Club*, had a place in Albufiera and Paul went horse riding with her and her husband. She remembers him playing a new song to them after dinner one evening, which was almost certainly 'Yesterday' with its words finally in place.

It has been suggested that the lyrics are about the loss of Paul's mother, and one line could possibly be read as that. If so, it was an unconscious element in the song's composition.

John was already familiar with the song when Paul took 'Yesterday' in to the recording session on 14 June. Paul played it for George Martin and asked once again if it was a known melody. George said there was a Peggy Lee tune called 'Yesterdays' but the title was all they had in common. The other Beatles liked the song but were a bit nonplussed what to with it.

> PAUL: I played it for George and Ringo and they said, 'Lovely, nice one.' Ringo said, 'I don't think I can really drum on that.' George said, 'Well, I'm not sure I can put much on it either.' And John said, 'I can't think of anything, I think you should just do it yourself. It's very much a solo thing.'
>
> So I did, just me and my guitar. Then George Martin had the idea to put the string quartet on it and I said, 'No, I don't think so.' He said, 'I've really got a feeling for it. I can hear it working.' So I said, 'Oh, a string quartet, it's very classical, I'm not interested really ...' But he cleverly said, 'Let's try it,' and I thought, that's fair enough. 'If we hate it,' he said, 'we can take it off. We'll just go back, it's very nice just with the solo guitar and your voice.'
>
> People tend to think that we did the music and George did all the arrangements. The thing people don't generally know was that me or John or whoever it was involved in the orchestral angle would go round to George's house or he would come round to ours, and we would sit with him, and I did on this. I

went round to George's house and we had a pleasant couple of hours, had a cup of tea, sat there with the manuscript paper on the piano.

He said, 'Okay, G.' And I played it to him. 'These are my chords.' He said, 'That's very nice.' See, what we do in rock 'n' roll is block out chords with one white note between them. But a classical composer writing for strings might leave the G there but would think that having one note on either side would be too closely grouped, it would make a string quartet sound like almost one instrument. So the trick is to separate them. The chord G is comprised of G, B and D. So your G might go down an octave and be on the cello. The B might stay where it is and you take the D up. I remember that on that session George explained to me how Bach would have voiced it in a choral voicing or a quartet voicing. And he'd say, 'This would be the way Bach would do it,' and he'd play it.

It would be my same chords but spread over the piano, rather than closely grouped. It was nice, I was getting lessons. I find out these little tricks as I go along. A course in it would teach me them all, but I can't be bothered doing that. I learn as I go along. Music is such a beautiful innocent thing for me, a magic thing, that I don't want it ever to smack of homework, that would ruin it all.

So George showed me this voicing, and I said 'lovely' and we did the whole song, very straight, for a string quartet. And there was just one point in it where I said, 'Could the cello now play a slightly bluesy thing, out of the genre, out of keeping with the rest of the voicing?' George said, 'Bach certainly wouldn't have done that, Paul, ha ha ha.' I said, 'Great!' That was what we often used to do, try and claim our one little moment. I mean, obviously it was my song, my chords, my everything really, but because the voicing now had become Bach's, I needed something of mine again to redress the balance. So I put a 7th in, which was unheard-of. It's what we used to call a blue note, and that became a little bit well known. It's one of the unusual things in that arrangement.

George Martin booked a string quartet for 17 June 1965. He had a policy of always getting the best, usually players that were known to

him, often from the London Symphony Orchestra. Tony Gilbert and
Sidney Sax played violins, Kenneth Essex played viola and Francisco
Gabarro played the cello.

PAUL: George was very good that way. He got a very good,
competent quartet, and they played and I really liked the result, I
thought it was smashing. I remember going down the Ad Lib the
evening after we'd recorded it, meeting Terry Doran down
there, and saying to Terry, 'Just done this great song.' He told
me afterwards, 'I thought you were just really swell-headed, I
couldn't believe your arrogance.' He said, 'Now I see what you
mean, though, you must have been quite excited after that.'

In addition to the string-quartet idea, Paul devised a plan to have
the arrangement for 'Yesterday' written out and taken to the BBC
Radiophonic Workshop, the experimental facility specialising in
electronic music for radio and television, which was then run by Delia
Derbyshire. The futuristic electronic signature tune for *Dr Who* was
made there. Paul had listened to a lot of electronic music with the
present author, Barry Miles, and George Martin had played them the
famous 1962 Bell Telephone Labs recording of an IBM 7090
computer and digital-to-sound transducer singing 'Bicycle Built for
Two' in a thick German-American accent, which they loved. (This
was also favourite late-night listening at Miles's flat.)

PAUL: It occurred to me to have the BBC Radiophonic
Workshop do the backing track to it and me just sing over an
electronic quartet. I went down to see them: I found the number,
said, 'Do you mind if I come down and see you? Six o'clock's
good,' wandered down. They were in Maida Vale, Little Venice
somewhere, near me, so it was very simple for me to just hop in
the car, have a look around. The woman who ran it was very
nice and they had a little shed at the bottom of the garden where
most of the work was done. I said, 'I'm into this sort of stuff.' I'd
heard a lot about the BBC Radiophonic Workshop, we'd all
heard a lot about it. It would have been very interesting to do,
but I never followed it up.

Chris Farlowe was a well-liked singer who had been on the London
rock scene since the late fifties when his group, the John Henry Skiffle

Group, won the all-England Skiffle Championship of 1957. All he needed was a break. Eric Burdon, in his autobiography *I Used to Be an Animal but I'm All Right Now*, tells how Chris Farlowe almost re-launched his career with 'Yesterday':

> One day he phoned me at my Duke Street pad. 'Hey Eric, how ya doin', it's Chris Farlowe here,' he said in his hoarse voice. I asked how he was getting on. 'Oh, I'm OK. 'Ere listen, you'll never guess what happened. Paul McCartney – you know Paul out of the Beatles?' Yes, I had heard of him. 'Well, he came round to our house in the middle of the night. I was out doing a show, but me mum was in and he left her a demo disc for me to listen to.'
>
> This was wonderful news. When was Chris going into the studio to cut this gift from the gods? 'Ah,' he growled. 'I don't like it. It's not for me. It's too soft. I need a good rocker, you know, a shuffle or something.'
>
> 'Yeah, but Chris,' I said. 'Anything to give you a start, man. I mean even if it's a ballad you should go ahead and record it.'
>
> 'No, I don't like it,' he insisted. 'Too soft.'
>
> 'So what are you gonna do with the song?'
>
> 'Well, I sent it back, didn't I?'
>
> 'What was the title of the song?'
>
> '"Yesterday",' he retorted.

Despite its enormous popularity, the Beatles refused to allow the release of 'Yesterday' as a single in Britain. As a rock 'n' roll band they felt that the release of a ballad would be bad for their image, and, more importantly, they didn't want to focus on one member of the group to the exclusion of the others, and all decisions in the Beatles had to have complete approval. In Hamburg Bert Kaempfert had once suggested making a recording as Paul and the Beatles but the idea was quickly rejected by the group.

> PAUL: That would have been getting above yourself. We were always watching each other for any signs of that. I remember showing up for a photo session once and I had a grey suit and the others had dark suits and they made fun of me. I didn't know what suits they were going to come in, but it was because I stood out from the group. It was such a democracy. So 'Yesterday'

would have meant that the spotlight would go on me, so we never did that. It wasn't released here as a single. In America maybe. We would allow it there because we weren't living there, we'd visit there, but that wasn't the same. But here, no way on earth.

It was released in the USA as a single in September 1965 and went to number one. When the Beatles played *The Ed Sullivan Show* on 14 August live before a television audience of 73,000,000 people, Paul sang the song backed by a string quartet from the New York Ed Sullivan Orchestra.

This was a period of increasing confidence for Paul and John as songwriters; a period of transition where they felt able to insert private references about sex and drugs into their songs, knowing that in many cases even George Martin would not catch on. A good example, one which combined both sex and drugs, was their next single, 'Day Tripper', co-written in October 1965 at Kenwood.

PAUL: This was getting towards the psychedelic period when we were interested in winking to our friends and comrades in arms, putting in references that we knew our friends would get but that the Great British Public might not. So 'she's a big teaser' was 'she's a prick teaser'. The mums and dads didn't get it but the kids did. 'Day Tripper' was to do with tripping. Acid was coming in on the scene, and often we'd do these songs about 'the girl who thought she was it'. Mainly the impetus for that used to come from John; I think John met quite a few girls who thought they were it and he was a bit up in arms about that kind of thing. 'She Said' was another one. But this was just a tongue-in-cheek song about someone who was a day tripper, a Sunday painter, Sunday driver, somebody who was committed only in part to the idea. Whereas we saw ourselves as full-time trippers, fully committed drivers, she was just a day tripper. That was a co-written effort; we were both there making it all up but I would give John the main credit. Probably the idea came from John because he sang the lead, but it was a close thing. We both put a lot of work in on it. I remember with the prick teasers we thought, That'd be fun to put in. That was one of the great things about collaborating, you could nudge-nudge, wink-wink a bit, whereas if you're sitting on your own, you might not put it in. You know, 'I'd love to turn you on', we literally looked at each other like, 'Oh, dare we do this?' It was a good moment, there was always good eye contact when we put those things in.

'Day Tripper' was scheduled to be the Beatles' next single – until 'We Can Work It Out' was recorded a few days later and was generally felt to be a more commercial track. John objected quite vociferously and eventually the record was marketed as a double A side, though shops soon reported that far more people came in asking for 'We Can Work It Out' than 'Day Tripper'.

Paul wrote 'We Can Work It Out' at Rembrandt, the five-bedroomed house he bought for his father in July 1964 in Heswall, Cheshire, on the peninsula overlooking the River Dee estuary. It was a large mock-Tudor house with a decent-size garden in a leafy suburb about 15 miles from Liverpool and cost Paul £8,750, a lot of money for the time. Paul spent a further £8,000 installing central heating and decorating. There was a piano in the dining room where Paul often tinkered with new tunes. If he was composing on the guitar, however, he would usually go to the back bedroom to get away from everyone.

PAUL: I wrote it as a more up-tempo thing, country and western. I had the idea, the title, had a couple of verses and the basic idea for it, then I took it to John to finish it off and we wrote the middle together. Which is nice: 'Life is very short. There's no time for fussing and fighting, my friend.' Then it was George Harrison's idea to put the middle into waltz time, like a German waltz. That came on the session, it was one of the cases of the arrangement being done on the session. The other thing that arrived on the session was we found an old harmonium hidden away in the studio, and said, 'Oh, this'd be a nice colour on it.' We put the chords on with the harmonium as a wash, just a basic held chord, what you would call a pad these days. The lyrics might have been personal. It is often a good way to talk to someone or to work your own thoughts out. It saves you going to a psychiatrist, you allow yourself to say what you might not say in person.

SIX

AVANT-GARDE LONDON

I see now that most people were just living these
really ordinary little lives while we were madmen
riding this incredibly psychedelic whirlwind. It seemed
very normal to us to be smoking a lot of pot and
flying around very late.

Paul McCartney

Lennox Gardens

DURING THE THREE YEARS HE LIVED AT WIMPOLE STREET, PAUL GOT TO
know not only Jane's circle of friends but Peter's friends as well.
Perhaps the most important among them was John Dunbar, who was
to be his initial conduit to what can loosely be described as the
London avant-garde scene. It was through John that Paul met the art
dealer Robert Fraser, became involved in starting Indica Bookshop
and Gallery, and was introduced to a demi-monde of writers, jazz
musicians and junkies. John and Marianne Faithfull's flat was a
gateway to an alternative London life. Paul: 'There used to be certain
places where you could light up a joint and not be frowned on: Brian
Jones's place, Robert's flat, Miles's house, my house, John Dunbar's.
This meant you could go there for the evening and just generally
hang there, and 29 Lennox Gardens was one of those early formative
little pads.'

During the time Peter Asher and his singing partner Gordon
Waller were still at Westminster School, Gordon had a girlfriend
called Jenny Dunbar, one of identical twins. Through Gordon, Peter
got to know Jenny and her family, who lived in Bentinck Street, just

two short blocks away from Wimpole Street. Jenny and her sister Margaret had an older brother, John, who had gone up to Cambridge to study natural science, changing to history of art for his final year. Peter and John found they had similar interests in film, art and music and soon became close friends. Being virtually next-door neighbours, they saw a great deal of each other and John got to know Peter's family. It was not long after this that Jane first met Paul when the Beatles played the Albert Hall. John Dunbar remembers her walking round to his parents' flat in Bentinck Street and telling him that she'd been out with Paul. Jane was only seventeen and seemed thrilled by this new development in her life.

John was a frequent visitor to Wimpole Street, and Paul soon got to know him. John's world was studenty and intellectual, something to which Paul had always been attracted, but John was also very cool – that was the word in the early sixties. John's preference in art was for Duchamp, Dubuffet and the School of Nice: Yves Klein, Arman, César. He liked Christo's wrapped objects and Arman's boxes – the cerebral end of modern art. His musical taste ran to Beethoven's late quartets, Chicago blues and the post-bebop jazz improvisations of Thelonius Monk, John Coltrane and Ornette Coleman. Having studied science at Cambridge as well as art, he was able to make connections between subjects that seemed at the time to offer remarkable revelations. There was no question but that John was hip. Paul was intrigued

John Dunbar was born in Mexico of a Russian mother, Tania, and a Scottish father, Robert. He spent his infancy in Moscow, where his father was posted during the war. His father had graduated from the Royal College of Art and after his spell in the foreign service set up the London School of Film Technique in Covent Garden, which at that time was the only place in Britain to teach the techniques of film-making. John grew up in an artistic, slightly bohemian household which gave the children self-confidence and encouraged them to be creative: John's older sister Marina became an architect and later built her own house, and after breaking up with Gordon Waller, Jenny married the American poet Ed Dorn and went to live in Colorado. John himself graduated from Churchill College, Cambridge, and began writing a regular column of art criticism for the *Scotsman*.

In different circumstances, he might have entered the academic world, but at this point in the sixties there were other powerful forces shaping up. John saw little of value happening in the art world, with only a very few galleries prepared to take risks and show work that was truly experimental or subversive. At Cambridge he had discovered soft drugs, though in the early sixties these were confined to a handful of students, usually those, like John, who also had in interest in progressive jazz and the literature of the Beat Generation. John was a charming, slightly vague character with a fondness for blue pinstripe suits with waistcoats and black horn-rimmed glasses. He wore his wiry black hair long to his collar in the fashion of the time and spoke a meta-hipster argot, partly of his own making, in which most nouns were rendered as the word 'scene'. He had a distinct twinkle in his eye and greatly enjoyed female company.

One day in March 1964, John arrived at 57 Wimpole Street with a schoolgirl called Marianne Faithfull. She had wide sensuous lips and looked out from under long silver-blonde hair. Her mother was the Baroness Erisso von Sacher-Masoch, an Austro-Hungarian aristocrat whose great-uncle was Baron Leopold von Sacher-Masoch, the author of *Venus in Furs* and from whom we got the term 'masochism'. Marianne's father was Dr Glynn Faithfull, a psychologist who lived in a utopian commune in Oxfordshire. For Marianne that weekend in London with John was memorable:

> It was the first weekend I had sex, the first weekend I met one of the Beatles, and the weekend I got discovered. John took me to meet Peter Asher, who was John's great friend. And that's how I met Jane and met Paul. He was incredibly good-looking and obviously a great beau.
>
> I was in Reading, at school, and I'd met John at the party after the Valentine's Ball at Cambridge. And John and I fell in love. Then John invited me up to stay with his parents in Bentinck Street, so I got on the train in Reading and came up, and I was seventeen and obviously, I guess, very very pretty. John was giving me a very good time, I mean, this was my London boyfriend, my first boyfriend at all, at all! And we had a very nice time and I met Paul McCartney that weekend at the Ashers'.
>
> It was a huge great big house in Wimpole Street, the biggest house I'd ever been in in my life apart from my father's, which

was a commune. And one family lived in this house, plus Paul McCartney. I was just stunned by it all. And I remember asking John, did Paul and Jane have sex? He just looked at me like I was stupid and said, 'Of course they do!'

In the evening we went to this party, at Adrienne Posta's. I was just speechless by then. Peter and Gordon had just done 'World Without Love', and I remember when we went in with Peter and Gordon there was a whole group of girls there. It was one of those parties with the Stones there and Andrew Oldham must have set all this up. And as we went in they thought John was John Lennon and I was Cynthia. And I went 'Wow!' Very pleased about this! Not knowing that once I got into this party I was going to be discovered by Andrew, which is what happened.

Paul: 'I knew Marianne directly she came out of the convent. I'd met her at the Ashers' house so I'd see her there socially. She was such a pretty, virginal little thing. Then I remember reading an interview with her and she said, "I want to experience anything and everything," and I remember thinking, Ooh, hold on now, Marianne. Come on, girl – straight out of the convent to anything and everything?'

But Marianne was to get her dreams; and it was Andrew Loog Oldham, the manager of the Rolling Stones, who got them for her. He recognised that her looks would go a long way in establishing her as a sixties pop icon and had enough experience in record production to know that echo chambers and double-tracking could build even the most imperfect voice into something good enough for a pop record. 'With a name like yours you should be making records,' he said, and within six weeks she was in the studio.

At the party for the actress Adrienne Posta's birthday, Marianne had fleetingly met Mick Jagger and Keith Richards, whom she dismissed as 'vulgar and spotty'; however, it was to Mick and Keith that Andrew Oldham turned to write a song to launch her career. Legend has it that he asked them to write a ballad for a convent schoolgirl: 'I want a song with brick walls all around it and high windows and no sex.' The truth of the matter is that Mick and Keith already had a song called 'As Time Goes By' and all they did was change the title to 'As Tears Go By'. It was a curious choice for a seventeen-year-old girl to sing because the lyrics are written from the point of view of an older woman, but with Marianne's beauty, Oldham knew he had a winner.

Marianne herself recognised that her fabulous looks helped. Looking back, she now describes her own appearance on *Juke Box Jury* as like 'an angel with big tits'. It only took a few TV appearances to make her a star. 'As Tears Go By' reached number nine in the charts and even made 22 in the *Billboard* top 100.

Meanwhile John Dunbar was happily hitch-hiking around Greece, unaware that anything had come of Marianne's poppy weekend in London. He arrived back in the country to find her face all over the music papers and Marianne with money to spend, indulging her taste for luxury. She had made a new set of friends while John was away, but she went back to him, despite his cynical dismissal of the pop scene.

A feature of the music business then was to capitalise on chart success by going on tour, the opposite of today's practice where a tour is used to promote a record. Marianne went out on a series of typical pop packages. On the first she starred alongside the Hollies, and she had an affair with Allan Clarke from the band. This was followed shortly by the Gene Pitney tour, during which she and Gene Pitney had an affair which reached the gossip columns.

Her next tour was with Roy Orbison, but her affairs had unnerved John Dunbar and in a grand romantic gesture he took a train to Wigan, the next port of call for the Roy Orbison tour, found Marianne and proposed to her on Wigan pier. She accepted. Marianne wrote: 'I saw myself as a good girl and suddenly I was being very promiscuous. The convent girl reappeared. I started to think I was a bad woman, a whore and a slut. I'd better get married and then I'd be good again.'

Marianne had moved from her mother's house in Reading to a spacious flat at 29 Lennox Gardens, off Pont Street, in Knightsbridge. The living room overlooked a semicircular private garden of mature trees. Marianne bought a beautiful formal dining table, silverware and elegant wineglasses. Everything was done properly and in the best of taste. Harrods was, after all, just around the corner.

Her second single did not do well but Marianne's third, 'Come and Stay with Me' again put her in the top ten, reaching number four in March 1965. There seemed every reason to think that her career in pop music was going well. As far as John Dunbar was concerned it was all frivolous rubbish and she should enjoy it while it lasted before going on to a more serious career in acting.

John and Marianne were married on 6 May 1965 in Cambridge, where John had still to take his finals. Peter Asher was best man and the guests included Peter's girlfriend, the singer Millie Small, Gordon Waller and Jennifer Dunbar and many of John's student friends. Paul was absent, busy filming *Help!* Marianne was eighteen and already three months pregnant. She and John spent their honeymoon in Cornwall.

The flat at 29 Lennox Gardens soon became a regular hang-out for John's friends, most of whom were scroungy students with nowhere to stay, and in the beginning it was a meeting of two distinct worlds: that of the elegant Knightsbridge pop star and her circle of arrangers, producers, publicists and music-business friends; and John with his scurrilous counter-cultural gang of beatniks, artists and drug takers. There was always someone in the living room, reading the art magazines or slumped in the corner rolling a joint; blues, jazz or Indian music coming from the huge speakers. Marianne: 'There were very few friends of John's that I could even talk to or relate to, that weren't completely mad. The only one I really liked was Mason Hoffenberg. I don't know why I loved Mason so much, I just did. He made me laugh. But Sandy Bull and John's artists were dreadful.'

Mason Hoffenberg was the wisecracking American hipster who co-wrote *Candy* with Terry Southern. A junkie, he stayed at Lennox Gardens for months, delivering long Lenny Bruce-style raps filled with hip talk and wonderful weird humour for his supper. (Ringo would later star in the film of *Candy*, playing the Mexican gardener.) Another long-term house guest was Charlie Moffett, the respected new-wave drummer from Fort Worth, Texas, who spent 1965–66 touring Europe with his old schoolfriend Ornette Coleman.

Another regular in the living room was Taff, a get-away driver friend of John Dunbar's, who was very impressed with Paul's Aston Martin DB4, which he always referred to as the 'D-B Far-Out'. Once, when Paul was visiting Lennox Gardens, Taff borrowed it to collect Marianne Faithfull from the airport. The police clocked the car doing over 130 mph on the way out, and over 120 on the way back, but were unable to catch it.

For Paul, in 1965, this scene presented another alternative lifestyle, as different again from the Asher household as the Ashers' had been from Jim McCartney's little suburban house in Liverpool. He spent a lot of time there.

PAUL: My main recollection of Lennox Gardens is a rather chilling thing, being at John Dunbar and Marianne's house when one of their friends came around who was a heroin addict. And we are in the corner smoking a little bit of pot here. And he is over there, and suddenly he pulls out a big red rubber tube thing and he tightened his arm up, putting a tourniquet on. And he's tapping, and he's got needles and he's got spoons and he's got a little light. And I'm going, 'Uhhhhhh!' You get the kind of shock of horror through you, I thought, 'My God, fucking hell! How did I get here? I'm in a room with a guy who's shooting up!' He had a big rubber tourniquet, which smacked to me of operations. I'd always been fearful of red rubber as a kid. And me mum was a nurse, so enemas and things, it was all red rubber. Very frightening sort of thing to me, not pleasant at all, that shit. We couldn't look at him.

Then next week I said, 'What happened to Sandy?' John said, 'He died.' He was dead the week after. That really ended the period, heralded the end really for me. You've got to be very confident of yourself, because otherwise the peer pressure to take drugs is impossible. Let's face it, you're meeting a lot of really groovy guys, man, in the rock 'n' roll world. These are groovy dudes. And, 'What, you don't do this? What are you, not as old as us? Or you're not as hip or something?'

JOHN DUNBAR: I was probably kidding. I do remember that Sandy *nearly* died. What he would do is, in those days you could get this National Health coke from John Bell and Croyden which was totally utterly pure, like if you spilled some it took like ten minutes to settle, each flake would flutter down, it would be like all over the room. And also when it's finished, it's actually not finished, it's all over the glass phial. You just wash it out and shoot it up. And he totally OD'd and I remember it was really unpleasant. He was in really bad shape, on coke. Fixing, mainlining an overdose of coke. But he didn't die.

The incident made a lasting impression on Paul, but the scene at Lennox Gardens was not all about sex and drugs.

JOHN DUNBAR: We talked a lot about the music, all of the time. We used to play stuff and record stuff. Old blues, Jimmy Reed, Muddy Waters, all the old blues blokes. Most of them were dead then, let alone now. John Mayall was around a lot then, who was also totally into that blues stuff. His dad had a huge collection of blues records in Manchester in the fifties. Mason lived there, six months, maybe it only seemed like that but he lived there for a while. Shaun Philips, Donovan, Marc Bolan, he was called Mark Feld then, everybody who was around came around.

Paul would often bring music with him when he arrived at Lennox Gardens.

I used to prepare tapes in the Ashers' house. I used to have a couple of Brenell tape recorders I got through Dick James's son. I used to experiment with them when I had an afternoon off, which was quite often. We'd be playing in the evening, we'd be doing a radio show or something, and there was often quite a bit of time when I was just in the house on my own so I had a lot of time for this. I wasn't in a routine. I could stay up till three in the morning, sleep through till two in the afternoon, and often did. It was a very free, formless time for me. Formative yet formless. I didn't have to be up for the baby, at that time there was none of that. So I would sit around all day, creating little tapes.

I did one once called 'Unforgettable' and used the 'Unforgettable' – Nat King Cole – 'Is what you are ...' as the intro. Then did a sort of 'Hello, hello ...' like a radio show. I had a demo done by Dick James of that, just for the other guys because it was really a kind of stoned thing. That was really the truth of it. You knew you'd be round someone's house later that evening and if you had an interesting piece of music, it would be quite a blast, whether it be Ravi Shankar or Beethoven or Albert Ayler, as I remember being quite into him too.

In 1995, Paul used this same idea as the format for a radio series called *Oobu Joobu* – inspired by Alfred Jarry's character Père Ubu – that he made for the American network Westwood One. In the promotional video for the series, Paul explained, 'We started off by getting hold of a few favourite records of mine, and looking for out-takes and rehearsal tapes from some of the recordings we'd done. After saying some silly things into the microphones, we finally edited the whole thing down into what you're going to hear as *Oobu Joobu* – which we think of as wide-screen radio.'

Some of Paul's earliest experiments in 1965 were made by running the tape backwards, a technique he used almost immediately on Beatles songs.

PAUL: After the 'Unforgettable' thing I got into tape loops. I would do them over a few days. I had a little bottle of EMI glue that I would stick them with and wait till they dried. It was a pretty decent join. I'd be trying to avoid the click as it went through but I never actually avoided it. If you made them very well you could just about do it but I made 'em a bit hamfisted and I ended up using the click as part of the rhythm. I would put them on and overdub on them. There was a superimpose head on the machine that you could take off. It normally wiped everything that came through in order to make room for the new recording, but if you took it off, it didn't wipe. With a loop you had to work very fast. You couldn't review what you'd done because every time it went through it recorded again. Even if there was no new sound it would record an invisible layer of silence, so the quality was going.

I worked out a few rules for it; if you wanted something to remain, you had to do it last. You couldn't have your good idea first. If you wanted background sounds, this was okay because they would fade back, get quieter and quieter and quieter. And you had to know when to stop. Very like painting.

I used to make loops mainly with guitar or voices, or bongos, and then I'd record them off on to this other Brenell so that I had a series of loops. It would start with a thing that sounded like bees buzzing for a few seconds, then that would slow down and then an echo would kick in and then some high violins would come in, but they were speeded-up guitar playing a little thing, then behind them there would a very slow ponderous drone. Quite a nice montage sound collage. The guitar would sound like seagulls. They were great little things and I had great plans for them, they were going to be little symphonies, all made with tape loops done by vari-speeding the tape. I'd run the whole thing off my Brenell onto a cassette. That's when I compiled it all together. Then I would take this finished tape over to John Dunbar's. We used to have those little Philips cassette recorders that had just been invented, and we found that you could plug them into the regular stereo system with the big speakers. This little thing would run for five or ten minutes and then I had some Julian Bream music after that, 'Courtly Dances' from Benjamin Britten's opera *Gloriana*, which is a great guitar piece, and that would go a good quarter of an hour. I'd be like a DJ. So it was like a fucking album! And these were wild, pretty wild moments, we used to play them endlessly.

And you'd light up a joint and maybe have a glass of wine or something, and that was it, you were off for the evening. It was our equivalent of going to the pub. And you would just sit around on bean bags or nice comfy armchairs. Bean bags I think was the order of the day, great big bean bags! You'd listen to the music, and talk a bit, and maybe listen to it again, and so on. And so that was what we used to do.

I was into a lot of those things, which was very strange because I was at the same time known as the cute Beatle, the ballad Beatle or whatever. I hate to think what I was known as. John was the cynical one, the wise Beatle, the intellectual. In fact at that time it was wildly in reverse. John would be coming in from Weybridge; he'd sit and he used to tell me he was jealous: 'God, man, I'm so fucking jealous!' He had to break free – which is what he did, later.

Sometimes the company assembled in Lennox Gardens would experience a great urge to make music. Since most of them were non-musical and therefore restricted to percussion instruments, all of Marianne's gleaming copper-bottomed pots would be dragged in from the kitchen and used as bongos. The ensuing cacophony was usually held in shape by at least one person able to play guitar or at least keep time on one of the few proper instruments in the flat.

Another favourite occupation was playing wineglasses: wetting the rims of wineglasses and rubbing them gently to produce a clear ringing note, which could be changed by putting different amounts of liquid into the glass. Five or six people could produce some beautiful slow variations, sitting on the floor, stoned as could be. Several years later Paul made the track called 'Glasses' on the first solo *McCartney* album using this method.

Paul was always on the lookout for new techniques; new ways of making sounds, particularly those which utilised unorthodox sound sources. Paul: 'Stockhausen used to use those kind of techniques a little bit and he had a thing called *Gesang der Jünglinge,* which was my big favourite plick-plop piece of his.' Stockhausen's electronic composition *Gesang der Jünglinge* was written 1955–56, and brought together both sung notes and electronically produced ones into a single sound, exactly the kind of new idea that Paul could work with for the Beatles.

> PAUL: I finally had time to allow myself to be exposed to some of the stuff that had intrigued me for a long time, since my mid-teens really, when I'd started to read about artists' experiences and that kind of culture, an inquiring culture. I might have just been reading about Madame Blavatsky or André Breton, whatever it was, all these strange little strands, but it started to awaken in me the sense that this kind of bohemian thing, this artistic thing was possible. So I used to take a lot of time for those pursuits, because it was so well balanced on the other side with straight Beatle stuff. And it was nice for this to leak into the Beatle stuff as it did.

One evening in August when Paul was visiting Lennox Gardens, Marianne told him that she planned to record 'Yesterday'. They had a long discussion about how she was going to treat the song and she explained that her producer and musical director Mike Leander had plans for an elaborate orchestration using a large chorus. Paul kept pointing out that since the *Help!* album had been released on 6 August, a number of cover versions of 'Yesterday' were already in the works and warned her that the most important thing was to get her version out before Matt Monro released his.

Paul was keen for Marianne to have a hit with 'Yesterday', both because she was a friend and because he had made a vague promise to give her a song, on which he had not yet delivered.

I knew Marianne so it was natural that I would be asked to write a song at some point. I did write a song but it was not a very good one. It was called 'Etcetera' and it's a bad song. I think it's a good job that it's died a death in some tape bin. Even then I seem to remember thinking it wasn't very good. There was always the temptation to keep your better songs for yourself and then give your next-best songs to other established people, so when it was someone like Marianne, who at that time was a newcomer, those people would tend to end up with fairly dreadful offerings of mine.

I suppose, thinking back on it, after 'As Tears Go By' maybe they were looking for more sort of a 'Yesterday', something more poignant, more baroque. I probably thought, well, this is really all I've got at the moment. I'll send it round and hope it's all okay, and maybe they'll put a baroque thing on it and that'll make it okay. She probably did 'Yesterday' because they figured, Well at least it's better than 'Etcetera'.

Paul went to Marianne's recording session at Decca studios but doesn't remember if he contributed anything to it: 'Those kind of sessions tended to be off duty for me. So I might be in a little bit of a party mode and just sort of swinging by a couple of sessions that evening.' Marianne certainly wouldn't have welcomed outside suggestions, even from a Beatle.

When Paul came down to my sessions and would say 'Why don't you do this?' or 'Overdub that' or 'Do it backwards,' I would look at him and I wouldn't say anything, but thinking, How dare you come down to my session and say ...? He came down to quite a few of them. And I took his suggestions sometimes, but somewhat grudgingly ... Because I wasn't a generous, easy-going person. I don't like people coming down to my sessions telling me what to do!

Marianne's version of 'Yesterday' was finally released on 22 October 1965 and Paul did all he could to promote it. Granada Television had proposed a big-budget fifty-minute television special called *The Music of Lennon and McCartney*, featuring Peter and Gordon, Billy J. Kramer, Cilla Black and other top stars famous for singing their songs, with the Beatles themselves introducing the acts and miming to 'Day Tripper' and 'We Can Work It Out'. Marianne:

'Paul really helped me by putting me on the thing that the Beatles did with Granada. It was really great, because he started it off.' Paul began the song alone, sitting on a stool, strumming his guitar and singing, then after a half-minute the song faded into Marianne's version, complete with choir and orchestra.

Marianne was eight months pregnant with Nicholas and in those days it would have been considered shocking to see a pregnant woman on television, particularly an entertainer. In what was probably a historic first, Paul insisted that she be allowed to go on the programme – though the cameras filmed only her head and shoulders or angled views from above. Marianne: 'It was very very nice of him and it was one of the things that really brought me into all that world. But Matt Monro had the hit.' Nonetheless, Marianne's version charted at number 36.

After Marianne gave birth to their son Nicholas on 10 November 1965 at the London Clinic, her mother, the Baroness Erisso, began to spend more and more time in Lennox Gardens. Marianne, her mother, Nicholas and his nanny Maggie would be busy with the baby in the kitchen and bedroom, while at the other end of the corridor, John and his friends were taking LSD, smoking pot and hanging out in the living room. Marianne: 'There was a complete split, with my mother and the nanny and one life going on, and then there was all this other stuff. It was extraordinary, it was as if the two didn't see each other.'

John and his friends were actually engaged in serious discussions. Since John was disillusioned by most of the art galleries in London, he had decided to start one of his own. He talked about it for some time but now it was actually going to happen. He, Peter Asher and a bookseller called Miles were going to start an experimental bookshop and gallery and call it Indica. It was going to blow everyone's minds.

Indica

John Dunbar, Peter Asher and Miles were confident that their new avant-garde art gallery and bookshop would be a success because there were so few outlets for new and experimental art and literature in London. In the mid-sixties, only two bookshops in London carried little mimeographed poetry magazines, small-press publications and the works of disestablishment poets: the Turret Bookshop, which

Bernard Stone operated from a tiny room on Kensington Church Walk and which focused on British poetry; and Better Books, a large Charing Cross Road bookshop owned by Tony Godwin, the legendary editor-in-chief at Penguin Books, which concentrated more on obscure Beat Generation writings and art. Better Books held poetry readings and screenings of avant-garde films by Bruce Connor or Kenneth Anger and experimental art installations and 'Happenings' in the basement. When Godwin announced that he was going to sell the shop to Hatchards, the staff feared that all this would come to an end. The manager of the paperback department, Barry Miles, the author of this book, usually known simply as Miles, decided to open his own shop. Paolo Lionni, a friend of the American poet Gregory Corso, introduced him to John Dunbar, who he knew was thinking of opening an art gallery.

In September 1965, after a dinner at Bianchi's on Frith Street, John and Miles decided to combine forces since they had similar interests in art and literature: John was well read in the Beat Generation, which was Miles's speciality, and Miles had studied painting at Gloucestershire College of Art. John approached Peter Asher for the start-up capital since Marianne, very sensibly as it turned out, said she wouldn't lend it to him. The three of them formed a company called MAD (Miles, Asher and Dunbar) Limited to run the venture. Peter lent John and Miles £600 each and put in £600 himself. With this meagre amount, Indica was started.

John began scouting for premises and one night, at the Scotch of St James Club with Marianne, he noticed that the building next door was for rent. Number 6 Mason's Yard consisted of one large square room on the ground floor, with a small office taking up one corner, and a larger gallery space in the basement which extended out beneath the pavement. Meanwhile Miles was buying stock for the new bookshop, concentrating mostly on American small-press imports, books by Beat Generation writers and more serious avant-garde literature, since they had not the resources nor space to carry a full range of literature. The books were delivered to Wimpole Street, where Mrs Asher gave them the room next to the music room in the basement to organise the stock while the gallery-bookshop was prepared for opening.

Paul was the bookshop's first customer. He would sometimes go down to the basement at night and browse among the piles of books to find something to read, leaving a note for them to be put on his account. Anselm Hollo's *And It's a Song*, Ed Sanders' *Peace Eye* poems, *Drugs and the Mind* by DeRopp and *Gandhi on Non-Violence* were Indica's first sales, a selection which gives a good indication of Paul's interests at the time and the range of the bookshop's stock.

Meanwhile the bookshop had to be shelved and the gallery painted and carpeted. Wood was ordered from Phillip Weisberg's timber yard on Goodge Place and John and Miles, having no vehicles of their own, arrived to pick it up in Paul's Aston Martin. Weisberg wrung his hands in mock despair. 'I just don't understand you lads. You spend hours complaining about the price of four by two, wasting my precious time, then you arrive to collect it in a car that costs three years' wages? Wassa matter with you? Whose car is that? Why doesn't he buy the wood?'

Back at Mason's Yard, Ian Sommerville, William Burroughs's ex-boyfriend and collaborator on his books *Nova Express* and *The Ticket That Exploded*, was installing a ring main for the lighting and power. Meticulous to the point of mania, he carefully sanded the battening, then painted it red, white and blue before attaching it to the wall beneath the shelves where it would not, in any case, be seen. It was several days before Ian appeared with any actual electrical wire. He was accompanied in his work by Ian Whitcomb's 'You Turn Me On (Turn On Song)', repeated endlessly on his Philips cassette machine, rather as Andy Warhol would play 'Sally Go Round the Roses' by the Jaynetts while he painted.

Ian was living with his boyfriend Alan Watson in William Burroughs's apartment at Dalmeny Court, Duke Street, St James's, virtually overlooking Mason's Yard, and Alan would often drop by to see Ian. Alan had bright-yellow hair of a rather unnatural hue and wore tight hipster pants, cut so low that they were little more than two legs with a belt. He would sashay across the yard, hand on hip, blowing kisses at the workmen engaged in building the new Cavendish Hotel which backed on to the yard from Jermyn Street. The workmen would play football in the yard during their tea breaks and Alan would call out gaily, 'Score a goal for me, boys!' They enjoyed the joke and whistled and hooted back at him. Alan worked in the canteen at Scotland Yard and would dance on the tables for the enjoyment of the constabulary. He and Ian had a stormy relationship with their host, Burroughs, who was still in love with Ian despite having left him for a prolonged visit to New York the previous year, having given no indication that he was coming back. For Burroughs, living with Alan had its ups and downs: he was a good cook but he also played opera constantly, which was not one of Bill's favourite forms of culture. Paul was to get to know Ian and Alan quite well when Ian acted as the tape operator for a demo studio that Paul built.

The poet Pete Brown also joined in the labour, hammering and painting, uttering his inventive curses – 'By St Enid's toenail!', 'God's teeth!' and the like – as he hit his thumb or jabbed himself. He originally became involved because he was keen on the idea of a bookshop that held poetry readings. However, it was soon obvious that this one was not just another version of Better Books. Pete: 'I would be painting away and look over my shoulder and there would be Paul McCartney sawing wood.'

Pete was secretly lusting after Jane Asher, who also dropped in from time to time, and he even wrote a screenplay for her perusal. Over the weeks Pete arrived later and later, to appear eventually only half an hour before lunchtime, murmuring hopefully, 'Any chance of a spot of nosh then?' before everyone retired to Gus's café, a worker's café on the opposite corner of the yard which sold some of the worst food in London and was patrolled by the largest and greasiest black cat anyone had ever seen. Later in 1966, after working with Graham Bond, Pete teamed up with Jack Bruce and wrote the lyrics for 'Wrapping Paper', 'White Room', 'Sunshine of Your Love', 'I Feel Free' and a number of other hits for Cream, which enabled him to form his own band, Piblokto.

Jane donated the shop's till. It was Victorian, a long oblong wooden box with a small window set in the top to write on the till roll. As a little girl she used to play shops with it. The bookshop opened in February 1966, and at the end of the first year's trading the till roll went to the accountant along with the paying-in books, but the accountant reported a tremendous discrepancy between the two. It turned out that one of the accountant's assistants had carefully added up all Jane's childhood purchases which filled the first half of the till roll: 6 eggs £1.12.6d; 1 loaf of bread 1/6d ... all written in Jane's childhood hand. John and Miles refused to pay for the accounts and the accountant issued a writ against them; Indica's lawyer, however, advised calm and prudence and tapped his nose knowingly. Sure enough, the next week the accountant fled the country, leaving a trail of debts.

On one occasion the shop was overwhelmed by Beatles fans. Paul and Jane rushed into the shop, slamming the door behind them, and scurried downstairs to the gallery. Seconds later a mob of fans and tourists pressed themselves against the windows, staring in as if everyone inside was a caged animal. Paul and Jane had been at a nearby store buying coloured thread for a dress when a crowd gathered. Though they walked quickly, the crowds grew alarmingly and they were out of breath when they arrived. They ordered a cab to take them to Albemarle Street, their next destination, less than two blocks away. When the black cab arrived, the driver muttered, 'I thought it was someone like you lot. Anyone else would have been able to walk there.' Thereafter, John whitewashed the window to prevent people from staring in until the bookshop was open.

Paul would put in a day's work whenever he had time, mixing the 'green gunge' needed to fill in holes and cracks in the plaster, sawing wood and painting the walls with white paint. This caused Peter a slight discomfort because he sometimes used Indica as a venue for interviews in order to give the shop publicity; there were often surrealistic tableaux of young female interviewers seriously asking Peter his favourite colour and what colour hair he preferred in girls ('fair' when interviewed by a Scandinavian magazine, 'black' when the interviewer was Japanese), while at the same time their eyes kept straying across to Paul, who would be winking or raising his eyebrows at them behind Peter's back as he sloshed paint on the wall and 'The Turn On Song' blasted out and book reps and John's artists all vied for attention.

Paul helped draw the flyers which were distributed to announce the opening and even designed the wrapping paper. He kept it a big secret. Peter was consumed with curiosity because Paul had locked himself in his room for two days and wouldn't let anyone in and was acting in a most mysterious way. He had drawn a typographical design based on the name and address of Indica with the lettering crossing like the Union Jack. He sneaked the artwork out of Wimpole Street and gave it to a printer to make 2000 sheets as wrapping paper. It was not until the shop was about ready to open that he arrived and presented his surprise gift. *16* magazine in the USA ran a photograph of it and the shop was inundated with letters from American Beatles fans wanting sheets mailed to them, usually enclosing American stamps, which were of little use.

Meanwhile in the basement gallery John carefully carved and polished a wooden banister rail, laid brown hessian ex-Ideal Home Exhibition carpeting and prepared a series of mixed shows to give the public an idea of the type of work Indica intended to present. A good example of the kind of bafflement he had to contend with is seen in Jonathan Aitken's 1967 book *The Young Meteors*, in which Aitken describes visiting one of the group shows at Indica and seeing, among other things, the work of Barry Flannigan, Takis, and Christo's wrapped objects:

> One establishment that makes no attempt to woo the provincial buyers is the way-out Indica Gallery ... it is run by 24-year-old John Dunbar, a Cambridge graduate, who has filled the gallery with the most bizarre paintings ever to be described as 'art'. Handbags, lumps of cement, pieces of machinery, and odd scraps of miscellaneous bric-à-brac all glued together on a canvas and priced at £200, is the sort of thing one finds on the walls of Indica. Equally strange is the proprietor himself, Dickensian gold-rimmed glasses perched precariously on the end of his nose, his face covered by enough spare long hair to weave a carpet ...

The first proper exhibition at the gallery was by the kinetic-art 'collective' the Groupe de Recherche d'Art Visuel de Paris, featuring neon sculpture, light boxes and Op Art constructions by François Morellet, Le Parc, Garcia Rossi, Sobrino, Stein and Yvaral. It opened on 4 June 1966. Julio Le Parc's work was influenced by fairgrounds and circuses; he made distorting spectacles and hand-held mirrors that warped the reflection like a fun-fair hall of mirrors. One of his works was displayed outside in Mason's Yard: a set of unstable black wooden boxes. When you stood on them they wobbled alarmingly like precarious stepping stones across a stream. One morning, Westminster council dustmen mistook them for rubbish and carted them away, never to be seen again.

While the Indica show was on, Julio Le Parc won the prize for painting at the Venice Biennale. He fainted, and Indica found itself launched into the limelight by actually having a show of the Biennale winner mounted at the time.

John returned from Venice and set about dealing with the professional art world. One day an overweight American walked into the gallery. 'I'm a big American art collector,' he said.

'I'm a little English art dealer,' John giggled.

The prices for Le Parc's work seemed low and rather arbitrary. Only after John sold a few did it turn out that Julio had put joke prices on the pieces – £10 on one work – not for one moment expecting John actually to sell any of them.

The word spread, and people began to show up to see the shows and buy books. Miles was sent a sticker by the Mac Meda Destruction Company, an underground surfer gang, members of the Pump House crowd who hung out at Windansea Beach in La Jolla, California. How they ever heard of Indica remains a mystery. The enclosed note said, 'Put this decal in your window, and Tom Wolfe will come and see you.' They put the sticker on the window, and about a week later, Tom Wolfe walked in the door wearing his trademark white suit and high collar. When told he was expected, he was astonished. He had spent time with the surfers, and his essay 'The Pump House Gang' would be the title story of his second book in 1968, but he didn't even remember telling any of them he was going to London. However, there he was, obviously drawn to Indica by the magic sticker. No one else seemed in the least surprised.

One afternoon in late March 1966, Paul arrived at Indica with John Lennon. John wanted a book by what sounded like 'Nitz Ga'. It took Miles a few minutes to realise that he was looking for the German philosopher Nietzsche, long enough for John to become convinced that he was being ridiculed. He launched into an attack on intellectuals and university students and was only mollified when Paul told him that he had not understood what John was asking for either, and that Miles was not a university graduate but had been to art college, just like him. Immediately friendly again, John talked about Allen Ginsberg and the Beats, laughing about his school magazine the *Daily Howl*: 'Tell Ginsberg I did it first!' Miles found him a copy of *The Portable Nietzsche* and John began to scan the shelves. His eyes soon alighted upon a copy of *The Psychedelic Experience*, Dr Timothy Leary's psychedelic version of the *Tibetan Book of the Dead*. John was delighted and settled down on the settee with the book. Right away, on page 14 in Leary's introduction, he read, 'Whenever in doubt, turn off your mind, relax, float downstream.' He had found the first line of 'Tomorrow Never Knows', one of the Beatles' most innovative songs.

Ken Weaver, the drummer with the Fugs, sent Miles a copy of their first album, *The Village Fugs*, from New York. Paul wanted to hear it and, since Indica had no record player, everyone followed Paul into Mason's Yard to the locked entrance of the Scotch of St James nightclub located next door to Indica. After a lot of ringing and banging, the manager was roused; he protested that the club was closed, but was unable to refuse a Beatle, whose presence in the club at night guaranteed good business. The club looked very seedy in the daytime. There were no windows, but the bare light bulbs used to light the place up for cleaning revealed just how flimsy and tacky all the furnishings were. The Fugs album was placed on the DJ's turntable, housed in an old carriage, and the discordant lyrics of 'Slum Goddess from the Lower East Side' and Tuli Kupferberg croaking his way through 'Supergirl' filled the club. 'My God! What's that filth?' yelled the manager, shocked that Paul would want to listen to such smutty lyrics, but Paul was amused. Afterwards, whenever pushy tourists called upon him to sign an autograph, he wrote 'Tuli Kupferberg', the name of the Fugs' percussionist.

Paul's own taste in art and literature veered towards the proto-surreal. In art he was attracted to the dream landscapes of Giorgio de Chirico, Paul Delvaux and Salvador Dali and he admired the paintings of Max Ernst, but it was the work of René Magritte that gave him the most pleasure. The Surrealists had always acknowledged a debt to the work of the turn-of-the-century playwright Alfred Jarry, and in literature it was Jarry's work that struck a particular chord with McCartney. While driving to Liverpool in his Aston Martin in January 1966, Paul had heard a BBC Third Programme production of Alfred Jarry's *Ubu Cocu* (Ubu Cuckolded). 'It was the best radio play I had ever heard in my life, and the best production, and Ubu was so brilliantly played. It was just a sensation. That was one of the big things of the period for me.'

Not long afterwards, in July 1966, Bill Gaskill revived Jarry's *Ubu Roi* (King Ubu), first staged in Paris in 1896, at the Royal Court Theatre in Sloane Square. The director, Iain Cuthbertson, cast the veteran vaudevillian Max Wall in the lead. Though he was fifty-eight years old, it was his début in the straight theatre and one of the most successful examples of the Royal Court's experiments with casting across traditional 'legitimate' borders. The young David Hockney designed the sets and costumes. Paul and Jane were not very excited by the production, though Jane thought the idea of Max Wall playing the lead was inspired. Paul preferred *Ubu Cocu* to the better-known *Ubu Roi* and even began to consider staging his own version of it and writing music for the production, an idea he still entertains. He read more Jarry, particularly his writing on the subject of 'pataphysics – the French art and literary 'science' created by Jarry and described by Eugène Ionesco as 'anarchy raised to the level of metaphysics'. It was an early form of Surrealism, which is why Paul was attracted to it. Famous 'pataphysicians included Marcel Duchamp and Jean Dubuffet, and Jarry had a profound effect on the Theatre of the Absurd writers Raymond Queneau, Boris Vian and Ionesco, though membership of the College of 'Pataphysics itself was generally used as an excuse for elaborate banquets rather than any artistic ventures.

Paul's interest was sparked first by the radio play, then the stage performance. His antennae were out and after reading a number of Jarry's play scripts Paul had taken enough from Jarry to utilise him in his work with the Beatles; not in a big production number, which might puzzle or mystify people, but in a subtle reference. Miles had recently been made a member of the College of 'Pataphysics and awarded the *Ordre de la Grande Gidouille* for ''pataphysical activity'. The rock band Soft Machine held the Chair of Applied Alcoholism for the English Isles and there were a few other members of the College in Britain but it was not exactly a well-known literary movement.

> PAUL: Miles and I often used to talk about the 'pataphysical society and the Chair of Applied Alcoholism. So I put that in one of the Beatles songs, 'Maxwell's Silver Hammer': 'Joan was quizzical, studied 'pataphysical science in the home ...' Nobody knows what it means; I only explained it to Linda just the other day. That's the lovely thing about it. I am the only person who ever put the name of 'pataphysics into the record charts, c'mon! It was great. I love those surreal little touches.

That gesture summed up Paul's approach to the avant-garde and the ways in which he chose to incorporate the new ideas he was encountering into his work with the Beatles.

PAUL: That was the big difference between me and John: whereas John shouted it from the rooftops, I often just whispered it in the drawing room, thinking that was enough.

Hanson Street

In the programme for Paul's 1989 World Tour, Paul wrote:

John's ended up as the one that's the avant-garde guy because he did all that with Yoko. Well, actually quite a few years before he'd ever considered it, when he was living out in the suburbs by the golf club with Cynthia and hanging out there, I was getting in with a guy called Miles and the people at Indica. I used to be at his house a lot of nights, just him and his wife, because he was just so interesting, very well-read. So he'd turn you on to Burroughs and all that. I'd done a little bit of literature at school but I never really did much modern. I find this very interesting because it's something I realise I didn't put around a lot at the time, like I helped start *International Times* with Miles, helped start Indica Bookshop and Gallery where John met Yoko ...

Barry Miles and his then wife Sue were living at 15 Hanson Street in the middle of London's garment district, a five-minute walk down New Cavendish Street from Wimpole Street, into another world. Hanson Street now is a very mixed neighbourhood but then it was in the centre of a working-class Jewish quarter, mostly made up of the women who worked in the sweatshops scattered throughout the area. Whereas Paul's Aston Martin was inconspicuous in his part of Marylebone, in Hanson Street it attracted considerable attention parked outside the kosher butcher across the street.

Miles and Sue first met Paul in August 1965 at Wimpole Street when John Dunbar, Peter Asher and Miles started Indica and began to assemble the stock of the bookshop in the basement of the Asher household. After a day's work unpacking and cataloguing books, Miles and Sue would join Peter in his room at the top of the house and sometimes stay for dinner. At some point during their first meeting with Paul, Sue Miles mentioned that she had just made a batch of hash brownies using the recipe for 'Haschich Fudge, (which anyone could whip up on a rainy day)' (sic) in the *Alice B. Toklas*

Cookbook. Alice, who was Gertrude Stein's lover, enthused over the fudge: 'it might provide an entertaining refreshment for a Ladies' Bridge Club ...' she wrote. She was given the recipe by the painter Brion Gysin, who neglected to tell her you had to bake them. Sue, who later became a professional chef, did bake hers. The next day Miles came home from work to find Paul sitting on the work counter in the kitchen, talking to Sue, nibbling on a brownie.

Flat 8, on the second floor, looked rather like student accommodation: walls painted white, covered with paintings and collages, furniture rescued from the street or bought second-hand, including an impossibly hard *chaise longue*, a large wooden work table that doubled as a dining table, and four French café chairs, obtained from Pete Townshend's mother, who dealt in antiques. The flat was filled with books, with a heavy emphasis on the Beat Generation: Allen Ginsberg had stayed there that summer when he had appeared at the Royal Albert Hall poetry reading and was followed shortly afterwards by Lawrence Ferlinghetti. Miles introduced Paul to the work of William Burroughs and Allen Ginsberg and lent him copies of *Evergreen Review*. The discussions ranged from 'pataphysics to Buddhism and drugs.

Most of the records in the flat were avant-garde jazz – John Coltrane, Albert Ayler, Sun Ra, Cecil Taylor, Ornette Coleman – and works by Karlheinz Stockhausen, John Cage, Luciano Berio, Morton Subotnick and other electronic-music composers. Paul particularly liked Albert Ayler's free-form tenor-saxophone playing: sweeping screams and wails which helped define the nascent Black Power movement. He bought some of Ayler's albums for himself and enjoyed the puzzled look on George Martin's face when he put on *Spirits* or *Bells* and filled the room with Albert's honks and squeals. William Burroughs's spoken-word album *Call Me Burroughs* was a great favourite for late-evening listening when people were stoned; Paul heard Burroughs's cold, flat Mid-Western voice reading from *The Naked Lunch* before he saw the book.

The discussion often focused on the nature of music and the possibilities of electronic music and random sound; the way boundaries were being tested in jazz by Ayler, Coleman, the saxophone chords of John Coltrane and the orchestration of Sun Ra; the musical environments being created by Terry Riley and Steve Reich, and the wide-ranging experiments of the French *musique concrète* composers

Pierre Henry and Pierre Schaeffer in the late forties and fifties who were producing sound collages.

> PAUL: We sat around. We got wrecked together. We discussed all these crazy ideas together. We put down these lines of research together. I'd come home from an exciting crazed sort of think meeting with Miles, a stoned think tank, which was great fun and I'd love it and I'd be very enthusiastic about all these ideas and I used to tell John about this stuff. I'd spew 'em all out the next day. John would say, 'Wow, wow, wow! Well, why don't you do that? Why don't you do that?' I remember saying to him I had an idea for an album title, *Paul McCartney Goes Too Far*. He said, 'Fantastic! Do it! Do it!' He always wanted me to do that.
>
> I remember one of our ideas was to master two pieces of music on to a record, have two albums on one record, and all you would do in the future was switch out one of them with your brain. You'd say, 'I'm not listening to the Beethoven, I'm listening to the Beatles,' but they would be both going on. So this was ... cheap, cheerful, good value for money. You had to have the mental control to be able to switch one of them out ... Last night it happened, my album *Paul Is Live* was playing and *Neighbours* was on the telly, and the two playing together totally reminded me of the sixties! Linda said, 'God in heaven, that's terrible!' and I said, 'I rather like it.'

On 24 February 1966, Paul went with Miles and Sue to hear the Italian electronic composer Luciano Berio, then a lecturer at the Juilliard School of Music in New York, give a talk at the Italian Cultural Institute on Belgrave Square. Paul had heard Berio's *Thema (Omaggio a Joyce)* (1958) at Miles's house. On it Cathy Berberian, the American mezzo-soprano, reads the beginning of Chapter 11 of James Joyce's *Ulysses* and Berio's music consists entirely of this reading cut up, superimposed, speeded up, and reduced to loop tapes which sometimes spin so fast they sound like a tree full of starlings. No instruments were used. Paul was more interested in the idea and approach than in the actual piece.

At the lecture, Berio played a tape of his new piece *Laborintus 2 (Un Omaggio a Dante)*, which develops certain themes in Dante's texts, combining them with biblical texts as well as the work of

T. S. Eliot, Ezra Pound and Edoardo Sanguineti. During the intermission, Paul was able to have a few words with Berio but the Italian embassy staff clustered around so closely that serious conversation was difficult. The meeting may have sparked Berio's interest in the Beatles since, not long afterwards, his wife Cathy Berberian released an album called *Beatles Arias* in which she gave full glorious operatic treatment to such numbers as 'Here, There and Everywhere', 'Help!' and 'Ticket to Ride'. Berio also made some settings of Beatles material which were sung by Les Swingle Singers, the French choral group whose work varied from popular songs to the most difficult of experimental music.

Of all the modern composers Paul encountered during this period, John Cage had the most influence on him. Though he didn't hear a great deal of the music, the ideas behind the music were a frequent subject of discussion; and you don't actually need to hear *4'33"* to get the gist. This notorious 1952 composition for piano lasting four minutes and thirty-three seconds contains no notes at all but is divided into three movements designated by the closing and reopening of the keyboard lid. The piece is silent, except of course for the sounds made by the audience themselves – coughs, sniffs, breathing – and the ambient room sound, distant traffic, air conditioners, police sirens. It was the ultimate demonstration of Cage's belief that all noise belongs to the realm of musical sound and that even sounds not intended by the composer are perfectly legitimate parts of a composition.

In *Silence*, Cage reprinted a 1957 lecture entitled 'Experimental Music' in which he said:

> Try as we may to make a silence, we cannot. For certain engineering purposes, it is desirable to have as silent a situation as possible. Such a room is called an anechoic chamber ... a room without echoes. I entered one at Harvard University ... and heard two sounds, one high and one low. The engineer in charge ... informed me that the high one was my nervous system in operation and the low one my blood in circulation. Until I die there will be sounds. And they will continue following my death. One need not fear about the future of music.

Since all and every noise was equally eligible for use in a musical composition, Cage and his accompanist David Tudor began to introduce unorthodox sound sources. At a lecture by John Cage given at Columbia Teachers' College in March 1959, David Tudor introduced several radios as noise elements, randomly spinning the dials to make short bursts of broadcasts or static to augment his piano. One record, the 1959 album *Indeterminacy*, was often on the record player at Miles's place when Paul was visiting. On it Cage reads ninety stories accompanied by David Tudor on piano and electronic sounds which sometimes drown the voice completely.

John Cage's leading disciple in Britain was the composer Cornelius Cardew. A professor of composition at the Royal College of Music, Cardew spent two years as Karlheinz Stockhausen's assistant, working with him on a huge orchestral work, and had worked with John Cage and David Tudor in Europe, where he had prepared a version of Cage's *Fontana Mix* for guitar. It was at one of Cardew's free-form performances with AMM, early in 1966, that Paul first heard Cage's theories put into practice.

AMM was probably the most experimental group of the sixties, consisting of Cornelius Cardew on piano, cello and transistor radio, Lou Gare on tenor saxophone and violin, Eddie Provost on drums, xylophone and other percussion, Keith Rowe on electric guitar and transistor radio and Lawrence Sheaff on cello, accordion, clarinet and transistor radio.

A musical happening was already in progress when Paul, Miles and Sue finally found the unmarked basement room at the Royal College of Art where AMM held their weekly sessions. In addition to conventional instruments there were tape recorders, signal-generating equipment, electric tools, drills and electric toys which were allowed to run loose or to vibrate in a controlled environment such as a steel tray. There were whistles and a siren. There was no division between performers and audience, all sounds constituted part of the piece being performed, whether they originated from the members of the group or the audience of a dozen or so people sitting on the floor. Every scratch, honk, chair squeak and bump was received with the utmost attention. There were no melodies and no rhythms. Sometimes there was nothing to listen to except silence. As Cardew wrote, 'An AMM performance has no beginning or ending. Sounds outside the performance are distinguished from it only by individual sensibility.'

Cardew did not touch the keyboard of the piano; in fact, he rarely even touched the exposed strings of the piano. Most of the time he sat on the floor by one of its legs, which he occasionally tapped with a small piece of wood, his head inclined to one side, listening intently.

From time to time Paul contributed by running a penny along the coils of the old-fashioned steam radiator that he was sitting next to on the floor. After the intermission, he used the penny to tap on his pint-glass beer mug. The atmosphere of the performance was one of exceptional seriousness with an almost painful degree of attention to sound, lacking humour in every sense except for the half-smile on Cardew's face.

Paul didn't find the performance musically satisfying, but neither did the participants, who said afterwards that it was not a good evening. Paul observed that obviously the existence of such groups, challenging all normal concepts of the necessity for time signatures, rhythm and melody, was important and said, 'You don't have to like something to be influenced by it.' Whereas John Lennon would have probably felt that they were putting him on, Paul understood their serious purpose but told the organiser Victor Schonfeld, 'It went on too long.'

It quickly became apparent that it made more sense to separate out Indica Bookshop from Indica Gallery. One of the reasons for being in the St James area was to be among the other galleries, and it did not do the work justice to expect visitors to go through a crowded bookshop and down to the basement to see the art. Besides, the large crowds which gathered for art openings also had a tendency to steal the books. In the summer of 1966, Indica Books moved to new premises at 102 Southampton Row, near the British Museum and all the Bloomsbury bookshops, allowing the gallery to take over the ground floor of the Mason's Yard property. There was room in the back of the bookshop for a gallery annexe, and one of the first shows there was of musical sculpture by the Frères Bachet, which all the Beatles attended at one time or another.

The bookshop was huge and when Miles and his old friend John Hopkins – usually known as 'Hoppy' – decided to start an underground newspaper, to be called *International Times* (*IT*), the unused basement of Indica Books seemed the ideal place for the editorial office. The paper soon ran into trouble financially and Paul suggested to Miles, 'If you interview me, then you'll be able to get advertising from record companies.' Rather than do a conventional interview, Miles just taped an afternoon's conversation at Paul's house, during which they discussed fame, spiritual matters, drugs and electronic music. It was transcribed and printed as a straightforward question and answer in the best Warholian tradition, with no introduction or summing-up. It was picked up by the underground press syndicate and reprinted all over the world, from the *San Francisco Oracle* and the *Georgia Straight* to obscure underground outfits in Sweden and Holland. 'You should go and do one with my friend George,' said Paul, and so George Harrison became the second person interviewed by *IT* and devoted his entire interview to discussing Hinduism and Zen. Pop stars liked the straight Q & A interview presentation because press interviews at that time were mostly paraphrase with very little direct quotation and their words were always changed to suit the purpose of the journalist. *IT* gave them a vehicle to state their views.

Paul was correct in thinking that interviews with musicians would enable *IT* to get record-company ads, but the paper was still broke and often unable to pay the printer or its staff. Paul helped out financially, and was thanked by being given a credit in the staff box under the name of 'Ian Iachimoe'. This was the 'secret' name that Paul suggested his friends use when writing to him to make their letters stand out from all the fan mail. It was the sound of his own name played backwards on a tape recorder. He even used it himself: the original manuscript of 'Paperback Writer', which was written in the form of a letter, ends with 'Yours sincerely, Ian Iachimoe'. Paul was happy to lend a hand in laying out the paper and there was one evening when Paul, together with the Beat poet Harry Fainlight, took time out before dinner to draw a half-page psychedelic ad for Indica Books in order to meet the printer's deadline the following morning. It was published in issue 16. Such were the times.

Montagu Square

One thought to emerge from sitting around stoned in Miles's flat was how great it would be to have access to all the experimental work going on, to be able to hear poetry readings and free-form concerts on record. Paul felt that it would be a good idea to have a small demo studio available for poets and avant-garde musicians to record their work; that if these people were given access to recording facilities, then a lively exchange of tapes would happen. Poets in Liverpool would be able to hear the latest developments in beat music from London, and vice versa; rock musicians could send their work in progress to fellow musicians in the USA, and so on. The idea was that some of the most interesting tapes could be released on a cheap-label album, possibly monthly like a magazine. It was just one of the many projects that later helped inspire Apple; this one, in particular, was realised with the launch of the Zapple label two years later.

Rather than jump right in with a studio and staff and enormous costs, Paul proposed that he set up a basic recording unit and see how it went from there. Even the most basic facility needed premises, however, and someone to operate the equipment. Miles suggested his friend Ian Sommerville as an ideal tape operator for the project. Paul had already met him a number of times when Ian installed the electrical wiring for Indica in Mason's Yard and suggested meeting to talk about it. They got together in Miles's flat in Hanson Street in the early days of spring 1966, and in the course of a pleasant evening Ian explained the principles of free-floating equations and the mechanics of producing hallucinations using flickering lights. Paul said Ian was clearly the man for the job and that he would buy the necessary equipment and find a place to accommodate it.

Ringo had a flat that he was not using at 34 Montagu Square, on the corner with Montagu Place, just a few blocks from Wimpole Street. It was a converted ground floor and basement in a Regency terrace five doors from Anthony Trollope's old house. French windows opened to a small yard at the back and the flat was reached by narrow stone steps leading from a gate in the iron railings on the street, making it self-contained. Paul rented it from Ringo to use as a studio.

Ian went to Teletape, a hi-fi shop on Shaftesbury Avenue, and bought a pair of Revox A77s, a pair of huge Revox speakers, a small mixer, microphone stands, a selection of microphones, an editing block and a stock of tape, charging it all to Paul. The equipment looked slightly incongruous in the flat, which Brian Epstein's interior designer, Ken Partridge, had decorated in early-sixties camp pop-star style with purple watered-silk wallpaper, silk curtains and lead-streaked mirrors.

Ian and his boyfriend Alan quickly moved into the flat and

established themselves. Though Paul had not expected this, it did make sense as the studio was most likely to be used in the late evening when anyone else would have gone home unless specifically booked. This way people could just make a quick phone call and drop by. It became another of the 'little pads to hang out in'. John Dunbar, Christopher Gibbs, Robert Fraser, Miles, the film-maker Antony Balch and others were frequent visitors and, though many a stoned evening was recorded, very little in the way of avant-garde experiment was actually put on tape. Aside from Paul himself, William Burroughs probably used the studio more than anyone else, conducting a series of stereo experiments with Ian known as the 'Hello, Yes, Hello' tapes.

Ian Sommerville was a mathematician, thin and birdlike with high cheekbones, pale parchment skin and a nervous habit of running his fingers through his hair that made it stand on end. He had been William Burroughs's boyfriend for most of the sixties, living with him first in the Beat Hotel in Paris, where he had used his scientific training to help Bill and the painter Brion Gysin develop their cut-up technique. This had originally been a way of composing new texts by cutting up old ones and randomly juxtaposing them to find new word lines and associations. Ian helped them to apply the same method to tape recordings and film.

In those days everything was recorded reel to reel. They began by using Brion Gysin's Uher tape recorder. 'I did a number of experiments with that,' said Burroughs, 'lots of them with Ian Sommerville following Brion's experiments, all sorts of cut-ups, musical cut-ups and sleep recordings. They weren't supposed to be works, it was not an art proposition at all.'

Bill and Ian experimented with backward tapes and superimposed recordings made at different speeds upon each other. A second tape recorder enabled them to overdub as well as just drop in new material. Together they developed something called 'inching' in which the tape was manually pulled across the tape heads while recording or overdubbing material. Ian bought a throat microphone to use in recordings of subvocal speech; music and other non-text material was introduced. They became adept at laying down a backing track: a BBC Third Programme lecture or a recording of room conversation made a good base to superimpose upon. Bill would read fragments from his texts or from newspaper reports, or drop in random extracts from different radio broadcasts.

Paul was interested in all this because it tied in so neatly with the tape-loop experiments that he had been conducting with his Brenells. Burroughs's cut-up tapes became another of the new elements that ultimately contributed to Paul's input in the music of the Beatles: to the eventual use of fragments of radio broadcasts, animal sounds and the other collage elements which occur throughout the *Sgt. Pepper* period. For now, though, he used the studio for other things.

> PAUL: In our conversations, I thought about getting into cut-ups and things like that and I thought I would use the studio for cut-ups. But it ended up being of more practical use to me, really. I thought, let Burroughs do the cut-ups and I'll just go in and demo things. I'd just written 'Eleanor Rigby' and so I went down there in the basement on my days off on my own. Just took a guitar down and used it as a demo studio.

> WILLIAM BURROUGHS: I saw him there several times. The three of us talked about the possibilities of the tape recorder. He'd just come in and work on his 'Eleanor Rigby'. Ian recorded his rehearsals so I saw the song taking shape. Once again, not knowing much about music, I could see he knew what he was doing. He was very pleasant and prepossessing. Nice-looking young man, fairly hardworking.

> PAUL: Occasionally Burroughs would be there. He was very interesting but we never really struck up a huge conversation. I actually felt you had to be a bit of a junkie, which was probably not true. He was fine, there never was a problem, it just never really developed into a huge conversation where we sat down for hours together. The sitting around for hours would be more with Ian Sommerville and his friend Alan. I remember them telling me off for being a tea-head. 'You're a tea-head, man!' 'Well? So?'

This was rich, coming from Ian, who told Miles that when he was living with Burroughs in the Arab quarter of Tangier, he slept on a pillow stuffed with finely chopped marijuana: 'No twigs, just the leaves and flowers. It was as soft as feathers. That perfume is the best

sleeping pill, man, you have such beautiful dreams and it is a joy to
wake up to that smell.'

Paul: 'William did some little cut-ups and we did some crazy tape
recordings in the basement. We used to sit around talking about all
these amazing inventions that people were doing; areas that people
were getting into like the Dream Machine that Ian and Brion Gysin
had made. It was all very new and very exciting, and so a lot of social
time was taken up with just sitting around chatting.'

In the end nothing came of it. No one used the studio to make
tapes, largely because Ian got it into his head that he was working
exclusively for Paul and put off everyone else who approached him
for studio time. Paul took one of the Revoxes and gave all the
remaining equipment to Ian. Ian moved out and the flat remained
empty until December 1966 when Ringo let Jimi Hendrix, Chas
Chandler and their respective girlfriends stay there for three months
while they looked for a place of their own. Jimi trashed the flat by
throwing paint at the walls while on acid, so Ringo had it painted
white. His next tenants, John and Yoko, finally gave Ringo's landlord
legal grounds to terminate his lease. In October 1968, a well-
publicised police raid led to the pot conviction that would later cause
John so much trouble in obtaining his American green card. Ringo's
lawyers worked out a deal. Paul, John and Yoko, Jimi Hendrix and
William Burroughs: 34 Montagu Square clearly qualifies as a
candidate for one of the blue marker plaques that the City of
Westminster fixes to buildings of historical interest.

Paul's life was not all avant-garde music and drugs; at the same time
as investigating Luciano Berio, he was learning about the blues. This
he did through the blues veteran John Mayall, whose group the
Bluesbreakers was a training ground for the likes of Eric Clapton,
Peter Green and Mick Taylor.

> PAUL: John Mayall's was another hangout, not very often, but a
> few times after a club he'd still be around and we'd go back to
> his house. He was a blues DJ, fantastic collection. I think his dad
> had been into it and passed it on to his son. John would sit me
> down in a good position for the stereo – 'Can I get you a glass of
> wine?' – and you'd get cooled out there and sit back in the chair,
> and he literally would DJ it from his corner; banks of records. He

first played me B. B. King. 'Have you heard this one, man? This is great, you know, B. B. King.' 'No, who's he?' 'Oh, you haven't heard? Oh, let's check out BB.' It'd be great stuff, live recordings of BB and girls screaming in the audience, like the Beatles. He was playing beautifully, very early and precise, exciting electric guitar. So John would play you some great great blues; Buddy Guy he'd play a lot. Then he'd play me some early Eric Clapton stuff, which was: 'God, it's amazing!' You could really see where Eric was getting some of the stuff from but Eric was making his guitar sound like a violin. It was a great education.

Mount Street

Paul first met the art dealer Robert Fraser in the spring of 1966, at John and Marianne's apartment in Lennox Gardens. This was shortly before Robert and John went to the Venice Biennale together, for which they were planning their joint strategy. Fraser represented Harold Cohen, who was one of the five young British artists to be shown at the British pavilion. Paul listened to their art talk and was impressed by Fraser's ideas. In the course of a few more encounters Paul and Robert became rather unlikely friends. Robert was a nervous Old Etonian homosexual with a fantastic eye for art. He was also a heroin addict. Paul was interested in art but was mainly attracted to Surrealism, which was not one of Robert's strong points, though as an art dealer he was happy to be of service.

Paul visited Robert's gallery and would often drop by his flat to see who was there and what was happening. Robert was a superb host; he always mixed the latest drinks, had the best drugs, and a room full of interesting people. Through Robert, Paul entered the world of art; he met Andy Warhol, Claes Oldenburg, Peter Blake and Richard Hamilton and, in the course of listening to their conversations, he learned a great deal about art appreciation. Paul: 'The most formative influence for me was Robert Fraser. Obviously the other Beatles were very important but the most formative art influence was Robert. I expect people to die so I don't feel a loss but there's a vacuum where he used to be.'

Eton had given Robert a halting, rather arrogant, aristocratic stutter and he was ramrod-straight from his army days. During the sixties Robert was thin and dapper, his black hair brushed back in a modified Elvis Presley cut complete with long, thick sideburns. Black thick-framed glasses threatened to overbalance his slender frame and he wore suits with trousers so impossibly tight that he had to bend almost double in order to pull the wad of notes from his pocket to tip the doormen at clubs. In 1967 Cecil Beaton described him in his diaries as having 'the usual pallor, the five-o'clock shadow, the tie badly in need of a pull up, and hair'. Though in later years alcohol and age brought the fleshy jowls of his father to his face, his characteristic lopsided smile remained.

Robert Hugh Fraser was born in London in August 1937 and grew up at 67 Cadogan Place, an elegant six-floor townhouse in a Regency terrace in which his parents lived until he was nineteen. His father, Lionel Fraser, was a self-made man who rose to become one of the leaders of the City of London financial establishment. Lionel Fraser was a golf-playing, teetotal Christian Scientist. He also had an interest in writing – his autobiography *All to the Good* was published in 1963 – and, more importantly, he was an art lover. In 1958 he joined the board of trustees of the Tate Gallery. His wife shared his interest and after Lionel's death in January 1965 she continued to serve as head of the Friends of the Tate Gallery.

Robert first showed his rebellious nature at Fan Court, a residential prep school near Chertsey in Surrey. When he was eight years old, his mother was telephoned by the anxious headmaster asking her to come at once. Robert had somehow obtained a paperback of Willie Gallacher's *The Case for Communism*, and was calling in such eloquent terms for the downfall of capitalism that he was having a profound effect on his fellow pupils. He had produced his own pamphlet, *Communism v. Capitalism*, which contained such phrases as 'The noose tightens round the capitalist's neck' and 'Capitalists have nothing to offer but further security to the upper classes'. Mummy talked him out of it and he willingly surrendered his copy of Gallacher.

In 1950 Robert joined his older brother Nicholas at Eton; his name had been put down the day after he was born. His best friend there was Christopher Gibbs, a man of impeccable taste who was to become that rare thing, a trend-setting antique dealer. He and Robert had much in common. Christopher: 'Robert was already firmly established in the raffish side of Eton life at the time I got there but we discovered each other soon after and I remember him coming to see me. "I'm told you've got some drawings by Sir Edwin Landseer in your room," was Robert's opening gambit. Which I think I did have, for some odd reason, but anyway we became friends.'

Robert's insight and unconventional reasoning in the field of art developed rapidly. On his wall at Eton he had a reproduction of a Monet and on the back was Robert's appraisal, written at the age of fourteen, of why this was an important picture. But Robert and Eton were not a good match. As Robert's father delicately put it:

> For some boys school is like the Elysian fields, for others it is a perpetual trial and a drag. This probably sums up the different sentiments of our two sons. Nicholas went on to King's College, Cambridge, whereas Robert, having to do National Service, was posted to the Grenadiers as a guardsman. Finding the Brigade unwilling to adapt itself to his personal idea of discipline, he was commissioned to the King's African Rifles and served a cooling period in Uganda with that first-class African regiment.

Robert later claimed that his sergeant in Uganda was Idi Amin, who during his presidency of Uganda snacked on human limbs stored in his refrigerator.

It was Robert's mother Cynthia who supported his desire to become an art dealer. First he learned the essentials of the business at one of the auction houses, then he went to work for the Wildenstein Gallery in New York, where he was first exposed to the latest trends in both modern art and drugs. Christopher Gibbs: 'He always had a nose for the scene, so to speak, always knew what was going on and a relentless pull towards the slightly seamy. He was always amused by all kinds of rascals and I suppose that his sex life became much more rich and varied through America.'

He returned to Britain in April 1962 and formed a liaison with a young French art dealer called Michel du Warenne. Warenne was dark with very short hair and Latin good looks. He had known many artists but, more crucially, he knew a lot of old ladies who had known artists. Warenne's specialty was in distracting them with flattery while spiriting their Max Ernsts out of the door. Robert began to spend a lot of time with him in Paris.

Robert opened his gallery on 15 August 1962 at 69 Duke Street, just a few blocks from his home. The Robert Fraser Gallery was one of the most interesting of the new wave of purpose-built commercial galleries. It was designed by Cedric Price and had blank walls, with no mouldings or skirting to distract the eye.

His taste at the time was still moulded by Michel du Warenne. Christopher Gibbs: 'When Robert started his gallery in London, Michel Warenne was very much around, very much directing him, and Robert was getting rather impatient with this "flitty frog telling me what to do. . .".' It was du Warenne who persuaded Robert to open the gallery with a Jean Dubuffet show. Robert's parents were among his best customers and through him made some very serious purchases, including Matisse, Magritte and Max Ernst, Odilon Redon, Peter Blake, and modern American artists such as Ellsworth Kelly and Andy Warhol. Robert exhibited the work of Bridget Riley, Clive Barker, Derek Boshier, Peter Blake, Claes Oldenburg, Roy Lichtenstein, Ed Ruscha, Cy Twombly, Arman, Yves Klein, Wolf Vostell and Matta, often giving them their first British shows.

Robert moved to an apartment at 20 Mount Street, on the second floor above Scott's Oyster and Lobster Bar in Mayfair, and set up his salon. The large, sparsely furnished living room was used as an adjunct to the gallery and contained several large day beds in silver-lacquered wood with writhing marine beasts carved at each end. There were some grand black leather chairs from Italy with silvered backs made from interlaced branches. Christopher Gibbs: 'Some of these things had come from Michel Warenne, who was obviously crazy about Robert. Robert treated him with a certain contempt and roughed up these splendid gifts. He would paste a drawing on to the black leather or stick a few Christmas decorations on it.'

The walls were white for displaying paintings but the lighting was subdued: paintings could be lit with halogen lamps (the latest thing) but there were also Tiffany lamps and candles. Robert was constantly adjusting and orchestrating the lighting as he stalked about the room, laying out the most fashionable cocktails or Nepalese Temple Balls hashish. There was always plenty to drink and lots of grass. A passage led to the bedroom, bathroom and a kitchen where Robert's silent Moroccan manservant Mohammed spent his time, though food was generally delivered by the Chinese take-away.

At first Robert frequented the gay Soho scene, centred on Muriel Belcher's Colony Room club, where his friend Francis Bacon held court, and the Rockingham Club off Shaftesbury Avenue, which was the only truly gay club in London at the time. He got to know Lionel

Bart and the Soho theatrical scene and they all came to Mount Street. Then, in 1964, a fashion model introduced him to the young photographer Michael Cooper.

Robert Fraser wrote about him when he died:

> Michael was the first 'pop' personality that I had met and he was very strong in showing me the direction that I should take in developing the gallery. He brought my attention to the fact that photography was an art. Like a lot of photographers, Michael had this feeling that his mission in life was to be a film-maker rather than a photographer, and he did have some great ideas. He had a very high opinion of himself. At every level he thought he was God's gift ...

Through his friendship with Michael Cooper, Robert began to move into a hipper, younger, more drug-oriented world. Christopher Gibbs: 'Michael Cooper was a very important formative influence because Michael was very bored with all these old steamer people and rough boys and such. He thought it was not interesting, so, they were kind of disposed of ... and on would come the new lot, new people who were doing things in movies, music ...'

Part of the new lot was Paul McCartney. He remembers it well:

> It was a big posh flat. There would always be a bunch of various friends around, as there were at John Dunbar's, and people I didn't necessarily know, who would be from the upper classes, not from our group. There might be Lord Londonderry, someone like that, and there were Bonham-Carters. There were a few of these sort of people with double-barrel names who I would say 'Hi' to but they were generally tripping or a little bit too out of it, actually, for my liking. I liked to sit and giggle and get a bit stoned and then go home. They wanted to stay the week – often. For me, at that time, the limit was joints. Later it moved to coke, but that was later, shortly before *Sgt. Pepper*. I was introduced to coke through Robert, who was messing around in the upper echelons of drugs, including heroin.

By 1966 the crowd at Robert's included a complete cross-section of the London scene; everyone from Sid Caesar, the American comedian, then famous for the film *It's a Mad Mad Mad Mad World*, to the screenwriter Terry Southern, then in London for the making of *Casino Royale*. Keith Richards, Brian Jones and Anita Pallenberg could often be found lounging in their crushed velvet and antique lace on Robert's day beds. Photographers, artists, musicians and old school friends sampled Robert's drugs and disported themselves upon his antique rugs. School chums included the Ninth Marquess of Londonderry, who played drums at Eton and whose wife Nicolette was one of the last débutantes to be presented to the Queen.

They all gathered at Mount Street, in the kind of social mix of East End photographers and West End aristocrats that so characterised the sixties. As far as Robert was concerned, background didn't matter as long as the person was someone special. Christopher: 'Robert was a "principal only" person. He wasn't interested in people who were appendages of somebody else. He really wasn't interested in the also-rans, people who were quietly going along doing something. They had to have some sort of star quality, even if it wasn't visible, it had to be something there.'

PAUL: I didn't necessarily know everyone there but I was one of the crowd and I would just sit with whoever I knew, in my corner of the room. With Robert's thing of course there would be gayness. But there was no open gayness, if there was to be gayness it would be a quiet phone call that Robert would go and take in the bedroom or something. That was one of the good things, actually, because I knew he was gay and he knew I wasn't gay so we were quite safe in our own sexuality, we could talk to each other. Actually I remember one of the most touching conversations we had was about his mum and dad. I said, 'My mum died when I was young but I think my dad's great. He's a real fine man and I've got a lot of respect for him and I'm not ashamed to admit it.' Feeling slight peer pressure as I did admit it. And he said, 'Well uh uh uhg. I feel the same way about my mother. I love my parents!' and we had a little moment where we both admitted we loved our parents, which then was not the kind of thing you did. I don't think I ever had it with the Beatles, it certainly was not a common thing.

Robert clearly orchestrated his evenings to ensure that guests like Paul didn't encounter anyone or anything that might alienate them: for they were, after all, potential customers as well.

CHRISTOPHER GIBBS: Robert was a sort of catalyst figure to all those people. He netted them and it was fairly effortless. They were well ready to be netted and they thought it was great fun, or sensed it was the hippest scene around and things would be revealed which were quite unfamiliar territory and very intriguing and all that, and I don't think they were disappointed. Also I think Robert did try and sell them things, too, and I certainly think Paul bought some very good things from him.

Paul saw a lot of Robert during 1966 and in the period leading up to the release of *Sgt. Pepper* in 1967.

PAUL: The way Robert lived, which became the way I lived for a couple of years and which I now figure for a rather aristocratic way of life, would be that he'd ring early in the day and say, 'What are we doing for dinner tonight?' It all hinged round dinner. Once he'd had dinner fixed, then he could fill in the rest of the day. It all worked around the event. Robert generally liked to eat down Chelsea: King's Road, Fulham Road area. The San Lorenzo, the Trattoria.

As well as dinner or hanging out at Mount Street, Paul would often put in an appearance at the gallery. 'Once I got to know Robert, a nice thing would be going to the gallery and helping install an exhibition. Just sit around and smoke a bit of pot while somebody else was installing the exhibition. Helping. Play a little music for him. At Indica we did a lot of that too and a lot of fun we had.'

Through Robert Fraser, Paul got to meet many of the artists and film-makers who passed through London, one of whom was the leading New Wave Italian film-maker Michelangelo Antonioni, director of *L'Avventura*, *La Notte* and *L'Eclisse*. Paul: 'I remember the word around town was "There's this guy who's paying money for people to come and get stoned at some place in Chelsea", and of course in our crowd that spread like wildfire. It was Antonioni. He was doing *Blow-Up* and everyone was being paid, like blood donors, to smoke pot.' It was April 1966, and Antonioni was using Christopher Gibbs's exquisite apartment on Cheyne Walk, overlooking Chelsea Bridge, as the set for his orgy scene. Beautiful long-haired people in tattered lace and velvet sat around on Moroccan cushions, leaning against medieval tapestries and carved screens as Antonioni, out-of-place in his light-blue Italian suit, tried not to destroy the atmosphere with his lights and cameras.

Christopher took Antonioni round to visit Robert Fraser at a time when Paul happened to be there.

> He was just there at Robert's one evening. And Keith Richards and myself just happened to be there, and I'd brought some little home movies of mine. I used to have a projector that would flick pictures very slowly: click, click, click. So instead of 25 frames a second, a cat would just move flip, flop, flip, and we'd play sitar music or Beethoven or Albert Ayler, who was a great favourite. It was very very slow but it created a hypnotic mantra kind of effect. I showed Antonioni these movies and he was quite interested. They lasted about quarter of an hour, it was really a five-minute flick but we showed it so slow.

The Beatles used to rent their own film projectors so that they didn't have to brave the cinema crowds. Robert was fascinated and immediately picked up on the idea.

> PAUL: It was a showbizzy thing which came from more the Hampstead crowd. You'd rent a movie from a movie house and you'd have an evening for your children, 'We're showing *Jason and the Argonauts* tonight.' Ringo used to do it a lot, every night he'd just hire a movie. Robert rather liked that and turned it more into an art thing. So he would hire Bruce Connor's *A Movie*, Kenneth Anger, he'd pull in the harder West Coast stuff. I liked it, it was very liberating.

In September of that year, Robert had his first serious brush with the law. He put on a show of collages and drawings by the American pop artist Jim Dine, assisted in some cases by Eduardo Paolozzi. But a retired general from Weybridge, making his way down Duke Street, found that by peering through the window of the gallery he could just discern a collage of a graffitied gift-wrapped penis, one of Dine's comments on Swinging London. The outraged general went to the police and the gallery was raided. The police removed twenty-one Dine drawings and closed the exhibition. Robert was prosecuted and appeared before the Marlborough Street Magistrates' Court charged under the Vagrancy Act on the grounds that the Dine exhibition could be seen from the street. (The Vagrancy Act was designed to stop veterans from the Napoleonic Wars from displaying their wounds on the street as beggars.) In court Robert was unrepentant. Detective-Sergeant Beale, who led the raid and brought the charges, claimed to have been shocked and outraged. Robert replied, 'I'm certainly not bothered by the opinion of a tuppeny-ha'penny policeman. I consider these pictures to be as pornographic as Cézanne.' He was fined £20 with 50 guineas costs. The notoriety of the Jim Dine case only gave the gallery more cachet.

In October 1966 Robert put on an exhibition of multiples by Richard Hamilton of Frank Lloyd Wright's Guggenheim Museum in New York. Paul helped hang the show and bought one of the pieces. He also arranged for John Lennon to come to the opening, which was possibly the first time that Robert and John met. Several years later Robert was to show some of John's work.

From the day it opened, the Robert Fraser Gallery had been a critical success but there were always problems with money. Robert had always depended on someone else's money or bank guarantee, and the gallery stock usually belonged to someone else. There were always a lot of things on consignment as it would have been impossible to survive on selling from a monthly solo show. The big problem was that Robert rarely paid anyone so he was always having to find new people to borrow stock from. His artists suffered the most and many of them left him because he did not pay them for work he had sold.

> CHRISTOPHER GIBBS: The thing one never remembers about Robert is that he was capable, on a fairly regular basis, of doing the most terrible things to you. Anything that was to do with money, you'd be screaming and biting your lip and rolling about on the floor and saying, 'I'm never going to see this creep again!', and then three months later you'd have completely forgotten the crime, which hadn't been cleared up, it was still there. There was a litter of corpses all the way through one's relationship with Robert. Quite amazing things he used to do. And he would look at you, if you asked him to pay, look at you very startled and outraged, you know.

Paul was one of those Robert touched up for money from time to time. 'I'd lend him a bit of money here and there and he wouldn't give it me back. He was a bit notorious with money, Robert.' The artist

Brian Clarke, who would be Robert's best friend through the late seventies and eighties, also had financial run-ins with him:

> There's a lot of artists think that Robert was a crook. And I know better than a lot of people about this because Robert and I did more deals than any of his other artists ever did. And he always intended to pay, but sometimes he didn't get round to it. I should have seen the writing on the wall the first night Robert took me for dinner. He took me to Soho and we were walking past a restaurant when a Chinese chef ran out into the street in Gerrard Street with a cleaver and he pinned Robert by the throat against the wall. He held the cleaver over him and said, 'You don't pay me my money, I split your head!' Robert pushed him out of the way, grabbed hold of me by the collar and said, 'Leg it!' and we went running down the street. Then finally we stopped and Robert said, 'He must be mad. I've never seen that man before in my life.' And I believed it! And of course it was just one of many restaurateurs that wanted to kill Robert.
>
> He was terribly grand. He told me the proudest moment of his life was when he got his first chequebook and issued all sixty cheques in twenty-four hours and they all bounced. He was so cavalier with money and it did get infuriating.

The money went on boys and an expensive heroin habit. Robert had been hooked since 1965 and, like many junkies, was keen to get others to try it. There was a lot of heroin around at the time, both on the aristocratic Chelsea scene and in the rock world. Pure heroin was available on prescription in Britain and there were doctors all over Mayfair who were happy to prescribe. Heroin jacks cost £1 each: cheap unless you were getting through twenty a day, as Robert was at the height of his addiction. (The average wage at the time was £15 a week.) It would have been impossible for Paul not to have been exposed to it.

> PAUL: I was very frightened of drugs, having a nurse mother, so I was always cautious, thank God as it turned out, because I would be in rooms with guys who would say, 'Do you want to sniff a little heroin?' and I would say, 'Well, just a little.' I did some with Robert Fraser, and some of the boys in the Stones who were doing things like that. I always refer to it as walking

through a minefield, and I was lucky because had anyone hit me with a real dose that I loved, I would have been a heroin addict.

Robert Fraser once said to me, 'Heroin is not addictive. There's no problem with heroin addiction, even if it is addictive, you've just got to have a lot of money. The problem with heroin is when you can't pay for it.' Which of course is absolute bullshit! You're a junkie, of course you are. This was the way he put it to me and for a second I was almost taken in but then my northern savvy kicked in and said, 'Now don't go for all of this. This is all very exotic and romantic but don't go for all of it.' There was always a little corner, at the back of my brain, that 'knock! knock! knock!' on the door – 'Stop!'

A lot of his friends messed around with heroin. A lot of his lords and ladies were heroin addicts and had been for many many years. And give Robert his due, he knew I wasn't that keen. He knew I wasn't a nutter for that kind of stuff. So I did sniff heroin with him once, but I said afterwards, 'I'm not sure about this, man. It didn't really do anything for me,' and he said, 'In that case, I won't offer you again.' And I didn't take it again. I was often around it when they'd all be doing it. They'd repair to the toilet and I'd say, 'I'm all right, thanks, no.' One of the most difficult things about that period was the peer pressure to do that.

Cavendish Avenue

In 1965, Paul had begun looking for a place of his own in central London. One of the problems was that he wanted a freehold property, whereas much of central London was only available on long leases, at the end of which the building reverted to the landowner.

I'd looked at a house in Chester Terrace, because with the Beatle money I could afford a good big house. Well, I got blocked there by Jack Hylton, who said, 'We don't want this kind ... the fans'll be around all the time.' The irony of it! A bloody bandleader saying, 'We don't want 'im here. We don't want musicians, trash, cabaret ...' But he was right. There were fans. So I looked at the other end of Regent's Park where Harold Pinter had a

house. It was great looking at all this amazing real estate. It
improved my knowledge of London buildings.

So when I moved it was to St John's Wood, but it was in the
middle of London, I still was enthralled with London. London
to me was the setting for all the Dickens I ever read. St John's
Wood was where they dropped off their mistresses in their
carriages. I loved the sense of history and so I was eager to stay
there, to be near the theatre, to be near everything. Really the
only reason we moved to the country was to bring the kids up.

He found a three-storey Regency house in Cavendish Avenue,
hidden away behind Lord's Cricket Ground in a quiet residential
street with an original Victorian pillarbox which leaned at a slight
angle at the corner. The old queen's monogram was thick with official
red paint. The house was set back from the street, protected by a high
wall and large black metal gates. There were steps leading to the front
door, which was flanked by columns. To the side was a garage for
Paul's cars: the Aston Martin and a souped-up Mini with black
windows and a wide wheelbase.

Paul bought the house on 13 April 1965 for £40,000. He hired
John and Marina Adams to fix up the place. Marina was John
Dunbar's elder sister, and her and her husband's first job as architects
had been the carpentry in Peter Asher's room. Paul loved Wimpole
Street, so it was only natural that he would use the same people,
people that he knew. 'It was the strangest briefing I've ever had,' said
John Adams. 'Paul said he wanted to have the smell of cabbage
coming up from the basement, which was obviously something he
associated with the Asher house.' Though he was a millionaire, he
was unused to spending money on something like property and
initially wanted to spend only £5,000 to do up the house. In the end it
cost £20,000 and his greatest extravagance was the Victorian
streetlamp he had installed in the front drive.

Work on the house took much longer than expected but eventually,
in late March 1966, Paul was able to move in. His possessions were
brought over from Wimpole Street and as a thank-you present for
having him live there for two and a half years, Paul had the outside of
Wimpole Street decorated.

Wimpole Street remained very much the model, and in the
beginning, Cavendish Avenue had a similar feel to the Ashers'. John

Dunbar: 'There was a kind of salon round at the Ashers', there were three kids, and they had a lot of people around all the time. Cavendish Avenue was kind of like Wimpole Street. Obviously with a lot more room and it was Paul's own place.' At Wimpole Street he had never been able to entertain his friends in privacy, or reciprocate when people invited them to dinner except by taking them to a restaurant. Paul began life in Cavendish Avenue with a series of dinner parties and people round for lunch or afternoon tea.

Tea, with sandwiches and a large cake, was served by the housekeeper in the living room, a light, airy room taking up the whole back of the house. French windows opened on to a terrace and a flight of stone steps led to the long, tree-filled garden. A low bookcase ran along one wall to the open fireplace and the wall above it slowly filled with Magrittes and eventually housed one of the two drum faces made for the *Sgt. Pepper* cover; the one Paul has differs slightly from the one eventually used. An enormous prototype videotape recorder, one of five given to the Beatles and Brian Epstein by the BBC for them to try out, stood next to an experimental BBC colour monitor. A few hours of colour television each week, on one channel only, was introduced in Britain in July 1967 (just in time for that year's Wimbledon – Paul's Aunty Jin came to stay and though he offered her Centre Court tickets to Wimbledon, she preferred to stay home and watch the tennis on colour television). Paul liked to tune it away from the two available channels to receive colour static.

In the corner near the French windows stood a tambour, an Indian drone instrument. In his storage room in the basement there were wooden statues, great carved bedheads and other items picked up when the Beatles made a three-day stop-over in India in 1966 on their way home from Manila. Next to the tambour was the Takis sculpture made from two aircraft wing lights welded to tank antennas that Paul bought from the Takis show at Indica Gallery in November 1966. Paul: 'People used to think it was a burglar alarm. We used to call it Peter and Gordon because one was a red light, and the other with a white light was a bit taller.' The lights clicked on and off at intervals. It was part of a series known as *Signals* which utilised industrial objects and forms. To turn mechanical and military paraphernalia into objects of beauty had a particular appeal to the anti-materialistic, anti-military sixties generation. The transformation of military uniforms into the psychedelic costumes of Sergeant Pepper's Lonely Hearts

Club Band or the dragoons' jackets of Jimi Hendrix came from the same sensibility.

The wall opposite the fireplace had a built-in floor-to-ceiling bookcase containing two record players, tape equipment and a concealed movie screen which would appear magically from the top of the unit in the best James Bond style. Unfortunately the screen nearly always stuck and had to be pulled down manually, and one of the record players was inevitably broken.

> PAUL: The stereo didn't work, all our stereos never worked, I remember going to see Jimmy Page, the kind of guy you think, He'll have a great stereo, and his was broken. We were all so flaky. Once one wire came out, that was the end of it. I had electric curtains upstairs in the bedroom, but they were like a Hornby double-O train set, not at all like James Bond which it was supposed to be. They've got a lot to answer for, those James Bond films. My Aston Martin's another.

Also on the ground floor Paul installed an open-plan kitchen and a formal dining room dominated by a huge round steel-faced wall clock.

> PAUL: The clock in Cavendish Avenue is the great big one from outside the Army and Navy Club in Pall Mall. I saw it in *What's On*, which always used to have an 'Antique Corner'. It was on view at Philips auctioneers. And I liked it and had a place made in the wall for it. My thing was that it had just come from one of those big gentlemen's clubs, and in the sixties that sort of stuff was breaking down. We were sweeping it out of the way. So it was something from another era. The clothes became like that too. Biba, uniforms, the vestiges of Empire. It didn't worry me that the Empire was crumbling. I thought it was a good thing. I was very pleased to see all that old regime get out. It was just, wow, I can actually have a clock that has seen that much history! And it's lovely. It's a big one, it's much too big for the room.

Above the fireplace hung a *Monarch of the Glen* commissioned from the British pop artist Peter Blake. The Beatles first met Blake through the photographer Robert Freeman who did the sleeve for *With the Beatles*, and Paul asked Robert Fraser, who represented Peter, to get him one of Peter's pictures. Peter asked him what kind of picture he wanted, because he had done various kinds of paintings, but Paul just said he wanted 'a sort of key one'. They talked and Peter asked Paul what his favourite picture was. On a recent visit to Scotland Paul had bought an old brown picture of Highland cattle in a stream and Peter half-joked, 'You ought to have a nice stag with that, like *Monarch of the Glen* or *Stag at Bay*.' Paul agreed.

Peter traced the original of Sir Edwin Landseer's *Monarch of the Glen* to Messrs John Dewar & Sons Ltd, whisky manufacturers, who have used it in innumerable advertisements. Landseer was Queen Victoria's favourite painter and *Monarch of the Glen* was originally conceived as part of the decorative scheme for refreshment rooms at the House of Lords. When this fell through, it spent fifty years in private collections before Thomas Dewar bought it in 1916. Peter made a more or less straight copy of it; a rare example of his use of an entire image, rather than collaging different pop elements. In the corner, using his signature stencilling, Peter wrote 'After "The Monarch of the Glen" by Sir Edwin Landseer. Peter Blake 1966.' Later he received a postcard from Paul saying, 'Picture is nice but the lettering is not – would you take it off?' but Peter refused.

> PAUL: I didn't like the lettering which he put in the bottom corner, I thought it was such a good painting it stood on its own. I thought this rather spoiled it, having to say 'After Sir Edwin Landseer' but of course it's the Pop Art, it's what makes it Pop Art now. It's possibly the best bit of the painting. And I've since said to him, 'Well, you were completely right, of course. I was stupid.' I just never had seen that before. I'd never commissioned a picture before. That's the truth of it. It's beautiful, and he did a fantastic job, took forever and ever, as he does, but it was fabulous.

There was a large dining table with an antique lace tablecloth, which was always beautifully set with all the appropriate cutlery, but it had a plastic salt cellar and pepper shaker in the centre. Paul owned silver ones but insisted on using the cheap ones, mainly to annoy the housekeeper, Mrs Kelly, and her husband, who had previously worked for gentry and let it be known, not very subtly, that they regarded their new position as a step down in the world. The husband had initially attempted to continue his role as gentleman's gentleman by laying out Paul's clothes each morning until Paul made it abundantly clear that this was not required. Every time they set the table the silver cruet was laid and each time Paul replaced it with the plastic one. Paul fired them for selling their story to an Australian magazine

The window on the staircase still had its original glass from the 1840s and gave quite a distorted view because the glass was so uneven. Paul insisted that the glass remained untouched when the house was renovated. The master bedroom had a large walk-in cupboard behind the bedhead and was very luxurious.

On the top floor, in what were originally the servants' rooms, Paul had his den, the music room. The music room had a hessian wall, a sixties design fad very popular at the time. With its accumulation of bongos, drums, guitars and other instruments, it became one of the main hanging-out rooms in the house. There were microphones and a Revox A77 tape recorder which Paul used to produce a long-drawn-out echo that made even the stoned bongo playing of his non-musician friends sound terrific. It was here he wrote many of his best-loved songs, seated at the piano, gazing out of his window over the front yard to the big black double gates. 'Penny Lane', 'Getting Better' and 'Hey Jude' were to be written in this music room, and it was here that Paul and John worked on many of the songs for *Sgt. Pepper*, John pacing restlessly round the room in his dirty white sneakers or the two of them laughing uproariously together. It was also where people sometimes just hung out of an evening.

A large chrome Paolozzi sculpture called *Solo* dominated the music room. Paul had bought it from Robert Fraser and he lent it to the Royal Academy for their major Pop Art retrospective in 1990. The Scottish-Italian artist Eduardo Paolozzi, one of the leading figures in the British Pop Art movement, had a previous connection with the Beatles: he taught Stuart Sutcliffe painting at Hamburg State Art College in 1961–1962, after Stuart left the Beatles to live with Astrid Kirchherr. Paul is still in touch with Paolozzi, who is occasionally to be seen at Paul's parties.

One day Paul mentioned to Miles that he wanted the door of the music room's built-in cupboard painted with little scenes in the panels and a decorative border. Miles proposed his friend Peter Simpson as the ideal artist for the job. Paul and Pete reached an agreement and a week or so later the door was delivered to Pete's studio. He spent months on the work, applying layers of gesso and polishing it with a shark's tooth in the correct Renaissance manner before painting each panel in exquisite detail. Pete could not be hurried.

An upright piano painted in an exploding psychedelic rainbow by the design team of Binder, Edwards and Vaughan, stood by the window of the music room. Paul: 'It was a Knight piano that I had them paint, a small upright; they have a short string length, they're more like cabaret pianos but they're very easy, the best of that type. So they did my piano, which is still my magic piano.' Paul had a replica of it made and painted which he used on his World Tour of 1990–91. David Vaughan met Paul through the Guinness heir Tara Browne, who offered to take him round to Paul's and introduce him. 'What's he like as a person?' asked David. 'He's the most intelligent man I've ever met,' Tara told him. They drove over to Cavendish Avenue in Tara's Buick 6, which Binder, Edwards and Vaughan had painted in psychedelic colours. Paul was very impressed by the car and suggested that they might like to paint his upright piano.

David Vaughan had seven years of art college behind him, finishing up at the Slade School of Art in London. David: 'From a very early age I could see angels wrapped round doorways. I wanted public art, mosaics, courtyards with statues, a longing for something that was different from the stark reality I was brought up into; which was absolutely nowt. No culture.' He was a fervent believer in community art so rather than producing easel paintings for the few, he concentrated on customising cars and furniture, painting murals, designing wallpaper and fabrics. 'I wanted to use paint to break down the establishment, that's how we saw it.'

He immediately tried to involve Paul in his plans to redecorate all the youth clubs in the north of England with psychedelic murals. David: 'We had a few rows about it. He used to lecture me, he said, "The trouble with you is that you came down here fighting." I said, "I didn't." He said, "Yes, you did. And about that piano. When will it be ready?"' The piano took a while to customise because it had no back on it. They had to make one from plywood and prepare the surface before painting it with a sunburst. Paul missed his piano and tried to hurry them up.

DAVID: He said, 'I want that piano for tonight.' I said, 'Well, it's ready but you won't be able to use it tonight.' He said 'Why not?' I said 'Because it needs retuning. We've just put a back on it.' 'Ah. Good thinking, good thinking.' He give us a few points for that. So he got his piano back. It was £250. I said, 'It'll be about 300 quid.' He said, 'I've heard that one before!' I said, 'I'm not trying to rip you off just because you've got some loot. I'm just saying, the original quote was without the back. That'll be a bit extra, that's all.' He wouldn't let anybody take advantage of him, and he knew if anybody was trying to pull the wool over his eyes.

David became a frequent visitor to Cavendish Avenue, initially with Tara, then, after the latter's death, alone or with his children. Paul liked children and would sometimes take David's daughter Sadie to nearby London Zoo. Once, when Paul and John Lennon were working in the music room, David took them a cup of tea. David: 'I can still picture the pair of 'em, the look of astonishment on their faces when I walked in with a cup of tea, because nobody ever thought, "Well, these two poor buggers might need a brew." Nobody thought of them like that ...' Despite David's attempts to involve Paul in his plans to change the world, Paul obviously enjoyed his company. He even lent him the keys to his sheep farm in Kintyre, bought in 1966 at his accountant's suggestion as a retreat from the pressures of stardom, and told David to take his kids there for a holiday.

On one occasion Robert brought Andy Warhol and a group of his friends over to visit Paul at Cavendish Avenue. Paul: 'We watched *Empire*, which is something like three hours of one building, which is pretty tough going – it's a good job we were into pot because we couldn't have handled it otherwise! It was one of his very long films. It went on. In fact, if I had seen that coming I would have probably said to Robert, "Oh no, don't let's see that one. Have you got anything else?"'

Paul had been warned that the film would require two projectors so he hired an extra one. He was also told that they must start at exactly the same time, but Andy just casually turned one on and then the other. To Paul it seemed that it didn't really matter if they were in synch.

He was just showing 'em any old way. It was daring but it was laborious to watch. Very very boring. Endlessly boring. I must say it was not a great evening out. The people in the room being bored with you and Andy being enigmatic at the back of it all.

It was nice to have Andy there. He was a very shy, quiet guy. I got the impression he didn't want to say too much in case it came out stupid. I hate to say it but it created an air of incredible mystery. He seemed like a nice bloke. I remember we had dinner at the Baghdad House in Fulham Road. The great attraction there was they let you smoke hash downstairs because it was Baghdad and everything, so we sat around a table and had yoghurt and honey and various Iraqi things.

Mick Jagger often called at Cavendish Avenue and it was Paul and Mick who often checked with each other to make sure that the Beatles and the Stones didn't release a new single within the same few weeks, which would have split sales and jeopardised both their chances of reaching number one. After Marianne Faithfull left John Dunbar in January 1967 to live with Mick at Harley House on Marylebone Road, just across Regent's Park from Paul's house, they would often come to visit Paul together.

> MARIANNE: We would go and see them a lot, but I don't remember him coming to us. Mick always had to come to his house, because he was Paul McCartney and you went to him. Paul never came to us. I was always very curious about how Mick saw him, how Mick felt about him. It was always fun to watch. There was always rivalry there. Not from Paul, none at all. Paul was oblivious, but there was something from Mick. It was good fun. It was like watching a game on the television.

Mick was one of the people who spent time hanging out in the music room upstairs. Paul: 'I believe I turned Mick Jagger on to pot in my little music room at Cavendish Avenue, which is funny because everyone would have thought it would have been the other way round.' It made Paul part of a lineage connecting the sixties youth movement with the American Beat Generation of the forties and fifties; a *noblesa* of potheads descending along the hipster tradition: Mick Jagger was introduced to pot by Paul McCartney, who was introduced to pot by Bob Dylan, who was introduced to pot by Al Aronowitz, who was introduced to pot by Allen Ginsberg, who was introduced to pot by some Puerto Rican sailors in a brothel in New Orleans in 1945.

Mick and Paul discussed the idea of a jointly owned recording studio for the exclusive use of the Beatles and the Stones. At the time it was a great idea which everyone liked, but putting the idea into reality was another matter and it was quietly forgotten. The Stones would later buy their own mobile studio to record their endless tours, and the Beatles eventually built their own studio in Savile Row, but by the time it was finished, the group had broken up. Paul never used it and John Lennon was living in the USA, never to return.

One of the first things Paul did on moving in was buy an Old English sheepdog puppy. He called her Martha, and she became the inspiration for one of Paul's best-loved songs. She grew huge, with tangled hair.

> PAUL: Martha was my first ever pet. I never had a dog or a cat at home. My parents both went out to work, which was why we couldn't have any, even when one terrible day they were giving away free puppies! Just a hundred yards away from where we lived. We came screaming home, my brother and I, 'They're giving 'em away! We can get one if you tell us now, we can go and get one, we've chosen the one we want!' They said, 'You can't have one, son. Me and your mum go out to work and it wouldn't be fair on a dog.' 'We'll look after it, we'll do it.' 'You're at school.' 'Well, we'll come back at lunchtime. Surely?' 'No, no, no.' Crying crying crying. We just couldn't understand because they were free! We could understand not buying one because we weren't that well off, but passing up a freebie puppy! He was quite firm about stuff like that and I suppose he was right.

Paul drove out to get Martha from Ann Davis, a breeder in High Wycombe. The dog was like a huge tangled ball of wool and kept bumping into things because her hair covered her eyes until they tied it up in ribbon. Paul: 'She was a dear pet of mine. I remember John being amazed to see me being so loving to an animal. He said, "I've never seen you like that before." I've since thought, you know, he wouldn't have. It's only when you're cuddling around with a dog that you're in that mode, and she was a very cuddly dog.' Paul has had

Old English sheepdogs ever since, and keeps three at his house in Sussex.

Martha spent a lot of her time snuffling after Thisbe the cat. In Shakespeare's *A Midsummer Night's Dream*, a group of Athenian workmen – the 'mechanicals' – led by Bottom the weaver, attempt to stage a play called *Pyramus and Thisbe*. The Beatles performed a short extract from this play within a play for the Jack Good TV show *Around the Beatles* in May 1964. John played Thisbe, Paul played Pyramus, George was Moonshine and Ringo appeared as Lion. Thisbe was to feature in a number of Paul's home movies, peering round doors and jumping down steps; she was soon joined by three more of her kind.

> PAUL: I had a litter of cats called Jesus, Mary and Joseph. Jesus ran off, Joseph stuck around for a long time, and Mary had kittens. We put the kittens in this little box and I remember me and Brian Jones stayed up all night, looking at the kittens. I got the word 'God' from three symbols on the side of the box: one of them was a moon, the G; O was the sun, and the star was like the D. And somehow it read, 'God'. I had this live-in couple called the Kellys who would wake you up early in the morning like everything was just going normally and we had just stayed up all night and it was like, 'Go away please!' It was just amazing because we were actually watching what went on. Instead of saying, 'Oh yes, we've got kittens, ain't they marvellous? There they are, cuddly cuddly, now I'm going to go and do something important,' we took five hours with these kittens. Now they call it 'Stop and smell the flowers'. They say you should do more things like that in a stressful life.

By the time they moved to Cavendish Avenue, Paul and Jane were growing increasingly apart. In October 1965 Jane had joined the Bristol Old Vic and was deeply involved in her career as an actress. She spent most of her time in Bristol, leaving Paul free to enjoy London as a single man. The majority of Jane's friends were in the theatre. She did not take drugs and clearly felt increasingly alienated from Paul's drug-taking friends. The relationship hung on, in part, *because* they were apart so often: if Jane was in a play, Paul would not see much of her unless he attended a performance, and Paul himself was often out of town, touring with the Beatles or at late-night recording sessions, television recordings, official receptions and other Beatles activities. They really only saw each other properly on special occasions like holidays – skiing in Klosters in March 1966 just before moving into Cavendish Avenue, and in November on safari together in Kenya – when they would reaffirm their relationship; but the underlying trend was apart.

> PAUL: During that period with Jane Asher I learned a lot and she introduced me to a lot of things, but I think inevitably when I moved to Cavendish Avenue, I realised that she and I weren't really going to be the thing we'd always thought we might be. Once or twice we talked about getting married, and plans were afoot but I don't know, something really made me nervous about the whole thing. It just never settled with me, and as that's very important for me, things must feel comfortable for me, I think it's a pretty good gauge if you're lucky enough. You're not always lucky enough, but if they can feel comfortable then there's something very special about that feeling. I hadn't quite managed to be able to get it with Jane.

Magritte

It was not until he had his own house that Paul began collecting art. Robert Fraser took an active role in building Paul's collection. Paul: 'I was very interested in Magritte and Robert was interested in my interest in Magritte and he said, "Well, I know this gallery owner Iolas who's his dealer in Paris."' So, some time early in 1966, Paul and Robert flew to Paris. They checked into the Plaza Athénée on the Avenue Montaigne in the heart of *haute-couture* Paris, one of the most fashionable and snobbish hotels in France.

Going on a trip with Robert caused a few comments from Paul's friends.

> PAUL: Because he was gay, it raised a few small-minded eyebrows and funnily enough, one or two of them were from within the Beatles: 'Hey, man, he's gay, what you going off to Paris with him for? They're gonna talk, you know. Tongues are going to wag.' I said, 'I know tongues are going to wag, but tough shit.' I was secure about my sexuality. I always felt this is

fine, I can hang with whoever I want and it didn't worry me. I mean, we didn't share a room or anything.

I love Paris. I can always go to Paris, it never alters for me, it's my student dream. I'm an artist if I go to Paris; the smell of Gitanes, the women with hair under their arms and the way they've kept the buildings. I can get into all my fantasies.

Alexandre Iolas was an old friend of Robert's from the Paris gay scene and had arranged a small dinner party in their honour at his apartment above his gallery on Boulevard St-Germain.

PAUL: Robert and I went over and had a very pleasant time. Iolas was a very urbane Parisian, a very nice man. There were a couple of other people there, including an older woman, it was very social. Just French friends of Iolas.

He had a couple of Nicholas Monro's free-standing sheep which you used to see in houses in the sixties; people used to have them as sculptures. He had a couple of those and, also by Monro, he had a whacking great rhino, a full-sized rhinocerous, it was a cocktail cabinet. He would open the rhinocerous's side and serve drinks, and we would all go, 'Hah, hah, very funny!' It was like a talking point. And after dinner and a couple of drinks, we wandered downstairs, where the whole place was just full of Magrittes. I was in seventh heaven. He was Magritte's agent and I had my pick of Aladdin's cave. Now being a sensible lad, I only chose two oils. They were about 30 × 40, decent-size pictures, the most expensive of which was £3,000.

I bought a big oil called *Gloria*, which was an upturned carp. When you look sideways at it it looks like a big hooded figure with one eye but when you look the other way at it it's a carp, it's a fish, in the shadows inside a castle keep and outside is the sky and clouds where we all want to be. I bought another, called *The Countess of Monte Cristo*, which is a painting showing a painted bottle alongside two ordinary wine bottles, very Magritte, very Surrealist. I didn't know he painted actual bottles themselves till much later so I thought this was just a joke, the girl is on the bottle. A bottle came up at a studio sale. Paul Simon bought one, I know because I've visited him and seen it.

I wish I'd bought more now but the ones I got were very good. And then over the years I've started to get this and that. It was lovely, lovely to be able to look through them all and looking back I remember I saw *Ceci n'est pas une pipe* (This Is Not a Pipe), one of the new series, which I nearly bought. I liked that a lot. It was the first time I'd heard of it. I liked the whole idea, 'This is not a pipe.' 'Why?' 'It's a painting of a pipe.' 'Oh yes, of course!' That's one of the big things I got from him.

My view now is that he was probably the greatest of the Surrealists. At the time I thought he was damn good but that there were more important Surrealists, but now I don't think there are. Who is there? De Chirico? Dali? I personally don't like their stuff quite as much. Of course we were very into all the legends: how Magritte painted from nine until one and then had his lunch. Robert went to see him with Michael Cooper, and the greatest photograph of Michael Cooper's is of the bell push. It just says 'R. Magritte'.

Magritte died in August 1967 and was survived by his widow Georgette, who in the mid-eighties held a series of studio sales. At the final sale, Linda bought a mixed lot, including Magritte's old double-sided easel, as a Christmas present for Paul, who had started painting himself in 1983. It came with a few blank canvases, some brushes, his palette and a small painting table with a drawer and a shelf. There was an old paints box full of wedges for stretchers, tubes for tablets which originally contained cortisone and other drugs he needed but which he had re-used to store tacks and paperclips. There were even boxes of charcoal labelled '*très mou*', '*dur*' and '*très dur*' in his distinctive cursive hand. Somehow Linda managed to keep it a secret until 25 December.

Paul was delighted.

It was lovely. I use the easel. It was very intimidating the first time, massively intimidating. What was most intimidating was putting one of the canvases on the easel; a beautiful linen canvas with a beige-coloured back whereas I'd mainly used white Winsor & Newton canvases. This was a more pro canvas. A Belgian canvas. I felt I had to paint guys in bowler hats or roses filling rooms or something. Then I thought, What would he have wanted? He would have wanted me to use it. Go to it, my son. Paint it! So I did one of my comic characters and painted away and felt great about it. It got over the block immediately.

I've got his spectacles too. I've recently had the spectacles mended because they are so fabulous, just round horn-rimmed spectacles. I mean, they themselves are icons. And you know what? They work great if I'm ever having trouble with fine print. I was warned by the optician to come back when I was forty-seven. I have been fighting it, I can still read without glasses, but if it's *Middlemarch*, there's an awful lot of words on that page. Or the fine print on certain shampoo bottles, then I have to either borrow Linda's specs or go to Monsieur Magritte's, which work perfectly. It's quite trippy because I'm such an admirer of his.

Magritte was to provide one of the images that are for ever associated with the Beatles.

PAUL: It always seems to have been summer. All the memories seem to be of gardens, leaves in full bloom, grass very long, flies in the air, things humming. And I remember one of those times. I was out in the garden at Cavendish Avenue with a camera team filming Mary Hopkin and we were down by the folly at the bottom of the garden when Robert arrived and was let in by the housekeeper. When we came in he'd gone, but the big door to the garden was open and there on the table in the living room, Robert had propped a Magritte against a vase. A Magritte painting of the big green apple which we were later to use as the Apple.

That's where it all came from, this one painting; a big, beautifully painted green apple in a frame. And written across it, in his beautiful Magritte writing, on one of his lovely brown backgrounds, it says, '*Au revoir.*' Robert knew I'd want it, knew we could come to an arrangement about the money, and he just propped it up there and left. That's conceptual! That's cool. He knew it was safe. He knew we were out there and he didn't want to disturb us, so that was probably Robert's greatest conceptual deed. I still remember the glee of walking in and going, 'Yeah!' That would be a magic moment in anyone's book.

SEVEN

Making the Albums

When the mood of the music changes, the walls of
the city shake.

Plato

Rubber Soul

TWO ALBUMS ABOVE ALL COMPLETED THE BEATLES' TRANSITION FROM A
singles band to studio band: *Rubber Soul* and *Revolver*. There was a
complex maturity in the work; songs like John's 'Nowhere Man' dealt
with lack of self-confidence and Paul's 'I'm Looking Through You'
was no longer a simple love song, but about a problematic
relationship. A playful humour was often in evidence too, and a wide-
ranging experimentation in the musical arrangements: George on
sitar, Paul playing fuzz bass, George Martin's double-speed baroque
piano ... The period of *Rubber Soul* and *Revolver* produced some of
the most beautifully crafted of all the Beatles songs. Both John and
Paul were at peak performance. John may not have been perfectly
happy and 'Help!' may have been a literal cry for help, but compared
to his later insecurities and drug addiction, this was a calm period for
him. These songs are the bedrock on which the Lennon–McCartney
songwriting reputation rests: songs like 'Day Tripper', 'Drive My
Car', 'Norwegian Wood' and 'Paperback Writer', confident songs
written at the height of fame and success, halcyon days when they
were undisputed kings of the rock 'n' roll world.

With each new album, the Beatles further consolidated their
control over their output, at least in Britain. They had a big say in
which tracks to release as singles, had effective approval over cover
art and now took to naming their own albums, usually using a play on

words: *Rubber Soul* was a reference to rubber-soled shoes as well as soul music, whereas *Revolver* did not mean a gun, but something that revolves, like a record. Johnny Dean, editor of *Beatles Monthly*, was with them on the night of 24 June 1966 in a Munich hotel room when they named the latter. At first they had all four wanted to call it *Abracadabra*, but someone had already used it. *Pendulums* and *Fat Man and Bobby* were other ideas. Ringo suggested having a joke with the Rolling Stones by calling it *After Geography* since the Stones had just done *Aftermath!* John proposed *Beatles on Safari* and Paul came up with *Magic Circle*. John changed this to *Four Sides of the Circle* and *Four Sides of the Eternal Triangle*, which somehow led them to *Revolver*.

Described by George Martin as 'the first album to present a new, growing Beatles to the world', *Rubber Soul* was recorded in October and November 1965. It opens with 'Drive My Car', a humorous rocker with an ingenious role-reversal that is typical of John and Paul's songs of the period. Paul arrived at John's house in Weybridge with the tune in his head but with very bad lyrics.

> PAUL: The lyrics were disastrous and I knew it. Often you just block songs out and words just come into your mind and when they do it's hard to get rid of them. You often quote other songs too and you know you've got to get rid of them, but sometimes it's very difficult to find a more suitable phrase than the one that has insinuated itself into your consciousness. This is one of the songs where John and I came nearest to having a dry session. The lyrics I brought in were something to do with golden rings, which is always fatal. 'Rings' is fatal anyway, 'rings' always rhymes with 'things' and I knew it was a bad idea. I came in and I said, 'These aren't good lyrics but it's a good tune.' The tune was nice, the tune was there, I'd done the melody. Well, we tried, and John couldn't think of anything, and we tried and eventually it was, 'Oh let's leave it, let's get off this one.' 'No, no. We can do it, we can do it.' So we had a break, maybe had a cigarette or a cup of tea, then we came back to it, and somehow it became 'drive my car' instead of 'gold-en rings', and then it was wonderful because this nice tongue-in-cheek idea came and suddenly there was a girl there, the heroine of the story, and the

story developed and had a little sting in the tail like 'Norwegian Wood' had, which was 'I actually haven't got a car, but when I get one you'll be a terrific chauffeur'. So to me it was LA chicks, 'You can be my chauffeur', and it also meant 'you can be my lover'. 'Drive my car' was an old blues euphemism for sex, so in the end all is revealed. Black humour crept in and saved the day. It wrote itself then. I find that very often, once you get the good idea, things write themselves. So that was my idea and John and I wrote the words, so I'd go 70-30 on that to me.

The same black humour crept into 'Norwegian Wood', which ends with the girl's flat being burned. John had begun it in February 1965 while on a skiing holiday with Cynthia and George Martin and his wife Judy in St Moritz in Switzerland. When he returned, Paul came over for a writing session in John's music room in the attic at Kenwood. This is another example of a song more or less writing itself, beginning with a classic Beatles play on words: 'having' a girl and being 'had'.

PAUL: I came in and he had this first stanza, which was brilliant: 'I once had a girl, or should I say, she once had me.' That was all he had, no title, no nothing. I said, 'Oh yes, well, ha, we're there.' And it wrote itself. Once you've got the great idea, they do tend to write themselves, providing you know how to write songs. So I picked it up at the second verse, it's a story. It's him trying to pull a bird, it was about an affair. John told *Playboy* that he hadn't the faintest idea where the title came from but I do. Peter Asher had his room done out in wood, a lot of people were decorating their places in wood. Norwegian wood. It was pine really, cheap pine. But it's not as good a title, 'Cheap Pine', baby. So it was a little parody really on those kind of girls who when you'd go to their flat there would be a lot of Norwegian wood. It was completely imaginary from my point of view but in John's it was based on an affair he had. This wasn't the décor of someone's house, we made that up. So she makes him sleep in the bath and then finally in the last verse I had this idea to set the Norwegian wood on fire as revenge, so we did it very tongue in cheek. She led him on, then said, 'You'd better sleep in the bath.' In our world the guy had to have some sort of revenge. It could have meant I lit a fire to keep myself warm, and wasn't the décor of her house wonderful? But it didn't, it meant I burned the fucking place down as an act of revenge, and then we left it there and went into the instrumental.

George had become very interested in Indian music and it was his first sitar solo. It's in waltz tempo 3/4 time, it's a quirky song, like an Irish folk song; John liked that, we liked that. So it ended up on the session with George's sitar on it. It's 60-40 to John because it's John's idea and John's tune. But I filled out lyrically and had the idea to set the place on fire, so I take some sort of credit. And the middle was mine, those middle eights, John never had his middle eights.

There is another play on words in the title of Paul's 'You Won't See Me', which uses the popular subject of a young woman's refusal to answer a young man's phone calls.

PAUL: Normally I write on a guitar and have full chords, or on the piano and have full chords, but this was written around two little notes, a very slim phrase, a two-note progression that I had very high on the first two strings of the guitar: the E and the B strings. I had it up on the high E position, and I just let the note on the B string descend a semitone at a time, and kept the top note the same, and against that I was playing a descending chromatic scale. Then I wrote the tune for 'You Won't See Me' against it. I changed it but it was still a two-note thing but instead of it going down I pushed it up and then came down again; just a slight variation. It was 100 per cent me as I recall, but I am always quite happy to give John a credit because there's always a chance that on the session he might have said, 'That'd be better.' To me it was very Motown-flavoured. It's got a James Jameson feel. He was the Motown bass player, he was fabulous, the guy who did all those great melodic bass lines. It was him, me, and Brian Wilson who were doing melodic bass lines at that time, all from completely different angles, LA, Detroit and London, all picking up on what each other did.

John wrote 'Nowhere Man' after a night out. He told *Playboy*: 'I'd spent five hours that morning trying to write a song that was meaningful and good, and I finally gave up and lay down. Then "Nowhere Man" came, words and music, the whole damn thing, as I lay down.' When Paul arrived at Kenwood, John was still asleep on the *chaise longue* in his glass-sided den.

> PAUL: When I came out to write with him the next day, he was kipping on the couch, very bleary-eyed. It was really an anti-John song, written by John. He told me later, he didn't tell me then, he said he'd written it about himself, feeling like he wasn't going anywhere. I think actually it was about the state of his marriage. It was in a period where he was a bit dissatisfied with what was going on; however, it led to a very good song. He treated it as a third-person song, but he was clever enough to say, 'Isn't he a bit like you and me?' 'Me' being the final word. That was one of John's better ones.

'The Word' was the first of the Beatles overtly love and peace songs; the word in question was 'Love', which in 1965 made it one of the first hippie anthems. It was a song that John and Paul wrote together at Kenwood. It was their normal practice to scribble songs down, with many annotations and changes, and afterwards make a fair copy each. After writing 'The Word' they rolled a joint, and instead of their usual lyric sheet, they produced a psychedelic illuminated manuscript using coloured crayons.

Paul: 'We smoked a bit of pot, then we wrote out a multicoloured lyric sheet, the first time we'd ever done that. We normally didn't smoke when we were working. It got in the way of songwriting because it would just cloud your mind up – "Oh, shit, what are we doing?" It's better to be straight. But we did this multicolour thing.' When Yoko Ono first arrived in Britain, before she met John, she turned up at Paul's house asking for manuscripts to give to John Cage for his fiftieth birthday. Cage collected musical scores. Paul told her that he always kept his original manuscripts, but not long afterwards she asked John to give her one and he chose the multicoloured fair copy of 'The Word' as a birthday gift. It is reproduced in John Cage's *Notations*, a selection of the scores he had been collecting for the Foundation of Contemporary Performance Arts to show the diversity of notation in modern music.

Also on *Rubber Soul* was 'Michelle', destined to become one of the most played songs on the radio of all time. It was one of Paul's oldest melodies, written when he was still at the Liverpool Institute.

PAUL: 'Michelle' was a tune that I'd written in Chet Atkins' finger-pickin' style. There is a song he did called 'Trambone' with a repetitive top line, and he played a bass line whilst playing a melody. This was an innovation for us; even though classical guitarists had played it, no rock 'n' roll guitarists had played it. The first person we knew to use finger-pickin' technique was Chet Atkins, and Colin Manley, one of the guys in the Remo Four in Liverpool, who used to play it very well and we all used to stop and admire him. Later John learned how to do it folk-style from Donovan or Gypsy Dave, which he used on 'Julia'. I never learned it. But based on Atkins's 'Trambone', I wanted to write something with a melody and a bass line on it, so I did. I just had it as an instrumental in C.

There used to be a guy called Austin Mitchell who was one of John's tutors at art school and he used to throw some pretty good all-night parties. You could maybe pull girls there, which was the main aim of every second; you could get drinks, which was another aim; and you could generally put yourself about a bit. I remember sitting around there, and my recollection is of a black turtleneck sweater and sitting very enigmatically in the corner, playing this rather French tune. I used to pretend I could speak French, because everyone wanted to be like Sacha Distel, or Juliette Greco was actually who you wanted to be like, even though she was a girl, because she had the feel of it all: that French existential thing, they were all in turtlenecks and black and down the bohemian clubs. It was bohemia! So I used to sit around and murmur. It was my Maurice Chevalier meets Juliette Greco moment: me trying to be enigmatic to make girls think, 'Who's that very interesting French guy over in the corner?' I would literally use it as that, and John knew this was one of my ploys.

Years later, John said, 'D'you remember that French thing you used to do at Mitchell's parties?' I said yes. He said, 'Well, that's a good tune. You should do something with that.' We were always looking for tunes, because we were making lots of albums by then and every album you did needed fourteen songs, and then there were singles in between, so you needed a lot of material. So I did.

Paul had kept up his friendship with Ivan Vaughan, the man who introduced him to John. Ivan and Paul had much in common; they were even born on the same day in Liverpool. Ivan's wife Jan taught French, and one day when they were visiting Paul at Wimpole Street, he asked Jan for some help with the lyrics.

PAUL: I said, 'I like the name Michelle. Can you think of anything that rhymes with Michelle, in French?' And she said, '*Ma belle.*' I said, 'What's that mean?' 'My beauty.' I said, 'That's good, a love song, great.' We just started talking, and I said, 'Well, those words go together well, what's French for that? Go together well.' '*Sont les mots qui vont très bien ensemble.*' I said, 'All right, that would fit.' And she told me a bit how to pronounce it, so that was it. I got that off Jan, and years later I sent her a cheque around. I thought I better had because she's virtually a co-writer on that. From there I just pieced together the verses.

The other interesting point was there's a very jazzy chord in it: 'Michelle, ma *belle.*' That second chord. That was a chord that was used twice in the Beatles: once to end George's solo on 'Till There Was You' and again when I used it in this. It was a chord shown to us by a jazz guitarist called Jim Gretty who worked behind the counter at Frank Hessey's where we used to buy our instruments on the never-never in Liverpool. So Jim Gretty showed us this one great ham-fisted jazz chord, bloody hell! George and I learned it off him.

John had been listening to Nina Simone's 'I Put a Spell on You', which repeats the line, 'I love you, I love you ...' and when Paul hummed the song through to John, he suggested using those words, with the emphasis changed to the word 'love', as a middle eight.

PAUL: The 'I love you, I love you, I love you' wasn't in the original. The original was just the chorus. That sounds like Nina Simone, I can see that. I'll give him ten points for that.

I remember 'Michelle' particularly. Because it was only on four little tracks, it was very easy to mix. There were no decisions to make, we'd made them all in the writing and in the recording. We would mix them, and it would take half an hour, maybe. Then it would go up on a shelf, in a quarter-inch tape box. And that was it. That was the only thing we ever did to 'Michelle'. We never remixed it for dance, we never did a funky mix. That was the end of it and it's still around and it's still a popular song, still clocking up numbers on the little tachometer or whatever it is they've got: four million broadcast performances. From that one little thing. Minimum effort, minimum expense, minimum everything. It's lovely, absolutely the best way to do it. I advise young groups these days, write 'em great, rehearse them up so you know 'em, have a good relationship between yourselves and go in and record them the simplest possible way that you can, mix it that day and have done with it. I wish I could take my own advice.

I saw David Bailey down the Ad Lib not long after it came out and he said, ''Ere, that "Michelle". It *is* tongue in cheek, you *are* joking with that, aren't you?' He thought it was a parody of a French song, which in many ways it is. He thought that was funny.

I said, 'Fuck off!', quite taken aback that he thought it was a joke. I was very insulted. But I knew what he meant

When asked what his contribution to 'What Goes On' was, Ringo replied, 'About five words.' It was an old song written by John before they had a recording contract but which they never played live. Since it was important to have Ringo sing at least one song on each album, John dusted it off and Paul and Ringo wrote a new middle eight for it.

'Girl' was composed during one of Paul and John's writing sessions out at Kenwood.

PAUL: It was John's original idea but it was very much co-written. I remember writing 'the pain and pleasure' and 'a man must break his back', it was all very working-on-the-chain-gang. My main memory is that John wanted to hear the breathing, wanted it to be very intimate, so George Martin put a special compressor on the voice, then John dubbed it.

It was always amusing to see if we could get a naughty word on the record, 'fish and finger pie', 'prick teaser', 'tit tit tit tit'. The Beach Boys had a song out where they'd done 'la la la la' and we loved the innocence of that and wanted to copy it, but not use the same phrase. So we were looking around for another phrase, so it was 'dit dit dit dit', which we decided to change in our waggishness to 'tit tit tit tit', which is virtually indistinguishable from 'dit dit dit dit'. And it gave us a laugh. It was to get some light relief in the middle of this real big career that we were forging. If we could put in something that was a little bit subversive then we would. George Martin might say, 'Was that "dit dit" or "tit tit" you were singing?' 'Oh, "dit dit", George, but it does sound a bit like that, doesn't it?' Then we'd get in the car and break down laughing. So I credit that as being towards John but I put quite a bit in. It wasn't one that he came in with fully finished at all.

'I'm Looking Through You' was a song provoked by the difficulties of Paul's stormy relationship with Jane, who insisted on putting her acting career first and continued to spend most of her time in Bristol. Written in Paul's attic room at Wimpole Street, surrounded by the evidence of Jane and her family, the lyrics are unusually specific and personal for Paul, who normally preferred to universalise his songs.

> PAUL: As is one's wont in relationships, you will from time to time argue or not see eye to eye on things, and a couple of the songs around this period were that kind of thing. This one I remember particularly as me being disillusioned over her commitment. She went down to the Bristol Old Vic quite a lot around this time. Suffice it to say that this one was probably related to that romantic episode and I was seeing through her façade. And realising that it wasn't quite all that it seemed. I would write it out in a song and then I've got rid of the emotion. I don't hold grudges so that gets rid of that little bit of emotional baggage. I remember specifically this one being about that, getting rid of some emotional baggage. 'I'm looking through you, and you're *not there!*' I think it's totally my song. I don't remember any of John's assistance.

Of all the songs jointly credited to Lennon and McCartney, there are only two that are the subject of contention. In interviews given to *Hit Parader, Newsweek, Playboy, Rolling Stone* and various other magazines, John described his role in the creation of most of the Beatles' songs, though his comments were not always consistent. Paul's recollections in this book were made without reference to

John's published comments and in only two cases was there substantial disagreement: on 'In My Life' and 'Eleanor Rigby'.

PAUL: I'll give my memories of writing 'In My Life'. I arrived at John's house for a writing session and he had the very nice opening stanzas of the song. As many of our songs were, it was the first pangs of nostalgia for Liverpool; not that we longed to return there but, like everyone, you look at your youth, as Maharishi used to say, through a golden glass, and it looks much better than it was. 'Remember those times when we used to walk with guitars and strum at night?' and they were good but they sound much better in retrospect, it was just walking along the street with a guitar. Once the Beatles had happened, us two little waifs walking along strumming quite openly on the street suddenly becomes a romantic legend, something they would definitely not miss in a film. That was what John had. But as I recall, he didn't have a tune to it, and my recollection, I think, is at variance with John's. I said, 'Well, you haven't got a tune, let me just go and work on it.' And I went down to the half-landing, where John had a Mellotron, and I sat there and put together a tune based in my mind on Smokey Robinson and the Miracles. Songs like 'You've Really Got a Hold on Me' and 'Tears of a Clown' had really been a big influence. You refer back to something you've loved and try and take the spirit of that and write something new. So I recall writing the whole melody. And it actually does sound very like me, if you analyse it. I was obviously working to lyrics. The melody's structure is very me. So my recollection is saying to John, 'Just go and have a cup of tea or something. Let me be with this for ten minutes on my own and I'll do it.' And with the inspiration of Smokey and the Miracles, I tried to keep it melodic but a bit bluesy, with the minors and little harmonies, and then my recollection is going back up into the room and saying, 'Got it, great! Good tune, I think. What d'you think?' John said, 'Nice,' and we continued working with it from then, using that melody and filling out the rest of the verses. As usual, for these co-written things, he often just had the first verse, which was always enough: it was the direction, it was the signpost and it was the inspiration for the whole song. I hate the word but it was the template. We wrote it, and in my memory we tagged on the introduction, which I think I thought up. I was imagining the intro of a Miracles record, and to my mind the phrases on guitar are very much Smokey and the Miracles. So it was John's original inspiration, I think my melody, I think my guitar riff. I don't want to be categorical about this. But that's my recollection. We then finished it off and it was a fine song which John sang.

John told *Playboy*: 'Paul helped me write the middle-eight melody. The whole lyrics were already written before Paul even heard it. In "In My Life" his contribution melodically was the harmony and the middle-eight itself.' An existing manuscript of an early version shows that the lyrics went through a tremendous number of changes, with very few lines remaining from the original text. Commenting on Paul's claim to have written the music, the musicologist Ian MacDonald observes in *Revolution in the Head*: 'its angular verticality, spanning an entire octave in typically wide – and difficult – leaps, certainly shows more of his touch than Lennon's, despite fitting the latter's voice snugly. (As for the middle eight, there isn't one, the song alternating between its verse and an extended chorus.)'

Paul: 'I find it very gratifying that out of everything we wrote, we only appear to disagree over two songs.'

Of the remaining songs on *Rubber Soul*, 'Wait' was written in the Bahamas, during the filming of *Help!*, and was originally intended for the soundtrack album. The Beatles had a little house near the sea where they hung out whenever they had a day off from filming or if there was time between shoots. One of the people they met in the Bahamas was the actor Brandon de Wilde, a former child star who appeared in *Shane* in 1953 at the age of eleven as well as a TV series called *Jamie*. He managed to make the transition to adult roles and starred in *Hud* with Paul Newman in 1963. He was a member of the Peter Fonda, Dennis Hopper group of Hollywood hard-livers who liked to hang out and get stoned. He died in a car crash in June 1972 and was the subject of Gram Parsons's moving requiem 'In My Hour of Darkness'. Paul: 'He was a nice guy who was fascinated by what we did. A sort of Brat Pack actor. We chatted endlessly, and I seem to remember writing "Wait" in front of him, and him being interested to see it being written. I think it was my song. I don't remember John collaborating too much on it, although he could have.'

John's 'Run for Your Life', written at Kenwood, was probably more about himself and his own affairs than macho advice to a two-timing girlfriend. It was based on the line 'I'd rather see you dead, little girl, than see you with another man', which John took from Elvis Presley's 1955 'Baby, Let's Play House'. It was one of his confessional songs, transposed from first to third person to veil the message. Paul: 'John was always on the run, running for his life. He was married; whereas none of my songs would have "catch you with another man". It was never a concern of mine, at all, because I had a girlfriend and I would go with other girls, it was a perfectly open relationship so I wasn't as worried about that as John was. A bit of a macho song. It was largely John's.'

The single 'Paperback Writer' was the fourth song recorded during the sessions for *Revolver* and fits perfectly between the two albums. It even has a nod to the Beach Boys' *Pet Sounds* in its complex vocal harmonies. Paul had the idea for the song while driving out to John's house.

PAUL: You knew, the minute you got there, cup of tea and you'd sit and write, so it was always good if you had a theme. I'd had a thought for a song and somehow it was to do with the *Daily Mail* so there might have been an article in the *Mail* that morning about people writing paperbacks. Penguin paperbacks was what I really thought of, the archetypal paperback.

I arrived at Weybridge and told John I had this idea of trying to write off to a publishers to become a paperback writer, and I said, 'I think it should be written like a letter.' I took a bit of paper out and I said it should be something like 'Dear Sir or Madam, as the case may be ...' and I proceeded to write it just like a letter in front of him, occasionally rhyming it. And John, as I recall, just sat there and said, 'Oh, that's it,' 'Uhuh,' 'Yeah.' I remember him, his amused smile, saying, 'Yes, that's it, that'll do.' Quite a nice moment: 'Hmm, I've done right! I've done well!' And then we went upstairs and put the melody to it. John and I sat down and finished it all up, but it was tilted towards me, the original idea was mine. I had no music, but it's just a little bluesy song, not a lot of melody. Then I had the idea to do the harmonies and we arranged that in the studio.

The B-side was 'Rain'.

PAUL: 'Rain' was a co-effort with the leaning slightly towards John. I don't think he brought the original idea, just when we sat down to write, he kicked it off. Songs have traditionally treated rain as a bad thing and what we got on to was that it's no bad thing. There's no greater feeling than the rain dripping down your back. The most interesting thing about it wasn't the writing, which was tilted 70-30 to John, but the recording of it.

'Rain' was recorded on 4 April 1966. They played the backing track faster than normal and then slowed the whole thing down so that it dropped a tone, making the bass very low and the drums very heavy. Paul: 'The drums became a giant drum kit. If you slow down a footstep it becomes a giant's footstep, it adds a few tons to the weight of the person. So we got a big, ponderous, thunderous backing and then we worked on top of that as normal, so that it didn't sound like a slowed-down thing, it just had a big ominous noise to it. It was nice, I really enjoyed that one.'

Ringo: 'I think I just played amazing. I was into the snare and the hi-hat. I think it was the first time I used this trick of starting a break by hitting the hi-hat first instead of going directly to a drum off the hi-hat.'

Revolver

Despite an entirely phoney rivalry between the Beatles and the Rolling Stones, promulgated by music journalists to give themselves something to write about, there was actually no contest between the two groups in anything other than chart positions. The real contender was always Brian Wilson, the composer and arranger of the Beach Boys. Like Paul, Brian was the bass player. Unlike Paul, however, he usually wrote alone or with a shifting series of collaborators. Brian Wilson watched the Beatles with an eagle eye, noting each new development, each experiment, and pushing himself to equal or better it. He had managed to reach the top several times in charts dominated by British Invasion groups but commercial success was not his main interest, though it was for the other Beach Boys. Brian wanted to match the Beatles on an artistic level. In a 1995 television documentary by Don Was, Brian described how the group would gather in prayer: 'We prayed for an album that would be a rival to

Rubber Soul. It was a prayer, but there was some ego there ... and it worked. *Pet Sounds* happened immediately.'

Paul regarded *Pet Sounds* as one of the greatest popular-music albums ever made and was effusive in its praise, particularly for the way in which it proved that the bass player need not play the root note of a chord but can weave a melody around it of its own. He recommended the album to everyone he met. Throughout the industry, everyone who cared about the actual music instead of the money was astonished at what Brian Wilson had pulled off. When the album threatened to stiff in Britain, Andrew Loog Oldham, the Rolling Stones' manager, took the unprecedented step of taking out full-page advertisements in the music press to announce that *Pet Sounds* was the greatest album ever made. For someone with no financial interest in the band or its record company, this was an extraordinary gesture, typical of Oldham, which had the required effect. That morning, every minor executive in the music business sent a secretary out to buy a copy to see what all the fuss was about. Unfortunately for Brian, his rivals were already at work recording *Revolver*, which was to 'push the envelope' of popular music so far into new realms of experimentation that it could no longer be performed on stage. By the time *Pet Sounds* was released in July, the next stage in the music revolution was already half recorded. The first session for the *Revolver* album was held at Abbey Road on 6 April 1966.

The album opens with 'Eleanor Rigby', which Paul wrote on the upright piano in Mrs Asher's music room in the basement of Wimpole Street. Mrs Asher had found someone from the Guildhall School of Music to give Paul piano lessons; it was an idea that he often toyed with but, as before, he was not interested in putting in the homework necessary and also still had a nagging doubt that it might inhibit his composing technique to know the 'right' way to do things. Paul: 'I wrote it at the piano, just vamping an E-minor chord; letting that stay as a vamp and putting a melody over it, just danced over the top of it. It has almost Asian Indian rhythms.' Paul played the tune for his piano teacher but had no name for the tune.

When he gets a good melody, Paul often just blocks it in with any old words that spring to mind. Paul often dropped in on Donovan, since he and his flatmate Gypsy Dave lived nearby in Maida Vale, and Donovan remembered hearing it in its unfinished state.

One day I was on my own in the pad running through a few tunes on my Uher tape recorder. The doorbell rang. It was Paul on his own. We jammed a bit. He played me a tune about a strange chap called 'Ola Na Tungee'.

'Ola Na Tungee/Blowing his mind in the dark/With a pipe full of clay/No-one can say.'

It was 'Eleanor Rigby' but the right words had not come yet. Lots of songwriters put in any old words to sketch in the lyric.

Back at Cavendish Avenue Paul carried on tinkering with the lyric:

I was just mumbling around and eventually came up with these words: 'Picks up the rice in a church where a wedding has been'. Those words just fell out like stream-of-consciousness stuff, but they started to set the tone of it all, because you then have to ask yourself, what did I mean? It's a strange thing to do: most people leave the rice there, unless she's a cleaner. So there's a possibility she's a cleaner, in the church, or is it a little more poignant than that? She might be some lonely spinster of this parish who's not going to get a wedding, and that was what I chose. So this became a song about lonely people.

I knew quite a lot about old people. I was a Boy Scout and I often visited local pensioners as a good deed. I used to think it was the right thing to do – I still do, actually – but what I'm saying is, I wasn't ashamed to go round and ask someone if they wanted me to go to the doctor's for them or to help old ladies across the road. It had been instilled into me that that was a good deed. So I sat with lots of old ladies who chatted about the war and all this stuff, and also, as I fancied myself as a writer, a part of me was getting material. There was a corner of my brain that used to enjoy that kind of thing, building a repertoire of people and thoughts. Obviously writers are always attracted to detail: the lonely old person opening her can of catfood and eating it herself, the smell of the catfood, the mess in her room, her worrying always about cleaning it up, all the concerns of an old person.

I'm told that there's a gravestone with Eleanor Rigby on it in the graveyard in Woolton where John and I used to hang out, but there could be 3000 gravestones in Britain with Eleanor Rigby on. It is possible that I saw it and subconsciously remembered it, but my conscious memory was of being stuck for a name and liking the name Eleanor, probably because of Eleanor Bron, who we knew and worked with around that time. I'd seen her at Peter Cook's Establishment Club in Greek Street, then she came on the film *Help!* so we knew her quite well, John had a fling with her. I liked the name Eleanor. I wanted a genuine second name. I'm big on names, always have been, so I was very fussy to get the correct name and I was in Bristol on a visit to see Jane Asher at the Old Vic, and just walking round the dock area I saw an old shop called Rigby, and I thought, Oooh, It's a very ordinary name and yet it's a special name, it was exactly what I wanted. So Eleanor Rigby. I felt great. I'd got it! I pieced all the ideas together, got the melody and the chords, then took it out to John because I hadn't finished all the words. And he and I worked on it.

I had Father McCartney as the priest just because I knew that was right for the syllables, but I knew I didn't want it even though John liked it so we opened the telephone book, went to McCartney and looked what followed it, and shortly after, it was McKenzie. I thought, Oh, that's good. It wasn't written about anyone. A man appeared, who died a few years ago, who said, 'I'm Father McKenzie.' Anyone who was called Father McKenzie and had any slim contact with the Beatles quite naturally would think, Well, I spoke to Paul and he might easily have written that about me; or he may have spoken to John and thought John thought it up. John wanted it to stay McCartney, but I said, 'No, it's my dad! Father McCartney.' He said, 'It's good, it works fine.' I agreed it worked, but I didn't want to sing that, it was too loaded, it asked too many questions. I wanted it to be anonymous. John helped me on a few words but I'd put it down 80-20 to me, something like that.

In February 1972, at the height of his estrangement from Paul, John told *Hit Parader*, 'I wrote a good deal of the lyrics, about 70 per cent,' and he later stuck to this, telling *Playboy*, 'The first verse was his and the rest are basically mine ...' John's friend Pete Shotton was there during Paul's visit when the name McKenzie was found in the phone book, and though his book *John Lennon in My Life* often credits Lennon with ideas originating with the other three Beatles, in this instance he says, 'Though John was to take credit, in one of his last interviews, for most of the lyrics, my own recollection is that "Eleanor Rigby" was one "Lennon–McCartney" classic in which John's contribution was virtually nil.' It seems as though John backed himself into a corner and couldn't find a way to save face, because a less likely John Lennon composition would be hard to find.

Paul recorded most of the demo versions of 'Eleanor Rigby' at the experimental recording studio that he had set up in Marylebone. One of the people who heard the song in all its different stages was William Burroughs, who admired how much narrative Paul was able to pack into just a few lines. Paul also played it to Marianne Faithfull and Mick Jagger after they had rejected his offer of 'Etcetera'. Paul: 'Marianne was much more interested in "Eleanor Rigby" but I had to say, "No, I want that one."'

Paul regarded 'Eleanor Rigby' as something of a breakthrough in his songwriting; a move away from the strictly poppy side of music into more thoughtful lyrics.

PAUL: I remember thinking to myself, What am I going to do when I'm thirty? Thirty was the big age. Will I still be in a group? I remember being round at John Dunbar's house, having a very clear vision of myself in a herringbone jacket with leather elbow patches and a pipe, thinking 'Eleanor Rigby', this could be a way I could go, I could become a more serious writer, not so much a pop writer. It was the first inklings of what I'm starting to get into now, writing a solo piano piece, writing a piece for classical orchestra or the *Liverpool Oratorio*. I never did get into it then, I just stayed in pop. But I remember imagining myself with the patches, thinking, Yes, it wouldn't be bad actually. Be quite a good thing – at the terrible old age of thirty.

'Eleanor Rigby' was also released as a single and, like their previous eleven singles, it went to number one.

Paul: 'One day I led the dance, like "Paperback Writer", and another day John would lead the dance, like "I'm Only Sleeping". It was nice, we weren't really competitive as to who started the song, but the good thing was if he wrote a great "Strawberry Fields", I'd try and write a "Penny Lane". So we kept each other on our toes.' Often Paul would be John's morning alarm call. Living at Wimpole Street had meant that he was involved in the famous Asher diary, which inevitably meant he got up earlier than John and packed more into each day. John led a more relaxed suburban life but if he went to dinner in London or to a club, living so far from town meant that he returned home very late. Paul would arrive at midday or the early afternoon and wake him up, which was where John got the idea for 'I'm Only Sleeping'.

Paul: 'It was a nice idea, there's nothing wrong with it. I'm not being lazy, I'm only sleeping, I'm yawning, I'm meditating, I'm having a lay-in – the luxury of all of that was what it was about.' The song was written and arranged in one writing session, co-written but from John's original idea.

Though these were work sessions, they would also take time out for a friendly chat. The discussion that day was how to deal with pot and children, because they found themselves trying to hide it from Julian and keep him from seeing what they were doing. It was a new problem for Paul because he had no children, but Julian was of an age when John had to decide how to deal with it. They agreed it was best not to roll up and smoke openly in front of him but to keep it as something they did in private.

For Paul, the most exciting thing that happened with 'I'm Only Sleeping' was during the recording rather than in the writing. They were taping George's guitar solo and the tape operator put the tape on tails out.

PAUL: It played backwards, and, 'What the hell is going on?' Those effects! Nobody knew how those sounded then. We said, 'My God, that is fantastic! Can we do that for real?' So George Martin, give him his due, being amenable to ideas like that, being quite experimental for who he was, a grown-up, said, 'Yes. Sure, I think we can do that.' So that was what we did and that was where we discovered backwards guitar. It was a beautiful solo actually. It sounds like something you couldn't play.

'Here, There and Everywhere' also had its genesis in John's sleeping patterns. In this case Paul arrived at Kenwood for a songwriting session and John was still in bed. Since it was a nice June day, Paul asked someone to make him a cup of tea and went to sit by John's swimming pool while he waited.

I sat out by the pool on one of the sun chairs with my guitar and started strumming in E, and soon had a few chords, and I think by the time he'd woken up, I had pretty much written the song, so we took it indoors and finished it up. But it's very me, it's one of my favourite songs that I've written. Jazz people used to pick it up because they like the chord structure.

'Here, There and Everywhere' has a couple of interesting structural points about it: lyrically the way it combines the whole title: each verse takes a word. 'Here' discusses here. Next verse, 'there' discusses there, then it pulls it all together in the last verse, with 'everywhere'. The structure of that is quite neat. And I like the tune. John might have helped with a few last words. When I sang it in the studio I remember thinking, I'll sing it like Marianne Faithfull; something no one would ever know. You get these little things in your mind, you think, I'll sing it like James Brown might, but of course it's always you that sings it, but in your head there's a little James Brown for that session. If you can't think how to sing the thing, that's always a good clue: imagine Aretha Franklin to come and sing it, Ray Charles is going to sing it. So that one was a little voice, I used an almost falsetto voice and double-tracked it. My Marianne Faithfull impression. So I would credit me pretty much 80-20 on that one.

John described 'Here, There and Everywhere' as 'one of my favourite songs of the Beatles' and told *Hit Parader*, 'This was a great one of his.' The Beatles wrote many beautiful love songs: George's 'Something', John's 'Girl', Paul's 'And I Love Her', enough for EMI to issue a double album simply called *Beatles: Love Songs*.

The range of songs was extraordinary; it is hard to conceive that the same hand was behind 'Yellow Submarine'.

PAUL: I was laying in bed in the Ashers' garret, and there's a nice twilight zone just as you're drifting into sleep and as you wake from it; I always find it quite a comfortable zone, you're almost asleep, you've laid your burdens down for the day and there's this little limbo-land just before you slip into sleep. I remember thinking that a children's song would be quite a good idea and I thought of images, and the colour yellow came to me, and a submarine came to me, and I thought, Well, that's kind of nice, like a toy, very childish yellow submarine. I was thinking of it as a song for Ringo, which it eventually turned out to be, so I wrote it as not too rangey in the vocal. I just made up a little tune in my head, then started making a story, sort of an ancient mariner, telling the young kids where he'd lived and how there'd been a place where he had a yellow submarine. It's pretty much my song as I recall, written for Ringo in that little twilight moment. I think John helped out; the lyrics get more and more obscure as it goes on but the chorus, melody and verses are mine. There were funny little grammatical jokes we used to play. It should have been 'Everyone of us has all he needs' but Ringo turned it into 'everyone of us has all *we* need.' So that became the lyric. It's wrong, but it's great. We used to love that.

Donovan recalls that he helped out on a lyric on the same occasion that Paul sang him the unfinished 'Eleanor Rigby': 'He played one about a Yellow Submarine. He said he was missing a line and would I fill it in. I left the room and returned with this: "Sky of blue and sea of green/in our Yellow Submarine." It was nothing really, but he liked it and it stayed in.'

Since 'Eleanor Rigby' was finished and arranged for a string octet by the end of April, this must have been early in the month or late March. Once the backing track was down, another session was arranged to add the sound effects. George Martin had made his name producing comedy records with the Goons and Peter Sellers, and sound effects were one of his specialities. Alf Bicknell, the Beatles' driver, rattled old chains while the Rolling Stone Brian Jones tapped his glass. John blew bubbles through a straw in a bucket of water and he and Paul improvised Goonish nonsense, 'Full stern ahead, Mr Bosun', in the studio's echo chamber. The result was not only a much-loved children's record but a novelty record of such universal appeal that it was taken up both as an anthem by the peace movement in the USA and as a pub sing-along favourite in Britain along with 'Knees Up, Mother Brown'.

'She Said She Said' had its origins in something that the actor Peter Fonda said. The Beatles were holed up in a house in Benedict Canyon, Los Angeles, during their summer 1965 American tour. Surrounded by police and thousands of fans, two of whom tried to land in the garden in a helicopter, the besieged Beatles had no choice but to party at home. Roger McGuinn and Dave Crosby from the

Byrds were there as well as Peter Fonda. They had spent the afternoon watching Jane Fonda's *Cat Ballou* (described by Pauline Kael as 'uneven, lumpy, coy and obvious'), which John had hated. Afterwards John and George used the occasion to take an acid trip. George sat out on the deck with Fonda and told him he felt that he was dying. Fonda, an old hand at tripping out, calmed him, saying there was nothing to fear and that all he had to do was relax. He said that when he was a child he had almost died on the operating table and told George, 'I know what it's like to be dead.' John was passing and heard him. He had already had enough of the Fondas from watching *Cat Ballou* and snapped, 'Who put that shit in your head?' before turning to an aide and demanding 'Get this guy out of here.' However, John obviously filed away the phrase for later use.

It was a song that Paul liked. 'Very much John. It's a nice one. I like the title "She Said She Said", which I think was made up on the session. John brought it in pretty much finished, I think. I'm not sure but I think it was one of the only Beatle records I never played on. I think we'd had a barney or something and I said, "Oh, fuck you!" and they said, "Well, we'll do it." I think George played bass.' (EMI studio records do not mention this.)

The big hit of the summer of 1966 in England was the Lovin' Spoonful's 'Daydream' and it spawned a number of sound-alike songs such as 'Lazy Sunday Afternoon' by the Small Faces and the Kinks' 'Sunny Afternoon'. 'Good Day Sunshine' by the Beatles was another.

> PAUL: It was really very much a nod to the Lovin' Spoonful's 'Daydream', the same traditional, almost trad-jazz feel. That was our favourite record of theirs. 'Good Day Sunshine' was me trying to write something similar to 'Daydream'. John and I wrote it together at Kenwood, but it was basically mine, and he helped me with it.
>
> 'And Your Bird Can Sing' was John's song. I suspect that I helped with the verses because the songs were nearly always written without second and third verses. I seem to remember working on that middle-eight with him but it's John's song, 80-20 to John.

'For No One' was written in March 1966 when Paul and Jane were on their skiing holiday in Klosters, Switzerland. They had rented a chalet high above Klosters, about half a mile from the town.

PAUL: It was very nice and I remember writing 'For No One' there. I suspect it was about another argument. I don't have easy relationships with women, I never have. I talk too much truth.

Paul and Ringo were the only Beatles present for the recording, with Paul playing bass, piano and harpsichord. Dennis Brain, the premier horn player in Britain, was originally booked to play the French horn solo. As usual, George Martin did not stint in hiring the best session players for the Beatles and in this case there was an element of excitement looking forward to that session. Unfortunately, Dennis Brain died in a car crash before the session and Alan Civil took his place, both on the session and as Britain's top player. Paul hummed the melody that he wanted the French horn to play and George Martin wrote out the score. When it was finished, George pointed out to Paul that the high note went just beyond the top of the horn's range and showed him the reference book used for orchestral writing which showed the top notes of orchestral instruments. George Martin said, 'But you know, these good players, they can play above the range.' Paul said, 'Let's try him then.'

PAUL: George was in for the crack, he liked that. He said, 'It'll work, it'll work.' On the session Alan Civil said, 'George?' and looked at us both. He said, 'George, you've written a D,' and George and I just looked at him and held our nerve and said, 'Yes?' And he gave us a crafty look and went, 'Okay.' We did the same trick on 'Penny Lane' with David Mason on the piccolo trumpet, and he almost never forgave me for it because the only thing people ever asked him to do after that was high trumpet stuff.

On the release of the album there was considerable speculation about the identity of 'Dr Robert', with many of the London *cognoscenti* taking it as a reference to Robert Fraser, who was always a walking pharmacy. In fact, the name was based on the New York Dr Feelgood character Dr Robert Freymann, whose discreet East 78th Street clinic was conveniently located for Jackie Kennedy and other wealthy Upper East Siders from Fifth Avenue and Park to stroll over for their vitamin B-12 shots, which also happened to contain a massive dose of amphetamine. Dr Robert's reputation spread and it was not long before visiting Americans told John and Paul about him.

> PAUL: John and I thought it was a funny idea: the fantasy doctor who would fix you up by giving you drugs, it was a parody on that idea. It's just a piss-take. As far as I know, neither of us ever went to a doctor for those kind of things. But there was a fashion for it and there still is. Change your blood and have a vitamin shot and you'll feel better.

'Got to Get You into My Life', which Paul wrote after the Beatles had first been turned on to marijuana by Dylan, was one of the first records on which the Beatles used brass. Paul: 'We got some cool horn players, and they played some really good screaming high stuff and got into the spirit of it.' Paul hired two members of Georgie Fame's Blue Flames for the job: Eddie Thornton on trumpet and Peter Coe on tenor sax. The other musicians, Ian Hamer and Les Condon on trumpet and Alan Branscombe on tenor sax, were session jazzmen. John, who knew the concealed meaning of the song, always particularly liked the lyrics, possibly for that reason. He told *Playboy* in his characteristic way: 'I think that was one of his best songs, too, because the lyrics are good and I didn't write them.'

George had two tracks on *Rubber Soul* – 'Think for Yourself' and 'If I Needed Someone' – and three on *Revolver*: 'Love You To', 'I Want to Tell You' and 'Taxman', which incidentally featured a guitar solo by Paul. Though outnumbered by Lennon and McCartney, George was becoming a third significant songwriter in the group.

The album ended with their first great psychedelic song, 'Tomorrow Never Knows', a hint of things to come.

> PAUL: I remember John coming to Brian Epstein's house at 24 Chapel Street, in Belgravia. We got back together after a break, and we were there for a meeting. George Martin was there so it may have been to show George some new songs or talk about the new album. John got his guitar out and started doing 'Tomorrow Never Knows' and it was all on one chord. This was because of our interest in Indian music. We would be sitting around and at the end of an Indian album we'd go, 'Did anyone realise they didn't change chords?' It would be like 'Shit, it was

all in E! Wow, man, that is pretty far out.' So we began to sponge up a few of these nice ideas.

This is one thing I always gave George Martin great credit for. He was a slightly older man and we were pretty far out, but he didn't flinch at all when John played it to him, he just said, 'Hmmm, I see, yes. Hmm hmm.' He could have said, 'Bloody hell, it's terrible!' I think George was always intrigued to see what direction we'd gone in, probably in his mind thinking, How can I make this into a record? But by that point he was starting to trust that we must know vaguely what we were doing, but the material was really outside of his realm.

'Tomorrow Never Knows' was recorded on 6 April 1966 during the first session for the *Revolver* album. As well as Ringo's rock drumming, the backing track had a tambour drone fading in and out. John said he wanted his voice to sound like the Dalai Lama singing from the top of a mountain, an effect that was achieved by George Martin putting his voice through the Leslie speaker of the Hammond organ. A Leslie rotates inside a cabinet to give a swishing effect when picked up by another microphone and it did sound as if John's voice was coming from somewhere across the void. A normal guitar solo in the middle of all this would have been inappropriate; the track needed something really special. This was where Paul came in. He realised that his experiments with tape loops could be put to use on a Beatles number and suggested that he do a tape solo for it. That night he set to work, making a large selection of loops, sometimes varying their lengths. The next day's session was in the afternoon, from 2.30 to 7.15 p.m., so Paul walked over to Abbey Road, carrying them in a plastic bag.

Paul: 'People tend to credit John with the backwards recordings, the loops and the weird sound effects, but the tape loops were my thing. The only thing I ever used them on was "Tomorrow Never Knows". It was nice for this to leak into the Beatle stuff as it did.'

From making his 'little symphonies', Paul knew pretty much how it would sound. He wanted to put on as many of the tapes as possible at the same time and fade them in and out, placing them in different parts of the stereo spread. Five seperate tape machines were used to simultaneously play Paul's tape loops in the control room of Studio Two. Men with white coats shook their heads in disbelief and stood before their BTR3s, each with its little loop of quarter-inch tape going round, held in tension with a pencil or a glass tumbler as it passed through the capstans, past the playback head, endlessly repeating itself, fed through the mixer on faders. These were manned by the Beatles while George Martin controlled the stereo positioning, creating a montage of tape loops, fading in and out, overlaid and repeating; a tapestry of interwoven sounds, each one a little musical event in itself.

> PAUL: We ran the loops and then we ran the track of 'Tomorrow Never Knows' and we played the faders, and just before you could tell it was a loop, before it began to repeat a lot, I'd pull in one of the other faders, and so, using the other people, 'You pull that in there,' 'You pull that in,' we did a half random, half orchestrated playing of the things and recorded that to a track on the actual master tape, so that if we got a good one, that would be the solo. We played it through a few times and changed some of the tapes till we got what we thought was a real good one.
>
> I think it is a great solo. I always think of seagulls when I hear it. I used to get a lot of seagulls in my loops; a speeded-up shout, hah ha, goes squawk squawk. And I always get pictures of seasides, of Torquay, the Torbay Inn, fishing boats and puffins and deep purple mountains. Those were the slowed-down ones.

In *Summer of Love: The Making of Sgt. Pepper*, George Martin comments that 'it is the one track, of all the songs the Beatles did, that could never be reproduced: it would be impossible to go back now and mix exactly the same thing: the "happening" of the tape loops, inserted as we all swung off the levers on the faders willy-nilly, was a random event.'

Brian Wilson tried to follow *Revolver*, but unlike Lennon and McCartney, he was saddled with a conservative band who just wanted to stick to the old money-making formula. Having been told by Mike Love that *Pet Sounds* was crap, Brian became progressively more isolated from the other Beach Boys. The release of *Sgt. Pepper* finally destroyed his ambition to produce the greatest rock 'n' roll album ever. He abandoned his current project, *Smile*, and spent the next two years in bed.

EIGHT

SERGEANT PEPPER

Changing the lifestyle and appearance of youth
throughout the world didn't just happen – we set out
to do it; we knew what we were doing.

John Lennon, 1972

Nouvelle Vague

THE BEATLES PLAYED THEIR LAST ADVERTISED PUBLIC CONCERT ON 29
August 1966 at Candlestick Park, just outside San Francisco. The
next day they returned exhausted to the rented villa in Beverly Hills
they had been using as their base and, on the 31st, left for Britain.
The pressures of fame and tour fatigue had taken their toll. The 1966
American tour had been a harrowing experience: beginning in
Chicago, they had played ten stadium shows in a row before their first
day off. They were exhausted and determined never to tour again.
Most of their newer songs were unsuitable for public performance
because they used studio effects or orchestration impossible to
reproduce on stage; they were sick of playing to audiences that did
nothing but scream and didn't listen to the music. And in the South,
religious fanatics were burning Beatles records and the Ku Klux Klan
had issued death threats because John told journalist Maureen Cleave
that in terms of popularity, the Beatles were bigger than Jesus.

PAUL: I must admit we didn't really take it too seriously at all, we
just thought, Yes, well, you can see what it is. It's hysterical low-
grade American thinking. There is high-grade American thinking, which we know and appreciate: we like Lenny Bruce, we
like Jack Kerouac, we like the painters, et cetera, we see the high

free thinking. But we know there's this Elmer Gantry undercurrent. And of course that's exactly who got hold of it all, so there were record burnings, which of course echoed Hitler's book burnings. We always used to point out that to burn them, you've got to buy them, so it's no sweat off us, mate, burn 'em if you like. It's not compulsory to play 'em. So we took a balanced view of it, but I will never forget in one of the places down South, we pulled in there in the coach and there was this little blond-haired kid, he could have been no older than eleven or twelve, who barely came up to the window, screaming at me through the plate glass, banging the window with such vehemence. I thought, Gosh, I wonder how much he knows about God? He's only a young boy. It can only be what he's been fed, but he's been fed that we are the anti-Christ or something. This was the face of a zealot!

It wasn't that that made us stop touring, it wasn't the woman who predicted Kennedy's death saying we were going to die on a flight into Denver; we still got on the plane. We didn't listen to stuff like that, we still went ahead. But at the end of that particular tour it had started to become less enjoyable. There were all these other things to contend with, plus the screaming rather than someone watching the chords, and the craftsmanship going a bit. We began to lose respect for the live act, and everyone started to become a bit disgruntled. I was holding on, thinking, no, no, no. You can't just not do it, you know? You should just do it and work it all out. But in the end there was one lousy concert [St Louis, Missouri, 21 August 1966]: it was raining and we had a couple of bits of corrugated iron over us. It looked like a mud hut in the middle of somewhere and there were people miles away cheering. They were all in the rain, we were in the rain, it was a really miserable day. There was danger of the stuff all blowing us up with the water on the amps, and it was like, 'Oh, God, who needs this?' And finally, we finished the show. Everyone was in a bit of a mood, but we did the show, I'm not sure how much the audience would have known we were in a mood. We did the show and piled into the back of one of these chrome-lined panel trucks; they were always empty, and we'd pile into this terrible empty space, on this tour which had become spiritually rather empty, and this empty playing, and on that one occasion, I said, 'Okay,' and I let off a bit of steam, swore a bit and said, 'Oh, well, I really fucking agree with you. I've fucking had it up to here too!' And the guys said, 'Well, we've been telling you for weeks, man!' But finally they had my vote.

Back home in Cavendish Avenue that September, Paul still felt wound up from the tour and decided to take a driving holiday in France. But even in France, the least pop-conscious nation in Europe, Paul could not venture on to the street without squealing fans appearing from nowhere and taxi drivers demanding autographs. He decided to travel incognito, disguised so that he would not be recognised.

He went on his own, arranging to meet his roadie, Mal Evans, under the town clock in the centre of Bordeaux in two weeks' time, and then drove his new dark-green Aston Martin DB5 to Lydd airport in Kent, which used to do an air car-ferry service to France. The cars went in the belly of a fat-bellied cargo plane and their drivers went upstairs for a drink to calm their nerves during the bumpy 45-minute flight. 'Then you went and did your passports and they just drove your car off like a big posh hotel,' Paul said. 'It was great seeing your car come out, and also I was pretty proud of the car. It was a great motor for a young guy to have, pretty impressive.'

After French customs Paul put on his disguise. When the Beatles were making *A Hard Day's Night*, he had asked Wig Creations, the film make-up company, if they would make him a moustache. 'They measure you and match the colour of your hair, so it was like a genuine moustache with real glue. And I had a couple of pairs of glasses made with clear lenses, which just made me look a bit different. I put a long blue overcoat on and slicked my hair back with Vaseline and just wandered around and of course nobody recognised me at all. It was good, it was quite liberating for me.'

Paul had first tried out his disguise on the other Beatles, with complete success, during their July 1964 visit to Stockholm.

PAUL: We'd arrived in the afternoon and everyone was just settling in. I put on this disguise and picked up a camera and went around and knocked on the guys' doors. I knocked on George's and he came to the door, quite grumpy, you know,

'Yeah?' and I'd never seen him like that before. I said, 'Peresi, yea? Peresi?' A made-up foreign language, like someone who couldn't speak English. And he said, 'What d'you want? What d'you want?' He was quite curt with me, he was getting quite nasty actually, so I just changed the accent, 'Paresi, George, paresi, can't you tell, it's Paul speaking. It's me!' and I went into my real accent. And he goes, 'Fuckin' hell!'

Brian Epstein was in the bath with his door open when Paul wandered in.

I had a camera round my neck so I looked like a guy pestering people for photos and I had a little card I was flashing. It was one I'd been given by Wesley Rose of Acuff and Rose, the music publishers, and I was impressed by it because it was see-through red plastic. So I pulled this out and said, 'Paresi, paresi?' Brian said, 'Yes, can I help you?' I said, 'Paresi? Mr Epsteini? Photo?' He said, 'No, no, no, not now. Look, can't you see I'm in the –' 'No, no, no, Brian, can't you tell it's me?' Freaked him out.

Paul's plan was to drive to Paris, then head for Bordeaux, following the Loire down from Orléans, stopping off at the chateaux along the way. 'I was a little lonely poet on the road with my car.' His isolation was increased by his inability to speak French; he got by mainly on gestures, imitation and phrase-book sentences.

PAUL: It was an echo of the trip John and I made to Paris for his twenty-first birthday, really. I'd cruise, find a hotel and park. I parked away from the hotel and walked to the hotel. I would sit up in my room and write my journal, or take a little bit of movie film. I'd walk around the town and then in the evening go down to dinner, sit on my own at the table, at the height of all this Beatle thing, to ease the pressure, to balance the high-key pressure. Having a holiday and also not be recognised. And re-taste anonymity. Just sit on my own and think all sorts of artistic thoughts like, I'm on my own here, I could be writing a novel, easily. What about these characters here in this room?

In addition to keeping a journal record – now lost – he made a film of his trip, trying out a few experimental techniques of his own invention. Paul had been making home movies for more than a year.

He had filmed his friends, his cats and his dog. Two of the films, *The Defeat of the Dog* and *The Next Spring Then*, were described at the time in *Punch* magazine:

> They were not like ordinary people's home movies. There were over-exposures, double-exposures, blinding orange lights, quick cuts from professional wrestling to a crowded car park to a close-up of a television weather map. There were long still shots of a grey cloudy sky and a wet, grey, pavement, jumping Chinese ivory carvings and affectionate slow-motion studies of his sheepdog Martha and his cat. The accompanying music, on a record player and faultlessly synchronised, was by the Modern Jazz Quartet and Bach.

In March 1966 Paul ran a competition in a little underground magazine called the *Global Moon Edition of the Long Hair Times*, the direct forerunner of *International Times*, edited by Miles and produced by John Hopkins on his own hand-cranked offset-litho machine. Paul, using his pseudonym Ian Iachimoe, offered twenty guineas for a film script:

> Ian Iachimoe, the Polish 'new wave' film director, is offering a prize of 20 guineas to anyone who can supply the missing link in the following script. The dialogue is not needed, just the idea. Here is the outline of the story:
>
> A woman (age 35–45) is fanatical about cleanliness. She is amazingly houseproud and obsessional about getting rid of dirt. This carries over in her dress, looks, and so on.
>
> Something happens to make her *have* to crawl through a great load of dirt, old dustbins and so on. Good old honest dirt. *What is this something?*
>
> The story continues with the woman's mind being snapped by her experiences with dirt. She goes mad and her obsession gets even worse.
>
> What is needed is the idea. What could have caused her to become involved with filth. (She is not forced to do it, but chooses to do it herself.)
>
> Send all answers, as many as you like, to Ian Iachimoe, c/o Indica Books & Gallery. 6 Mason's Yard, Duke St, St James's. London SW1. WHI 1424

This competition is for real – it seems strange but it is real.

PAUL: The thing about cleanliness could be my mother, who was a nurse and was very hygienic. She was amazingly house proud, she was almost obsessive about getting rid of dirt. So if I was analysing it, that would be the first thing I'd go to.

Twenty guineas was a lot of dough! I was very interested in making films. I used to have a few images that I stored to use if I ever did make a film. I suppose I was thinking of New Wave French directors, or New Wave Polish in this case. I remember I had an image of breaking an egg into an ashtray, a very full, very dirty ashtray. That was a shot that was always on my mind. I think it was the natural perfection of the egg breaking into the really slobby man-made mess of the all the ciggies and stuff. I was interested in the contrast.

Then I had a thought about the sound of fire being very similar to the sound of applause and I wanted to do something with that. So I had a lot of unrelated ideas. I suppose it culminated in 'Magical Mystery Tour'. That was about the nearest I got to it.

All of Paul's home movies were subsequently stolen by fans who broke into Cavendish Avenue and exist now only in the memory of those who saw them.

On his drive through France, Paul concentrated on filming images that he knew would look good when he superimposed over them.

Kodak 8 mm was the one, because it came on a reel. Once it became Super-8 on a cartridge you couldn't do anything with it, you couldn't control it. I liked to reverse things. I liked to reverse music and I found that you could send a film through the camera backwards. Those very early cameras were great.

If you take a film and run it through a camera once, then you rewind it and run it through again, you get two images, superimposed. But they're very washed out, so I developed this technique where I ran it through once at night and only photographed points of light, like very bright reds, and that would be all that would be on the first pass of the film. It would be like on black velvet, red, very red. I used to do it in my car so it was car headlights and neon signs, the green of a go sign, the red of a stop, the amber.

The next day, when it was daylight, I would go and shoot and I had this film that was a combination of these little points of light that were on a 'black velvet' background and daylight. My favourite was a sequence of a leaning cross in a cemetery. I turned my head and zoomed in on it, so it opened just with a cross, bingo, then as I zoomed back out, you could see the horizon was tilted at a crazy angle. And as I did it, I straightened up. That was the opening shot, then I cut to an old lady, facing away from me, tending the graves. A fat old French peasant who had stockings halfway down her legs and was revealing a lot of her knickers, turning away, so it was a bit funny or a bit gross maybe. She was just tending a grave so, I mean, I didn't need to judge it. I just filmed it. So the beautiful thing that happened was from the previous night's filming. There she is tending a grave and you just see a point of red light appear in between her legs and it just drifts very slowly like a little fart, or a little spirit or something, in the graves. And then these other lights just start to trickle around, and it's like Disney, it's like animation!

One thing I'd learned was that the best thing was to hold one shot. I was a fan of the Andy Warhol idea, not so much of his films but I liked the cheekiness of *Empire*, the film of the Empire State Building, I liked the nothingness of it. So I would do a bit of that.

There were some sequences I loved: there was a Ferris wheel going round, but you couldn't quite tell what it was. And I was looking out of the hotel window in one French city and there was a gendarme on traffic duty. There was lot of traffic coming this way, then he'd stop 'em, and let them all go. So the action for ten minutes was a gendarme directing the traffic: lots of gestures and getting annoyed. He was a great character, this guy. I ran it all back and filmed all the cars again, it had been raining so there was quite low light in the street. So in the film he was stopping cars but they were just going through his body like ghosts. It was quite funny. Later, as the soundtrack I had Albert Ayler playing the 'Marseillaise'. It was a great little movie but I don't know what happened to it.

All the films were silent, but Paul created soundtracks by playing records.

> We discovered that if you put a home movie on, and put a record on at a random point, the record would synchronise with the music. At a number of points it would synchronise magically and at a number of points it would run out of synch. My theory was that in a movie there are probably fifty points that are moving at any time: the cat's tail, the cat's paws, the leaves, the bit of sunlight, the door which was opened and the person that walks through. The arms of the person, the feet of the person, the head turning; there are a lot of points in a movie that were moving; even the camera sometimes. Sometimes it's just the camera that's moving. Camera wobble and the lights will give you movement. And I figured that your eye synchronised these points of movement with the movement in the music, so fast sitar music was always very good for it. It would link up and, because it was Indian, it would suggest an exotic feel to the movie.

Paul was making his films using techniques which were being developed in parallel by many other experimental film-makers. Superimposition itself had been used throughout the history of film since Georges Méliès first invented it. René Clair's *Le Fantôme du Moulin Rouge* in 1924 and Jo Gerçon and Hershell Louis's *The Story of a Nobody* in 1930 were important early works using the technique. Ian Hugo's 1952 *Bells of Atlantis*, based on Anaïs Nin's *The House of Incest*, a film with many similarities to Paul's shorts, helped to usher in the New American Cinema of the late fifties and early sixties. There the technique was used repeatedly in the films of Ron Rice, Storm de Hirsch, Harry Smith, Barbara Rubin, Carl Linder and most notably Stan Brakhage, whose *Dog Star Man* (1959–64), *Prelude* (1961) and *Art of Vision* (1961–65) were among the masterpieces of the movement.

Paul could not have been influenced by these film-makers since very few of their films had been shown in Britain at the time; but he shared with them the sixties desire to push the boundaries, and in exploring the possibilities of film he came up with similar results. In an interesting turn of the circle, however, Paul's views on superimposition and film-making were to be cited at length by Jonas Mekas, the leading theoretician of the New York underground film movement. Mekas had a weekly column called *Movie Journal* in the then radical *Village Voice* which chronicled the doings of the New York experimental film-makers. In the course of reviewing a collective show by twenty different experimental film-makers at the New York Cinematheque in his column for 9 March 1967, Mekas quoted from an interview Paul had done with Miles for the *International Times*. Mekas wrote:

> It was a visionary show and one that marks a very important direction in cinema and I will attempt to indicate this direction with a few quotes. The quotes will be from Max Heindel, the mystic who died in 1919; Paul McCartney, the Beatle; and the Gospel of Thomas (uncovered in 1945 in a ruined tomb in Upper Egypt).
>
> Paul McCartney (in the *International Times*, No 6 – you can buy it at the 8th Street Bookshop):
>
> With everything, with any kind of thing, my aim seems to be to distort it. Distort it from what we know it as, even with music and visual things, and to change it from what it is to what it could be. To see the potential in it all. To take a note and wreck it and see in that note what else there is in it, that a simple act like distorting it has caused. To take a film and superimpose on top of it so you can't quite tell what it is any more, it's all trying to create magic, it's all trying to make things happen so that you don't know why they've happened. I'd like a lot more things to happen like they did when you were kids, when you didn't know how the conjuror did it, and were happy to just sit there and say, 'Well, it's magic!' ... The only trouble is, that you don't have the bit that you did when you were a kid of innocently accepting things. For instance, if a film comes on that's superimposed and doesn't seem to mean anything, immediately it's weird or it's strange, or it's a bit funny to most people, and they tend to laugh at it. The immediate reaction would be to laugh. And that's wrong! That's the first mistake and that's the big mistake that everyone makes, to immediately discount anything they don't understand, they're not sure of, and to say, 'Well, of course, we'll never know about that.' ... There's all these fantastic

theories people put forward about 'it doesn't matter anyway' and it does, it does matter, in fact that matters more than anything, that side of it.

In France meanwhile Paul reached Bordeaux and decided to have a night out on the town before meeting up with Mal. He went to a disco, but his disguise was so good and he looked so drab and ordinary that they wouldn't let him in.

I looked like old jerko. 'No, no, monsieur, *non*' – you schmuck, we can't let you in! So I thought, Sod this, I might as well go back to the hotel and come as him! So I came back as a normal Beatle, and was welcomed in with open arms. I thought, Well, it doesn't matter if I've blown my cover because I'm going to meet Mal anyway, I don't have to keep the disguise any longer. Actually, by the time of the club I'd sort of had enough of it. Which was good. It was kind of therapeutic but I'd had enough. It was nice because I remembered what it was like to not be famous and it wasn't necessarily any better than being famous.

It made me remember why we all wanted to get famous; to get that thing. Of course, those of us in the Beatles have often thought that, because we wished for this great fame, and then it comes true but it brings with it all these great business pressures or the problems of fame, the problems of money, et cetera. And I just had to check whether I wanted to go back, and I ended up thinking, No, all in all, I'm quite happy with this lot.

Paul had arranged to meet Mal Evans at the Grosse Horloge, on the corner of cours Victor Hugo and rue St James.

PAUL: We met up, exactly as planned, under the church clock. He was there. I figured I'd had enough of my own company by then. I had enjoyed it, it had been a nice thing. Then we drove down into Spain but we got to Madrid and we didn't know anyone; the only way would have been to go to a club and start making contacts. So we thought, This is not going to be any fun, and rang the office in London, and booked ourselves a safari trip.

They flew off to Kenya on safari. Mal Evans's home movies were later released on video and show Paul filming all the way through

Spain and on safari in Africa, but the films themselves have long since disappeared.

Sgt. Pepper

Paul, with Mal Evans, had a relaxing safari in Kenya, visiting the Ambosali Park at the foot of Mount Kilimanjaro, and staying at the exclusive Treetops Hotel, where the rooms are built up among the branches of ancient trees. Their final night in Africa was spent at a YMCA in Nairobi before returning to London on 19 November 1966. It was on the flight back that Paul came up with the idea for Sergeant Pepper's Lonely Hearts Club Band.

It was a long plane journey but rather than sleep Paul stayed awake writing and playing with ideas. The freedom he had experienced while driving through France in disguise at the beginning of the holiday had given him the idea of creating a new identity for the Beatles: by not being the Fab Four they could try something new, experiment, and show the fans that they had grown up.

PAUL: We were fed up with being the Beatles. We really hated that fucking four little mop-top boys approach. We were not boys, we were men. It was all gone, all that boy shit, all that screaming, we didn't want any more, plus, we'd now got turned on to pot and thought of ourselves as artists rather than just performers. There was now more to it; not only had John and I been writing, George had been writing, we'd been in films, John had written books, so it was natural that we should become artists.

Then suddenly on the plane I got this idea. I thought, Let's not be ourselves. Let's develop alter egos so we're not having to project an image which we know. It would be much more free. What would really be interesting would be to actually take on the personas of this different band. We could say, 'How would somebody else sing this? He might approach it a bit more sarcastically, perhaps.' So I had this idea of giving the Beatles alter egos simply to get a different approach; then when John came up to the microphone or I did, it wouldn't be John or Paul singing, it would be the members of this band. It would be a freeing element. I thought we can run this philosophy through the whole album: with this alter-ego band, it won't be us making all that sound, it won't be the Beatles, it'll be this other band, so we'll be able to lose our identities in this.

The first thing Paul needed was a name for the Doppelgänger-Beatles. This was the heyday of fantastically named groups: the Nitty Gritty Dirt Band, Country Joe and the Fish, Lothar and the Hand People, Big Brother and the Holding Company, Quicksilver Messenger Service, the Bonzo Dog Doo-Dah Band. Precedents for extravagance were not hard to find.

PAUL: Me and Mal often bantered words about which led to the rumour that he thought of the name Sergeant Pepper, but I think it would be much more likely that it was me saying, 'Think of names.' We were having our meal and they had those little packets marked 'S' and 'P'. Mal said, 'What's that mean? Oh, salt and pepper.' We had a joke about that. So I said, 'Sergeant Pepper,' just to vary it, 'Sergeant Pepper, salt and pepper,' an aural pun, not mishearing him but just playing with the words.

Then, 'Lonely Hearts Club', that's a good one. There's lot of those about, the equivalent of a dating agency now. I just strung those together rather in the way that you might string together Dr Hook and the Medicine Show. All that culture of the sixties going back to those travelling medicine men, Gypsies, it echoed back to the previous century really. I just fantasised, well, 'Sergeant Pepper's Lonely Hearts Club Band'. That'd be crazy enough because why would a Lonely Hearts Club have a band? If it had been Sergeant Pepper's British Legion Band, that's more understandable. The idea was to be a little more funky, that's what everybody was doing. That was the fashion. The idea was just take any words that would flow. I wanted a string of those things because I thought that would be a natty idea instead of a catchy title. People would have to say, 'What?' We'd had quite a few pun titles – *Rubber Soul*, *Revolver* – so this was to get away from all that.

Back in London, Paul put the idea to the other Beatles.

PAUL: They were a bit bemused at first, I think, but they said, 'Yeah, that'll be great.' There wasn't any hard sell needed. Everyone was into it. It was a direction for an album. I had the name so then it was, 'Let's find roles for these people. Let's even get costumes for them for the album cover. Let them all choose what they want.' We didn't go as far as getting names for ourselves, but I wanted a background for the group, so I asked everyone in the group to write down whoever their idols were, whoever you loved. And it got quite funny, footballers: Dixie Dean, who's an old Everton footballer, Billy Liddle's a Liverpool player. The kind of people we'd heard our parents talk about, we didn't really know about people like Dixie Dean. There's a few like that, and then folk heroes like Albert Einstein and Aldous Huxley, all the influences from Indica like William Burroughs, and of course John, the rebel, put in Hitler and Jesus, which EMI wouldn't allow, but that was John. I think John often did that just for effect really. I first of all envisioned a photograph the group just sitting with a line of portraits of Marlon Brando, James Dean, Einstein and everyone around them in a sitting room, and we'd just sit there as a portrait.

We were starting to amass a list of who everybody's favourites were, and I started to get this idea that Beatles were in a park up north somewhere and it was very municipal, it was very council. I like that northern thing very much, which is what we were, where we were from. I had the idea to be in a park and in front of us to have a huge floral clock, which is a big feature of all those parks: Harrogate, everywhere, every park you went into then had a floral clock. We were sitting around talking about it, 'Why do they do a clock made out of flowers?' Very conceptual, it never moves, it just grows and time is therefore nonexistent, but the clock is growing and it was like, 'Wooah! The frozen floral clock.'

So the second phase of the idea was to have these guys in their new identity, in their costumes, being presented with the Freedom of the City or a cup, by the Lord Mayor in all his regalia, and I thought of it as a town up north, standing on a little rostrum with a few dignitaries and the band, above a floral clock. We always liked to take those ordinary facts of northern working-class life, like the clock, and mystify them and glamorise them and make them into something more magical, more universal. Probably because of the pot. So we would be in presentation mode, very Victorian, which led on from the portrait. When Peter Blake got involved, the portrait idea grew. We had the big list of heroes: maybe they could all be in the crowd at the presentation!

Sgt. Pepper is often described as the first concept album, but it was not initially conceived as such. There was never the intention to make a themed album, a 'northern' album, or present a mini-opera as the Who did later. Though both *Rubber Soul* and *Revolver* had experimental tracks, Paul's notion of the group being Sergeant Pepper's Lonely Hearts Club Band, rather than the four mop tops, liberated the Beatles to range across the musical landscape. Paul: 'With our alter egos we could do a bit of B. B. King, a bit of Stockhausen, a bit of Albert Ayler, a bit of Ravi Shankar, a bit of *Pet Sounds*, a bit of the Doors; it didn't matter, there was no pigeon-holing like there had been before.' It freed them from their public image and allowed them to take a new, unfettered direction; it gave them the distance necessary to attempt something as extraordinary as 'A Day in the Life'.

Only later in the recording did Neil Aspinall have the idea of repeating the 'Sgt. Pepper' song as a reprise, and the Beatles and George Martin begin to use linking tracks and segues to pull it all together, making it into more of a concept album.

Recording sessions for the Beatles' new album began on 24 November 1966. 'Strawberry Fields Forever' and 'Penny Lane' were the first and third songs completed, with 'When I'm Sixty-Four' in between; but Paul does not remember any overt decision by himself and John to write songs with a northern theme, even though these first two would indicate a concept album along those lines. As it happened, Brian Epstein decided that the Beatles needed a new single and both tracks were pulled for this, though initially the single was to be 'Strawberry Fields Forever' backed with 'When I'm Sixty-Four'. The Beatles' practice at the time was to never put singles on albums.

John wrote 'Strawberry Fields Forever' in Almería, Spain, while he was filming *How I Won the War* with Richard Lester. It is a memory song, about the Salvation Army hostel near his home in Liverpool.

PAUL: I've seen Strawberry Fields described as a dull, grimy place next door to him that John imagined to be a beautiful

place, but in the summer it wasn't dull and grimy at all: it was a
secret garden. John's memory of it wasn't to do with the fact that
it was a Salvation Army home; that was up at the house. There
was a wall you could bunk over and it was a rather wild garden,
it wasn't manicured at all, so it was easy to hide in. The bit he
went into was a secret garden like in *The Lion, the Witch and the
Wardrobe* and he thought of it like that, it was a little hide-away
for him where he could maybe have a smoke, live in his dreams a
little, so it was a get-away. It was an escape for John.

Perhaps inspired by John's nostalgia, Paul then wrote 'Penny
Lane':

I think we wrote them round about the same time, we were often
answering each other's songs so it might well have been my
version of a memory song but I don't recall. It was childhood
reminiscences: there is a bus stop called Penny Lane. There was
a barber shop called Bioletti's with head shots of the haircuts you
can have in the window and I just took it all and arted it up a
little bit to make it sound like he was having a picture exhibition
in his window. It was all based on real things; there was a bank
on the corner so I imagined the banker, it was not a real person,
and his slightly dubious habits and the little children laughing at
him, and the pouring rain. The fire station was a bit of poetic
licence; there's a fire station about half a mile down the road, not
actually in Penny Lane, but we needed a third verse so we took
that and I was very pleased with the line 'It's a clean machine'. I
still like that as a phrase, you occasionally hit a lucky little phrase
and it becomes more than a phrase. So the banker and the
barber shop and the fire station were all real locations.

There is 'a shelter in the middle of the roundabout' at Smithdown
Place, known to the locals as the Penny Lane Roundabout, where
Church Road meets Smithdown Road. It is now occupied by a café,
but was then used as a place to meet people or shelter while waiting
for a bus.

PAUL: John and I would often meet at Penny Lane. That was
where someone would stand and sell you poppies each year on
British Legion poppy day; where John and I would put a shilling

in the can and get ourselves a poppy. That was a memory. We fantasised the nurse selling poppies from a tray, which Americans used to think was puppies! Which again is an interesting image. I was a choirboy at a church opposite called St Barnabas so it had a lot of associations for me.

When I came to write it, John came over and helped me with the third verse, as often was the case. We were writing childhood memories: recently faded memories from eight or ten years before, so it was a recent nostalgia, pleasant memories for both of us. All the places were still there, and because we remembered it so clearly we could have gone on.

On the corner of Smithdown Place, next to the bank, stood the showroom of photographer Albert Marrion, who took the first official portraits of the Beatles – chosen by Brian Epstein because he had done the pictures for Clive Epstein's wedding. The window displayed formal portraits, including one mounted artistically upon an easel. Paul: 'I often used to stop in front of Albert Marrion's, who did high-class photography and wedding photos; we once had our picture taken by him, so there could have been a fourth verse about a photographer, but the song was finished before we needed any more characters. Penny Lane was a place with a lot of character and a lot of characters, good material for writing.'

Paul wrote 'Penny Lane' in the music room at Cavendish Avenue, on the piano which had recently been painted with its psychedelic rainbow by David Vaughan. In December 1966, about the same time as he delivered the piano, Vaughan asked Paul if he would contribute some music for a couple of *Carnival of Light Raves* that Binder, Edwards and Vaughan were promoting at the Roundhouse as part of their idea of bringing art to the community, in this case in the form of light shows, experimental music and films. David: 'I asked Paul to do it and I thought he would make more of it than he did, I thought this was a vehicle for him, if anything was. My trouble is, I expect everybody to drop everything. I forget other people have got things on.'

Amazingly, perhaps, Paul agreed to make a contribution, despite being in the middle of the recording sessions for *Sgt. Pepper*. So it was that on 5 January, after overdubbing a vocal on 'Penny Lane', the Beatles under Paul's direction freaked out at Abbey Road, producing an experimental tape just under fourteen minutes long. The tape has no rhythm, though a beat is sometimes established for a few bars by the percussion or a rhythmic pounding on the piano. There is no melody, though snatches of a tune sometimes threaten to break through. The Beatles make literally random sounds, although they sometimes respond to each other; for instance, a burst of organ notes answered by a rattle of percussion. The basic track was recorded slow so that some of the drums and organ were very deep and sonorous, like the bass notes of a cathedral organ. Much of it is echoed and it is often hard to tell if you are listening to a slowed-down cymbal or a tubular bell. John and Paul yell with massive amounts of reverb on their voices, there are Indian war cries, whistling, close-miked gasping, genuine coughing and fragments of studio conversation, ending with Paul asking, with echo, 'Can we hear it back now?' The tape was obviously overdubbed and has bursts of feedback guitar, schmaltzy cinema organ, snatches of jangling pub piano, some unpleasant electronic feedback and John yelling, 'Electricity.' There is a great deal of percussion throughout, again much of it overdubbed. The tape was made with full stereo separation, and is essentially an exercise in musical layers and textures. It most resembles 'The Return of the Son of Monster Magnet', the twelve-minute final track on Frank Zappa's *Freak Out!* album, except there is no rhythm and the music here is more fragmented, abstract and serious. The deep organ notes at the beginning of the piece set the tone as slow and contemplative.

DAVID: That organ is exactly how I used to see him. I used to picture him as a maniac from the seventeenth century: one of those brilliant composers who'd suddenly been reincarnated into this century, let loose with modern technology. A lot of people thought Paul McCartney was shallow. I didn't see him as that at all, I saw him as very very deep. He had this open fire with a big settee in front of it, there would be no lights on, and he'd be playing music at top volume. I used to sit there watching him for hours. I think that's the real him; this real deep, dark ... I thought, Who knows what he could do if they'd leave him alone for a bit? Because he could absorb a lot without encountering any mental block, he could express that Machiavellian, European horror.

The sleeve was beginning to come together in Paul's head so he wrote a song to go with it, once more using the north as a jumping-off point. Paul: 'I started writing the song: "It was twenty years ago today, Sergeant Pepper taught the band to play ..." Okay, so I was leading myself into a story. What was this about? Well, he's some guy, then, and I always imagined him as associated with a brass band; we've always liked brass bands. So again it was northern memories.' 'Sgt. Pepper' was Paul's song, with little or no input from John. It acted as an overture to the album and, by announcing Ringo as Billy Shears, introduced the notion that the members of Sergeant Pepper's band were alter egos for the Beatles, something that was not followed through overtly in the rest of the album.

'With a Little Help from My Friends' was tailored specifically for Ringo.

> PAUL: This was written out at John's house in Weybridge for Ringo; we always liked to do one for him and it had to be not too much like our style. I think that was probably the best of the songs we wrote for Ringo actually. He was to be a character in this operetta, this whole thing that we were doing, so this gave him a good intro, wherever he came in the album; in fact it was the second track. It was a nice place for him, but wherever it came, it gave us an intro. Again, because it was the pot era, we had to slip in a little reference: 'I get high!'
>
> It was pretty much co-written, John and I doing a work song for Ringo, a little craft job. I always saw those as the equivalent of writing a James Bond film theme. It was a challenge, it was something out of the ordinary for us because we actually had to write in a key for Ringo and you had to be a little tongue in cheek. Ringo liked kids a lot, he was very good with kids so we knew 'Yellow Submarine' would be a good thing for Ringo to sing. In this case, it was a slightly more mature song, which I always liked very much. I remember giggling with John as we wrote the lines 'What do you see when you turn out the light? I can't tell you but I know it's mine.' It could have been him playing with his willie under the covers, or it could have been taken on a deeper level; this was what it meant but it was a nice way to say it, a very non-specific way to say it. I always liked that.

'With a Little Help from My Friends' was picked up by Denny Cordell and Joe Cocker. Joe was sitting on the outside toilet at his parents' house at Tasker Road, Sheffield, when he got the idea of performing the song as a waltz, full-blown, anthemic, a celebration of sixties ideas of communalism, peace and smoking dope. It became his best-known song as well as his first big hit.

PAUL: Denny Cordell gave me a ring and said, 'We love that song that Ringo sings but we've got this treatment of it that we really think would be great, singing it very bluesy, very crazy, slow it right down.' I said, 'Well, great, try it, and let me hear what you do with it.' He came over to see us at Apple studios at Savile Row and played it and I said, 'Wow, fantastic!' They'd done a really radical treatment of it and it's been Joe's staple diet for many a year. Then it was taken on by John Belushi, who used to do a Cocker impression, and so taken even further by Belushi, so it has good memories, that song. It became the theme tune to the very good American series about growing up in the sixties called *The Wonder Years*, so it's been picked up and used a lot, that song, but it really started just as a co-written song crafted for Ringo.

'Lucy in the Sky with Diamonds' was one of the fastest songs on the album to record: one day to record the backing tracks, one to overdub the instrumentals and vocals, and a final day to mix. It was also one of the most controversial tracks because, unbeknown to the Beatles at the time, the title contained the initials 'LSD', resulting in it being banned from many airwaves around the world. Certainly the song was about acid, but the reference in the title was unintentional.

PAUL: I went up to John's house in Weybridge. When I arrived we were having a cup of tea, and he said, 'Look at this great drawing Julian's done. Look at the title!' He showed me a drawing on school paper, a five-by-seven-inch piece of paper, of a little girl with lots of stars, and right across the top there was written, in very neat child handwriting, I think in pencil, 'Lucy in the Sky with Diamonds'. So I said, 'What's that mean?', thinking, Wow, fantastic title! John said, 'It's Lucy, a friend of his from school. And she's in the sky.' Julian had drawn stars, and then he thought they were diamonds. They were child's stars, there's a way to draw them with two triangles, but he said diamonds because they can be interpreted as diamonds or stars. And we loved it and she was in the sky and it was very trippy to us. So we went upstairs and started writing it. People later thought 'Lucy in the Sky with Diamonds' was LSD. I swear we didn't notice that when it came out, in actual fact, if you want to be pedantic you'd have to say it is LITSWD, but of course LSD is a better story.

The title lettering was probably written out in copybook child script by Julian's teacher, since Julian was only four years old. The picture was of Lucy O'Donnell, the little girl who sat next to him in one of the old-fashioned school desks at Heath House School, a private nursery in Weybridge.

John said that the psychedelic imagery was inspired by the 'Wool and Water' chapter of Lewis Carroll's *Through the Looking Glass*: '... she found they were in a little boat, gliding along between banks: so there was nothing for it but to do her best.' It also captures the languid shifting imagery of the book's final poem:

> A boat, beneath a sunny sky,
> Lingering onward dreamily
> In an evening of July –

PAUL: John had the title and he had the first verse. It started off very *Alice in Wonderland*: 'Picture yourself in a boat, on the river ...' It's very Alice. Both of us had read the Alice books and always referred to them, we were always talking about 'Jabberwocky' and we knew those more than any other books really. And when psychedelics came in, the heady quality of them was perfect. So we just went along with it. I sat there and wrote it with him: I offered 'cellophane flowers' and 'newspaper taxis' and John replied with 'kaleidoscope eyes'. I remember which was which because we traded words off each other, as we always did ... And in our mind it was an Alice thing, which both of us loved.

The Beatles' biographer Hunter Davies recounts that he was with Paul while he walked his dog Martha on Primrose Hill, near Paul's home in St John's Wood in the spring of 1967, when Paul remembered the phrase 'It's getting better' that Jimmy Nichol used to use all the time. (Nichol was the drummer who had taken Ringo's place for five days in Denmark and Australia in 1964 when Ringo was ill.) By the time John arrived for a writing session, Paul had the music to accompany the song title. Paul doesn't remember the moment the idea occurred.

PAUL: I just remember writing it. Ideas are ideas, you don't always remember where you had them, but what you do remember is writing them. Where I start remembering it is where I actually hit chords and discover the music, that's where my memory starts to kick in because that's the important bit; the casual thought that set it off isn't too important to me.

'Getting Better' I wrote on my magic Binder, Edwards and Vaughan piano in my music room. It had a lovely tone, that piano, you'd just open the lid and there was such a magic tone, almost out of tune, and of course the way it was painted added to the fun of it all. It's an optimistic song. I often try and get on to optimistic subjects in an effort to cheer myself up and also, realising that other people are going to hear this, to cheer them up too. And this was one of those. The 'angry young man' and all that was John and I filling in the verses about schoolteachers. We shared a lot of feelings against teachers who had punished you too much or who hadn't understood you or who had just been bastards generally. So there are references to them.

It's funny, I used to to think of the bad grammar coming from Chuck Berry but it's actually more Jamaican, like writing in slang. It just appeared in one of the verses, it felt nice, it scanned nicely, rather than 'I used to be an angry young man', '*me* used ...' We'd always grab at those things, lots of precedents with Elvis, 'ain't never done no wrong'. At school the teachers would have said, 'Isn't it terrible grammar?' and you'd say, 'Yeah, isn't it great?'

There is an account of the writing of 'Getting Better' which mistakenly has Paul sitting in the studio, singing 'It's getting better all the time' and John bursts in and responds with the line 'Couldn't get much worse'. In fact, Paul and John rarely took unfinished songs to the studio; though they sometimes used expensive studio time for rehearsal, they would not have kept the other members of the group and the engineering staff waiting while they finished a song. The story is a conflation of two separate events: John and Paul writing 'Getting Better' at Cavendish Avenue, and a much later recording session for the song 'Ob-La-Di Ob-La-Da' at Abbey Road. Paul described with relish how John came up with the sarcastic rejoinder as they added the words to Paul's music at Cavendish Avenue.

I was sitting there doing 'Getting better all the time' and John just said in his laconic way, 'It couldn't get no worse,' and I thought, Oh, brilliant! This is exactly why I love writing with John. He'd done it on a number of other occasions, he does a Greek chorus thing on 'She's Leaving Home', he just answers. It was one of the ways we'd write. I'd have the song quite mapped out and he'd come in with a counter-melody, so it was a simple ordinary story.

The part of the story where John bursts into the studio occurred during the recording of the White Album, when John arrived late at Abbey Road as Paul was running through 'Ob-La-Di Ob-La-Da' on the guitar with the others. John ran in, threw himself down in front of the piano, asked which key they were in and immediately began pounding out the aggressive piano line that gave the final recording its energy. Paul: 'That became the song, and we all went, "Oh yeah!"'

Another inaccurate but frequently told story is that 'Fixing a Hole' was about heroin. This track is actually about marijuana. Like 'Got to Get You into My Life', it is described by Paul as 'another ode to pot', the drug that got him out of the rut of everyday consciousness and gave him the freedom to explore.

PAUL: 'Fixing' later became associated with fixing heroin but at that time I didn't associate it really. I know a lot of heroin people thought that was what it meant because that's exactly what you do, fix in a hole. It's not my meaning at all. 'Fixing a Hole' was about all those pissy people who told you, 'Don't daydream, don't do this, don't do that.' It seemed to me that that was all wrong and that it was now time to fix all of that. Mending was my meaning. Wanting to be free enough to let my mind wander, let myself be artistic, let myself not sneer at avant-garde things. It was the idea of me being on my own now, able to do what I want. If I want I'll paint the room in a colourful way. I'm fixing the hole, I'm fixing the crack in the door, I won't allow that to happen any more, I'll take hold of my life a bit more. It's all okay, I can do what I want and I'm going to set about fixing things. I was living now pretty much on my own in Cavendish Avenue, and enjoying my freedom and my new house and the salon-ness of it all. It's pretty much my song, as I recall. I like the double meaning of 'If I'm wrong I'm right where I belong'.

The funny thing about that was the night when we were going to record it, at Regent Sound Studios at Tottenham Court Road. I brought a guy who was Jesus. A guy arrived at my front gate and I said 'Yes? Hello' because I always used to answer it to everyone. If they were boring I would say, 'Sorry, no,' and they generally went away. This guy said, 'I'm Jesus Christ.' I said, 'Oop,' slightly shocked. I said, 'Well, you'd better come in then.' I thought, Well, it probably isn't. But if he is, I'm not going to be the one to turn him away. So I gave him a cup of tea and we just chatted and I asked, 'Why do you think you are Jesus?' There were a lot of casualties about then. We used to get a lot of people who were maybe insecure or going through emotional break-downs or whatever. So I said, 'I've got to go to a session but if you promise to be very quiet and just sit in a corner, you can come.' So he did, he came to the session and he did sit very quietly and I never saw him after that. I introduced him to the guys. They said, 'Who's this?' I said, 'He's Jesus Christ.' We had a bit of a giggle over that.

Most books about the Beatles' songs attribute 'Fixing a Hole' to Paul doing a bit of do-it-yourself to the roof of his Scottish farmhouse, but this is not the case. Paul; 'It was much later that I ever got round to fixing the roof on the Scottish farm, I never did any of that till I met Linda. People just make it up! They know I've got a farm, they know it has a roof, they know I might be given to handyman tendencies so it's a very small leap for mankind ... to make up the rest of the story.'

On 27 February 1967, the *Daily Mail* newspaper ran a story headlined 'A-Level Girl Dumps Car and Vanishes'. Seventeen-year-old Melanie Coe, studying for her A-level examinations at Skinner's Grammar School in Stamford Hill, London, ran away from home leaving behind a mink coat, diamond rings and her own car. 'I cannot imagine why she should run away, she has everything here,' her father was quoted as saying.

PAUL: John and I wrote 'She's Leaving Home' together. It was my inspiration. We'd seen a story in the newspaper about a young girl who'd left home and not been found, there were a lot of those at the time, and that was enough to give us a story line. So I started to get the lyrics: she slips out and leaves a note and then the parents wake up and then ... It was rather poignant. I like it as a song, and when I showed it to John, he added the Greek chorus, long sustained notes, and one of the nice things about the structure of the song is that it stays on those chords endlessly. Before that period in our songwriting we would have changed chords but it stays on the C chord. It really holds you. It's a really nice little trick and I think it worked very well.

While I was showing that to John, he was doing the Greek chorus, the parents' view: 'We gave her most of our lives, we gave her everything money could buy.' I think that may have been in the runaway story, it might have been a quote from the parents. Then there's the famous little line about a man from the motor trade; people have since said that was Terry Doran, who was a friend who worked in a car showroom, but it was just fiction, like the sea captain in 'Yellow Submarine', they weren't real people.

George Harrison said once he could only write songs from his personal experience, but they don't have to exist for me. The feeling of them is enough. The man from the motor trade was just a typical sleazy character, the kind of guy that could pull a young bird by saying, 'Would you like a ride in my car, darlin'?' Nice plush interior, that's how you pulled birds. So it was just a little bit of sleaze. It was largely mine, with help from John.

This was the first Beatles track arranged by someone other than George Martin. Paul was getting very keen on the possibilities of orchestral settings and felt that 'She's Leaving Home' would be best suited by this type of arrangement.

PAUL: I rang George Martin and said, 'I'm really on to this song, George. I want to record it next week.' I'm really hot to record it,

I've got one of those 'I've got to go, I've got to go!' feelings and when you get them, you don't want anything to stop you, you feel like if you lose this impetus, you'll lose something valuable. So I rang him and I said, 'I need you to arrange it.' He said, 'I'm sorry, Paul, I've got a Cilla session.' And I thought, Fucking hell! After all this time working together, he ought to put himself out. It was probably unreasonable to expect him to. Anyway, I said, 'Well, fine, thanks George,' but I was so hot to trot that I called Mike Leander, another arranger. I got him to come over to Cavendish Avenue and I showed him what I wanted, strings, and he said, 'Leave it with me.' It is one of the first times I actually let anyone arrange something and then reviewed it later, which I don't like as a practice. It's much easier if I just stay with them. Anyway he took it away, did it, and George Martin was very hurt, apparently. Extremely hurt, but of course I was hurt that he didn't have time for me but he had time for Cilla.

In his book George Martin wrote, 'I couldn't understand why he was so impatient all of a sudden. It obviously hadn't occurred to him that I would be upset.'

Paul: 'It didn't work out badly. I don't like the echo on the harp, but that must be George rather than Mike Leander, or, to give him his due, it might have been one of us saying, "Stick some echo on that harp." You just can't tell.'

'She's Leaving Home' became one of the best loved and most moving songs the Beatles ever did. Oddly enough, the Beatles do not play on the song at all, just as they didn't on 'Yesterday'. 'She's Leaving Home' was sung by Paul and John with nothing but a string backing: a harp, four violins, two violas, two cellos and a double bass. The lyrics struck a particular chord at a time when unprecedented numbers of young people were running away from home, heading for communes and squats, setting up home together with lovers, going on the hippie trail. In the USA especially, tens of thousands were taking Timothy Leary's advice and 'turning on, tuning in and dropping out', heading for Haight-Ashbury in San Francisco, New York's Lower East Side, West Hollywood and Venice, wherever the bohemian quarter, looking for alternatives to the materialism their parents' generation offered.

'Being for the benefit of Mr Kite!' was taken almost entirely from a

Victorian circus poster. The poster, advertising a performance by Pablo Fanque's Circus Royal to be held at the Town Meadows, Rochdale, on 14 February 1843, was bought by John from an antique shop in Sevenoaks, Kent, when the Beatles were filming a promotional clip for 'Strawberry Fields Forever' on 31 January 1967. All the main characters of the song feature on the poster: for example, Mr Henderson, who announced his intention to leap 'through a hogshead of real fire … Mr H. challenges the World!' The evening was advertised as 'Being for the Benefit of Mr Kite'.

> PAUL: 'Mr Kite' was a poster that John had in his house in Weybridge. I arrived there for a session one day and he had it up on the wall in his living room. It was all there, the trampoline, the somersets, the hoops, the garters, the horse. It was Pablo Fanque's fair, and it said 'being for the benefit of Mr Kite'; almost the whole song was written right off this poster. We just sat down and wrote it. We pretty much took it down word for word and then just made up some little bits and pieces to glue it together. It was more John's because it was his poster so he ended up singing it, but it was quite a co-written song. We were both sitting there to write it at his house, just looking at it on the wall in the living room. But that was nice, it wrote itself very easily. Later George Martin put a fairground sound on it.

The fairground sound, suggested by John, was a brilliant piece of production work on George Martin's part. George had an enormous amount of experience using sound effects, most of it predating the Beatles, but in this instance he took a leaf out of their book. Using the same random principles that Paul had used in selecting the loop tapes for 'Tomorrow Never Knows', he made a tape up in the William Burroughs–Brion Gysin tradition. He described the event in *Summer of Love*, his account of the making of *Sgt. Pepper*. Taking a collection of steam organ recordings, he instructed the tape operator Geoff Emerick to transfer them all on to one tape:

> 'Geoff,' I said, 'we're going to try something here; I want you to cut that tape there up into sections that are roughly fifteen inches long.' Geoff reached for the scissors and began snipping.
> In no time at all we had a small pyramid of worm-like tape fragments piled up on the floor at our feet. 'Now,' I said, 'pick

them all up and fling them into the air!' He looked at me. Naturally, he thought I'd gone mad ...

'Now, pick 'em up and put them together again, and don't look at what you're doing,' I told Geoff ... When I listened to them, they formed a chaotic mass of sound ... it was unmistakably a steam organ. Perfect! There was the fairground atmosphere we had been looking for. John was thrilled to bits with it.

Paul originally wrote the tune for 'When I'm Sixty-Four' when he was sixteen in Liverpool and revived it for the album.

PAUL: 'When I'm Sixty-Four' was a case of me looking for stuff to do for *Pepper*. I thought it was a good little tune but it was too vaudevillian, so I had to get some cod lines to take the sting out of it, and put the tongue very firmly in cheek. 'Will you still need me?' is still a love song. 'Will you still look after me?', okay, but 'Will you still feed me?' goes into *Goon Show* humour. I mean, imagine having three kids called Vera, Chuck and Dave! It was very tongue in cheek and that to me is the attraction of it. I liked 'indicate precisely what ...' I like words that are exact, that you might find on a form. It's a nice phrase, it scans.

It's pretty much my song. I did it in rooty-tooty variety style. George Martin in his book says that I had it speeded up because I wanted to appear younger but I think that was just to make it more rooty-tooty; just lift the key because it was starting to sound a little turgid. George helped me on a clarinet arrangement. I would specify the sound and I love clarinets so 'Could we have a clarinet quartet?' 'Absolutely.' I'd give him a fairly good idea of what I wanted and George would score it because I couldn't do that. He was very helpful to us. Of course, when George Martin was sixty-four I had to send him a bottle of wine.

Next up was 'Lovely Rita', one of Paul's fantasy stories.

PAUL: 'Lovely Rita' was occasioned by me reading that in America they call traffic wardens 'meter maids', and I thought, God, that's so American! Also to me 'maid' had sexual connotations, like a French maid or a milkmaid, there's something good about 'maid', and 'meter' made it a bit more official, like the meter in a cab; the meter is running, meter maid. Hearing that amused me. In England you hear those American phrases and they enter our vocabulary. We let them in because we're amused, it's not because we love them or want to use them, it's just because it's funny. 'Rita' was the only name I could think of that would rhyme with it so I started on that, Rita, meter maid, lovely Rita. And I just fantasised on the idea.

Paul wrote the words while walking near his brother Michael's house in Gayton, in the Wirral near Liverpool, which looks out over the estuary of the River Dee to Holywell in Wales.

PAUL: I remember one night just going for a walk and working on the words as I walked. This was about the time that parking meters were coming in; before that we'd been able to park freely, so people had quite an antagonistic feeling towards these people. I'd been nicked a lot for parking so the fun was to imagine one of them was a bit of a easy lay, 'Come back to my place, darlin'.' It somehow made them a figure of fun instead of a figure of terror and it was a way of getting me own back.

It wasn't based on a real person but, as often happened, it was claimed by a girl called Rita who was a traffic warden who apparently did give me a ticket, so that made the newspapers. I think it was more a question of coincidence: anyone called Rita who gave me a ticket would naturally think, 'It's me!' I didn't think, Wow, that woman gave me a ticket, I'll write a song about her – never happened like that.

The parking-meter warden was actually named Meta Davies, who claimed, several years after the album was released, that she had just completed a parking ticket for Paul's car, parked somewhere near his house in St John's Wood, when he appeared. She had signed with her full name and he asked if her name was really Meta and told her it would be a good name for a song. Though not Rita, the combination of Meta and 'meter' may have provided an unconscious spark of an idea. There is also the possibility that the song was already written and Paul was just being friendly.

They began work on John's 'Good Morning' on 8 February, but continued to fiddle with it until the very last. The animal effects were not added until 28 March and the final mixing did not take place until mid-April. It is a song about suburban torpor.

PAUL: This is largely John's song. John was feeling trapped in suburbia and was going through some problems with Cynthia. It was about his boring life at the time, there's a reference in the lyrics to 'nothing to do' and 'meet the wife'; there was an afternoon TV soap called *Meet the Wife* that John watched, he was that bored, but I think he was also starting to get alarm bells and so 'Good morning, good morning'.

The title line itself was taken from a Kelloggs Cornflakes television advertisement. John's inspiration usually came from events in his life but his life had become so circumscribed that suburban lassitude and watching a lot of TV had become his main source of stimulation.

PAUL: When we came to record it we used Sounds Incorporated to do a big sax thing; they were friends of ours who had been on tour with us. But we still felt it needed something more manic so we decided to use a lot of sound effects on the fade. The great thing about working at EMI Abbey Road was that anything you needed was within reasonably easy reach. EMI was so multi-dimensional they had everything covered and we took advantage of all this. We used Daniel Barenboim's piano that he'd just recorded on; they would sometimes lock it but we would just ask, 'Can you unlock it?' and they'd say, 'Sure.' That was used on the big chord at the end of 'A Day in the Life'. There were so many grand pianos laying around, there were Hammond organs, there were harmoniums, there were celestes, and there was a sound-effects cupboard which they used for doing plays and spoken-word albums. George Martin said, 'There is a library, what do you want?' and we said, 'What have you got?' so we got the catalogue. 'Right, elephants, cock-crowing, the hunt going tally-ho, we'll have that ...'

The sound effects added to 'Good Morning, Good Morning' were taken from the EMI sound-effects tapes 'Volume 35: Animals and Bees' and 'Volume 57: Fox-hunt', each placed, at John's insistence, in order of ability to eat, or at least frighten, its predecessor.

Sound effects were also put to good use in the 'Sgt. Pepper' title song, where audience applause and laughter were overdubbed to give the impression of a live performance.

PAUL: We had an audience laughing on the front of 'Sgt. Pepper'. It had always been one of my favourite moments; I'd listened to radio a lot as a kid, and there had always been a moment in a radio show, say with somebody like Tommy Cooper, where he would walk on stage and he'd say hello, and they'd laugh, and he'd tell a joke, and they'd laugh, and there would always be a moment in these things, because it was live radio, where he wouldn't say anything, and the audience would laugh. And my imagination went wild whenever that happened. I thought, What is it? Has he dropped his trousers? Did he do a funny look? I had to know what had made 'em laugh. It fascinated me so much, and I'd always remembered that, so when we did 'Pepper' there's one of those laughs for nothing in there, just where Billy Shears is being introduced they all just laugh, and you don't know what the audience has laughed at.

The audience track came from a 1961 live recording George Martin made of a performance of *Beyond the Fringe*, a comedy revue starring Dudley Moore, Peter Cook, Alan Bennett and Jonathan Miller. Paul: 'We sat through hours of tapes, just giggling, it was just hilarious listening to an audience laugh. It was a great thing to do actually.' The orchestra tuning up, used on the same track, was a recording of the musicians preparing for 'A Day in the Life'.

A Day in the Life

Studio One at Abbey Road is a cavernous aircraft hangar of a place, used almost exclusively for classical recording, as large as a concert hall with enough space for several symphony orchestras to spread out. Sir Edward Elgar, Sir Thomas Beecham, Sir Malcolm Sargent, Sir John Barbarolli and Yehudi Menuhin all recorded there. It is strictly functional space: a vast expanse of parquet flooring littered with movable sound baffles and bits of scaffolding, grey walls which might once have been white, covered by scores of large square sound baffles like a sixties sci-fi movie and studded with speaker cabinets, part of the Ambiophonic feedback system. Had Sir Malcolm looked in on 10 February, 1967, he would have been in for a shock: the studio was filled with balloons, and flower children in tattered lace and faded velvet tripped around the room blowing rainbow bubbles. Three Rolling Stones – Brian Jones, Keith Richards and Mick Jagger – accompanied by Marianne Faithfull paraded in King's Road psychedelic finery, with flowing scarves, crushed velvet and satin trousers and multicoloured boots. Donovan, the cosmic troubadour, Graham Nash, the only psychedelic member of the Hollies, the Monkee Mike Nesmith, Patti Harrison (George's wife) and dozens of other friends milled around the edge of the room. The four Dutch designers known as the Fool arrived dressed as characters from the Tarot, carrying tambourines and bells, while the mighty Abbey Road air conditioners worked hard to control the rich fragrance of joss sticks and marijuana. At the centre stood George Martin and Paul McCartney, preparing to conduct a symphony orchestra, who were being asked, to their astonishment and for the first time in their careers, to improvise.

The orchestra and George Martin had been asked to attend in full evening dress, which the Beatles also promised they would wear. The Beatles did not keep their word but the orchestra and George Martin looked very smart in their tuxedos. In order to get them into the mood to play something unconventional and to encourage in them an element of playful spontaneity, the Beatles went among the players handing out party favours. Mal Evans had been sent to a joke shop on Great Russell Street and returned with plastic stick-on nipples, plastic glasses with false eyes, rubber bald pates, some with knotted handkerchiefs balanced on them, huge fake cigars, party hats and streamers: David McCallum, the leader of the London Philharmonic, wore a large red false nose; Erich Gruenberg, the leader of the second violins, had on a pair of flowery paper spectacles and held his bow in a large gorilla paw; the bassoon players, Alfred Waters and N. Fawcett, had balloons attached to their instruments which inflated and deflated with each note, raising a laugh from George Martin. Several film-makers with hand-held cameras circled the room.

The Beatles were recording 'A Day in the Life', one of their most experimental tracks but also one of the most beautiful and satisfying. It is a perfect example of a successful Lennon–McCartney collaboration but also encapsulates the results of Paul's two years of interest and experimentation in avant-garde circles. At the count-in the orchestra began to play a long free-form chord over twenty-four bars, with each player beginning at his lowest possible note and slowly moving up the scale to his highest, at the same time going from pianissimo to fortissimo, while the sound was fed back into the studio by the one hundred Ambiophonic speakers around the walls, filling the space with a massive wall of sound, more like a live concert than a recording session.

Paul: 'It was a song that John brought over to me at Cavendish Avenue. It was his original idea. He'd been reading the *Daily Mail* and brought the newspaper with him to my house. We went upstairs to the music room and started to work on it. He had the first verse, he had the war, and a little bit of the second verse.'

John Lennon told *Rolling Stone*: '"A Day in the Life" – that was something. I dug it. It was a good piece of work between Paul and me. I had the "I read the news today" bit, and it turned Paul on. Now and then we really turn each other on with a bit of song, and he just said "yeah" – bang, bang, like that. It just sort of happened beautifully ...'

> PAUL: The verse about the politician blowing his mind out in a car we wrote together. It has been attributed to Tara Browne, the Guinness heir, which I don't believe is the case, certainly as we were writing it, I was not attributing it to Tara in my head. In John's head it might have been. In my head I was imagining a politician bombed out on drugs who'd stopped at some traffic lights and he didn't notice that the lights had changed. The 'blew his mind' was purely a drug reference, nothing to do with a car crash. In actual fact I think I spent more time with Tara than John did. I'd taken Tara up to Liverpool. I was with Tara when I had the accident when I split my lip. We were really quite good friends and I introduced him to John. Anyway, if John said he was thinking of Tara, then he was, but in my mind it wasn't to do with that.

Tara Browne was the son of Lord and Lady Oranmore and Browne, whose great-grandfather was the brewer Edward Guinness. Tara went to Eton and, had he lived, would have inherited £1,000,000 at the age of twenty-five. A charming, likeable boy, with a wide grin and his hair brushed forward in a Beatle cut, he was a great friend of Brian Jones and often stayed overnight tripping on LSD with Brian, Keith Richards and Anita Pallenberg at Brian's flat in Courtfield Road. In the book *Shutters and Blinds* Anita described one trip with him: 'I remember being with Tara Browne on one of the first acid trips. He had a Lotus sportscar and suddenly near Sloane Square everything went red. The lights went red, the trees were flaming and we just jumped out of the car and left it there.'

Tara died in the early hours of the morning of 18 December 1966, while on his way to visit David Vaughan, who was painting a design on the front of Tara's Kings Road shop Dandy Fashions. He smashed his Lotus Elan into the back of a parked van while swerving to avoid a Volkswagen which had pulled out in his path in Redcliffe Gardens in Earls Court. He was twenty-one. The coroner's report on his death was issued in January 1967.

John told *Playboy*: 'I was reading the paper one day and noticed two stories. One was about the Guinness heir who killed himself in a car. That was the main headline story. He died in London in a car crash. On the next page was a story about four thousand potholes in the streets of Blackburn, Lancashire, that needed to be filled.' The pot-hole story appeared in the 7 January 1967 issue of the *Daily Mail*.

PAUL: We looked through the newspaper and both wrote the verse 'how many holes in Blackburn, Lancashire'. I liked the way he said 'Lan-ca-sheer', which is the way you pronounce it up north. Then I had this sequence that fitted, 'Woke up, fell out of bed ...' and we had to link them. This was the time of Tim Leary's 'Turn on, tune in, drop out' and we wrote, 'I'd love to turn you on.' John and I gave each other a knowing look: 'Uh-huh, it's a drug song. You know that, don't you?'

'Yes, but at the same time, our stuff is always very ambiguous and "turn you on" can be sexual so ... c'mon!'

As John and I looked at each other, a little flash went between our eyes, like 'I'd love to turn you on', a recognition of what we were doing, so I thought, Okay, we've got to have something amazing that will illustrate that.

When we took it to the studio I suggested, 'Let's put aside twenty-four bars and just have Mal count them.' They said, 'Well, what are you going to put there?' I said, 'Nothing. It's just going to be, One, chunk chunk chunk; two, chunk chunk chunk; three ...' And you can hear Mal in the background doing that. He counted down and on bar twenty-four he hit the alarm clock, Brrrrrr! It was just a period of time, an arbitrary length of bars, which was very Cage thinking. I'm using his name to cover all the sins, but that kind of avant-garde thinking came from the people I had been listening to.

Next they had to come up with something to put in the gap. The twenty-four bars had been recorded with increasing amounts of reverberation on Mal's voice so by the last bar there was a tremendous echo on it. Paul also added discordant piano chords over Mal's countdown when he recorded the grand opening chords and piano track for the song. The basic tracks were recorded on 19 and 20 January 1967, with Ringo adding a new drum track on 3 February. Paul: 'We persuaded Ringo to play tom-toms. It's sensational. He normally didn't like to play lead drums, as it were, but we coached him through it. We said, "Come on, you're fantastic, this will be really beautiful," and indeed it was.'

It was not until another week had passed, during which they worked on Paul's title song 'Sgt. Pepper's Lonely Hearts Club Band' and made promo films of 'Penny Lane' and 'Strawberry Fields Forever', that they returned to 'A Day in the Life'. By now, Paul had decided what to do with the twenty-four bars. He asked George Martin for a symphony orchestra. The Beatles had never used one before, and, as a company man, George Martin immediately thought of the cost. He describes his reaction in *Summer of Love*:

> 'Nonsense,' I replied. 'You cannot, cannot have a symphony orchestra just for a few chords, Paul. Waste of money. I mean you're talking about ninety musicians!' ... Thus spake the well-trained corporate lackey still lurking somewhere inside me. Yet my imagination was fired: a symphony orchestra! I could see at once that we could make a lovely sound.

Paul told him what he wanted to do with it and in the end they settled on half an orchestra, forty-one players, which they could then double-track to make a whole.

> PAUL: First we wrote out the music for the part where the orchestra had proper chords to do: after 'Somebody spoke and I went into a dream ...' big pure chords come in. But for the other orchestral parts I had a different idea. I sat John down and suggested it to him and he liked it a lot. I said, 'Look, all these composers are doing really weird avant-garde things and what I'd like to do here is give the orchestra some really strange

instructions. We could tell them to sit there and be quiet, but that's been done, or we could have our own ideas based on this school of thought. This is what's going on now, this is what the movement's about.' So this is what we did.

I said, 'Right, to save all the arranging, we'll take the whole orchestra as one instrument.' And I wrote it down like a cooking recipe: I told the orchestra, 'There are twenty-four empty bars; on the ninth bar, the orchestra will take off, and it will go from its lowest note to its highest note. You start with the lowest note in the range of your instrument, and eventually go through all the notes of your instrument to the highest note. But the speed at which you do it is your own choice. You've got to get from your lowest to your highest. You don't have to actually use all your notes but you've got to do those two, that's the only restriction.' So that was the brief, a little avant-garde brief.

The orchestra, consisting mostly of members of the New Philharmonia, was unaccustomed to ad-libbing.

PAUL: So we had to go round and talk to them all, seeing them all separate: 'Wot's all this, Paul? What exactly d'you ...'

'In your own speed ...'

'What do you mean, any way I want?'

'Yeah.' The trumpets got the idea rather easily. I said, 'You can do it all in one spurt if you like. But you can't go back. You've got to end at your top note, or have done your top note.'

It was interesting because you found out the internal character of an orchestra; for instance, all the strings went together like sheep, all looked at each other to see who was going up. 'If you're going up, so am I!' They tried to go up together as a bank. Trumpets had no such reservations whatsoever, trumpets are notoriously the guys who go to the pub because you need to wet your whistle, you need plenty of spittle. So they were very free.

This did actually get a little organised by George Martin. I didn't want that amount of restriction on them and in my instructions to them I didn't give it, but George, knowing a symphony orchestra and their logic, decided to give them little signposts along the way.

The guests moved to the sides of the studio. The two conductors raised their batons – George Martin in evening dress and Paul McCartney in a red butcher's apron and a purple and black psychedelic paisley shirt – and recording began.

The orchestra played the chord through five times in all, and each take was very different. Then George Martin and his team had to synchronise it with their original four-track master since they did not have an eight-track machine. The engineer Ken Townshend lashed up a method of starting all the tape machines simultaneously using a 50-hertz signal, but even then the synchronisation wasn't quite perfect and on the final mix the orchestra can just be heard going in and out of time.

> PAUL: And it became what's been referred to as a 'musical icon'. It's a very famous sound bite and of course John loved it. It was great to bring those ideas to it but this is the difference between me and Cage: mine would just be in the middle of a song as a little solo; his would be the whole thing. So we did this, and it was a great session.

If there was ever an example where up-to-date equipment would have improved a recording, it is 'A Day in the Life'. Because EMI was still using antiquated four-track equipment, nine years after American record companies such as Atlantic had switched to eight-track, George Martin was constantly forced to transfer one track to another in order to record the next layer of sound. As well as taking up a tremendous amount of studio time, each transfer multiplies the signal-to-noise ratio, introducing tape hiss: two copies creates four times the amount of hiss but a third copy increases it by nine times, so George Martin was constantly juggling tracks and worrying about keeping a track free. There is a lot of hiss and noise on 'A Day in the Life', as a pair of decent headphones will show. George Martin and his engineers did a brilliant job considering that they were working in a museum, but the sound quality would have been better had it been recorded on modern equipment. It was typical of EMI that when they did finally decide to upgrade, they opted for an eight-track instead of buying one of the sixteen-track machines that had already become standard throughout the industry. By then, however, rock groups had become accustomed to using the top-of-the-line equipment in the independent studios, and EMI had to replace the eight-track with a sixteen within a year.

'Experimental' or 'avant-garde' are often derogatory terms in popular journalism, as if the experiment was going to be performed upon the public rather than on the art form. John Lennon was deeply suspicious of any conscious intellectual attempt to bend or break the rules. Only later, when he was with Yoko, did he relax and accept that most attempts to challenge the rules were perfectly valid even if they were on occasion pretentious. In September 1969, in a recorded conversation with Miles, John said how Yoko had helped him see that he wasn't stupid.

> 'She wouldn't have loved a dummy, which I was beginning to think I was, so that helped. Of course she goes through the same thing, but I could help her in the same way, once I got over my intellectual reverse snobbery about avant-garde and that sort of thing, which I *had* to get over.'
> MILES: 'You've still got it to an extent.'
> JOHN: 'Sure, sure. I can't help it. It will take a long time to wear off, but I'm getting better.'

Paul's attitude was almost the complete opposite. He had an open mind about even the most extreme avant-garde experiments, though that did not necessarily mean he liked the art or music produced. In the two-year period leading up to *Sgt. Pepper* he was at his most inquisitive and receptive, listening to every type of music, going to art openings and attending experimental plays. He would go to see John, his head filled with the latest ideas. John would accept them from Paul, and took many of them on board, but it was not a good time for John and he was happy to let Paul take over the running of the ship. He told Miles: 'I was still in a real big depression in *Pepper* and I know Paul wasn't at that time. He was feeling full of confidence, but I wasn't. I was going through murder.'

One of the reasons the Beatles were such an exceptional group was that they did not rest on their laurels. Rather than stay with the simple pop-music formula of their early work, the period of Beatlemania, they pushed the boundaries of their music, making each album more complex than the one before, although never enough to alienate the fans. They were the first group to make rock 'n' roll an art form and show the other bands what could be done with it.

They were also the first to examine the whole spectrum of modern music, to see what was happening in other musical forms and incorporate any ideas that might be useful to Beatles music – a Post-Modernist shopping trip which passed effortlessly from genre to genre. George Harrison introduced elements of traditional Indian music, which became an important part of their later work. With 'Nowhere Man' and 'Help!', John Lennon's lyrics became more confessional, less poppy. Ringo's drumming became more sophisticated: according to Phil Collins, his drum fills on 'Day in the Life' would be impossible to duplicate. As a country-and-western music lover, Ringo was responsible for the country twang to some of the numbers, usually those written specially for him by John and Paul.

Paul gleaned musical ideas and influences from every part of the cultural spectrum, from classical music to avant-garde, music hall to the cutting edge of modern jazz. He was first exposed to classical music by the Ashers and George Martin, leading eventually to the string arrangements on 'Yesterday' and, 'Eleanor Rigby' and the French horn and piccolo trumpet solos on 'For No One'. Sometimes the influence was direct; for instance, when Paul was working on 'Penny Lane' he used a number of flutes, piccolos, trumpets and a flugelhorn for the backing track, but he remained dissatisfied with the results. Then he saw the English Chamber Orchestra playing, from Guildford Cathedral, Bach's Second Brandenburg Concerto in F Major on the BBC television show *Masterworks*. David Mason was playing piccolo trumpet. Mason was telephoned the next morning and summoned to Abbey Road for that evening's session. Meanwhile while he was there Paul composed on the spot a perfect solo for him to play in the middle eight. He sang it to George Martin, who transcribed it for B-flat piccolo trumpet. David Mason played it and 'Penny Lane' was complete.

George Martin was quite comfortable using radio clips and tape collages on tracks like 'Strawberry Fields Forever' and 'I Am the Walrus' because of his vast experience in making spoken-word recordings with Peter Sellers, Spike Milligan and the other Goons, which utilised a tremendous number of special sound effects. It was an area that George was very interested in and very good at. He had also experimented with electronic sound, and in 1962 even released a single on Parlophone, 'Time Beat', under the name of Ray Cathode, consisting of a few live musicians over an electronic rhythm track created at the BBC Radiophonic Workshop.

Tracing the paths of ideas is not an exact science. Sometimes, however, their route is known. The fragment of a live BBC broadcast of *King Lear* which appears in the mix at the end of 'I Am the Walrus' was the direct result of Paul telling John about John Cage using randomly tuned radios in his compositions. John had a radio set up and began twiddling the knob. Since the BBC had a monopoly over radio broadcasting, it wasn't long before he came upon a reading of Shakespeare that he liked. Paul: 'I had been talking to John about this. Having been turned on myself, naturally I would turn the guys on to it. Not claiming any credit, it's just that I was listening to more of that stuff.'

Tape montage seemed to be an idea that was being worked on simultaneously by a number of different people in different areas: John Cage and Luciano Berio had been working with it as a form of music since the late fifties, while William Burroughs and Brion Gysin had quite independently been conducting similar experiments, also since the late fifties, approaching it as a form of literature. Though they had not been released commercially, Paul had access to Burroughs's tapes through Miles and Ian Sommerville, the tape engineer who made most of them.

It was left to George Martin to sequence the tracks and prepare the album for release. Significantly, the mono mix took three times longer to do than the stereo. Stereo was still something new in Britain and few people had the equipment to play it. *Sgt. Pepper* was essentially conceived of and recorded as a mono release apart from some tricky stereo panning on the sound effects. After mixing, the sleeve still needed some work but as far as the Beatles were concerned there was only one small thing left to record.

In the sixties, the playing arm of most record decks would stick in the centre run-off groove, making an unpleasant scraping sound. In their quest to provide the best-value album ever, the Beatles even addressed themselves to this and on 21 April they went to Abbey Road for the final recording session of the album.

PAUL: It was a problem when the record came to an end and no one could be bothered to get up and turn it off. 'I know, we should put something on that!' I could handle that, because that'll be a mantra! That's fine. I can handle five hours of that and if nobody gets up, it won't bore us. Hours of random tape was recorded but we just chose one little bit that we liked: 'Couldn't really be any other; Couldn't really be any other; Couldn't really be any other,' something like that. And we knew that that's what it said, but you see how legends and rumours grow, because I remember some kids coming round to Cavendish Avenue and asking about the swearing on it.

I had this very open house then, because I was living on my own. If American fans came over, I'd just invite them in for a cup of tea and we'd have a chat. It was like you were a guru, and you sensed a bit of that yourself, because often you would get the nutters coming and you didn't want to just turn them away so you felt you had to try and explain to them, 'No, Mr Kite is a fictitious character, we made him up.' 'Yes, but I am Mr Kite.' 'I know what you're saying, but as far as we're concerned, really, we didn't write it about you. You should know that. We wrote it actually off a circus poster and it's a fictitious name.' 'Yes, but I am Mr Kite. I am a patient under R. D. Laing.' I used to get a lot of R. D. Laing's people, he must have sent 'em round. I used to talk to 'em, you know. Something I might not think of doing now, with a family and kids. I had Billy Shears, I had Mr Kite, to both of them I had to explain nicely over a cup of tea. I had quite a few visitors there, but these kids came in one day and said, 'What's all that swearing when it goes backwards on the end of the loop about?' I said, 'No, it doesn't, it says, "It really couldn't be any other."' They said, 'It does do it, though, we've done it.' I said, 'No, it bloody doesn't.' I said, 'Well, come in, look, we'll get my record player.' We put the record on, then you could turn the turntable backwards. It probably hurt the motor, but you could turn it backwards, and sure enough, it said something like 'We'll fuck you like Superman; We'll fuck you like Superman. We'll fuck you like Superman.' I said, 'Oh, my Gawwd!' That kind of stuff does happen. That's why you can explore the accident. But that was far out. We had certainly had not intended to do that but probably when you turn anything backwards it sounds like something ... if you look hard enough you can make something out of anything.

Art into Pop: The *Sgt. Pepper* Sleeve

As the recording sessions for *Sgt. Pepper* had progressed, so too did the work on the sleeve. First came Paul's initial concept of the Beatles standing before a wall of framed photographs of their heroes. One of his pen-and-ink drawings shows the four Beatles, all sporting moustaches, wearing long military-band jackets complete with epaulettes, holding brass-band instruments: Paul has an E-flat bass, the same brass instrument that his grandfather played; John holds a clarinet, George a trumpet and Ringo a kettle drum. John has a sash and Ringo a medal. They stand in an Edwardian sitting room with a wall of framed photographs behind them and a few trophies and shields. To the left of the framed photographs is a pin-up poster of Brigitte Bardot in one of her famous late-fifties poses: kneeling with her hands behind her head. By some oversight, Brigitte did not make it on to the final album sleeve.

Next, Paul made a series of pen-and-ink drawings of the Beatles being presented to some dignitaries in front of a floral clock. Paul: 'I did a lot of drawings of us being presented to the Lord Mayor, with lots of dignitaries and lots of friends of ours around, and it was to be us in front of a big northern floral clock, and we were to look like a brass band. That developed to become the Peter Blake cover.'

Many of Paul's friends had ideas for the sleeve, in particular John Dunbar, who thought that a totally abstract picture with no text or explanation would be a great idea: 'People will know what it is, man, people will know what it is!' But Paul was unconvinced and thought that the idea was too radical. He explained to John that the Beatles had fans from nine to ninety years old, and though the group in their mid-twenties would get it, many of the others wouldn't. Paul: 'It was probably just as well because it was confusing enough for people anyway, but I think the cover made it on its own, and it became a very famous cover.'

Paul showed his drawings to Robert Fraser, who immediately suggested that the Beatles should get a 'real' artist to execute the sleeve and suggested Peter Blake. Paul agreed that it would be a perfect project for Peter, so he and Robert went to Peter's house in west London to discuss it with him.

Peter Blake's Pop Art has the nostalgic quality of English popular culture: circus artistes, wrestling posters, strippers, Victorian toys, seaside piers, 'What the Butler Saw' machines and naughty postcards, even when he is painting Elvis, Bo Diddley, the Beatles, the Lettermen or LaVern Baker. His work is painterly, always brilliantly drawn, but based on the folk-art style of inn signs, painted barges and fairground rides. There is a sense of the accumulation of centuries of memorabilia, household scrapbook mementoes and Victorian advertising. He painted his first comic strip in 1957 and was one of the founders of the Pop Art movement. The *Sgt. Pepper* cover as conceived by Paul, with its English popular cultural imagery, its collage of heroes and whiff of nostalgia, could have been custom-made for Peter Blake.

> PAUL: So I took the little drawings of the floral clock and the Lord Mayor and all our heroes, which was like the end design, and we went to see Peter. He lived in a little suburban house in an ordinary row; a very cosy house with lots of things everywhere like an antique shop. All the walls were loaded with pictures, the corridor to the next room and up to the bedroom was filled with tattooed-lady pictures – he had a lot of those.

There were posters of Hilda Beck and Tarzan the wrestler. Works by other artists, including columns by Joe Tilson and a Richard Smith painting, filled the walls.

> All Peter's early stuff was there: the Wrestlers, the little boy with badges, the pin-ups, his great works, work by other pop artists. His picture of the Beatles was there too, so it was like 'Oh, hey!' It's difficult to say anything, because when it's the Beatles it's not a portrait of you, it's a portrait of your legend. It's difficult to comment, so I think we just bantered about it. I told him I thought it was very good. He got a cool likeness of me at the time, so I was able to compliment him on it, but mainly I was looking around for my own interest really. We talked about Elvis and Gene Vincent and stuff like that that was the real deep common denominator.

Peter Blake was then married to the American artist Jann Haworth,

Unfinished drawing by Paul of a map showing the location of Indica Books and Gallery in Mason's Yard, to be used as a flyer.

Indica under construction in January 1966 (l to r) Miles, John Dunbar, Marianne Faithfull (holding an electric plug), Peter Asher and Paul McCartney. [*Graham Keen*]

Front page of *The International Times*, January 16 1967.

Wrapping paper, designed and printed by Paul as a surprise present when Indica opened in February 1966.

William Burroughs. [*Graham Keen*]

Cornelius Cardew. [*Frazer Wood*]

Peter Blake. [*Camera Press*]

Michelangelo Antonioni. [*Keystone*]

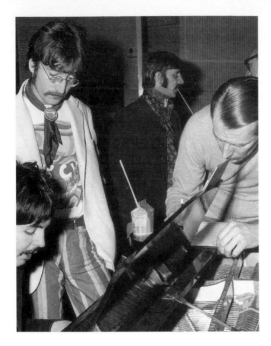

Working with George Martin
on *Sgt. Pepper.* [*Apple*]

Recording *Sgt. Pepper.*
The alarm clock was
used by Mal Evans on
'A Day in the Life'.
[*Apple*]

At Michael Cooper's Chelsea studio to photograph the sleeve for *Sgt. Pepper*. Front row: Neil Aspinall, George Harrison, John Lennon, Robert Fraser, Paul McCartney, Ringo Starr, Michael Cooper. Seated: Cooper's son Adam. [*Michael Cooper / Apple*]
Linda meets Paul for the second time at the *Sgt. Pepper* party. [*Keystone*]

Posed photograph from the party at Brian Epstein's house to launch *Sgt. Pepper*. [*Linda McCartney*]

This advertisement is sponsored by SOMA*

the law against marijuana is immoral in principle and unworkable in practice

The signatories to this petition suggest to the Home Secretary that he implement a five point programme of cannabis law reform :

1 THE GOVERNMENT SHOULD PERMIT AND ENCOURAGE RESEARCH INTO ALL ASPECTS OF CANNABIS USE, INCLUDING ITS MEDICAL APPLICATIONS.

2 ALLOWING THE SMOKING OF CANNABIS ON PRIVATE PREMISES SHOULD NO LONGER CONSTITUTE AN OFFENCE.

3 CANNABIS SHOULD BE TAKEN OFF THE DANGEROUS DRUGS LIST AND CONTROLLED, RATHER THAN PROHIBITED, BY A NEW AD HOC INSTRUMENT.

4 POSSESSION OF CANNABIS SHOULD EITHER BE LEGALLY PERMITTED OR AT MOST BE CONSIDERED A MISDEMEANOUR, PUNISHABLE BY A FINE OF NOT MORE THAN £10 FOR A FIRST OFFENCE AND NOT MORE THAN £25 FOR ANY SUBSEQUENT OFFENCE.

5 ALL PERSONS NOW IMPRISONED FOR POSSESSION OF CANNABIS OR FOR ALLOWING CANNABIS TO BE SMOKED ON PRIVATE PREMISES SHOULD HAVE THEIR SENTENCES COMMUTED.

Jonathan Aitken
Tariq Ali
David Bailey
Humphry Berkeley
Anthony Blond
Derek Boshier
Sidney Briskin
Peter Brook
Dr. David Cooper
Dr. Francis Crick, F.R.S.
David Dimbleby
Tom Driberg, M.P.
Dr. Ian Dunbar
Brian Epstein
Dr. Aaron Esterson
Peter Fryer
John Furnival
Tony Garnett
Clive Goodwin
Graham Greene
dsh
Richard Hamilton
George Harrison, M.B.E.
Michael Hastings
Dr. J. M. Heaton
David Hockney
Jeremy Hornsby
Dr. S. Hutt
Francis Huxley
Dr. Brian Inglis
The Revd. Dr. Victor E. S. Kenna, O.B.E.
George Kiloh
Herbert Kretzmer

Dr. R. D. Laing
Dr. Calvin Mark Lee
John Lennon, M.B.E.
Dr. D. M. Lewis
Paul McCartney, M.B.E.
David McEwen
Alasdair MacIntyre
Dr. O. D. Macrae-Gibson
Tom Maschler
Michael Abdul Malik
George Melly
Dr. Jonathan Miller
Adrian Mitchell
Dr. Ann Mully
P. H. Nowell-Smith
Dr. Christopher Pallis
John Piper
Patrick Procktor
John Pudney
Alastair Reid
L. Jeffrey Selznick
Nathan Silver
Tony Smythe
Michael Scho...
D...

DISCLAIMER—Signatures should in no w... or support of its aims or objectives.
*SOMA is applying for recognition as a comp... Trust. It is being formed to examine withou... moral, social and philosophical aspects of he... reference to the effects of pleasure-giving dru... discussion on the mechanisms, potentialities an... ness and will publish its findings. Contributor... postal orders should be made payable to SOMA, ... ant, 20, Fitzroy Square, W.1.

"All laws which can be violated without doing anyone any injury are laughed at. Nay, so far are they from doing anything to control the desires and passions of man that, on the contrary, they direct and incite men's thoughts toward those very objects ; for we always strive toward what is forbidden and desire the things we are not allowed to have. And men of leisure are never deficient in the ingenuity needed to enable them to outwit laws framed to regulate things which cannot be entirely forbidden. . . . He who tries to determine everything by law will foment crime rather than lessen it."—Spinoza

The herb Cannabis sativa, known as 'Marihuana' or 'Hashish', is prohibited under the Dangerous Drugs Act (1965). The maximum penalty for smoking cannabis is ten years' imprisonment and a fine of £1,000. Yet informed medical opinion supports the view that cannabis is the least harmful of pleasure-giving drugs, and is, in particular, far less harmful than alcohol. Cannabis is non-addictive, and prosecutions for disorderly behaviour under its influence are unknown.

The use of cannabis is increasing, and the rate of increase is accelerating. Cannabis smoking is widespread in the universities, and the custom has been taken up by writers, teachers, doctors, businessmen, musicians, scientists, and priests. Such persons do not fit the stereotype of the unemployed criminal dope fiend. Smoking the herb also forms a traditional part of the social and religious life of hundreds of thousands of immigrants to Britain.

A leading article in The Lancet (9 November, 1963) has suggested that it is "worth considering . . . giving cannabis the same status as alcohol by legalizing its import and consumption . . . Besides the undoubted attraction of reducing, for once, the number of crimes that a member of our society can commit, and of allowing the wider spread of something that can give pleasure, a greater revenue would certainly come to the State from taxation than from fines. . . . Additional gains might be the reduction of inter-racial tension, as well as that between generations."

The main justification for the prohibition of cannabis has been the contention that its use leads to heroin addiction. This contention does not seem to be supported by any documented evidence, and has been specifically refuted by several authoritative studies. It is almost certainly correct to state that the risk to cannabis smokers of becoming heroin addicts is far less than the risk to drinkers of becoming alcoholics.

Cannabis is usually taken by normal persons for the purpose of enhancing sensory experience. Heroin is taken almost exclus...
reality. By prohibiting cannabis Parliam...
where heroin could occasion...
otherwise have...
n...

at a moment of national anxiety". In recent months the persec... of cannabis smokers has been intensified. Much larger fines a... increasing proportion of unreasonable prison sentences sugges... the crime at issue is not so much drug abuse as heresy.

The prohibition of cannabis has brought the law into disreput... has demoralized police officers faced with the necessity of enforci... unjust law. Uncounted thousands of frightened persons have arbitrarily classified as criminals and threatened with arrest, victimia... and loss of livelihood. Many of them have been exposed to ... contempt in the courts, insulted by uniformed magistrates an... to suffer in prison. They have been hunted down with Alsatian do... stopped on the street at random and improperly searched. The Na... Council for Civil Liberties has called attention to instances... drugs have apparently been ' planted ' on suspected cannabis sm... Chief Constables have appealed to the public to inform on their... bours and children. Yet despite these gross impositions and the... to civil liberties which they pose the police freely admit that they... been unable to prevent the spread of cannabis smoking.

Abuse of opiates, amphetamines and barbiturates has bec... serious national problem, but very little can be done about it se... as the prohibition of cannabis remains in force. The police do no... the resources or the manpower to deal with both cannabis an... dangerous drugs at the same time. Furthermore prohibition prov... potential breeding ground for many forms of drug abuse and gan... ism. Similar legislation in America in the 'twenties brought th... of both alcohol and heroin under the control of an immensely po... criminal conspiracy which still thrives today. We in Britain mu... lose sight of the parallel.

MEDICAL OPINION

"There are no lasting ill-effects from the acute use of mar... and no fatalities have ever been recorded. . . . The causal relati... between these two events (marihuana smoking and heroin addicti... never been substantiated. In spite of the once heated interchanges... members of the medical profession and between the medical pro... and law enforcement officers there seems to be a growing agr... within the medical community, at least, that marihuana do... directly cause criminal behaviour, juvenile delinquency, sexual excit... or addiction."

Dr. J. H. Jaffe, in The Pharmacological Basis of Therapeutics, L. Goodman... Gillman, Eds., 3rd Ed. 1965

"Certain specific myths require objective confrontation since... wise they recurrently confuse the issue, and incidentally divert the... and attention of police and customs and immigration authori... directions which have very little to do with facts and much more... with prejudiced beliefs. The relative innocence of ... rijuana t... parison with alcohol is one such fact ...] a com... myth."

Dr. David Stat...
Tim...
...lly sp...
...mo...
...ed ap...
...s and...
...s co...
...as...
...r,...
...it...

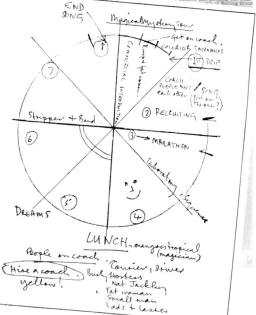

Paul's 'scrupt' for *Magical Mystery Tour*.

Richard Hamilton. [*Camera Press*]

Jimi Hendrix. [*Hulton Getty*]

Pete Brown. [*Graham Keen*]

John Hopkins. [*Graham Keen*]

who also exhibited at Robert Fraser's gallery. She made life-size stuffed figures of off-beat characters. Two of her waxwork dummies sat on the settee. One memorable show included a collection of oversize teddy bears, each with John Betjeman's face, some of whom were having a teddy bears' picnic. John Betjeman was the British Poet Laureate, best known for his poems on country churches and his celebration of English suburbia. As Paul explored Peter and Jann's house, he came across some of her Betjeman teddy bears in a drawing room filled with potted plants: 'Jan had a big Californian surfer, one of her models, standing there, but the Betjeman was the most memorable. I love Betjeman as well, he was so sweet. I would like to have hung out with him but I never got to meet him.'

Peter Blake looked the archetypal artist, with a pointed beard and dressed in Levi jacket and jeans, then virtually impossible to obtain in Britain, where the fashion of wearing jeans had not yet caught on and Levis were available only from one of two import shops. He had what Paul called a 'precise English gentlemanly scholarly twinkle in the eye'. They got on well.

PAUL: I remember asking him for painting hints. I asked him to give me a couple of lessons but it just fell by the way. Recently he said, 'Oh, did I? Oh, I would have, I'd have been pleased to.' But I really wanted little hints, like how do you get a hair off the canvas when it gets on there?

So, I showed him my little drawings and said, 'Look, we're on a little hill like this, and we have a floral clock there, what can we do with this? This is my idea so far, you can mess it round, I'm not fixed. I'd love your input.' And from there it grew. Now that Peter was involved, Robert actually had a role; it led Robert to becoming an unofficial art director on the project.

The idea did get a bit metamorphosed when Peter was brought in; they changed it in good ways. The clock became the sign of the Beatles in front of it, the floral clock metamorphosed into a flower bed. Our heroes in photographs around us became the crowd of dignitaries, and it was them that was presenting us with something, except no one was getting presented with something any more. So the idea just crystallised a bit. Which was good. It took a lot of working out but it's one of the all-time covers, I think, so that was great.

Finding photographs of everyone on the list was the first problem. First of all, Neil Aspinall went looking for portraits of everyone on the list as it stood before Peter Blake was involved. The list he brought into Indica Bookshop read as follows:

Yogas, Marquis de Sade, Hitler, Nietzsche, Lenny Bruce, Lord Buckley, Aleister Crowley, Dylan Thomas, James Joyce, Oscar Wilde, William Burroughs, Robert Peel, Stockhausen, Aldous Huxley, H. G. Wells, Einstein, Carl Jung, Beardsley, Alfred Jarry, Tom Mix, Johnny Weissmuller, Magritte, Tyrone Power, Karl Marx, Richmal Crompton, Dick Barton, Tommy Hanley, Albert Stubbins, Fred Astaire.

George's list had been composed of nothing but Indian gurus, including his favourites: Babaji and Paramahansa Yogananda. John's list ran from de Sade to Oscar Wilde; he later added Lewis Carroll and Edgar Allan Poe. A cut-out of Hitler, who was on his list, was made and removed from the set up only just before the photo session began. Paul's list ran from William Burroughs to Fred Astaire. Ringo said he would go along with whatever the others chose. Peter Blake added W. C. Fields, Tony Curtis, Dion, Shirley Temple, Sonny Liston and the sculptor H. C. Westerman. Robert Fraser suggested Terry Southern and the American artists Wally Berman and Richard Lindner.

In the end, the list departed very much from the original concept; for various reasons people got dropped and others, who had little to do with the Beatles, were added. Brigitte Bardot, who is drawn ten times larger than any other hero in Paul's original sketch, does not appear but Diana Dors, a pale English imitation from the same era, does. Magritte and Alfred Jarry similarly did not appear, though they were on earlier lists. The project was taking on a life of its own.

PAUL: Then we had a few meetings and we decided it might need to be a gatefold thing because we started to need space. George Martin in his book says *Sgt. Pepper* was going to be a double album but they didn't have enough material. I'm not sure that's true. I think it was always going to be single album but we ran out of space for the artwork rather than have too little material. We suddenly had an art project here and people want canvases, you know.

It quickly became obvious that the outdoors municipal environment was no longer appropriate and that it would be much easier to shoot the cover in a studio. Robert Fraser recommended that the ex-*Vogue* photographer Michael Cooper take the picture and that the set should be built in his studio in Flood Street, Chelsea. Behind most of Robert's suggestions, there was an ulterior motive. In this case Robert happened to be in business with Michael Cooper and had set up the Flood Street photographic studio with him as a business venture the previous year. Michael Cooper took all the photographs for Robert's gallery and Robert steered as much business through the studio as possible.

PAUL: So we had the cover pretty much covered. There was a lot of running to and fro. I went out a couple of times to Peter's and he came to Cavendish Avenue a couple of times. Robert would say, 'Do you mind if we do this?' or 'This would be great,' and 'Peter would like to do this,' 'Peter wants to go to Madame Tussauds and he wants to use your waxwork models and Sonny Liston's.' So it was great, great, great. It was really developing fine. The Rolling Stones were friends of us all, and I think Robert thought that it would be a great harmonious gesture to actually acknowledge them on our record cover because everyone thought the Beatles and the Stones are always bitching at each other, so that would be far out. There were millions of ideas like that. Peter knew a lot of fairground painters who paint roundabouts and sideshows, so he got somebody to do the bass drum specially for it. We just developed it. It was a nice art project. It was great.

Everything was done by consensus between Paul, the other Beatles, Robert, Peter and Jann. John went with Robert to see Peter Blake early on, but did not get very involved, partly because he was living out of town. Brian Epstein had been against a 'group photograph' idea from the beginning and had little to do with the sleeve, although when it came to getting copyright clearance to use the likenesses of the famous crowd, it was his office that was given the job. Brian had become heavily involved with the sixties drug scene and spent the four months *Sgt. Pepper* took to record either on holiday or in the Priory, an expensive residential drug-rehabilitation centre in Putney, London. He left the clinic long enough to launch the album with a

party at his house on Chapel Street but returned to the Priory after
the party. His long-suffering assistant Wendy Hanson had already
resigned in desperation because drugs had made him impossible to
deal with. He had to hire her on a freelance basis specifically to get the
copyright clearances for the album since no one else at NEMS was
capable of doing it.

EMI were not very pleased with the sleeve idea either. They were
concerned about the copyright implications of using the likenesses of
so many famous people, and very concerned about the idea of using
Mahatma Gandhi in the line-up, which they felt, probably correctly,
could lead to unpleasant political repercussions in India, a country
where EMI had a very large domestic market controlled by their
subsidiary, the Gramophone Company of India (Private) Limited of
Dum Dum. Since the Beatles were making literally millions of pounds
in profits for the company, they merited a personal visit from the
EMI chairman Sir Joseph Lockwood.

PAUL: They just wouldn't let Gandhi be on the cover and Sir Joe
Lockwood came round to my house to tell me this personally.
He said it could be taken as an insult in India. I always got on
particularly well with Joe, I liked him a lot. I think he was a very
clever man and found him a very charming bloke with a sense of
humour. So it never got heavy with Joe. He always had his
young personal-assistant guy with him, very charming. It was
unusual for us, who'd not seen the head of a big company like
that that at close hand; with a private life, just to the side of it all.
You were seeing power in high places.

So he came round. And he said, 'Oh, er,' smirking a bit. 'We
have some problems on this. I'm afraid they've sent me around.'
And he said, 'There are going to be a lot of problems on all these
people, all these faces, because everyone has the right to their
own likeness and you can't just put them on a cover. They're
going to sue us. We're going be up to our eyeballs in lawsuits.'
I said, 'No, you won't.' He said, 'We will.' I said, 'They'll all
be pleased to be on it.' I said, 'What you should do is ring them
all and ask 'em! Have you rung them all?' 'No.' I said, 'Well, ring
Marlon Brando, or his agent, and say, the Beatles would love
him to be on this little montage, on the front. It's nothing
detrimental or anything. It's a homage that the Beatles are doing

to these people. Explain it. I would think they would be pleased to be on it. It's a big thing being on a Beatle cover ...' 'Mmmm,' he said. 'We'll get a lot of letters.' So I said, 'Well, everyone you get a letter from, let me know and it'll have to come out of royalties, so cover your ass legally but just let us get on with it.' Which he did.

In *Abbey Road*, the official history of the studios, written by Brian Southall, Sir Joseph Lockwood said:

I told them they would have to take Gandhi out as he was a holy man and that they would have to get permission from each of the people included in the picture before we would agree to its use. They gave us an indemnity for 10 million dollars royalties in the light of any legal action and set about contacting the people. The first telegram they sent was to Leonard Bernstein, who said he would be 'delighted' to be on the sleeve and the remarkable thing is that we have never had a single claim on that record even though the Beatles didn't bother to contact everybody.

PAUL: EMI is very like the BBC or the government. It's a giant institution and I've always found that one of its charms. Some people hate that kind of thing, but I don't. I like the BBC. I always imagine Britain without the Beeb would be a very different place. Sometimes that kind of stuff's central to your civilisation. Iraq hasn't got a Beeb, has it? For all its dreadfulness and for all its terrible cobwebbiness, there is an amazing machine in place there. I value that kind of stuff. We used the Beeb like a giant loudspeaker, loudhailer. We were there often and they would put out our music to all the country, then often it would get on the World Service, so you knew you were getting round the world with it. So it was a great machine to plug into. One of the original clean machines.

The idea for the *Pepper* thing to me was to give as much as you could. All of us Beatles remembered going to the record shop when we were kids; Saturday mornings was my free time to go and shop, school the rest of the week and homework etcetera, but Saturday morning I had my pocket money, and I'd saved up and I used to go into the record department of Lewis's and there'd be girls with beehives sitting round dreamily listening to Johnny Mathis sing 'A Certain Smile', and you'd come in and riffle through the 45s and 78s; originally it was 78s and then as we grew up it became 45s, and EPs. And I'd been burned once or twice. I remember buying a record called 'Rock Pile' by Ray Charles. I loved 'What'd I Say', but this was an instrumental. It was the Ray Charles Orchestra, it might not have even been by Ray Charles, so I'd spent this sacred money, this long-saved pocket money, and I'd blown it on a piece of shit. I once bought a Little Richard record which consisted of one live track of his and the rest consisted of this Buck Ram Orchestra, and I hated that. We all hated that. So by the time we got to *Pepper*, we thought, we'll make the album we always wanted to make. We'll really do it all this time. We're in no hurry. There's no tour we have got to be on, we're getting stoned, we're feeling great; we were being cool about this whole thing. We wanted it to be very very full of value.

I wanted a great cover, I wanted it packed with images. I wanted something I could read on the bus back from Lewis's, because that's what I used to do. I'd take it out of its brown paper bag and read it. And I could read some albums for half an hour and just look at the graphics. It was the age of sleeve notes. So we wanted to pack it with goodies. One of the ideas was to have an envelope and in it we were going to have things like they used to hand out in comics: we wanted transfers you could stick on yourself, because we had those when we were kids. It was all childhood memories.

I had to fight at EMI even for things like the thickness of the cardboard. EMI were always trying to give me less and less thick cardboard. I said, 'Look, when I was a kid, I loved my records, the good ones, and I wanted to protect them and thick cardboard would keep my records. That's all I want to do is give the kids who buy our stuff something to protect our records.' 'Well now, Paul, we can't do it, the volume you boys sell at. If we can save point oh oh pence … And you can't tell the difference.' 'I bloody can! That's a thin piece of cardboard!' But I got my thick cardboard. I was always arguing for things like that. It somehow fell to me. Later people put me down for that, 'Oh, he was always the pushy one, the PR one.' The truth was, no other fucker would do it! And it had to get done, and I was

living in London and I could hop in a taxi and go down
Manchester Square and say, 'I'll be down in ten minutes to talk
to you about the cardboard.'

Our idea was to give people a record, which is a damn fine
record, you get a thick cover, which lasts and lasts for years and
years, you get a cover you can read for ever, you get goodies,
freebies, and 'all yours for the price of a regular record'! That's
what we wanted to do. They kept saying, 'No, that'll increase the
price,' so the envelope of little sticky things had to become more
practical. So that became the insert with *Sgt. Pepper* on it that
you could take off and make into a badge, the moustache and
the bass drum. That became the practical way they could give it
to us. We fought like devils, I tell you. But I see no reason why
you shouldn't fight for things like that. It was like, 'We're the
Beatles, it's not as if we're some shitty act. We're making you a
lot of money. It's not as if you couldn't give us a little bit back.
All we're trying to do is give people a great deal, they'll buy more
because it's a great deal and they'll come back for the next one,'
so it all seemed very wise to us.

The idea of giving their fans extra value made Paul and John decide
that instead of having sleeve notes, they would print the lyrics of the
songs on the sleeve. The music-publishing company immediately
objected, thinking, probably correctly, that it would cut the sales of
sheet music. It was the first time anyone had done this with lyrics,
though until then the vast majority of pop groups did not write their
own material so for most of them the question did not arise. The
Beatles didn't realise that this was a ground-breaking exercise. Paul
thinks it was probably the idea of Gene Mahon, a designer whom
they hired as a co-ordinator on the project. 'He was a nice Irish guy
who was at an ad agency who we found to help pull it all together
because we had Michael Cooper, we had Robert, Peter, Jann, Neil
and all of us to get together.'

Gene Mahon was working at a new advertising agency called Geer
Dubois. It became Gene's job to do most of the hard work on putting
the sleeve together; working from the agency's offices, he and a
colleague, Al Vandenberg, selected most of the photographs and
supervised the enlargements. Robert Fraser and Michael Cooper
were much too grand to do such work, and also too out of it on junk

most of the time (like Robert, Michael was also a junkie). It was Gene Mahon who pulled the line from the lyrics and inserted it as the final credit on the back sleeve: 'A splendid time is guaranteed for all.'

The Fool

When it was decided that the record needed a gatefold sleeve in order to accommodate the insert, the Beatles hired a Dutch group known as the Fool to paint a scene for the inner spread. The Fool consisted of Simon Posthuma and Marijke Koger, who arrived in London from Amsterdam, via Morocco, at the end of 1966. Not long afterwards they were joined by Josje Leeger, also from Amsterdam, and an Englishman, Barrie Finch, who worked for Brian Epstein's Saville Theatre and met them when he commissioned them to do a concert poster. The hippie philosophy had been seized upon wholeheartedly by the young Dutch: they smoked more pot, held bigger love-ins in the Vondel Park, listened to more interminable guitar solos and dressed more exotically than any other hippies on earth, and Simon and Marijke were no exception

Simon was twenty-eight, tall, well-built, with long dark wavy hair and a Van Dyke nose. He dressed in full-sleeved silk blouses, gold chains, red knee-length boots with patterned Turkish pants billowing over the top, often topped off with a full-length red cloak. He was a painter and very much the mentor of the group. He was prone to deliver long bouts of hippie philosophy, though his English was not as good as Marijke's. She was twenty-three and had been a commercial artist in Holland. Her long red hair was worn in bangs held in place by multicoloured headscarves. Over her tiny miniskirt she wore layer after layer of brightly patterned silk blouses, waistcoats, brocaded jerkins and silk coats, as well as a tangle of ethnic jewellery. They were vegetarians, teetotal, and studied Rudolf Steiner and other esoteric philosophers. They were followers of the Dutch medium Josef Rudolf, but also had their own Hindu swami. Most of all, they studied the Tarot. Simon told the *Sunday Times*: 'You are what you made yourself and every race and nationality is joined. There is a general spiritual revival going on and we should be governed by people who have regard for our spiritual life. In future people will have more leisure and they will have to develop their inner eye. They will want to get to know the supreme power: love!'

PAUL: Originally it was just Simon and Marijke, and later they called themselves the Fool. I used to know Marijke, she was a quite striking-looking girl. She used to read my fortune in Tarot cards, which was something I wasn't too keen on because I didn't want to draw the death card one day. I still don't like that kind of stuff because I know my mind will dwell on it. I always steered a bit clear of all that shit, but in fact it always used to come out as the Fool. And I used to say, 'Oh, dear!' and she used to say, 'No no no. The Fool's a very good card. On the surface it looks stupid, the Fool, but in fact it's one of the best cards, because it's the innocent, it's the child, it's that reading of fool.' So I began to like the word 'fool', because I began to see through the surface meaning. I wrote 'The Fool on the Hill' out of that experience of seeing Tarot cards.

Simon and Marijke had produced a couple of psychedelic posters: one of Bob Dylan in the current style of Aubrey Beardsley on acid, and another simply spelling out 'Love' in swirling lettering among stylised figures. They rented a small shop front on Goswell Street, off New Cavendish Street, to sell North African jewellery and clothes, psychedelic posters, joss sticks and books of esoteric philosophy.

For the *Sgt. Pepper* centrefold Simon and Marijke painted a dream landscape of stylised mountain peaks and wonderful birds, like an LSD-influenced Chinese willow-pattern design. The sky was rainbowed with two oval panels for text, one of which was filled with stars and comets. A further empty panel had a flower border with a peacock draping its tail over the side. Tiny figures of the Beatles peeped out from among the flora. The style was Euro-psychedelic, owing much to Mucha, Beardsley, art nouveau and nineteenth-century children's book illustration. Unfortunately they got the dimensions wrong, but even with a border added, the work looked somehow second-rate. The Beatles, however, loved it.

PAUL: They had done a drawing that was going to be the whole centrefold and Robert said, 'Uh-uh, it's no good. It's not good art.' And we said, 'Oh, it's fabulous, man! You know, it looks great! Here we are, we're going to be smiling out of the clouds and it's all colourful.' And he said, 'Yes, but they don't draw well. It, it, it's not good,' and he just wouldn't allow it. I said, 'Tough shit, it's our record, you may be a consultant, man, but it's not your record and the Beatles want it.' I think what let them down was the drawing. The colours were very nice and their clothes were smashing, patchwork and velvet and all that, but actual draughtsmanship was what Robert was talking about. And he refused to allow it, which was very ballsy because he actually didn't have the right. We said, 'We just won't do it your way,' and right to the end almost it was going to be the Fool cover. We resisted that for quite a few days. And I've since seen it and I know he was quite right about it.

At Michael Cooper's studio at 4 Chelsea Manor Studios, Flood Street, SW3, the set took two weeks to assemble. The photographs were enlarged, hand-tinted and glued to hardboard sheets to be cut out as silhouettes. Figures arrived from Madame Tussauds and from Jann Haworth. The Beatles' Sergeant Pepper uniforms were made and delivered to them at Abbey Road, where they tried them on and wore them for part of a session.

On 30 March 1967, the day of the shoot, Clifton Nurseries in St John's Wood, where Paul bought his plants for Cavendish Avenue, delivered the potted plants. They did not bring enough flowers for even a small floral clock so the delivery boy made a guitar with them instead. Gene Mahon sat in a side room, rolling joints. The Beatles and their friends and associates arrived and the shoot began. Robert suggested the Beatles have a series of portrait shots done at the same time as the front-cover photo session, because that would make a much better centre spread. They also shot the back-cover picture to use with the lyrics. There was a rumour, part of the 'Paul is dead' madness, that Mal Evans replaced Paul in the back-cover shot, but since this is taken from the same session as the front sleeve, and Mal was about twice as big as Paul, this is impossible.

When Robert handed them the portraits from the Michael Cooper session, he said, 'No, really. This should be it. It just ties in so much better,' and the Beatles finally agreed to replace the Fool's artwork with the portrait. The Fool were asked to do the inner sleeve instead, which was not normally designed at all. They made an abstract wave pattern printed in different shades of maroon, which fitted well with the rest of the sleeve.

PAUL: The inside cover was now to be the portrait, which Robert thought was very strong, for a number of reasons. One of the things we were very much into in those days was eye messages. I had seen a thing on TV about eye contact in apes, and I'd become fascinated by this whole idea that you don't look at each other. I'd thought this was a way to get a breakthrough here on acid and this became a sort of party game we used to play then. I used to play it all the time with Mal and John, you get a feedback. Quite trippy.

I remember later John and Yoko looking at each other for hours in the studio because it became a thing for bonding, it became almost necessary. John and Yoko looking at each other for hours and hours – 'It's gonna be all right! It's gonna be all right! It's gonna be all right! It's gonna be all right!' – using that as a mantra. Funky games. So with Michael Cooper's inside photo, we all said, 'Now look into the camera and really say "I love you!" Really try and feel love, really give love through this! It'll come out, it'll show, it's an attitude.' And that's what that is, if you look at it you'll see the big effort from the eyes.

The money men at EMI were horrified when they saw the bill for the sleeve. Their usual budget for a sleeve photograph was £25, perhaps rising to £75 for an act as big as the Beatles. Copyright and retouching fees for the cut-out heroes came to £1,367.13.3d. Robert Fraser and Michael Cooper's fees amounted to £1,500.12.0d, out of which Peter Blake was given £200. Sir Joe Lockwood told Robert Fraser that he could have hired the whole of the London Symphony Orchestra for what it cost.

It was worth it. The *Sgt. Pepper* sleeve became an immediate popular culture icon. David Mellor, commenting on it in his book *The Sixties Art Scene in London*, said:

> The wall of faces of cult heroes are like badges covering a jacket. This album cover was, among other things, an evocation of popular memory – with the civic, parkland space in the foreground and the souvenir 'kit' inside the record sleeve, the entirety formed the apotheosis of Blake's assemblage style, which was now feeding back into popular commercial design and packaging.

Certainly as far as Peter Blake was concerned the feedback was complete: he was now responsible for one of the cultural icons that previously he would have used as his subject matter. Pop had become Art.

Sgt. Pepper was released on 1 June 1967 and critical reaction was virtually unanimous in its praise. Almost the only seriously dissenting voice was Richard Goldstein in the *Village Voice*, and even his critical appraisal admitted that it was better than 80 per cent of all other music around. The underground press raved, and *Crawdaddy* magazine ran a seventeen-page review by the editor Paul Williams, written high on acid. It seems that he liked it. Timothy Leary said, 'I declare that John Lennon, George Harrison, Paul McCartney and Ringo Starr are mutants. Evolutionary agents sent by God, endowed with mysterious powers to create a new human species.' And the English music press finally discovered that producers have a lot to do with making records.

PAUL: When *Sgt. Pepper* came out, the reviews said, 'George Martin's finest album' and 'Svengali-like George Martin', and we went, 'What? What!' It was a piss-off for us because we'd put our heart and soul into it, all this work, and not to detract from George, but it was not good enough that he should get the credit. I mean, this was not George's direction. However much George helped, and he was massive on that album, it was our direction. So I think there's been a slight resentment, certainly on Ringo's part, certainly on George's part, on my part and certainly a very vociferous one on John's part, which was: Hey, George Martin was great. He's a lovely guy and we all loved him, but don't get the idea for one minute that he did it. OK, he was the producer, fine, and you have to give the producer credit, but he couldn't have made this album with Gerry and the Pacemakers, so it's not just George Martin.

He knew those technical things, he was a great help, and we learned a lot of tricks from him: knowing to slow something down to half speed when it was too difficult to play, then play it down an octave and it would be absolutely perfect when it comes back up. And he did arrangements and could play the piano.

The main point was that George was the grown-up, not on drugs, and up behind the glass window, and we were the kids, on drugs, in the studio. He was somebody completely different, an alien force really, performing his wartime role as the Fleet Air Arm observer from behind the glass window. When he was doing his TV programme on *Pepper*, he asked me, 'Do you know what caused *Pepper*?' I said, 'In one word, George, drugs. Pot.' And George said, 'No, no. But you weren't on it all the time.' 'Yes, we were.' *Sgt. Pepper* was a drug album.

The influence of *Sgt. Pepper* on other musicians was enormous. Virtually all the West Coast psychedelic bands cite it as a milestone in their development. But the first tribute from a fellow musician came from Jimi Hendrix. Paul had first seen the Jimi Hendrix Experience at the Bag o'Nails on 11 January 1967.

PAUL: It would be one of his first gigs in London. Jimi was a sweetie, a very nice guy. I remember him opening at the Saville on a Sunday night, 4 June 1967. Brian Epstein used to rent it when it was usually dark on the Sunday. Jimi opened, the curtains flew back and he came walking forward, playing 'Sgt. Pepper', and it had only been released on the Thursday so that was like the ultimate compliment. It's still obviously a shining memory for me, because I admired him so much anyway, he was so accomplished. To think that that album had meant so much to him as to actually do it by the Sunday night, three days after the release. He must have been so into it, because normally it might take a day for rehearsal and then you might wonder whether you'd put it in, but he just opened with it. It's a pretty major compliment in anyone's book. I put that down as one of the great honours of my career. I mean, I'm sure he wouldn't have thought of it as an honour, I'm sure he thought it was the other way round, but to me that was like a great boost.

Even the sleeve of *Sgt. Pepper* was influential, not only in showing what could be done with record sleeves as a vehicle for illustration and artwork, but sparking a series of copies and parodies. The Rolling Stones did a pale imitation with *Their Satanic Majesties Request*, even using Michael Cooper to photograph the sleeve; but the first parody came from Frank Zappa. Zappa was in London in September 1967 to play the Royal Albert Hall and to promote his second album, *Absolutely Free*. He was using the Indica Bookshop as his unofficial headquarters and told Miles he would like to do a parody of the *Sgt.*

Pepper sleeve on his next album. Miles called Paul for him from a back office during an MGM Records press reception for the Mothers, and they talked.

> PAUL: As I remember it, he rang me up and said, 'We want to do an album parodying the *Pepper* cover. I want to do a cover similar to it but with dustbins and garbage and stuff. I'm ringing to see if you have any objection.' I said, 'Well, no, I haven't but sometimes there are copyright problems. It's outside my jurisdiction. I can say, "Hey, Frank, go for it, man!" but then somebody in the lawyers' department of EMI might say, "We don't allow this." You'll have to speak to those people yourself, but as far as I'm concerned, yes, you've got my blessing.' I rang up my office and said, 'Frank Zappa wants to do this. Try and help him if you can.' And then I'm not sure what happened. I assumed he'd done it but then years later I heard him saying, 'Oh, he wouldn't let me do it.'

Frank Zappa, coming from the rough and tumble of small independent labels in Los Angeles, could not have understood how a group as famous as the Beatles could still be powerless in the face of a record company as large and old as EMI. They got away with many things at EMI, but not everything. 'Even with all our clout,' Paul said, 'sometimes they just say no.' In this instance, it seems that MGM-Verve Records, Frank Zappa's label, did not even approach EMI for permission to parody the cover, though it is unlikely that a parody would have constituted an infringement of copyright. MGM thought it would slow their release date and involve expensive lawyers, so they reversed the sleeve, putting the parody heroes and letters made from vegetables inside and the portrait shot as a wrap-around on the outside – a situation that was not rectified until the album, called *We're Only in it for the Money*, came out years later on CD.

NINE

The Walrus Was Paul

You're a genius all the time

Jack Kerouac

Magical Mystery Tour

WITH SGT. PEPPER FINISHED, PAUL DECIDED TO PAY A SURPRISE VISIT to Jane on her twenty-first birthday on 5 April. She was touring the USA with the Bristol Old Vic playing *Romeo and Juliet*. On 3 April 1967, two Air France officials arrived at Cavendish Avenue to pick up Paul and Mal Evans, and not long afterwards they touched down at Orly Airport, Paris. From there they took a direct flight to Los Angeles. Paul had intended to bring a copy of the photograph for the sleeve of *Sgt. Pepper* to show Jane but he forgot. He also forgot to check if his American visa was still valid so it took a half-hour to get him through immigration in Los Angeles. Travelling in style, they hired Frank Sinatra's private Lear jet to fly to San Francisco, which was experiencing its first snow in forty-two years. Here they showed up unannounced at the Fillmore Auditorium, where the Jefferson Airplane happened to be rehearsing. Paul accompanied Marty Balin and Jack Casady to the apartment on Oak Street they shared with their road manager Bill Thompson. Paul played them the acetate of *Sgt. Pepper* he was bringing for Jane and told them about a wonderful new guitarist called Jimi Hendrix. They attempted a jam session, but Paul, being left-handed, found it hard to play Casady's bass upside down. The members of the Airplane toked up on DMT mixed with pot, which Paul decided to forgo. Jack Casady drove them back to their hotel and next day Paul and Mal flew on to Denver.

Paul had his movie camera with him and it was two days later, while filming in a Denver park, that he came up with using a mystery tour as the basis for a television special. Ideas fell quickly into place and it became a magical mystery tour: a typical Beatles combination of northern working-class culture and taking the fans on an acid trip. On 9 April, the Old Vic company flew out to continue their tour of America, and Paul and Mal took Frank Sinatra's Lear jet back to Los Angeles.

> PAUL: I used to do a lot of amateur filming and from my interest in that it was a very small step for me to say, 'Well, if we hired a film cameraman and we told him where to shoot, then we're starting to film, aren't we? As long as we know that we want to go over Westminster Bridge backwards, he'll be able to do that. I can convey it to him.' So, the idea tumbled together that we'd hire a bus, take a bunch of people out and start trying to make up something about a magical mystery tour.
>
> It used to just be called a mystery tour, up north. When we were kids, you'd get on a bus, and you didn't know where you were going, but nearly always it was Blackpool. From Liverpool, it was inevitably Blackpool and everyone would go, 'Oooo, it was Blackpool after all!' Everyone would spend time guessing where they were going, and this was part of the thrill. And we remembered those. So much of the Beatles' stuff was a slight switch on a memory; in 'Penny Lane', the nurse and the barber and the fireman were just people we saw on a bus route, but this time they'd be with us. So we'd always just heighten the reality to make a little bit of surreality. That we were interested in.

There was also an element of Ken Kesey and the Merry Pranksters in the idea. In 1964 Kesey and his cohorts had painted a 1939 International Harvester school bus in psychedelic colours and taken it on a transcontinental tour of the USA, dispensing LSD along the way and filming and recording every dramatic encounter, intending to make a movie called *The Merry Pranksters Search for a Cool Place*. The film never materialised but the bus trip became the stuff of legend, eventually being written up by Tom Wolfe in *The Electric Kool-Aid Acid Test*.

Paul picked up the idea again on the overnight flight back to England on 11 April with Mal. He borrowed a notepad from a stewardess and made notes for the lyrics of the title song; then he began to plan out the film, using a circle to represent the sixty minutes of a television special and slotting in various ideas for events.

John later complained that Paul took over and led the Beatles after Brian died, but no doubt if John had come up with some suggestions of his own instead of drifting in a haze of heroin and LSD, then the others would have been equally responsive. As it was, even before Brian's death, virtually everything the Beatles did from *Sgt. Pepper* onwards was initially proposed by Paul, though Beatles democracy never faltered and all projects had to have approval from all four members of the group.

In the *Rolling Stone* interviews with Jann Wenner, John spoke about *Magical Mystery Tour* as very much Paul's idea. 'He set it up and he had worked it out with Mal and then he came and showed me what his idea was and this is how it went, it went around like this, the story and how he had it all, the production and everything. He said, "Well, here's the segment, you write a little piece for that." And I thought, fuckin' Ada, I've never made a film, what's he mean, write a script?'

In fact Paul discussed the project in some detail in April 1967 with Brian Epstein before *Sgt. Pepper* was even released. Sitting next to Paul on the big settee in Paul's living room, Brian went over all aspects of the project, pausing every few minutes to make a note on a pad of paper. Paul had now reworked his original notes to show the whole sixty-minute film as a pie chart divided into segments. Brian could translate this, as he could all Beatles commands, into specific timetables of booked studios, rehearsal halls, rented equipment, tea for forty-five people and everything else they needed, without the Beatles even suspecting what degree of organisation was actually called for to satisfy their often obscure and demanding requests.

Occasionally Brian would interrupt to say that one of the other Beatles could add something to a scene. He was very concerned that they all had an equal part of the action – 'We must find more for Ringo to do,' 'George could do a song here' – and appeared very enthusiastic and excited about the plan. The Beatles were no longer touring and their latest album had not yet been released so Brian had very little to do on their behalf. He was clearly pleased to be involved in a new major project which would utilise his skills. Had Brian not died, his management skills would have made *Magical Mystery Tour* a great deal easier to make; he would have booked film studios, dealt with unions, hired catering facilities and hotels just as if the Beatles were on tour. He did some preliminary work on the project; for instance, the cinematographer Peter Theobald, who worked on the film as technical director, was recommended by the film critic Peter Wollen after Brian Epstein telephoned the British Film Institute to ask for their recommendations.

It is probably because Brian assumed that he would be producing the film that his American company, Beatles USA Ltd, was registered as the owner of the copyright. Though Brian's percentages, and the way he had cut himself in for 25 per cent of their record royalties for seven years after his management contract would expire, left much to be desired, the title registration of *Magical Mystery Tour* was probably legitimate, given that he was expecting to have some heavy expenses in setting up the project.

It was very simple idea – to get on a bus with a few friends, drive around, improvise a few scenes and film everything that happened – but it would bring the Beatles before their hungry public again and it would also provide the vehicle for some new songs. It was not as good as a full-length film but it was a good structure for a television special. Brian liked it and John was quickly converted to the idea, which had many similarities to the initial concept of *Sgt. Pepper*. John and Paul spent an afternoon at Cavendish Avenue writing the title tune. Though they were still putting the finishing touches to *Sgt. Pepper*, beginning 25 April the Beatles spent five sessions recording and mixing the *Magical Mystery Tour* title track, complete with trumpets.

PAUL: 'Magical Mystery Tour' was co-written by John and I, very much in our fairground period. One of our great inspirations was always the barker. 'Roll up! Roll up!' The promise of something: the newspaper ad that says 'guaranteed not to crack', the 'high class' butcher, 'satisfaction guaranteed' from 'Sgt. Pepper'. 'Come inside,' 'Step inside, Love'; you'll find that pervades a lot of my songs. If you look at all the Lennon–McCartney things, it's a thing we do a lot.

I used to go to the fairgrounds as a kid, the waltzers and the dodgems, but what interested me was the freak shows: the boxing booths, the bearded lady and the sheep with five legs, which actually was a four-legged sheep with one leg sewn on its side. When I touched it, the fellow said, 'Hey, leave that alone!' These were the great things of your youth. So much of your writing comes from this period; your golden memories. If I'm stuck for an idea, I can always think of a great summer, think of a time when I went to the seaside. Okay, sand sun waves donkeys laughter. That's a pretty good scenario for a song.

John and I remembered mystery tours, and we always thought this was a fascinating idea: getting on a bus and not knowing where you were going. Rather romantic and slightly surreal! All these old dears with the blue rinses going off to mysterious places. Generally there's a crate of ale in the boot of the coach and you sing lots of songs. It's a charabanc trip. So we took that idea and used it as a basis for a song and the film.

Because those were psychedelic times it had to become a magical mystery tour, a little bit more surreal than the real ones to give us a licence to do it. But it employs all the circus and fairground barkers, 'Roll up! Roll up!', which was also a reference to rolling up a joint. We were always sticking those little things in that we knew our friends would get; veiled references to drugs and to trips. 'Magical Mystery Tour is waiting to take you *away*,' so that's a kind of drug, 'it's *dying* to take you away' so that's a *Tibetan Book of the Dead* reference. We put all these words in and if you were just an ordinary person, it's a nice bus that's waiting to take you away, but if you're tripping, it's dying, it's the real tour, the real magical mystery tour. We stuck all that stuff in for our 'in group' of friends really.

Magical Mystery Tour was the equivalent of a drug trip and we made the film based on that. 'That'll be good, a far-out mystery tour. Nobody quite knows where they're going. We can take 'em anywhere we want, man!' Which was the feeling of the period. 'They can go in the sky. It can take off!' In fact, in the early script, which was just a few fireside chats more than a script, the bus was going to actually take off and fly up to the magicians in the clouds, which was us all dressed in red magicians' costumes, and we'd mess around in a little laboratory being silly for a while.

The Beatles were in no real hurry to begin filming and intended to finish off one or two other little projects and have their summer holidays before turning their attention to *Magical Mystery Tour*. One of these was a live television broadcast to a potential viewing audience estimated at half a billion. The BBC had come up with the idea of using the newly installed satellite relays to connect the national television networks of countries all around the world. As the BBC put it, 'for the first time ever, linking five continents and bringing man face to face with mankind, in places as far apart as Canberra and Cape Kennedy, Moscow and Montreal, Samarkand and Söderfors, Takamatsu and Tunis'. The Beatles were chosen to represent Britain in the show, which was to be called *Our World*. Rather than play one of their existing hits, or something off *Sgt. Pepper*, they composed a new single specially for the programme.

Paul: '"All You Need Is Love" was John's song. I threw in a few ideas, as did the other members of the group, but it was largely ad libs like singing "She Loves You" or "Greensleeves" or silly little things at the end and we made those up on the spot.' Knowing that millions of the viewers would not understand English, John kept the chorus as simple as possible. It was the philosophy of *Sgt. Pepper* and the era reduced to five words. Paul: 'The chorus "All you need is love" is simple, but the verse is quite complex, in fact I never really understood it, the message is rather complex. It was a good song that we had handy that had an anthemic chorus.'

It took five days of recording and mixing to get the song right but Paul's bass, John's vocal, George's solo and Ringo's drums, as well as the orchestra, were all broadcast live during the event. The Beatles invited Brian Jones, Keith Richards, Mick and Marianne and dozens of other friends to the session, which was staged as a party in Studio One at Abbey Road. The single was released two weeks later and became a hit all around the world.

Other events conspired to delay work on the *Magical Mystery Tour* film: *Sgt. Pepper* was released, the Beatles started Apple and met the Maharishi, and Brian Epstein died, all in a matter of months. On 1 September 1967, four days after Brian Epstein's death, the Beatles met at Cavendish Avenue to plan their future. They put their trip to the Maharishi's ashram in India on hold, but decided to continue with the various Apple projects and keep working on *Magical Mystery Tour*. Alistair Taylor and his wife were dispatched for a weekend at the seaside in Eastbourne to make sure that mystery tours still existed, otherwise no one would know what they were talking about. It turned

out that they did, so Alistair's next task was to go back to Eastbourne
and find a gaudily painted seaside coach. Recording sessions were
booked at Abbey Road for the next week and plans made to begin
filming in two weeks' time.

Not much work had been done on the film in the five months since
they recorded the title track, except for recording one more song for
the soundtrack, Paul's 'Your Mother Should Know', made on 22 and
23 August. It was recorded at Chappell Recording Studios on
Maddox Street, presumably because Abbey Road was not available at
short notice. The second night marked Brian Epstein's last-ever visit
to a Beatles recording session.

> PAUL: I dreamed up 'Your Mother Should Know' as a
> production number. I thought, Well, okay, at least we'll sing one
> or two songs for real. I wrote it in Cavendish Avenue on the
> harmonium I have in the dining room there. My Aunty Jin and
> Uncle Harry and a couple of relatives were staying and they
> were in the living room just across the hall, so I just went to the
> dining room and spent a few hours with the door open with
> them listening. And I suppose because of the family atmosphere
> 'Your Mother Should Know' came in. It's a very music-hall kind
> of thing, probably influenced by the fact that my Aunty Jin was
> in the house.
>
> I've always hated generation gaps. I always feel sorry for a
> parent or a child that doesn't understand each other. A mother
> not being understood by her child is particularly sad because the
> mother went through pain to have that child, and so there is this
> incredible bond of motherly love, like an animal bond between
> them, but because we mess things up so readily they have one
> argument and hate each other for the rest of their lives. So I was
> advocating peace between the generations. In 'Your Mother
> Should Know' I was basically trying to say your mother might
> know more than you think she does. Give her credit.

When it came time to film 'Your Mother Should Know', they
decided to pull out all the stops.

> PAUL: The big prop was that great big staircase that we danced
> down, that was where all the money went: in that particular shot
> on that big staircase. I said, 'Sod it, you've got to have the Busby

Berkeley ending,' and it is a good sequence. Just the fact of John dancing; which he did readily. You can see by the fun expression on his face that he wasn't forced into anything.

People read significance into the fact that I had a black carnation on. The truth of the matter was they'd only brought three red ones. There'd been a mistake, as there often is with film crews, and they'd brought three red ones and a few black ones, and for some reason, I said, 'Well, you have them.' I wasn't trying to make a special point or anything, but it became part of the 'Paul is dead' legacy afterwards. We choreographed the whole thing, we organised it all. We got local scouts and RAF cadets and just said, 'You march across here,' we just did it, we just made it up as we went along. And the best thing I remember, the day we did all that, was doing a thing with the crowd at the end of it, which hardly made it into the movie but was a great shot. I got right up on the crane, miles above all these people, and the whole frame was filled with people looking up at you. It was like an audience looking up at you. We called it 'the sea of faces' when we were editing it. It comes in a very quick shot a couple of times. There was no edge to the frame; you could only see people in the camera. That was my fond memory of that day.

Aside from the two songs ready for the soundtrack, the Beatles had little else prepared. John had spent an afternoon in his swimming pool thinking up ideas for the script. He thought it might be fun to get everyone blind drunk, including himself, naturally, and film that. He came up with a quiz game but it was too corny an idea and he rejected it, along with an idea of playing *Candid Camera* in an out-of-the-way village, pretending to be the Beatles.

John could only think of one person he would like to see on the bus, and that was Nat Jackley, who had always been a hero of the Beatles. He did funny walks, which in music hall are officially known as Eccentric Dancing. He worked in the tradition of the music-hall stars Wilson, Keppel and Betty, Billy Dainty and Max Wall. Paul: 'There's all sorts of swings they can do. It looks very gawky, very funny, and it's very hard to do well. It's a great skill. So we thought, Ah, Nat Jackley. He's great. He just looks funny. He's got a little Hitler moustache, little cloth cap and he's a beanpole of a man. John

particularly admired him.' Nat Jackley was hired to play the Rubber
Man.

They knew from their first two films that they needed to record the
songs for the film in order to be able to mime to them. The recording
of John's 'I Am the Walrus' began on 5 September.

> PAUL: John worked with George Martin on the orchestration and
> did some very exciting things with the Mike Sammes Singers,
> the likes of which they've never done before or since, like getting
> them to chant, 'Everybody's got one, everybody's got one ...',
> which they loved. It was a session to be remembered. Most of
> the time they got asked to do 'Sing Something Simple' and all
> the old songs, but John got them doing all sorts of swoops and
> phonetic noises. It was a fascinating session. That was John's
> baby, great one, a really good one.

Recorded only nine days after Brian Epstein's death, John sounds
in real pain: 'I'm crying!' Far from being light-hearted nonsense
verse, John's lyrics are a desperate howl of frustration. (The 'Eggman'
in the lyrics is almost certainly Eric Burdon, who was known to his
friends as 'Eggs' because he was fond of breaking eggs over naked
girls during sex. In Eric's autobiography he describes an orgy in
Mayfair, following an evening at the Scotch of St James, in which
John Lennon watches him break amyl nitrate capsules under the
noses of two half-naked girls and follow this up with two raw eggs.
John is quoted as encouraging him, 'Go on, go get it, Eggman. Go for
it. I've been there already, it's nice.')

The next session began with Paul recording a demo version of 'The
Fool on the Hill' and laying down basic rhythm tracks for George's
'Blue Jay Way', written when he had a couple of hours to kill because
Derek Taylor had become lost in the canyons in a Los Angeles fog
trying to find Blue Jay Way, where George was staying. In the film
George sits cross-legged on the floor, his expensive cars behind him,
playing a keyboard chalked on the concrete floor like a pavement
artist or an Indian beggar, while the camera does various clever tricks
using prisms, still used today in rock videos.

The fourth track was an instrumental, their first, called 'Flying',
recorded on 8 September, which shows that they had an inkling of
what they were intending to shoot. So far they had recorded tracks
written by John, Paul and George. 'Flying' was democratically

credited to all four of them, including Ringo, making the film, at least at this stage, very much a joint project.

PAUL: 'Flying' was an instrumental that we needed for *Magical Mystery Tour* so in the studio one night I suggested to the guys that we made something up. I said, 'We can keep it very very simple, we can make it a twelve-bar blues. We need a little bit of a theme and a little bit of a backing.' I wrote the melody. The only thing to warrant it as a song is basically the melody, otherwise it's just a nice twelve-bar backing thing. It's played on the Mellotron, on a trombone setting. It's credited to all four, which is how you would credit a non-song.

With the title track and 'Your Mother Should Know', they now had six songs, enough to begin filming.

Paul was always very involved in the sequencing of tracks on albums and in the running order of radio and television shows. He would plan them like a pie chart, cutting up slices of the cake. 'I would say, "that first five minutes is yours, you can do that, we'll have a song here, then I'll do the next five minutes and I'll do a sort of funny thing, then we'll have a number here ..."' He had planned *Magical Mystery Tour* in much the same way with the same diagram that he and Brian Epstein had worked on months before: a single sheet of paper with a circle divided into eight numbered segments:

1. Commercial introduction. Get on the coach. Courier introduces.
2. Coach people meet each other / (Song, Fool On The Hill?)
3. marathon – laboratory sequence.
4. smiling face. LUNCH. mangoes, tropical.(magician)
5. and 6: Dreams.
7. Stripper & band.
8. Song.
END.

There was a cast list: 'People on coach: Courier, driver, Busty hostess, Nat Jackley, Fat woman, small man, lads & lasses.' There was one further note: 'Hire a coach. yellow!' There was no plot, no dialogue and no organisation.

PAUL: We got Neil and Mal, our trusty roadies, to hire a driver and coach and paint our logo on the side: 'Magical Mystery Tour'. We hired a bus full of passengers, some of which were actors. I got a copy of *Spotlight* and selected all the actors from there. I said, 'There's a fat lady. What's her name? Jessie Robbins. Look up her agent. Book her.' 'There's a guy, Derek Royle, looks like he could do Jolly Jimmy Johnson, the courier.' Derek Royle was a good actor who could do athletics, he could do somersaults and stuff, so I knew there would be a bit of mileage in that, we could get him to do some somersaults. Then there was the pretty stewardess, Mandy Weet, who was a bit busty. I must admit, in casting those busty girls there was always a little bit of ulterior motive. It's just the thrill of being able to say, 'Oh, could you stand up please? Could you turn round?' It was just pure libertine casting there. They were all from a copy of *Spotlight*.

We got those people, then we got Ivor Cutler. I knew Ivor, I'd seen him on telly with his very dour Scottish accent, which I like very much, and he used to play this little Indian hand harmonium. He had a song I liked called 'I'm Going in a Field', just a lovely little song. I used to want to record that with him. How I got to know him was, I looked him up in the phone book and rang him up one night. I said, 'Hello, Mr Cutler. My name's Paul McCartney. I'm one of the Beatles. I'm a great admirer of yours. Would you like to come out to dinner?' 'This is very surprising, why are you asking me out?' 'Because I like you.' 'Oh, oh. Oh, very well then. Yes, I wouldn't mind.' He's very precise-spoken Scottish fella, very quiet but real entertaining, real nice bloke. Very sensitive. We went out to dinner. It was very nice. So in the film he became Buster Bloodvessel and he was very good and very helpful. He made that name up. 'Buster, Buster, I could be Buster Bloodvessel.' 'Yes, that's brilliant, got that!' The big fat guy in a band called Bad Manners later used the name.

There were four cameramen and a sound man, a technical adviser and various technical assistants, many of them friends, such as Gavrik Losey, the son of the film director Joseph Losey. Like Jean-Luc Godard's *Breathless*, it was, literally, made on the run; and in its very freedom of form it reflects the improvisational tradition of John

Cassavetes's 1959 *Shadows*, where much of the dialogue was improvised on camera. *Magical Mystery Tour* belongs in its openness to chance and experiment to the time in which it was made; it shows an appreciation – albeit undigested – of the French New Wave, particularly the films of Godard, and a familiarity with the underground movies of Bruce Connor, Kenneth Anger, Antony Balch, Stan Brakhage and others, which Paul had seen at Robert Fraser's flat and at the UFO Club.

> PAUL: We literally made it up as we went. I felt this would be a very bold and a very challenging thing to do. I felt it would be the best thing for us, because we'd had a couple of film scripts and it wasn't that easy to get a perfect writer who could just come up with *a Hard Day's Night* thing, so in the spirit of the times, I thought, Well, we could just go places and arrange people on hills and just film them – 'Do this,' 'Run through there' – and cobble together some sort of story as you went along, because, after all, the theme of a mystery tour is just that: that you don't know where you're going anyway. So we thought we'd take this to the extreme and literally not know what film we were making. And that was part of the buzz.
>
> So we headed off down to Cornwall. We paired a couple of people together: 'Okay. You're the love interest, you two. So whenever we get off the bus, you hold her hand, or be loving. Just develop your little thing.' Personally I just tried to keep an eye on it and tried to be very solicitous, as I thought a director ought to be, with all the actors. I tried to soothe any sort of doubts they had, and believe me they had millions, because I don't think they'd been on a film like this before.

For the actors, as for the symphony orchestra playing without music notation to guide them on 'A Day in the Life', this was relatively new territory, but to the Beatles, veterans of thousands of live performances where improvisation in response to audience reaction was the key to survival, it held no fears. From their first two films they knew something of the techniques required; from countless press conferences, interviews and television shows they had confidence in the spontaneous wit which had contributed greatly to their reputation.

Typically, the film got off to a late start. In the early sixties, when the Beatles toured the country with Helen Shapiro, Tommy Roe and Chris Montez, it was traditional for the tour bus to set out from Allsop Place, a service road of garages and back entrances to the huge Chiltern Court apartment building behind Baker Street tube station. Paul decided to start the Magical Mystery Tour from there, just like a rock 'n' roll touring show. Unfortunately the coach was still being painted in its new livery and, on 11 September 1967, it arrived two hours late for its 10.45 a.m. departure. Thirty-three passengers climbed aboard, plus a film crew, and set out for the West Country, picking up John, George and Ringo in Virginia Water on the way. It was not until they were on the coach that most of the actors realised that they were expected to improvise. Paul: 'I explained to them on the coach what we were trying to do. I went round them all ...'

The filming was not as chaotic as has sometimes been made out. They had already recorded the six soundtrack songs so they knew they had to film sequences to go with them and that alone would account for a substantial portion of the film.

PAUL: We had to have a beginning, so I'd shot it with that in mind. I knew that we had to have Ringo shuffling up the street with his old mum, the fat lady, and getting on the bus and that would start us off. That was an opening. Once we got on the bus we could let the bus take off and then all sorts could happen. And we knew we had to have something to finish, so 'Your Mother Should Know', being the big production number, seemed an okay way to finish, and looking back on it, I am pretty proud of that.

It was mainly John and I doing it. We were the main forces, pretty much as usual, I suppose. I think it was generally considered I was directing it. For instance, I'd hold all the meetings in the evening with Peter Theobald and the cameraman. 'What did you get today?' 'Did you end-slate it?' and all this. I became used to the way of doing it. I enjoyed the organisational thing of it all, and it was fairly easy-going. Obviously it wasn't as tough as directing a major feature.

The first overnight stop was at the Royal Hotel in Teignmouth, Devon, almost 200 miles from London. The next day they made numerous short stops to film before arriving at the Atlantic Hotel in

Newquay, Cornwall, where they abandoned the idea of moving to a different location each day and booked themselves in for three nights. There, on 13 September, they filmed Nat Jackley.

> PAUL: We were down in Cornwall, so I said, 'Well, how about you do the Nat Jackley thing now, John? When it's done, we can get rid of him.' But John didn't really prepare anything and hadn't thought up much for him to do. Nat just walked from person to person and it wasn't very funny and I think he quite resented it. He was never going to understand what we were doing; we were drug-children and he was an old-school music-hall, vaudeville performer. Nat did not like how he came out in the film. He was amongst our most vociferous critics when they all came looking for us. And I can't blame him really because it didn't exactly enhance his career.

First John had Nat Jackley chase young women in bikinis around the Atlantic Hotel's swimming pool, then chase them along the cliffs at nearby Holywell. Both of these sequences were lost on the cutting-room floor.

John had more luck with his other dramatic scene. Paul: 'I remember him telling me one morning, "God, I had the strangest dream." I said, "Come on then. Remember it and we'll film it." He said, "Oh, okay. I was a waiter, and I'm shovelling spaghetti on this person." I said, "Fantastic, that's on!"'

John found a perfect crimson waiter's jacket and a small black bow tie and slicked his hair back with Brylcreem with long bushy sidies and a pencil moustache, transforming himself into an obsequious waiter complete with flashing smile over clenched teeth. Paul: 'He allowed himself to make some fun of his stepfather Alfred Dygens, who we unkindly called "Twitchy" Dykans, who was a waiter. I sensed a little transference of thought there. We did talk about that hair and the little moustache.' In the film John uses a shovel to pile spaghetti on the Fat Lady's plate until the table is filled to overflowing. It is one of the most successful non-musical scenes in the film.

One musical interlude which unfortunately was not filmed occurred in a small pub in the Cornish fishing village of Perranporth. Spencer Davis and his family happened to be on holiday there when they saw a news item on the television showing the tour bus stuck on a narrow bridge outside Widecombe on their way to Cornwall. The AA and local police all had to help push and pull, among rising tempers, before the trapped vehicle was freed. Spencer Davis telephoned the Atlantic Hotel and the next day Paul, Ringo, Neil Aspinall and others drove over from Newquay to visit him in Perranporth. Spencer Davis reports in *Blinds and Shutters*: 'I invited some of them back to the pub in the evening ... There was a piano in the corner and Paul stuck a pint of beer on the top and started playing. People hadn't even noticed that he was in there. There was one girl who looked and said, "The piano player, look who it is!" It was so funny to see the reaction on their faces.' Paul led the pub sing-along until past 2 a.m., working his way through every pub standard in the book except 'Yellow Submarine', which he refused to play.

No one had thought to book time at Shepperton or any of the large film studios so much of the film was shot at West Malling Air Station, near Maidstone, Kent, the only large stage the Beatles were able to get at short notice. It was here that John's 'Aunt Jessie's Dream' sequence with the spaghetti was filmed, as were most of the songs. The aerodrome was originally built during World War II as a US Army Airforce base and still had thirty-two enormous concrete blast-deflecting shields designed to protect parked bombers from anything but a direct hit. They proved to be useful in filming 'I Am the Walrus'.

PAUL: They were big tall concrete structures that we could get people up on the top of, waving their arms. We gave people rubber egg-head skull caps, and we had a walrus. It was all directly from *Alice in Wonderland*, the walrus, the carpenter and all that surrealist stuff. John had just written 'I Am the Walrus' and it was decided therefore it should go in the film. It is one of John's great songs and it is very Lennon.

Even now I'm a bit shy to say I was the director of *Magical Mystery Tour* although it was the fact: it was me that was first up in the morning, me that virtually directed the whole thing. So being the *de facto* director, I would go and say good night to everyone. Just to check on the team. I was saying good night to John in the hotel in Cornwall and saying thanks for doing the Nat Jackley thing. I was standing at the door and he was in bed, and we were talking about the lyrics of 'I Am the Walrus', and I remember feeling he was a little frail at that time, maybe not going through one of the best periods in life, probably breaking up with his wife. He was going through a very fragile period. You've only got to look at his lyrics – 'sitting on a cornflake waiting for the van to come'. They were very disturbed lyrics.

For the instrumental 'Flying', they decided that the music demanded a sequence of aerial shots: clouds and landscapes seen from the air. The film producer Denis O'Dell, who was to become the head of Apple Films, was already working for the inchoate Apple at the time. He had been part of the production team on Stanley Kubrick's 1963 *Dr Strangelove*, and remembered that they had hours of aerial shots taken while flying over the Arctic to get the final scenes where B-52s cross the pole to drop their nuclear bombs on Russia. He told Paul, 'I can get you some out-takes,' and did. They edited them together and tinted them to make it look unlike *Strangelove*.

Unfortunately the colour filters over the black and white originals turned the grey cloud shots even more grey and formless when the film was broadcast in monochrome on British television, so the 'Flying' section proved very boring viewing and contributed greatly to the adverse reception that *Magical Mystery Tour* ultimately received.

Paul edited the film with Roy Benson, one of the film editors on *A Hard Day's Night*. Paul: 'He and I got our heads together and I said, "Well, look, we've shot all this, and we've got clapper boards on some of it." He said, "Not on everything?" I said, "No, no. No, some of it we just shot, but I'm sure it synchs."' But not all of it did, and the biggest problem came with the musical segment 'Fool on the Hill', one of the major scenes in the film.

Paul, Mal Evans and the cameraman Aubrey Dewar had flown to Nice, on the Côte d'Azur, to film it on 30 October. Paul forgot to take a passport or any money but still managed to get through customs. 'I told them, "You know who I am so why do you need to see a photograph of me in a passport?"' They checked into a hotel and hired a taxi driver, who woke them up at 3.30 in the morning.

PAUL: We just asked the local taxi driver, 'Where is a good place to see the sunrise from?' Nice was fairly easily accessible. It had good mountain scenery and I figured we might get a good clear sunrise down there. It was the right time of the year. We all piled in the taxi and drove up into the mountains behind Nice. It took us about an hour and sunrise was in about half an hour. We unpacked the stuff from the boot, loaded up his camera, set up the tripod where we knew the sun would rise, and waited in the freezing cold. I had a big long black coat on and we just waited until the the sun arose. And I just danced around and he filmed it.

I just ad-libbed the whole thing. I went, 'Right, get over there: Let me dance. Let me jump from this rock to this rock. Get a lot of the sun rising. Get a perfect shot and let me stand in front of it.' I just had a little Philips cassette to mime to and roughly get the feeling of the song. There was no clapper because there was no sound. Just my cassette. I said, 'We'll lay in the sound of "Fool on the Hill" afterwards.' I'm miming sometimes, but of course it should be in synch, that's what clappers are for. I didn't know these small technicalities, and also I wasn't that interested in being that precise.

We stayed until the sun went down. As the day went on, the light got worse. It got to be harsh daylight, so we got less material in the daytime. We basically used all the dawn stuff. And that was it. It was very spontaneous, as was the whole of *Magical Mystery Tour*. Later, when we came to try to edit it all, it was very difficult because I hadn't sung it to synch.

We shouldn't have really had just one cameraman, it was anti-union. That was another reason to go to France. The unions wouldn't have allowed it in Britain, nor probably in France, but they didn't know we were doing it. It was just the four of us; there was none of this grips, best boy, gaffer, none of that. In fact, our biggest danger was that the film didn't conform with one union rule.

'Fool on the Hill' was mine and I think I was writing about someone like Maharishi. His detractors called him a fool. Because of his giggle he wasn't taken too seriously. It was this idea of a fool on the hill, a guru in a cave, I was attracted to. I remember once hearing about a hermit who missed the Second World War because he'd been in a cave in Italy, and that always appealed to me.

I was sitting at the piano in at my father's house in Liverpool hitting a D 6th chord and I made up 'Fool on the Hill'. There were some good words in it, 'perfectly still', I liked that, and the idea that everyone thinks he's stupid appealed to me, because they still do. Saviours or gurus are generally spat upon, so I thought for my generation I'd suggest that they weren't as stupid as they looked.

It was written before or during the *Sgt. Pepper* sessions the year before, because he first played it to John at Cavendish Avenue in March 1967 when they were working on 'With a Little Help from My Friends'. John told him to write it down but Paul assured him that he wouldn't forget it.

Paul had set aside two weeks to edit the film. It took eleven. Paul: 'So I got started with Roy but of course I now realised it was a nightmare for him. Without the clapper boards to synch it, it was murder!' They hired an editing suite from Norman's Film Productions on the corner of Wardour Street and Old Compton Street, on the second floor above a shop. Paul: 'The guys were dropping in and out, and someone was making a blue movie in the back room, and we'd go in and say, 'How's it going?' Just like being film-makers. I mean, once you were doing it day after day for eleven weeks, that was exactly what you were. Very boring.'

There was ten hours of material to choose from, which meant that the majority of scenes did not get used in the 53-minute film. However, this 10-1 ratio was quite reasonable considering that the average was 8-1. In comparison, Howard Brookner's film *William Burroughs*, which was shot in more or less the same way, had a 40-1 shooting ratio, so the Beatles were in fact more organised than many critics have alleged.

Paul took the film to the BBC because he wanted it to be screened nationwide, rather than selling it to all the separate commercial channels and possibly not having it shown in some parts of the country. Because of this, the BBC had him at a negotiating disadvantage. 'I went down to see Paul Fox, who was head of that department,' Paul remembered. 'We talked and he seemed to want to show it, such was our popularity and so on. He said, "Pretty strange film", and I said, "Well, it is, but you know, people like that." ' Fox offered him the derisory sum of £9,000.

PAUL: I said, 'Well, that's not an awful lot. I think you'll probably get more viewers than will warrant that as a fee,' but I thought, Well, sod it, that's not really the important thing. Then he said, 'But there's one thing I want taken out.' I said, 'What?' thinking, Oh, what have we done? Some drug reference or something a little bit naughty in there? What Paul Fox wanted out of the final edit was a scene with Ivor Cutler and the fat lady, Jessie, running around on the beach to the sound of some schmaltzy orchestral version of 'All My Loving', which he thought was insulting to old people. I thought it was a very romantic scene: Ivor running in circles around Jessie Robbins so that his footprints drew a heart shape in the sand around her and it was a little love scene. It was a completely innocent little romantic scene where they were just running on the beach somewhere down Cornwall. We just stopped the coach and I just said, 'Right, everyone, go and have lunch and we'll just do a little scene down here. Come on, Ivor, Jessie, camera,' and we went down on the beach and just made up this little scene. There was no groping or grappling or anything, but he wanted that out.

This was a typical piece of BBC prudery of the time. They had already banned 'I Am the Walrus' because of the reference to a girl taking her knickers down, but to censor a sequence of Ivor Cutler and Jessie Robbins kissing was the BBC at its worst – an act that would now be regarded as discriminatory towards both fat people and older people. The kiss itself was done with great taste, though perhaps with not enough build-up, in a sequence that lightly parodied Louis Malle's overhead shots in *Les Amants* (1958), which also included a Brahms string sextet. Paul Fox's delicate sensitivities were ultimately overruled within the BBC, because when the programme was repeated in 1979 the offending sequence was reinstated. The 1989 video version is also uncensored.

PAUL: I thought, as I still do, that the Beeb can give big viewing coverage to something. So their big viewing figures were on Boxing Day, which was when we wanted to do it. We wanted to take over the Bruce Forsyth slot. He was always on: 'Hello, everyone, happy Christmas! Had enough Christmas dinner?' We thought we'd had enough of all of that. We wanted to make a change, so we wanted that same big audience slot, which we got. We walked into the jaws of the lion with that, quite naïvely, quite willingly. It was probably a mistake really in retrospect because those people probably wanted Bruce Forsyth: everybody's had too much turkey and sherry and they're sitting back and they just want, 'Bring me sunshine ...' 'Oh, I like that,' 'Oh, they're funny.' They just want comedy, a few girls kicking their legs up and so on. But because we knew that was the peak time in Britain for people to watch telly, we wanted to have our thing shown then. The kids wanted us, so for the kids it was cool, but it got slated very heavily. It probably would have been wiser, in retrospect, to have it shown late on a Friday night and in colour.

We could have aimed it at the Bruce Forsyth thing; if we'd just gone on in our suits and played our songs and had a few guests. But we weren't into anything remotely like that and we'd made this little film of our own.

The BBC transmitted the film in black and white at 8.35 p.m. on 26 December 1967, Boxing Day evening. It was repeated in colour on 5 January 1968, but few people in Britain had colour sets, which had only been introduced six months before. It was very much a colour film and lost a great deal of its impact in monochrome. Viewers were also puzzled by the lack of a proper narrative or sequence of events since it was, literally, a mystery tour.

The critics, particularly on the tabloids like the *Daily Mail* and *Daily Mirror*, used it as an excuse to savage the Beatles for what they saw as the Beatles advocating LSD, for signing the legalise-pot advertisement, and for their promotion of underground, psychedelic and hippie culture in general, which Fleet Street found immensely threatening. They knew on an instinctive level that a culture is something you live in, not just write about, and were scared of the changes they saw coming. 'If they were not the Beatles, the BBC would not have fallen for it,' said the *Daily Mirror*. 'Blatant rubbish,' said the right-wing *Daily Express*. Only the *Guardian* understood what the Beatles were trying to do, reviewing the film in glowing terms: '... the whole was an inspired freewheeling achievement and "I Am the Walrus" has a desperate poetry by which we will be remembered, just as an earlier desperation is remembered through Chaplin.' The following day the *Guardian* journalist Keith Dewhurst defended the Beatles' position after the rest of Fleet Street erupted in fury: 'My amazement is for the way in which the film has been dismissed as pretentious rubbish with no attempt to analyse content.'

PAUL: They were all looking for the plum-pudding special. That's what they were expecting, and they very much didn't get it! This very much wasn't that, loves, we weren't even intending giving you that. We were giving it to the young kids. We figured there would be young kids looking on Boxing Day. Why shouldn't they see something far out? I understand that Steven Spielberg and some of the guys in film school thought it was really cool and it was quite influential on their early stuff. Probably just the fact that it was so free. You get people like that appreciating and analysing it. Just the fact that we had the balls to go out there and had the sheer determination and persever-ance to go and make it, I think validates it all now.

So vociferous was the criticism at the time that Paul went on *The David Frost Show* before a live television audience the day after it was shown to defend the film against his critics and told the London *Evening Standard*: 'I suppose if you look at it from the point of view of good Boxing Day entertainment, we goofed really.'

The American *Daily Variety* in its inimitable style headlined: 'Critics and Viewers Boo: Beatles Produce First Flop with Yule Film.' But was it a flop? The film cost £40,000 to make and, as *Time* magazine reported, it grossed $2,000,000 in rentals to American colleges alone, quite apart from the soundtrack album grossing $8,000,000 in its first ten days of release. Television companies in dozens of countries around the world bought the rights to show it. In America, where it was seen in cinemas in glorious colour rather than on black and white television, it had a much more favourable reception among its largely younger audience.

Paul: 'I put a lot of work into the film but it was credited as directed by the Beatles. In actual fact, like it, love it or hate it, it was me that directed it so I really had to carry the can when it got bad reviews, but by the same argument, I can now take the credit for the cool little film that I still think that it is.'

The film had six songs, too many for an EP but too few for an album. In Britain, EMI opted for a curious compromise and issued a double EP as a small book of stills from the film with the records in a pocket on each cover. In the USA, where EPs were virtually unknown, Capitol released the songs as an album, padding it with the Beatles' most recent singles: 'Hello Goodbye', 'Strawberry Fields Forever', 'Penny Lane', 'Baby, You're a Rich Man' and 'All You Need Is Love'. This was in turn imported back into Britain by EMI, who eventually gave in to public demand and released it themselves.

Added to the soundtrack album was the Beatles' latest single, 'Hello Goodbye', the end chorus of which was used over the closing credits of the film.

> PAUL: 'Hello Goodbye' was one of my songs. There are Geminian influences here I think: the twins. It's such a deep theme in the universe, duality – man woman, black white, ebony ivory, high low, right wrong, up down, hello goodbye – that it was a very easy song to write. It's just a song of duality, with me advocating the more positive. You say goodbye, I say hello. You say stop, I say go. I was advocating the more positive side of the duality, and I still do to this day.

In his book *Yesterday*, Alistair Taylor says he was present at Cavendish Avenue when Paul got the first idea for 'Hello Goodbye'. He had asked Paul to explain exactly how he wrote songs:

> Paul marched me into the dining room, where he had a marvellous old hand-carved harmonium. 'Come and sit at the other end of the harmonium. You hit any note you like on the keyboard. Just hit it and I'll do the same. Now whenever I shout out a word, you shout the opposite and I'll make up a tune. You watch, it'll make music.' ...
>
>   'Black,' he started. 'White,' I replied. 'Yes.' 'No.' 'Good.' 'Bad.' 'Hello.' 'Goodbye.'

John had wanted 'I Am the Walrus' to be the A side of the Beatles' next single, but it was not as commercial as 'Hello Goodbye' and was relegated to the B side. 'Hello Goodbye' became the Beatles' best-selling single since 'She Loves You', with seven weeks at the top of the English charts.

The other single included on the soundtrack album was 'Baby, You're a Rich Man', the B side of 'All You Need Is Love'. John had an incomplete song called 'One of the the Beautiful People', based on the press articles about the emerging hippies, who had not yet been given that sobriquet. Paul already had the chorus, 'Baby, you're a rich man ...', so the two were joined together, much as they had fitted the two parts of 'A Day in the Life'.

PAUL: 'Baby, You're a Rich Man' was co-written by John and me at Cavendish Avenue. 'Tuned to a natural E' is a line I remember us writing, a slight pun on the word 'naturally' – 'natural E'. There was a lot of talk in the newspapers then about the beautiful people. That was what they called them, so we figured, well, the question then was, how does it feel to be one of the beautiful people?

We recorded it at a rather exciting recording session at Olympic, in Barnes, where Keith Grant mixed it, instantly, right there. He stood up at the console as he mixed it, so it was a very exciting mix, we were really quite buzzed. I always liked that track.

The late-night session was held on 11 May 1967 and ran from 9 p.m. until 3 a.m. Some of the Rolling Stones were there at the session, and the Beatles' chronicler Mark Lewisohn reports that one of the tape boxes has '+ Mick Jagger?' written on it, suggesting that they joined in the chorus at the end.

Magical Mystery Tour has stood up remarkably well over the years and can now be seen as an influence on many strands in popular culture. It gave expression to many of the ideas that were current in the sixties, particularly in its freedom from formal convention and belief in the validity of random events. It was a sort of road movie, made two years before Peter Fonda and Dennis Hopper's *Easy Rider* popularised the genre. More significantly, it was the vehicle for a number of prototype rock videos, some of which, like 'Fool on the Hill', could be shown on MTV in the mid-nineties and look as if they were freshly made. This is an area where the Beatles have received little credit, but in which they were the undisputed ground-breakers. If nothing else, the musical scenes make *Magical Mystery Tour* a memorable film and justify the claim that the Beatles invented the pop video as a form.

It has long been said that Dick Lester's film sequence of the Beatles singing 'I Should Have Known Better' in the guard's van of the train in *A Hard Day's Night* was the prototype pop video. They followed this up with the surreal film clips for 'Strawberry Fields Forever', which came complete with colour superimpositions, and 'Penny Lane' with its disjointed cut-up editing. *Magical Mystery Tour* contains five hermetic film sequences (not counting 'Flying') which provide the template for virtually every pop video made since, from the camera-through-a-prism of 'Blue Jay Way' to the surreal clowning and jump cuts of 'I Am the Walrus'. The intercut costume changes in the film made to accompany the single 'Hello Goodbye' (on the album but not in the film) have also become standard fare for rock-video makers.

In this the Beatles can be seen as Post-Modernist artists of the avant-garde: appropriating the out-takes from *Dr Strangelove*; dispensing with script, conventional narrative, or even any clear idea of director; collaging variety songs with hard rock 'n' roll. Just as they freed themselves from the image of the Beatles by becoming Sergeant Pepper's Lonely Hearts Club Band, now they were transforming their entire background. All the popular-cultural symbols of working-class identity – fairground barkers, coach trips, couriers and holiday-camp hostesses (Mandy Weet as the stewardess was essentially playing a Redcoat; the bus became Butlins on wheels); standing jokes about fat ladies, army sergeants, crooners, Jack-the-lads at strip shows, pub sing-alongs – all were mind-bendingly metamorphosed into a psychedelic free-for-all, complete with dwarves, contortionists, star-lets and the Beatles themselves. No wonder it gave the Boxing Day audience dyspepsia.

Paul: 'If we did have to justify it, I think "I Am the Walrus" alone makes it. It's the only time John ever sang "I Am the Walrus" on film, so right there it's historical. There's quite a few good little musical scenes: "Blue Jay Way", "Fool on the Hill", "Your Mother Should Know". This is a good start, isn't it?'

John agreed and is quoted in conversation with Paul by Anthony Fawcett in his book *John Lennon, One Day at a Time*, saying:

I don't regret *Magical Mystery*, I think it was great, I think it'll prove that in the end. I just think that it was a good piece of work and we were fucked up by cameramen, but that's not important because you probably think it was more fucked up than I do, because you like professionalism, y'know. But I enjoyed the fish-

and-chip quality of *Magical Mystery*. The fact that we went out with a load of freaks and tried to make a film is great, you know?

Magic Alex

An awful lot of strange people came into the Beatles' orbit. There was, for instance, the TV repair man who persuaded John Lennon that he could build him a flying saucer. As the Magical Mystery Tour bus meandered around Britain, all group shots showed a new addition to Beatles circles standing smiling and waving in the centre – a young Greek who came to be known as Magic Alex. He entered their lives via Indica and John Dunbar.

On 24 November 1966, a show opened at the Indica Gallery by the Greek sculptor Takis Vasilakis. He worked with magnetic elements: metal objects suspended on wires held in space at strange angles by electromagnetic fields, military compasses, flashing lights and tank antennas. Paul bought one of the *Signals*, two flashing lights on metal wands, and so did John and George. Ringo allegedly had his chauffeur knock one up in the garage. A frequent visitor to the show was Takis's ex-wife Liliane Lijn, who was also a sculptor. She and John Dunbar became friends and he went to see her work: large hinged metal panels that could be arranged in different configurations on the floor. He liked it and in March 1967 she too had a show at the Indica Gallery.

Liliane introduced John to a friend of hers, a 21-year-old Greek called John Alexis Mardas who had entered England as a student but now worked as a television repairer for Olympic Electronics. To the London lads at the TV repair shop he was known simply as Yanni Mardas. In his spare time he built a box with a group of small lights on the front that flashed on and off in a random pattern. It was just a fun object with no practical application but seemed incredibly amusing to someone on an acid trip. Despite his thick accent, Alexis could spin a tale and told John Dunbar about the fantastic ideas he had for new inventions. However, when he learned that John had studied science as well as art at Cambridge, he quickly toned down his suggestions to ideas that were practical.

'He was quite cunning in the way he pitched his thing,' John Dunbar remembered, 'because he knew that I knew all that kind of stuff. He wasn't a complete charlatan in the sense that he didn't know anything. He did. And he knew enough to know how to wind people up and to what extent. He was a fucking TV repairman: Yanni Mardas, none of this "Magic Alex" shit!'

At the time, however, John Dunbar was quite taken by Mardas and they became good friends. John was working with a number of kinetic artists and thought that it might be a good plan to combine some of his own artistic ideas with Alexis's inventions and knowledge of electronics. He suggested that he and Alexis form a partnership to exploit Alexis's ideas, with John setting up the jobs and getting publicity. Though Marianne Faithfull had by this time left John for Mick Jagger, John still saw her when he went to collect their son Nicholas for weekends, and in the course of these visits he inevitably saw a fair amount of Mick Jagger. The first job he arranged was for Alexis and himself to do the lights on a three-week Rolling Stones tour of Europe which began on 25 March 1967 in Örebro, Sweden, and took them all through Germany, Austria and Italy to finish at the Athens football stadium on 17 April.

Alexis and John's contribution was a system of spotlights that Alex had designed which not only would respond electronically to the rhythm of the music but would change colour with the pitch and tone. 'It didn't always work,' John recalls, 'but it worked quite a lot of the time.' The Stones, however, were not impressed and John began looking for other sponsors.

John Dunbar was still seeing a great deal of John Lennon, taking a lot of acid with him, so he was the most obvious person to approach for funds. After Marianne had left him, Dunbar moved first into Indica Gallery itself, then found himself a flat on Bentinck Street, across the road from his parents' flat. John Lennon would sometimes visit and Paul also stopped by. Around the fireplace the wall was covered with doodles and signatures to which both John Lennon and Paul had contributed – it was a very sixties pad. Dunbar recalls taking acid with both of them there. Not long after he moved in, Alexis Mardas joined him to share the rent, and consequently soon got to know Lennon. John Lennon was enormously taken by Alexis's ideas and gave him the sobriquet Magic Alex. Alex quickly ingratiated himself and moved to protect Lennon from any influence other than his own, including that of John Dunbar.

Paul remembers how Alexis joined the Beatles' circle:

We were all meeting one morning in my house before a recording session or something, and John showed up with Alex, like two little flower children with necklaces on and bouncing blond hair and John with his sporran, the little money-bag pouch he used to have. I remember John sitting on the floor in front of me saying, 'This is my new guru: Magic Alex.' That was how he arrived. John named him. And a little voice inside me went, 'Hmmmm. Oh, wow, gosh! I hope that's right, John. That's a very sweeping statement, you know.' Okay, 'Guru in what way?' 'Oh, you know.' I think John wasn't all that keen on the idea of just automatically getting hooked with an Indian guru, a teacher, that would show you the path. But he saw the wisdom of such an idea, of such an apprenticeship. So he'd probably been talking to Alex, chatting about all these far-out things and suddenly thought, You're my new guru! This is the future! So we all got to meet Alex and he was fun, and Alex became part of the group.

Because John had introduced him as a guru, there was perhaps a little pressure on him to try and behave as a guru. I didn't treat him that way, I thought he was just some guy with interesting ideas: 'Alex, there you go, mate.' And let him do his guru stuff, whatever he wanted to do. We didn't really call anyone's bluff, it would have been a bit too aggressive. So we just let him get on with it.

Alex's original ideas were all theoretically possible given the existing technology, though the computing power needed at that time would have made them prohibitively expensive: they included a telephone that you told whom you wanted to call, which dialled the number using voice recognition, and one that displayed the telephone number of an incoming call before you answered, both of which were already in prototype at the Bell Telephone labs in New York, though the Beatles didn't know that. From these he moved on to greater flights of imagination: an X-ray camera that could see through walls, so you could see people in bed or in the shower. A force field that would surround a building with coloured air so that no one could see in. A force field of compressed air that would stop anyone rear-ending your car. A house that would hover in the air, suspended on an invisible beam like something out of a Flash Gordon movie – which may well have been where he got the idea.

George Harrison commented in his autobiography:

> What Magic Alex did was pick up on the latest inventions, show them to us and we'd think he'd invented them. We were naïve to the teeth … I was going to give him the V12 engine out of my Ferrari Berlinetta and John was going to give him his, and Alex reckoned that with those two V12 engines he could make a flying saucer. But we'd have given them to him – 'Go on, go for it!' – daft buggers.

Paul: 'He would sit and tell us of how it would be possible to have wallpapers which were speakers, so you would wallpaper your room with some sort of substance and then it could be plugged into and the whole wall would vibrate and work as a loudspeaker – "loudpaper". And we said, "Well, if you could do that, we'd like one." It was always "We'd like one."'

Most of the Beatles' friends were not impressed with Alexis. He did not like to discuss his ideas with anyone who knew anything about science or electronics, such as George Martin, because they might demonstrate to John why they wouldn't work. It seemed very much that Alexis had a subscription to *Popular Science* and the Beatles didn't. In retrospect Paul agreed:

> It certainly could have been just that! I think, to give him his due, he knew a little more than that but I wouldn't put that past him because that was the kind of thing he was able to tell about. And we would say, 'But is it really possible, or is this just some sort of theory?' and he would insist that it was really possible. You would be able to have telephones that responded to voices, etcetera, and he said, 'It's possible now, the technology is around but nobody's really putting all this together.'

The Greek Islands

The technological future wasn't Alex's only passport to the group. One of John Lennon's big fantasies was that the Beatles, their friends and staff would all live in a protected compound on an island, free from outside interference. Derek Taylor described John's vision in his autobiography:

> The four Beatles and Brian would have their network at the centre of the compound: a dome of glass and iron tracery not unlike the old Crystal Palace over the mutual creative/play area, from which arbours and avenues would lead off like spokes from a wheel to the four vast and incredibly beautiful separate living units. In the outer grounds, the houses of the inner clique: Neil, Mal, Terry and Derek, complete with partners, families and friends ...

Marianne Faithfull remembered Paul's reaction to the idea:

> John wanted them all to live together on an island. I remember him talking about it, saying, 'What has to happen is that all of us, the Beatles ...' and of course for Paul this was a nightmare, the last thing Paul wanted to do was live on some fucking island, whether it was in Ireland or Greece, wherever it was, with John, George and Ringo and their wives and their roadies, and Mal and Neil, all on an island. This was John's vision and they all had to do this. And of course Paul was, 'Yeechhhhhh.' There were going to be a few other people, like John Dunbar. But it was just awful for Paul and I remember him talking about this and saying, 'Well, I guess they'll never get it together.' Paul was really much more sophisticated than John ever was.

Alex seized on John's dream as a way to get involved with the Beatles and their finances. He quickly sold the idea to John that the Beatles' compound should be on a Greek island. Greece had been taken over in April 1967 by a fascist military junta. Democracy had been suspended, anyone opposed to the junta was hunted down and tortured, the press was strictly censored and thousands of politicians, students and intellectuals were leaving the country. Long hair and rock 'n' roll had been banned. Naturally, the press of the Western democracies was unanimous in its denunciation of the imposition of military rule. To Alex it was obvious that having the Beatles buy a Greek island would help counter the negative press that the military regime was attracting.

Alex claimed that his father was a high-up member of the secret police, though this may have been another fantasy. His boasting about a connection to the military junta did little to endear him to the Beatles' other friends, who thought he was exploiting John Lennon's gullibility. But John wanted his Beatles commune, so Alistair Taylor from Brian Epstein's office flew out to look at real estate with Alexis. After several false starts, they found the perfect place: the island of Leslo, of about 80 acres, with four idyllic beaches and four smaller habitable islands surrounding it – one for each Beatle. The entire property was for sale for £90,000, including a small fishing village of traditional white-painted houses grouped around a harbour filled with brightly coloured fishing boats and 16 acres of olive groves.

Alistair Taylor reported back and on 20 July 1967, George and Patti, Ringo and Neil flew to Athens, followed two days later by Paul and Jane, John and Cynthia with Julian, and Patti's sixteen-year-old sister Paula, Alistair Taylor and Mal Evans. Maureen remained in Britain because she was in the last stages of pregnancy. They were welcomed with open arms by Alex's father. According to Peter Brown, Alex had done a deal with the Greek authorities that if the Beatles were given diplomatic immunity – that is to say, their bags would not be searched and their drugs would not be found – then the Beatles would pose for press photographs for the Ministry of Tourism.

PAUL: Alex invited John on a boat holiday in Greece, and we were all then invited. There was some story of buying a Greek island or something. It was all so sort of abstract but the first thing we had to do is go to Greece and see if we even liked it out there. The idea was get an island where you can just do what you want, a sort of hippie commune where nobody'd interfere with your lifestyle. I suppose the main motivation for that would probably be no one could stop you smoking. Drugs was probably the main reason for getting some island, and then all the other community things that were around then – 'Oh, we'll paint together. We'll do this. I'll chop wood.'

I think that if you're going to write a great symphony or you're going to rehearse the greatest string quartet in the world, it's fair enough to cut yourself off. It's just a practical matter; give yourself lots of time and if you're going to do that, then why shouldn't it be in Greece? It was a drug-induced ambition, we'd just be sitting around: 'Wouldn't it be great? The lapping water, sunshine, we'd be playing. We'd get a studio there. Well, it's possible these days with mobiles and ...' We had lots of ideas like that. The whole Apple enterprise was the result of those ideas.

The Beatles hired a luxury yacht to cruise among the islands but it was held up by a storm off Crete so they were delayed in Athens for a few days. Alex arranged a few sightseeing trips to keep them from being bored, but he also kept the Greek tourist authorities informed of their timetable so wherever they went there were crowds of people following. Alistair Taylor wrote: 'Once on a trip to a hill village, we came round a corner of the peaceful road only to find hundreds of photographers clicking away at us.' The Beatles accepted an invitation from the Oxford University Dramatic Society to attend a performance of *Agamemnon* by Aeschylus on 23 July at the theatre at Delphi, the ancient Greek shrine on the lower southern slopes of Parnassos overlooking the gulf of Corinth. It could have been a delightful trip, but once again, Alexis had given the tourist authorities advance notice and they broadcast their upcoming attendance at the performance on Athens Radio. Consequently, when they arrived in Delphi, they were assailed by crowds and persistent journalists. They retired to their Mercedes limousine and returned to Athens immediately without seeing the play.

The yacht, the MV *Arvi*, finally arrived. It had twenty-four berths and a crew of eight, including the captain, a chef and two stewards. First they went island-hopping, spending the days swimming, sunbathing, making music and taking drugs. Then they set sail to inspect the potential Beatles island commune. After a full day exploring the island, planning where the recording studio would be located and who would have which island for their dream houses, Alistair Taylor was told to fly straight back to London and arrange to buy the property. This was at a time when it was difficult to transfer money out of Britain and the Beatles had to apply to the government for permission to spend £90,000 abroad. Taylor eventually got the clearance but by then the Beatles' enthusiasm had cooled.

PAUL: We went on the boat and sat around and took acid. It was good fun being with everyone, with trippier moments. For me the pace was a bit wearing. I probably could have done with some straight windows occasionally, I'd have enjoyed it a bit more. But nothing came of that, because we went out there and thought, We've done it now. That was it for a couple of weeks. Great, wasn't it? Now we don't need it. Having been out there, I don't think we needed to go back. Probably the best way to not buy a Greek island is to go out there for a bit.

In the meantime, the value of their £90,000 worth of property dollars had risen so when Alistair Taylor sold them back to the government, the Beatles made £11,400 profit on the deal.

'It's a good job we didn't do it,' Paul said, 'because anyone who tried those ideas realised eventually there would always be arguments, there would always be who has to do the washing-up and whose turn it is to clean out the latrines. I don't think any of us were thinking of that.'

Expanding the Field of Consciousness

Paul first took LSD in 1966 with his friend Tara Browne. Tara lived in Eaton Row, a quiet dead-end mews in Belgravia just off Eaton Square, and was often to be seen in Sibylla's and the Bag o'Nails with his girlfriend Suki Potier. At the end of an evening, Paul had gone back to Tara's mews house with Patrick, a dancer on the *Ready Steady Go!* TV show; Viv Prince, drummer with the Pretty Things; and several girls.

PAUL: Tara was taking acid on blotting paper in the toilet. He invited me to have some. I said, 'I'm not sure, you know.' I was more ready for the drink or a little bit of pot or something. I'd not wanted to do it, I'd held off like a lot of people were trying to, but there was massive peer pressure. And within a band, it's more than peer pressure, it's fear pressure. It becomes trebled, more than just your mates, it's, 'Hey, man, this whole band's had acid, why are you holding out? What's the reason, what is it about you?' So I knew I would have to out of peer pressure alone. And that night I thought, well, this is as good a time as any, so I said, 'Go on then, fine.' So we all did it.

We stayed up all night. It was quite spacy. Everything becomes more sensitive. Later, I was to have some more pleasant trips with the guys and outdoors, which was nicer. I was never that in love with it all, but it was a thing you did. I remember John saying, 'You never are the same after it,' and I don't think any of us ever were. It was such a mind-expanding thing. I saw paisley shapes and weird things, and for a guy who wasn't that keen on getting that weird, there was a disturbing element to it. I remember looking at my shirtsleeves and seeing they were dirty and not being too pleased with that, whereas normally you wouldn't even notice. But you noticed and you heard. Everything was supersensitive.

We sat around all evening. Viv Prince was great fun. Someone said, 'Do you want a drink?' And every one would say, 'No thanks, don't need drink, this is plenty.' If anything, we might smoke a joint. But Viv demolished the drinks tray: 'Oh yeah, a drink!' Cockney drummer with the Pretty Things. 'Orrright, yeah! Nah, does anyone want a drink? I fink I'll 'ave one of them.' And he had the whisky and he had everything. He was having a trip but his was somehow a more wired version than anyone else's. In the morning we ended up sending him out for ciggies.

Then one of the serious secretaries from our office rang about an engagement I had; she had traced me to here. 'Um, can't talk now. Important business' or something. I just got out of it. 'But you're supposed to be at the office.' 'No. I've got 'flu.' Anything I could think. I got out of that one because there was no way I could go to the office after that.

Then I had it on a few of occasions after that and I always found it amazing. Sometimes it was a very very deeply emotional experience, making you want to cry, sometimes seeing God or sensing all the majesty and emotional depth of everything. And sometimes you were just plain knackered, because it would be like sitting up all night in a train station, and by the morning you've grown very stiff and it's not a party any more. It's like the end of an all-nighter but you haven't danced. You just sat. So your bum might be sore, just from sitting. I was often quite wiped out by it all but I always thought, Well, you know, everybody's doing it.

This is why I am always keen to warn people about peer pressure. I've certainly experienced it. It was quite freaky but I guess it was something I wouldn't want to have missed in many ways. I had mixed feelings about it, certainly, but we took it and in songs like 'Lucy in the Sky with Diamonds', when we were talking about 'cellophane flowers' and 'kaleidoscope eyes' and 'grow so incredibly high!', we were talking about drug experiences, no doubt about it.

Paul took his second trip with John. On Tuesday 21 March 1967, during the *Sgt. Pepper* sessions, John, Paul and George were overdubbing vocals on to a track of 'Getting Better' in Studio Two at Abbey Road. John took out the little silver art nouveau pill box that he had bought from Liberty's and rummaged among his pep pills. Paul: 'He would open it up and choose very precisely: "Hmm, hmmm, hmmm. What shall I have now?" Well, by mistake this night he had acid, and he was on a trip.'

John went upstairs to the control room to tell George Martin that he was feeling unwell. George Martin reports the incident in *Summer of Love*; 'He suddenly looked up at me. "George," he said slowly, "I'm not feeling too good. I'm not focusing on me." "Come on, John," I said. "What you need is a breath of fresh air. I know the way up to the roof."' Just as John was explaining how amazing the stars were looking, Paul and George came rushing out on the flat roof. They knew that John was tripping and when they found out where George had taken him they ran anxiously to restrain him in case he thought he could fly off the unguarded parapet.

John told *Rolling Stone*: 'I never took it in the studio. Once I did, actually. I thought I was taking some uppers, and I was not in the state of handling it … I suddenly got so scared on the mike. I said, "What is it? I feel ill …"'

The session was cancelled. For some reason John did not have his car there, and in any case did not want to travel while having a bad trip, so Paul took him back to Cavendish Avenue.

PAUL: I thought, Maybe this is the moment where I should take a trip with him. It's been coming for a long time. It's often the best way, without thinking about it too much, just slip into it. John's on it already, so I'll sort of catch up. It was my first trip with John, or with any of the guys. We stayed up all night, sat around and hallucinated a lot.

Me and John, we'd known each other for a long time. Along

with George and Ringo, we were best mates. And we looked into each other's eyes, the eye contact thing we used to do, which is fairly mind-boggling. You dissolve into each other. But that's what we did, round about that time, that's what we did a lot. And it was amazing. You're looking into each other's eyes and you would want to look away, but you wouldn't, and you could see yourself in the other person. It was a very freaky experience and I was totally blown away.

There's something disturbing about it. You ask yourself, 'How do you come back from it? How do you then lead a normal life after that?' And the answer is, you don't. After that you've got to get trepanned or you've got to meditate for the rest of your life. You've got to make a decision which way you're going to go.

I would walk out into the garden – 'Oh no, I've got to go back in.' It was very tiring, walking made me very tired, wasted me, always wasted me. But 'I've got to do it, for my well-being.' In the meantime John had been sitting around very enigmatically and I had a big vision of him as a king, the absolute Emperor of Eternity. It was a good trip. It was great but I wanted to go to bed after a while.

I'd just had enough after about four or five hours. John was quite amazed that it had struck me in that way. John said, 'Go to bed? You won't sleep!' 'I know that, I've still got to go to bed.' I thought, now that's enough fun and partying, now … It's like with drink. That's enough. That was a lot of fun, now I gotta go and sleep this off. But of course you don't just sleep off an acid trip so I went to bed and hallucinated a lot in bed. I remember Mal coming up and checking that I was all right. 'Yeah, I think so.' I mean, I could feel every inch of the house, and John seemed like some sort of emperor in control of it all. It was quite strange. Of course he was just sitting there, very inscrutably.

Though *Sgt. Pepper* is always regarded as a drug album, the only member of the group really taking a lot of drugs was John. Paul probably only had two acid trips during the three months the album took to record and only took it about four or five times altogether. The others, too, rarely used anything stronger than pot. The one hard drug used during the making of *Sgt. Pepper* was cocaine, then not

widely in circulation. It featured in old blues songs – 'Cocaine, goin'
round my brain.' It had been fashionable in society circles in the
twenties; Johnny Cash had sung about it; but outside of a few hip
musicians and artists, it was not easily available until the end of the
sixties.

Inevitably it was Robert Fraser who introduced Paul to cocaine.
Robert always had a selection of drugs with him when he came down
to the *Sgt. Pepper* sessions. He usually had two test tubes, the sort
used in chemistry labs, one containing cocaine and the other
speedballs: a mixture of cocaine and heroin. He offered them around
freely and though the Beatles stayed well clear of the speedballs,
others of their visitors were happy to indulge.

PAUL: He walked in with a little phial of white powder. 'What's
that?' 'Cocaine.' 'Shit, that smells just like what the dentist used
to give us.' To this day, I swear as kids in Liverpool we were
given cocaine to deaden the gums. People say no, that will have
been Novocaine, but I think that was much later. I recognise the
smell from the dentist; it's a medical smell coke can have.
Anyway, that was my first thought about it.

I liked the paraphernalia. I liked the ritualistic end of it. I was
particularly amused by rolling up a pound note. There was a lot
of symbolism in that: sniffing it through money! For *Sgt. Pepper*
I used to have a bit of coke and then smoke some grass to
balance it out.

So Robert introduced me to it, and I know the other guys
were a bit shocked at me and said, 'Hey, man, you know this is
like, "now you're getting into drugs". This is more than pot.' I
remember feeling a little bit superior and patting them on the
head, symbolically, and saying, 'No. Don't worry, guys. I can
handle it.' And as it happened, I could. What I enjoyed was the
ritual of meeting someone and them saying, 'Have you seen the
toilets in this place?' And you'd know what they meant. 'Oh no,
are they particularly good?' And you'd wander out to the toilets
and you'd snort a bit of stuff. Robert and I did that for a bit. It
wasn't ever too crazy; eventually I just started to think – I think
rightly now – that this doesn't work. You've got to put too much
in to get too little high out it. I did it for about a year and I got off
it.

I'd been in a club in London and somebody there had some and I'd snorted it. I remember going to the toilet, and I met Jimi Hendrix on the way. 'Jimi! Great, man,' because I love that guy. But then as I hit the toilet, it all wore off! And I started getting this dreadful melancholy. I remember walking back and asking, 'Have you got any more?' because the whole mood had just dropped, the bottom had dropped out, and I remember thinking then it was time to stop it.

I thought, this is not clever, for two reasons. Number one, you didn't stay high. The plunge after it was this melancholy plunge which I was not used to. I had quite a reasonable childhood so melancholy was not really much part of it, even though my mum dying was a very bad period, so for anything that put me in that kind of mood it was like, 'Huh, I'm not paying for this! Who needs that?' The other reason was just a physical thing with the scraunching round the back of the neck, when it would get down the back of your nose, and it would all go dead! This was what reminded me of the dentist. It was exactly the same feeling as the stuff to numb your teeth.

I remember when I stopped doing it. I went to America just after Pepper came out, and I was thinking of stopping it. And everyone there was taking it, all these music business people, and I thought, no.

Apart from John's accidental trip, the Beatles never took acid in the studio. Most of their recording, from *Help!* onwards, was assisted by cups of tea, fish and chips or Chinese take-aways, and maybe marijuana. Pot was illegal and though the police must have known that the Beatles used it, they had so far ignored the fact. Throughout the sixties, until the police corruption trials of the early and mid-seventies, the Drug Squad was itself involved with the sale of drugs and so it was selective about whom it brought to trial. If money was paid to the right people, it was also possible to avoid a trial, or for the evidence, which in many cases the police brought with them, mysteriously to transform itself into a bag of oregano or talcum powder. By the beginning of 1967, many thousands of people were smoking pot, not just in London but all across the country, encouraged by the spread of sixties attitudes through rock 'n' roll songs, magazine articles, psychedelic layouts in teen magazines, the underground press and the grim warnings issued by parents, police and teachers. The big outdoor rock festivals, which were to spread the word even more efficiently by example and sample, had not yet been invented. The first one, at Monterey in California, was in June 1967.

At the same time, people were going to prison for six months or a year for simple possession of a small quantity of the drug. The situation was similar to Prohibition in the USA, with such a large percentage of the population breaking the law that respect for the law itself was diminishing. The law against marijuana had been introduced as part of a general prohibition against hallucinogenic and addictive drugs at a time when its use was virtually unknown in Britain. Now that so many people were using it, the situation had obviously changed and needed reassessment. In 1964 for the first time more whites than blacks were arrested for pot and by 1967 it was no longer contained within the West Indian and jazz communities, but had become a white middle-class problem. The situation was exacerbated by the sleazy end of Fleet Street running stories about 'drug orgies', particularly ones that hadn't happened.

It was against this background that some of the most prominent members of British society committed themselves to a call for a change in the law. They declared themselves to an outraged establishment with the publication in *The Times*, on Monday 24 July 1967, of a full-page advertisement headed: 'The law against marijuana is immoral in principle and unworkable in practice.' The extensive text opened by presenting informed medical opinion that marijuana was not addictive and had no harmful effects; and it sparked a resounding public debate.

> There are no long lasting ill-effects from the acute use of marijuana and no fatalities have ever been recorded … there seems to be growing agreement within the medical community, at least, that marijuana does not directly cause criminal behaviour, juvenile delinquency, sexual excitement, or addiction. Dr J. H. Jaffe, *The Pharmacological Basis of Therapeutics*. L. Goodman and A Gillman, eds. 3rd edn. 1965
>
> The available evidence shows that marijuana is not a drug of addiction and has no harmful effects … [the problem of marijuana] has been created by an ill-informed society rather than the drug itself. *Guy's Hospital Gazette* 17, 1967.

One of the three columns of text presented a petition which read:

The signatories to this petition suggest to the Home Secretary that he implement a five-point programme of cannabis law reform:

1. The government should permit and encourage research into all aspects of cannabis use, including its medical applications.
2. Allowing the smoking of cannabis on private premises should no longer constitute an offence.
3. Cannabis should be taken off the dangerous drugs list and controlled, rather than prohibited, by a new *ad hoc* instrument.
4. Possession of cannabis should either be legally permitted or at most be considered a misdemeanour, punishable by a fine of not more than £10 for a first offence and not more than £25 for any subsequent offence.
5. All persons now imprisoned for possession of cannabis or for allowing cannabis to be smoked on private premises should have their sentences commuted.

The petition was signed by sixty-five of the leading names in British society, including such luminaries as Francis Crick, the co-discoverer of the DNA molecule and a Nobel laureate; the novelist Graham Greene; and Members of Parliament, as well as the photographer David Bailey, the theatre director Peter Brook, broadcaster David Dimbleby, Dr R. D. Laing, Dr Jonathan Miller, the critic Kenneth Tynan and scientist Francis Huxley. The list contained medical and psychological doctors, several well-known artists and four Members of the Order of the British Empire, and Brian Epstein. The media reacted with horror and outrage, and questions were asked in Parliament. Who was responsible? Clearly not the unknown organisation SOMA, who had placed the ad? A page in *The Times* then cost £1,800, twice the average annual wage. The finger of suspicion pointed towards the Members of the Order of the British Empire.

The year 1967 was marked by a police crackdown on drugs. Many premises were raided and people arrested; some were able to buy their way out, others not. The most celebrated raid was upon Keith Richards' house in West Wittering, Sussex, where Mick Jagger, Marianne Faithfull, Christopher Gibbs, Robert Fraser and others had gathered for a country weekend. Another guest was David 'Acid King' Schneiderman, also known as Dave Britton, who was later alleged to have been in the pay of the *News of the World* as a police informer.

The house was under surveillance by the police, acting on a tip-off that drugs were being used on the premises, and it is generally thought that they waited for George Harrison and Patti to leave before launching their raid. Though the *News of the World* predictably denied that they had paid someone in the Stones camp to act as informer, it was widely believed that Schneiderman was the culprit. In the course of the famous bust (during which Marianne, who had just taken a bath, was wearing only a fur rug, and Christopher Gibbs the Pakistani national dress), Robert was chased through the garden and rugby-tackled by two policewomen, found to be in possession of twenty-four jacks of heroin and arrested. The police threw away all the cocaine, not knowing what it was, but took for analysis the bottles of Ambre Solaire suntan lotion and, inexplicably, all the bars of complimentary soap that Keith had brought home from hotels around the world. They pointedly ignored David Schneiderman's large aluminium briefcase, which was packed to the seams with every conceivable illegal substance.

Robert Fraser had the most to lose because he was in possession of heroin. Mick only had four legally obtained amphetamine tablets; and while Keith was told he would be liable for allowing his premises to be used, the only drugs actually found on the premises were in the pockets of Schneiderman, who was carrying two types of hash and a bag of grass.

Robert was anxious to get help, and according to the entirely unreliable 'Spanish Tony', a drug-dealer friend of the Stones, £8,000 was handed to the police in a bar in Kilburn. Spanish Tony: 'Not one word of the raid had appeared in any newspaper; no summonses had been issued; it was as though the raid had never happened …' In her autobiography Marianne Faithfull maintains that the story is 'a complete myth' and that no money changed hands.

The next weekend the *News of the World* ran a carefully worded article headed 'Drug Squad Raid Pop Stars' Party'. None of the other papers had the story because the police had not announced it and no charges had been brought. It was immediately picked up by the other Sunday newspapers for their later editions, and by the dailies on Monday.

On 10 May 1967, Mick, Keith and Robert appeared in court at Chichester in West Sussex, to be remanded on bail. That same day the police increased their pressure by raiding Brian Jones's flat at 1 Courtfield Road and arresting him for possession of pot. Now they had all three leading Rolling Stones.

The police crackdown on drugs and the underground continued when on 1 June 1967, John Hopkins, known to his friends as Hoppy, one of the founders of *International Times*, the organiser of the UFO Club, the famous *14 Hour Technicolour Dream* and other underground events, was sentenced to nine months in Wormwood Scrubs for possession of a small quantity of pot. He had been arrested on 30 December 1966, during a police raid on his flat in Queensway. The other defendants in the case, his flatmates and girlfriend, were cleared by the magistrates' court, but Hoppy elected to go to trial by jury. The judge, A. Gordon Friend, passed the stiff sentence after Hoppy explained to the court that pot was harmless and that the law should be changed. The judge told him, 'I have just heard what your views are on the possession of cannabis and the smoking of it. This is not a matter I can overlook. You are a pest to society.'

The following day there was an emergency gathering in the back room of the Indica Bookshop on Southampton Row to discuss tactics. Steve Abrams, who ran a drug-research organisation called SOMA, told the meeting that the best way to get the law changed would be to influence the committee that the government had set up two months earlier to examine the question of drugs and society. On 7 April that year, the Home Secretary Roy Jenkins had appointed Baroness Wootton of Abinger to head a separate 'Sub-committee on Hallucinogens' of the Advisory Council on Drug Dependence. Steve believed that it was possible to affect the deliberations of this committee by bringing the whole issue of soft drugs and the law into the public debate by running a full-page advertisement in *The Times*.

Steve was confident that if Baroness Wootton's committee

concentrated on the social and medical effects of marijuana alone, they would reach the same conclusion as the two previous major official studies: the Indian Hemp Commission of 1893–94 appointed by the government of India, and the Report by the Mayor's Committee on Marijuana, carried out for New York City Mayor LaGuardia in 1944, which had both concluded that marijuana was non-addictive and harmless.

The idea of placing such an advertisement was approved by the assembled underground activists as an excellent idea, particularly as Steve was prepared to do all the work in organising it; the main problem was where to find the money to finance the ad.

As the initial meeting in Indica's back room broke up, Miles telephoned Paul, who was horrified to hear that Hoppy had been jailed. Following on the arrests of Mick, Keith, Robert and Brian, it seemed as though the world was closing in on previously charmed lives.

The police had already tried once to close down *International Times* and there was a fear expressed at the meeting that Hoppy's arrest might herald a new attack on the paper. Paul advocated calm and said that he would get *IT* the best lawyers if that happened. Miles explained Steve Abrams's plan for an ad in *The Times* and Paul offered to put up most of the money. He said 'we', meaning the Beatles, and said to come over the next day.

It was a beautiful sunny day, and Paul had the french windows to the garden open wide to allow a slight breeze into the living room. Steve seemed to be in some trouble, pursing his lips, taking tiny little steps and muttering something about a chemical he had taken before the meeting being rather stronger than he expected. Nonetheless he had the idea very thoroughly worked out in his head, and named some important names whom he thought would sign the advertisement. Paul agreed to organise the money, told Steve that all the Beatles and Brian Epstein would put their names to it, and explained how to contact the other Beatles for their signatures. As Miles and Steve left, Paul offered Steve a copy of *Sgt. Pepper* from a big pile on a table to the right of the living-room door. 'No thanks, I've already heard it,' said Steve, and began to laugh. Paul smiled.

The trial of Mick Jagger, Keith Richards and Robert Fraser at Chichester Crown Court began on Monday, 27 June. On Thursday 30th, Judge Block pronounced sentence. Keith's was the worst: one year's imprisonment and £500 towards the costs for allowing his house to be used for smoking cannabis, even though he was a first offender, had not been found in possession, and the only person who had – Schneiderman – had not been charged and had mysteriously been allowed to leave the country. Mick was given three months in prison for possession of four amphetamine tablets, bought legally over the counter in Italy. Robert was given six months in jail for possession and £200 prosecution costs. He had been remanded in custody during the trial. Lord Chief Justice Parker had dismissed Robert's leave to appeal, saying,

> Where heroin is concerned the court is satisfied that, in the ordinary way, if there are no special circumstances, the public interest demands that some form of detention should be imposed ... Heroin has been termed in argument a killer, and it must be remembered that anyone who takes heroin puts themselves body and soul into the hands of the supplier. They have no moral resistance to any pressure being brought to bear on them.

Robert had no choice but to serve his time in Wormwood Scrubs.

That night there was a spontaneous demonstration outside the *News of the World* building; the first time anyone had demonstrated in Fleet Street since World War I. The police turned their dogs on the protesters, there was panic, a scuffle and six people were arrested. The demonstrations continued until the early hours of the morning when the daily papers were being put to bed, again highlighting the generation gap which caused the clash of attitudes: no one but young people would demonstrate at the dead of night.

The next day, Friday, Mick and Keith were released on bail and there were further demonstrations outside the *News of the World*. On Saturday night there were more demonstrations, this time with many arrests, including Hoppy's girlfriend Suzy Creamcheese. Mick Farren from *International Times* was beaten up by the police, as were many others. But the point had already been made; on the same day, William Rees-Mogg, the editor of *The Times*, published an editorial leader, headed 'Who breaks a butterfly on a wheel?,' condemning, in the politest possible terms, the sentences on Mick and Keith. In commenting upon the sentences before the appeal was heard, Rees-Mogg was making himself liable for contempt of court, but since the newspaper was *The Times* and his leader was couched in terms of public interest, he pulled it off. This opened the floodgates and virtually the whole of Fleet Street followed *The Times*'s lead in criticism of the harshness of the sentences, leaving the *News of the World* sidelined.

Robert's artists were horrified by his jail sentence and Richard Hamilton had the idea of keeping the gallery open by mounting a group exhibition to show their solidarity. Many artists, such as Bridget Riley and Harold Cohen, had left the gallery after arguments over money – Robert had not paid them for paintings he had sold – but the only one to refuse to send along an important work was Eduardo Paolozzi. Hamilton himself had been swindled by Robert, who had used some of his paintings as collateral for a Magritte; Magritte's dealer Alexandre Iolas kept the Hamiltons when Robert did not pay him. 'Robert was a charming, if not very convincing, liar,' said Richard Hamilton, 'but on the other hand, he had a wonderful eye for a painting, he adored art and loved what his artists were doing.'

The group show opened at the Robert Fraser Gallery on 10 June 1967. Robert subscribed to a cuttings agency which normally supplied press reviews of his art exhibitions. The tremendous publicity generated by the trial of Mick Jagger and Keith Richards meant that Robert's name appeared in literally hundreds of newspapers and a huge mound of clippings piled up at the gallery. Richard Hamilton used them as collage material to make his print series *Swingeing London*, which has as its central image a photograph of Fraser and Jagger handcuffed together. The Tate Gallery wanted to buy a copy, but Robert's mother, who headed the Friends of the Tate, intervened. Robert was outraged. After protracted arguments, the Tate did eventually buy one of the edition.

Meanwhile preparations for the pot ad were going ahead. It was trailed by Philip Oates's Atticus column in the *Sunday Times*, which revealed that all four Beatles would be among those contributing to the cost of the advertisement. Then, on the eve of publication, when Steve Abrams went to approve the proofs, the advertising manager, a Mr Davison, got cold feet and delayed publication until he checked that all those named had indeed signed. He also, not surprisingly, insisted on advance payment for the ad. Steve Abrams called up Peter Brown at Brian Epstein's office, who sent round a personal cheque for £1,800 made out to *The Times*. Paul had wanted to keep the source of the money a secret, fearing adverse publicity, but the information was in the *Evening Standard* Londoner's Diary the very next day. It was impossible to keep a secret like that in Fleet Street; the *Standard* reporter was told the source by his own editor.

The advertisement when it appeared caused a furore. It was debated in the House of Commons on the day of its publication. The minister of state Alice Bacon gave a speech in which she claimed that 97 per cent of heroin addicts 'started on cannabis', statistics which she appeared to have made up; and, in a rambling, racist speech, blamed the use of cannabis and LSD on the importation of Negro music and Indian spirituality. She told the House of her experience under the hair drier, where she had read a copy of *Queen* magazine: 'There is a very long article in it called "The Love Generation". I was horrified by some of the things I read in it.' She then read a quote by Paul McCartney to the House: 'God is everything. God is in the space between us. God is in the table in front of you. God is everything and everywhere and everyone. It just happens that I've realised all this through acid.' She contrasted Paul's statement to one by 'a little pop singer called Lulu' who said, 'People talk about this love, love, love thing as if you have to be on drugs before you can be part of it. In fact love is far older than pop and goes right back to Jesus. I'm a believer.' Though this view in no way contradicted Paul's statement, the minister of state commended Lulu for her views and castigated Paul for his. She did, however, say that the issues raised by the advertisement would be considered by the Wootton subcommittee, and she committed the government to taking the Wootton Report into consideration when framing new legislation.

On 31 July, a week after the advertisement appeared, Keith Richards's conviction for allowing his premises to be used for smoking pot was quashed on appeal, and Mick's prison sentence was reduced to a conditional discharge. The ad had specifically asked for the premises offence to be abolished and the publicity and debate generated may well have influenced the appeal court's decision.

Baroness Wooton's report reached the conclusion that 'the long-term consumption of cannabis in moderate doses had no harmful effects.' The report said 'the long-asserted dangers of cannabis are exaggerated and that the related law is socially damaging, if not unworkable'. And in a covering letter the committee said that they want to create a situation in which nobody is sent to prison for cannabis.

She presented her report on 1 November 1968 to Home Secretary James Callaghan. During his time in opposition Callaghan had been 'Sunny Jim, the Policeman's Friend', the paid parliamentary lobbyist for the Police Federation. He rejected the report, and defended his position when it was debated in Parliament. However, despite his unilateral dismissal of the Wootton Report, Callaghan actually had little option other than to implement its recommendations. New bipartisan legislation controlling psychotropic drugs was drafted and, as he had asked the Wootton subcommittee to remain sitting in an advisory capacity, he now had to agree to their insistence on the difference between hard and soft drugs, a distinction which had not previously been reflected in law. On 1 February 1970 the *Sunday Mirror* reported in a page-one leader headed 'Drug Law Shock. Jim Changes His Mind. Penalties for "Pot" Smokers to Be Cut':

> Mr Callaghan only a year ago championed the cause of holding the line against drug permissiveness … last year Mr Callaghan denounced what he called 'a notorious advertisement' in *The Times*, signed by many public figures including the Beatles, which urged that possessing cannabis should either be legalised, or at most punishable by a fine of not more than £25.

Callaghan had been outvoted in Cabinet Committee and the new Misuse of Drugs Bill implemented everything the Wootton Commit-tee recommended. The Labour Party lost the 1970 general election, but the legislation had been bipartisan and was re-introduced by Reginald Maudling for the Conservatives. The new Act reduced the maximum imprisonment on summary conviction to six months, and magistrates were advised that minor offences did not merit prison sentences, and that they should treat pot smokers with 'becoming moderation' and 'reserve the sentence of imprisonment for suitably flagrant cases of large-scale trafficking'. The courts stopped imposing custodial sentences for possession.

The situation in nineties Britain is that sentences such as those passed on Hoppy or Keith are virtually unknown unless large-scale dealing is involved or the sentence is concurrent with another, more serious charge and has been used to make the other charge stick. It has been estimated that several million people in Britain smoke pot from time to time. Steve Abrams's 1967 *Times* advertisement had repercussions that no one at the original meeting in the back room of Indica could have dreamed of. It was, of course, only part of the story, and the members of Baroness Wootton's Committee must be thanked for changes in the law that have kept thousands out of jail.

This was the first example of Paul's involvement in political lobbying, a skill which he would later apply with great success to saving his local hospital in Rye, Sussex, and in starting and funding the Liverpool Institute of Performing Arts. The Beatles signed and paid for the advertisement at his instigation. There was no high-profile posturing. He did not sit in a black bag or sing a song about it, just supported a traditional method of lobbying. In this instance quiet and effective work led to a change in the law – from which he himself benefited when police found pot plants growing on his Scottish farm in 1972.

TEN

THE MAHARISHI

Each man has within himself a great storehouse of
creative energy, peace and happiness ... In order to
feel the benefit of this storehouse, however, a man
must have access to it; he must know that it is there,
know how to reach it ...

Maharishi Mahesh Yogi, *Towards World Peace*

Meditation

PAUL: Looking back I feel that the Maharishi experience was
worthwhile. For me, then, it was the sixties, I'd been doing a
bunch of drugs, I wasn't in love with anyone, I hadn't settled
down. I think maybe I was looking for something to fill some
sort of hole. I remember at the time feeling a little bit empty. I
don't know whether it was spiritual or what, it was probably just
staying up all night and doing too many drugs. I was probably
just physically tired.

The whole meditation experience was very good and I still use
the mantra. I don't really practise it massively but it's always in
the back of my mind if I ever want to. For instance, when I was
in jail in Japan it came in very handy; I meditated a lot there and
it was very good. I wasn't allowed to write and I didn't want to
just sit there and do nothing. My brain was racing, as you can
imagine, so meditation was great. I found it very useful and still
do. I find it soothing and I can imagine that the more you were
to get into it, the more interesting it would get.

Whatever the ultimate value of the meditation experience for the

Beatles, the trip to visit the Maharishi in India in 1968 was an extraordinary period of creativity for them. Almost all the songs that would appear on the White Album and *Abbey Road* were composed in those few productive weeks. Even Ringo wrote a song – 'Don't Pass Me By'.

They collaborated with each other and jammed with other musicians who were there. They were for once without their usual protective Liverpool bubble; when they were touring, the only people the Beatles usually dealt with were their manager, their two road managers and their press officer, all from Liverpool. In India the company included musicians and celebrities as diverse as Donovan and his friend Gypsy Dave, Mike Love of the Beach Boys and the American flautist Paul Horn, Mia Farrow and her sister, and assorted meditators from all nations. Wives and girlfriends were also there, the womenfolk who were usually barred from touring and recording sessions. After six frenetic years as the four mop tops and Lords of Psychedelia, the Beatles sat in their brightly coloured Indian cotton shirts, quietly meditating or strumming guitars, surrounded everywhere by hibiscus and frangipani, black crows flapping in the treetops and squealing monkeys tumbling through the branches of the surrounding jungle.

Of all the Beatles, George Harrison had always been the one most attracted to Eastern ideas, both musically and philosophically. His introduction to the sitar came unexpectedly during the making of the film *Help!* The director Dick Lester and the screenwriter Charles Wood set up a scene in which a trio of Indian musicians play a selection of Beatles hits while the group are eating in an Indian restaurant. An arranger did his best to transcribe English music notation for tabla, flute and sitar, and as the musicians were making their first hilarious attempt to sight-read 'A Hard Day's Night', George appeared, intrigued by the unusual sound. He began fiddling with the sitar and soon learned the rudiments. A few months later, in October 1965, he played sitar on 'Norwegian Wood', released on *Rubber Soul*. His sensitive, haunting playing intrigued Brian Jones, who quickly learned enough to play the sitar on 'Paint It Black', one of his triumphs with the Stones. Sales of sitars soared. That same year, 1965, George met Ravi Shankar, the greatest of Indian sitar virtuosos, at dinner in the home of Mr Anghadi, who ran the Asian

Music Circle in London. Not long afterwards, Ravi visited George in Esher and gave him a quick sitar lesson with John and Ringo looking on.

In July 1966, on their way back to Britain after their tour of Hong Kong and Japan, the Beatles stopped off briefly in New Delhi, hoping to get away from Beatlemania. George had originally planned to stop over in India for a few days to buy a sitar, and, as he didn't want to go alone, had asked along their road manager Neil Aspinall. However, by the time the Beatles tour got to Japan, the other Beatles decided that they wanted to stop over in India too. But in Manila, they had inadvertently caused offence by not attending a reception given by Imelda Marcos, the wife of the Philippines dictator Ferdinand Marcos. They had to struggle on to their plane through crowds of jeering Filipinos, carrying all their equipment. Their concert fees were confiscated and their chauffeur, Alf, was beaten up.

In George's autobiography *I Me Mine*, he recalls:

> By the time we had got through the Manila experience, nobody wanted to get off the plane when it arrived in Delhi, they thought 'no thanks, no more changes, let's get home!' They didn't want to go through some other strange country and so I said to Neil, 'Are you still coming?' and he said 'Yes,' so we got our hand baggage and prepared for Delhi and then a steward or stewardess came down the plane and said: 'Sorry, we've already sold your seats to London, so you'll have to get off' and so they all got off. We all did.

As crowds of Indian fans tried to get past the two massive turbaned Sikhs guarding suite 448 of the Oberoi Hotel, the Beatles slipped out of the back door and over to the premises of Rikhi Ram and Sons, sitar makers, on Connaught Circle, where they all ordered sitars from the overwhelmed and delighted proprietor, Mr B. D. Sharma.

Two months later, George returned to India with Patti, checked into the Taj Mahal Hotel in Bombay and spent six weeks studying sitar with Ravi Shankar. Shankar himself claimed that after seven and a half years of study with his teacher Ustad Alludin Khan, he had not yet fully mastered the nineteen-stringed instrument; however, after six weeks, he pronounced George 'an apt pupil'. But George was not intending to play classical Indian ragas, he just wanted to be proficient enough to play on Beatles songs, and told the press, 'I've got no illusions about being a sitar player ...' When Shankar arrived in London that October, George was at the airport to meet him wearing Indian clothes. Shankar, who had been educated in Paris, was wearing a smart European suit.

George told Miles in 1967:

Ravi's my musical guru ... But then later I realised that this wasn't the real thing, this was only a little stepping stone for me to see, because through the music, you reach the spiritual part ... My stepping stones have led me to become a Hindu ... It's a good vibration which makes you feel good. Those vibrations that you get through yoga, cosmic chants, it's such a buzz. It buzzes you out of everywhere. It's nothing to do with pills or anything like that. It's just in your own head. It buzzes you right into the astral plane.

As yet, George had taken no personal guru, though he was very influenced by the work of Vivekananda. The other Beatles were intrigued and showed great sympathy and respect for his interest and commitment to Hinduism, but Indian philosophy remained primarily George's interest. Paul told *NME* in August 1967: 'In some ways I envy George because he now has a great faith. He seems to have found what he's been searching for.'

George and Patti attended Ravi Shankar's concert at the Hollywood Bowl on 4 August 1967, and the day before George gave a press conference with Ravi to help promote the event. It was during this trip that George wrote 'Blue Jay Way', another song in which he used the sitar to particularly good effect. The sound of the instrument was becoming a profound element in the Beatles' work.

While in California, encouraged by Patti Boyd's sister Jenny, who was living in Haight-Ashbury, George and Patti visited San Francisco to see the hippie scene for themselves. George had read about it, but was expecting something like the King's Road, Chelsea, with small shops and artisans. He was very disappointed:

San Francisco is great, there are so many great people there. But there are so many, you know, *bums*, too, spoiling a great idea. It's lovely but it's going bad because a lot of people there believe the answer is to take drugs and drop out. And they drop out on to the pavement, hoping God's going to manifest himself and take them off with him. Well, he's not. That's not being hip. Anything further from hip, in fact, I've never seen, because they're just fooling themselves. I mean, even if they just worked chopping wood, they're nearer to God than by dropping on to the pavement. You don't need drugs, you see. The first trip you see that you don't need acid. At least, that's how it was with me. There's high, and there's high, and to get really high – I mean, so high that you can walk on the water, that high – that's where I'm going. The answer isn't pot and it isn't acid. It's yoga and meditation and working and discipline, working out your karma.

Patti Boyd's interest in Eastern philosophy and meditation had been stimulated by the six weeks they spent in Bombay, so when a friend asked her to go with her to a lecture on Transcendental Meditation at Caxton Hall, she was very keen. Even though the lecture wasn't very stimulating, she asked to be put on the mailing list. When she saw that the Maharishi Mahesh Yogi was giving a series of talks in the ballroom of the London Hilton, she enthused about him to George. George told the other Beatles, and so 24 August 1967 found George and Patti, John, Paul and Jane all sitting in a row near the front. Others were rather put off by the fact that tough-looking bodyguards in expensive business suits stood guarding each side of the stage, in great contrast to the Maharishi himself, who was surrounded only by flowers. For the Beatles, security guards were of course a familiar part of the landscape.

PAUL: We saw that Maharishi was on one of his voyages round the world. We'd seen him years before on a Granada TV current-affairs programme. There he was, just a giggling little swami who was going around the world to promote peace. So when he came around again and somebody said there was a meeting, we all went, 'Oh, that's that giggly little guy. We've seen him. He's great.' We wanted to try and expand spiritually, or at least find some sort of format for all the various things we were interested in: Indian music, Allen Ginsberg, poetry, mantras, mandalas, tantra, all the stuff we'd seen. It made us in a mood to inquire.

I think there was a little bit of emptiness in our souls, a lack of spiritual fulfilment. We were seeing all this stuff on acid, what I still think were DNA wheels: great big multicoloured chains of things. When you see the pictures of DNA, it looks remarkably like what I used to see in my head. So that made sense to me, that you can actually perceive your own DNA. We were glimpsing bits of bliss and we wanted to know, and I guess I still do, how best to approach that.

So Maharishi came to a hall in London and we all got tickets and sat down near the front row. There were a lot of flowers on the stage and he came on and sat cross-legged. And he looked great and he talked very well and started to explain, and I still think his idea is fine.

The lecture was followed by a press conference, after which John, Paul, George and their party were granted a ninety-minute private audience. 'Expansion of happiness is the purpose of life, and evolution is the process through which it is fulfilled,' said the Maharishi. He believed it was the duty of everyone to be happy to serve the purpose of creation. He believed the endless wandering of the mind was a search for happiness among external objects but that only by coming into contact with the source of thought itself could true bliss be achieved.

For the media, the Maharishi was the yogi sent from Central Casting: the liquid eyes, twinkling but inscrutable with the wisdom of the East, the long flowing beard and cascading ringlets. The giggling guru with his huge smile, bunches of flowers and holy-man robes looked like an oriental Santa Claus, later lampooned as Mr Natural by the American cartoonist Robert Crumb. Though they were sceptical of his spiritual message, the media nonetheless seized upon him because of his pro-establishment, anti-drug message, to which young people seemed to be listening.

The Maharishi presented his philosophy to the Beatles using the analogy of a flower with its roots in the earth, a stem and a beautiful head. He told them to think of themselves as the head of the flower, the visible manifestation of creation. Then to consider the sap, the source of the flower's energy. Water and nutrients in the soil are drawn up to make the flower head from a reservoir of goodness in the earth. With humans, the physical body is the flower head but the sap that feeds it is spiritual energy.

PAUL: He said that by meditating, you can go down your stem and, just like the sap, reach the field of nutrients which he called the pool of cosmic consciousness, which was all blissful and all beautiful. The only mistake we make, and he didn't put it quite like this, was we fuck up all the time. We don't reach it. We're all so busy playing guitars, or talking politics or reading other people's words or whatever it is, we don't take time ... Maharishi doesn't believe in a creator God. And all of that found a certain sympathy in our minds. We liked him.

The Maharishi's message struck a chord and the Beatles, George in particular, were anxious to learn more. They made arrangements to travel to Bangor, in North Wales, the next day in order to attend the weekend initiation seminar that the Maharishi was holding there. This would give them the mantras they needed to begin his meditation method.

The Maharishi had a degree in physics and studied Sanskrit and Hindu scriptures with Swami Guru Dev, who became his spiritual master. In the early fifties he began working as an employee of Shankararacheraya of Jyotirpeeth, the founder of his order. When Shankararacheraya died, there was an unseemly struggle for leadership between the two senior priests of the order, but while their lawyers argued their grievances in court, the Maharishi surreptitiously took over, adopted the title of 'Maharishi' and has never looked back.

His teachings are very Westernised versions of ancient Vedic knowledge, simplified so much that they would be derided in Uttar Pradesh. However, it was not his message but his organisation that was most criticised by other Hindu teachers, who felt the Maharishi was violating the most basic principles of the faith. According to Hindu tradition, anyone who presents themselves at an ashram requesting to be taught meditation is given free instruction as well as free food and board. As in any monastery, it is a rigorous life, rising with the dawn and living in spartan conditions.

The Maharishi changed all this: he suggested a one-off payment of one week's earnings from his students. He provided luxurious – by Indian ashram standards – accommodation for his wealthy clients, and turned away poor students if their places were needed for richer ones. He developed close contacts with right-wing Indian politicians, who gave him their approval; the *Bhagavad-Gita* teaching that it is better to accept than question, better to meditate than act, suited them very well. By the late fifties he was ready to take his message abroad and in 1959 he opened his first centre in Britain. By the time the Beatles went to see him, he had established about 250 meditation centres in about fifty countries. He was an expert at publicity and, knowing that television was crucial, always ensured that he was newsworthy. It was, after all, on television that the Beatles first saw him.

The next day they all went to Bangor by train to attend the Maharishi's meditation seminar: John, Paul, George and Ringo, accompanied by Patti, Jane and Maureen, Mick Jagger and Marianne Faithfull. Cynthia was barred from joining the train by a policeman who thought she was a fan, and so Neil Aspinall had to drive her there. It was really George's idea, though the others were interested enough to get the basic instruction in meditation. Paul told a friend at the time: 'George wants it. What one of us wants, the others go along with.' The Maharishi had not had time to make special arrangements so the Beatles finished up sleeping in a rented schoolroom like everyone else.

PAUL: We went to Bangor for a weekend to learn how to meditate, and we were initiated there. It was a bit funny going to those camps because it was like going back to school. Just the nature of it meant staying in a classroom and we'd been used to our nice comfortable homes or hotels so to be staying in an old school on a camp bed was a little bit disconcerting. Then trying to learn to meditate. It's not that easy, you don't just pick it up like that, it's an effort and you've got to be involved, so it was like going back to school. And of course the food was all canteen food. But we were interested enough to learn the system, which we did.

The actual ceremony in Bangor when we got given the mantra was nice. You had to wait outside his room as he did people one by one, and then you got to go into the inner sanctum, just a room they'd put a lot of flowers in and a few drapes around, and lit a few joss sticks. You had to take some cut flowers to Maharishi as some sort of offering. It was all flowers with Maharishi, but flowers were the symbol of the period anyway so it was very easy. So you got your flowers, you

took your shoes off and went into a darkened room where
Maharishi was. It was quite exciting. It reminded me of Gypsy
Rose Lee's tent in Blackpool – 'Come inside!' – Santa's grotto or
something. Maharishi explained what he was going to do, he
said, 'I'll just do a few little bits and pieces ...' however he put it,
of this and that, little incantations for himself, then he said, 'I will
just lean towards you and I'll just whisper, very quietly, your
mantra.' He gives you your mantra and he's only going to say it
once and you repeat it once, just to check you've got it, and he
says, 'Yes, that's it.' And he said, 'The idea is that you don't
mention that to anyone ever again, because if you speak it, it will
besmirch it to some degree; if you never speak it, then it's always
something very special.'

But I must admit, I have spoken it, to Linda. At one point we
decided that to reaffirm our faith in each other I would even tell
her that, but that's the only time I've spoken it, once, to Linda. I
know, I know, I've completely blown it, man! But I don't think
you're really not allowed to. It's not like a chant, I think it's just
generally a pretty good idea if you don't voice it, and I go along
with that.

I asked Maharishi, 'Am I supposed to see this word? Or am I
supposed to hear this word?' and it was hear it. But he said, 'You
can repeat this at any speed, slow, fast, or anything. Try it at
various speeds.' I remember one of the ways I could get into it
was visually. Mind you, if you follow this through and look at
Buddhism, they eventually imagine mandalas and the whole
tantric thing. But I remember one of my little aids to meditation
was imagining someone on a gate with a straw out of his mouth,
just chewing, that feeling of being very very calm. You get nice
peaceful images like this and, obviously, to spend twenty
minutes out of your day doing that rather than sleeping or eating
or shouting at someone was not a bad idea and that was basically
all I thought of it all.

Brian Epstein

Brian Epstein had been invited to come with the Beatles to Bangor
and had agreed to join them there after the August Bank Holiday.
Brian, a complex, vulnerable man, had been having a particularly bad

time. Earlier that month he had sat the traditional Jewish *shiva* for his late father in Liverpool and was now very worried about his mother's health and state of mind. He had only recently come out of the Priory Clinic, where he had tried with some, but not much, success to kick amphetamines and rid himself of acute insomnia. Contributing to his worries was the fact that his management contract with the Beatles was coming up for renegotiation on 30 September. Though he was fairly sure that they wanted him to continue with them, he also knew that his management fee would be reduced from 25 per cent to the more usual 10, now that they were no longer touring.

On Friday, 25 August, Brian invited Geoffrey Ellis and Peter Brown, who both worked for him, down to Kingsley Hall, his country house near Uckfield in Sussex, for the bank-holiday weekend. It was his first social event since his father's death. When a gang of rent boys failed to show up, Brian drove back to London to find some 'action', leaving his friends to continue without him. The next day he telephoned at five o'clock in the afternoon from his Chapel Street flat, sounding very groggy. Peter Brown suggested he take the train down to the country rather than drive under the influence of Tuinals. Brian said he would have some breakfast, read that day's mail and watch *Juke Box Jury* on television, then he would telephone to tell them which train to meet. He never called.

The inquest revealed that he had taken six Carbrital sleeping pills in order to sleep. This was probably not an unusual amount for Brian, but it meant that his tolerance had come close to a lethal level. Brian was pronounced dead of an accidental overdose. There were all manner of rumours surrounding the cause of death, from suicide to accidental suffocation at the hands of a guardsman – Brian had a very colourful sex life which often left him bruised and battered. He had made a previous attempt at suicide but it is unlikely that his death was anything other than a genuine accident.

The Beatles were strolling in the school grounds in Bangor after a late Sunday lunch when the pay phone on the wall of their dormitory began to ring. Peter Brown, from Brian's office, had made Patti Harrison swear to telephone him with a number when they reached Bangor so that he could reach the Beatles in the event of an emergency. The phone continued to ring and eventually Jane Asher went inside to answer it. 'Get Paul to the phone,' said Peter Brown.

Jenny Boyd has described the intense feelings of everyone present at the seminar: 'While we were in Wales we learned that Brian Epstein had died in London. It was an incredible experience; first the experience of the meditation, then the incredible sadness of Brian's death. Brian had been the bridge between Lennon and McCartney. It really felt like the Beatles ended that weekend, and everyone felt it.'

> PAUL: We were shocked with the news of Brian's death, which was terrible. We checked with Maharishi: 'What do you do, man? Look, this great guy's dead ...' He said, 'Well, we'll just have to send him great vibrations. There's nothing more you can do, just have to meditate and feel good ourselves. There's no more you can do.' So that slightly placated us. It helped a little bit, in my own mind. I can't speak for anyone else. Then eventually we went off, sorrowed by the news of Brian's death. It was shattering, sad, and a little frightening. We loved him.

The Beatle probably most affected by Brian's death was John. Not long after Brian's death, he said:

> With Brian dying it was sort of a big thing for us and if we hadn't had this meditation it would have been much harder to assess and carry on and know how we were going. Now we're our own managers, now we have to make all the decisions. We've always had full responsibility for what we did, but we still had a father figure, or whatever it was, and if we didn't feel like it, well, you know, Brian would do it. It threw me quite a bit. But then the Maharishi talked to us and, I don't know, cooled us out a bit.

Though John normally appeared the most cynical, least vulnerable of the Beatles, Brian's death undermined his confidence. Years later he told *Rolling Stone* magazine: 'I knew that we were in trouble then. I didn't really have any misconceptions about our ability to do anything other than play music and I was scared. I thought, "We've fuckin' had it!"' John probably used Brian more as a father figure than the others and with Brian gone, John turned for help to the nearest authority figure, which happened to be the Maharishi, and focused all his hopes on him. The Maharishi had hoped that the Beatles would become converts but was not prepared for such sudden acceptance. Soon John and George were equal in their expectations of him and had elevated him to a position that he didn't want and was probably incapable of fulfilling. Paul and Ringo remained interested but that was the extent of it.

The press was uneasy with many of the countercultural heroes of the sixties and in particular waged a campaign against Dr Timothy Leary, whose message of using drugs as a path to greater awareness was anathema to them. By contrast they loved the Maharishi because he preached the exact opposite, even if it did come from a slightly suspect oriental source. He was opposed to the use of drugs and told his audience, 'It is not good to quit school. We should stay in school and learn,' and 'We should obey the parents. They know what is best.' He was against nuclear disarmament and supported the war in Vietnam.

In America, where he concentrated his efforts, many students were shocked by his attitude. When they asked him if they should resist the draft to avoid killing fellow humans, the Maharishi replied, 'We should obey the elected leaders of the country. They are representatives of the people and have more information at their disposal and are more qualified to make the right decisions.' His politics were those of the American establishment. In fact, many of his meetings in the USA broke up because his youthful audience walked out, appalled at his message. After a meeting at UCLA in September 1967, one student commented, 'If his opinions reflect what twenty years of meditation will do for you, I estimate that forty will raise you to the stature of Hitler!'

The Beatles may have been quite casual in their investigation of the Maharishi; John and George perhaps naïvely expected him to slip them the answer to the meaning of existence, but they tempered this with a healthy Liverpudlian irreverence – an irreverence which was unfortunately lacking in many of the young people who attended his lectures purely because he was the Beatles' 'guru'. Miles, who was writing for the underground paper *International Times*, did some background research into the Maharishi and asked Allen Ginsberg, who had lived in India for several years, what he knew about him. When Miles warned Paul and John that he had connections with right-wing politicians in India and that his students were expected to give him one week's wages per annum, John's characteristic response was, 'Ain't no ethnic bastard gonna get no golden castles out of me, if that's what you think!' Nor did he; Lennon never paid him a penny.

But neither was John moved by the criticism from other Hindu teachers. 'So what if he's commercial? We're the most commercial group in the world!'

The Maharishi was very quick to use the Beatles' name to promote his cause. In November 1967, he released his own album, promoted in ads as 'Maharishi Mahesh Yogi, the Beatles' Spiritual Teacher, speaks to the youth of the world on love and the untapped source of power that lies within'. Even before the Beatles went to Rishikesh, he had announced that they would join him in a TV special for the ABC network in America. Twice Peter Brown had to inform the ABC lawyers that the Beatles were not appearing on his show, but the Maharishi insisted that he could deliver them. Peter Brown flew to Malmö, Sweden, where the Maharishi was encamped, but a few days later ABC called to say he was still confirming their participation. Eventually Paul and George, accompanied by Peter Brown, flew to Malmö and finally convinced him that he must not use their name without authority in his promotions. The Maharishi just nodded and giggled. George defended him, saying the Maharishi was not a worldly man, but the fact was that the Maharishi had been touring the world since 1958, rather longer than they had. The Beatles did agree to appear in a film to promote his Indian centre, but when Neil Aspinall flew to Rishikesh to negotiate the deal, he was surprised to find that the holy man had a full-time accountant on hand and was very sophisticated in negotiating percentage points and profit splitting.

Because of the publicity generated by the Beatles, and fanned by the Maharishi's own press people, his smiling face was on the cover of virtually every mass-market magazine in America: *Time, Life, Newsweek, Look, Esquire,* the *New York Times* Sunday Supplement, and on specialist magazines from *Ebony* to *Dance Magazine.* He appeared on *The Johnny Carson Show* and at Madison Square Garden. Through the Beatles he gained thousands of new followers.

Rishikesh

The period after Brian's death was one of confusion and uncertainty. The Maharishi could offer not only solace but a refuge – and perhaps a solution. George had become more and more interested in Hinduism and was now a firm believer in the notion of a cycle of karma and rebirth. It was he and John who were perhaps most keen on the idea and devised the plan of the Beatles all going to India for further meditation practice at the Maharishi's ashram in the foothills of the Himalayas. Paul was enthusiastic and Ringo went along for the ride.

> PAUL: John and George were going to Rishikesh with the idea that this might be some huge spiritual lift-off and they might never come back if Maharishi told them some really amazing thing. Well, being a little bit pragmatic, I thought in my own mind, I'll give it a month, then if I really really like it, I'll come back and organise to go out there for good, but I won't go on this 'I may never come back' thing, I won't burn my bridges. That's very me, to not want to do that. I just see it as being practical, and I think it is.

The sceptical expression on Jane's face in photographs taken as she and Paul listen to the Maharishi's lectures suggests that she may have been dubious about the whole venture.

After a number of delays caused because the filming and editing of *Magical Mystery Tour* took far longer than they had expected, the Beatles were finally able to make enough time to go to India. Their roadie Mal Evans went out first in order to organise transport for John and George. Their excess luggage cost £200. George and Patti, Patti's sister Jenny, John and Cynthia took the flight to Delhi the next day, arriving on 16 February 1968. Mal met them at the airport with Mia Farrow, who had flown to India with the Maharishi from New York three weeks earlier and had already elected to become part of the Beatles' entourage. Mal had organised three ancient, battered taxis for the 150-mile drive from Delhi to Rishikesh.

Paul and Jane, Ringo and Maureen arrived at 8.15 on the morning of the 19th after an overnight flight, attracting much more press attention. A film crew was on hand as they stepped from the plane after the exhausting twenty-hour flight, jet-lagged from the five time zones. Mal Evans and Raghvendra from the ashram placed garlands of red and yellow flowers around their necks in the traditional token of greeting. Ringo's arm was hurting from the required shots, so their first move was to find a hospital. Their driver lost his way and finished up in a dead end in the middle of a field, followed by a whole convoy of press cars. One of them came to the rescue and took them to the hospital.

Paul and Jane took one car and Ringo and Maureen another.

PAUL: There was an Indian driver and Raghvendra from the camp in front and me and Jane Asher in the back and it was long and it was dusty and it was not a very good car and it was one of those journeys, but great and exciting. I remember these Indian guys talking in what was obviously an Indian language and I was starting to doze off in the car in the back because once you were two hours into the journey the tourism had worn off a little. It was fascinating seeing naked holy men and the kind of things you just don't see unless it's late-night Soho, and the ones you tend to see in Soho tend to be covered in shit and very drunk. I slipped into sleep, a fitful back-of-the-car sort of sleep. It was quite bumpy, and the guys were chattering away, but in my twilight zone of sleeping it sounded like they were talking Liverpool. If you listened closely, it so nearly slid into it. There was like a little segue into very fast colloquial Liverpool. And I was thinking, Uh, where the fuck am I? What? Oh, it's Bengali, and I would just drop off again. 'Yabba yabba, are yer comin' oot then, lad?' It was a strange little twilight experience. It was a long journey.

Rishikesh is about 150 miles north-east of Delhi, halfway to Tibet. On the way they passed through Hardiwar, one of the seven sacred cities of the Hindus, filled with temples and ashrams, monkeys and sacred cows, and from there into the foothills of the Himalayas to an area studded with Hindu pilgrim centres. The Academy of Transcendental Meditation occupied a guarded compound on a flat ledge, 150 feet up the side of a mountain above the fast-flowing Ganges, full to overflowing from the rainy season, which had just ended. There were wonderful views out over the sacred river to the small town of Rishikesh on the opposite bank and to the plains beyond. The centre was reached by a modern suspension bridge built across the river, which had a big sign, 'No camels or elephants', but the students tended to use the open ferryboat that ploughed back and forth across the muddy river. The ashram was surrounded on the other three sides by jungle-covered mountains filled with howling monkeys, peacocks and brightly coloured parrots.

The students lived in six solidly built stone cottages set in groups along an unsurfaced road. Each bungalow contained five self-contained rooms furnished with two four-poster beds, a dressing table and chairs, new rugs on the floor and walls and modern bathroom facilities with hot and cold running water, though sometimes the water supply broke down. Surrounding the buildings were flowering shrubs and plants, tended by an old gardener. It was simple, clean and very peaceful. 'It was back to Butlins holiday camp,' Paul thought, 'you all had your own chalet. It was like all these camps are, it was a Boy Scout camp really except not under canvas, it had these little flat-roofed huts; for some reason it suggested a Butlins chalet to me. Quite nice, nothing fancy at all.'

The ashram had a staff of about forty people, including a construction crew, a printing works, cooks and cleaning staff. The room service was first-class and there was even a masseuse on hand. There were no bugs but there were flies.

PAUL: Ringo didn't like the flies, but it doesn't bother me too much. Maureen, Ringo's wife, apparently had every fly spotted. She knew the six flies that were in the room. There would be one above the door lintel; she knew that one was going to get her. And then there was one just by the window. She knew it and she hated it. Whereas I would just tend to take a broader view, 'Ah yes, it's India, innit? They got flies here.'

John Lennon told the story of how one day Maureen, who had a great interest in things magical, could not stand the flies any more and gave them a thunderous black look and the flies dropped dead around her.

A path led from the row of cottages down towards the Ganges, past the lecture hall to the two dining rooms. While the Beatles were there, a swimming pool was under construction next to the lecture building. Beyond the kitchens there was a heated dining room for use if the weather was bad, but they normally took their meals in a glass-walled dining room, open to the sky, near the cliff over the river. There they were sheltered from the sun by a canopy of leaves from creepers trained across a wooden trellis and were often joined at their meals by monkeys, which roamed around the tables and made off with the toast.

They sat on benches at a long communal table, covered with plastic tablecloths held down by jars of jam and bowls of fruit. Breakfast was served from 7 a.m. until 11 a.m.: porridge, puffed wheat or cornflakes, fruit juice, tea or coffee, toast, marmalade or jam, brought by young Indian servants. 'The idea was you'd all wake up at a certain time and you'd all go for breakfast,' Paul explained. 'You'd sit outside all together and chat about this and that, have a bit of breakfast, a communal thing.' Breakfast was followed by meditation practice, with no rules or timetable. Lunch and dinner both consisted of soup followed by a vegetarian main dish.

John and George were already vegetarians so for them the diet was nothing strange. Paul liked the Indian cuisine but the spices were too strong for Jane. Ringo had spent long periods in hospital with peritonitis as a child and found the food much too hot for his taste. Mal Evans assembled a stock of eggs so that he could cook Ringo fried, boiled, poached or scrambled eggs, and Ringo himself had resourcefully brought along a suitcase of baked beans, just in case. The local water was safe to drink as it came cold and fresh from a mountain spring. At first they boiled it to be on the safe side. The Maharishi never ate with his students, preferring to stay in his bungalow.

They had enrolled in a teachers' course in Transcendental Meditation (TM), designed to give the student enough information to pass the method on to others. There were ninety-minute lectures at 3.30 and 8.30 with students describing their meditation experiences and the Maharishi answering their questions. Most of the time was taken up by meditation itself.

Because they arrived late, the Beatles were three weeks behind the other students, and Paul and Ringo four days behind John and George, so the Maharishi gave them extra tuition and lectures in the afternoons. These took place in the open air, sometimes on chairs on the grass and other times on the flat sun roof of his bungalow. If it was a cool day, they would go to his bungalow and sit on cushions. Big Mal Evans had his own chair because he was unable to cross his legs comfortably.

PAUL: It felt ordinary. By anybody else's standards it certainly didn't look ordinary; it was the front page of the *Daily Mail*, and you can't call that ordinary, can you? But it felt ordinary, like the ordinariness of an Edward Hopper painting. That quality he gets: it's streets I've seen, it's corners I've been on, it's people I know, the old bald janitor with the waistcoat.

It was quite nice. It was a bit strange being away from home in a sort of camp, but I found the experience was very interesting and I was quite into the meditation. We'd had the introduction to it in Bangor where Maharishi had done his little bit. I'm glad when I talk about meditation to people today and we talk about Transcendental Meditation, I can say, 'Well, I got my mantra from Maharishi.' Nowadays if you do it you'll get your mantra from one of his followers, who'll take you through the ceremony. So it's kind of nice to have got it from the horse's mouth, as it were. Slipped it to me, yeah.

One thing slightly impressed me was, being a good British person, whenever I went to a hot place I would get sunburned. Stay out in the sun too long, not realising, which the Brits never seem to do. Take me shirt off, get a nice lobster tan, and really be in pain the rest of the day and probably have to drink in the evening to try and anaesthetise it. Then fall asleep and just hope for the best.

But this time, I got sunburned in the morning and come lunchtime I was going, 'Oh, my God, it's going to be the burning lobster thing.' But I meditated for a couple of hours and low and behold, the lobster had gone. I often wondered whether it was just the fact that I'd calmed myself, whereas normally I'd go running around with a shirt on, irritating it, or I'd go to a dance and really rub it, whereas now I was just sitting very quietly with it for three hours. But it certainly didn't bother me.

The meditation sessions were increasingly long, they were as long as you could handle. It was a very sensible thing. He basically said, 'Your mind is confused with day-to-day stress so I want you to try and do twenty minutes in the morning and twenty minutes in the evening.' That's what they start you on. Twenty minutes in the morning is not going to hurt anyone. You sit still, I suppose you regulate your breathing and, if nothing else, you rest your muscles for twenty minutes. It's like a lie-in. That's pretty good. The meditation helps your productivity that day. And then twenty minutes in the evening; I used to liken it to sitting in front of a nice coal fire that's just sort of glowing. That sort of feeling, that very relaxed feeling, a twilight feeling which I quite like. Are you dreaming or are you awake? There's a nice little state that they recognise halfway between it.

My best experience of the whole time, which doesn't sound much but which was very pleasant, came when I was meditating. Some of us were called into little like Bible-study groups, but these were just meditation-study groups, good ones. A few of us would sit around on little chairs on the roof of the building Maharishi lived in and talk to him about meditation.

People would complain, saying, 'Anything we can do about the crows? They aren't 'alf distracting.' And he'd say, 'Well, we can only shoot them.' And we'd say, 'Oh no, maybe not; you know, leave 'em.' So you had to deal with it yourself. I didn't mind, I figured it's got to be part of the deal, you can't shoot everything that breathes and makes a noise just because you want to meditate. I thought, I'm not sure they've got the spirit of this here. Really. Then it was 'Maharishi, it's too noisy where I am to meditate,' and he'd say, 'Ah, don't worry about it. If you meditate well it'll go away anyway.'

Then we'd meditate and he'd leave us. After one of those sessions, I remember having a great meditation, one of the best I ever had. It was a pleasant afternoon, in the shade of these big tropical trees on the flat roof of this bungalow. It appeared to me that I was like a feather over a hot-air pipe, a warm-air pipe. I was just suspended by this hot air, which was something to do with the meditation. And it was a very very blissful feeling. It took you back to childhood when you were a baby, some of the secure moments when you've just been fed or you were having your nap. It reminded me of those nice, secure feelings. And I thought, Well, hell, that's great, I couldn't buy that anywhere. That was the most pleasant, the most relaxed I ever got, for a few minutes I really felt so light, so floating, so complete.

The difficulty, of course, is keeping your mind clear, because the minute you clear it, a thought comes in and says, 'What are we gonna do about our next record?' 'Go away!' Meditate, mantra mantra mantra. 'I still want to know what we're doing on this next record.' 'Please go away, I'm meditating, can't you see?' There's inevitably all sorts of little conversations you can't help getting into.

Maharishi used to give some very good advice, things that I suppose tied in with Vedic traditions. He would always translate it into a particular Englishy kind of phrase, like 'The heart always goes to the warmer place,' which I've ever since always found to be a very reassuring thought. I think at the time I half suspected that, being the perverse spirit that it is, my ego would want go to the thing that's bad for me. You tend to suspect your darker side, I suppose. But he was quite reassuring: 'No, your heart always wants to go to the warmer place.' Little things like that: the story of the snake which, when you look at it closely, turns out to be a piece of string and your fears were unfounded.

Sometimes Maharishi would ask us questions about how best to advance this system of meditation and we'd try and clue him in on how we thought it would best go down, try and give him some advice. Maharishi was very practical, he liked to know how to do things the simplest Western way. He would ask what kind of car they should use and you'd say, 'A Mercedes is a good practical car, not too flash, pretty flash, it'll get you there, it'll tend not to break down.' 'This is the car we should have!' It was all done like that, it wasn't 'Rolls-Royces are very nice, Maharishi. You could have a couple of them on what you're earning.' It wasn't that, it was very practical. He wanted to know what was the strongest car that won't break down and that they would get the best wear out of. I never minded that. He never had a fleet of them like some of these other guys, and of course he only ever wore this cheesecloth, so you couldn't accuse him of being into Armani suits or anything. So I couldn't see what he was doing with his money, if he was hoarding it somewhere. To this day he still sits around in a cheesecloth, pushing TM. I don't think he does have a big swinging penthouse in Hong Kong. I've never suspected him of that. And I never saw him come out of his house for the whole month. He was always meditating. I don't think he raved it up at all. Let's put it this way, there were no spoils. If a cheesecloth is a spoil, then that was it.

We would go down and get some breakfast, then go for a short walk around or read a book or something. Then you might do another twenty minutes. But they increased the sessions, so now you could do an hour. And then you'd go and talk to someone or talk to Maharishi. In the evenings there generally was a question-and-answer session. There was a hall, like a school hall with a stage. There would be about a hundred people from all walks of life: there was a guy from Brooklyn, there were the celebs, there were teachers from England. It was a bit the swotty crowd, bit the Youth Hostel Association crowd. And you think, Well, it would be. We're talking about pursuing meditation here, it is going to be a little bit art mistresses and religious instruction and Buddhists. They were actually a very nice crowd.

During their first week there, John and Cynthia, George and Patti had thrown themselves wholly into meditation, so by the time Paul, Jane, Ringo and Maureen arrived, they were ready to let off steam a bit. They took afternoons off to sunbathe on the banks of the Ganges and to go sightseeing. A number of other celebrities flew in. Donovan came with his old friend Gypsy Dave in pursuit of Jenny Boyd. He wrote 'Jennifer Juniper' to win her over, but though Jenny and Patti later opened a boutique of the same name, his overtures came to nothing. 'I liked him,' she remembers, 'but I didn't want a boyfriend.' She later married Mick Fleetwood of Fleetwood Mac.

Donovan described the scene when he arrived:

We took taxis at the airport, monkeys were leaping about on the roof. Some hours later we arrived at the village of Rishikesh and the luggage was loaded on to oxen, we took mules, and even walked the last part up a ravine to the ashram gates. We were all amazed at the sights and sounds of the Indian atmosphere. We checked into stone bungalows and went down to see the Yogi in his modern bungalow. We all stood around as Maharishi sat cross-legged on his deerskin. John decided to break the awkward silence, went up to our Yogi, patted him on the head and said, 'There's a good Guru.' We all broke up with laughter. This Liverpudlian humour was always evident, it glued them together in all their fame.

Mia Farrow was already there, described by Paul as 'a quiet little thing in a sort of Nehru jacket'. She was getting over her 1966 marriage to Frank Sinatra. 'That must have been fun, a year with Sinatra,' Paul commented. 'No wonder she needed to meditate.' Her

brother John and her nineteen-year-old sister Prudence were travelling with her, and Prudence became the inspiration for one of John
Lennon's best-loved songs.

PAUL: Prudence Farrow got an attack of the horrors, paranoia,
what you'd call these days an identity crisis, and wouldn't come
out of her Butlins chalet. We all got a little bit worried about her
so we went up there and knocked. 'Hi, Prudence, we all love
you. You're wonderful!' But nobody could persuade her out. So
John wrote 'Dear Prudence, won't you come out and play ...'
He went in and sang it to her and I think that actually did help.
We walked up to her chalet, a little delegation, and John sang it
outside her door with his guitar. And she looked out, she
improved after that. It was a turning point. I think it was quite
sensitive of John to realise that she needed showing that she was
okay, for someone to tell her that she was all right. You know, if
you're used to McDonald's and Howard Johnson's, India is a
little bit different. Looking at it now, from a nineties perspective,
there was probably a lot of therapy needed for a lot of the people
there. We were all looking for something. Obviously you don't
go to Rishikesh if you're not looking for something. It's a long
schlep otherwise. Prudence probably needed to talk about it
rather than meditate.

John Lennon told *Playboy*: 'Mia Farrow's sister, who seemed to go
slightly balmy, meditating too long, wouldn't come out of the little hut
we were living in. They selected me and George to try and bring her
out because she would trust us.' Prudence has no memory of ever
hearing the song in India, but Paul Horn has said that she was in a
semi-catatonic state from almost continuous meditation, against the
Maharishi's wishes, and didn't even recognise her own brother at the
time, so her memory is probably faulty.
Mike Love from the Beach Boys was also resident.

PAUL: Mike Love sat in his place and did meditation, but what I
found amusing there was that I saw him rather as the
quartermaster of the camp. Because we'd all brought our
cameras and film cameras and little tape recorders, and we were
using a lot of movie film and we'd run out. He was to my mind
the resourceful American who decided he'd hire a taxi and go to

New Delhi, he'd buy up lots of the Kodak film that everyone needed, so he became like the quartermaster's stores to me. You'd go to his place and say, 'You got any Kodak, Mike?' He'd say, 'What do you want, Kodak II or Kodacolor?' And behind one of the curtains and in one of the wardrobes of his little Butlins chalet, he had a lot of movie film. He reminded me of a dealer. He had film and batteries and things like that, all the requirements. There wasn't a camp shop so he became the camp shop. It's like when the American army goes anywhere, there's always one guy who can get you stuff. I think he might have even had booze in there. 'Hey, man. Come to Mr Love!' It was a great time, we all enjoyed it, we were all pretty friendly with each other and enjoyed Mike Love's company, and everyone's company; all in all it was good fun. Mike Love's now something big in TM, the way only Californians can get serious.

There was another established musician among the other medita-tors. Paul: 'Paul Horn the flute player was there. I got quite friendly with Paul, he was very nice. He later went on to record an album at the Taj Mahal and he was hatching that plan there.' Paul Horn and Patti Harrison shared a birthday (he was some fourteen years older), and the occasion was celebrated with a party. Paul gave him an Indian *kurta*, a long cotton shirt, which Paul had painted with the words 'Paul' on the front, with some stars and dots, and 'Jai Guru Dev' – 'Long live Guru Dev', the Maharishi's own guru – on the back. The Maharishi arrived and chanted the appropriate prayers, then the company sang 'Happy Birthday' and the party began. George played a couple of ragas on his sitar and followed this with a rendering of 'God Save the Queen' accompanied by Paul playing the tambour, a bass drone instrument that Donovan had bought that morning. The evening ended with a conjurer and fireworks.

The fact that the Beatles were at the ashram was of course well known to the world press – two Fleet Street reporters had accompanied John and George over on the flight – but there was really very little for them to report. The Beatles gave them a few photo opportunities and then retreated beyond the guarded gates of the compound.

PAUL: The camp compound had a wire fence all around it, which was handy later, for the press decided they wanted to have pictures of everything that we did. They would catch us walking past the gates so we started to avoid that area and they didn't get in much. They got a few pictures of us but we didn't feel too pestered.

We went down to the village one evening when they were showing a film; the travelling cinema came around with a lorry and put up a screen. It was a very pleasant Indian evening so Maharishi came, everyone came, and we all walked down as a procession. And it was very very pleasant; walking along in the dust slightly downhill through a path in the jungle from the meditation camp with my guitar and singing 'Ob-La-Di Ob-La-Da', which I was writing, accompanying the procession on the way. Of course 'Ob-La-Di Ob-La-Da' has got no connection with meditation except 'Life goes on ...', it's a little story about Desmond and Molly. In actual fact, I think they quite enjoyed it. Maharishi quite liked someone strolling along singing.

I had a friend called Jimmy Scott who was a Nigerian conga player, who I used to meet in the clubs in London. He had a few expressions, one of which was, 'Ob la di ob la da, life goes on, bra.' I used to love this expression. Every time we met he'd say, 'Ob la di ob la da, life goes on, bra.' Or somebody would say 'Too much' and he'd say, 'Nothing's too much, just outta sight.' At some point in our existence we'll probably find that he was a great guru. He sounded like a philosopher to me. He was a great guy anyway and I said to him, 'I really like that expression and I'm thinking of using it,' and I sent him a cheque in recognition of that fact later because even though I had written the whole song and he didn't help me, it was his expression.

It's a very *me* song, in as much as it's a fantasy about a couple of people who don't really exist, Desmond and Molly. I'm keen on names too. Desmond is a very Caribbean name. It could have been Winston, that would have been all right. Jimmy Scott had his own band. He died a few years ago, but he was a real cool guy.

Jimmy Anonmuogharan Scott Emuakpor came to Britain in the fifties and had been playing around the London club scene ever since. His catch-phrase 'Ob la di ob la da' is Yoruba for 'Life goes on'. Jimmy played congas on the track when the Beatles recorded it for the

White Album. He died in 1986 in his mid-sixties, a victim of British racism. He was strip-searched at London airport immigration and kept naked in a cell for two hours. He developed pneumonia and died in hospital the next day.

> PAUL: I wrote quite a few songs in Rishikesh and John came up with some creative stuff. George actually once got quite annoyed and told me off because I was trying to think of the next album. He said, 'We're not fucking here to do the next album, we're here to meditate!' It was like, 'Ohh, excuse me for breathing!' You know. George was quite strict about that, George can still be a little that way, and it's like, 'Oh come on, George, you don't have a monopoly on thought in this area. I'm allowed to have my own views on the matter.'
>
> I was doing a song, 'I Will', that I had as a melody for quite a long time but I didn't have lyrics to it. I remember sitting around with Donovan, and maybe a couple of other people. We were just sitting around one evening after our day of meditation and I played him this one and he liked it and we were trying to write some words. We kicked around a few lyrics, something about the moon, but they weren't very satisfactory and I thought the melody was better than the words so I didn't use them. I kept searching for better words and I wrote my own set in the end; very simple words, straight love-song words really. I think they're quite effective. It's still one of my favourite melodies that I've written. You just occasionally get lucky with a melody and it becomes rather complete and I think this is one of them; quite a complete tune.

Donovan's memory is a little different:

I don't think I helped with the lyrics. He is very productive and will always take over the writing in a jam. From listening to the lyrics now, I can hear that Paul no doubt threw together the words for this tune when he got to the studio after India. I may have helped with the shape of the chords and encouraged the imagery from tunes I wrote then in India. The descending movements of my songs may have encouraged Paul to write differently.

It was an extremely productive period for all the Beatles and

between them they wrote more than forty songs while they were
there, more than enough to justify the trip by any standards. For the
first time in years John's brain was free from drugs and the music
poured from him: 'Julia', 'Dear Prudence', 'The Continuing Story of
Bungalow Bill', 'Mean Mr Mustard', 'Across the Universe', 'Cry
Baby Cry', 'Polythene Pam', 'Yer Blues' and, during the first few jet-
lagged days when he was unable to sleep, 'I'm So Tired'.

PAUL: 'Mean Mr Mustard' was very John. I liked that. A nice
quirky song. I don't know what it was about. 'Across the
Universe' is one of John's great songs. It had special words. I
remember John singing 'Bungalow Bill' in Rishikesh. This is
another of his great songs and it's one of my favourites to this
day because it stands for a lot of what I stand for now. 'Did you
have to shoot that tiger?' is its message. 'Aren't you a big guy?
Aren't you a brave man?' I think John put it very well. Funnily
enough, John wasn't an overt animal activist, but I think by
writing this song he showed that his sentiments were very much
that way. One of the nice things about Beatles songs is that in
many cases they do seem to stand the test of time and this is an
example of one that's getting better with time. It's becoming
more and more relevant. If you look at veal crating and listen to
this song, or look at the hunting of nearly extinct species like
tigers and rhinos, well, this is a very good song. In that context
it's fabulous.

'So Tired' is very much John's comment to the world, and it
has that very special line, 'And curse Sir Walter Raleigh, he was
such a stupid git.' That's a classic line and it's so John that
there's no doubt that he wrote it. I think it's 100 per cent John.
Being tired was one of his themes, he wrote 'I'm Only Sleeping'.
I think we were all pretty tired but he chose to write about it.

John came up with a massive TV scenario! A big TV show. I
came up with calling the next album *Umbrella,* an umbrella over
the whole thing. I think this was the point at which George got
annoyed at me because we mixed the two things. John and I'd
do a lot of chatting.

DONOVAN: Some afternoons we would gather at one of our pads
and play the acoustic guitars we had all brought with us. Paul
Horn, the American flute wizard, was there. John was keen to

learn the finger-style guitar I played and he was a good student. Paul already had a smattering of finger style. George preferred his Chet Atkins style. John wrote 'Julia' and 'Dear Prudence' based on the picking I taught him.

PAUL: The interesting thing for me on 'Julia' is the finger-picking style. He learned to finger-pick off Donovan or Gypsy Dave, I think John said it was Gypsy Dave but the two of them were fairly inseparable and they both would have known it, and if they were both sitting down picking, then who is to know? It was a folk picking style, and he was the only one in the band who could ever do that properly. I made my own variation. Once you can do it, it's really very handy, it's a useful style. Actually I should learn it, never too late. That was John's song about his mum, folk finger-picking style, and a very good song.

Paul was equally prolific and wrote fifteen songs while he was at the ashram, including 'Wild Honey Pie', 'Rocky Racoon' and 'Back in the USSR'. Mike Love says he helped with the chorus on 'Back in the USSR', which was in part a parody of the Beach Boys as well as Chuck Berry's 1959 hit.

MIKE LOVE: I was sitting at the breakfast table and McCartney came down with his acoustic guitar and he was playing 'Back in the USSR', and I told him that what you ought to do is talk about the girls all around Russia, the Ukraine and Georgia. He was plenty creative not to need any lyrical help from me but I gave him the idea for that little section ... I think it was light-hearted and humorous of them to do a take on the Beach Boys.

PAUL: 'Back in the USSR' was my take-off of Chuck Berry's 'Back in the USA'. It's a typical American thing to say when they're away: 'I miss my doughnuts and my Howard Johnson's and my launderettes and I miss the convenience of the Hyatt Hilton and it's just so much better back home and the TV's got more channels ...' So I thought, Great, I'll do a spoof on that. This'll be someone who hasn't got a lot but they'll still be every bit as proud as an American would be. It's tongue in cheek. This is a travelling Russkie who has just flow in from Miami Beach; he's come the other way. He can't wait to get back to the Georgian mountains: 'Georgia's always on my mind'; there's all sorts of little jokes in it. It's a jokey song, but it's also become a bit of an anthem now. Every time Billy Joel goes to Russia, he plays it. Probably my single most important reason for going to Russia would be to play it. It was a good song and I liked it a lot. I remember trying to sing it in my Jerry Lee Lewis voice, to get my mind set on a particular feeling. We added Beach Boy style harmonies.

'Mother Nature's Son' was inspired by a lecture on nature given by the Maharishi but mostly written in Liverpool when they got back. The same lecture inspired John to write a piece called 'I'm Just a Child Of Nature', which he later turned into 'Jealous Guy'. Many of the songs written in India, however, had a more informal genesis in rooftop sing-alongs with George playing sitar and Mike Love, Donovan, Paul and John on guitars. Paul wrote 'Rocky Raccoon' sitting on the roof of the ashram with John and Donovan helping out. It sounds like a story being told to friends.

PAUL: 'Rocky Raccoon' is quirky, very me. I like talking blues so I started off like that, then I did my tongue-in-cheek parody of a western and threw in some amusing lines. I just tried to keep it amusing, really; it's me writing a play, a little one-act play giving them most of the dialogue. Rocky Raccoon is the main character, then there's the girl whose real name was Magill, who called herself Lil, but she was known as Nancy.

There are some names I use to amuse, Vera, Chuck and Dave or Nancy and Lil, and there are some I mean to be serious, like Eleanor Rigby, which are a little harder because they have to not be joke names. In this case Rocky Raccoon is some bloke in a raccoon hat, like Davy Crockett. The bit I liked about it was him finding Gideon's Bible and thinking, Some guy called Gideon must have left it for the next guy. I like the idea of Gideon being a character. You get the meaning and at the same time get in a poke at it. All in good fun. And then of course the doctor is drunk.

I'm not sure if I took my tape recorder, we often didn't, we often worked on songs as if they were poems and carried them in our heads. Which is actually the best way because you can revise them at any time, because you know them. It was a difficult song to record because it had to be all in one take, it would have been very hard to edit because of the quirkiness of the vocal, so I had to do couple of takes until I got the right sort of feel. But it was fun to do.

From time to time the Maharishi would organise day trips to Dehra Dun or other nearby towns in order that the meditators did not get too cut off from everyday reality, though usually they would make their own arrangements. These included fairly frequent appearances of the Beatles and their wives and girlfriends at Nagoli's restaurant in Dehra Dun.

PAUL: The camp got a little bit constricting to someone like me who always wanted to get out of school. I used to sag off and go into the Liverpool Cathedral graveyard. We would go and sunbathe and smoke loose ciggies, which were called 'Loosies' (Lucys) at 2d a time from the tuck shop. So when I got out to Maharishi's I got a bit constricted and I found a way I could bunk out of the camp. Because you weren't allowed to go out, you actually had to ask permission, 'Can I go into New Delhi, Maharishi?' 'Why?' I was standing there, tending to think, Why not? – you know, I thought, I'm going to sag off. So I got down to the Ganges a few afternoons. I remember playing by the banks of the Ganges, which was rather nice, just like a kid, it was such a nice day. I just thought, I'd rather be on holiday.

Donovan remembers a similar incident. 'After the day's meditation we would all gather for the evening lecture by Maharishi. One night Paul and I were having an illegal cigarette by the lecture hall. Maharishi approached, surrounded by his usual admirers. Paul saw him coming and said, "Quick, lads, fags out. Here comes teach!"'

PAUL: We were in India almost as tourists. We asked him, 'Can people fly? Can people levitate? We've seen it in all the books and stuff.' And he said, 'Oh yes, people can, yes.' We said, 'Can you?' He said, 'No, I personally have not practised this art.' We said, 'Well, who could?' He said, 'I believe there might be someone three villages away from here.' We said, 'Can we get 'im?' There was an element of, 'We're on holiday, after all. We've come all this way, could we have a levitation display? It would be great to see people do it.' And he half thought of fixing one up but nothing ever materialised. What materialised years later is an actual flying course, a *siddi*. Which I suspect slightly. I've seen it, the Natural Law commercial for the election had a few people bunny-hopping, lotus position. What we always imagined was you actually lift off. So I'm a bit sceptical about that. But the interesting point I'm making was that when we asked him, Maharishi did not know about it, did not know anyone who did it, was not able to provide one; so it certainly was not a high priority. Now they've modified their approach to include that, and it's an expensive little course. I know a couple of people who've been on the course who say they can fly, but let's put it this way, I've never seen 'em. I always say to them, 'Get me a film of you flying for one minute and I can guarantee you *News at Ten* tonight with that.

We said it as a tourist thing. 'Eh, you got any of them snake charmers then, Swami? Can you do the Indian rope trick?' There was a slight aspect of that, we were just Liverpool lads. Let's face it, this was not the intercontinental Afro-Asian study team; this was not a group of anthropologists.

Despite the occasional similarity to school or camp, there were some truly magical moments. One night there was a torchlight procession down to the River Ganges, where they piled into two boats. Mia Farrow, Donovan, Mike Love, the Maharishi, all the Beatles and their wives and girlfriends made their way slowly upstream, then the engines were cut and the boats allowed to drift downstream under a clear, starry sky. Mike Love produced a set of pipes, Paul picked up his guitar and everyone sang.

PAUL: One day Maharishi needed to get to New Delhi and back for something, so someone suggested a helicopter. When it arrived we all trooped down, a bouncing line of devotees, coming down a narrow dusty track to the Ganges, singing, being delightful. Very like the Hare Krishnas, marvellous, chatting away. We got down to the Ganges, the helicopter landed and then they asked, 'Does anyone want a quick go before Maharishi takes off?' John jumped up. 'Yea, yea, yeah, yeah!' John got there first, and there was only room for one.

Paul was puzzled since John had been in a helicopter many times before; the Beatles had often used them to arrive and depart from large arenas.

> So later I asked John, 'Why were you so keen? You really wanted to get in that helicopter.' 'Yeah,' he said, 'I thought he might slip me the answer!' Which is very revealing about John. I suppose everyone is always looking for the Holy Grail. I think John thought he might find it. I think it shows an innocence really, a naïvety. It's quite touching really.

Ringo and Maureen were the first to leave. When they broke the news to the Maharishi just before lunch one morning, the Maharishi was quite shocked. 'He first suggested that perhaps we should go off somewhere and then come back,' Ringo said, 'but we wanted to come home. It was like a hundred reasons which formed into one thing.' They hated the food and missed their children and left promising to send the rest of the Beatles a care package of cine film. Ringo told the waiting press that the ashram was 'a bit like Butlins', but defended the Maharishi against continuing speculation that he was a con man.

> No, it is not a gigantic hoax. A lot of people are going to say that I left because I was disillusioned by it all but that just isn't so. The Academy is a great place and I enjoyed it a lot. I still meditate every day for half an hour in the morning and half an hour every evening and I think I'm a better person for it. I'm far more relaxed than I have ever been. You know, if you're working very hard and things are a bit chaotic, you get all tensed up and screwed up inside. You feel as if you have to break something or hit someone. But if you spend a short while in the mornings and evenings meditating, it completely relaxes you, and it's easier to see your way through problems. If everyone in the world started meditating, then the world would be a much happier place.

However, a few weeks after getting back, he admitted that his regime had broken down somewhat: 'At the moment I meditate every day. Well, I might skip the odd day if I get up late or arrive in town late or something.'

Paul left on 26 March with Jane, thoroughly satisfied with the experience.

I came back after four or five weeks knowing that was like my allotted period, thinking, No, well, no, I won't go out and become a monk but it was really very interesting and I will continue to meditate and certainly feel it was a very rewarding experience.

Ringo and Maureen had only stayed for two weeks. John and Cynthia, George and Patti, the ones who had all along been the most interested, remained, intending to finish the course. The problem was, too many people had a vested interest in the Beatles remaining their old selves. 'Then Magic Alex arrived,' Jenny Boyd remembered. 'He came because he didn't approve of the Beatles' meditating, and he wanted John back. He made friends with another girl in our party, and I could see them walking the grounds of the ashram together, obviously cooking something up.' Alex had been introduced to the others as John's guru and he could see that his position was about to be usurped by the Maharishi, particularly if John gave up drugs permanently. Alex's fantastic inventions would have been far less believable if John was straight.

In her autobiography Cynthia Lennon wrote:

Alexis and a fellow female meditator began to sow the seeds of doubt into very open minds ... Alexis's statements about how the Maharishi had been indiscreet with a certain lady, and what a blackguard he had turned out to be gathered momentum. All, may I say, without a single shred of evidence or justification. It was obvious to me that Alexis wanted out and more than anything he wanted the Beatles out as well.

Meditation over a prolonged period makes the meditator extremely sensitive and very open to suggestion. John and George were in a state of utter confusion, not knowing whether to believe Alexis's accusations or have faith in the Maharishi. In the event, the Maharishi was not even given a chance to answer his accuser, whereas Alexis spent the night reinforcing the doubts and fears that he had planted in their minds.

Things came to a head very quickly. Cynthia Lennon reports: 'Out of confusion and accusation came anger and aggression ... The Maharishi had been accused and sentenced before he even had a chance to defend himself ... the following morning, almost before any of us had a chance to wake up, Alexis set the ball in motion by ordering taxis to take us to the airport. That was how quickly things got out of hand.' Alexis was determined to consolidate his victory and was not about to have John and George talk to the Maharishi.

In Jenny Boyd's account she writes, 'Poor Maharishi. I remember him standing at the gate of the ashram, under an aide's umbrella, as the Beatles filed by, out of his life. "Wait," he cried. "Talk to me." But no one listened. We went back to the hotel in Delhi and George and John tried to decide what to do. "Should we tell the world that the Beatles made a mistake?" John asked. "He isn't what's happening at all." Everyone was so disappointed.'

The Maharishi had no idea why they were leaving, and why the atmosphere was so charged and unpleasant. All John Lennon would tell him was, 'If you're so cosmically conscious as you claim, then you should know why we're leaving.' Just to rub it in, John wrote the song 'Sexy Sadie' about the Maharishi while they were waiting in the dining area for the taxis to arrive. Alex was so anxious to get John away from the Maharishi that even in Delhi he vetoed the idea of booking seats on the first available flight the next day, insisting that they could just make the night flight which was due to leave in an hour. He would not feel secure until they had all left India.

Paul was surprised to see them back in England so soon.

I got back, fine, and wondered what was going to happen with the other guys. For a week or so there I didn't know if we'd ever see 'em again or if there ever would be any Beatles again. What happened amazed me. They all came storming back and they came round to Cavendish Avenue, it must have been for a recording session, we often used to meet there. It was a big scandal. Maharishi had tried to get off with one of the chicks. I said, 'Tell me what happened?' John said, 'Remember that blonde American girl with the short hair? Like a Mia Farrow look-alike. She was called Pat or something.' I said, 'Yeah.' He said, 'Well, Maharishi made a pass at her.' So I said, 'Yes? What's wrong with that?' He said, 'Well, you know, he's just a bloody old letch just like everybody else. What the fuck, we can't go following that!'

They were scandalised. And I was quite shocked at them; I said, 'But he never said he was a god. In fact very much the opposite, he said, "Don't treat me like a god, I'm just a meditation teacher." There was no deal about you mustn't touch women, was there? There was no vow of chastity involved. So I didn't think it was enough cause to leave the whole meditation centre. It might have been enough cause to say, 'Hey, excuse me? Are you having it off with a girl? In which case, should we worry about this or is this perfectly normal?' And to tell the truth, I think they may have used it as an excuse to get out of there. And I just said, 'Oh yes, okay.' But in my mind it was like, well, he never pretended to be anything but a guy, and as far as I'm concerned there's nothing wrong with someone making a pass at someone. Perhaps they had been looking for something more than a guy and found he wasn't a god, whereas I'd been looking at a guy who was saying, 'I'm only giving you a system of meditation.'

John wrote 'Sexy Sadie' about it. Righteous indignation! I remember being quite shocked with that. It's really funny, John's reaction to this sexual thing. I mean, maybe say, 'Hey, we thought he was better than that,' but it seemed a little prudish to me, to do that. So I was quite glad I'd left the week before. I mean, even if they found him in bed, what is this? Anyway, it ended in disarray and that was the reason given. And it became public that we didn't like Maharishi but I never felt that way particularly and I know George is still involved with him.

Originally 'Sexy Sadie' was called 'Maharishi': 'Maharishi, what have you done?' etc. But George persuaded John to change the title and he made the suggestion of 'Sexy Sadie' to protect the innocent. I think George was right. It would have been too hard and it would have actually been, as it turned out, rather untrue, because it was Magic Alex who made the original accusation and I think that it was completely untrue.

PAUL: A week before the British elections of 1992, the ones where the Maharishi's Natural Law Party took double-page ads in all the papers, George asked me to stand as the Natural Law Party Member of Parliament for Liverpool. Just one week before the last general election. George rang me giggling from LA. He said, 'I've been up all night and you may think this is a bit silly, but Maharishi would like you, me and Ringo to stand as

Members of Parliament for Liverpool.' He said, 'We'll win.' I said 'Yeeeessss!' He said, 'It'll be great.' I said, 'Why, what'll we do?' He said, 'Well, we'll introduce meditation for everyone.' I said, 'Wait a minute, this is a quite far-out idea this, you know.' I think, as George's wife pointed out to him, he just wouldn't want the work. If you send George a bunch of papers, he says, 'I'm not looking at that!', but if you're an MP, you've got to look at those papers, there's no getting round it. But it was quite funny. I said, 'George, let's get one thing straight. No way am I gonna do it. I don't want to put a damper on, I don't want to rain on your parade or anything. You do it if you want. I'll support you. I'll back you up. But there's no way in heaven I am going to stand as a Member of Parliament a week before the election! You've gotta be kidding!' Well, they put 230 candidates out and I think every one of them lost their deposit. That may be a slight exaggeration but I don't recall any of them getting in. It showed they had a bit of dough, though. But they were talking mad things. George was saying, 'You know places like Bradford and Blackburn or Southall where they have a big Indian community? They're going to bring in Indian guys, holy men, people like that to be candidates.' He said, 'Well, they'll definitely win in all those Indian communities.' There was lots of talk, it was talk.

Looking back on his experience in India twenty-five years later, Paul said, 'I always thought I learned what I wanted to learn there. I took it just as a skill like riding a bike. I didn't then disbelieve. Now I say to my own kids, "Go and get a mantra, because then if you ever want to meditate and you're on some hilltop somewhere, you'll know how to do it." I'm not sure you have to go into it any deeper than that myself.'

ELEVEN

APPLE

A goodly apple rotten at the heart.

Shakespeare, *The Merchant of Venice*

Cavendish Avenue

'CAVENDISH AVENUE BECAME WHAT I USED TO THINK OF AS MY bachelor pad,' Paul said. 'There would be lots of people around there. If you wanted to hang out, and you were living in London and couldn't think of anything to do, you'd ring me and say, "What you doing?" So quite a strange assortment of people came through here. Some of my relatives would be staying upstairs, then there might be Mick and Marianne, just because it was a good place to hang. It was a cool place.'

All the old gang whose flats and houses Paul used to frequent would drop in at Paul's place: Robert Fraser, John Dunbar, Miles, Tara Browne, Mick Jagger, Marianne Faithfull, Ivan Vaughan, John Lennon, Stash de Rollo, Brian Jones, visiting pop musicians like Mickey Dolenz of the Monkees, film people, artists and old Liverpool chums were soon making themselves at home in the living room or the upstairs music room, 'Paul's mad room', as it was called by the girl fans who camped at his gates.

MARIANNE: Paul was much more accessible. John [Lennon] never was accessible, whether it was in Weybridge or whether it was in some house with Yoko, or whether it was in some house in New York, John was out of it for me, or for most of us, anyway. He used to do a lot of drugs with John Dunbar but hardly anyone ever saw John Lennon at all. Whereas everybody who came to town went to see Paul, and you could always be sure of a welcome.

When Jane was home, this inevitably caused tensions. She and her friends were not into drugs; Paul and his friends were. Jane was determined to continue her career as an actress, whereas Paul thought that she might give it up and devote herself to him. They were at an impasse, but there was still so much friendship between them that neither of them wanted to admit that it wasn't working out, so they let it continue. When Jane was there they would have dinner parties for George Martin and his wife Judy, Mick and Marianne would come round, and Jane would entertain her friends from the theatre. Normal life went on – but it went on mostly apart.

The marathon recording sessions for *Sgt. Pepper* had begun on 24 November 1966. These often lasted until two or three in the morning, so Jane made her own social arrangements, having theatre people over for dinner or going out by herself. By the time the sessions finished, on 1 April 1967, she had already started the extended tour of the USA with the Bristol Old Vic which would keep her away until 29 May. For these six crucial months at the height of their careers, she and Paul were apart. They were essentially living in different worlds.

Linda

On 15 May 1967, Paul was out on the town.

The night I met Linda I was in the Bag o'Nails watching Georgie Fame and the Blue Flames play a great set. Speedy was banging away. She was there with the Animals, who she knew from photographing them in New York. They were sitting a couple of alcoves down, near the stage. The band had finished and they got up to either leave or go for a drink or a pee or something, and she passed our table. I was near the edge and stood up just as she was passing, blocking her exit. And so I said, 'Oh, sorry. Hi. How are you? How're you doing?' I introduced myself, and said, 'We're going on to another club after this, would you like to join us?'

That was my big pulling line! Well, I'd never used it before, of course, but it worked this time! It was a fairly slim chance but it worked. She said, 'Yes, okay, we'll go on. How shall we do it?' I forget how we did it, 'You come in our car' or whatever, and we all went on, the people I was with, and the Animals, we went on to the Speakeasy.

It was the first evening any of us had ever heard a record called 'A Whiter Shade of Pale' with words about feeling seasick. The lyrics were all very strange and poetic and the theme was a famous Bach theme but we didn't know that. We just thought, God, what an incredible record! It was a sort of marker record. It was a benchmark. And we were all trying to guess who it was. So we had to go to the booth and ask, 'What was that one you just played?' and he said, 'Oh yes, "Whiter Shade of Pale" by Procol Harum.' 'Procol what? Is it Latin or something?' And there were rumours went around about what that meant. So all the mystery of the evening.

LINDA: I first met Paul at the Bag o'Nails. The Animals were old friends because I'd photographed them so much in New York, so when I came to London they took me out; and we went to see Georgie Fame at the Bag o'Nails. And that's where Paul and I met. We flirted a bit, and then it was time for me to go back with them and Paul said, 'Well, we're going to another club. You want to come?' I remember everybody at the table heard 'A Whiter Shade of Pale' that night for the first time and we all thought, Who is that? Stevie Winwood? We all said Stevie. The minute that record came out, you just knew you loved it. That's when we actually met. Then we went back to his house. We were in the Mini with I think Lulu and Dudley Edwards, who painted Paul's piano; Paul was giving him a lift home. I was impressed to see his Magrittes.

They met again four days later at the launch party for *Sgt. Pepper*, an exclusive affair for a dozen journalists and a dozen photographers held at Brian Epstein's house at 24 Chapel Street, Belgravia. Linda Eastman was in London to take photographs for a book called *Rock and Other Four Letter Words* on which she was collaborating with the journalist J. Marks. She was only given a $1,000 advance, all of which went on her travel costs, but the resulting pictures, virtually impossible to see in the final book because of poor design and printing, now form a major part of her sixties portfolio and have

become well known, particularly through the books *Linda McCart-*
ney's Sixties and *Linda's Pictures*. The deal that Bantam Books had
offered her was so bad that Linda's father, the lawyer Lee Eastman,
had advised her not to do it.

> LINDA: I said, 'Don't tell me not to do it, are you kidding? I'm
> going to go photograph all these groups.' So we were in London
> to take pictures for this book. I'd always wanted to photograph
> Stevie Winwood because I loved Spencer Davis, I loved Stevie
> Winwood, and the Beatles. I'd pretty much photographed
> everybody else. But it was up to me, it's not like Marks rang up
> people and said, 'I'm with Bantam Books. We want to take your
> picture.' Nothing was organised, so I had to do it. I took my
> portfolio around to NEMS at Hille House, and Peter Brown
> looked at it. I'd met Peter when he and Brian Epstein came to
> New York, we had mutual friends. So I took my portfolio and
> asked him to show it to Brian. Brian liked it a lot and wanted to
> buy some of the pictures, which I loved. I gave them to him in
> the end. He said, 'Yes, you can photograph the Beatles.' So I got
> to go to this press conference at Brian's house for *Sgt. Pepper*. I
> got one good photo that I liked, which is that thumbs-up one.
> The rest are just like everyone else's photographs, but for that
> one I said, 'Oh, come on, guys! You know?' and that shows at
> least they were relating, because if you believe the press you'd
> never think John and Paul ever related.

In the photograph John and Paul are shaking hands, John with
thumbs up, and the other two laughing. It shows all four in a very
good-natured mood. Linda used it on the back cover of her *Sixties*
book. Though she was getting on well in London and meeting lots of
people, Linda had a four-year-old daughter, Heather, waiting for her
in New York, so as soon as her photographic assignment was
completed she flew straight home.

When Jane returned from the USA after her tour with the Bristol Old
Vic in June 1967, she is reported as saying, 'Paul had changed so
much. He was on LSD, which I knew nothing about. The house had
changed and was full of stuff I didn't know about.' Despite her
reservations about LSD, she looked happy and relaxed in the
photographs taken during the trip to buy a Greek island six weeks

later, even though most people on the boat were tripping the whole time.

A few weeks before the Greek voyage, Miles brought Allen Ginsberg round to visit Paul at Cavendish Avenue. Mick Jagger and Marianne Faithfull were already there, Marianne dressed in transparent white, Mick in a frilly shirt and a white silk scarf so long it trailed across the carpet. He lay draped over the rocking chair with one leg over the arm and told them he had just bought the film rights to Walter M. Miller's post-apocalyptic novel *A Canticle for Leibowitz*. 'I rather fancy myself as the old monk flapping round the desert in me robes!' he said, fluttering his hands.

Allen Ginsberg had a full rabbinical beard, long hair and was wearing a Tibetan oracle ring and Yoruba beads. Paul: 'I remember him coming round to my house with his harmonium and sitting cross-legged, giving us a little prayer or two. He was charming. The big thing I remember him for was his poetry and his harmonium, his chanting and his singing.' They discussed LSD, and Paul told Allen that the Beat Generation and the local eccentrics on the streets of Liverpool had a lot in common. Mick had been reading Eliphas Levi and for an hour they compared Eastern mysticism and Western ritual magic. It was a typical sixties Cavendish Avenue discussion. As they talked, Paul idly opened some of the parcels that fans had sent him. There was always a sack or two of fan mail waiting in the hall sent over by the fan club in case he felt like browsing through it. In one package there was a red satin shirt and he found some coloured marker pens and began drawing psychedelic paisley patterns on it. When it came time to go, Paul gave the shirt to Allen, saying, 'A present from Swinging London.' Though it was rather too small for him, Allen nevertheless wore it to the Legalise Pot Rally in Hyde Park the next day.

In the living room Paul had a large-scale wooden model of the meditation chapel that he was having built at the end of his garden. It was a glass geodesic dome, like a transparent igloo. A circular platform could be made to rise up into the dome so you were completely surrounded by the glass. It was a perfect place to lie and look at the stars or sit and meditate. Paul took Allen for a walk in the garden to see where it was going to be built. 'Build it out of wood,' Allen advised him. 'You might want to take it down one day.'

PAUL: It was a bit too late by then, they were bringing the concrete and the bricks the next day. But I now tell that story because I think it was quite a wise thought. It hadn't occurred to me then that I might want to take it down. The funny thing is that now it's got Groucho Marx's circular bed in it and my kids suspect my motives. I say, 'It was a meditation dome, I promise you.' They say, 'Yeah, Dad. Sure! So why has it got a great big round bed in it?' And I tell them, well, that's there because Alice Cooper came to see it, when it was a meditation dome, as part of the tour round the house. And he said, 'I've got just the bed for this in LA.' I said, 'What you talking about?' He said, 'Groucho Marx gave me a round bed that was his, and this is the place for it.' And of course it fits exactly. It's changed the vibe of the whole thing; it's not easy to meditate on a big Hollywood bed, you feel more like getting laid!

Alice Cooper first met Groucho Marx on his eighty-fourth birthday in the outdoor garden of the Polo Lounge at the Beverly Hills Hotel. Groucho loved embarrassing people and when he found that Alice didn't take drugs, he immediately called to the waiter, 'Dope! Do you have any dope for my friend? He needs dope,' while Alice squirmed in his seat. They became good friends. In his autobiography *Me, Alice*, Alice wrote:

> Groucho came to visit me at my old house one night but I didn't have any furniture and he refused to sit on the floor. The next day he sent me a round bed that he had slept in for five years. 'I never had any luck in it. Maybe you will,' the note read. Some time later Groucho and I decided to give the bed to Paul and Linda McCartney as an anniversary present. We sent it them in London, with a big brass plaque on the head board that says, 'May all your stains be large ones. From Groucho and Alice.'

Also that month, Brian Jones sat in on a Beatles session at Abbey Road; the only time that the friendship between the two groups resulted in a Stone appearing on a Beatles record. On 10 May 1967, Brian Jones had been busted. Paul had always been close to Brian and understood how worried and anxious Brian must be. He had called to commiserate with him and invite him to come to a Beatles recording session. Three weeks later, on 8 June, Brian showed up at the studio.

PAUL: He arrived at Abbey Road in his big Afghan coat. He was always nervous, a little insecure, and he was really nervous that night because he's walking in on a Beatles session. He was nervous to the point of shaking, lighting ciggy after ciggy. I used to like Brian a lot. I thought it would be a fun idea to have him, and I naturally thought he'd bring a guitar along to a Beatles session and maybe chung along and do some nice rhythm guitar or a little bit of electric twelve-string or something, but to our surprise he brought his saxophone. He opened up his sax case and started putting a reed in and warming up, playing a little bit. He was a really ropey sax player, so I thought, Ah-hah. We've got just the tune.

John had arrived one night with this song which was basically a mantra: 'You know my name, look up the number. You know my name, look up the number.' And I never knew who he was aiming that at, it might have been an early signal to Yoko. It was John's original idea and that was the complete lyric. He brought it in originally as a fifteen-minute chant when he was in space-cadet mode and we said, 'Well, what are we going to do with this then?' and he said, 'It's just like a mantra.' So we said, 'Okay, let's just do it.'

Even though it was fifteen minutes long, it didn't have much substance, it just droned on. So we put it to one side. Then it became a standing joke, a running gag that whenever we'd go to try another song, if we were feeling in a silly mood, we'd say, 'Well, let's do another version of "You Know My Name, Look Up the Number".' It was very easy to do a version of because it didn't have a mound of lyrics to remember. So we did the other versions: we did the nightclub singer, Dennis O'Bell parodying Apple film executive Denis O'Dell, which was me singing, which is a pretty funny piss-take of that kind of thing. It became one of my favourite Beatle records just because we had so much fun putting it together.

The words, like many of John's lyrics, were a found object. John told *Playboy*: 'That was a piece of unfinished music that I turned into a comedy record with Paul. I was waiting for him in his house and I saw a phone book on the piano with the words, "You know their NAME? Look up their NUMBER."' John's original idea for it was as a

Four Tops type of song but, though it has similar chord changes, it soon developed in a different direction.

PAUL: I remember at one point we asked Mal to shovel a bucket full of gravel as a rhythmic device. We had a bit of a giggle doing those kind of tracks. Mal also played the anvil on 'Maxwell's Silver Hammer' and came in very useful on 'Yellow Submarine' to turn various devices. He rang the alarm clock on 'Day in the Life'. He was always in the studio if we needed an extra hand. I remember we had one thing that required a sustained organ note, 'Being for the Benefit of Mr Kite', so I said to Mal, 'Look, that's the note. I'll put a little marker on it. When I go "There", hit it.' Which he did. And I said, 'When I shake my head, take your finger off.' So for that kind of a part, he was very helpful. And so on 'You Know My Name, Look Up the Number', Brian plays a funny sax solo. It's not amazingly well played but it happened to be exactly what we wanted. Brian was very good like that.

Brian always had a pleasant word. We always got on like a house on fire. He had a good old sense of humour, I remember laughing and giggling a lot with him. And we would play jokes on him. I remember being in Hyde Park, coming back from John's house in his big chauffeur-driven Rolls-Royce. John had a microphone he could use with the speakers mounted under-neath the car. We were driving through the park, and ahead of us was Brian's Austin Princess. Everyone used to go around in these big Austin Princesses then, it was a sign you were a pop star. You automatically got one of those. We could see his big floppy hat and blond hair and we could see him nervously smoking a ciggy in the back of the car. So John got on the mike and said, 'Pull over now! Brian Jones! You are under arrest! Pull over now!' Brian jumped up. 'Fucking hell!' He really thought he had been busted. He was shitting himself! Then he saw it was us. And we were going, 'Yi, yi, yi. Fuck off!' giving V-signs out of the car window. So it would be that kind of humour most of the time, really, although you'd sometimes get a chance to quietly talk about music.

Brian was a nervous sort of guy, very shy, quite serious, and I think maybe into drugs a little more than he should have been because he used to shake a little bit. He was lovely, though. I remember being in a car with Chris Barber and I was driving and someone else in the car saying, 'Bloody Brian. On bloody heroin,' and we said, 'Yeah, maybe he is on heroin but we're supposed to be his friends and you can't go around slagging him off.' I think a lot of people used to get a bit annoyed with him but he was smashing. I never really knew his particular tastes, because we'd just meet people on one level: the musician and friend level with a bit of soft drugs generally, and we tended to see the nice side of people.

On Jane's return from America, she and Paul made a last-ditch stand to consolidate their relationship. Jane, unusually, even accompanied Paul to a recording session on 20 July 1967 to see the trumpeter and trombonist Chris Barber, the man who popularised traditional jazz in Britain. He was recording 'Cat Call', an early instrumental of Paul's which had been a part of the Beatles' playlist down the Cavern. Paul can be heard singing in the chorus and shouting 'Please play it slower!' at the end.

PAUL: I knew Chris Barber because he was always down all the clubs. He was from the generation before us but his love of blues meant he would be likely to want to get up and jam with Hendrix and play a bit of trombone. His wife, the jazz singer Ottilie Patterson, strangely enough had been a patient of the doctor who'd owned my house in Cavendish before I bought it. There had been stories of this guy painting the house in midwinter, wearing just a pair of shorts, so I was obviously carrying on quite a rich tradition at this place. I'd said, 'Well, come round for a cup of tea tomorrow.' When Ottilie saw the house, she said, 'Oh yes, this used to be the waiting room' – which is now the kitchen – and 'This was the consulting room.' Chris Barber was a good musician and a good fun, interested guy. He was not patronising. With a few jazz musicians at that time it was, 'Mmm, rock 'n' roll ...' They felt like they knew more scales than we did, or they could read music, unlike us, but not Chris.

Two days after the session, Jane accompanied Paul to Greece with the other Beatles. In August Jane was with him on the trip to Bangor to be initiated by the Maharishi, and during the difficult days following Brian's death she was clearly a great source of strength and comfort to him; someone familiar and safe he could trust and confide in; someone with all the attributes of a wife. They spent the first three weeks of December alone together in Paul's remote Scottish farm-house and four days later, on Christmas Day, 1967, they announced to Paul's family – perhaps slightly to their own surprise – their engagement.

Apple Corps

The year 1967 had been a great one for Paul. He was the prime mover during the recording of *Sgt. Pepper* and the *de facto* director of *Magical Mystery Tour*. The Beatles had had three more hit singles, been seen by 400,000,000 people on the *Our World* TV show, and had set in motion plans to start their own record company, which was to be known as Apple.

Apple came into existence in April 1967 because the Beatles' tax advisers told them that if they didn't put money into a business, they would have to pay £3,000,000 in tax. Apple Corps was to be the holding company, with a series of subsidiary companies engaged in different business activities: Apple Records, Apple Music, Apple Films, Apple Publishing, Apple Electronics and so on. The boutique was to be run by Apple Retail, headed by John Lennon's old school friend Pete Shotton, who was already running a supermarket on Hayling Island, bought for him by Lennon.

The company logo was suggested by the painting by René Magritte, *Le Jeu de mourre* ('The Guessing Game'), that Robert Fraser had left casually propped up on Paul's living-room table in the summer of 1966. It was one of Magritte's last works, painted that same year, shipped by his dealer to Robert not long after the paint dried. Paul, 'We were sitting around at EMI wondering, "What shall we call this thing?" We were looking through names, A is for Apple, B is for Banana, C is for Caterpillar, and we though, Yeah. Like a schoolbook. A is for Apple. That should be the name of the company. Then I thought, Wow, that Magritte apple is very much "an apple", a big green apple, you know. I told the ad man about it.'

The Apple logo was designed by Gene Mahon, known around the

Apple press office as Gene Gluv. He told the journalist Jonathon Green:

> Designing the Apple label was a relatively straightforward job. What I brought to it was the idea that it can stand as a pure symbol. Let it never have any type on, put all that on the other side of the record – just designer stuff really. And the apple that had the information on it should be sliced, to give a light surface on which to put type … I said to McCartney, 'It's a green apple, a big Granny Smith' and he said, 'Oh, good!'

Apparently there were legal requirements which meant that the record company had to detail the record's contents on both sides of the disc – or so EMI said – so the purity of the idea was quickly compromised. However, work on the design progressed. The Beatles went off to India and came back. The photographer Paul Castell's transparencies of apples were narrowed down and one was finally selected. For some reason the die-transfers for the master printing were made in New York. Finally the designer Alan Aldridge, the man responsible for the illustrated books of Beatles lyrics, drew the copyright lettering which surrounds the label. The project took all of six months. Paul: 'So that painting of Magritte's, the "*Au revoir*", became the basis for that image. That was a great visit of Robert's.'

It turned out that the Beatles already owned a four-storey redbrick building at 94 Baker Street, on the corner of Paddington Street; one of the many investments made on their behalf by their financial advisers. This was immediately requisitioned by the Beatles, who used the ground floor for a boutique and the upper floors of offices as a temporary location for Apple Corps.

'Apple is not in competition with any of the underground organisations, rather it exists to help, collaborate with and extend all existing organisations, as well as to start many new ones,' Paul told Miles in 1967. Some of the underground boutiques, head-shops and music clubs had begun to get anxious about the Beatles' far-reaching plans. No need to be worried, said Paul. 'The idea is to have an "underground" company above ground, as big as Shell BP or ICI but with no profit motive. The profits to go first to the combined staff, so that everyone who needs a Rolls-Royce can have one, then, after that, we'll give them away to anyone who needs help.' The beginnings of

Apple were firmly rooted in the ideas of the hippie underground counter-culture of the time: informed by drugs, mysticism and the ideas surrounding *International Times*, Indica, Release, the UFO Club and other underground institutions which had varying degrees of self-management or collective ownership. Clearly in its original idealistic form it could not, would not, work, and it didn't. It was several years later that Richard Branson started his Virgin group using a watered-down version of the plan, to great success.

Even though he was unable to sell them an island, Alex continued to spin his fantasies about scientific inventions, and less than a month after they returned to London, he was employed by the Beatles to head Apple Electronics. At an Apple board meeting of 24 August 1967, with Paul and John both present, it was agreed to pay Alex a wage of £40 a week, plus 10 per cent of the profit made on his inventions with a minimum of £3,000 a year. As a TV repairman he had probably been earning a maximum of £15 a week. The boat trip had enabled Alex to ingratiate himself further with John Lennon and, though John Dunbar was involved in the early stages of Apple Electronics, Alex quickly elbowed him out of any further involvement.

John Dunbar: 'By then, Mardas had completely taken over John and the Apple recording scene. Alex got money off them and started up this workshop to build them a studio. But Mardas absolutely shut me out. It was one of those scenes. I just thought, Oh, fuck it, if it's going to be like that …'

Paul: 'So we formed Apple Electronics after having talked about all these things for a while, to just see if he could make any of them. Just to do some research into the whole thing. We didn't really apply ourselves like a great electronics company would and really smack 'em down and really work on it and put a lot into the development of one of these things.'

Apple Electronics rented a garage on Boston Place behind Marylebone Station in the centre of London, and the Beatles would sometimes drop by to see how he was doing, but there was nothing really to see. Just an oscilloscope from his TV-repair days, and a few tools on a bench, and, naturally, an expensive stereo and an expensive car parked outside.

PAUL: As I say, this was John's doing. This was John's guru, but we were all fascinated by the talk, which was rather sci-fi but the idea being that you could do it now. In the sixties there was this feeling of being modern, so much so that I feel like the sixties is about to happen. It feels like a period in the future to me, rather than a period in the past.

I was just going along with the thing. We committed ourselves with Apple Electronics to make the little gadgets of tomorrow: the wallpaper loudspeaker, the phone that would respond to voice commands. We were thinking this could happen in five years, whereas it's taken a little longer. A lot of it is still not on-line but I think it's accepted that it will be, so we weren't being stupid, but we were probably overreaching. We were thinking, if he's got a little place, he may be able to come up with something. Then we'd involve some big electronics giant and say, 'Come on, Grundig, we've patented this. Surely you'll want this? You could make it great.' We were on to all those sort of schemes but I don't think it was so much to make money as to move things ahead. So the scientific ideas would be available.

We were doing the wallpaper speakers so we could have them! Then I think it just ran on. Our friends would want them too, so that'd be a few more, and then, why not let everyone have them? I'm trying to remember why we even bothered getting involved now. Hopefully for all the right reasons. So we were committed to this electronics company which we registered and he was in some back room trying to develop something, I'm not sure what. I was a bit suspicious. 'Well, what's he got then? What is it we're working on? Is it the loudpaper?' I always sensed that there wasn't going to be a product there, and it was a bit of a wild-goose chase and we'd move on from that to the next thing.

Just as Magic Alex got his electronics company, so the Fool got a boutique. They had dressed some of the Beatles and their wives and girlfriends for the *Our World* television programme, decorated the chimneypiece and outside walls at Kinfauns, George's bungalow in Esher, and painted John's favourite piano, though, it must be said, not as well as Paul's had been painted by Binder, Edwards and Vaughan. 'We started an Apple clothes shop because we were now dressing in such interesting clothes,' Paul explained, 'and the Fool were making a lot of them. So we said, "Could you make a few pieces that we could take to other people and they could manufacture stuff to your designs?"' The Fool quickly made the Apple boutique into a showcase for their ideas, and no one else's.

Simon Posthuma, the leader and spokesman for the Fool, described how the shop would be: 'It will have an image of nature, like a paradise with plants and animals painted on the walls. The floor will be imitation grass and the staircase like an Arab tent. In the windows will be seven figures representing the seven races of the world, black, white, yellow, red, etc. There will be exotic lighting and we will make it more like a market than a boutique.'

The idea was that everything in the store was for sale; including the furniture, display cases and light fittings. The Beatles said it was to be 'a beautiful place where beautiful people can buy beautiful things'. In addition to adults' and children's clothes, the shop would sell inflatable chairs, hand-painted psychedelic furniture, small musical instruments like flutes and tambourines, Moroccan jewellery and the Fool's own paintings, posters and greetings cards. At the Beatles' expense, all four members of the Fool, accompanied by Pete Shotton, spent ten days in Marrakesh buying fabrics and antiques, eating majoun and smoking hashish. With the exception of the few things they brought back with them, most of the goods they bought were 'lost in the post', if they were ever shipped at all.

Simon told the *Sunday Times*: 'When they used to open shops it was just after the bread of people, not after turning them on. We want to turn them on. Our ideas are based on love. If you're doing things for people you must be part of the people, not set yourself up as something extraordinary.' Despite this other-worldly attitude to money, the Fool managed to spend something like £100,000 of the Beatles' money. Their previous boutique, a converted barber's shop in Amsterdam called the Trend, had gone bust because of their enormous personal expenditure.

About a hundred outfits were completed and in production before the shop opened; among them were an orange embossed velvet coat with long sleeves, puffed at the elbow, narrow at the wrist, at ten guineas, brocade trouser suits, outdoor coats of heavy tapestry and, at seven guineas, minidresses with long skirts which could be added for evening wear. Marijke and Josje's designs combined elements from many cultures and ethnic traditions. Talking to the press before the boutique opened, Marijke said, 'All the people of the earth are forced to come together now and this expresses itself even in fashion. Our ideas come from every country – India, China, Russia, Turkey. And from the sixteenth to the twenty-first century. There's a bit of everything.'

The clothes looked more like fancy-dress costumes than anything one could wear day to day: court jester crossed with harlequin crossed with Peter Pan, rainbow colours, zig-zag hems, Kate Greenaway layers of flowing fabrics, ballet tights and operatic coats for flower children.

MARIJKE: It is a gradual evolution for the people who will wear our clothes, as it was for us. We have been dressing like this for eight years but gradually we have added things. Boys and girls can't go to offices dressed quite like we are. But we have made velvet suits for boys and dresses for girls that they could begin to wear everywhere. And gradually they will begin to add extra things – a pretty bodice on top of something they may already have – and they will learn to be more creative. That's how it should be, for them to do something too.

Simon insisted that all the labels for the clothes be woven from pure silk. When Pete Shotton refused to authorise this extravagance, Simon threw a tantrum and Shotton took the matter to John Lennon. In his book *John Lennon in My Life*, Shotton told how he explained to John that from a business point of view it was sheer insanity because the labels would cost more to make than the clothes themselves. He wrote that John replied, 'Oh, just do it the way he wants. Remember, Pete, we're not business freaks, we're artists. That's what Apple's all about – artists ... so fucking what, anyway. If we don't make any money, what does it fucking matter?' It was this approach to Apple which ensured the boutique's demise.

It took the manufacturers Gublick and Schlickstein weeks to get Simon's silk labels exactly right; each design they submitted was always marred by some imperceptible flaw, causing Simon to erupt in temperamental rage, the very opposite of the love vibes he normally beamed at the Beatles.

The Fool wanted a psychedelic mural to cover the entire building but the City of Westminster planning authorities refused permission. Rashly, they decided to ignore officialdom and the weekend before the shop was to open, scaffolding was erected over the front of 94 Baker Street and a team of art students created a huge bearded genie, grinning up the street, surrounded by swirling moons and stars in rainbow colours. It lasted three weeks before the council told them they would send their own workmen over to repaint and charge Apple for the privilege. But the mural was there for the opening.

In the meantime, Magic Alex had received a large sum of money to work on an artificial sun which was going to hover over Baker Street and light up the sky during the boutique's gala opening. Needless to say, at 8.16 p.m. on Monday, 4 December 1967 (the time John Lennon had decreed for guests to arrive for the grand opening), there was no sign of the artificial sun. For some reason Paul and Ringo were also absent and missed the fashion show 'at 8.46 sharp'. In fact, the opening was so crowded that half the stock was trampled under foot as people struggled back outside for air. Even a BBC commentator fainted from heat and lack of oxygen.

The shop opened at the height of the Christmas season and was packed with shoppers from the moment it opened its doors. The stock literally flew off the shelves. The problem was, most of it was not paid for. A knowledge of the retail trade was not a qualification to work at the Apple boutique. To smoke as much dope as John Lennon, however, would get you hired. Since it would have been terribly unhip to complain about a shoplifter, the stock disappeared by the armload, much of it taken by the assistants themselves. Pete Shotton was still vainly trying to keep the enterprise afloat but wrote, 'Even the Fool eventually had to be taken severely to task for their constant expropriation of Apple property; having worn out their welcome with the Beatles, Simon, Marijke, and Josje subsequently split for America. Within seven months the boutique was to lose almost £200,000.'

After this inauspicious start as shopkeepers, during which the Fool got their Rolls-Royce, the chastened, wiser Beatles concentrated on getting the other Apple companies off the ground, in particular the record division. Neil Aspinall began to look for a headquarters building to house the many Apple companies and in the meantime office space was rented above a bank at 95 Wigmore Street, an uneventful eight-storey 1940s office block on the southeast corner of Duke Street, chosen in part because EMI, the Beatles' record company and Apple's distributors, was only one street away on Manchester Square. They remained here until the first week of September 1968, when most departments were transferred to 3 Savile Row, leaving only the accountants behind.

Music would be the core business, with Apple Publishing, Apple Films and other related companies as spin-offs. The magazine, the school, the chain of shops, all fell by the wayside and the Apple boutique was closed not long afterwards with the Beatles giving the entire stock away. They began by tempting Ron Kass away from his job as head of Liberty Records International to run the Apple Records division. Peter Asher was appointed the head of A & R. The protective Liverpool bubble that had served so well in the past was extended to Apple: Neil Aspinall, then twenty-six years old, was made managing director; the 33-year-old Alistair Taylor, who had witnessed their original contract with Brian Epstein, was made office manager; Tony Bramwell, twenty-three, who had previously worked for Brian, became Denis O'Dell's assistant at Apple Films; the 32-year-old Peter Brown had previously worked as Brian Epstein's personal assistant, and now performed the same role for the Beatles with his customary aplomb; Terry Doran, a 'man from the motor trade', a friend of Brian Epstein's from the fifties, was made head of Apple Music; the 36-year-old Derek Taylor, somewhat inaccurately described by Michael Braun in *Love Me Do* as 'a reporter given to Italianate suits and talking out of the side of his mouth', who had acted as publicist for the Beatles in 1964–65, was repatriated from Los Angeles to run the press office; and their roadie Mal Evans continued to be on hand as the Beatles' PA during the interminable recording sessions which occupied them for most of the year. They were almost all from Liverpool; people whom the Beatles had known and trusted for a long time. Between them they created a unique institution.

In the difficult course of translating the idea of Apple into reality, it was surprising how much of the original optimism and energy remained; there was an atmosphere of tremendous excitement during the early days of 1968 when the record division was being set up. Peter brought in James Taylor and the Modern Jazz Quartet. George Harrison wanted to release Delaney and Bonnie, and all the Beatles wanted to sign Harry Nilsson. Initially, the record division worked as it was intended: they signed the people they liked, produced their records and played on their albums. It was like an extended musical family. The main problem was money.

The press office appeared at first glance to be the most obvious source of profligate spending, but a few cartons of cigarettes and a large alcohol and hashish bill was nothing compared to the first-class air fares, luxury hotels and nights of expensive schmoozing in fashionable nightclubs that the heads of other departments were charging. Yet for the price of a well-stocked bar, the Beatles became the hippest people in town: everyone who was anyone in the music business dropped by Apple to say hello. Within a few months of the office opening, Eric Clapton, members of the Jefferson Airplane, members of the Doors, members of the Mamas and Papas, Canned Heat, Jim Webb, Terry Stamp, Peter Sellers, Dean Stockwell, Diana Rigg, as well as the owners of Elektra Records, A & M Records and Track Records had all enjoyed the hospitality of the press office. Often as not, none of the Beatles was there to say hello, but the press office acted as their public face and did it for them. Visitors felt as if they had been in their presence and went away happy. Entertaining this many people was an exhausting business, as Derek Taylor commented in the house magazine: 'We've had many guests at Apple, friends. Can't remember any of them. Very stoned, you see. Affects the memory.'

As far as the press were concerned, Paul and Jane entered 1968 as the same fabled couple that they had gushed over four years earlier during the days of Swinging London. They were often seen out on the town, smiling at the cameras; on 21 May, for instance, they had lunch with the singer Andy Williams and his French wife Claudine Longet and that evening attended his final Royal Albert Hall show and the end-of-the-show party afterwards. Paul was able to keep several balls in the air at once, as the logo of his company, MPL, shows. (Paul's logo is of a juggler keeping a sun, a moon and a planet aloft.) He remained interested in the glamorous show-business side of London as well as in the cosmic awareness preached by the Maharishi. His relatives still came to stay and he still saw old friends. Most of all, he continued to write songs.

Paul's ideas on love, marriage and the role of women were formed in the pre-feminist fifties and reflected the northern working-class attitudes of the time. However, unlike many, if not most, male rock 'n' roll lyrics from the period, his songs were never misogynist or overtly exploitative, though they often portrayed a healthy, lusty sexuality. He could never write 'Under My Thumb' or 'Yesterday's Papers'. His songs about women were often thoughtful and appreciative, like 'Lady Madonna', released on 15 March 1968.

PAUL: 'Lady Madonna' started off as the Virgin Mary, then it was a working-class woman, of which obviously there's millions in Liverpool. The people I was brought up amongst were often Catholic; there are a lot of Catholics in Liverpool because of the Irish connection and they are often quite religious. When they have a baby I think they see a big connection between themselves and the Virgin Mary with her baby. So the original concept was the Virgin Mary but it quickly became symbolic of every woman; the Madonna image but as applied to ordinary working-class woman. It's really a tribute to the mother figure, it's a tribute to women. 'Your Mother Should Know' is another. I think women are very strong, they put up with a lot of shit, they put up with the pain of having a child, of raising it, cooking for it, they are basically skivvies a lot of their lives, so I always want to pay a tribute to them.

There's an interesting film director called Alison Anders who did a lot of small-budget films in Los Angeles, who says if you look at my songs there's a great support for the female and that is what made her able to write feminine characters for her screenplays. And she cites many of them in my songs, more than I even knew.

'Lady Madonna' was me sitting down at the piano trying to write a bluesy boogie-woogie thing. I got my left hand doing an arpeggio thing with the chord, an ascending boogie-woogie left hand, then a descending right hand. I always liked that, the juxtaposition of a line going down meeting a line going up. That was basically what it was. It reminded me of Fats Domino for some reason, so I started singing a Fats Domino impression. It took my voice to a very odd place. Richard Perry got Fats to do it. I probably told Richard Perry that it was based on Fats. Recently [1994] I was writing the words out to learn it for an

American TV show and I realised I missed out Saturday; I did every other day of the week, but I missed out Saturday. So I figured it must have been a real night out.

On 11 May 1968, Paul and John, accompanied by Neil Aspinall, flew to New York for four days to launch Apple Records and its associated companies in the USA. John brought along Magic Alex to talk about Apple Electronics. The press interviews were held at the St Regis but an afternoon press conference took place on the 14th at the Americana Hotel, where Linda was able to contact Paul again. Linda: 'I was taking pictures and we started talking. He said, "We're leaving, give me your number," and I remember writing it on a cheque. When I got back to the apartment he'd rung.'

Paul was busy that night – they were staying with their New York attorney Nat Weiss on East 73rd Street and most of their time was taken up by a round of interviews, television and business meetings – but he arranged to see Linda the next day by inviting her to ride out to the airport with them. 'Did I want to come along for the ride? I took a bunch of pictures; one of John was used for the cover of *Eye* magazine but the light was not good in the PanAm waiting room. Anyway, we got to know each other in a car ride a bit; I'm sitting in the middle with my camera bag in between John and Paul. Who knows what was going on?' Paul flew off to London and Linda returned to Manhattan in the limo with Nat Weiss and Neil Aspinall, but five weeks later Paul called her. He was arriving in Los Angeles on 20 June for the Capitol Records sales convention.

In the days before answering machines, people like Linda had an answering service. Calls were automatically re-routed and answered by telephone operators. Inevitably they got to know the intimate details of their clients' lives.

> LINDA: It was like having a friend. Different friends. You could tell it was, like, black women living up in Harlem. They'd go, 'Hi, Linda, So-and-so called tonight ...' We'd talk and it was great. So this night it was 'Paul McCartney called and so-and-so called.' Well, that was interesting. Then he called back and said he was going to Los Angeles, staying at the Beverly Hills Hotel, did I want to come out for two days? Now I don't like flying, but

then it was like, 'Sure, okay!' 'Diana, my friend, could you look after Heather for two days?'

Heather was looked after, that's all I cared about, and then I booked a ticket at the travel agent right on the corner of Madison by my apartment. Paid for it myself. It wasn't like, 'You send me a ticket and I'll come out.' Got on the plane going to LA, there were these two hairdressers and another girl and we started talking, and they had some pot on this plane and we were all smoking. Things you just wouldn't do now! Paul had just said 'I'm here if you show up,' so I showed up.

Paul had brought along his school friend Ivan Vaughan, the man who introduced him to John Lennon and who was supposedly going to start an Apple school. Tony Bramwell from the Apple office was also there. Ivan was the only one at home when Linda arrived and he let her into the bungalow. When he first got to Los Angeles, Paul had been seeing Winona Williams, an old friend of David Bowie and Jimi Hendrix whom Paul knew from the London club scene, but with Linda's arrival she was quickly disposed of.

LINDA: So at first I was at the Beverly Hills on my own. I remember this beautiful smell of orange blossom or jasmine in the air. We hung out there for a couple of days, it wasn't long at all. I spent a lot of time with Ivan because Paul was doing a lot of press at the Capital convention. Ivan and I just got on like that, it was such a great rapport. Tony Bramwell was with some stewardess and it was all chicks chicks chicks.

It was a short visit. Paul and his entourage returned to London and Linda flew back to New York.

Back in London Paul had his time cut out for him at Apple. The Fool and the Apple boutique had become a big problem. Pete Shotton had been replaced at Apple Retail by John Lyndon, who as early as January 1968 had informed the Fool that there was to be no more expenditure without written authority. Further correspondence with the Fool's business manager Simon Hayes ensued, and in March, Lyndon finally informed Hayes that if the Fool removed any more garments from Canel's workshops he would have no alternative but to exclude them from the premises. Seeing that they had sucked the apple dry, the Fool now moved to New York, where they extracted a large advance from Mercury Records, very sensibly inserting a clause in their contract excluding anyone from Mercury from the recording sessions, 'because they wanted to vibrate with the engineer'. The head of Mercury A & R is said to have literally vomited when he heard the final results, but by then the Fool had already moved on, having arranged to paint the 'biggest psychedelic mural on earth' on the side of the theatre where *Hair* was playing in Los Angeles. There was nothing foolish about the Fool.

John Lyndon was briefly succeeded as manager of the Apple boutique by an angelic-looking *I Ching* and Tarot-card reader called Caleb, who cast daily horoscopes for John and whose readings determined all important business decisions at Apple Corps. But the Beatles were 'getting fed up with being shopkeepers' and on 31 July 1968, after ransacking the shelves themselves, they gave away the stock and shut up shop. Caleb ended up in a lunatic asylum. Paul: 'At least when the boutique fell through, to our credit we gave all the stuff away. We just gave the stuff away and closed it.'

Jane missed most of the excitement of setting up Apple because she was still spending most of her time in Bristol. She and Paul had been together for five years, during which time they had both grown and changed dramatically. In the end the relationship came to an abrupt halt. Jane came home unexpectedly from Bristol and found Paul in bed with someone else. A frosty Margaret Asher came over and took away her clothes, cooking pots and ornaments. On 20 July 1968, Jane appeared as one of the guests on *Dee Time*, then BBC Television's most popular talk show, and told the British public that their engagement was over. 'I haven't broken it off,' she told Simon Dee, 'but it is broken off, finished.'

> PAUL: I don't remember the breakup as being traumatic, really. I remember more one time when she was working at the Bristol Old Vic and she'd got a boyfriend in Bristol and was going to leave me for him. That was wildly traumatic, that was 'Uhhhh!' Total rejection! We got back together again but I had already gone through that when we eventually split up. It seemed it had to happen. It felt right.
>
> I liked her a lot and we got on very well. She was a very intelligent and very interesting person, but I just never clicked.

One of those indefinable things about love is some people you click with and some people who you should maybe click with, you don't. Whatever.

Marianne Faithfull, however, never felt the relationship was a lasting one:

> I never remember them getting on very well, Jane and him, it was sort of like an act almost, and I can quite see that he would be much happier with Linda because with Jane it would have been very difficult. I love watching people living their domestic life and seeing how that goes. I always thought Jane and Paul were very tense. I do remember very clearly an evening at Cavendish Avenue where she wanted the window shut and he wanted the window open. That really was like a Joe Orton play. It was fucking great. I sat there all night watching Jane get up and open it, and Paul close it, and it was just like, nothing was said. And quite soon after that they split up, which of course I could have told anyone they would.
>
> Paul: 'I got cold feet. It was that, and a few other personal things.'

Not long after they split up, on 29 October 1968, Jane appeared with Victor Henry in the fourth revival of John Osborne's *Look Back in Anger* at the Royal Court Theatre. This was so successful that it transferred to the Criterion Theatre in the West End on 10 December. It was the watershed in her stage career. In a 1986 interview in *Plays and Players* she said, 'It was the first time I took myself seriously.' The critics agreed, calling her performance 'her dramatic coming of age'. It established her on a par with Paul in her chosen profession.

Meanwhile, refurbishment began on 3 Savile Row, which Apple bought for £500,000 in June 1968. 'I had asked Neil to look for a great London building,' Paul explained, 'And he found it, 3 Savile Row, Lady Hamilton's London residence, which Nelson bought for her. I thought, If nothing else, that's a good London building.' It was a magnificent listed town house, part of a once uniform terrace built between 1733 and 1735 running the length of the east side of Savile Row, and conveniently close to Nelson's house on Bond Street for him to drop round on Lady H. whenever the urge took him. *The Survey of London* says that number 3 has good interior features, as indeed it did until a later phase of Apple's history when Allen Klein was to move in and rip the building apart to build a recording studio in the basement. Initially, however, it was beautifully restored, its marble fireplaces cleaned and the ceiling mouldings revealed beneath countless coats of paint. Carpets and mirrors all reflected the building's eighteenth-century origins.

Paul was determined to get Apple Records off to a good start and as well as writing 'Hey Jude', the Beatles' first Apple release, he produced the second release, 'Those Were the Days' by Mary Hopkin.

Mary Hopkin

Paul first heard of Mary at his father's house in Liverpool in May 1968. The model Twiggy and her manager Justin de Villeneuve had just driven up in their new car and came to dinner. They were eating pudding when the conversation turned to television talent-discovery shows. Paul wondered whether anyone ever got discovered, really discovered on discovery shows. Twiggy said she had seen a great singer on *Opportunity Knocks*, a seventeen-year-old Welsh girl called Mary Hopkin with a high, clear voice. 'She'll win next week,' Twiggy said. 'Don't worry, you'll see her again, I'll bet.'

Paul: 'So I tuned in next week to see her and she did have a very nice, very soft, well-controlled Welsh voice. And she looked very pretty, young girl, blonde, long hair, so I thought, Okay. Quite right. We should sign her for Apple, maybe make an interesting record with her.'

Next day, several other people mentioned her and it looked as if Mary had made quite an impact. That day Paul had lunch with Twiggy and Derek Taylor at a smart restaurant in Fulham. Twiggy again enthused over Mary. Back in the office, someone got Mary's telephone number from the television company. In his memoirs Derek Taylor reports how he rang her at her home in Pontardawe near Swansea in South Wales. '"Paul McCartney for you," I said to the sound of much sweet disbelief and mellifluous Welshness. (It can't be! Oooh, is it really? Well, I never.) "Paul here," said the great man ...'

In an article in *Melody Maker* to promote the record, Paul wrote:

This beautiful little Welsh voice came on the phone and I said: 'This is Apple Records here; would you be interested in coming down here to record for us?' She said: 'Well, er, would you like to speak to my mother?' and then her mother came on the line and we had a chat and two further telephone conversations and later that week Mary and her mum came to London. We had a nice lunch and went to Dick James' studios in Oxford Street and I thought she was great. She sang a lot of songs on tape and I knew she was great ... she seemed to mean what she sang. Most impressive. But at the same time I thought she was very Joan Baez – a lot of Joan's influence showed. We chatted and I said, 'Look, it would be nice, we should maybe sign if you like us and you like the look of the whole thing.' Well, it didn't look too crazy then, obviously we looked all right because she did sign.

Paul has always had a good ear for a catchy tune, and once he has heard it, it remains with him. Three or four years earlier he heard Gene and Francesca Raskin, an American architect and his wife who had an amateur cabaret act, sing 'Those Were the Days' at the Blue Angel cabaret club in Berkeley Square, and it stuck in his mind. Paul tried to get someone to record it at the time because he thought it was so good. He suggested it to the Moody Blues but nothing came of it, and later in India he played it to Donovan, who loved it but didn't get round to recording it. Paul thought that it would be perfect for Mary. He played it to her and she liked it. Paul didn't remember the names of the singers but he called the Blue Angel and they were able to look it up. Paul wrote to Gene Raskin and sent a tape of the tune. 'I asked, "Who wrote that?" and he said, "Well, we did. It's a Russian melody but arranged by us and we put the words to it."'

David Platz at Essex Music, the publishers of the song, had no lead sheets or demos but he contacted Raskin, who quickly wrote a lead sheet. Paul and Peter Asher, whose job it was to look after Hopkin, found an arranger and Paul decided to produce the record himself. They went into the studio in mid-July 1968. Paul showed Mary how he thought the song should be done. 'I thought it was very catchy, it had something, it was a good treatment of nostalgia. She picked it up very easily; as if she'd known it for years.' At first she sang it as if she didn't mean it, and in fact it must have been difficult for a seventeen-year-old to sing 'those were the days' convincingly since she had no adult past; the song was intended for an older singer. Paul: 'After a few tapes, I kept showing her the way she should sing it and generally worked on it and suddenly she got it and we just put a tambourine on it and went home.'

The B side, 'Turn, Turn, Turn', they recorded in one take and the record was released on 30 August 1968 as Apple 2. The Beatles' 'Hey Jude' was the first record on Apple, but EMI insisted that it keep their catalogue number. Paul used his influence to get Mary on to *The Ed Sullivan Show* in the USA and *The David Frost Show* in Britain. 'Those Were the Days' reached number one in the UK, toppling 'Hey Jude' from that position. In the USA, where 'Hey Jude' kept it from top, it reached number two. It was an auspicious beginning for both Mary and Apple Records. To make sure that Mary made as big an impact abroad as he hoped she would in Britain, Paul produced Italian, French, German and Spanish-language versions of Mary's 'Those Were the Days' in the same way that the Beatles recorded German versions of their records in the early days.

Anxious to follow up her success with 'Those Were the Days', Paul made an album with Mary: fourteen tracks, mostly pop standards and show tunes which Mary had never heard of and didn't particularly like. Paul: 'I basically did a lot of tunes that were my favourites that I thought she'd be good at.' He did Ray Noble's 1933 hit 'Love Is the Sweetest Thing', recreating Al Bowlly's arrangement in modern stereo, George Olsen's 1932 'Lullaby of the Leaves' and the 1927 George Gershwin hit 'Someone to Watch Over Me'. 'Inchworm' was originally sung by Danny Kaye in the 1956 film *Hans Christian Andersen*, which Paul saw as an adolescent, and the old standard 'There's No Business Like Show Business' came from the 1949 Broadway show *Annie Get Your Gun*.

Mary's favourite tracks on the album were the three written by Donovan, which were closer to her own folk tradition; she had been singing in folk clubs around Swansea for several years. Two tracks, 'Lord of the Reedy River' and 'Voyage of the Moon', Donovan wrote specially for her; a third, 'Pebble and the Man (Happiness Runs)', he had already recorded. Donovan and Paul played acoustic guitars on all three tracks. Paul also asked Harry Nilsson for a song. He sent her

'The Puppy Song', which went on to become one of Harry's own best-loved numbers.

> PAUL: She was a very nice girl and good fun to work with. It was all done at EMI. Just go in, do a couple of songs. Then Linda took her down to Kew Gardens and took the cover photograph. I got in touch with Valentines, the postcard makers, and said, 'Will you please make a postcard of this?', which they did for that one summer: a limited edition of postcards. It was rather home-made, a pleasant album to make.

Paul wrote the track listing on the postcard and mailed it to Apple. The card, with stamp and postmark, became the liner information and gave the album its title: *Postcard*. The album was launched on 13 February 1969 with a reception at the revolving restaurant at the top of the Post Office Tower, then London's tallest building. Paul and Linda stayed to the end, showing the assembled journalists that Apple was really behind its artists. Jimi Hendrix, Donovan and other luminaries made an appearance.

Naturally Mary needed a follow-up to 'Those Were the Days'. Over in Cavendish Avenue Paul quickly wrote one called 'Goodbye'.

> PAUL: I didn't have in mind any more Russian folk songs so I just wrote one for her. I thought it fit the bill. It wasn't as successful as the first one but it did all right. My main memory of it is from years later, going on a boat trip from the north of Scotland to the Orkney Islands. The skipper of the boat was called George, and he told me it was his favourite song. And if you think of it from a sailor's point of view, it's very much a leaving-the-port song. He had the strangest Scottish accent, almost sort of Norwegian, as the Orkneyans do. He was quite proud of the fact that that was his favourite song.

'Goodbye' entered the British charts at number five, but didn't make it to the top.

'After "Goodbye", Mary and I didn't work together again,' Paul said. 'She wanted to do a more folky album, and I felt that if she wanted to do that I wasn't really interested in producing it. I don't think it was a very good idea in the end.' The album, *Earth Song/Ocean Song*, was produced by Tony Visconti, whom she married in 1971. After that, she more or less left the business to have children, though she made appearances on records as diverse as David Bowie's *Low* in 1977 and an entire album sung in Welsh, *The Welsh World of Mary Hopkin*, in 1979.

The whole point of having your own record company was that you could release any record you liked. Paul indulged his love of brass-band music and made a single with the Black Dyke Mills Band, the best brass band in the land, playing one of his own compositions called 'Thingumybob', a theme tune for a TV series starring Stanley Holloway. It was one of the first four Apple releases. George Harrison was also heavily involved on the production side. The third Apple record released was 'Sour Milk Sea' by Jackie Lomax, written and produced by George. Jackie was an old friend of the Beatles from Liverpool, where he played in the Undertakers. George produced his first album, *Is This What You Want?*, and the follow-up single 'New Day', on which Ringo played drums. Paul produced the B side, 'Thumbin' a Ride', and played drums on it. Apple also released *Wonderwall Music*, a film soundtrack written by George which he recorded partly in London, partly in Bombay, with Indian musicians. He later told Paul that the studio had a sign which commanded: 'No spitting on the walls.' Later, in 1969, George was to produce Billy Preston's first album, *That's the Way God Planned It*, and a follow-up, *Encouraging Words*, in 1971.

The other major signing to Apple was James Taylor. His group the Flying Machine had acted as a backing band for Peter Asher when he toured America with Peter and Gordon. When Peter was appointed head of A & R for Apple, James was one of the first people he thought of signing. Paul played drums on the track 'Carolina on My Mind' from James's first album, which was issued as a single. James was a good example of the talent that Apple discovered but were unable to develop.

Ringo's contribution to Apple was quite surprising: he introduced a young classical composer called John Taverner to the label. Taverner was the brother of Roger Taverner, who had been doing some building work for Ringo. His first long work, *The Whale*, had received a rapturous reception at the 1968 Royal Albert Hall Proms, and when Ringo heard a tape of the BBC broadcast he quickly contacted Taverner at his parents' house in north London. The bemused composer, who barely knew who Ringo was, soon found himself at

Savile Row, signing his first recording contract. The Apple connection was enough to guarantee airplay on the BBC Third Programme and launch his career, but commercial success remained elusive, largely because Derek Taylor in the Apple press office hadn't the faintest idea how to promote 'underground classical music' as Ringo described it. Nonetheless, *The Whale* and the subsequent *Celtic Requiem* were both challenging and worthwhile contributions, very much in Apple's original spirit. Ringo so liked *The Whale* that he later reissued it on his own Ring O' Records label. John took no part in developing the Apple artist roster, though he did produce a string of Plastic Ono Band records and later acted as William Randoph Hearst to Yoko Ono's Marion Davies, producing a stream of Yoko Ono records, none of which sold in any quantity.

Apple placed ads in the underground papers and the music press, asking people to send them tapes. They arrived by the sackload, so many that most of them were never played. There was some discussion with the Rolling Stones about a jointly financed recording studio. It was reported at the time that Mick Jagger and Paul had had preliminary talks but no one now remembers what took place.

> PAUL: It's possible we talked to them about Apple – 'Hey, we'll get the Stones on our label.' The thinking behind it was very excited, which was, Well, if we get Donovan, and we've got the Beatles, and we get James Taylor, and then we get a couple of others, maybe the Stones might even want to come on. And what if some of the really cool American bands like the Byrds want to come, because we're good friends with them? We figured that all our friends would eventually join us. It would be the freest thing. It would be a revolution in the recording business. We'll give them all decent deals. And a lot of that did happen. It was enough for me to be enjoying what we were doing, to be making good music, to be making good friends, and just getting on. And if we had a hit, great. Donovan never did sign with us; but that was the dream. The housekeeping was what let us down and in the end it was just a free-for-all.

Despite all this activity, Paul also found time to produce 'I Am the Urban Spaceman' by his friends the Bonzo Dog Band using the name Apollo C. Vermouth. It was to be their only top-ten hit.

Unlike the other Beatles, John took relatively little part in the launch of Apple. He was in the middle of his divorce from Cynthia at the time. He had put Kenwood up for sale and moved into Ringo's unused flat in Montagu Square, where he retreated into a soporific heroin haze with his new girlfriend, Yoko Ono.

Yoko Ono

Among the artists who spent time hanging out at Indica Gallery were Yoko Ono and her husband Tony Cox. John Dunbar and Miles knew her work with the New York-based Fluxus art group, with which she had been associated since 1960. Indica also stocked her limited-edition book *Grapefruit* and had some of the Fluxus boxes and posters containing her work on the shelves. Yoko arrived in London with Tony in September 1966 to take part in the Destruction in Art Symposium. She soon familiarised herself with the London art scene and it didn't take her long to persuade John Dunbar that he should give her a show, particularly since she said she had a sponsor who would pay for the catalogue and posters. Her work fitted well with other shows John had put on and an exhibition was planned.

Unlike the big commercial Bond Street galleries, John Dunbar liked to keep things loose and not schedule art shows very far ahead. That way he could respond to what was going on and slot in new things whenever he wanted. Yoko's show Unfinished Paintings and Objects opened on 9 November 1966, less than six weeks after she first walked into the gallery. The day before the vernissage Tony Cox, the gallery manager Geneviève Morgan, Miles and his wife Sue, and a few others were sitting around in the basement as Yoko put the finishing touches to the show. She was dressed in her usual black sweater, black trousers and shoes, with her long black hair hanging over her shoulders like a bell tent: very much the Greenwich Village bohemian. A joint was making the rounds when John Lennon dropped in to see John Dunbar. The two Johns were good friends, their relationship cemented by drugs, including one legendary week-long acid trip during which they visited an uninhabited island off the west coast of Ireland that Lennon happened to have bought after seeing it advertised as for sale by auction.

John Dunbar introduced John to Yoko and they both went downstairs to the basement to see the show. All the objects were white or transparent, with one exception: the *Add Colour Painting, 1966*, where the viewer was allowed one colour to add to the painting. A white chair was provided with the painting to hold the paints and brushes. *Apple* consisted of an apple on a transparent Perspex stand and the catalogue featured a photograph of John Dunbar eating it – or an earlier version of it. Another item, *Pointedness* from 1964, was a small sphere on a Perspex stand.

John Lennon was intrigued by a painting mounted on the ceiling. He could just see a word written on it in tiny letters. A magnifying glass to enable the viewer to read it hung from a string attached to the frame, reached by a white stepladder which stood beneath. John climbed up and was pleased to find the mysterious word was 'Yes'. Another work that interested John was *Painting to Hammer a Nail In*, a piece dating from 1961, of which this was the sixth version Yoko had made. John wanted to hammer a nail in it then and there but Yoko objected, wanting to keep her painting pristine until the official opening the next night. John Dunbar persuaded her to relent but Yoko told Lennon it would cost him five shillings. 'Suppose I drive an imaginary nail in for five imaginary shillings,' retorted Lennon, entering into the spirit of the exhibition. This he did and no visible money changed hands. Throughout the viewing, Yoko had linked her arm around John's as she explained the works and when he made a move to go, she asked him to take her with him. John had been up for three days and was on his way back to Kenwood. He politely declined, climbed in the back of his black-glass chauffeur-driven S.S. Cooper-Mini, and sped off across the cobbles of Mason's Yard. Yoko made sure that they met again.

She bombarded John with letters and postcards filled with poems and short performance pieces. He was intrigued. He enjoyed the quirky, surreal aspect of her art. They met from time to time, though John was initially interested in her purely as an artist – she was considerably older than he and could not have been further from John's conventional beauty stereotype of Brigitte Bardot. But the letters kept coming and he became fascinated by her ideas, which he recognised as having a lot in common with his own. When the Beatles went to visit the Maharishi in India, John arranged for her letters to reach him without Cynthia knowing.

By spending two months in deep meditation in India, John brought his deepest problems to the surface but he was unable to resolve them: the contradiction between his family life and his life as a rock star with all the drugs and groupies was too great. Had he stayed with the Maharishi until the end of the course, he might have avoided some of the pain, but by terminating the instruction abruptly, he was left hanging in thin air. During the weeks at the camp, he had been receiving daily letters from Yoko, though nothing sexual had yet happened between them. He was very attracted by her but he felt tremendous guilt about breaking up his marriage: doing to Julian what his own parents had done to him, repeating the pattern.

The Maharishi had given John and Cynthia a beautiful suit of Indian clothes for them to give to Julian on his upcoming birthday, causing John to experience a wave of love and affection for his family. Cynthia wrote in her autobiography:

> On leaving the Maharishi, John held my hand. He was overjoyed.
>
> 'Oh Cyn,' he said, 'won't it be wonderful to be together with Julian again. Everything will be fantastic again, won't it? I can't wait, Cyn, can you?'
>
> I found it hard to believe that I was hearing John speak from the heart about our family for the first time in what seemed like years. It filled me with love and hope for the future.

But her happiness was short-lived. On the plane returning to London, after walking out on the Maharishi, John began drinking heavily and told Cynthia of all the other women he had slept with during their marriage: the groupies and the whores but in particular the ones she knew personally, her friends and the wives of friends. When he got back to Kenwood, he went on an orgy of drink and drugs, mostly LSD, trying to bury the thoughts and feelings that the meditation had allowed to rise to the surface.

The meditation had essentially precipitated a nervous breakdown, which was not helped by John's tremendous drug intake. On 18 May 1968, he summoned a meeting of the Beatles at Apple and announced to them that he was Jesus Christ, a revelation that they accepted with equanimity. This was before the plague of acid casualties, but it was obvious that John was literally going off his head and the others were very worried about him. Yoko meanwhile had been keeping up her relentless flow of postcards and letters. The night after he told the other Beatles that he was the Saviour, he finally called Yoko and told her to come over. They took acid together and spent the evening recording the electronic collage later released as *Two Virgins* before making love for the first time. The tape, consisting of simple superimpositions and tape echo, was made on the pair of linked Brenells that John had asked Paul to set up for him in his music room, using the same system that Paul used for the loop tapes for 'Tomorrow Never Knows'.

John was completely bowled over by Yoko. In his fragile state, the rush of emotion and the power of the feelings released astonished him. When Cynthia arrived back from holiday the next day, she found Yoko wearing her dressing gown and John looking sheepish.

No sooner had they got together than John and Yoko were strung out on heroin. Yoko first encountered heroin when the Beatles were away in India. John had already been introduced to it by Robert Fraser, who, though unsuccessful in persuading Paul of the delights of junkie life, had much better luck with John. India had left John in a delicate and shaky state; heroin would take the pain away. Fortunately John had the strength to kick it eventually but like many junkies, he had trouble admitting to himself that he was hooked – sniffing is no different from injecting as far as addiction goes – and he blamed his addiction on other people.

John told Jann Wenner: 'I never injected it or anything. We sniffed a little when we were in real pain. We got such a hard time from everyone, and I've had so much thrown at me and at Yoko, especially at Yoko ... We took H because of what the Beatles and others were doing to us. But we got out of it.' John and Yoko began spending a lot of time with Robert Fraser.

When he came out of jail early in 1968, Robert had begun to rebuild his life. He had lost his flat on Mount Street and had been blackballed from his club, White's, where his father had been a member before him. 'I only ever used it to cash cheques, anyway,' said Robert dismissively. He went around to all his old friends, reaffirming friendships, testing the water, seeing who was a genuine friend and who not. Christopher Gibbs had visited him in the Scrubs, taking with him Lady Nico Londonderry, who expressed disappointment that he didn't have arrows printed on his prison uniform. Paul had also written to Robert in jail and invited him over to Cavendish Avenue as soon as he got out. Robert visited shortly after his release.

Paul: 'He was standing close to me and I remember thinking, God, that's jail soap! It actually smelled. And it was one of my fears, in jail in Japan, that I'd come out smelling of jail.'

Robert got a new flat on Mount Street, this time across from the Connaught Hotel, much larger and grander than the previous one, with higher ceilings, better able to show off the work. The gallery entered a new era, with shows by artists more in keeping with the late sixties. He showed the Cadillac painted in psychedelic patterns by the Binder, Edwards and Vaughan design team which had inspired Paul to commission them to customise his piano, but the show did not go down very well. Robert: 'I got a lot of criticism for that car, I must say.'

Robert was said by some to have lost the cutting edge that so characterised his gallery in the early and mid-sixties and was accused of simply putting on fashionable shows. However, there were a few artists from before who could afford to remain with him, like Richard Hamilton, who continued to show his latest work. Yoko had attended all the openings at the Robert Fraser Gallery from the moment she arrived in London and had lost no time in asking him for a show. He turned her down, and commented to Paul, 'This woman is pretty pushy. This is a woman who wants to really get known, you know? She's got her own career.' Though he had originally rejected Yoko's request for a show, Robert now offered one to John – the You Are Here show, which opened on 1 July 1968, six weeks after John and Yoko got together. It was essentially Yoko's show by default since many of the ideas were hers.

The Apple staff assembled a large group of collection boxes for the blind, for the Spastics Society and other similar charities, and filled the gallery space with them. It was in line with John's sick humour, the jokes about cripples and deformity which also informed his writing. There were 365 balloons released, each with a ticket reading 'You are here. Please write to John Lennon c/o the Robert Fraser Gallery', and a message written on circular white canvas which read 'You are here'. Robert: 'The John Lennon show was very poorly received. Looking back on it, it did have a certain pretentious element. It was fun. I don't know if it was art. It wasn't popular.'

As might be expected, Apple's greatest success came with Beatles records, beginning with Paul's 'Hey Jude'.

PAUL: 'Hey Jude' was a song which I originally thought of whilst driving my car out to visit Cynthia and Julian Lennon after John's divorce from them. We'd been very good friends for millions of years and I thought it was a bit much for them suddenly to be *personae non gratae* and out of my life, so I decided to pay them a visit and say, 'How are you doing? What's happening?' I was very used to writing songs on my way out to Kenwood because I was usually going there to collaborate with John. This time I started with the idea 'Hey Jules', which was Julian, don't make it bad, take a sad song and make it better. Hey, try and deal with this terrible thing. I knew it was not going to be easy for him. I always feel sorry for kids in divorces. The adults may be fine but the kids ... I always relate to their little brain spinning round in confusion, going, 'Did *I* do this? Was it me?' Guilt is such a terrible thing and I know it affects a lot of people and I think that was the reason I went out. And I got this idea for a song, 'Hey Jude', and made up a few little things so I had the idea by the time I got there. I changed it to 'Jude' because I thought that sounded a bit better.

I finished it all up in Cavendish and I was in the music room upstairs when John and Yoko came to visit and they were right behind me over my right shoulder, standing up, listening to it as I played it to them, and when I got to the line 'The movement you need is on your shoulder', I looked over my shoulder and I said, 'I'll change that, it's a bit crummy. I was just blocking it out,' and John said, 'You won't, you know. That's the best line in it!' That's collaboration. When someone's that firm about a line that you're going to junk, and he says, 'No, keep it in.' So of course you love that line twice as much because it's a little stray, it's a little mutt that you were about to put down and it was reprieved and so it's more beautiful than ever. I love those words now, 'The movement you need is on your shoulder.' Of course I now feel that those are terribly deep words; I've had letters from religious groups and cults saying, 'Paul, you understand what this means, don't you? The wherewithal is there, whatever you want to do ...' And it is a great line but I was going to change it because it sounded like a parrot or something; not entirely logical. Time lends a little credence to things. You can't knock it, it just did so well. But when I'm singing it, that is when I think of

John, when I hear myself singing that line; it's an emotional point in the song.

The end refrain was never a separate song. I remember taking it down to a late night hashish-smoking club in a basement in Tottenham Court Road: the Vesuvio club. We were sitting around on bean bags as was the thing. I said to the DJ, 'Here's an acetate. Do you want to slip it in some time during the evening?' He played it, and I remember Mick Jagger coming up: 'Fuckin' 'ell, fuckin' 'ell. That's something else, innit? It's like two songs.' It wasn't intended to go on that long at the end but I was having such fun ad-libbing over the end when we put down the original track that I went on a long time. So then we built it with the orchestra but it was mainly because I just wouldn't stop doing all that 'Judy judy judy – wooow!' Cary Grant on heat!

There is an amusing story about recording it. We were at Trident Studios in Soho, and Ringo walked out to go to the toilet and I hadn't noticed. The toilet was only a few yards from his drum booth, but he'd gone past my back and I still thought he was in his drum booth. I started what was the actual take, and 'Hey Jude' goes on for hours before the drums come in and while I was doing it I suddenly felt Ringo tiptoeing past my back rather quickly, trying to get to his drums. And just as he got to his drums, boom boom boom, his timing was absolutely impeccable. So I think when those things happen, you have a little laugh and a light bulb goes off in your head and you think, This is the take! and you put a little more into it. You think, oh, fuck! This has got to be the take, what just happened was so magic! So we did that and we made a pretty good record.

John regarded it as the best record Paul ever made and thought it was written about him; that Paul was giving him permission to break up their 'marriage' and get together with Yoko instead. He told *Playboy*:

> I always heard it as a song to me. If you think about it ... Yoko's just come into the picture. He's saying, 'Hey Jude' – 'Hey John'. I know I'm sounding like one of those fans who reads things into it, but you can hear it as a song to me. The words 'go out and get her' – subconsciously he was saying, 'Go ahead, leave me.'

On a conscious level, he didn't want me to go ahead. The angel in him was saying, 'Bless you'. The devil in him didn't like it at all because he didn't want to lose his partner.

This is an attractive reading of the lyrics even though Paul had disagreed and said that the song was more about himself: Paul in his Aston Martin, making the familiar drive to John's house in the country where they always wrote songs, thinking of all the changes in their lives: John's divorce, his own ambivalence over Jane. Both Paul and John were skilled at entering a half-trance state which enabled them to access material from their unconscious. The lyrics are universal; many readings are possible.

'Hey Jude' was the Beatles' most successful single, selling more than 5,000,000 copies worldwide in six months; 7,500,000 in four years. It was number one in the USA for nine weeks, as well as going to number one in Britain and ten other countries. At seven minutes and nine seconds, it was also the Beatles' longest single, with four minutes devoted to the fadeout. It got Apple Records off to a tremendous start. The only thing that marred its success was a conflict between Paul and George Harrison over the guitar part.

PAUL: I remember sitting down and showing George the song and George did the natural thing for a guitar player to do, which is to answer every line of vocal. And it was like, 'No, George.' And he was pretty offended, and looking back, I think, Oh, shit, of course you'd be offended. You're blowing the guy out. I said, 'No, no. You come in on the second chorus maybe, it's going to be a big build this.'

That's the difficulty of a group. You are not the director bossing around a dance company where they naturally expect you to boss them around. You're just a guy in a very democratic unit; which a group, at best, is. We were all equal in voting, our status within the group was equal. We were joking when we made the *Anthology*: I was saying, 'I realise I was a bossy git.' And George said, 'Oh no, Paul, you never did anything like that!' With a touch of irony in his voice, because obviously I did. But it was essential for me and looking back on it, I think, Okay. Well, it was bossy, but it was also ballsy of me, because I could have bowed to the pressure.

'The Lovely Linda'

With Jane no longer even nominally resident, Cavendish Avenue
rapidly collapsed. In the living room a big jar of pot sat on the
mantelpiece, books and records piled up all over the floor and the
plywood model of the meditation dome became chipped and scarred
with cigarette burns, tiny tangles of dog hair sprouting from the
corners where Martha had pushed past. Miles recorded a visit some
time in 1968 in his journals. He and Paul had been discussing Zapple,
the proposed spoken-word label that Apple Records were going to
launch. At one point he and Paul were laughing loudly:

> A beautiful girl looked in to see what the laughter was about, but
> Paul said we were talking business and she left. There were
> several semi-clad girls walking about the house. 'It's terrible,' he
> said, gesturing. 'The birds are always quarrelling about some-
> thing. There's three living here at the moment.' The jostling for
> position must have been something to see. 'And there's another
> one, an American groupie, flying in this evening. I've thrown her
> out once, had to throw her suitcase over the wall, but it's no
> good, she keeps coming back.' He gave a resigned look and
> laughed.

Though he was not lacking female company, Paul was on the
lookout for someone special and already had his eye on Linda. Before
Jane walked out of his life, they had spent time together in both New
York and Los Angeles; now there was nothing to stop him from
inviting her over to stay. After a day of madness in the office, Paul
was getting fed up with a night of madness at home as well.

> LINDA: And then I got a phone call: 'Why don't you come over?'
> It was September. I remember Heather was just going to start
> Dalton and my parents were so furious with me. She got into
> Dalton. It would have been great. It was really good for Heather;
> I wish she had had that kind of life, instead of this crazy life.
> Dalton and then do well at school, go to university, whatever.
> But I had no feeling of responsibility, I must have been quite
> irresponsible to think that a five-year-old kid is starting school
> for the first time, and I'm buzzing off leaving her. It was one of
> those, 'Oh, can you stay with Ella for a few weeks? And not tell

anybody and not talk to anybody and I'll buzz off to London.' I was led to feel guilty by my parents, my father and stepmother.

I'm going to London now, so I get on the plane. I must have said something because somebody picked me up at the airport. I got there and I arrived at this house and it was a dark house, a lot of brown, a lot of dark colours, a bachelor's house, a man's house. I remember nothing worked, the TV barely worked, the stereo was broken, nothing worked. I remember the green velvet settee, which I called a couch at the time. But it could still be there, it hasn't changed that much. I remember seeing Apple white labels piled up, the Brenells, you could see that Paul was totally into making music.

I didn't know how long I was staying. I arrived that night, I remember the lights, I didn't know the house. I remember lying on the settee and just meditating. It was so quiet I could hear the fridge turn on and the motor run. There was nothing in it and I'm a real picker of food, but there was nothing in it. I think there was a Findus steak.

But I was in somebody else's house, somebody I didn't even know that well. This was like a freaky experience but I took it in my stride because I did a lot of things like that through this period. In fact, from the day I got divorced, it was like my life again and I took advantage of it.

PAUL: We re-met in a pretty funky way. I said, 'Come on over, then,' and she arrived the night when we were doing 'Happiness Is a Warm Gun'. She arrived at the house and phoned, and I had Mal go round to check that she was all right. She remembers the fridge had half a bottle of sour milk and a crust of cheese, a real British fridge. She just couldn't believe the conditions I was living in.

Paul got in very late. The sessions for 'Happiness Is a Warm Gun' were booked between 23 and 26 September 1968 from 7.00 p.m. until 2.00 a.m. but they tended to run on through the night and the mono mix of the song was made between 5.00 and 6.15 a.m. on the 25th.

LINDA: I stayed for a few weeks, while they were finishing the White Album. In the beginning I didn't go to the studio a lot. I didn't feel right. I went a lot when they were mixing it and took a lot of pictures. What I liked about Paul when I lived there in London was the books that were around and painting. Paul would say, 'Let's paint,' and he and Ivan Vaughan would get paints and go down in the basement and the three of us would paint on the canvas. It was fun. Paul is so much more cerebral than people think, because he was quote 'the cute Beatle'. I hate this 'Was it John or was it Paul?' thing because they were both talented. They were both artists. They are equal for number one.

PAUL: When we first met, it would be late at night after a session or something and I would be trying to unwind and so we would go for a drive around London in the late-night clear streets, two in the morning or something, and she'd say, 'Try and get lost.' And I'd say, 'That goes against every fibre in my body. As a driver, the one thing you never try and do is get lost!' She said, 'Try it.' And I'd try it; 'For you I'll try it.' So I'd turn off little streets round Battersea and down little back streets – 'Hey, this is great' – but pretty soon you'd see a big sign, 'West End'. Signs everywhere. It's actually very difficult to get lost round London. We used to end up in the greatest of places that I'd never been to before. We never did get lost. So that kind of freedom was part of our thing; still is, actually.

The song 'Two of Us' on the *Let It Be* album was written on one of these drives after Linda came to live in London. They bundled Martha into the back seat and drove the Aston Martin out beyond Esher and Weybridge to the country near Cobham where the M25 motorway now rings London, picking up sandwiches on the way. They found a side road and drove down it, found another side road and tried to get as remote and away from it all as possible. They found a secluded spot to park near a wood and Linda got out to take some photographs. One of her pictures shows the song actually being composed: Paul with a day's growth of stubble, wearing a white open-necked shirt and his $10 thrift-shop herringbone coat, sitting half in the driver's seat, strumming his acoustic guitar.

PAUL: We'd just enjoy sitting out in nature. And this song was about that: doing nothing, trying to get lost. It's a favourite of mine because it reminds me of that period, getting together with Linda, and the wonderfully free attitude we were able to have. I had my guitar with me and I wrote it out on the road, and then maybe finished some of the verses at home later, but that picture is of me writing it.

A couple of things really struck me about her: I liked her as a woman, she was good-looking with a good figure and so physically I was attracted to her, but her mental attitude was, and still is, quite rebellious because she was brought up in this rather lofty, well-to-do world. It wasn't huge conspicuous wealth, but relative to me it was huge wealth. She was the kind of kid who would hang out in the kitchen with the black maids, learning to cook, and she didn't like all the socialising, 'Hello, how are you, I'm the younger daughter of the family.' She used to keep out of the way of all that, so to this day she doesn't like big, rich, empty houses. There was a lot of that where she came from. She was more likely to go on to the empty plot behind the big rich house when the big rich people didn't know she was there in the woods and up-end rocks looking for salamanders. This was one of the big things we had in common because I used to do a lot of that when I was a kid, we both shared a love of nature. That became one of our big links.

Linda had this wonderful free attitude. She used to hate the word 'compromise' and she hated the word 'cope', she never really had to deal with those words and she had been a very free spirit all her life. She'd been a bit of a rebel at home and something of a black sheep as far as education was concerned, whereas her family had all been extremely academic. She was an artist and was not cut out to be an academic.

Linda allowed Paul to be Paul Everyman, not the famous Beatle but a person.

PAUL: I remember very early on apologising because I was so tired, I said, 'I'm really tired, I'm sorry.' She said, 'It's allowed.' I remember thinking, Fucking hell! That was a mind-blower. I'd never been with anyone who'd thought like that: 'It's allowed.' And it was quite patently clear that it was allowed to be tired. I think I'd trained myself never to appear tired. Always to be on the ball. 'Sorry I'm yawning. I'm sorry,' which is complete bullshit. It's a Beatles thing, you had to be there, you had to be on time.

Zapple

With the record label established, the Beatles now turned their attention to Zapple, intended as the home for experimental and spoken-word releases. It was named by John Lennon, not, as Frank Zappa thought, after him, but in the same spirit that the original name was chosen: 'A is for Apple. Z is for Zapple' – the other end of the alphabet. It was essentially an extension of the experimental demo studio that Paul had set up with the help of Ian Sommerville in Ringo's old flat back in the spring of 1966. Paul saw Zapple as the point of connection between Apple and Indica Bookshop and he and John appointed Miles as the *de facto* label manager. The idea was to issue a series of very cheap spoken-word albums, possibly monthly like a magazine. Miles prepared a list of people to record, most of whom were in the USA, and took it over to Cavendish Avenue in November 1968. 'Great!' said Paul. 'Get it together! Get an assistant and go out there and record them.'

The original list included Allen Ginsberg, Lawrence Ferlinghetti, Michael McClure, Richard Brautigan, Charles Olson, Kenneth Patchen, Henry Miller, Charles Bukowski, William Burroughs, Simon Vinkenoog, Ed Sanders, Ken Kesey, Anaïs Nin, Aram Saroyan, Anne Waldman, with a note to look into the possibility of reissuing Lord Buckley and Lenny Bruce. It was enough to keep the label going for a while. Not every album would necessarily be devoted to just one person's work; the idea was sometimes to record a live reading featuring a number of poets, like the Poetry Project group around St Marks Church in New York, or the Liverpool Scene group of Adrian Henri, Brian Patten, Roger McGough and so on.

Nor was it intended to concentrate entirely on poetry and literature: electronic music, avant-garde performances, lectures, anything off-beat, Beat, experimental or strange would be considered. One idea was to record the thoughts of various world leaders, and large packages of Beatles albums and Apple releases were shipped off to Mao Tse Tung, Fidel Castro, Indira Gandhi and others, together with an invitation to record a spoken-word album explaining their philosophy to a worldwide audience of young people. Another idea was to record conversations: William Burroughs discussing drugs; the Beatles discussing their latest album. Paul thought the latter notion was a good one because it could be obviously tied in with publicity. In the days before bootleg records, it prefigured the idea of journalists releasing interview tapes as records, which began with David Wigg's *The Beatles Tapes* in 1976. The poets, however, were seen as the easiest way to get the system in place. Miles left for New York in January 1969 to record the first batch.

The first album recorded was of the poet Charles Olson reading from his new book *Maximus IV, V, VI,* as well as parts of the *Mayan Letters* and other works. It was made over a five-day period at Charles's house in Gloucester, Massachusetts, recording at night, because Olson never got up before 6 p.m. and also because it was quiet then and the recording would not be spoiled by the sound of trucks gunning and slithering their way through the deep snowdrifts of the New England winter. Olson died a year later and this was the only 'studio' album he ever made.

Next came Ken Weaver, the drummer with the Fugs and a brilliant raconteur. He planned an album of Texspeak: homilies, humour and bar talk in a Texas accent. Much of the material recorded appeared in his 1984 book *Texas Crude. The How-To on Talkin' Texan.* Tuli Kupferberg, the percussionist with the Fugs, already had an album out of his readings from bizarre advertisements, and the remaining Fug, Ed Sanders, was down for a future poetry album.

Charles Bukowski was still working at the Post Office in January 1969 and was still virtually unknown. He had not yet done any public readings and was nervous of reading with anyone around. Because of this, a field recording was made: Miles set up a professional tape recorder and microphone in his living room in a run-down section of Los Angeles, showed him how to use it and left him a pile of blank tapes. A week later he had filled them all, and accidentally erased some by trying to record 'on the other side'. It was his first professional recording.

Meanwhile, John and Yoko had been thinking about the series and sent a telegram asking if Gregory Corso and Diane di Prima could be added to the list. They were both well-known Beat Generation poets but the suggestion obviously came from Yoko.

Three studio recordings were made at Golden State Recorders on Harrison Street in San Francisco. One was of the Beat poet Lawrence Ferlinghetti, owner of City Lights Books and publisher of Allen Ginsberg's *Howl*. In the fifties Ferlinghetti had made some pioneering records of poetry with jazz and his 1958 book *A Coney Island of the Mind* was the biggest-selling poetry book in the USA, having sold more than 500,000 copies. Lawrence's work is designed more for reading aloud than for the page, so this was a good opportunity for him to get his recent work out.

Michael McClure was originally selected on the strength of his 'Lion Poem', where he roared at the lions in the San Francisco Zoo and they roared back; a very powerful recording that Miles planned to include on the album. Michael now decided that he wanted to make an album with Freewheelin' Frank of the Hell's Angels with himself playing an autoharp given to him by Bob Dylan, and Frank banging a tambourine and reading his satanic poetry. Unfortunately Frank insisted on having his chopper with him in the studio, causing one or two delays in the recording.

Richard Brautigan recorded a selection of poems and stories, often giving the words a heightened reality with sound effects – a stereo recording of the actual stream referred to in 'Trout Fishing in America', for instance. Hours of tape of Richard talking on the telephone and sitting around the kitchen drinking beer with his buddy Price were recorded. The resulting album was called *Listening to Richard Brautigan*. Each poet had signed a contract issued by Ron Kass and all that remained was to edit the tapes.

Zapple was launched on 3 February 1969. A press release from Jim Mahoney & Association, Public Relations Company of Los Angeles, explained what the Beatles intended the new label to do:

> Beatles to introduce Zapple, new label and recording concept, on May 1. The label will be called Zapple and it will emphasize a series of 'spoken word' albums and some music releases of a more wide-ranging and esoteric nature. Price of the Zapple albums will generally be $1.98 or $4.98 depending on the type of release.
>
> Zapple will be a division of Apple Records, which is headed by Ron Kass, who is also chief executive for all Apple music activities. Supervising the Zapple program will be Barry Miles, a British writer-intellectual in his late 20s.
>
> The first three releases on the Zapple label are now being pressed and include:

1. A new John Lennon–Yoko Ono album entitled *Unfinished Music No.2 – Life With The Lions*;

2. A George Harrison composed-produced electronic music album which was recorded with a Moog;

3. A spoken-word album recorded by poet-writer Richard Brautigan.

Other well-known writer-poets already committed to Zapple releases include: Lawrence Ferlinghetti – America's best selling 'serious' poet; poet-playwright Michael McClure; veteran literary figures Kenneth Patchen and Charles Olson and poet-essayist Allen Ginsberg. Additionally, Zapple will release one of the late Lenny Bruce's last concerts as an album.

It is the hope of Apple Corps Ltd. that the new label will help pioneer a new area for the recording industry equivalent to what the paperback revolution did to book publishing.

The company is now studying new market ideas for the label, which it hopes to eventually retail in outlets where paperback books and magazines are sold. University and College outlets will also be emphasized in Zapple's distribution plans.

Discussions are now in progress with several world figures as well as leaders in the various arts and sciences to record their works and thoughts for the label. The Beatles plan to tape several discussion sessions amongst themselves as an album release – probably for the fall. It is assumed that Zapple will have little difficulty attracting those people who might not normally record albums because of the general educational tone of the project ...

In December 1968, Ken Kesey, the author of *One Flew Over the Cuckoo's Nest*, arrived at Apple. He and the Merry Pranksters had travelled America in his psychedelic bus driven by Neal Cassady, organising the famous Acid Test dances and attempting to blow everyone's mind. Kesey was accompanied by two Hell's Angels – Frisco Pete and Billy Tumbleweed – plus sixteen hangers-on who had been told by George Harrison in San Francisco that Apple would look after them. They were expected because George Harrison had sent round a memo:

Hell's Angels will be in London within the next week on the way to straighten out Czechoslovakia. There will be 12 in number, complete with black leather jackets and motorcycles. They will undoubtedly arrive at Apple and I have heard that they might try to make full use of Apple's facilities. They may look as if they are going to do you in but are very straight and do good things, so don't fear them or uptight them. Try to assist them without neglecting your Apple business and without letting them take control of Savile Row. December 4, 1968.

Derek Taylor lent Kesey a tape recorder and told him to go out and record a street diary of his visit to London, but because Miles was in the USA, no one was there to encourage him or give him direction, and the project went nowhere though the tape recorder did. Two gleaming Harley-Davidsons had preceded the arrival of Frisco Pete and Billy Tumbleweed by air freight at a cost to Apple of £250, and were now parked in Savile Row, attracting curious glances from the gentlemen on their way to be measured for suits identical to the ones they were already wearing. The Angels and their hangers-on took over the Apple guest lounge and hung out, terrifying people and drinking the place dry. Everyone was too scared to tell them they couldn't live there indefinitely, so George Harrison, who had not yet visited his guests, finally came into the office and pointedly asked them when they would be leaving. They got the picture and left peaceably, taking only a few souvenirs.

The guest lounge was also home to a family of American hippies: Emily, her husband Frank and their four children. Emily had received a psychic message during an acid trip instructing her to take John and Yoko to Fiji, and was camping out at Apple until John and Yoko had time to see her. Shirley and Janet from the kitchen refused to enter the room because Emily spent most of her time naked. It was hard to run an efficient record company when several dozen Americans were using the second floor as a crash pad and there was a permanent party going on.

The plug was finally pulled on Zapple by Allen Klein while Miles was in the middle of a second recording trip to America. Two tracks of what would eventually become *Allen Ginsberg Tunes William Blake's Songs of Innocence and Experience* had already been recorded at Capitol studios, New York, when overnight the label ceased to exist. John and Yoko's *Unfinished Music* and George's *Electronic Music* had been released. *Listening to Richard Brautigan* had reached acetate stage and a sample sleeve had been made up. It was eventually released on EMI-Harvest in America with a modified sleeve. Charles Olson's album was released after his death on Folkways Records. Some of Ferlinghetti's tracks later surfaced on Fantasy Records, but the album as originally planned was never released. The label was folded before the Michael McClure, Ken Weaver and Charles Bukowski tapes could be edited. The two Allen Ginsberg tracks were frozen in Capitol's tape vaults so Ginsberg began his album over again in an independent studio with Miles producing. This time it was leased to MGM Records, which by then had Ron Kass as its chief executive and Peter Asher as its A & R man.

Apple can be seen to divide into three phases. The first, the original vision, involved an Apple Foundation, the Apple School and other fanciful organisations. This initial phase was based at Baker Street above the boutique and was seen mainly as a way of avoiding tax. Close on a million pounds was spent on the Apple boutique, Apple Electronics, and buying and fitting up Savile Row. Money flowed out of Apple like a river for trips to New York, expensive lunches, air fares and top-of-the-line office equipment. The two other distinct phases can be labelled as pre- and post-Allen Klein. Before Allen Klein, Hell's Angels, mystics and musicians were encouraged to hang out and join the fun, and Paul was the only Beatle who attempted to economise and control spending. Post-Allen Klein came when their accountants pointed out how bad the situation was, causing the other Beatles to panic and get in Klein to clean up the act.

The Beatles managed to avoid most of the day-to-day madness of Apple by first going to India, then disappearing into Abbey Road to record *The Beatles*, or the White Album, as it is universally known. In the early days of Savile Row, Paul was the Beatle most often seen in the building, in part because he was the only one who could just hop on a bus to get there. Apple had always been more of Paul and John's baby than George and Ringo's, but by the time Apple Records was up and running, John was distracted by his new, all-consuming love affair with Yoko and had no time to produce anyone else's records even though he and Yoko were by then living in Ringo's flat in Montagu Square, quite close to Apple. Until the autumn of 1968 they only appeared at Savile Row for business meetings. Mostly they sat in their basement, utterly absorbed in each other, living on champagne, heroin and caviar in what John described as 'a strange cocktail of love, sex and forgetfulness'.

Over at Apple, it didn't take long for Paul to identify a tremendous drain on resources: anything not bolted down was immediately stolen and one of the office boys was even caught stealing the lead off the roof, dragging it out of the building in mail sacks and passing it to an accomplice parked up the road. Paul particularly objected to the permanent party going on in Derek Taylor's press office. Most bands made do with an independent press officer to represent them: the Rolling Stones, for instance, used Les Perrin's office, but the Beatles were running their own record company and were responsible for promoting the other acts on Apple as well as themselves. It is true that the Apple press office quickly became a haven for Fleet Street hacks, drunken rock journalists and underground press writers who dropped by for a quick joint. The drink and drugs bill was astronomical; as the December 1968 in-house magazine slyly commented, 'Lebanese export companies, we learn, are pleased by the amount of business we are putting their way.' However, the cost of the press department was as nothing compared to the entertainment expenses of some of the directors, who were known to spend thousands of dollars for a few days at a top New York hotel, or the Beatles' own expenses. For instance, whenever John and Yoko visited, Yoko ordered a pot of caviar costing £60, about five weeks' wages for one of the cooks who served it.

The work of the press office was not restricted to publicity: Derek, his two assistants and the 'house hippie' were also used by the Beatles every time they wanted something done. Someone had to blow up 400 balloons for John and Yoko's show at the Robert Fraser Gallery; the house hippie was dispatched to spend the day at Duke Street. John and Yoko wanted to send two acorns to every world leader as a peace gesture; John asked the press office to get them. The problem was, it was the wrong time of year for acorns. Weeks were spent digging in Hyde Park and Regents Park to find acorns hidden by squirrels for the winter, and many that were found were mouldy. In desperation they appealed to the public. Someone offered to sell them some at £1 each. Special boxes had to be bought, labels printed, addresses found ...

There was only one really noticeable cut-back in press-office expenses. The nameless in-house magazine they published was terminated after just two issues when Derek violated confidentiality by printing a bunch of inter-office memos, including one referring to a Swiss bank account.

PAUL: We just didn't know how to run it. I had theories but they were too mill-owner for everyone. I tried to cut down on the staff, which is what any sensible person would have done, but the era was not a cut-down-on-the-staff era; the massive cut-backs and the belt-tightening came later. I wanted Apple to run; I didn't want to run Apple. I wanted Apple to be reasonably efficient and to take in more money than it was spending, but even though we had 'Hey Jude', 'Let It Be' and 'Those Were the Days' and big successes like that, our spending more than matched it. I just saw it as a recipe for disaster and in fact that's what it was.

That period for me felt like I was in an *Alice in Wonderland* scenario. I would say, 'Now what's to be done here? Ah, I know, cut spending.' That would start in my brain as a reasonable assumption but by the time it reached my mouth, it was like the devil was speaking. It was like a traitorous utterance. I once did try and get rid of one of the secretaries in Derek's place. She was a very nice-looking girl, that was the problem, I probably should have chosen someone not as good-looking. I said, 'Look, Derek, you really don't need however many secretaries it was, this is really just the press club. It's like an annexe to a Fleet Street bar. And people are just coming in here to hear you pronounce on this and that, and the drinks bill for the press office!' But immediately George came into the office: 'You're not going to do that. You can't do that!' 'But we're losing money. We've got to do something!' 'No, you're not doing it, and if you do, we'll immediately reinstate her.'

So I started to think my logic was suspect and that to try and make money was a suspect act. It was a rather uncommunist thing to do, an ignoble thing to try and make it work. And anything I said seemed to come out wrong. I really couldn't say anything without feeling I was being devious. And yet I knew I wasn't.

I remember saying something to John once. He was doing his finances funny, and he'd been charging personal stuff to Apple.

Someone warned me that he was going to get into a real problem and I remember saying to him, 'Look, I'm not trying to do anything, I'm really trying to help you ...' and as I said it I heard my devilish voice, like 'I'm trying to trick you!' I said, 'Look, John. I'm right.' And he said, 'You fucking would be, wouldn't you? You're always right, aren't you?' So to be right was wrong! He admitted I was right but to be right didn't bring any rewards, it brought scorn, and so it became very very difficult to do anything, it really just became impossible, so I started to get very very nervous and paranoid about everything.

During the third phase, post-Allen Klein, everything was turned upside down. The money tap was turned off. Half the staff lost their jobs and the remaining employees were fearful. Ron Kass was fired and John and Yoko established themselves in his newly vacated office on the ground floor and began their peace campaign, allowing anyone who wanted to interview them to do so. Paul bowed out and spent most of his time with Linda and their first child together, Mary. They had an extended vacation before Mary's birth, and retired to Scotland not long after it, leaving Apple in the hands of John, Yoko and John's latest guru, Allen Klein.

TWELVE

THE WHITE ALBUM

Celebrity is a mask that eats into the face.

John Updike, 'Self-Consciousness'

Five Months at Abbey Road

THE BEATLES WERE APPLE'S GREATEST ASSET, AND THEY BEGAN recording their first album for their own label not long after the record division was set up. There had not been a proper Beatles album since *Sgt. Pepper*. *Magical Mystery Tour* had only six new tracks and didn't really count. There had also been a soundtrack album to the cartoon film *Yellow Submarine*, but that only had two new Beatles tracks on it: Paul's 'All Together Now' and John's 'Hey Bulldog'.

'All Together Now' was a number in the music-hall tradition.

PAUL: When they were singing a song, to encourage the audience to join in they'd say 'All together now!' so I just took it and read another meaning into it, of we are all together now. So I used the dual meaning. It's really a children's song. I had a few young relatives and I would sing songs for them. I used to do a song for kids called 'Jumping Round the Room', very similar to 'All Together Now', and then it would be 'lying on your backs', all the kids would have to lie down, then it would be 'skipping round the room', 'jumping in the air'. It's a play away command song for children. It would be in G, very very simple chords, only a couple of chords, so that's what this is. There's a little subcurrent to it but it's just a sing-along really. A bit of a throwaway.

I remember 'Hey Bulldog' as being one of John's songs and I

helped him finish it off in the studio, but it's mainly his vibe. There's a little rap at the end between John and I, we went into a crazy little thing at the end. We always tried to make every song different because we figured, Why write something like the last one? We've done that. We were always on a staircase to heaven, we were on a ladder so there was never any sense of stepping down a rung, or even of staying on the same rung, it was better to move one rung ahead. That's why we had strange drum sounds using tables and tops of packing cases. We'd say to Ringo, 'We heard that snare on the last song.' Whereas now, a drummer just sets up for a whole album, he keeps the same sound for his whole career! But we liked to be inventive. It seemed to us to be crucial to never do the same thing twice, in fact, as they say now, 'They never did the same thing once!'

The Beatles, or the White Album as fans usually call it, was eagerly awaited: how could they top *Sgt. Pepper*? The answer was to go in the other direction: from an exciting, cluttered sleeve, bursting with energy and dense imagery, to the clean serenity of a pure white cover, printed only with a number and a small embossed name. The shining blank double sleeve was a precursor of the other famous white double album, the world's first rock 'n' roll bootleg, *Great White Wonder* by Bob Dylan. Similarly, instead of the long, self-conscious title *Sgt. Pepper's Lonely Hearts Club Band*, they went for the ultimate reduction: *The Beatles*, an album title that, oddly enough, they had not used before. And the contents, though not as extreme a contrast as Bob Dylan's switch from the amphetamine-driven *Blonde on Blonde* to the austere country of *John Wesley Harding*, had a starkness and simplicity which showed both their maturity and experience as composers and, for about half of the songs, the calm and sober conditions under which they were composed in India. Even the experimental tracks, of which there were many, were approached with the confidence and directness of old hands at the game.

The four sides contained thirty new songs: a huge amount of material, too much for the critics to digest at once because as usual each track was treated as a separate unit and given its most suitable arrangement and instrumentation, varying from string quartet to heavy rock combo. The Beatles never just played their way through an album's worth of new songs as a four-piece rock band in the way the Stones and most other groups did. This is part of what made them unique.

Recording began on the 30 May 1968, with John's 'Revolution 1', which was then just called 'Revolution', a simple little pop tune with its political lyrics rendered unthreatening by the use of a corny doo-wop chorus and a brass section playing Beach Boys style chords. This was the first of John's three songs with 'Revolution' in the title. The ending of this slow ballad was so drawn out that John cut it off and used the last six minutes as the basic track for the notorious sound collage 'Revolution 9'. 'Revolution 9' is probably more of a Yoko Ono record than a Beatles track, though it has some similarities to the fourteen-minute 'Carnival of Light' tape that Paul had made with the Beatles eighteen months before, and uses his loop-tapes technique.

John told *Playboy*: 'It was somewhat under [Yoko's] influence I suppose. Once I heard her stuff – not just the screeching and howling but her sort of word pieces and talking and breathing and all this strange stuff – I thought "My God". I got intrigued, so I wanted to do one.' Yoko had performed many times with John Cage in New York and was very familiar with this type of work.

Paul was in New York when 'Revolution 9' was made and George and Ringo's only contribution was to shout a few words which are buried in the mix. Three years later, when John was in his Maoist political phase, he described his intentions, saying, 'I thought I was painting in sound a picture of revolution – but I made a mistake. The mistake was that it was anti-revolution.' He was being interviewed by the left-wing theoreticians Tariq Ali and Robin Blackburn for *Red Mole*, so he probably tailored his explanation to what he thought they would like to hear. It is hard to see how the track related to revolution, one way or another, since it is the type of sound collage that avant-garde poets and composers had been making for the previous twenty years, combining fragments of conversations usually panned across the stereo arc, bits of symphonies, loop tapes, talking and shouting, usually with full echo. It sounds very much like a home tape and would probably have been on a John and Yoko solo album like *Two Virgins* had it been recorded a little later. The other Beatles and George Martin all tried their best to persuade John to leave it off the album. Thus the personality problems which were to dog this album, caused largely by John's insistence that Yoko be always at his side, and Yoko's unwanted comments on the songs, were endent from the very beginning of the sessions

John's description of the making of 'Revolution 9' sounds similar to the way Paul's solo on 'Tomorrow Never Knows' was made. He told *Playboy*:

> It has the basic rhythm of the original 'Revolution' going on with some twenty loops we put on, things from the archives of EMI. We were cutting up classical music and making different size loops, and then I got an engineer tape on which some test engineer was saying, 'Number nine, number nine, number nine.' All those different bits of sound and noises are all compiled. There were about ten machines with people holding pencils on the loops – some only inches long and some a yard long. I fed them all in and mixed them live. I did a few mixes until I got one I liked. Yoko was there for the whole thing and she made decisions about which loops to use.

The song, just called 'Revolution', which was used as the B side of 'Hey Jude', was faster than the doo-wop version and recorded with maximum volume and distortion with all the VU meters jammed over in the red. It was originally planned as the A side of their first Apple Records release, but, much to John's chagrin, 'Hey Jude' was voted more likely to succeed. Both the slow and fast versions had the same set of lyrics.

> PAUL: It was a great song, basically John's. He doesn't really get off the fence in it. He says you can count me out, in, so you're not actually sure. I don't think he was sure which way he felt about it at the time, but it was an overtly political song about revolution and a great one. I think John later ascribed more political intent to it than he actually felt when he wrote it.
>
> They were very political times, obviously, with the Vietnam war going on, Chairman Mao and the Little Red Book, and all the demonstrations with people going through the streets shouting 'Ho, Ho, Ho Chi Minh!' I think he wanted to say you can count me in for a revolution, but if you go carrying pictures of Chairman Mao 'you ain't gonna make it with anyone anyhow'. By saying that I think he meant we all want to change the world Maharishi-style, because 'Across the Universe' also

had the change-the-world theme. I remember John talking to Maharishi about it and Maharishi wanted more optimism, 'Meditation will change your world,' he didn't want 'nothing's going to change your world,' that sounded too negative. But we refused to do that because it sounded better the other way. But 'Revolution' was obviously a highly political song and a great one. John was just hedging his bets, covering all eventualities. The album version was a really good recording, the hottest recording we ever did. It's good that it comes right after 'Helter Skelter' because those two qualify as the most raucous Beatles songs on record.

Paul wrote 'Blackbird' at his farm in Scotland. Shortly afterwards, on a warm summer night back in London, he sat next to the open window of his top-floor music room and sang the song, accompanying himself on acoustic guitar. For the fans gathered in the darkness beyond his gates this unwitting free concert was the sort of magical moment that made their vigil worthwhile.

PAUL: The original inspiration was from a well-known piece by Bach, which I never know the title of, which George and I had learned to play at early age; he better than me actually. Part of its structure is a particular harmonic thing between the melody and the bass line which intrigued me. Bach was always one of our favourite composers; we felt we had a lot in common with him. For some reason we thought his music was very similar to ours and we latched on to him amazingly quickly. We also liked the stories of him being the church organist and wopping this stuff out weekly, which was rather similar to what we were doing. We were very pleased to hear that.

I developed the melody on guitar based on the Bach piece and took it somewhere else, took it to another level, then I just fitted the words to it. I had in mind a black woman, rather than a bird. Those were the days of the civil-rights movement, which all of us cared passionately about, so this was really a song from me to a black woman, experiencing these problems in the States: 'Let me encourage you to keep trying, to keep your faith, there is hope.' As is often the case with my things, a veiling took place so, rather than say 'Black woman living in Little Rock' and be very specific, she became a bird, became symbolic, so you could apply it to your particular problem.

This is one of my themes: take a sad song and make it better, let this song help you. 'Empowerment' is a good word for it. Through the years I have had lots of wonderful letters from people saying, 'That song really helped me through a terrible period.' I think that the single greatest joy of having been a musician, and been in the Beatles, is when those letters come back to you and you find that you've really helped people. That's the magic of it all, that's the wonder, because I wrote them with half an idea that they might help, but it really makes me feel very proud when I realise that they have been of actual help to people.

The blackbird itself was taken from an ornithological record in the EMI sound archives. Paul: 'He did a very good job, I thought. He sings very well on that.'

'Everybody's Got Something to Hide Except Me and My Monkey' very much reflected the early days of John and Yoko's life together at Montagu Square. It was one of John's more experimental songs, but still retained the confessional element that characterised much of his best work. When he and Yoko appeared in public together for the first time, on 15 June, the press had a feeding frenzy and more or less camped out in Montagu Square. John and Yoko spent a few days at Cavendish Avenue in order to get away from them, spending their evenings quietly watching television or, on one occasion, eating hash cookies that Yoko baked. Paul was often out in the evenings. He and John still felt a deep friendship between them, but Paul felt uncomfortable around John and Yoko because they were so focused on each other to the exclusion of everyone else. Their drug use also made communication difficult. It was around this time that 'Everybody's Got Something to Hide Except Me and My Monkey' was recorded. 'Monkey' or 'monkey on the back' was forties and fifties jazz-musician argot for heroin addiction.

PAUL: He was getting into harder drugs than we'd been into and so his songs were taking on more references to heroin. Until that point we had made rather mild, rather oblique references to pot or LSD. Now John started to be talking about fixes and monkeys and it was a harder terminology which the rest of us weren't into. We were disappointed that he was getting into heroin because we didn't really see how we could help him. We just hoped it wouldn't go too far. In actual fact, he did end up clean but this was the period when he was on it. It was a tough period for John, but often that adversity and that craziness can lead to good art, as I think it did in this case.

You could almost be forgiven for thinking 'Good Night' was mine, because it's so soft and melodic and so un-John. I believe John wrote this as a lullaby for Julian, and it was a very beautiful song that Ringo ended up singing to the accompaniment of a big string orchestra. I think John felt it might not be good for his image for him to sing it but it was fabulous to hear him do it, he sang it great. We heard him sing it in order to teach it to Ringo and he sang it very tenderly. John rarely showed his tender side, but my key memories of John are when he was tender, that's what has remained with me; those moments where he showed himself to be a very generous, loving person. I always cite that song as an example of the John beneath the surface that we only saw occasionally. I think that was what made us love John, otherwise he could be unbearable and he could be quite cruel. Now that I'm older, I realise that his hostility was a cover-up for the vulnerability that he felt, and if you look at his family history it's easy to see why. But this is an example of that tender side. I don't think John's version was ever recorded.

George Martin's Hollywood arrangement, which uses a large string section and the Mike Sammes Singers, is perfect for this sentimental ballad. Ringo is the only Beatle on the track.

'Cry Baby Cry' was another of John's songs from India. 'Because John had divorced Cynthia and gone off with Yoko,' Paul explained, 'it meant that I'd hear some of the songs for the first time when he came to the studio, whereas in the past we checked them with each other.' This was an example of such a song. John described it as 'a piece of rubbish' and said he got the lyric from an advertisement but Paul liked it.

Paul came up with the idea for 'Helter Skelter' in Scotland after reading an interview with Pete Townshend in which he described the Who's new single, 'I Can See for Miles', as the loudest, rawest, dirtiest and most uncompromising song they had ever done.

PAUL: I was always trying to write something different, trying to not write in character, and I read this and I was inspired, Oh, wow! Yeah! Just that one little paragraph was enough to inspire me; to make me make a move. So I sat down and wrote 'Helter Skelter' to be the most raucous vocal, the loudest drums, et cetera et cetera. I was using the symbol of a helter skelter as a ride from the top to the bottom – the rise and fall of the Roman Empire – and this was the fall, the demise, the going down. You could have thought of it as a rather cute title but it's since taken on all sorts of ominous overtones because Manson picked it up as an anthem, and since then quite a few punk bands have done it because it is a raunchy rocker.

I went into the studio and said, 'Hey, look, I've read this thing. Let's do it!' We got the engineers and George Martin to hike up the drum sound and really get it as loud and horrible as it could and we played it and said, 'No, it still sounds too safe, it's got to get louder and dirtier.' We tried everything we could to dirty it up and in the end you can hear Ringo say, 'I've got blisters on my fingers.' That wasn't a joke put-on: his hands were actually bleeding at the end of the take, he'd been drumming so ferociously. We did work very hard on that track. Unfortunately it inspired people to evil deeds.

Charles Manson, the psychopathic killer responsible for seven murders including that of the actress Sharon Tate, blamed LSD and the Beatles' White Album for the series of killings his 'Family' committed in August 1969. Manson was obsessed with the Beatles and, like many disturbed Beatles fans, thought they were directing secret messages to him via their songs. In Manson's case, he thought the messages were ordering him to kill, and that 'Helter Skelter' was the uprising in which blacks would murder a third of the world's population. It was also the name his followers used for a murder spree. In his rambling statement at the conclusion of his murder trial on 19 November 1970, he told the judge and jury:

Like, Helter Skelter is a nightclub. Helter Skelter means confusion. Literally. It doesn't mean any war with anyone. It doesn't mean that those people are going to kill other people. It only means what it means. Helter Skelter is confusion. Confusion is coming down fast. If you don't see the confusion coming down fast, you can call it what you wish. It's not my conspiracy. It is not my music. I hear what it relates. It says 'Rise!' It says 'Kill!' Why blame it on me? I didn't write the music. I am not the person who projected it into your social consciousness.

There were five tracks on the White Album that Manson played more than others: 'Blackbird', 'Piggies', 'Revolution 1', 'Revolution 9' and 'Helter Skelter', though for Manson virtually every one of the thirty tracks brimmed with hidden significance. Even the fact that the sleeve was white was prophetic.

Manson's interpretation of the Beatles' lyrics was a twisted affair also heavily dependent on the Book of Revelation of John 9, which he equated with John's 'Revolution 9'. In the biblical Revelation, St John says, 'So the four angels held were set loose to kill a third of mankind. They had been held ready for this moment, for this very year and month, day and hour ...' To Manson the Beatles were the four angels. At the beginning of Revelation 9, John sees an angel [star] fall to earth:

and the star was given the key of the shaft of the abyss. With this he opened the shaft of the abyss; and from the shaft smoke rose like smoke from a great furnace, and the sun and the air were darkened by the smoke from the shaft. Then over the earth, out of the smoke, came locusts ...

Locusts, in Manson's mind, meant beetles. The fallen angel with the key was, of course, himself. He had also found an abandoned mine shaft in the desert north of Los Angeles about which he span many a fancy tale to his brainwashed followers, claiming it was the shaft in Revelation 9. Manson's exegesis of Beatles lyrics was a supreme example of obsessional interpretation and would have been hilarious had the results not been so tragic. Manson taught his followers that the White Album prophesied that the black races would rise up and murder the whites but that Manson and his Family would be saved. To him, 'Rocky Raccoon' was about a 'coon', a black man. 'Happiness Is a Warm Gun' was the Beatles telling the blacks that the time had come to fight, and the lyrics to 'Blackbird' spelled it out even more clearly. With headphones on, Manson was able to hear the command to 'Rise!' hidden in the mix of John and Yoko's sound collage urging the blacks to rise up; in fact it was John shouting

'Right' from the original 'Revolution' tape. The white enemy was identified in 'Piggies', which is why the Family scrawled the words 'Death to Pigs' in blood on the wall after killing Rosemary and Leno LaBianca with knives and forks 'in the dead of night', and 'Pig' on the door of Sharon Tate's home. The words to 'Helter Skelter' showed Manson and the Family emerging from the shaft to take over after Armageddon. Manson expected the murders to be the long-awaited signal for the blacks to begin their bloody uprising and was surprised that riots did not follow.

Vincent Bugliosi, Deputy District Attorney for Los Angeles, whose book *Helter Skelter* is the standard work on the trial and Manson's cult, questioned Manson about his beliefs. 'We both know you ordered those murders,' he told him. 'Bugliosi,' Manson replied, 'it's the Beatles, the music they're putting out. They're talking about war. These kids listen to this music and pick up the message. It's subliminal.' It was complete madness.

> PAUL: I seem to remember writing 'Mother Nature's Son' at my dad's house in Liverpool. I often used to do that if I'd gone up to see him. Visiting my family I'd feel in a good mood, so it was often a good occasion to write songs. So this was me doing my mother nature's son bit. I've always loved the song called 'Nature Boy'; 'There was a boy, a very strange and gentle boy ...' He loves nature, and 'Mother Nature's Son' was inspired by that song. I'd always loved nature, and when Linda and I got together we discovered we had this deep love of nature in common. There might have been a little help from John with some of the verses.

By the third month of recording, tensions began to develop. George Martin was now working as an independent producer and was much in demand from other clients. As a consequence he was not always available and the Beatles found themselves essentially producing their own sessions. There were acrimonious exchanges with the studio staff and among themselves, and with no one in proper charge, the sessions drifted into pointless repetition of takes.

Though court proceedings to disband the Beatles did not begin until the last day of 1970, it is possible with hindsight to see that the real separation began during the recording of the White Album, at the very peak of their recording career, precipitated by the arrival of Allen Klein and by John's obsession with Yoko to the exclusion of the other three Beatles. John's insistence that Yoko accompany him everywhere, even when he went to the lavatory, exacerbated the hairline cracks in the group relationship, turning each one into a fissure. Beatles music was created in part by spontaneous magic: an almost telepathic sympathy for each other's musical sensibilities which enabled them to predict each other's response, gauge each other's ideas from hearing the most fragmentary musical reply as well as the usual hermetic language of signs and catch-words that musicians develop after playing with each other over a long period of time. Only Mal and Neil were allowed access to their protective Liverpool bubble; even George Martin could not penetrate without permission. The addition of Yoko to the sessions violated this space.

> JOHN: When I met Yoko is when you meet your first woman and you leave the guys at the bar and you don't go play football any more and you don't go play snooker and billiards. Maybe some guys like to do it every Friday night or something and continue that relationship with the boys, but once I found *the* woman, the boys became of no interest whatsoever, other than they were like old friends. You know, 'Hi, how are you? How's *your* wife?' ... The old gang of mine was over the moment I met her. I didn't consciously know it at the time, but that's what was going on. As soon as I met her, that was the end of the boys, but it so happened that the boys were well known and weren't just the local guys at the bar.

The main problem was that the other Beatles weren't just the guys at the bar, they were his colleagues at work as well. No one objected to Yoko socially – it was none of their business whom he went out with – but to bring her to work as well, every day, was a situation that most people, not just the Beatles, would not have tolerated.

John's heroin addiction made the recording of the White Album difficult because he was on edge, either going up or coming down. The other Beatles had to walk on eggshells just to avoid one of his explosive rages. Whereas in the old days they could have tackled him about the strain that Yoko's presence put on recording and had an old-fashioned set-to about it, now it was impossible because John was in such an unpredictable state and so obviously in pain. Yoko sat right next to him while he played, ordering Mal Evans to fetch her food and drinks and, worst of all, adding her unasked-for comments and musical suggestions, thoroughly inhibiting the other Beatles. Most of John's attention was focused upon her instead of the other three Beatles. The Fab Four had become the Fab Five without the other three ever being asked if they wanted a fifth Beatle. Yoko managed to irritate the other Beatles in a myriad of small ways. Paul: 'When she referred to the Beatles, she called them "Beatles": "Beatles will do this. Beatles will do that." We said, "*The* Beatles, actually, love." "Beatles will do this. Beatles will do that." I mean, she even took our personal pronoun off us, you know? [laughs]' Despite what John and Yoko later told reporters, it was not racism or sexism that made the others hate her; the fact is, anyone in that position would have made the other Beatles self-conscious and inhibited their musical spontaneity.

The reasons for John and Yoko's behaviour were obviously complex. Junkies sometimes need the close proximity of their drug partners in order to feel secure. During the latter part of recording the White Album, Yoko was pregnant, which is another reason why John wanted her by his side, but unfortunately she had a miscarriage on 21 November.

John got very bored working on 'Ob-La-Di Ob-La-Da', a song which he disliked intensely and which seemed to him to take too long. Even though outside musicians had been brought in to play a brass arrangement, Paul was not satisfied with the version they made and insisted on starting over again. The next day he began again from scratch but eventually decided the first remake was the best, featuring as it did John's loud blue-beat piano intro.

It has been said that this track was the cause of much acrimony but Paul has a different recollection:

PAUL: I remember being in the studio with George and Ringo, struggling with an acoustic version of the song. John was late for the session but when he arrived he bounced in, apologising, in a very good mood. He sat down at the piano and instantly played the blue-beat-style intro. We were very pleased with his fresh attitude. It turned us on and turned the whole song around. He and I worked hard on the vocals and I remember the two of us in the studio having a whale of a time.

'Ob-La-Di Ob-La-Da' was completed on 15 July and the next day the balance engineer Geoff Emerick, who had worked with them for years, quit because he could not stand the tension, arguments, swearing and bickering in the studio any longer.

The atmosphere improved a bit for the next few weeks while they recorded Ringo's 'Don't Pass Me By', John's 'Sexy Sadie', 'Good Night' and 'Everybody's Got Something to Hide Except Me and My Monkey'. Matters were helped by an interlude at Trident Studios in St Anne's Court in Soho to record 'Hey Jude'. The Beatles had used this independent studio to record Apple artists like James Taylor because Trident had an eight-track facility whereas, even in the summer of 1968, EMI was still plodding along with four tracks. (They had an eight-track which they were 'testing' but they had not told the Beatles about it in case they wanted to use it, tying it up for months.)

The epic project continued and more tracks were finished.

PAUL: When John first went with Yoko I think it focused his musical tastes and put a slightly more avant-garde slant on them, so that you were getting things like 'Happiness Is a Warm Gun' and 'Yer Blues'. We all liked blues but 'Yer Blues' was John's: John's lyrics, John's whole song as far as I recall. We were always looking for a different way to record things and next to the control room in number-two studio in Abbey Road where we were working there was a little tape room. It was quite a small room, about ten feet by four feet, a poky cupboard really that normally had tapes and microphone leads and jack plugs in it. And we said, 'Can we record in there?' And George Martin said, 'What, the whole band?' We said, 'Yes! Let's try it!' We'd always liked being on stage at the Cavern and places like that because small stages push you together as a band and you're shoulder to shoulder, instead of being spread out over a huge stadium stage where you wonder, 'Who is that playing guitar over there?' We liked being in close contact with each other, we felt it added to the power of our music, and it did.

The main worry engineers normally had was separation of instruments so that if later we wanted to hear more drums or a little less, we had control over it so we could pull it back or lift it. To do that you had to get separation from all the other instruments, otherwise you brought up the guitars when you brought up the drums. So they were worried about separation but what we did was turn the amplifiers to the wall and put a microphone in there, so we actually got amazing separation on them. Ringo came in with his drum kit and I had the bass and everything and we just played as a band. John just stood there and sang the vocal. He did a little work afterwards on the vocal but that was it; we actually did it shoulder to shoulder in this tiny little cupboard and it worked out very well. The engineers were surprised to find out how much separation they had. It was cool; I always remember that track for that.

On 7 August, they began work on George's 'Not Guilty'. After recording 46 takes, they finally packed it in at 5.30 in the morning. The next day they reached take 101, the first time they had passed the hundred mark. After two more days' work on the track and a preliminary mix, it was abandoned and was not heard of again until George's 1979 solo *George Harrison* album. Shortly afterwards, George upped and left for Greece without telling the others, causing them to cancel a session at short notice and reschedule work while he was away.

At the same time, Paul and John were having words and a very frosty atmosphere developed between them, possibly over a song called 'What's the New Mary Jane', a heavily Yoko-inspired track that John said he co-wrote with Magic Alex. John and George were the only Beatles playing on it. It is a discordant meandering tune that goes nowhere but probably sounds good if you are very high. The basic song has certain similarities to 'You Know My Name, Look Up the Number' but perhaps lacks its humour and sophistication. Most of the six-minutes-plus track is taken up with a long ending, similar to 'Revolution 9', featuring Yoko's 'voice modulation' and a lot of random noodling on the piano. John tried to release it a year later as a Plastic Ono Band track 'backed by a group' but the other Beatles would not allow him. Considering Paul's opposition to the inclusion of 'Revolution 9' on a Beatles album, and the fact that he had been purposely not including similar self-indulgent pieces of his own on Beatles albums, it is likely that this would have been cause for a dispute.

Brian Epstein was found dead at his apartment in Chapel Street,
27 August 1967. [*Dezo Hoffmann / Apple* and *Apple*]

The Beatles are given a private audience with the Maharishi Mahesh Yogi in Bangor [*Apple*]

The suspension bridge over the Ganges leading to the Maharishi's ashram. [*Apple*]

Cavendish Avenue. (Note Magritte's *Au Revoir*, which inspired
the logo for Apple Records.) [*Linda McCartney*]

The 40-foot-high psychedelic painting by The Fool, which covered the front of the Apple boutique for two weeks in December 1967. [*Keystone*]

Always on hand, Neil Aspinall and Mal Evans. [*Linda McCartney*]

Early days at Apple Records: Left: the group in the meditation dome in Paul's garden at Cavendish Avenue. [*Apple*]

Right: recording 'Hey Jude' at Trident Studios in Soho, the first record released by their own label. [*Apple*]

Mixing the
'White Album'
at Abbey Road.
[*Linda McCartney*]

Putting together the medley on side two of *Abbey Road*.
[*Linda McCartney*]

Artists and Writers:
Allen Ginsberg at the Albert Hall,
1995 [*Marc Atkins*];
Willem de Kooning in his studio
[*Linda McCartney*];
Alfred Jarry, inventor of
'pataphysics.

Paul and Linda with
Heather, visiting
Ringo on the set of
Magic Christian,
March 1969.
[*Pictorial Press*]

Paul with Mary.
[*Linda McCartney*]

Six days later, according to the engineer Ken Scott, who was recording the brass overdub session for Paul's 'Mother Nature's Son', 'Everything was going really well, and then John and Ringo walked in, and for the half-hour they were there, you could have cut the atmosphere with a knife.' Apparently the sudden tension evaporated immediately they left.

George arrived back from Greece on 21 August, but the next day, as they began to lay down the backing track for 'Back in the USSR', Paul ticked Ringo off over a fluffed tom-tom fill. They had already argued about how the drum part should be played. Ringo was unhappy with the atmosphere in the studio; he did not like Yoko being there, and Paul's criticisms finally brought matters to a head. Announcing that he couldn't take any more, Ringo quit the group. He flew down to the Mediterranean and spent a fortnight on Peter Sellers's yacht, thinking about his future.

While he was away, the remaining three members quickly cut 'Back in the USSR' with Paul playing drums, and Paul also played drums on John's 'Dear Prudence', recorded a week later. When Ringo returned on 3 September, he may have been expecting a row but instead he found his drum kit wreathed in flowers and a banner saying 'Welcome back'. The next day, working with the director Michael Lindsay-Hogg at Twickenham Film Studios, the Beatles filmed a series of promo clips for 'Hey Jude'. Everyone was on his best behaviour. A good time was had by all and much of the animosity seemed to melt away.

Sessions continued without a summer break. George brought in Eric Clapton to play lead on his 'While My Guitar Gently Weeps'. After this they recorded John's 'Glass Onion'.

PAUL: He and Yoko came round to Cavendish Avenue and John and I went out into the garden for half an hour, because there were a couple of things he needed me to finish up, but it was his song, his idea, and he worked on the arrangement with George Martin. It was a particularly good arrangement, I think. It was a nice song of John's. We had a fun moment when we were working on the bit, 'I've got news for you all, the walrus was Paul.' Because, although we'd never planned it, people read into our songs and little legends grew up about every item of so-called significance, so on this occasion we decided to plant one.

What John meant was that in *Magical Mystery Tour*, when we came to do the costumes on 'I Am the Walrus', it happened to be me in the walrus costume. It was not significant at all, but it was a nice little twist to the legend that we threw in. But it was John's song. I'd guess I had minor input or something as we finished it up together.

It was rare for the Beatles to make up a song in the studio, but on 8 September that is what happened. Paul had been the first to arrive at the session, getting to Abbey Road shortly after 5.00 p.m., and though they probably had something in mind to record, he began jamming at the upright piano in Studio Two. It quickly turned into a bouncy rock number and by 9.00 p.m., they had already laid down twenty takes of the backing track to 'Birthday'.

PAUL: We thought, 'Why not make something up?' So we got a riff going and arranged it around this riff. We said, 'We'll go to there for a few bars, then we'll do this for a few bars.' We added some lyrics, then we got the friends who were there to join in on the chorus. So that is 50-50 John and me, made up on the spot and recorded all on the same evening. I don't recall it being anybody's birthday in particular but it might have been, but the other reason for doing it is that, if you have a song that refers to Christmas or a birthday, it adds to the life of the song, if it's a good song, because people will pull it out on birthday shows, so I think there was a little bit of that at the back of our minds.

George Martin was away so his assistant Chris Thomas produced the session. His memory is that the song was mostly Paul's: 'Paul was the first one in, and he was playing the birthday riff. Eventually the others arrived, by which time Paul had literally written the song, right there in the studio.' Everyone in the studio sang in the chorus and it was 5 a.m. by the time the final mono mix was completed.

John found an American gun magazine lying around in the studio with a picture of a smoking gun on the cover. The lead article, which John didn't read, was called 'Happiness Is a Warm Gun in Your Hand'. John: 'I thought, what a fantastic, insane thing to say. A warm gun means you've just shot something.'

Paul: 'It's very similar to "Bungalow Bill" in that it's a piss-take of all the people who really do think happiness is a warm gun. There's a great vocal on it, good lyrics, and it's a very interesting song because it changes tempo a lot, it's quite a complex piece. It's very Lennon.'

Both Paul and George were reported as saying 'Happiness Is a Warm Gun' was their favourite track on the album, and John himself liked it. John: 'I consider it one of my best. It's a beautiful song and I really like all the things that are happening in it.'

PAUL: I was thinking the other day how poignant it was that John, who was shot in such tragic circumstances, should have written this song.

Both John and I had a great love for music hall, what the Americans call vaudeville. I'd heard a lot of that kind of music growing up with the *Billy Cotton Band Show* and all of that on the radio. I was also an admirer of people like Fred Astaire; one of my favourites of his was 'Cheek to Cheek' from a film called *Top Hat* that I used to have on an old 78. I very much liked that old crooner style, the strange fruity voice that they used, so 'Honey Pie' was me writing one of them to an imaginary woman, across the ocean, on the silver screen, who was called Honey Pie. It's another of my fantasy songs. We put a sound on my voice to make it sound like a scratchy old record. So it's not a parody, it's a nod to the vaudeville tradition that I was raised on.

For 'Wild Honey Pie', we'd very recently done John's 'Yer Blues' where we'd packed ourselves into a cupboard, so we were in an experimental mode, and so I said, 'Can I just make something up?' I started off with the guitar and did a multitracking experiment in the control room or maybe in the little room next door. It was very home-made; it wasn't a big production at all. I just made up this short piece and I multitracked a harmony to that, and a harmony to that, and a harmony to that, and built it up sculpturally with a lot of vibrato on the strings, really pulling the strings madly. Hence, 'Wild Honey Pie', which was a reference to the other song I had written called 'Honey Pie'. It was a little experimental piece.

The song 'Martha My Dear' was written entirely by Paul, and, like 'Yesterday', had none of the other Beatles playing on it. It began life as a piano exercise.

PAUL: When I taught myself piano I liked to see how far I could
go, and this started life almost as a piece you'd learn as a piano
lesson. It's quite hard for me to play, it's a two-handed thing, like
a little set piece. In fact I remember one or two people being
surprised that I'd played it because it's slightly above my level of
competence really, but I wrote it as that, something a bit more
complex for me to play. Then while I was blocking out words –
you just mouth out sounds and some things come – I found the
words 'Martha my dear'.

So I made up another fantasy song. I remember George
Harrison once said to me, 'I could never write songs like that.
You just make 'em up, they don't mean anything to you.' I think
on a deep level they do mean something to me but on a surface
level they are often fantasy like Desmond and Molly or Martha
my dear. I mean, I'm not really speaking to Martha, it's a
communication of some sort of affection but in a slightly
abstract way – 'You silly girl, look what you've done,' all that sort
of stuff. These songs grow. Whereas it would appear to anybody
else to be a song to a girl called Martha, it's actually a dog, and
our relationship was platonic, believe me.

The song was written in October 1968, when Martha was already
three years old, and recorded at Trident Studios in Soho, using a
brass band and a string section.

Towards the end of making the White Album, the Beatles were in
such a hurry to meet the deadline that they often had two studios in
use at once. On one day, 9 October, John and George had some ideas
to improve the mix of 'The Continuing Story of Bungalow Bill' and
were working on it with the engineer, Ken Scott in Studio Two.
Meanwhile Paul went into Studio One with another engineer,
Ken Townshend, and laid down the basic track of the short rocker
'Why Don't We Do It in the Road', to which he added lead vocals,
acoustic guitar and a piano overdub.

The next night, while John and George were engrossed in
overdubbing strings on to 'Piggies' and 'Glass Onion', Paul and Ken
Townshend again absented themselves, this time to Studio Three.
Paul got Ringo to come with him to add a drum track. The bass,
handclaps and electric guitar were all laid down by Paul.

PAUL: The idea behind 'Why Don't We Do It in the Road' came from something I'd seen in Rishikesh. I was up on the flat roof meditating and I'd seen a troupe of monkeys walking along in the jungle and a male just hopped on to the back of this female and gave her one, as they say in the vernacular. Within two or three seconds he hopped off again, and looked around as if to say, 'It wasn't me,' and she looked around as if there had been some mild disturbance but thought, Huh, I must have imagined it, and she wandered off. And I thought, bloody hell, that puts it all into a cocked hat, that's how simple the act of procreation is, this bloody monkey just hopping on and hopping off. There is an urge, they do it, and it's done with. And it's that simple. We have horrendous problems with it, and yet animals don't. So that was basically it. 'Why Don't We Do It in The Road' could have applied to either fucking or shitting, to put it roughly. Why don't we do either of them in the road? Well, the answer is we're civilised and we don't. But the song was just to pose that question. 'Why Don't We Do It in the Road' was a primitive statement to do with sex or to do with freedom really. I like it, it's just so outrageous that I like it.

John regarded the song as one of Paul's best and was upset that Paul had not asked him to work on it. His irritation still showed twelve years later when he complained to *Playboy*: 'That's Paul, he even recorded it by himself in another room ... I can't speak for George but I was always hurt when Paul knocked something off without involving us.' Paul countered this by telling Hunter Davies the next year, 'Anyway [John] did the same with "Revolution 9". He went off and made that without me. No one ever says all that.'

It was not a deliberate attempt to sidestep John. The pressure to complete the album was so great that John would not have had time to work on 'Why Don't We Do It in the Road' even if Paul had asked him. Contrary to some critical comment, the track had nothing to do with John Sinclair and the MC5's rallying cry, 'Sex and drugs and fucking in the streets!' Paul: 'The spirit of the times meant that a lot of us were thinking similar things, just doing it in different ways. It's a great track, isn't it? Good vocal, though I say it myself.'

After a marathon twenty-four hour session, utilising studios One, Two and Three as well as listening rooms 41 and 42, the huge double album was finally mixed and sequenced at 5 p.m. on Thursday, 17 October by John and Paul working with George Martin. Ringo was not present and George had already flown to Los Angeles to produce Jackie Lomax's album *Is This What You Want?* for Apple.

Richard Hamilton

Having used Peter Blake for the *Sgt. Pepper* sleeve, the Beatles decided to continue the tradition and use another established artist for their double album. Again the motivating force was Robert Fraser. He suggested Richard Hamilton, the actual inventor of Pop Art, which is generally thought to have started with his collage *Just What Is It That Makes Today's Homes So Different, So Appealing?* shown at the Whitechapel Gallery's This Is Tomorrow show in 1956. Richard Hamilton had studied at the Royal Academy and the Slade School and, at forty-five, was considerably older than the Beatles. He was, however, in touch with events on the pop scene.

Paul knew Richard Hamilton's work and owned one of his multiple editions of the Frank Lloyd Wright *Guggenheim Museum*.

PAUL: Robert had said, 'What about Richard?' I knew his work, I knew *Just What Is It That Makes Today's Homes So Different, So Appealing?*, so I said, 'Let's see how it goes. He might hate the idea.' And Richard started to get into it so I got encouraged and thought that he would be good to do it. Because, even though I admired Robert, I couldn't just take his word for it.

Robert arranged for Richard Hamilton to meet Paul at Apple in Savile Row, where he was kept waiting in an outer office so long that he was on the point of leaving when Paul appeared. 'I tried to get him interested in the whole thing,' Paul said. 'I laid out what it was we'd got. We'd got an album coming out, we hadn't really got a title for it. "I'd like you to work on the cover. We've done *Sgt. Pepper*. We've worked with a fine artist before and I just had a feeling you might be right."' Richard described the meeting in the Michael Cooper *Blinds and Shutters* book:

Since Sergeant Pepper was so over the top, I explained, 'I would be inclined to do a very prissy thing, almost like a limited edition.' He didn't discourage me so I went on to propose a plain white album; if that were too clean and empty, then maybe we could print a ring of brown stain to look as if a coffee cup had been left on it – but that was thought a bit too flippant. I also suggested that they might number each copy, to create the ironic situation of a numbered edition of something like five million copies. This was agreed, but then I began to feel a bit guilty at putting their double album under plain wrappers; even the lettering is casual, almost invisible, a blind stamping. I suggested it could be jazzed up with a large edition print, an insert that would be even more glamorous than a normal sleeve.

The white cover with blind-stamped name, printed number and an art print inside did become the final design concept but the sleeve went through a number of stages to reach that. Paul: 'Richard asked, "Has there been an album called *The Beatles*?" so I referred back to EMI and they said, "No. There's been *Meet the Beatles*, introducing the Beatles in America, but there'd never been an album called *The Beatles*." So he said, "Let's call it that"; which is the official title of the White Album.'

One early idea substituted an apple stain for the coffee ring on a blank cover.

PAUL: Richard had a friend from Iceland, the artist Diter Rot, who used to send him letters smeared in chocolate, and Richard liked that a lot, so then the idea grew; he said, 'Well, maybe we could do something like that with an apple. We could bounce an apple on a bit of paper and get a smudge, a very light green smear with a little bit of pulp.' But we ended up thinking that might be hard to print, because inevitably if these things do well, there are huge printings in places like Brazil and India and anything too subtle like a little apple smear can be lost, can just look like they printed it crappy. So that idea went by the wayside.

So now he was saying, 'Let's call it *The Beatles* and have it white, really white.' I was saying, 'Well, I dunno. It's a great concept, but we are releasing an album here. This is not a piece of art for a rather élite gallery, this is more than that. I see the point. It's a nice idea, but for what we were to people, and still are, it doesn't quite fit, we're not quite a blank space, a white wall, the Beatles. Somebody ought to piss on it or smudge an apple on it for it to become the Beatles, because a white wall's just too German and marvellous for us.' So the idea then emerged to do the embossing. 'Maybe if we emboss the word "Beatles" out of the white, that'll be good. We'll get a shadow from the embossing but it's white on white. It's still white. That'll be nice.' But I still wanted something on the white, an idea, like the apple smudging.

Then Richard had the idea for the numbers. He said, 'Can we do it?' So I had to go and try and sell this to EMI. They said, 'Can't do it.' I said, 'Look, records must go through something to put the shrink wrap on or to staple them. Couldn't you just have a little thing at the end of that process that hits the paper and prints a number on it? Then everyone would have a numbered copy.'

I think EMI only did this on a few thousand, then just immediately gave up. They have very very strict instructions that every single album that came out, even to this day, should still be numbered. That's the whole idea: 'I've got number 1,000,000!' What a great number to have! We got the first four. I don't know where mine is, of course. Everything got lost. It's all coming up in Sotheby's I imagine. John got 00001 because he shouted loudest. He said, 'Baggsy number one!' He knew the game, you've gotta baggsy it.

It was a very radical way to package the album. Richard Hamilton saw it, not as an art statement, but as a way of competing with the lavish design treatments of most post-*Sgt. Pepper* sleeves. Richard: 'Most people, among them Yoko, think it was Yoko's idea. It was at the time when Yoko was really moving into the Beatle business and putting her oar in strongly. But my contact with the project was only through Paul – even EMI was held off.'

The poster insert also posed problems, some of which Richard attempted to head off in its design. His control over the image would cease at an early stage because printing would take place simultane-ously all over the world. He decided to send positives from a process-engraving company in Amsterdam to all the countries where the poster would be printed. The plates would made in those countries and proofs sent to London for his approval. After that it was a matter of luck, and naturally the quality of the printing deteriorated with each subsequent printing. But first the poster had to be designed. Richard asked Paul to collect a selection of photographs of the Beatles.

PAUL: He said 'Have you got any old photos of the Beatles? They must all have family photos from when they were young, or any nice photos. Get me a lot of source material.' So I acted as the middleman. I went to the guys and said, 'Childhood photos, what have you got? Look in your cupboards. New photos if you want. Whatever you like,' and they brought in stuff from the bottom drawer that their mums had kept, along with their old rent books, all the old baby pictures. I told him, 'My wife's a photographer. She's got some pretty cool stuff. Would you like to look at that?' He said, 'Yes,' so I took that out to him as well.

Each day for the next week, Paul drove from St John's Wood to the artist's house in Highgate, where he lived with his girlfriend Christine. 'Richard was always very welcoming,' Paul thought, 'good fun, always a broad smile. You noticed his large nose and his bald head with the wisps of hair either side and the little cap he used to wear. Richard was very easy to get on with, a nice sly sense of humour, very pleasant.'

They would walk from the house to his modern functional studio next door, passing two sculptural steel garden chairs on the way. Unlike that of most painters, his work space was spotlessly clean: steel shelving units housing books and boxes against bare white concrete-block walls, bright concealed lighting illuminating the work space, a twenty-four hour clock flipping over the minutes. As a print-maker he needed a dust-free work space. The easily damaged prints from his project to recreate Duchamp's *Great Glass* were stacked against the walls, and any dust settling on wet ink would spoil a print. There was a modern plastic telephone and a Braun hi-fi; Hamilton was always at the forefront of good design. Paul: 'It was very clean, uncluttered, clear, everything was very precise. There wasn't lots of paint everywhere. It was what I'd think of as a very German interior to the studio, very Bauhaus, very sixties modern, but it wasn't particularly striking, it was clearly just a workplace.'

Watching an artist at work was of great interest to Paul because it was quite different from the rock 'n' roll world where teams of people are needed for everything except the actual writing of the song.

PAUL: I enjoyed the ambience of art, it was much more laid back than ours. We were always working. We'd write a bit of music, quickly. We'd go and record it, quickly. It's done. You never sing it again. It's like premature ejaculation, it's all rather quick. But art was much more solitary so I was enjoying this very much. I went out there every morning, regular as clockwork, off to work, and this was like, 'Oooh, God, working with Richard Hamilton!' because I was a bit of an admirer of his. I'd bought one of his Guggenheim things. This is one of the great experiences of my life. It didn't seem like work. I just dossed around while he did the work. Such an easy job because I just had to respond.

The first three or four days were spent sorting the images, which he laid out on a ten-foot-long work table.

PAUL: He started laying them out, sorting them. Ones he liked, ones he didn't like, ones that worked together, darker ones, lighter ones, themes, this against that, things he thought he might be able to use. Sorting the shapes in a painterly way. And it was fascinating for me because there's nothing like just watching.

We got on very well. It was always very pleasant, he would say, 'Shall we have tea now, shall we have coffee?' We established a routine, something like twelve till four or five each day; a good three- or four-hour session. Hamilton was a meticulous worker, with every decision carefully considered.

RICHARD HAMILTON: I paint so slowly. One or two paintings a year is as much as I can get through: on occasions only one in three years. If I make a couple of marks by the end of the day I'm happy ... The only reason I make pictures is because there is some idea which can be expressed. Unless you've got an idea and seek the means of communication, there's no value in painting. Every move you make should be a conscious decision towards an objective.

Once he had selected the pictures he wanted, Hamilton had copies made of some because they weren't necessarily all the right size; there were some he wanted to use but he required smaller prints. Then he set up an easel with a sheet of paper the actual size that the poster was going to be. As he explained in *Collected Words*, there were a number of technical problems to be allowed for in the poster:

> Because the sheet was folded three times to bring it to the square shape for insertion into the album, the composition was interestingly complicated by the need to consider it as a series of subsidiary compositions. The top right and left hand square are front and back of the folder and had to stand independently as well as be a double spread together. The bottom four squares can be read independently and as a group of four. They all mate together when opened up and used as wall decoration. I tried to think of the print as one which would reach and please a large audience, but there were some arcane touches which only the Beatles' more intimate associates were likely to smile at. Its standards are those of a small edition print pushed, with only some technical constraints, to an edition of millions.

PAUL: Again he'd just sit there, looking at it, sorting it out, put this on, take that off. I would just sit there enjoying watching what he was doing, thinking, I see why he's done that. That's good. Wow! Not sure I agree with that, then, five minutes later, Oh, I see. With a good artist there's always a bit of that. He worked carefully, methodically, always a little joke here and little bit of this there. He cut prints up. They weren't used just as they were. If he'd have an area of black in the bottom left-hand corner of a picture that was not doing anything, he'd cut that out to let another picture show through. So they weren't all necessarily rectangular, they were often little shapes he'd scissored before he glued them on.

In the evenings sometimes we'd hang around or go into his house. Linda has a photo of him in front of the Chairman Mao picture that he had at the time. Very pleasant company, the talk would be about art and music. I'd give him my gossip, he'd give me his. Very straightforward.

By the end of the week, all the pictures were in place.

PAUL: He'd done it and it was looking really good and I said,

'Well, that's it, wow! Shall I just take it now?' But it wasn't finished yet. The great moment was when he'd done the whole thing, when he'd filled the whole space densely with images, and got his composition right, then he took pieces of white paper that he'd cut out, and placed them strategically on the poster. And my mind couldn't comprehend that, and I went, 'Wait a minute! That's going to block out a bit of picture.' And he said, 'Yes, but if you look at it, it's only blocking out that little black bit there,' he said, 'and you'll be able to see through this negative space. You'll be able to see through the poster. It'll give it depth.' And sure enough it does. If you look at the poster you'll see the final thing he put on was four or five little bits of negative space: these white shapes he'd made, a white triangle or something that just fitted the area where he didn't want to obscure that face. I remember being very impressed; it was the first time that I'd ever seen that idea. I would have never thought of that. It was beautiful. That was cool. For me that was a great lesson that I was getting from the hands of someone like Richard Hamilton; a whole week of his thoughts. No mean teacher, man! Great education.

The Beatles was released on 30 November 1968 and not only lived up to expectations but is regarded by many as their greatest album. Not only had they a follow-up to *Sgt. Pepper*, they had again exceeded all expectations – and with thirty new songs. Their new single, 'Hey Jude', wasn't even on the album. They had total, apparently effortless dominance of the pop-music scene. It seemed they could do no wrong – but they were already breaking up.

Sometime in New York City

Linda Eastman grew up in a wealthy New York family. She spent most of her time in Scarsdale, where she went to high school, and made occasional shopping trips to Manhattan with her mother. Linda's father Lee Eastman was a show-business lawyer and it was common for Linda and her brother John to find Hoagy Carmichael, Tommy Dorsey or Hopalong Cassidy at the dinner table. Lee's walls were hung with the work of Franz Kline, Willem de Kooning, Robert

Rauschenberg, Richard Lindner and other painters whom he represented.

Lee was a self-made man who got himself a scholarship to Harvard when he was sixteen years old. The son of Russian Jewish immigrants to New York, he had a tremendous drive and ambition. Instead of joining a large legal partnership, he set up his own office and built his own reputation.

> PAUL: He was very patriarchal. Linda would try and avoid him on the street if she was with one of her long-haired friends because he wouldn't approve. He didn't approve when a photograph of her in Harlem with the Animals appeared in *Ebony* magazine because he had a lot of very high-powered white clients who might have disapproved. It was one of his clients who pointed it out to him. He wasn't prejudiced but it was a social thing. He aspired higher. I think he wanted a kind of Kennedy dynasty thing. There was a lot of that about then. They thought it was glamorous. It was like smoking: they hadn't realised it could be bad for you. I remember when I first met John Eastman, I asked him, 'What do you want to do? What's your ambition in life?' He said, 'To be the president of the United States of America,' which fairly soon after that he didn't want to do. They were very preppy. Very aspirational.

Most of this was lost on Linda, who cared more for animals than for position and power. By nature she is intuitive, spontaneous, a daydreamer: all good qualities for a photographer, but not for an intellectual or a business tycoon. She was close to her mother Louise, an independently wealthy woman with an income from the Linder department stores, but when Linda was eighteen years old, Louise was killed in a plane crash. This would become another bond between her and Paul.

Linda moved to Tucson, where she studied art and history. There is a myth that both Linda and Yoko Ono attended Sarah Lawrence, which was true of Yoko but not of Linda, whose brief academic career was at the University of Arizona. She was not exceptional academically and did not particularly enjoy it. It was an uncertain period of her life, she was grieving her mother and trying to find her place in the world. She married a young geology student named Mel See, with whom she had a daughter, Heather, but the marriage was a mistake and they soon split up. Linda: 'Then I grew up. My life began again with this new freedom.' She met Hazel Archer, the woman who first introduced her to photography, who remains a friend to this day. She showed Linda pictures by Dorothea Lange, Walker Evans and Ansel Adams. Linda was delighted; she had not known photography could be art. Hazel Archer's advice was simple: 'Borrow a camera, get a roll of film and take pictures.'

'Photography made me a different person because it was something I loved doing and just nothing else mattered,' Linda said. 'I could just take my camera and go, probably like Diane Arbus felt when she was walking taking pictures. I had that feeling. Even though I had a child I still felt single. It's different when you're married and you've got to go cook dinner. I could just go, go anywhere.' She learned her craft entirely by trial and error, and sometimes the errors produced wonderful results. Her early pictures were of Heather and of the mountains and deserts of Arizona.

The Royal Academy of Dramatic Art was performing a season of Shakespeare in the Desert and Linda went along with a friend who was reporting on it for a local newspaper. One of the actors asked her to take some publicity shots of him, and the first photograph she ever had published appeared in *Spotlight*, the British directory of actors.

Though she enjoyed the dramatic beauty of the Arizona landscape, Linda missed the energy and stimulation of her hometown. She missed the Museum of Modern Art and the leisure section of the Sunday *New York Times*, the yellow cabs and the pot-holes. In 1965 she packed up and went back to New York. Her father had recently remarried so when she returned to the parental home with a child, he quickly informed her that it was time she got a job and her own apartment.

Finding a decent apartment in New York City, then as now, is a difficult exercise. There is no point in answering advertisements because those have all gone; the only way is through a friend or to walk the streets. She decided she wanted to live on the Upper East Side of Manhattan and went out looking. One doorman thought there was an apartment coming up in his building. The woman had planned to advertise her apartment in the newspaper the next day. It was an L-shaped room and the woman, who was, like Linda, divorced with a child, had built a divider in it to make a tiny one-bedroom apartment. It was at 140 East 83rd Street on the southwest corner of Lexington Avenue, just three blocks from the Metropolitan Museum of Art and Central Park, in a safe, expensive neighbourhood, ideal for a single young mother with a child. It was $180 a month, reasonable rent for a building with a doorman in that area in the mid-sixties. It was on the edge of Yorkville, which was then still a distinctly Middle European and German neighbourhood with beer halls, pastry shops and shop signs written in German.

Now that she had the apartment, it was time to get a job. On her father's insistence she had once taken a typing course so she had a skill. She tried several times to pass the Condé-Nast typing test but always failed. One day she was passing the old Hearst building on 56th and Madison, and decided to try them. Fortunately the Hearst Corporation didn't have a typing test. When she asked if they had any jobs going, they offered her a job as receptionist at *Town and Country*. She earned $65 a week after tax.

First thing each day she took Heather to a nursery school on the West Side, then took a bus back to the East Side, where she had to get to *Town and Country* by 9.00 a.m. Her job required that she be the first one in the office. At 5.00 p.m. she made the journey in reverse. This arrangement lasted about a year. One advantage of the job was that the Hearst building was only a few blocks from the Museum of Modern Art on 52nd Street so she was able to spend her lunch breaks in the photographic department.

Town and Country used most of the top photographers in the country and, sitting in reception, Linda got to know them all. 'I never got to go on any of the shoots or anything, I just got to sit there and open letters.' The June 1966 *Town and Country* was a débutante issue which featured the Rolling Stones on the cover posing with the débutante Alexandra E. Chase dressed in a yellow evening gown. (The Stones' American marketing managers played down their rebellious image in the USA and built up the English angle.) David Bailey flew over to shoot it in the studio of his friend Jerrold Schatsberg, his New York counterpart on the fashion photography scene.

Because they had given the Stones a cover, *Town and Country* were automatically on the mailing list for an invitation to the press launch for *Aftermath*, released earlier that month, which the Stones were promoting with an American tour. Unless letters were addressed to individuals, it was Linda's job to open them. She quickly hid the press pass in her drawer. The Stones had been barred by fourteen New York hotels so they were using a yacht, the SS *Sea Panther*, as their floating headquarters. Their new business manager Allen Klein had arranged a press conference on the yacht for 24 June 1966, the day after they flew in from London, giving the journalists time to interview the Stones individually over a working lunch as the yacht sailed up and down the Hudson. Unfortunately that left no room for the photographers on board as well. Klein's press officer Betsy Doster could not take some and not others, so she tried to leave them all behind at the West 79th Street Marina. Linda refused to take no for an answer and the Stones, particularly Mick Jagger, so enjoyed the ensuing argument that they told Betsy to let her stay, almost costing Betsy her job.

As the only photographer on board, Linda had an amazing exclusive. All the journalists approached her for photographs to accompany their interviews and gave her their cards. The pictures turned out well. Linda: 'I remember once a week someone would phone and say, "Mr Klein would like to buy those negatives," and I'd say, "He can use whatever he wants but no chance." I was so desperate to take pictures, I would have done a deal if they'd said beforehand and they would own the negatives but they didn't, it was all so quick. So due to this Rolling Stones thing I quit my job and became a photographer.'

One of the journalists who wrote about the boat trip and used Linda's pictures was the Australian rock critic Lilian Roxanne from the *Sydney Morning Herald*. She began to use Linda's pictures for her column and they became good friends. Another was the journalist Danny Fields, who worked for *16* magazine and also commissioned sleeves for Elektra Records. The Blues Project asked her for a set of publicity pictures. Linda was so keen to get into the business that she said, 'You pay for the film and I'll do it.' It was a small scene and she soon had more than enough work to live on.

This was a time when someone like Al Kooper could play with Dylan, the Blues Project and Blood, Sweat and Tears and also hold down a job at Columbia Records as an A & R man. Rock music then, unlike now, was the vehicle for social protest: lyrics were analysed in meticulous detail and the release of each new album was a major event. It was a brief, precious period when the business had not yet become an industry, the really big money was not yet being made, rock festivals had not yet been invented and the Beatles were the only group ever to play stadiums. There were no lasers, no computerised lights or dry ice, and bands like the Doors, Jefferson Airplane and the Grateful Dead had not yet released albums.

Musicians jammed with one another and sat in on recording sessions. There was a family feeling in the music community which extended beyond the musicians and their loved ones to include the road crews, photographers, publicists and journalists. This was partly in the nature of the business – clubs, late hours, music, good times, groupies – and partly because it was a pot-smoking society at a time when it was possible to draw a ten-year sentence for possession of one joint. If you were part of the scene, it didn't take long to become a trusted member of the fraternity. Clubs like Micky Ruskin's Max's Kansas City, Steve Paul's Scene or the photographer Jerry Schatsberg's Salvation were the village pumps for the music scene, where everyone knew everyone, gossip flowed, sexual liaisons were proposed or, in the case of Max's, often consummated right there in the famous back room.

LINDA: From being a nine to five flunky at *Town and Country*, my life changed overnight. I didn't have to rush as much. I had no assistant, I had no studio, but it was great. I'd walk through the Metropolitan Museum on my way downtown, walking through the park to take my film in. There is nobody in Central Park from nine to five, they're all at work, just squirrels, no people whatsoever. The park was like living in the country. I would walk around, smoking a bit of pot, having a good time, life was nice. I had calluses on my hands because I never took taxis and I always carried: I had portfolios, cameras, film to develop. And I was making money. That was the best part, because I made enough to pay the rent and put a little bit aside. When I got paid, that is, because a lot of times I didn't get paid.

Linda's pictures of Cream appeared in the first issue of *Rolling Stone* magazine. She photographed Simon and Garfunkel in the studio, the Mamas and Papas in their hotel and Jackson Browne on the Staten Island Ferry. She toured the Mid-West with the prototype heavy-metal band Blue Cheer. But mostly she shot pictures backstage, on stage or in Central Park. There are few rock photographers with such a complete portfolio of sixties stars, in most cases taken at the very beginning of their career, playing the New York clubs or the Fillmore East. Her portraits of Jim Morrison were done before *The Doors* was released. She photographed Zappa when he was living in Greenwich Village for a summer season at the Garrick Theater with the original Mothers of Invention. Linda always used natural light, never flash, which partially accounts for the intimate feeling of her portraits.

Rock 'n' roll was rapidly becoming big business. Wave after wave of British groups arrived in New York in the wake of the Beatles: first the Stones, followed by the Kinks, the Who, the Dave Clark Five, the Animals, Jeff Beck, the Yardbirds, Herman's Hermits, Peter and Gordon, Donovan and a host of others. In January 1965, British artists held twenty-seven positions in the US top 100, a percentage which remained roughly the same for most of the sixties.

> LINDA: A new generation was moving into the business and it turned into big business; even me as a photographer turned into big business. I was getting noticed so I was making big bucks, for me. I was getting $1,000 a page from *Life* magazine! I was doing editorial work for *Mademoiselle*, but at the point where I was getting big work, it was all becoming horrible. It was getting to be a real pressure on me because I didn't have an agent. I had just started interviewing agents around the time I started going out with Paul.

The fun had gone out of the business. Management began to take over. Groups everywhere were being exploited by the money men, the 'suits', as they were known. Linda was close to Jimi Hendrix and remembers how distraught he was because his manager would drag him out of a recording session to do an interview or attend to business, interrupting his creative work. Business was starting to come first and the music a poor second. Linda: 'I really hated the music industry but I thought, What will I photograph then to make money? Athletes and wildlife? Somebody said, "Athletes? That's worse than the music business." So I'm glad I didn't do that.'

She found herself once more in an untenable situation.

> LINDA: Right after I'd interviewed an agent, I decided 'No way.' As soon as I got my apartment it was like my world, I could just close the door and I thought, If I get agents, there's too much

going on. I used to just lie there, smoke a joint and watch TV. I had a kid, and I'd done so much stuff. I was just fed up with the rock world, it just started getting really boring for me. Heather was just about to start at Dalton, and I was thinking, What am I doing? It was then, in late September, that Paul called and said, 'Come over.'

Linda arrived in London in time to catch the recording of the last ten or so tracks for the White Album, though mostly she just went to the studio to watch the mixing. Unlike Yoko, she didn't offer her opinion. 'The Beatles were obviously going through a bad time,' Linda observed. 'Everybody was obviously growing up and growing away a bit. The Beatles was Paul's job; he and John were a creative team, but John was with Yoko. Paul never had any time alone with John. It was John and Yoko and the other Beatles.' After a few weeks living together at Cavendish Avenue, things were still going well between Paul and Linda, so the obvious next move was to go to New York and fetch Heather.

PAUL: I remember ringing Heather from the bedroom in Cavendish Avenue. Because of the time difference we were in bed and it was early evening there, and Linda talked to her. Heather had no idea it was Paul in the Beatles or anything, it was just 'this guy who I really like and who I've been with. Would you like to say hello to him?' So I got on the phone thinking, Oh, my God, if she hates me, this could be very very difficult, so I was slightly overfriendly probably. I said, 'Will you marry me?' She said, 'I can't, you're too old!' like kids do, but that broke the ice and I said, 'Oh yes, of course. I forgot that. Well, maybe I should marry your mummy. That'd be good.' It was this kind of conversation and we seemed to get on quite well and she was nice and I handed her back to Linda.

They flew to New York in the middle of October, as soon as the White Album was complete, and stayed for about ten days at Linda's apartment. New York in 1968 was Rock 'n' Roll City. Most of the record companies were still headquartered there; the drift to the West Coast began a little later. The club scene was a major source of new talent. The Fillmore East showcased all the best West Coast groups as well as the visiting British groups like the Who and Cream and blues singers like B. B. King and Muddy Waters, whose careers had been boosted by the so-called blues revival. Though Linda had just about overdosed on the rock 'n' roll business, it still played a big part in the energy and excitement of New York towards the end of the sixties.

Paul had only been to New York as a Beatle, riding in a limousine, trapped in a luxury hotel suite; he had never had time to explore the city. Now he walked the streets from Harlem to Battery Park, took the subway and buses and got to know neighbourhood bars. They went to movies and clubs, explored Chinatown and Little Italy. For a couple of weeks he lived Linda's life in New York.

PAUL: I had a full beard at that time so I wasn't very recognisable as Beatle Paul, inverted commas, 'I am a Beatle!' Linda would take me to thrift shops, and there was a big army and navy store that we went to on 125th Street where I picked up an old uniform with a couple of stripes so I looked a bit like a Vietnam vet. I looked like the guy who would mug you rather than the guy you'd want to mug, so I was really quite safe on the streets with that disguise. Nobody was going to see me as me and nobody really knew Linda. She wore very casual jeans and a beige jacket, like a photographer, so it wasn't a couple of very rich people walking round New York, it was more the kind of people you'd want to avoid, you'd let them go on the pavement. So it was good, we were very free consequently.

LINDA: On the subway he did get noticed and a few people started following us a bit, but then we'd just get on a train and lose them. Usually if anyone recognised Paul on the subway it was all 'Hey, man, groovy, peace' – they loved him. Black guys too, because we used to go up to Harlem a lot. I remember walking around Harlem and some guy asking Paul about 'Revolution', 'Did you guys really mean that song, how did you mean that? Were you being aggressive, were you not being aggressive?' I did not change my lifestyle one bit and Paul dressed down to my way of life. He was definitely funking out a bit. I remember he got this great old herringbone coat at a thrift shop on 3rd Avenue for $10. It was brilliant.

PAUL: We had a lot of fun together, getting together the first time. We were exploring each other and our surroundings and there was a lot of fun attached to that, just the nature of how we are, our favourite thing really is to just to hang, to have fun. And Linda's very big on just following the moment. We used to spend a lot of time just wandering around, going into bars, literally just exploring New York. New York has this great literary ambience. You could imagine Jack Kerouac or Norman Mailer or Dylan Thomas or William Burroughs hanging out in these little places rather than at the Carlyle. We never went to the Carlyle, it would more likely be Flanagan's Bar.

They did all the tourist things that Paul could never do as a Beatle. They went on the Staten Island Ferry and walked around Greenwich Village. If they saw an interesting church they would look inside. Any art gallery or museum they happened to pass they went in.

Linda did not cook much in those days except to feed Heather, so they ate out a lot, not at fashionable restaurants but home cooking in Little Italy, Chinatown or the German restaurants in Yorkville.

PAUL: There was a lovely little German restaurant nearby on 86th Street called the Forester's Arms where there were alcoves and it was very private. You could have a meal and be totally on your own. There was a bar just out of eyesight and you could hear all the tinkling and the fat old German lady would come and serve you. The food was very good, and we would just sit and chat, just with each other most of the time.

It was a very warm period for me in New York. I got to see a lot of art, got to hang out a lot, be myself a lot rather than having to do anything for anyone or be anywhere for someone. It was a very free period, just wake up in the morning, go for a cup of coffee, a walk through Central Park, look at the listings, see if anyone was playing jazz or if a good band was in the clubs.

They saw Joe Pass at the Guitar, but most of the time they went to Brad Pierce's club Ondine near the 59th Street Bridge, which featured live music and had the advantage of being within walking distance. There was a corny nautical motif and the club was nothing much to look at, but by the time the last set began at 2.15 a.m. the booths were crowded with everyone from Warren Beatty to Andy Warhol, Edie Sedgwick and the Factory crowd. It was the hippest club in Manhattan at the time. 'I've always loved New York from the time I first went there,' Paul said, 'but this really gave me a deep love of it. I'm quite at home in New York, and I know it very well by now.'

Linda's apartment was small. The living room doubled as a bedroom when the sofa-bed was extended, and there was a partition to give Heather a room of her own. The kitchen was tiny, like a hotel kitchenette. Linda's prints were not filed away but were stacked everywhere in untidy piles where people had looked through them. The apartment was on the tenth floor with a view out over the corner of 83rd Street. Paul: 'There was a liquor store opposite. Every morning we used to see the guy opening up, pulling back the criss-cross iron shutters. Heather used to spend a lot of time looking out the window at the street life.'

Paul has always loved children. He grew up surrounded by an extended Liverpool family of cousins, nieces and nephews so there was little danger of his not hitting it off with five-year-old Heather.

PAUL: When we did meet we got on quite well. She had a little tiger costume she used to crawl around in all the time, she was animal mad. I think in New York, your fantasy starts to take over, you've no space. So she was that tiger. Sometimes Linda would leave me with her when she had to go off and do something. I cooked her something one time and it was horrible! She still remembers it. A dreadful omelette apparently with everything in it. She was not impressed with my omelette. But we got on very well and I was able to sit on my own in the apartment playing guitar and she would just wander around being a tiger till Linda got back. We didn't have any major traumas, and she hadn't thrown a wobbler or anything, so that gave us the feeling that it might work.

Over the years Heather had had a very distinguished line-up of baby-sitters, including Al Kooper, Stephen Stills and Mike Bloom-field, but Paul was the most celebrated.

Though they could walk the streets with little trouble, the people in Linda's building soon noticed that a Beatle was living there. Linda: 'Heather used to go down in the lift to wait to go to school and there was an older woman and her husband in the building who used to stop and give her sweets. Her job was to decide whether people could adopt children or not but she'd never had kids. She was a weirdo, she was very Southern, and she didn't like the fact that Paul was living there. She used to give me a real tough time.'

They would shop at the A&P across the street, buy organic apple juice from the local health-food store, and, at Mimi's Pizza, Paul discovered the New York tradition of a slice to go. He looked up a few friends such as Bob Dylan, who was living in Greenwich Village, and Linda took a roll of pictures of Dylan and Sarah with baby Jessie sitting on her lap, but mostly the two of them just hung out together. Paul had always been concerned that being a Beatle had cut him off from normal life and ordinary people, but in New York he was able to walk around and go to clubs with the minimum amount of interference.

Of all the Beatles he was the only one who would still try to take buses or walk to Apple. He missed ordinary life. The two weeks in New York with Linda and Heather were a wonderful break from the pressures of London and all the problems of the group. Suddenly he had a normal life and a ready-made family.

PAUL: I remember being on the subway once and Linda said, 'Look, I've got to go to the dentist. You just take Heather up to the apartment, she knows the way from the subway.' So I was led up from the 83rd Street exit from the subway, and then Heather walked me along past a little shoe shop where we got her shoes, and then past the doorman, up in the lift. We had fun. I remember I was singing, 'Out of college, money spent, see no future, pay no rent, but oh, that lovely feeling, nowhere to go!' This was how it was then, it still is our favourite thing.

Linda was often doing something, she had her own life to lead, and I had much more time on my hands. She would have to take Heather to school, pick Heather up from school, cook the meal, certain things as a mother she had to do. And her womanliness impressed me, I'd never actually known anyone who was quite so much a woman. Linda was a very good mother. It was one of the things that impressed me about her was that she had the woman thing down, she seriously looked after her daughter. It seemed very organised to me, in a slightly dishevelled way. She was very kind-hearted too, so that finished it all off. And there was this slight rebelliousness. And I didn't have to hide the fact I was smoking pot, I didn't have to pretend.

Because I couldn't be open with a lot of people I met. I could be pretty open. I've been pretty open with most of my relationships, but with her I could be completely open. Our relationship has always been like that, painfully open sometimes. Sometimes you don't want the truth, but it's always a good idea.

One day they were walking down Mott Street in Chinatown when they saw a Buddhist temple with a sign which read, 'Buddhist weddings'. Paul grabbed Linda's arm and said, 'C'mon, let's go and get married.' Linda: 'I really didn't want to get married again. I was so newly not married again so I went, "No, no, *no!*" And we kept walking and it was like it was never said.' But the idea had been implanted. It was becoming obvious to Paul that here was a woman who could give him the love, the support and the family he wanted; an island of calm in the madness of the disintegrating Beatles.

PAUL: I remember saying to her, 'Can we go to the Apollo? Is that okay yet?' Because I'd always been in New York with the Beatles, and we'd been warned off Harlem. 'You can't go up there, man, it's just too tough for white people.' So she said, 'Sure, yes.' She'd be taking photos as well, so this wasn't just wasted time; wherever she went at that time she would just sling her camera, so she would always be taking pictures. So we took the train up to 125th Street. It was my first introduction to Harlem. I was still looking like a Vietnam vet, and we walked along 125th Street all the way over to the Apollo. Quite a way over. I just stood looking – 'Wow, this is the Apollo! Wow!' – just thinking about it. It was quite an empty street, it wasn't crowded, it must have been a weekday, midday, so most people were at work.

We went to the Apollo a number of times. The black guy at the box office said, 'Are you sure you want to go in?' I said, 'Yeah, it's okay.' He gave us a little warning. I think we were the only two little whiteys there.

They went to Harlem many times on this and subsequent trips to New York. On one visit they had their photograph taken at a little photo booth located right next door to the Apollo. Paul: 'The guy had no idea it was me, even though by this time I was clean-shaven. The guy just took the picture: "Watch the birdy. Come on, smile a little."

It's a real goofy photo against a backdrop of a little house. Very nice, slightly distorted, the lens maybe had to get twenty people in sometimes so there's a slight fisheye quality. We did things like that.'

The cashier gave them a timely warning. This was a period of high racial tension: there had been riots in nearby Newark and the Black Panthers had a strong Harlem chapter. Paul and Linda strolled right by the Panther headquarters on 125th Street past all the guys in berets hanging out on the street corner.

PAUL: The nearest I came to grief was waiting for Linda one day in 1970. She was going to take the train up and we were going to meet at the station. I was killing time before meeting her, just exploring Harlem, because the way I was dressing did afford me some kind of privacy, some invisibility. I didn't stick out, I just looked like a poor white guy.

I was watching a playground full of little kids through the railings. They were skipping rope and playing all their games and whereas we would have done 'Salt, vinegar, mustard, pepper ...', theirs were all like rhythm and blues: they sounded just like lyrics to me! I was beguiled. I was watching it for just a few minutes, really loving it, but this black guy just happened to be walking past and he said, 'You a teacher?' I said, 'No.' He said, 'What're you watching those children for?' I said, 'I'm from England, this is fascinating for me.' He said, 'If you ain't off this block in a quarter-hour I'm going to put you off.'

So now I'm walking alongside him like Ratso out of *Midnight Cowboy*, trying to keep up with him, and he was walking stronger and I was walking, trying to keep his attention, saying, 'Look, this is what gives you guys a bad name.' I said, 'I'm a tourist, I've come here, I love this whole place, I love the Apollo, I love these kids. I'm not a pervert, don't you try making me out as a pervert, don't go jumping to conclusions, I'm going to try and –' He said, 'Just get off the block, man, just get off the block.' And he peeled off.

He did a left, which left me on a corner with some little black kids who were playing. And I said, 'Did you see that? Did you see that? This guy's warned me off the block.' I said, 'That's really not good enough!' And I went into a record shop and this guy calmed me down, a black guy there, he says, 'Hey, man, we're not all like that. You know, it's okay. C'mon now. Hey, ain't you the guy that did "Let It Be"?' So he cooled me out, and then when Linda came I said, 'Look, let's not stay today. Let's go somewhere else.' Looking back on it it was quite a hairy thing to do but we were just in love and she wanted to show me Harlem.

Linda showed Paul her New York: the corner bars and diners, pizza joints and luncheonettes. Even now, if he is staying in a hotel, he will always take everyone out for a proper New York breakfast of waffles, pancakes, coffee or freshly squeezed orange juice. He learned to take Checker cabs – 'they're just groovier' – instead of the usual beaten-up Fords. She showed him where Andy Warhol's Factory was; she had visited a few times but found the crowd too drug-oriented for her liking. They visited Max's Kansas City and the Fillmore East, where she had spent so much time that she was virtually regarded as the house photographer. The Fillmore was a run-down theatre on 2nd Avenue in the Lower East Side. The owner Bill Graham's attitude was best summed up by the huge banner hanging outside which spelled 'Fillmore Esat'.

PAUL: I loved that. Nobody even checks to see whether it's spelled right or not. I can imagine Bill Graham probably saw it too late and said, 'Fuck it. The kids'll never notice.'

We would dip into all the facilities of New York. One night we went to Lincoln Center for a performance of *La Bohème* and didn't reckon it, just did not reckon it. The opening was all right. I just got bored. I thought, Bloody hell! Are we kidding ourselves? I said, 'Are you loving this?' She said, 'No, are you?' And because we were doing what we wanted, we walked out halfway through. It was quite difficult to do! I said, 'Shall we go then?' 'Oh, my God!' I said, 'Just walk out. We bought tickets, we can walk out. Just keep your head down and try not to let the people on stage see.' That was my main worry. There were a lot of students outside hoping for tickets, so we gave our stubs to a couple of students and they were able to get our seats. We also went to the famous Peter Brook *Midsummer Night's Dream*, all very white with people coming down little ropes. We walked out of that too. It just didn't grab us by the balls. It's hard to sit through a play that you're hating and your bum's got sore.

'We should have stayed there longer because it was great living how I lived in New York,' Linda said. 'We came back to London and I lived Paul's life. I'm not half as restrained in New York as I am in England.'

The first two weeks in New York were a turning point in the relationship. It was then that they made the decision to be together and raise a family.

PAUL: So we wandered round New York, getting tighter and tighter. We've always been very close and that was the beginning of it all. It was a great change in my life. I've always had quite serious relationships, I didn't have that many women. I had girlfriends and one-night stands a lot, the swinging sixties, sexual revolution. But this was the start of this new kind of relationship for me. I found it very liberating. I found it very good for me as a person. There was a newspaper headline, 'Linda and Paul, 9000 Nights of Love', because apart from when I was busted in Tokyo, we have pretty much spent every night together. Personally I never saw any reason to be somewhere that she wasn't.

After two weeks of exploring New York, Paul, Linda and Heather took a yellow cab to Kennedy Airport, bound for London. Paul had his guitar with him; in the early days in Liverpool he took his guitar with him everywhere and now that Beatlemania had subsided, he resumed the habit. (Later, when he was making *Ram*, he substituted a ukulele tuned like a guitar which was more convenient to carry around.) Paul was working on the song 'She Came in through the Bathroom Window' at the time, but still needed a final verse. He looked at the police identification panel mounted on the dashboard of the cab. There was a mug shot of the driver and his name, stencilled in large black letters: 'Eugene Quits'; beneath that was written 'New York Police Dept'. Paul: 'So I got "So I quit the police department", which are part of the lyrics to that. This was the great thing about the randomness of it all. If I hadn't been in this guy's cab, or if it had been someone else driving, the song would have been different. Also I had a guitar there so I could solidify it into something straight away.'

Paul, Linda and Heather arrived in London on 31 October 1968, and five days later drove to Scotland for a long stay at High Park Farm, the remote retreat Paul had bought some years before to escape Beatlemania. The farmhouse was virtually derelict: three rooms desperate for a lick of paint and some falling-down wooden outbuildings riddled with rat-holes. Paul: 'Linda said, "We could do this place up!" And I'd never thought of that, I thought it just stayed how you bought it. I just wasn't enterprising enough to actually think, We could clean this place up! Linda really turned me on to it. I quite liked it before, I liked its isolation and I liked the privacy and the end-of-the-world remoteness compared to a city.'

Some years before, Paul had had bought some second-hand furniture from Campbeltown, including an electric stove. He had made a couch by nailing together some wooden potato boxes and folding an old mattress over the top. The settee was named Sharp's Express after the variety of potato the boxes once contained. Now he installed concrete floors, pouring the concrete himself, and began to fix the place up properly.

The farm, as its name suggested, was high on a slope, near a small loch with a cairn beyond. It looked out from its hill to the distant white sand dunes of Machrihanish Bay, two or three miles to the west. Fourteen miles to the south was the rocky headland of the Mull of Kintyre, which Paul later popularised in the biggest-selling pop single in British history.

'Scotland was like nothing I'd ever lived in,' Linda said. 'It was the most beautiful land you have ever seen, it was way at the end of nowhere. To me it was the first feeling I'd ever had of civilisation dropped away. I felt like it was in another era. It was so beautiful up there, clean, so different from all the hotels and limousines and the music business, so it was quite a relief, but it was very derelict.'

Paul's relationship with Linda was finally discovered by the newspapers, who immediately invented one of the most enduring myths about Linda of all: that she was in some way related to the Eastman Kodak family. This was presumably concocted by Fleet Street tabloids connecting her surname with the fact that she was a photographer. Paul: 'We were once in a Los Angeles disco and this bloke crept up, kneeling in front of us, and he said, "Are you Eastman Kodak?" She said no and he said, "I'm glad you said that, because I am."' No matter how many times Linda denied it, it became part of McCartney mythology that he had married an heiress.

For eighteen months throughout 1967–68, the British journalist
Hunter Davies had been working closely with the group on an
authorised biography. Paul got on very well with him and gave him all
the help he could. When he finished the book, Davies rented a villa in
Praia da Luz in the Algarve and took his family off for a winter
holiday. He sent Paul a postcard, casually inviting him to come and
stay. Late at night on 11 December he was woken up by shouts and
pebbles on his window and was surprised to find Paul, Linda and
Heather standing there together with a puzzled cab driver waiting to
be paid. That evening Paul had decided on the spur of the moment to
take up Hunter's invitation. As there were no more planes that day,
Neil Aspinall hired a private executive jet to fly to tiny Faro airport.
Paul arrived with no Portugese escudos on him so Hunter had to pay
the cab driver. The Davies family's tranquillity was shattered as they
found themselves unexpectedly engulfed in the media circus that
followed the Beatles everywhere they went. So many journalists
arrived the next day from Lisbon, alerted by the airport, that Paul had
to give a press conference on the beach, but after that their request for
privacy was more or less respected except for the mound of gifts and
invitations which piled up at the villa, sent by fans and local traders –
another permanent feature of Paul's life as a Beatle.

It was in Portugal that Paul proposed marriage to Linda, around
the time Linda first discovered she was pregnant with Mary.

> PAUL: As our relationship solidified and we really started to feel
> very confident with each other, it was a question of 'Well, shall I
> get off the pill then?' and we talked about that, and I said,
> 'Yeah!' I don't know why. It wasn't like planning a family, it was
> more 'If you like. We could see what happened. If anything
> happened. That would be all right.' Then Mary was on the way,
> it was definitely not planned. And we decided, round about that
> point, to get married.
>
> I asked Lee for her hand in marriage: 'I'd like to marry your
> daughter.' He gave me a bit of a hard time, he tried to test me
> out: 'I hear Britain's sinking' and stuff. I said, 'I hear America's
> not doing too well either,' so there was a bit of that. He was
> rather strict. But I had a different attitude, being a self-made
> man I didn't have to kowtow to him. So if he would say
> something or come on a bit strong at dinner, I'd be able to say, 'I

don't agree with that at all.' I remember once, after we were married, he told Linda off at dinner, and I said, 'I'd prefer you didn't do that.' And he looked at me like, 'Who are you?' I said, 'I'm her husband and I'd really prefer it if you didn't do that. I don't think she needs that.' It was just like throwing a grenade into the middle of the table! I just took her hand and said, 'Right. Good night, everyone. Pleasant evening. Thank you very much,' and we left. We got outside and she giggled and said, 'I don't believe you just did that!' I said, 'I'm under no obligation to this man at all. You are, it's your dad. But I have no links with him except through marrying you. And I'm self-made and so is he. He's just a guy to me.' I think eventually he respected me for that. We had one or two sticky moments but I liked him a lot.

Linda: 'So instead of getting an agent I met Paul instead and got married. Or I was going through a transition then and didn't know quite what I was doing and he obviously didn't know quite what he was doing so we ended up marrying instead.'

Heather was enrolled in Robinsfield, a small private school in St John's Wood, very close to Cavendish Avenue. They could walk her to school in the morning provided there were not too many fans camped outside the front gate; more than three or four meant they had to drive.

PAUL: It was a pleasant little school. She didn't have an easy time settling in because she was American and the kids made fun of her. She had a very poignant little story. I said to her, 'Don't try and make friends with everyone, just sit around in a corner, reading a book, and they'll eventually come up to you.' She said, 'They never did, Dad.' She did that, and it didn't work. Gulp! I don't think she made too many friends there. She wasn't desperate or anything, she was just a little sad because she's an American kid and she's a very friendly person.

Heather was still very young so Paul and Linda felt her studies would not be disrupted too much by taking her on a winter holiday. Peter Brown had a friend with a house in Ramatuelle, a fortified medieval village in the south of France not far from the famous Pampelonne beach where Brigitte Bardot made *And God Created*

Woman. They explored the tiny village with its winding lanes and two or three shops and ventured into nearby swinging St Tropez.

Paul and Linda got married at Marylebone Registry Office on 12 March 1969 amid the usual press hysteria even though it was supposed to be a secret. Paul had been best man at his brother Michael's wedding, and Michael was to be Paul's best man. Unfortunately his train broke down on the way from Birmingham and he arrived an hour late. Though he assumed it was all over, he nonetheless asked the chauffeur of the Rolls-Royce that had been sent to meet him to go to the registry office anyway. TV crews and huge crowds of weeping fans indicated that Paul and Linda were still waiting for him. None of the other Beatles was there, though George and Patti Harrison attended the wedding lunch at the Ritz afterwards, arriving very late after being delayed by Sergeant Pilcher of the Drug Squad, who tried to ruin the day by raiding George's Esher residence.

A week later Paul, Linda and Heather flew to New York to spend three weeks with Paul's new in-laws. Paul's life had entered a new phase.

PAUL: We were crazy. We had a big argument the night before we got married and it was nearly called off. We were very up and down, quite funky compared to the eventual image of 'Twenty-five years of married bliss! Aren't they lucky for people in showbiz?' But we are. You get this picture of us swanning along in a little rowboat managing to avoid the white water, but we were right in the middle of that white water, man, so it's even more miraculous that we made it. But we did.

THIRTEEN

Let It Be

The music business is about 99 per cent no-talent losers who can't stand a winner in their midst. I'm a winner, and if they want to sour grape my success by calling me names, let them. I don't give a shit.
Q: Would you lie?
A: Oh sure.
Q: Would you steal?
A: Probably.
   Look … It's really like chess, knowing all the moves. It's a game, for Chrissakes, and winning is everything. It's a shame it has to get nasty sometimes.

Allen Klein, Playboy, 1971

Live on Film

THE STRAIN OF PRODUCING THE DOUBLE ALBUM IN TIME FOR Christmas under these conditions caused irreparable rifts in the group. With John interested only in Yoko and his own music, and with George Martin often busy elsewhere or on holiday, Paul had inevitably taken charge of the album, at different times alienating both George Harrison and Ringo. Another major stress factor as the Beatles entered 1969 was Apple, which had become a behemoth and was expanding virtually out of control because there was no one in overall charge of it. While trying to record the White Album they had also had to run Apple. They managed to close the boutique and put a stop to that outflow of funds. They bought 3 Savile Row and refurbished it, but unfortunately in the course of moving all the paperwork to the new building by taxi from Wigmore Street, all the tax records went missing, throwing their financial affairs into even more chaos.

Relations with their accountants, who might have been expected to sort out the problem, were not improved when they objected on moral grounds to the sleeve of John and Yoko's *Two Virgins* album which showed them naked. Yoko had appeared in public naked several times before, notably at one of Jean-Jacques Lebel's Happenings at the Knokke-le-Zoute Film Festival in Belgium earlier in 1968. The other Beatles were horrified, not because they were shocked by the nakedness, but because they thought the sleeve would damage the Beatles as a group, but John was in no mood to listen. A meeting was called between John and Yoko, Paul and Sir Joseph Lockwood, the head of EMI.

> John to Sir Joe: 'Well, aren't you shocked?'
> Sir Joe: 'No, I've seen worse than this.'
> John: 'So it's all right then, is it?'
> Sir Joe: 'No, it's not all right. I'm not worried about the rich people, the duchesses and those people who follow you. But your mums and dads and girl fans will object strongly. You will be damaged, and what will you gain? What's the purpose of it?'
> Yoko: 'It's art.'
> Sir Joe: 'Well, I should find some better bodies to put on the cover than your two. They're not very attractive.'

It was agreed that EMI would press the album for them but have nothing to do with its distribution, which was eventually effected by Island Records in the UK and Tetragrammaton in the USA. Peter Brown reported that 'Paul hated the cover beyond words' but Paul himself doubts this, saying he was obviously still in a conciliatory mood as he actually wrote the sleeve notes for them. In the avant-garde spirit that the album was made, Paul picked a line more or less at random from the *Sunday Express*: 'When two great Saints meet it is a humbling experience. The long battles to prove he was a saint.' Paul: 'It was a "found object".'

Sir Joe was right, of course: despite the evidence of their recent records, their signatures on the pot ad and the admission of taking LSD, most of the public still regarded them as those four nice lads from Liverpool. The *Two Virgins* cover blew that image right out of the water. It was perhaps an unconscious attempt to sabotage the Beatles, John's first move to set himself free. It certainly changed the public perception of the group and also had the effect of opening John and Yoko to tremendous public ridicule.

Bryce Hanmer, the Beatles' accountants, had what William Burroughs would call an 'orgasm of prurience' and refused to act for them any longer because of the sleeve. Harry Pinsker, the head of the company, resigned from the board of Apple and the Beatles' affairs were delegated to a junior partner, Stephen Maltz, who had worked with Apple in-house since its beginning. Maltz himself resigned at the end of October 1968, after writing a five-page letter to each of the Beatles, detailing the terrible financial trouble that they were storing up for themselves and pointing out that for every £10,000 spent, something like £120,000 had to come in because of their enormous tax exposure.

With the group apparently on the verge of collapse and about to go broke, Paul proposed that they go back on the road: not for a gruelling North American tour but possibly to play a few dance halls up north, to help them remember what it was like to be in a group and maybe recreate the bond between them. The idea was scoffed at, particularly by George, who had no intention of going back on stage. As a compromise, Paul suggested a single-venue gig. The group had enjoyed shooting the promotional film for 'Hey Jude' with a live audience so he suggested a one-hour live television show. This idea was grudgingly accepted. Several venues were suggested, including the Roundhouse in north London, the site of many *International Times* events, the latter days of the UFO Club and more recently the venue for concerts by the Doors and Jefferson Airplane. This was agreed and the Roundhouse was booked for 18 January 1969. The idea held for a while but was cancelled in favour of a proposal by Michael Lindsay-Hogg, whom they had hired to direct the filming. Lindsay-Hogg had made the dramatic promotional film of the Rolling Stones' 'Jumping Jack Flash' and done their *Rock 'n' Roll Circus*. He wanted to shoot the concert in the more dramatic setting of a Roman amphitheatre in Tripoli. This concept emerged when Lindsay-Hogg was sitting around at the Stones' Maddox Street office talking to Mick's assistant Peter Swales, wondering what he could do with the Beatles. Swales had the idea of filming in a Roman amphitheatre and the fully worked scenario, as originally endorsed by the Beatles, entailed Bedouins arriving at the empty site at dawn and setting up a camp fire; as the sun rose, the amphitheatre would slowly fill with people from all over the world, of all races and colours: a multicultural idea to promote world peace and brotherhood long before Coca-Cola did the same thing in their 'I'd Like to Teach the World to Sing' ads. Finally, as the sun set over the Mediterranean, the Beatles would come on. It was a fabulous idea which, rumour had it at the time, was scotched by Ringo, who did not want to film in North Africa after his bad experience with the food in India.

Denis O'Dell, head of Apple Films, suggested that even if they couldn't agree where to hold the concert they could at least begin by filming rehearsals, which could be used as part of the concert footage or as a separate television documentary. He had already booked Twickenham Film Studios from 3 February 1969 for Ringo, who was to co-star with Peter Sellers in the film *The Magic Christian* – Ringo's second film of a book by Terry Southern. Since the studios would be free until that time, O'Dell booked Twickenham for the Beatles for the month beginning 2 January.

It was much too soon. They were all exhausted from five months of recording the White Album, and they had also all spent studio time working on Apple projects with James Taylor, Mary Hopkin, Jackie Lomax and George's *Wonderwall* music. To begin recording again after only eleven weeks' respite was a big mistake. The problems created during the White Album had not gone away or even been addressed.

The cameras were instructed to roll at all times to record the between-take conversations and provide a mass of footage from which to choose in the editing stages. The Beatles jammed their way through more than a hundred songs, sometimes making them up on the spot – such as 'Suzy Parker' – but mostly playing old Beatles numbers, children's nursery songs, parts of their old Hamburg and Cavern Club repertoire or pub standards. The problem was that they hadn't played live in years and were extremely rusty; the rehearsal tapes are terrible, the group is ragged and out of tune and stays that way.

The differences were exacerbated by having to work to film-industry schedules, which meant a morning call from Mal at 8.30 a.m. It was a horrible experience for them all. John described it to Jann Wenner: 'I was stoned all the time and I just didn't give a shit …

We couldn't get into it ... It was a dreadful, dreadful feeling in Twickenham Studio, and being filmed all the time, you know. I just wanted them to go away. And we'd be there at eight in the morning and you couldn't make music at eight in the morning.'

That was not the only problem. The rehearsal film shows the palpable tension in the air as George, Paul and Ringo attempt to run through a song while Yoko distracts John by kissing him or whispering in his ear. It was virtually impossible for the cameras to get a shot of the four of them without Yoko. It was hardly an unreasonable request when they asked John if she could be less intrusive. It is not as if he would have tolerated such behaviour from any of them, but John was so besotted that he didn't see it that way, he couldn't see that he was breaking up the group. He told *Rolling Stone*:

> They were writing about her looking miserable in *Let It Be*. You sit through sixty sessions with the most big-headed, uptight people on earth and see what it's fuckin' like, and be insulted just because you love someone. And George, shit, insulted her right to her face in the Apple office at the beginning; just being 'straight forward' you know, that game of 'Well, I'm going to be upfront because this is what we've heard and Dylan and a few people said she's got a lousy name in New York, and you gave off bad vibes.' That's what George said to her and we both sat through it, and I didn't hit him. I don't know why ...

Yoko does in fact smile in the *Let It Be* footage, during rehearsals on the day George walked out. George had never been keen on the project and the film clearly shows the tense atmosphere between him and Paul, with George visibly irritated at being told how to play his solo. However, it was a blazing argument between George and John just before lunch on 10 January that caused George to leave. 'See you round the clubs,' he told the others before leaving the studio and driving home to Esher.

Without speaking, Paul, John and Ringo returned to their instruments after lunch. Yoko symbolically settled herself down on George's now vacant blue cushion and began wailing. The remaining Beatles joined in as her backing group: Paul rubbing his bass against the amplifier speaker to create feedback; John, with full feedback, banging the back of his guitar to create surges of noise and working his way through the Pete Townshend and Jimi Hendrix guitar-hero feedback stances; Ringo rolling and thrashing his kit. Yoko played 'air' as John called it. She ululated, screeched and warbled in a vocal version of the controlled shrieks of Albert Ayler or John Tchicai. The camera moved in for a close-up of her beatific smile.

It is hard to believe that Yoko was unaware of how intrusive her presence was. But as John Lennon explained it to Andy Peebles of the BBC, Yoko naïvely believed that the Beatles would happily admit her, as a fellow musician, to play along with them, even though she claimed never to have heard of them before she met John and had no background in rock 'n' roll. John: 'There were a couple of jam sessions in "Let It Be", with Yoko and the Beatles playing, but they never got in the movie of course ... She just wanted to join in everything.' John, on a different occasion, said, 'Yoko sees men as assistants,' and the belief at the time among Apple staff was that Yoko simply saw the Beatles as a way of launching her own career.

The next day was a Saturday. No one expected George to reappear and he didn't. The following Wednesday there was a long meeting in which George outlined his conditions for staying in the Beatles: no more filming at Twickenham, no concert in Tripoli, no television show, and the songs they had rehearsed to be used in a new album to be recorded at the studio that Magic Alex was building for them in the basement of Apple. They all agreed.

The finale for the documentary film was eventually provided by the famous rooftop concert of 30 January. There was no Roman amphitheatre, no equipment except stage monitors, no audience except the office workers who managed to scramble up onto the neighbouring rooftops and no effort for the Beatles. All they had to do was walk up one flight of stairs.

Despite the lack of the promised artificial sun at the Apple boutique opening, Magic Alex had managed to remain in favour. His next projects were to be a flying saucer and magic paint that would render objects invisible: clearly both highly marketable inventions. This time his Boston Place workshop suffered a mysterious fire just before he unveiled his masterworks. It would obviously take months before he could produce new working prototypes so he bought himself another stay of execution.

Alex had been complaining for months that the equipment in EMI was out of date, that the Beatles were being fobbed off with second-rate facilities; he boasted that he could design and build a seventy-two-track studio for them that would be the most advanced facility on earth. It must have come as a shock when they finally called his bluff and asked him to do just that, though not without some serious misgivings being voiced by George Martin. Martin wrote in his autobiography *All You Need Is Ears*:

> I confess I tended to laugh myself silly when they came and announced the latest brainchild of Alex's fertile imagination. Their reaction was always the same, 'You'll laugh on the other side of your face when Alex comes up with it.' But of course he never did ... The trouble was that Alex was always coming to the studios to see what we were doing and to learn from it, while at the same time saying, 'These people are so out of date.' But I found it very difficult to chuck him out, because the boys liked him so much. Since it was very obvious that I didn't, a minor schism developed.

> PAUL: When we came to do something like a studio, or something electronic, if you've got a company called Apple Electronics, how could you bypass it? How could you not ask him to be involved? So Alex said, 'Yes, of course I can do a studio. Of course I can!' Whereas I would think, Of course I can do this. I can oversee it, with a team of very good engineers that I could talk to. I'm not sure Alex had a team of very good engineers. It was all a little bit of a solo effort and people like George Martin, being the voice of reason, would be tearing their hair out at that kind of thing. But Alex was Apple Electronics and he'd promised faithfully he could do it, so you had to give him a chance at it. You can't bring someone else in and say, 'This is the proper person,' because then the insinuation is, 'Why isn't the proper person running our company?' It would have all got much too close to home, I think. So that was one of those things. And in the end it was gutted.

George Harrison: 'Alex's recording studio at Apple was the biggest disaster of all time. He was walking around with a white coat on like some sort of chemist but didn't have a clue what he was doing. It was a sixteen-track system and he had sixteen little tiny speakers all around the walls. You only need two speakers for stereo sound. It was awful. The whole thing was a disaster and had to be ripped out.'

John Dunbar: 'It was absurd. If you'd had a few Revoxes you'd have done better ... He'd charge them thousands and buy the stuff second-hand. But John just wouldn't listen at that stage; I mean, it was Magic Alex, then Maharishi, then this, then that ...'

The studio was unusable. There was an eight-track Studer tape recorder but no mixing desk for it. There was no soundproofing, so the lower vibrations of loud conversations in other rooms seeped in. The floorboards of the room above creaked whenever anyone walked over them; if someone ran it sounded as if the roof was falling in. Alex had built the studio right next to the heating plant for the entire building so recording would have been interrupted every time the central-heating unit fired up. But in fact no recording was actually possible at all because he had completely neglected one vital point. Alex had forgotten to make connecting ports between the control room and the studio, which meant that there was no way of getting microphone leads from the studio to the mixing desk. George Martin borrowed a pair of four-track mixing consoles from EMI and the microphone cables were run down the corridor with the door open, with consequent leakage. Martin was so fed up with what he regarded as the Beatles' *folie de grandeur* that he left much of the recording to engineer/producer Glyn Johns, though Johns's final mixes were never released. John finally had to accept not only that Alex had not delivered, but that he didn't know the first thing about recording technology. The studio was eventually torn out without ever being used. Magic Alex disappeared. Not one of his ideas had ever materialised.

Let It Be

In her essay 'On Literature and Art', Camille Paglia applies Heinrich Wölfflin's analysis of early, high and late styles of painting to the career of the Beatles 'from the rough vigour of "Boys" and "Chains", through the shapely perfection of "Day Tripper", to the disintegrating sophistication of the studio bound *Sgt. Pepper* and *White Album*.

At the end of that tripartite pattern, major artists revolt, resimplify, as we see with Donatello and Picasso ...' The Beatles resimplified with *Let It Be* and *Abbey Road*. Paul's idea of playing small clubs to get the old magic back was part of this drift, something he would contrive later with Wings when he put together a pick-up group and went back out on the road.

The White Album itself was quite complex in its studio techniques, but it was a step towards simplicity, compared to *Sgt. Pepper*, as was its sleeve. *Let It Be*, as it was eventually called, was conceived of as an absolute return to basics. It was John's idea not to use any of the tricks of the modern recording studio, not even overdubs, but to play their new album live in the studio. George Martin: 'John said there was to be no echoes, no overdubs, and none of my jiggery-pokery. It was to be an "honest" album in that if they didn't get a song right the first time they would record it again and again until they did. It was awful, we did take after take after take. And John would be asking if Take Sixty-Seven was better than Take Thirty-nine.'

At first they were very rigorous in their approach but it quickly became apparent that their live sound was going to be rather thin without multitracking and overdubs, so when the American organist Billy Preston, whom they knew from Hamburg, stopped by Apple on the first day of recording, he was recruited by George Harrison to fill out the sound.

After a few days Yoko got bored with listening to the same song played over and over and brought in painting materials. Using Ringo's sound baffles as an easel, she pinned up paper and began to paint Japanese calligraphy. Though this is traditionally done with the paper horizontal and the brush held vertically above, Yoko painted Western-style at an easel, visible to everyone in the studio and particularly to the film cameras.

Nonetheless, things in the studio were not as bad as have sometimes been made out. The film *Let It Be* shows a number of moments when the band clicks and at least some of the old energy begins to flow. Paul's track 'Two of Us', written about Linda, was performed in the film by John and Paul, sharing the same microphone and behaving in every way as if the lyrics were about the two of them. They appear to be having a good time together, particularly when John ad-libs, 'Two of us wearing make-up.' Thus, with the cameras rolling, they began to make their twelfth album, which included, unusually for them, a new single – 'Get Back'.

'Get Back' was recorded on 27 January. It was basically Paul's song, composed in the studios at Twickenham for the now abandoned television show. Paul had a rough idea for the words and music and began jamming it out. John joined him and together they worked on some lyrics. Typically these were partly lifted from newspaper stories: in this case about the plight of Kenyan Asians, who were rushing to get to Britain before the passage of the Commonwealth Immigration Bill which would have denied them entry. Intended as a parody on racist attitudes, the line, 'Don't dig no Pakistani taking all the people's jobs!' was dropped early on as being too easily misconstrued. The rest of the third verse went through various changes, ending up in the final demos as:

> Meanwhile back at home too many Pakistanis
> Living in a council flat
> Candidate Macmillan tell me what your plan is
> Won't you tell me where it's at.

Meanwhile the fascist National Front was beating up Pakistanis on the streets and the right-wing politician Enoch Powell was predicting race war and 'rivers of blood' so, to avoid any possibility of inflaming the situation, the entire verse was ultimately dropped. As Paul later insisted, 'The words were not racist at all. They were antiracist. If there was any group that was not racist it was the Beatles'. But they did not want to be a hostage to misinterpretation. On a more frivolous level, the Jo Jo in the song was a fictional character. Paul: 'Many people have since claimed to be the Jo Jo and they're not, let me put that straight! I had no particular person in mind, again it was a fictional character, half man, half woman, all very ambiguous. I often left things ambiguous, I like doing that in my songs.'

'Don't Let Me Down', the B side of 'Get Back', was recorded at Apple with Billy Preston.

PAUL: It was a very tense period: John was with Yoko and had escalated to heroin and all the accompanying paranoias and he was putting himself out on a limb. I think that as much as it excited and amused him, at the same time it secretly terrified him. So 'Don't Let Me Down' was a genuine plea, 'Don't let me down, please, whatever you do. I'm out on this limb, I know I'm doing all this stuff, just don't let me down.' It was saying to Yoko, 'I'm really stepping out of line on this one. I'm really letting my vulnerability be seen, so you must not let me down.' I think it was a genuine cry for help. It was a good song. We recorded it in the basement of Apple for *Let It Be* and later did it up on the roof for the film. We went through it quite a lot for this one. I sang harmony on it, which makes me wonder if I helped with a couple of words, but I don't think so. It was John's song.

Some days produced a mass of new material: on 24 January, they recorded 'Two of Us', then still called 'On Our Way Home'; Paul's 'Teddy Boy', which was not used until the 1996 *Beatles Anthology* and which he later put on his first solo album; John's 'Dig It' and 'Dig a Pony', and even a quick burst of the old Liverpool pub song 'Maggie Mae', which slotted neatly into the final album.

One surprising song on *Let It Be* was 'One After 909', a relic of the earliest days of Paul and John's songwriting collaboration; in this case John's basic idea but worked on with Paul.

PAUL: It was a number we didn't used to do much but it was one that we always liked doing, and we rediscovered it. There were a couple of tunes that we wondered why we never put out; either George Martin didn't like them enough to or he favoured others. It's not a great song but it's a great favourite of mine because it has great memories for me of John and I trying to write a bluesy freight-train song. There were a lot of those songs at the time, like 'Midnight Special', 'Freight Train', 'Rock Island Line', so this was the 'One After 909'; she didn't get the 909, she got the one after it! It was a tribute to British Rail, actually. No, at the time we weren't thinking British, it was much more the Super Chief from Omaha.

'Dig It' was a studio improvisation led by John. The first take, which was not used, featured all four Beatles throwing in names – 'FBI, CIA, BBC, B. B. King' which is why they share the copyright credit. The master take lasted 12 minutes 25 seconds but only a tiny part edited from three quarters of the way through the recording was used for the album. Earlier parts of the track featured six-year-old

Heather on backing vocals and George Martin on maracas. The film *Let It Be* has more footage of this track being made but not the complete song and again, John certainly gives the impression of enjoying himself.

Paul had no input on 'Dig a Pony', which was entirely John's. Musically the song was quite complex and the group enjoyed the challenges presented in recording it.

Just as Paul had an inclusion in the middle of 'A Day in the Life', so John had one in the middle of Paul's 'I've Got a Feeling'. John's part – the 'Everybody had a ...' section – was a quite separately written song fragment, but it had the same tempo and was so well matched that they were able to link them together. John brought his section round to Cavendish Avenue and they finished the song together as an equal 50-50 collaboration. There is a myth that by this point in their career, Paul and John were no longer working together; it is true that they no longer got together as they used to for songwriting sessions, but they were certainly very supportive of each other's songs and still checked them with each other. 'I've Got a Feeling' is a good example of their continuing partnership.

> PAUL: Although John and I were very competitive, we liked each other's stuff, we wouldn't have recorded it so readily if we didn't. We still worked together, even on a song like 'Glass Onion' where many people think there wouldn't be any collaboration. Another is 'Ballad of John and Yoko', which John brought around to Cavendish Avenue for me to help finish the last verse he was having a bit of trouble with. He knew he could always leave a couple of sentences out, come and see me and we knew we would always finish them. It was a guaranteed solution.

For all the moments in which the old energy appears, however, the film *Let It Be* essentially shows all the Beatles looking worn out and at odds. It was by now obvious that John had virtually no interest in the band, and George's spiritual studies had provided a whole other life for him, working with both spiritual masters and Indian musicians: he was beginning to regard the group as a straitjacket. Ringo too was unhappy with the situation and had already walked out once. He had been building a solo career in films and getting a taste for a life where he was his own man. Paul was the one who most wanted the Beatles to stay together, but the more he tried, the more irritated the others became. The strain began to take its toll.

PAUL: This was a very difficult period. John was with Yoko full time, and our relationship was beginning to crumble: John and I were going through a very tense period. The breakup of the Beatles was looming and I was very nervy. Personally it was a very difficult time for me, I think the drugs, the stress, tiredness and everything had really started to take its toll. I somehow managed to miss a lot of the bad effects of all that, but looking back on this period, I think I was having troubles.

One night during this tense time I had a dream I saw my mum, who'd been dead ten years or so. And it was so great to see her because that's a wonderful thing about dreams: you actually are reunited with that person for a second; there they are and you appear to both be physically together again. It was so wonderful for me and she was very reassuring. In the dream she said, 'It'll be all right.' I'm not sure if she used the words 'Let it be' but that was the gist of her advice, it was 'Don't worry too much, it will turn out okay.' It was such a sweet dream I woke up thinking, Oh, it was really great to visit with her again. I felt very blessed to have that dream. So that got me writing the song 'Let It Be'. I literally started off 'Mother Mary', which was her name, 'When I find myself in times of trouble', which I certainly found myself in. The song was based on that dream.

For many people 'Let It Be' was to become an inspirational song, one that got them through the bad times in their lives. Paul is proud of the number of fans who, over the years, have written to thank him for writing it. It is a song that still goes down well in concert, and for which the audience shows its appreciation with candles, matches or even disposable lighters.

PAUL: Mother Mary makes it a quasi-religious thing, so you can take it that way. I don't mind. I'm quite happy if people want to use it to shore up their faith. I have no problem with that. I think it's a great thing to have faith of any sort, particularly in the world we live in. My mother was Catholic and she had me and my brother christened but that was the only religious thing we went through other than school, and occasional visits to church, where I sang in a surpliced choir. The first time I ever heard about religion really was when I was in hospital when I was eleven, and the sister on the ward lifted up my case sheet and said, 'What religion are you? It's not on here.' I said, 'I don't know.' She said, 'C of E?' I said, 'Probably.'

Looking back on all the Beatles' work, I'm very glad that most of it was positive and has been a positive force. I always find it very fortunate that most of our songs were to do with peace and love, and encourage people to do better and to have a better life. When you come to do these songs in places like the stadium in Santiago where all the dissidents were rounded up, I'm very glad to have these songs because they're such symbols of optimism and hopefulness.

'The Long and Winding Road' was written, like 'Let It Be', during the stormy recording sessions for the White Album in 1968 and reflects the dissension and troubled atmosphere within the band at the time. It was composed with Ray Charles in mind.

PAUL: It doesn't sound like him at all, because it's me singing and I don't sound anything like Ray, but sometimes you get a person in your mind, just for an attitude, just for a place to be, so that your mind is somewhere rather than nowhere, and you place it by thinking, Oh, I love that Ray Charles, and think, Well, what might he do then? So that was in my mind, and would have probably had some bearing on the chord structure of it, which is slightly jazzy. I think I could attribute that to having Ray in my mind when I wrote that one.

It's a rather sad song. I like writing sad songs, it's a good bag to get into because you can actually acknowledge some deeper feelings of your own and put them in it. It's a good vehicle, it saves having to go to a psychiatrist. Songwriting often performs that feat, you say it but you don't embarrass yourself because it's only a song, or is it? You are putting the things that are bothering you on the table and you are reviewing them, but because it's a song, you don't have to argue with anyone.

I was a bit flipped out and tripped out at that time. It's a sad song because it's all about the unattainable; the door you never quite reach. This is the road that you never get to the end of.

Allen Klein

In 1958 the singer Bobby Darin had a number-one hit with 'Splish Splash', followed a year later by Kurt Weill's 'Mack the Knife'. In 1962 he received a $750,000 advance from Capitol Records, making him the highest-paid pop singer in the world. At the party given to celebrate his signing to Capitol, a short, stocky figure with thick, black, wavy, brilliantined hair pushed his way through the crowd to Bobby Darin, whom he had never before met, and handed him a cheque for $100,000. 'What's this for?' Darin asked, puzzled.

'For nothing,' said Allen Klein.

Allen Klein was an accountant who had knocked about the music business since the late fifties. How he came to give the cheque to Bobby Darin is a perfect example of his flamboyant style. Determined to get Darin as a client, somehow he managed to get a look at the books. His own audit turned up a six-figure discrepancy. His deal for saying nothing was that he be allowed personally to deliver the cheque for the missing funds as 'for nothing'.

Darin was suitably impressed and, as Klein had hoped and planned, he fired his accountants and gave Klein his business. Klein immediately renegotiated the Capitol contract with some interesting new clauses. He wanted Capitol to sell the Trinity Music Publishing company to Darin for $350,000 cash. There were more than 700 songs in the Trinity catalogue of which only 70 were written by Darin. Capitol wanted Darin so badly they said yes. Within a year Darin was a millionaire and remained so, long after his career floundered and Klein had begun his empire-building. In many ways Klein was the first to recognise the importance to the singer-songwriter of keeping control of copyrights, though sadly his subsequent involvement with the Beatles was less successful in this respect.

Next he took on Sam Cooke, extracting nearly a million dollars from RCA just weeks before the singer was gunned down in December 1964. Klein's ability to ferret out money that was already owed to his clients was phenomenal. Most record companies were ripping off their artists so badly that all Klein had to do was nose around and threaten legal action. His trademark phrases 'I can get you double' and 'You want a million dollars? You got it!' were often true because his research had already shown that was the amount of money owed. It was money for nothing, but it took Klein to find it.

He helped get huge deals for the Animals, the Dave Clark Five and Herman's Hermits. He netted a fantastic contract with Decca for the Rolling Stones: a $1,250,000 advance against 25 per cent of wholesale; or about 75 cents an album. Compared to this, Brian Epstein's new deal for the Beatles with EMI – 15 per cent in Britain and 17.5 per cent in the USA – looked a mere pittance. Klein had his eye on the Beatles as far back as 1964 and rumour had it that he pulled the stops out on the Stones deal partly to impress the Beatles. They were the greatest rock 'n' roll band on earth and he had to have them.

The Allen and Betty Klein Company, ABKCO, was on the top floor of 1700 Broadway, a cut-price 41-storey sixties glass and steel tower five blocks from Columbus Circle in the centre of the entertainment business. (John Lennon's vituperative 1974 attack on Klein, the song 'Steel and Glass', is a reference to the building.) Klein had livened up the undistinguished architecture by installing a large door made from beaten copper, like a prop from the movie *Cleopatra*, to separate his large corner office from that of his ever-faithful personal secretary Iris Keitel, whose desk guarded the portal. He sat in the corner at a huge, conspicuously empty, kidney-shaped desk in an enormous leather chair in which he swivelled from side to side as he talked. Across from him were two walls of glass, filled with a panorama of skyscrapers and, between other towers, a view of Central Park.

In one of the outer offices lurked Pete Bennett – Peter Benedetto – a vast bulk of a man with a round Italian face, looking more like a bodyguard for Sinatra than the promo man responsible for getting the Beatles on the radio. This was the man who got Bobby Vinton to sing at the inaugural ball for President Nixon, a man proud to call the President his friend. He told *Rolling Stone*: 'I'm very active in Republican politics in Yonkers where I live. I promoted for the President in '68 on my spare time. I mean, whenever I'm calling a station about a record, I'm also promoting for Nixon.' It was ironic that John's 'Revolution' was being used to promote Nixon's election campaign; even more ironic that when John and Yoko moved to New York, they became great friends with Bennett while Nixon was simultaneously plotting to have John deported. With the introduction of Allen Klein into the Beatles equation, it was now inevitable that they would break up.

During an interview in 1968 with Ray Coleman, the editor of *Disc and Music Echo*, John casually said, 'Apple's losing money every week ... if it carries on like this, all of us will be broke in the next six months.' Though John assumed such a remark, which would have an adverse effect on Apple's business standing, was off the record, Coleman printed John's quote. In New York, Allen Klein read it and knew it was time to make his move. He flew to London and set about getting an introduction. The Apple publicist Derek Taylor gave him John's home telephone number. He called and left a message and on the night of 27 January, John and Yoko went to meet him in the Harlequin suite of the Dorchester Hotel, where he was staying.

John and Yoko were both impressed by Klein. He had done his homework and was able to run through the Beatles catalogue, identify songs that John had written and comment upon them. John was in need of all the encouragement and flattery he could get. He was still in a fragile and uncertain frame of mind after systematically destroying his ego with LSD; typically John, he had done a very thorough job. Now he was in recovery and utterly susceptible to this ego boost.

Though they seemed very different, John was able to relate to Klein. Klein had clawed his way to the top from an appalling background. He was born in Newark, New Jersey, in 1931. His mother died of cancer when he was two years old and his father, a kosher butcher, placed Allen and two of his three older sisters in an Orthodox Jewish orphanage because he was unable to look after them and run a business at the same time. Allen returned to his father's home when he was twelve years old and able to look after himself. His mother's youngest sister, Helen, was a tremendous influence on his life, acting as a surrogate mother, visiting him in the orphanage, giving him much-needed love and affection.

Only by sheer hard work and determination did Klein train himself as an accountant, working for a newspaper distributor by day and attending accountancy classes at Upsala College every evening. It is not surprising that John felt more empathy with this man than with the suave, wealthy Lee Eastman whom Paul was proposing as the man to take charge of the Beatles' affairs. Like John, Klein had effectively been abandoned by his father; like John, he grew up under the influence of an aunt rather than his mother. To John, Klein was a real working-class hero.

Apple has been described as many things – a complex tax arrangement, a way of spreading Beatles largesse among deserving new talent – but the original purpose behind it, which was put into operation four months before the death of Brian Epstein, was simply to appoint someone to take charge of the Beatles' financial affairs.

> PAUL: Apple was just to get a manager. It was in lieu of a manager. We hadn't had a manager after Brian. We realised we needed someone but getting that someone is very very difficult. In an ideal world, Mr X would appear out of the blue and would say, 'You're such a talented person that you ought to be freed to exercise your talent. I would therefore like to suggest that we put a group of people around you that will advise you on when to release your next record. Will advise on promotion. Will put a very good budget for the distribution and promotion together and you won't even have to think of it. Please take the day off.' Ahhhh! What artist wouldn't just die for that? Unfortunately they're not like that. So we set up Apple in order to put all our business affairs in one thing and then sign some good acts. It was 'Maybe we don't need to carry on like we've always carried on, maybe we could have more say in it all.' And John promptly had Lord Beeching over, who had reorganised the railways and done the railways in! But he was being promoted that year as Mr X. Mr Fix-it. You got any troubles with your business ... We were looking for someone like that.
>
> Beeching examined the financial records of Apple's various divisions and told John, 'Stick to music.'

Paul thought Lee Eastman 'would have been good businesswise, but of course, he had too much of a vested interest. He would have looked after me more than the others, so I understand their reluctance to get involved with that. And this is how Klein became Mr X.'

Lee Eastman sent his son John, the junior partner in Eastman and Eastman, who was fresh out of law school. Lennon has said that he would have probably agreed to Lee Eastman if he had come over in person.

With the advent of Allen Klein, everything changed. Klein had done his background preparation on Yoko as well as John, and was very careful to include her in every aspect of the discussion. By paying attention and giving her equal stature he gained her trust, which was the key to reaching John. John said later, 'We had him because Klein was the only one Yoko liked.'

One of the reasons she liked him was that he promised to get her an exhibition, a promise he fulfilled after they moved to the USA. This was a huge one-woman show held in the prestigious Everson Museum of Fine Arts in Syracuse, New York, scheduled to open on John's birthday on 9 October 1971. Normally such a show would be a retrospective of a lifetime's work gathered together from other museums and private collections. Yoko had only exhibited a couple of times and had sold virtually nothing. Her complete extant work would not have filled even one of the huge Everson galleries. In order to fill the huge spaces – 50,000 square feet consisting of seven galleries, a sculpture court and other rooms for installations – a team of people was hired to make art objects. The Everson Museum had allocated one sixth of its annual budget to the show but cost overruns meant that the Beatles, not just John, but all four of them, finished up paying $80,000 towards Yoko's exhibition – something that still rankles.

By the end of John and Yoko's conversation with Klein at the Dorchester, they had decided that he was their man. Even if the Beatles would not accept him, John was determined that Klein would represent him on a personal basis. Though Klein thought it a bit precipitate, John wrote a brief letter to Sir Joe Lockwood at EMI, Clive Epstein at NEMS, Dick James at Northern Songs and Harry Pinsker at Bryce Hanmer saying, 'I've asked Allen Klein to look after my things. Please give him any information he wants and full cooperation. Love. John Lennon.'

The other three Beatles had not been informed of John's meeting with Klein but listened carefully to his proposal that they should take him on as their new manager. George and Ringo were convinced. Paul was not. He had heard from Eastman about the case pending against Klein by the American tax authorities, which did not inspire confidence: tax was an area in which many groups had come unstuck in the past. The others were not concerned; perhaps in part because of that curiously rock 'n' roll attitude which says that if someone is really bad they must be good. 'Paradoxical thinking is part of the game in our art,' Paul explained. 'Rock 'n' roll specialises in that kind of, "This guy's a twerp. We've gotta have him on our team!" In rock 'n' roll you often stand things on their head.'

Word soon leaked out that John was consulting Klein and the rumours reached 46a Maddox Street, the Rolling Stones' office. The Stones had spent the previous year trying to extricate themselves from Klein's clutches but they were still not free. When Mick heard what was going on, he was concerned. He called his assistant Peter Swales into his office. Swales: 'Jagger gave me a note in an envelope to take over to Apple addressed to Paul. It was a warning, maybe in solidarity with him. It was to the effect of "Don't go near him, he's a dog. He's a crook."'

Paul: 'I called Mick Jagger and asked if he'd come round to Apple. We, the Beatles, were all gathered in the big boardroom there, and we asked Mick how Klein was, and he said, "Well, he's all right if you like that kind of thing." He didn't say, "He's a robber," even though Klein had already taken all the "Hot Rocks" copyrights off them by that time.' It sounds as if Jagger was a little intimidated at being summoned to Apple and faced by all four Beatles gathered around their huge oval table, and really didn't feel that he could advise them.

On 3 February, Allen Klein was appointed to conduct an audit of their financial affairs. The others outvoted Paul three to one at the board meeting and, presented with a *fait accompli*, Paul went along with it. Though Paul had opposed Klein's appointment, he recognised the need to have someone investigate the Beatles' finances and this was Klein's strongest area of expertise. But Paul did achieve one significant concession. All along he had moved to have the family firm of Eastman and Eastman appointed general counsel to the Beatles, so that there would at least be some check on Klein, and this was agreed to by the others. Lee and John Eastman formally became the Beatles' lawyers the following day, 4 February 1969.

For the next two months Klein sat in Apple surrounded by piles of papers while the staff, knowing his reputation, cowered in fear in their offices. As well as unravelling the confused money trails of their business, Klein himself slowly became more involved with the group's affairs. On 21 March he was appointed Apple's business manager and quickly began to 'rationalise' the staffing arrangements. With John's backing, he analysed every member of staff and was ruthless in clearing out those he considered inessential. The first to go were people who stood in Klein's way. Even Alistair Taylor, who had been with the Beatles since the day they signed with Brian Epstein, was fired. Ron Kass, who had done brilliant work in launching the label from nowhere, was dismissed with a golden handshake after a classic Klein disinformation manoeuvre. He questioned a cheque made out to Kass, and even though it was explained as covering cash Kass had advanced to Neil Aspinall in America, the seeds of doubt had been sown. Neil himself was fired, but here the Beatles objected and Klein relented when he realised that Neil did not pose a threat. A lot of dead wood was cleared away. At one point Peter Brown was ordered to fire ten people in one day. The remnants of Apple Retail were quick to go, as was Magic Alex. The kitchen staff went, so no one could get a cup of tea. Klein also fired the in-house multilingual translator so there was no one who could speak to the Japanese and European record-company executives who called up. The Beatles had always insisted on simultaneous release of Apple records in as many as twenty-seven countries and, since it was their label, they had to take care of the shipping of tapes, film for packaging and all the other details. Without a translator to talk to the art department in Sweden or Brazil, this quickly became a problem. Using Klein's logic, it would have made economic sense to close the press office and use an outside publicist, but Klein liked Derek Taylor because it was through him that Klein got to meet John, so Derek stayed.

In June, Peter Asher resigned to join Ron Kass, taking over MGM's A & R department. Peter told *Disc and Music Echo*:

> When I joined Apple the idea was that it would be different from the other companies in the record business. Its policy was to help people and be generous. It didn't mean actually I had a tremendous amount of freedom; I was always in danger of one Beatle saying, 'Yes, that's a great idea, go ahead,' and then another coming in and saying he didn't know anything about it. But it did mean that it was a nice company to work for. Now that's all changed. There's a new concentrative policy from what I can see and it's lost a great deal of its original feeling.

Peter became James Taylor's manager and immediately set about trying to get him released from the label since it appeared obvious that the only artists Allen Klein intended to promote were the Beatles. He asked Paul if they would tear up James's contract in the same spirit that they gave away all the clothes in the ill-fated Apple boutique.

PAUL: So James Taylor came and he and Peter said, 'We don't want to stay with the label. We like you, we like the guys, but we don't like this Klein guy and we don't like what's going to happen.' So I said, 'Why don't we just give him his album back and say, "There you go, man, you've made us some money, fabulous, thanks, peace." Like giving the clothes away?' But Allen Klein was very against that idea. 'You kidding? We've got his contract! We can hold this guy for ever. You're not going to give this guy his contract. Make him pay.' I said, 'No no no,' and the others, give them their due, said, 'No. We should just give him his contract back.' Klein was very sore about that but to our credit, we gave James Taylor his contract back. James is still one of my favourites, he's fabulous. He's gone on to do great things and I'm glad that our friendship is still intact. That's what was really important to me. Klein wasn't interested in that. He was just interested in winning winning winning.

Allen Klein was soon put through his paces when Dick James and Charles Silver surprised everyone and sold their 32 per cent of Northern Songs to Lew Grade's Associated Television. ATV already owned 3 per cent, and the deal now gave Grade a bigger share in the songwriting company than the Beatles' own 30 per cent. A massive financial battle for control of Northern Songs now commenced between the two sides, with Klein in the thick of it.

Unfortunately, at this moment when more than any other they needed to stick together, a major internal schism developed as Klein demanded 20 per cent of their income for his services. Paul thought this was far too much and also felt strongly that Klein should not get a percentage on deals that had been made before his arrival.

Things came to a head on 9 May 1969. The Beatles were booked in for a Friday-night session with the producer Glyn Johns at Olympia Studios in Barnes, but instead of recording, the session turned into an acrimonious argument about business. Klein had told the others that he had to have his three-year management contract signed immediately because he was flying back to New York the next day and had to present it to the board of his corporation.

PAUL: I said, 'He'll take 15 per cent. We're massive, we're the biggest act in the world, he'll take 15 per cent.' But for some reason the three of them were so keen to go with him that they really bullied me and ganged up on me. It sounds a bit wimpy but anyway they outvoted me on these issues. They said, 'He's got to have 20 per cent.' And Klein of course saw all this and said, 'I can't do it for any less than this. My board back in America won't allow it ...' Now the idea that Klein was run by some sort of board was a complete fiction. It was him and his assistant Peter Howard. Klein *was* the board, you only had to look on his letterhead. But they believed it.

They went, 'No, he's got to have a board meeting, he's told us. Tomorrow, Saturday.' I said, 'I've never heard of anyone doing any work on a Saturday, certainly not him.' They said, 'You're just stalling.' They were completely besotted with this guy. I said, 'No, I'm not. I want a good deal out of this guy. I don't think we should just run and jump into his arms. I'll wait to Monday before we ratify anything. My lawyer will be present on Monday. I happen to have a Jewish lawyer. What can I say to him? "Change your bloody religion, man, I need you"? You can't do that.' And they said, 'Well, we'll do it without you,' which they couldn't, that was why they needed me otherwise I don't think they'd have bothered showing up. So they said, 'Oh, fuck off!' and they all stormed off, leaving me with the session at Olympic.

Steve Miller happened to be there recording, late at night, and he just breezed in. 'Hey, what's happening, man? Can I use the studio?' 'Yeah!' I said. 'Can I drum for you? I just had a fucking unholy argument with the guys there.' I explained it to him, took ten minutes to get it off my chest. So I did a track, he and I stayed that night and did a track of his called 'My Dark Hour'. I thrashed everything out on the drums. There's a surfeit of aggressive drum fills, that's all I can say about that. We stayed up until late. I played bass, guitar and drums and sang backing vocals. It's actually a pretty good track.

It was a very strange time in my life and I swear I got my first grey hairs that month. I saw them appearing. I looked in the mirror, I thought, I can see you. You're all coming now. Welcome.

On the Monday negotiations began afresh and a compromise deal was worked out with Allen Klein.

PAUL: I agreed 20 per cent but I said, 'It can't be on everything, we've got an EMI contract, he can't just have 20 per cent of that.' They said, 'Okay, just on any increase he gets.' In other words, if he goes to Capitol and negotiates a new deal, he can have 20 per cent on the difference between the old deal and the new deal. I wasn't keen to have him but I thought that's fair. Everyone said, 'Okay, got a deal.' To give him his due, he was an energiser, but unfortunately he was an energiser who took too much in the end, for his pains.

Paul never did sign the management contract.

The financial imbroglios which followed were extremely complex and not helped by the fact that the Eastmans and Klein as well as Paul and the other Beatles were at loggerheads. Klein did make some remarkable deals on their behalf, as Paul conceded, particularly in his renegotiation of their contract with EMI/Capitol. As Paul's subsequent lawsuit showed, Klein made more money for them in eighteen months than Brian Epstein had during his entire period of management. The financial manoeuvring over the sale of NEMS, ATV, Northern Songs and the struggles between Allen Klein and the Eastmans were enough to fill an entire book: *Apple to the Core* by Peter McCabe and Robert D. Schonfeld.

LINDA: It was weird times. Allen Klein was stirring it up something awful. Between Allen Klein in one ear and Yoko in the other ear, they had John so spinning about Paul it was really quite heartbreaking. So stupid. It reminded me of the Eisenstein movie *Ivan the Terrible*; they were all whispering. It was like that with John; he was getting so bitter about Paul, and all Paul was saying was that he didn't want to sign a big management contract with Allen Klein. Nothing to do with anything else.

Abbey Road

Though *Let It Be*, or *Get Back* as it was still known at the time, had been intended as a live in the studio, warts and all, 'honest' recording, the three other Beatles were horrified at how ragged and thin it sounded. They were also sick of it. Not wanting to do any further work on it, they shelved the project until its companion film neared completion. Recording, however, continued. Since they no longer played live, the Beatles really only existed as an entity in the studio. The studio was their office, their factory, their workplace, and they were never absent from it for very long.

Despite the acrimonious disputes between them, the *Let It Be* sessions merged with very little gap into sessions for what was to become their next released album, *Abbey Road*. In addition, they were still producing other artists for their record company. One such was a band called the Iveys, discovered by Mal Evans. Paul never liked their name and encouraged them to change it. This they did, calling themselves Badfinger, but only after Apple released their first album, *Maybe Tomorrow*. Their first record as Badfinger was 'Come and Get It', written, produced and arranged by Paul. 'I wrote this very late one night at Cavendish Avenue,' Paul remembered 'leaving Linda in bed and saying, "I've got an idea for a song." I went downstairs and just whispered it into my tape recorder. I played it very quietly so as not to wake her. I knew it was a very catchy song.'

Paul cut a demo of 'Come and Get It' on 24 July 1969, before the other Beatles arrived to record the 'Sun King'/'Mean Mr Mustard' segue for *Abbey Road*. He recorded it first with himself singing at the piano, then overdubbed a double-tracked vocal, maracas, then drums and finally the bass line. He mixed it into stereo, and an acetate was cut for him to give to the group, all in one hour. Ringo was acting in the film *The Magic Christian*, so they were able to arrange for the song to be used as its theme tune and for Badfinger to record the soundtrack album.

> PAUL: I ran in and did it very very quickly with Phil MacDonald, the engineer. And I said to Badfinger, 'You should copy this faithfully.' They said, 'But we'd like to change it a little bit.' I said, 'No, it's absolutely the right arrangement.' They said, 'But —' I said, 'Change the B side, or change all the other stuff on the album, make those all yours, but please don't change this. I can guarantee it's a hit.'

Paul produced the record on 2 August at Abbey Road, making sure they followed his arrangement note for note, and sure enough it made number one in America. It was released in December 1969 in Britain and reached number four, launching yet another Apple act into instant stardom.

Paul: 'It was a sad story about Badfinger because they had Pete Ham with them, who was a very good songwriter and wrote a marvellous song for Nilsson called "Without You". Then he went and topped himself. Over management problems, apparently.'

Another single from the period between *Let It Be* and *Abbey Road* was 'The Ballad of John and Yoko'. John brought it round to Paul's house on 14 April 1969 for him to help complete. They quickly finished it off and went straight round to Abbey Road to record it. 'John was in an impatient mood so I was happy to help,' Paul said. 'It's quite a good song; it has always surprised me how with just the two of us on it, it ended up sounding like the Beatles.'

George was out of the country and Ringo was filming *The Magic Christian* but John wanted 'The Ballad of John and Yoko' out fast, like a piece of musical journalism. Paul and Linda had got married ten days before John and Yoko, and though neither invited the other Beatles to their respective ceremonies, they no doubt recognised the parallel paths in their lives. With John taking the vocal and playing lead and acoustic guitars, Paul sang back-up vocal and played everything else: drums, bass, piano and maracas. Despite their ongoing problems, some spark of the old friendship was still there. Here the musical partnership was in fine form and they played together with an intuitive understanding of what was needed. The old Beatles humour also resurfaced as they joked about the others not being there. Just before take four, John called out to Paul on the drums, 'Go a bit faster, Ringo,' to which Paul replied, 'Okay, George.' They did eleven takes and devoted the rest of the session to mixing it in stereo, the first Beatles stereo single. It was all over by 11 p.m.

Possibly buoyed up by the good feeling between John and Paul during work on 'The Ballad of John and Yoko', the sessions for *Abbey Road* went remarkably smoothly with only a few shouting matches. Putting the chaos of the *Get Back* sessions behind them, Paul had approached George Martin to produce an album 'like we used to', with the kind of feeling that they used to get in the earlier days. George Martin agreed, providing they really would cooperate and work with him like they used to do, so it was in the more disciplined atmosphere of earlier sessions that they produced what would be their final album.

Whereas each track on the White Album is considered the work of an individual Beatle, *Abbey Road* has a deceptive unity created by making the whole of side two into a medley. It was Paul's idea, and John was very happy about it at the time though he later claimed to have been opposed to it, but it pulled the whole album together, giving it a smooth pop surface. It showed too that the Beatles were still so prolific in their musical ideas that they could virtually give them away by combining eight separate song ideas – any one of which would have made a full-length number – into a seamless medley of Beatle music. And although the content of many of the tracks is sombre, there is overall a positive, upbeat feeling to the album given by the two songs about the sun – George's 'Here Comes the Sun', written in Eric Clapton's garden, and John's 'Sun King' – and by the warmth of 'Golden Slumbers' and the *Sgt. Pepper* humour of many of the medley fragments.

Unlike *Let It Be*, this record was in no sense cut live in the studio. The Beatles worked on it together only as much as they had on the White Album, appearing in the studio when absolutely necessary or to work on their own tracks. Another similarity with the White Album was the constant presence of Yoko Ono, even more conspicuous this time because she and John had been involved in a motoring accident in Scotland and she was ordered to bed by her doctors. Accordingly a huge double bed was delivered to the studio by Harrods and Yoko installed in it with a microphone suspended above her face in case she had any comments to make.

PAUL: This was one of the things that put a strain on the sessions. From their point of view, it was just that she had been ordered by a doctor to lie down and that John needed her to be with him. The three of us, we didn't quite get it. It was completely unusual for the Beatles to work in that way and it put a strain on it. Yoko has since told me that if for any reason she ever sat remotely nearer to me than to John, then he would give her hell when he got her home. 'You were sitting nearer to Paul than to me!' John was very paranoid in that way. One of the things most people don't know about John is that a lot of his genius was a cover-up for his paranoia.

The opening track on *Abbey Road* was 'Come Together', recorded in July 1969, a John Lennon song arranged by Paul.

> PAUL: He originally brought it over as a very perky little song, and I pointed out to him that it was very similar to Chuck Berry's 'You Can't Catch Me'. John acknowledged it was rather close to it so I said, 'Well, anything you can do to get away from that.' I suggested that we tried it swampy – 'swampy' was the word I used – so we did, we took it right down. I laid that bass line down which very much makes the mood. It's actually a bass line that people now use very often in rap records. If it's not a sample, they use that riff. But that was my contribution to that.

Paul recorded a lot of heavy breathing on the end but it is buried so deep in the mix as to be inaudible. John's copyright infringement was not overlooked by Morris Levy, owner of the Chuck Berry song. Though it was obviously only intended as an affectionate tribute to Berry, it got John into some very deep water in the early seventies when, as compensation, Levy persuaded him to release an album of rock 'n' roll songs available by mail order only through Levy's company Adam VIII Ltd.

A year after recording 'Come Together', when Paul released the news that the Beatles were effectively disbanded, he told the *Evening Standard*:

> I would love the Beatles to be on top of their form and to be as productive as they were. But things have changed. They're all individuals. Even on *Abbey Road* we don't do harmonies like we used to. I think it's sad. On 'Come Together' I would have liked to sing harmony with John and I think he would have liked me to but I was too embarrassed to ask him and I don't work to the best of my abilities in that situation.

George Harrison's beautiful ballad 'Something' was placed second on the album. Inspired by George's wife Patti and described by Frank Sinatra as 'the greatest love song of the past fifty years', it was the only Beatles song that Sinatra ever sang live, albeit introduced as a 'Lennon and McCartney composition'. It was George's only Beatles A side, and also the only time that a single was taken from an already released Beatles album. With versions by Ray Charles, Smokey Robinson and James Brown, it is one of the most covered Beatles songs. George had developed greatly as a songwriter and was now demanding equal time on albums for his compositions.

The fact that John and Paul did not give equal space to his songs on the albums had been a point of contention between them for some time. Anthony Fawcett recorded a conversation between the three of them at Apple in 1969 which showed John was feeling a twinge of guilt at their treatment of George:

> John to Paul: 'We always carved the singles up between us. We have the singles market, they [George and Ringo] don't get anything. I mean, we've never offered George "B" sides; we could have given him a lot of "B" sides, but because we were two people you had the "A" side and I had the "B" side.'
>
> Paul to John: 'Well, the thing is, I think that until now, until this year, our songs have been better than George's. Now this year his songs are at least as good as ours.'
>
> George: 'That's a myth, because most of the songs this year I wrote last year or the year before, anyway. Maybe now I just don't care whether you are going to like them or not, I just do 'em.'

The writing credits were shared more equally on *Abbey Road*, with George getting two tracks and Ringo one. The majority were, as ever, by John and Paul.

> PAUL: 'Maxwell's Silver Hammer' was my analogy for when something goes wrong out of the blue, as it so often does, as I was beginning to find out at that time in my life. I wanted something symbolic of that, so to me it was some fictitious character called Maxwell with a silver hammer. I don't know why it was silver, it just sounded better than Maxwell's hammer. It was needed for scanning. We still use that expression even now when something unexpected happens.

Paul's 'Oh! Darling' was placed next, a fifties-style rock 'n' roll ballad reminiscent of Jackie Wilson.

> PAUL: I mainly remember wanting to get the vocal right, wanting to get it good, and I ended up trying each morning as I came into the recording session. I tried it with a hand mike, and I tried it with a standing mike, I tried it every which way, and finally got

the vocal I was reasonably happy with. It's a bit of a belter, and if it comes off a little bit lukewarm, then you've missed the whole point. It was unusual for me, I would normally try all the goes at a vocal in one day.

John later commented, '"Oh! Darling" was a great one of Paul's that he didn't sing too well. I always thought I could've done it better. It was more my style than his.'

'Octopus's Garden' was Ringo's second song, written when he walked out on the Beatles during the White Album sessions and took his family to Sardinia. He was served octopus for lunch while out on Peter Sellers's yacht and, though he refused to eat it, he was intrigued when the captain told him how octopuses collect stones and shiny objects from the sea bed and build gardens with them.

Often regarded as the first real heavy-metal recording, John's 'I Want You (She's So Heavy)' achieved its much-copied massive guitar sound by John and George multitracking their guitars over and over in layers until John was satisfied it was heavy enough.

John's 'Because' was inspired by Beethoven's Moonlight Sonata. Yoko was a classically trained pianist but had stopped playing because her insensitive father had made fun of her small fingers and told her that her playing would never amount to anything. She went into musical composition but then focused on avant-garde art. Sometimes, however, she would play something for John, in this case Beethoven's Piano Sonata Number 14, Op. 27, No. 2. John was very taken with it. He was lying on the sofa listening and asked her if she could play the chords backwards. She tried and John wrote the music around her attempt, though it is more of a lift than a backwards version. It is sad that this, one of the most beautiful and fully realised of Beatles songs, should be one of the last things they recorded. The complicated three-part harmony which John, Paul and George sang together had to be thoroughly rehearsed. It was then overdubbed twice more, giving nine voices altogether. Both Paul and George said that it was their favourite track on the album.

Paul: 'I wouldn't mind betting Yoko was in on the writing of that, it's rather her kind of writing: wind, sky and earth are recurring, it's straight out of *Grapefruit* and John was heavily influenced by her at the time.' Later, when EMI were rationalising their instrument collection, Paul was able to buy the electric spinet which gives much of the characteristic sound to the track. He still has it in his recording studio along with many of the instruments used on *Sgt. Pepper* and Bill Black's stand-up double bass used on Elvis Presley's 'Heartbreak Hotel', bought for him as a birthday present by Linda on a visit to Nashville.

Though Paul would never have written a song like 'The Ballad of John and Yoko', his private life did filter through into his songs at a remove. 'You Never Give Me Your Money' is a good example. Paul: 'This was me directly lambasting Allen Klein's attitude to us: no money, just funny paper, all promises and it never works out. It's basically a song about no faith in the person, that found its way into the medley on *Abbey Road*. John saw the humour in it.'

'You Never Give Me Your Money' leads into the medley but is, in itself, a composite of at least three different fragments, ending with a reference to Paul and Linda's trips to purposely get lost in the country. It was written when they were together in New York. As on 'Tomorrow Never Knows', Paul brought in a selection of loop tapes for the segue into 'Sun King', providing an atmospheric cross-fade link that sounds like wind chimes.

'Sun King' came to John in a dream. It was an idea probably inspired by John reading, or reading a review of, Nancy Mitford's recent biography of Louis XIV of the same name. This leads to John's *Sgt. Pepper* fairground style 'Mean Mr Mustard', one of his throwaway pieces written in Rishikesh. It had its genesis in a newspaper article about a man who kept his money hidden in his rectum – something John naturally found very amusing but had to change for the song.

'Polythene Pam' was another of John's songs written in India and originally destined for the White Album. It was inspired by Stephanie, a girlfriend of the Beat poet Royston Ellis, whom the Beatles backed at Liverpool University in 1960. On 8 August 1963, the Beatles played at the Auditorium in Guernsey, the Channel Islands. Royston Ellis was working as a ferryboat engineer on the island and invited John to come back to his flat. John told *Playboy*: 'I had a girl and he had one he wanted me to meet. He said she dressed up in polythene, which she did. She didn't wear jackboots and kilts, I just sort of elaborated. Perverted sex in a polythene bag. Just looking for something to write about.' Royston Ellis told Steve Turner: 'We all dressed up in them and wore them in bed. John stayed the night with us in the same bed.' Paul remembered meeting Royston in Guernsey: 'John, being Royston's friend, went out to dinner with him and got pissed and stuff and they ended up back at his apartment with a girl who dressed herself in polythene for John's amusement, so it was a little kinky scene. She became Polythene Pam. She was a real character.' John: 'When I recorded it I used a thick Liverpool accent because it was supposed to be about a mythical Liverpool scrubber dressed up in her jackboots and kilt.'

Paul wrote 'Golden Slumbers' at Rembrandt, his father's house in Liverpool. Jim McCartney had remarried, giving Paul a stepsister, Ruth, and some of her sheet music was on the piano, including Thomas Dekker's lullaby 'Golden Slumbers'. 'I liked the words so much,' Paul said. 'I thought it was very restful, a very beautiful lullaby, but I couldn't read the melody, not being able to read music. So I just took the words and wrote my own music. I didn't know at the time it was four hundred years old.' It was first published in Dekker's *The Pleasant Comedy of Old Fortunatus* in 1603 so it was well out of copyright. Paul: 'I remember trying to get a very strong vocal on it, because it was such a gentle theme, so I worked on the strength of the vocal on it, and ended up quite pleased with it.'

'Carry That Weight', like 'You Never Give Me Your Money', was one of Paul's semi-autobiographical songs about the Beatles' business difficulties. 'I'm generally quite upbeat but at certain times things get to me so much that I just can't be upbeat any more and that was one of the times. We were taking so much acid and doing so much drugs and all this Klein shit was going on and getting crazier and crazier and crazier. Carry that weight a long time: like for ever! That's what I meant.'

By this time the atmosphere at Apple had soured irredeemably. At one time friends like Derek Taylor or Tony Bramwell could just wander into Beatles meetings, and the atmosphere was easy-going. Now they would be asked to leave.

PAUL: There was what my Aunty Jin would have called a bad atmosphere – 'Oh, I can feel the atmosphere in this house, love.' It wasn't difficult, she wouldn't have liked it there. It was 'heavy'. 'Heavy' was a very operative word at that time – 'Heavy, man' – but now it actually felt heavy. That's what 'Carry That Weight' was about: not the light, rather easy-going heaviness, albeit witty and sometimes cruel, but with an edge you could exist within and which always had a place for you to be. In this heaviness there was no place to be. It was serious, paranoid heaviness and it was just very uncomfortable.

It was fitting that the last track on the last recorded Beatles album should be called 'The End' (discounting 'Her Majesty', which was not listed on the original pressings). The track shows how the Beatles might have developed had they remained together: the extended drum solo and guitar-hero theatrics which were already developing among their contemporaries and which would became the main features of seventies 'rock' were already present in *Abbey Road*, including Ringo's only drum solo and a three-way guitar battle between John, Paul and George. Shakespeare ended his acts with a rhyming couplet so that the audience would know they were over. Paul: 'I wanted it to end with a little meaningful couplet, so I followed the Bard and wrote a couplet.'

The medley, or 'the Long One' as it was known in the studio, went through a number of changes before reaching its final order. The little fragment known as 'Her Majesty', which Paul wrote in Scotland, was originally placed after 'Mean Mr Mustard' but Paul decided it didn't work there and asked the tape operator John Kurlander to edit it out and throw it away. Following normal studio practice, he attached a long piece of leader tape to it to identify it as separate from the rest of the tracks and tacked it on the end of the reel. When an acetate was made of the medley, 'Her Majesty' was accidentally included. Paul liked it in its new position, and it was allowed to remain. This accounts for the long silence which precedes it, and the decaying chord with which it opens, which is in fact the last chord of 'Mean Mr Mustard'. Paul: 'That was very much how things happened. Really, you know, the whole of our career was like that so it's a fitting end.'

The lyrics to 'Her Majesty' are emblematic of how far apart John and Paul had become. Four months before John returned his MBE medal to the Queen, Paul was writing a few lines in her honour, even though they were tinged with irony. Paul: 'It was quite funny because it's basically monarchist, with a mildly disrespectful tone, but it's very tongue in cheek. It's almost like a love song to the Queen.'

The final track on *Abbey Road* to be completed was John's 'I Want

You (She's So Heavy)' on 20 August 1969. It was to be the last time that all four Beatles were together in the studio.

Ten days before that, the Beatles had assembled for a cover shot. They didn't have to go far, just outside Abbey Road studios. On 8 August the famous zebra-crossing photograph was taken by Ian Macmillan, based on a sketch by Paul. It was Paul's third Beatles sleeve in a row, and like *Sgt. Pepper* it was the subject of many parodies in years to come. It became such an icon that he even parodied it himself with his *Paul Is Live* album recorded in 1993.

Divorce

Linda was four months pregnant when they married. Since the birth would be in August, they took an early summer holiday beginning 15 May, and spent a month on the island of Corfu, on the west coast of Greece across from the heel of Italy, far away from the pressure of Apple and the sounds of corporate battles waged on their behalf by Allen Klein and John Eastman. They stayed in Benitses, then a sleepy fishing village a few miles south of Corfu Town, with the houses opening straight on to a tiny beach. It was here that Paul wrote 'Every Night', which appeared on his first solo album. Sadly, with the late-seventies 'development of Corfu' – the breezeblock hotels, late-night discos and lager louts on package holidays – the pretty little village of Benitses that Paul and Linda knew is now unrecognisable.

Mary McCartney was born on 28 August and was named after Paul's mother. With a new baby and a seven-year-old daughter to look after, Paul stayed away from the office, which he had grown to dislike since Klein had ensconced himself there, and his place was taken by John and Yoko.

By the time *Abbey Road* was completed, Allen Klein had reduced Apple to an ordinary management office. All the fine ideas were gone as well as most of the idealists. However, for those no longer fearful of losing their job, working at Apple was still better than working anywhere else. Jack Oliver, who had joined the company as Terry Doran's assistant at Apple Music, was, to his great surprise, promoted to replace Ron Kass as the head of the record division. He had no power since it was Klein who really ran the record company, so Jack whiled away the hours, engaged in a telex romance with the receptionist at Allen Klein's New York office. They never met but exchanged yards and yards of telex paper each day. The two expensive offices in the Capitol Tower at Hollywood and Vine, intended as the American headquarters of Apple, remained empty except for the two bored secretaries, who spent all day reading the trades and exchanging gossip with friends on the telephone.

John and Yoko moved into Ron Kass's vacated front office and ran an open house, giving the Apple press office plenty of fun things to do. Ever since John and Paul had gone on American television and effectively invited anyone with a good idea to come to them, Apple had been inundated with mad inventors, religious fanatics, hippie entrepreneurs, mystics, poets, playwrights, musicians and a man who thought he was Hitler. Since no one else was in a position to deal with them, Derek had to:

> Reception: 'There's a man here who says he's Hitler.'
> Derek Taylor; 'Christ, not that bastard again! All right, send him up.'

It was someone in Derek's office that fielded the telephone calls from Charles Manson and all the other fanatics who had decoded the album sleeves or lyrics to find secret messages addressed only to them. It was the press office that looked after the Hell's Angels George invited to come and stay, and the press office that had to try and explain John and Yoko's latest antics to puzzled journalists. There was a constant stream of reporters, not just from Fleet Street but from all over the world, not just newspapers and the music weeklies but women's magazines, *Time* and *Life*, television and radio stations from Los Angeles to Hong Kong, all needing interviews, photographs, quotes and stories. Popular interest in the Beatles remained as high as ever and was used by John and Yoko to further their peace campaign.

Even with Klein in charge, Apple still did not entirely operate like a normal company. The staff always had to expect the unexpected; they were told, for instance, that Yoko's daughter Kyoko must be allowed to do anything she wanted. One day she pulled all the plugs out of the telephone switchboard, cutting off international calls and bringing Apple Records business to a halt. The frustrated switchboard operator was almost fired because she dared to tell the precocious child to go away. On the surface, however, it might have looked as if Klein had saved the day. The haemorrhaging of money seemed to have been stopped; the Beatles were apparently getting on better than they had done; certainly *Abbey Road* was recorded in a better atmosphere than *Let It Be*. But underneath, tensions were still rising.

The one thing everyone concurred on was that Klein had done a good job in renegotiating the Beatles' contract with EMI/Capitol. After fierce negotiations, EMI agreed to increase the royalty on US records to an unprecedented 25 per cent of retail, to be paid directly by Capitol to Apple, a far higher royalty than any other group had ever attained. On this point, at least, John and Paul were in agreement and even John Eastman congratulated Klein on his negotiations. On 20 September 1969, all four Beatles gathered at Savile Row to sign the documents. It was then that John sprang his surprise on them.

> PAUL: We were all summoned to sign a new Capitol contract at Apple. We all went round to do it, and it got a little bit 'Well, why are we doing this? Are we sure the group is going to continue?' 'Oh, sure, it'll all continue.' 'Well, how's it going to continue? What are we going to do? Massive big shows?' Then I propounded the theory, 'I think we should get back to our basics. I think we've got out of hand, we've overwhelmed ourselves and I think what we need is to re-establish our musical identity and find out who we are again, and so we should go back to little gigs.' At that point John looked at me and said, 'Well, I think yer daft!' Which was a little bit of a show-stopper. He said, 'Well, I wasn't gonna tell you till after we'd signed the Capitol contract. Klein asked me not to tell you. But, seeing as you asked me, I'm leaving the group.' So everyone went, 'Gulp!' The weight was dropped, our jaws dropped along with it, everyone blanched except John, who coloured a little and said, 'It's rather exciting. It's like I remember telling Cynthia I wanted a divorce.' And I think from what he was saying there was an adrenalin rush that came with telling. So that was it. We signed the new Capitol deal in a bit of a daze, not quite knowing why we'd done it. That's my recollection.

For many years there was a spurious debate conducted in the music press and by 'Beatles experts' on 'Who broke up the Beatles?' Yoko was most often blamed. Sometimes Linda was proposed as the villain and Paul was frequently saddled with the role. It fact it was John who broke up the Beatles, as he often said in print. In his autobiographical essay 'The Ballad of John and Yoko', he wrote:

> Apart from giving me the courage to break out of the Stockbroker belt ... Yoko also gave me the inner strength to look more closely at my other marriage. *My real marriage.* To the Beatles, which was more stifling than my domestic life. Although I had thought of it often enough, I lacked the guts to make the break earlier ... I started the band. I disbanded it. It's as simple as that.

He wrote that when he finally got up the courage to tell the other three he wanted a divorce 'they knew it was for real, unlike Ringo and George's previous threats to leave'.

John never spelled out his reasons for leaving in any detail but his dissatisfaction with the group seemed to go as far back as the death of Brian Epstein. John had a much greater emotional involvement with Brian and was more shaken by his death than the others. Brian had been a substitute father to him and John saw his death as yet another abandonment, automatically associated with the deaths of his mother and Aunt Mimi's husband, Uncle George. Peter Brown reports that when Brian was in the Priory rehabilitation clinic for a sleep cure to get him off drugs, John sent a huge bouquet of flowers with a note saying, 'You know I love you, I really do ...', something that no other member of the group would have dreamed of doing.

After Brian's death, Paul tried to revitalise the group but John had lapsed into a state of lethargy. He had always been lazy, but now he spent virtually his whole time sitting around watching television, reading the papers, smoking pot or tripping. Consequently, when Paul came up with the idea of *Magical Mystery Tour*, John had no new material. In *John Lennon: One Day at a Time*, Anthony Fawcett quotes a taped conversation between John and Paul in September 1969, just before John left the group:

> JOHN: 'You'd come up with a 'Magical Mystery Tour'. I didn't write any of that except 'Walrus'; I'd accept it and you'd already have five or six songs, so I'd think, 'Fuck it, I can't keep up with that.' So I didn't bother, you know? And I thought I don't really care whether I was on or not, I convinced myself it didn't

matter, and so for a period if you didn't invite me to be on an album personally, if you three didn't say, 'Write some more 'cause we like your work', I wasn't going to fight!

John's paranoia was unjustified but nonetheless genuine. There had always been competition between John and Paul to get A sides. John fought hard to get 'Revolution' on the A side of Apple's first Beatles single but Paul won with 'Hey Jude'. To win, they had to convince the other Beatles and George Martin that their song was the more commercial, which in this case 'Hey Jude' obviously was. The problem came because John's productivity fell off dramatically at a time when Paul was building towards his artistic and commercial peak. On the early albums, the majority of songs were co-written, so the problem was not as acute. However, on *A Hard Day's Night*, when John was at the height of his powers, he effortlessly contributed seven of the songs, he and Paul co-wrote three and Paul only had three of his own. Following this, there was a rough balance between songs written mainly by John and those written mainly by Paul, but this balance was to change after Brian's death, particularly with *Magical Mystery Tour*.

John could not come to terms with the fact that Paul was now the *de facto* leader of the group. Though he personally liked the film, he hated the fact that *Magical Mystery Tour* was not his idea. He was also convinced that Paul got more studio time on his tracks that he did, an idea rubbished by George Martin, who has often said that if Paul got more time, it was because he was more meticulous, more prepared to take time getting the exact sound he wanted, whereas John couldn't be bothered. John could clearly have taken all the time he wanted to get a song right and sometimes did, as the many attempts at 'Strawberry Fields' show. In any case, it was an argument John should have had with George Martin, not with Paul. In *Summer of Love*, Martin wrote: 'The extremely difficult, John thought of as par for the course; only with the utterly impossible were you allowed to take more time. Once he had an idea, it had to be captured quickly. If it did not materialise in very short order, he tended to wander off and lose interest.' John's complaint to Paul was actually an attempt to get his songs on to albums without the usual democratic vetting by the others, as the conversation between John and Paul recorded by Anthony Fawcett in September 1969 reveals. John tells Paul:

If you look back on the Beatles' albums, good or bad or whatever you think of 'em, you'll find that most times if anybody has got extra time it's you! For no other reason than you worked it like that. Now when we get into a studio I don't want to go through games with you to get space on the album, you know. I don't want to go through a little manoeuvering or whatever level it's on. I gave up fighting for an A-side or fighting for time. I just thought, well, I'm content to put 'Walrus' on the 'B' side when I think it's much better ... I didn't have the energy or the nervous type of thing to push it, you know. So I relaxed a bit – nobody else relaxed, you didn't relax in that way. So gradually I was submerging.

Paul protested that he had tried to allow space on albums for John's songs, only to find that John hadn't written any. John explained, 'There was no point in turning 'em out. I couldn't, didn't have the energy to turn 'em out and get 'em on as well.' He then told Paul how he wanted it to be in the future: 'When we get in the studio I don't care how we do it but I don't want to think about equal time. I just want it known I'm allowed to put four songs on the album, whatever happens.'

This was something the other Beatles had always wanted to avoid, ever since John's insistence on including 'Revolution 9' on the White Album and his anger at their refusal to release the long, sound collage 'What's the New Mary Jane'. The other three Beatles wanted to retain a readily definable Beatles sound. Apple had already released *Two Virgins* and *Unfinished Music, Life with the Lyons* to mass derision and incomprehension, and plans were underway for *The Wedding Album*; understandably the other three wanted John's experiments to remain separate from his work with the Beatles. It was for this type of move, a cunning attempt to by-pass the Beatles democracy, that the others, much as they also loved him, regarded him as a 'manoeuvring swine', as Paul once put it.

Faced with John's declaration of intent to leave, the others were stunned. As they had done before, they decided the best course of action was to buy time. John was not in good shape: he was just coming off heroin (he was to record 'Cold Turkey' a week later) and there was always a possibility that a cleaned-up John Lennon might reconsider. For John to leave meant the end of the Beatles. It would have just about been possible to ride out the departure of George or Ringo since the group no longer played live, but the Beatles without John Lennon was inconceivable. At Allen Klein's request it was decided that the best plan of action was to tell no one. They needed time to think and they all hoped that John might change his mind. It had been known to happen. *Abbey Road* was released and publicised without a hint of the breakup leaking out.

John, normally the most painfully honest of the Beatles, continued to perpetuate the fiction that the group still existed. In an interview with *Rolling Stone* in January 1970, four months after he had left the group, John still worded his interviews to give the impression that the group still existed:

> RITCHIE YORKE: When you are about to record a new Beatles album, do you feel very excited about it? Does that old excitement still permeate the sessions?
> JOHN LENNON: Oh yeah, sure, sure. Everytime you go in the studio you get the whole thing all over ... the nerves and the light goes on and everything. It's still the same battle every time and the same joy.

Anyone who could read between the lines could have deduced that the Beatles no longer existed, but John was the only one giving interviews and wasn't saying it directly. The press preferred to believe the fiction, even though John as good as told them on several occasions. It did seem as though John was still unsure about the breakup. In January 1970 *New Musical Express* asked him if the Beatles would make another record and he told them:

> It just depends how much we all want to record together. I don't know if I want to record together again. I go off and on it ... In the old days, when we needed an album, Paul and I got together and produced enough songs for it. Nowadays, there's three of us writing prolifically and trying to fit it all into one album.
> We've always said we had fights, it's no news that we argue ... For instance, I don't give a damn about how 'Something' is doing in the charts – I watch 'Come Together' (the flip side) because that's my song. That is why I've started with the Plastic Ono and working with Yoko, to have more outlet. There isn't

enough outlet for me in the Beatles. The Ono Band is my escape valve. And how important that gets, as compared to the Beatles for me, I'll have to wait and see.

The one thing that was clear was the Beatles were no longer giving John what he needed from them.

PAUL: The Beatles was a gang, a family, an environment. It was very much a gentlemen's club, all of these things. We were each other's intimates. We knew things about each other that most other people didn't know. For all of us it was a family. I think it broke up because it couldn't give any more as a family. It had given security, warmth, humour, wit, money, fame, but there came a point where it didn't give bizarreness, it didn't give avant-gardeness, it didn't give ultimate spontaneity, it didn't give ultimate flexibility, it didn't give jumping off the cliff! I think for all of us it was a good thing that it broke when it did. But it was possibly the most useful to John. Well, it was John that broke the Beatles up.

Paul told the *Evening Standard* in April 1970: 'John's in love with Yoko and he's no longer in love with the other three of us.'

This was true, but with hindsight it is possible to look back and see that a graph of John's mental health suggests that far from being a destructive influence on John, it may have been Yoko who saved his life. John's long-term depression, precipitated by the death of Brian Epstein, had culminated in a series of week-long LSD sessions, during which he gobbled pills whenever he showed the slightest sign of coming down. No one had any experience of permanent acid damage at that time but had he not met Yoko, there is strong evidence that John might have joined the ranks of acid casualties such as Pink Floyd's Syd Barrett and Fleetwood Mac's Peter Green. The problem was that shortly after they got together, John got strung out on heroin, which, although it killed the pain and probably did stabilise him mentally for a while, also gave him all the classic behaviour symptoms of a junkie: it made him devious, paranoid and manipulative.

Junk further tested the bonds of the Beatles' friendship and even before John announced his leaving, they were hardly talking to each other. Their supposed disaffection was naturally exploited by the courtiers who whispered and plotted behind their backs, hoping to turn the situation to their advantage.

PAUL: When John and I used to meet during that period, he'd say, 'Do they try and set you against me like they try and set me against you?' And I'd say, 'Yes, often. People'll say, "Oh, did you hear that Lennon threw up before he went on stage in Toronto?"' They'd always tell me the juicy things, in case I wanted to go, 'Did he? What a bastard! Well, serve him right, ha, ha, ha.' We'd hear it just as gossip and derive some petty satisfaction from it, but on a deeper level it was like, 'Yes, but the amount of drugs he was on, he would be throwing up just with the drugs, never mind anything else. He might have tried to not have his heroin that day and I guess you're going to throw up.' The two of them were on heroin, and this was a fairly big shocker for us because we all thought we were far-out boys but we kind of understood that we'd never get quite that far out. I don't think people understand what was happening but there was a lot of affection still.

FOURTEEN

John

The heart stops briefly when someone dies,
a quick pain as you hear the news, & someone passes
from your outside life to inside. Slowly the heart
   adjusts
to its new weight, & slowly everything continues,
   sanely.

Ted Berrigan, 'Things to do in Providence'

Breaking Up Is Hard to Do

THREE WEEKS AFTER JOHN'S BLOCKBUSTER NEWS, PAUL RETIRED TO HIS farm in Scotland and stayed there until Christmas, insecure and bewildered, trying to come to terms with this new development, walking in the mists and drizzle of the Mull of Kintyre, wracking his brains for a solution.

> PAUL: I was going through a hard period. I exhibited all the classic symptoms of the unemployed, the redundant man. First you don't shave, and it's not to grow a groovy beard, it's because you cannot be fucking bothered. Anger, deep deep anger sets in, with everything, with yourself number one, and with everything in the world number two. And justifiably so because I was being screwed by my mates. So I didn't shave for quite a while. I didn't get up. Mornings weren't for getting up. I might get up and stay on the bed a bit and not know where to go, and get back into bed. Then if I did get up, I'd have a drink. Straight out of bed. I've never been like that. There are lots of people who've been through worse things than that but for me this was bad news because I'd always been the kind of guy who could really

pull himself together and think, Oh, fuck it, but at that time I felt I'd outlived my usefulness. This was the overall feeling: that it was good while I was in the Beatles, I was useful and I could play bass for their songs, I could write songs for them to sing and for me to sing, and we could make records of them. But the minute I wasn't with the Beatles any more it became really very difficult.

Three years later, Paul told a *Melody Maker* journalist:

Immediately after the breakup of the Beatles I felt, What am I going to do? I needed at least a month to think a bit. I went into a period of what everyone called being a recluse, a hermit in isolation. All sorts of little snide articles appeared saying: 'He's sitting up in Scotland, looking into his mirror, admiring his image.' It was not at all true. I was just planting trees. I was just getting normal again, and giving myself time to think. I never used to understand when they used to say, 'What are you going to do when the bubble bursts?' A joke question, and we always used to say 'Ha, ha, we'll burst with it.' I never once took that question in.

The bubble had burst and Paul felt trapped: bound by contract to a band that no longer existed and controlled by a manager he didn't trust. The root of the problem was an agreement signed by all four Beatles in July 1967 at the formation of Apple which bound them together financially for ten years. The profits from everything they did, with the exception of songwriting, were to be paid into Apple, which the four of them jointly owned. None of them was able to earn money separately so the profits from John's Plastic Ono Band activities were shared equally between the four of them, along with the royalties from George, Ringo and Paul's solo albums and Beatles royalties. It was advantageous for Ringo, whose *Sentimental Journey* sold a quarter the number of copies of Paul's first solo outing, but it was an agreement that reflected the share-and-share-alike philosophy that characterised Apple in its early days.

Times had changed, however, and with the group no longer in existence, Paul wanted out. In April 1970, he told the London *Evening Standard*:

Personally, I would like to see an independent panel of experts to work out how the Beatles could be given their independent finances – so that on their individual things they could get the rewards for their efforts. Beatles things would of course still be shared. We should all have our independent incomes and let us work out for ourselves the accompanying problems. Klein says it's impossible for tax reasons but I'm not convinced.

It was not surprising that Klein wanted to preserve the status quo. John had not yet produced a halfway commercial album and George's great creative breakthrough was only just beginning: his *All Things Must Pass* was not released until November 1970. Paul had always written the most commercial Beatles songs and it seemed likely that he would make the most commercial solo albums. As John, George and Ringo's manager, Klein did not want them to lose their share of Paul's royalties, or to lose his own percentage.

Apple had become a prison of Paul's own making.

PAUL: I was going through a bad time, what I suspect was almost a nervous breakdown. I remember lying awake at nights shaking, which has not happened to me since. One night I'd been asleep and awoke and I couldn't lift my head off the pillow. My head was down in the pillow, I thought, Jesus, if I don't do this I'll suffocate. I remember hardly having the energy to pull myself up, but with a great struggle I pulled my head up and lay on my back and thought, That was a bit near! I just couldn't do anything. I had so much in me that I couldn't express and it was just very nervy times, very very difficult. So I eventually went and said, 'I want to leave. You can all get on with Klein and everything, just let me out.' And they said, 'No, we're not going to let you go.' Because Klein had said, 'Look, he produced "Those Were the Days" and stuff.' Like James Taylor, same idea, 'Why let him go?' I remember having one classic conversation with George Harrison, I said, 'Look, George, I want to get off the label,' and George ended the conversation, and as I say it now I almost feel like I'm lying with the devil's tongue, but I swear George said to me, 'You'll stay on the fucking label. Hare Krishna.' That's how it was, that's how the times were.

I was having dreams that Klein was a dentist. I remember telling everyone and they all laughed but I said, 'No, this was a fucking scary dream!' I said, 'I can't be with the guy any longer.

He's in my dreams now, and he's a baddie.' He was giving me injections in my dreams to put me out and I was thinking, Fucking hell! I've just become powerless. There's nothing I can do to stop this rot. So I decided to just get out, but they wouldn't let me out, they held me to that contract.

Paul was already thinking about recording again. Never happy unless he was making music and with the Beatles not functioning, probably extinct, Paul began recording tracks for a solo album, beginning when he and Linda returned from Scotland just before Christmas 1969. Paul had had a Studer four-track installed at Cavendish Avenue in September but had to begin work without the benefit of a mixing desk or VU meters, which were not yet delivered. He had to guess whether he was recording at the right levels and not distorting but through trial and error he got the hang of it. With the exception of people from Apple and the engineering staff at Abbey Road and Morgan Studios in Willesden, very few people were aware that he was recording. Paul told *Rolling Stone* afterwards: 'We decided we didn't want to tell anyone what we were doing ... That way it gets to be like home at the studio. No one knows about it and there is no one in the studio or dropping by.' Linda would make the booking and they would arrive with sandwiches and a bottle of grape juice, put the baby on the floor, give Heather her toys, and start to make music. It felt like a holiday compared to the atmosphere that had attended Beatles recording sessions for the previous two years. Paul said at the time, 'I found that I was enjoying working alone as much as I'd enjoyed the early days of the Beatles.' The first track recorded was 'The Lovely Linda', a song written in Scotland.

Paul had been given a release date by Neil Aspinall and he built the project around meeting the various deadlines that entailed: handing in a final mix tape, designing and proofing the cover art, approving test pressings and so on. Working with the artist Gordon House and the designer Roger Huggett, whom he still uses, Paul and Linda put the entire thing together at home. Paul: 'I was feeling quite comfortable, the more I went on like this. I could actually do something again. Then I rang up Apple one day and said, "Still okay for the release date?" and they said, "No, we're changing it. You got put back now. We're going to release *Let It Be* first."' This was the final straw for Paul. He couldn't even get his own record released from his own record company without obtaining clearance from the other three Beatles and Klein.

> PAUL: They eventually sent Ringo round to my house at Cavendish with a message: 'We want you to put your release date back, it's for the good of the group' and all of this sort of shit, and he was giving me the party line, they just made him come round, so I did something I'd never done before, or since: I told him to get out. I had to do something like that in order to assert myself because I was just sinking. Linda was very helpful, she was saying, 'Look, you don't have to take this crap, you're a grown man, you have every bit as much right ...' I was getting pummelled about the head, in my mind anyway.

In his *Evening Standard* interview at the time, Paul said:

> The other day Ringo came around to see me with a letter from the others and I called him everything under the sun. But it's all business. I don't want to fall out with Ringo. I like Ringo. I think he's great. We're all talking about peace and love but really we're not feeling peaceful at all. There's no one who's to blame. We were fools to get ourselves in this situation in the first place. But it's not a comfortable situation for me to work in as an artist.

Allen Klein and John had decided to bring forward the release of *Let It Be* without telling Paul, and Paul eventually had to get George, as a fellow director of Apple, to authorise the release of *McCartney* for him on its original date, 17 April 1970.

The announcement that the Beatles had broken up is usually attributed to Paul, though he said little more than John had been saying in interviews for months – both were ambiguous, leaving the door ajar a little, just in case. It was the way that the news was delivered that made the difference.

> PAUL: I didn't want to do a press conference to launch the album because whenever I'd meet a journalist, they always floored me with one question: they'd say, 'Are you happy?' and it almost made me cry. I just could not say, 'Yes. I'm happy,' and lie through my teeth, so I stopped doing interviews. Peter Brown, who was at Apple at that time, said, 'What are you going to do

about publicity?' I said, 'I don't really want to do any.' He said, 'It's a new album. You'll kill it. Nobody'll even know it's out at all. You should do something.' I said 'Well, how do you suggest we do it?' He said, 'Maybe a questionnaire?' I said, 'Okay, look, you write some questions that you think the press wants to know. Send 'em over to me and I'll fill it out but I can't face a press conference.' So the questionnaire came, and Peter Brown realised that the big question was the Beatles so he put in a couple of loaded questions and rather that just say, 'I don't want to answer these,' I thought, Fuck it. If that's what he wants to know, I'll tell him. I felt I'd never be able to start a new life until I'd told people.

Peter Brown opened up with fairly standard press questions but at question 28 he asked:

Is this album a rest away from Beatles or start of a solo career?
PAUL: Time will tell. Being a solo album means 'the start of a solo career' ... and not being done with the Beatles means it's a rest. So it's both.
PETER BROWN: Have you any plans for live appearances?
PAUL: No.
PETER BROWN: Is your break with the Beatles temporary or permanent, due to personal differences or musical ones?
PAUL: Personal differences, business differences, but most of all because I have a better time with my family. Temporary or permanent? I don't know.
PETER BROWN: Do you foresee a time when Lennon–McCartney becomes an active songwriting partnership again?
Paul: No.

Paul roughed out a design for the album sleeve, using Linda's photographs, and Gordon House and Roger Huggett executed it. The questionnaire and an information sheet about the album were printed up on different-coloured paper stock and record-mailing envelopes were delivered to Cavendish Avenue. Paul and Linda sat at home stuffing the pink and yellow inserts into the albums, putting the albums into the envelopes, and addressing the envelopes to the press.

PAUL: We were actually enjoying ourselves like children, Linda and I, actually enjoying life for the first time in a while. And I had put the killer scoop in there, and then I just sent this out to the press. Only the press got the ones with the questionnaire in. I think some of the press thought this was how I was releasing the album, with this questionnaire in it, so a few people said, 'This is outrageous!' and John, I think, was very hurt.

I personally think he was hurt because he wanted to tell. I don't think it was anything more than that, I think it was just straightforward jealousy. He wanted to be the one, because he'd been the one to break up the Beatles and he hadn't had the nerve to follow it through because Klein had told him, 'Don't tell anyone. Keep this thing rolling as long as we can.' But we'd not seen each other for three or four months and I had been ringing, calling George and Ringo and asking 'Do you think we'll get back together?' 'Well, I don't know, what about John?' and I'd ring John. 'Oh no! Fucking hell!' So it was obviously not on. So I let the news out. So I was not loved for that by the other guys and that started a war between us.

The press, of course, not knowing that John had quit seven months earlier, thought that Paul was leaving the Beatles, precipitating the breakup, and went wild. The biggest, most successful act the world had ever known was breaking up. It was not long, however, before the true facts emerged: how first Ringo, then George had left and returned; and then finally John, never to return. Someone had to be responsible, someone had to take the blame. The press soon decided it was Yoko. Without Yoko John would not have gone through his 'avant-garde' phase and would have still wanted to play with the others instead of just doing nasty John and Yoko music. Certainly this was how the official Beatles biographer Hunter Davies saw it. He wrote in the *Sunday Times* that after John and Yoko got together, 'the rest of the Beatles didn't matter any more'. Yoko had broken up the beloved Beatles. His story went out over the wire services, producing many hundreds of newspaper articles worldwide with headlines like 'Beatles Expert Says Yoko Is Worm in Apple'.

The Beatles were no more. The last press release issued on their behalf was written by Derek Taylor and typed by his secretary Mavis Smith on 10 April, 1970:

Spring is here and Leeds play Chelsea tomorrow and Ringo and John and George and Paul are alive and well and full of hope.

The world is still spinning and so are we and so are you. When the spinning stops – that'll be the time to worry. Not before.

Until then, The Beatles are alive and well and the Beat goes on, the Beat goes on.

Breaking point came when Apple decided to release the long-delayed *Let It Be* album. In mid-April 1970, Paul told the *Evening Standard*:

> The album was finished a year ago, but a few months ago American record producer Phil Spector was called in by John Lennon to tidy up some of the tracks. But a few weeks ago, I was sent a re-mixed version of my song 'The Long And Winding Road', with harps, horns, an orchestra and women's choir added. No one had asked me what I thought. I couldn't believe it. I would never have female voices on a Beatles record. The record came with a note from Allen Klein saying he thought the changes were necessary. I don't blame Phil Spector for doing it but it just goes to show that it's no good me sitting here thinking I'm in control because obviously I'm not. Anyway I've sent Klein a letter asking for some of the things to be altered, but I haven't received an answer yet.

Nor did he. *Let It Be* was released on 8 May, with none of Paul's requests implemented.

George Martin was equally shocked when he heard what had been done to *Let It Be*. He told *Rolling Stone*:

> It was always understood that the album would be like nothing the Beatles had done before. It would be honest, no overdubbing, no editing, truly live … almost amateurish. When John brought in Phil Spector he contradicted everything he had said before. When I heard the final sounds I was shaken. They were so uncharacteristic of the clean sounds the Beatles had always used. At the time Spector was John's buddy, mate and pal … I was astonished because I knew Paul would never have agreed to it. In fact I contacted him and he said nobody was more surprised than he was.

Something that most critics missed was the way in which John had allowed his antagonism towards Paul to influence his sequencing of the album. 'Two of Us', Paul's song about Linda, introduced by John as 'phase one, in which Doris gets her oats', may not have been intentional, but his sarcastic attempt to deflate what he saw as the pomposity of 'Let It Be' by inserting a facetious clip before it of himself saying in a thick Liverpool accent, 'And now we'd like to do "'Ark the Angels Come,"' was certainly deliberate. The same can be said of other tracks. The critic Ian MacDonald went as far as to say, 'Lennon's crude bass playing on "The Long and Winding Road", though largely accidental, amounts to sabotage when presented as finished work.' Neither Paul nor George Martin was aware that Spector was working on the tapes, and with Paul living only minutes from EMI, it is indefensible that he was not contacted and offered a chance to put a decent bass line on one of his most beautiful compositions. As it is, Spector covered the poor playing with orchestral swirls and a heavenly chorus.

Paul decided he would sue Allen Klein, but John Eastman pointed out that Klein was not a party to any of the agreements, and had not even been involved when they were made. It always came back to the same thing: the only way out was to dissolve the Beatles partnership itself. Paul would have to break up the Beatles.

> PAUL: Talk about traumas! Not only was the Beatles broken up, this fabbest of groups and these nicest of people, the other three Beatles, these true buddies of mine from way way back, these truest friends of mine were now my firmest enemies overnight. Ever since I was a child I'd been in this group, I'd grown up in this group, this was my school, my family, my life. John Eastman said, 'You've got to do it this way, there's no other way.' I said, 'I can't do it! Can you imagine the perception of the world? I know what public relations I'm going to get. I know how the press will perceive it.' I was just trying to walk away from them and keep it low-key, but I couldn't. I knew I had to do it. It was either that or letting Klein have the whole thing, all the fortune we'd worked for all our lives since we were children.
>
> But we did rescue the Beatle millions. They had taken us long enough to earn and we hadn't screwed anyone to earn them and I always thought it was very clean money compared to the shipbuilders and the great sugar fortunes. No one *had* to buy our

records. We'd kept people in work at the vinyl factories, we'd worked for this, scraped our own fingers to the bone. So we felt good about that and I felt good about hanging on to it.

So, as the sanitised version of *Let It Be* followed his solo album up the charts, Paul's lawyers began building their case for the dissolution of the Beatles as a financial entity. Paul had finally decided to sue John, George and Ringo.

In Court

Preparation for the case took almost a year. Paul was in Los Angeles recording *Ram* when the case was finally given a court date.

PAUL: They called me and Linda back from LA: John Eastman said, 'You've got to be there every day in court.' I said, 'Whaaat?' But I realised it was make or break. And it was, it really was. The Beatles fortune was on the line. Not just mine, but theirs as well. Which is now how I can look back at it and think, Thank God I did that. If I had not had the nerve to sue them, none of us would have anything now.

On Thursday, 18 February 1971, Paul filed a writ in the Chancery Division of the High Court calling for the dissolution of the Beatles partnership and asking for accounts to be made of the partnership's dealings and a receiver to be appointed to oversee the partners' assets. The case was actively opposed by the other three Beatles, who wanted things to remain as they were with Klein in control. Paul and Linda attended every day of the proceedings. John Eastman told Paul he had to wear a suit and tie. Paul wore his Tommy Nutter suit, the one he wore on the cover of *Abbey Road*, but refused to wear a tie. Paul told him, 'That's too humiliating. I'm dressing up so they'll think I'm innocent. There's no way I'm doing that.' Paul had a full navy beard, like the sailor on the Players Navy Cut cigarette packet, and wore a white open-neck shirt. None of the other Beatles made an appearance.

Paul: 'I walked down to the Law Courts and sat on the second pew from the front, facing the judge. I turned round to look and right behind me was my counsel, David Hirst, QC, with his little glass of water, and then a couple of rows behind him, in a brown turtleneck sweater, was Allen Klein. I just looked at him, then turned away.'

It was quite a small courtroom, not at all what Paul had expected. His barrister David Hirst put on a brilliant show. He told Mr Justice Stamp:

> Mr Klein cannot be trusted with the stewardship of the partnership, property and assets ... Mr Klein has paid himself commission to which he is not entitled and is asserting an entitlement to even more ... Our confidence in Mr Klein has not been enhanced by the fact that on 29 January he was convicted on ten tax offences by a jury in a New York Federal District Court.

David Hirst explained to the judge that three things happened early in 1970 that made Paul decide to leave the group. The first was that Allen Klein tried to delay the release of Paul's solo album *McCartney* on the ground that it was in breach of the partnership agreement. In fact, their partnership agreement only prevented the Beatles from appearing alone or with other artists. There was nothing to prevent individual records being made. (The Beatles were not even aware that this partnership document existed until Klein found it, but in any case, these clauses in the partnership agreement had been regularly broken, mostly by John, who had performed with the Plastic Ono Band and released several albums with Yoko.)

Paul's second reason was that Allen Klein's company ABKCO altered Paul's 'Long and Winding Road' on the *Let It Be* album without consulting him. The third reason, David Hirst said, was that ABKCO, without any authority from Paul, had transferred the rights of the film *Let It Be* from Apple to United Artists.

On the third day of Paul's application for the appointment of a receiver, an affidavit from John Lennon was read out in which he said, 'I don't agree that after the touring ceased we began to drift apart.' Speaking of Allen Klein, John said, 'I wanted him as my manager. I introduced him to the other three. But if Paul is trying to suggest that I was rushing them and pushing him down their throats this is a wrong impression.' John ended by saying that Paul was behaving 'selfishly and unreasonably'.

Ringo's deposition said, 'Paul is the greatest bass guitar player in the world. He is also very determined. He goes on and on to see if he can get his own way. While this may be a virtue, it did mean that musical disagreements inevitably rose from time to time. But such disagreements contributed to really great products.' His statement ended by saying, 'My own view is that all four of us together could even yet work out everything satisfactorily.'

PAUL: Looking back on it now, I can say, 'Yes, okay, in the studio I could be overbearing.' Because I wanted to get it right! I heard tapes recently of me counting in 'I Wanna Hold Your Hand', which was our first number one in the States, and I'm being pretty bossy: 'Sssh, Sssh! Clean beginning, c'mon, everyone. One, two. No, c'mon, get it right!' and I can see how that could get on your nerves. But in any case, John didn't want to make any more Beatles records. He wanted a divorce.

Inevitably, much of the case centred on matters of tax and accounting. What concerned the court was that huge sums of tax were liable and no funds appeared to have been set aside to pay them. ABKCO had, however, paid its own commissions.

Seeing Klein in court changed Paul's feelings towards him. 'I felt he wasn't such a threat now. Once the ball is rolling you get a bit of an onward-going feeling. I would be there looking at the judge all the time and if ever there was a patent lie, I would do a shake of the head or something.'

The case revolved around Klein's competence to handle the Beatles' affairs. A pile of documents three feet high had been assembled for the case and Paul's team had diligently gone through them, piece by piece. In all of the documentation there emerged one piece of directly incriminating evidence: a cheque from Capitol Records. In his new deal with Capitol, Allen Klein had increased their royalty rate in the USA from 17.5 per cent to 25 per cent and so he was contractually entitled to 20 per cent of the 7.5 per cent increase. But Klein had charged commission of £852,000, which was 20 per cent of the whole 25 per cent royalty, £648,000 of which had already been paid to him at the time of the hearing. Paul claimed that this was at least £500,000 too high. 'And we got him!' Paul exclaimed. 'That was the only thing we caught him on, and we couldn't send him to jail for that, but at least we could get a judgment.'

Klein's defence was in the form of a letter dated January 1970 from John, George and Ringo, addressed to EMI and Capitol, instructing

them that royalties owed to Apple Records Inc. be paid directly to
ABKCO. The exact wording read: '20 per cent of all earnings on
records sold between September 1969 and April 1972, and then again
after January 1976.' Though signed by the three Beatles, it was never
implemented by Capitol and the first time Paul or his lawyers were
aware of it was after he issued the writ. This became another point of
contention, and Paul's lawyers argued that the other three did not
have the power to change Klein's percentage without Paul's agreement or knowledge. The Apple agreement which bound them
together demanded full rendering of information and that the
partners be 'just and faithful' to each other. Citing the original Apple
agreement, Mr Justice Stamp said that 'Apple was not a Frankenstein
set up to control the individual partners'. The judge was particularly
scathing about Allen Klein, whose testimony he described as 'the
prattling of a second-class salesman', and concluded that he was
unconvinced 'that there is now in the office a staff able to disentangle
the Beatles' affairs, or give the necessary directions to professional
men, or make the necessary administrative decisions'. In other words,
he distrusted Klein's ability to administer their affairs. He granted
Paul's application for a receiver to take over the running of the
partnership until a full trial could determine the long-term future of
the Beatles and their companies.

'So I got my freedom out of that,' Paul said. 'Funnily enough, we
couldn't get Klein because what he'd done wasn't actually a crime.'
Allen Klein went later to jail anyway on a separate, though related,
affair. In 1979 he was imprisoned for two months for not declaring
income from the sale of Apple promotional records between the years
1970 and 1972: the years spanning the court case. Most of this illegal
income came from selling promotional copies of the *Concert for
Bangla Desh* album, taking money which would have otherwise gone
to the charity if those albums had been bought through normal
channels.

PAUL: So anyway, what happened was I single-handedly saved
the Beatle empire! Ha! Ha! He said modestly. I can laugh about
it now; it was not so funny at the time. It certainly did not make
me the most popular man in Britain. It was very very traumatic
and there was no great joy in winning except I knew that justice
had been done, although in my case, personally, justice hadn't

been done because the others were continuing to slag me off. John was writing 'How do you sleep at night?' I felt I was doing it for the Beatles and that was what resulted. It was very tough. In the rough cut of that *Imagine* film there was some pretty tough stuff against me, you could see they were really bitter, they really thought I was to blame for all this stuff.

None of the Beatles were the sort of people ever to admit that they were wrong. This obduracy has been the cause of some of their biggest problems. Even after the other three Beatles changed their minds about Allen Klein and sued him themselves, they did not apologise or express any regrets for all the unpleasantness they had directed against Paul.

PAUL: In one meeting George did say, 'Well, you know, thanks for getting us out of that.' It was just one little sentence recognition of that hell I'd been through. It was better than nothing. But they never said, 'Hey, man, you really stuck your fucking neck out there. You had to sue us!' Anyone else suing the Beatles would have been immoral but for one of the Beatles to sue them, it was almost as if I was committing an unholy act. And I felt very much like that. I'd say it was probably the most difficult period in my life so far. So they didn't actually ever thank me and it would have been un-Beatle-like for them to thank me. Looking at it from the perspective of my age now, we were young. I would say we were children. We were the age of my children now, massively inexperienced in these dealings.

It took another six years fully to disengage the Beatles' affairs from Allen Klein, by which time he and the other three had sued and counter-sued each other, ending in January 1977 with Apple paying Klein $4,200,000. Apple continues to exist, run directly by a board of directors appointed by Paul, George, Ringo and Yoko and administered by Neil Aspinall.

PAUL: Apple is now a very successful company and one of the most successful things we did was copyright the name. Neil and the accounting people copyrighted the name Apple worldwide because we suspected that someone would nick it and put stuff out. Years later, when Apple Computers started, we went to them and said, 'Excuse us, we've got the name Apple. You can't trade under that name.' They said, 'We're very big now, we're going to be giants in the computer world.' We said, 'Well, we'll do a deal then,' and we did a deal for a large amount of money. Probably that one deal made more than Apple Electronics cost. Then Apple put a music chip in, so we went back to them because there was one proviso: they could use the name as long as they had nothing to do with music; they were Apple Computers and we were Apple Music. And then we settled for another very large amount of money, so actually the fact that we copyrighted the name Apple is one of the things that has made us the most amount of money. Housekeeping is very much in place now and Neil Aspinall turned out to be Mr X. I was in class with him, Neil is one of my longest contacts within all of this, so I'm very very glad to see Neil come out of it well.

So all the electronics and the clothes shop and all the peripheral things fell by the wayside. We were basically just trying to help young people but whereas we could help them with a vibe, when it came to the actual money it always got in a mess. The clothes weren't bad. The music wasn't bad. Many of the ideas we were engaged in, like the films and the spoken-word label, were good, but the trouble was, instead of being a highly efficient firm to allow people to go and do their thing, everyone spent their time dealing with the problems that were being generated.

How Do You Sleep?

With such an intense relationship between the four of them, it was not surprising that they found it hard to handle the breakup. The lifestyle and pressures associated with the major bands of the sixties took a heavy toll: Jim Morrison, Jimi Hendrix, Janis Joplin, Brian Jones, Pigpen, Bob Hite, Keith Moon ... virtually every top band lost a member, and heroin addiction was to plague many more, from Keith Richards to Eric Clapton, Brian Wilson, Pete Townshend and even Charlie Watts, damaging careers and causing pain. As the greatest, most pressured band of all, it is amazing that the Beatles came out of it so well.

PAUL: We lived out of each other's pockets for a long time. That was one of the great strengths of the band, that was why we were a tight little band. We could read each other very well through having gone through all these experiences. But when we actually had to break up we were so thick with each other that it was a bit painful. So we made the last album cover an exact replica of the first album cover. We were very conscious of having come full circle. That was it, goodbye.

The *Please Please Me* album cover had been taken on the stairwell at EMI Manchester Square by the veteran photographer Angus McBean. The Beatles commissioned a companion shot, showing them in maturity, to use on *Get Back* before the album was shelved. The two photographs were used as before and after shots on the Red and the Blue compilation albums: *The Beatles/1962–1966* and *The Beatles/1967–1970*. The staircase itself became a monument, an enormous piece of rock 'n' roll memorabilia. All EMI's new signings wanted their photograph taken on the stairwell, and it was carefully dismantled and transported to EMI's new headquarters when they moved to Brook Green, west London, in 1995.

The individual Beatles went through a difficult period with each other after the breakup. George had been on the ascendant as a songwriter during the last days of the group and now he blossomed. Though the antagonism between John and Paul was more public, the arguments between John and George appear to have been just as profound. John was very negative about George's three-album box set *All Things Must Pass*, and George was delighted to prove him wrong by selling millions of copies. There were other causes of disagreement between them. John originally agreed to appear with George and Ringo at the benefit concert for Bangladesh which George organised at Madison Square Garden, New York, but later insisted that Yoko be allowed to join them on stage. George had said from the beginning that Yoko was not included in his invitation and stuck to his guns. He had had enough of Yoko in the studio and for her to become, effectively, the fourth Beatle on stage was too much to ask. He was angry but not surprised when John bowed out and flew to Paris instead. John also promised to show up and join George at a few of the shows on George's solo American tour, but never did so. Apart from the personal bitternesses, the breakup of the Beatles as a financial entity provided many excuses for a good argument, particularly one occasion in December 1974, when the other Beatles all flew to New York to sign the final document in the dissolution of the group, only to find that John, who, by this time, was living there, refused to get out of bed that day 'because the stars aren't right'.

John and George's final disagreement came shortly before John's death when George published his autobiography *I Me Mine*, in which John Lennon is mentioned a mere eleven times. This is twice more than Paul but John was outraged and said so in *Playboy*: 'I was hurt by it ... By glaring omission in the book, my influence on his life is absolutely zilch and nil. Not mentioned. In his book, which is purportedly this clarity of vision of each song he wrote and its influences, he remembers every two-bit sax player or guitarist he met in subsequent years. I'm not in the book.' Sadly they had not reconciled their differences before John was murdered.

John's differences with Paul were more public, particularly after John's vitriolic attack on him in 'How Do You Sleep?' on the *Imagine* album. This track, which has been the subject of much comment and scrutiny, was later repudiated by John but at the time it was the cause of great hurt to Paul, who had no wish to launch a counter-attack and get into a slanging match with him. In fact, only about half the lyrics were actually by John. The remainder were by Yoko, and a couple of the lines were contributed by Allen Klein.

John and Yoko had by this time bought a large mansion called Tittenhurst Park in Ascot, near Windsor Great Park, a little deeper into the wealthy stockbroker belt than before but still quite close to George's and Ringo's houses.

One of those who witnessed the composition of 'How Do You Sleep?' was Felix Dennis, who was a house guest at Tittenhurst Park at the time. Dennis was one of the publishers of *Oz* magazine, and had been sentenced to jail at the Old Bailey for publishing obscene literature in the infamous 'school kids' issue of *Oz*. The trial had been front-page news for weeks. Felix and his two co-defendants were freed on appeal. The other two went abroad, leaving Felix to fend off the attentions of the press. John Lennon knew Felix and had recorded a benefit single, 'God Save Oz', for the *Oz* Defence Fund. Now the trial was over, John telephoned and invited Felix to Tittenhurst Park to get away from the media.

Felix was put up in the gatehouse and happened to be there when

John was recording the basic tracks for *Imagine* in his home studio. The album was being produced by Phil Spector, who had produced the *Oz* single. George and Ringo were also there, though Ringo was only visiting and does not play on the finished album. When Felix wandered in they were rehearsing 'How Do You Sleep?'

FELIX: They were writing the song as they performed it. And as these lyrics emerged, I remember Ringo getting more and more upset by this. He was really not very happy about this, and at one point I have a clear memory of his saying, 'That's enough, John.' There were two magnificent studio musicians, and they too were not very happy about it, but as usual, Lennon plowed his own furrow and he just didn't give a shit whether people liked it or not. It is absolutely true to say that Yoko wrote many of the lyrics. I watched her writing them and then watched her race into the studio to show John – which would often annoy the musicians, but she would race in there anyway, waving a piece of paper and show John she'd had an idea. He would say 'Great' or whatever, and he would add something to it, then he would come back and relax in the control room for a bit and they would confer together. They've both got appalling handwriting, writing in a great hurry.

He would think of a lyric, and then she would think of a lyric, and then they'd burst out laughing, they'd think that was absolutely hysterical. Some of it was absolutely puerile, thank God a lot of it never actually got recorded because it was highly, highly personal, like a bunch of schoolboys standing in the lavatory making scatological jokes and then falling about with laughter at their own wit. That was about the level of it but thank goodness in the end somebody obviously talked some sense to them, or they'd talked sense to each other. Maybe Ringo had got on to them and told them not to be so brutal. Some of the lyrics were a lot ruder than you will find on the final version.

To counterbalance that, even if it might have been very hurtful to Paul McCartney, I think that the mood in which it was written should be borne in mind, which was one of schoolboy for the hell of it. It's quite obvious that Paul must have been some sort of figure of authority in Lennon's life, because you don't take the piss out of somebody that isn't a figure of authority. The mood there wasn't totally vindictive. As I felt it, they were taking the piss out of the headmaster. A lot of giggling, a lot of laughing. They had one line about Paul's Little Richard singing. I don't know if this is true that Paul was always quite proud of his ability to sing like Little Richard; they were making reference to that. It never ended up on the final cut. Phil Spector never said a single word about the lyrics, but Ringo and other musicians there would remonstrate with him and say, 'Oh, for Christ's sake, John, that's a bit much, you know!' Sometimes he would agree and cross it out. All I can say, if he'd wanted to write something to really hurt Paul's feelings, they certainly compiled enough material to do so. If he'd had someone he could confide in, other than Yoko, I think they would have persuaded him to leave it in the vaults for posterity. It was a bit of a shame he ever let it out.

The song does focus on all John's resentment of Paul and it is no surprise to find in it a reference to 'Yesterday'; John never got over the fact that the two biggest Beatles songs, 'Yesterday' and 'Michelle', were solo efforts by Paul on which John did not even play. Allen Klein told Albert Goldman that after the line in 'How Do You Sleep?' that says the only song Paul wrote was 'Yesterday', John planned to scream, 'You probably pinched that bitch anyway!'

Klein was in the control booth with Phil Spector during the run-through at the Record Plant in New York, where the basic tracks were mixed and the final vocals added, and was so aghast at the potential libel involved that he demanded that John drop it. Klein himself improvised its anodyne replacement.

PAUL: When John did 'How Do You Sleep?', I didn't want to get into a slanging match. And I'm so glad now, particularly after his death, that I don't have that on my conscience. I just let him do it, because he was being fed a lot of those lines by Klein and Yoko. I had the option of going for equal time and doing all the interviews or deciding to not take up the gauntlet, and I remember consciously thinking, No, I really mustn't. Part of it was cowardice: John was a great wit, and I didn't want to go fencing with the rapier champion of East Cheam. That was not a good idea. And I also knew that those vibes could snowball, and you start off with a perfectly innocent little contest and suddenly you find yourself doing duel to the death with the Lennon figure and it's, Oh, my God, what have I carved out here? But it meant that I had to take shit, it meant that I had to take lines like 'All you ever did was "Yesterday".'

I always find myself wanting to excuse John's behaviour, just because I loved him. It's like a child, sure he's a naughty child, but don't you call my child naughty. Even if it's me he's shitting on, don't you call him naughty. That's how I felt about this and still do. I don't have any grudge whatsoever against John. I think he was a sod to hurt me. I think he knew exactly what he was doing and because we had been so intimate he knew what would hurt me and he used it to great effect. I thought, Keep your head down and time will tell. And it did, because in the *Imagine* film, he says it was really all about himself.

In that film John says, 'It's not about Paul, it's about me. I'm really attacking myself. But I regret the association, well, what's to regret? He lived through it. The only thing that matters is how he and I feel about these things and not what the writer or commentator thinks about it. Him and me are okay.'

John later described it as 'using somebody as an object to create something. I wasn't really feeling that vicious at the time, but I *was* using my resentment towards Paul to create a song.' John amplified on this explanation in one of his last interviews, recorded for BBC Radio by Andy Peebles two days before he was murdered:

> I used my resentment against Paul that I have as a kind of sibling rivalry resentment from youth, to create a song ... rivalry between two guys, I mean, it was always there, it was a creative rivalry, like there was a rivalry between the Beatles and the Stones, it was ... not a terrible vicious horrible vendetta ... I used my resentment and withdrawing from Paul and the Beatles and the relationship with Paul to write 'How Do You Sleep?' I don't really go round with those thoughts in my head all the time.

Paul knew this. Whereas some people were shocked and horrified at the way John would sometimes turn on them, Paul had known him since he was a kid. He had seen it all before: the drunken teddy boy kicking the art-school phone booth to pieces, fighting sailors in

Hamburg, answering back to anyone in authority and turning his vicious tongue on anyone who stood in his way. Paul and George had often been the subjects of John's scorn and vituperation, but they were also his closest buddies, his musical colleagues subject to a fierce personal loyalty, at least until Yoko came along. He never lost his respect for the other Beatles, despite the macho posturing in some of his interviews. It was all dumbshow.

'John and I were arguing about something and I was getting fairly heated,' Paul remembered. 'John just pulled his glasses down his nose and looked over the top and said, "It's only me," and then put them back again. Just a moment. I think that was very symptomatic of our whole relationship: John would let the barrier down and you'd get a couple of moments of deep reality, then he was defensive again.'

Despite the deep roots of their relationship, matters between John and Paul remained very bad for several years.

> PAUL: I would ring him when I went to New York and he would say, 'Yeah, what d'you want?' 'I just thought we might meet?' 'Yeah, what the fuck d'you want, man?' I used actually to have some very frightening phone calls. Thank God they're not in my life any more. I went through a period when I would be so nervous to ring him and so insecure in myself that I actually felt like I was in the wrong. It was all very acrimonious and bitter. I remember one time John said, 'You're all pizza and fairy tales.' I thought, What a great album title! I said, 'Well, if that's what I am, I'm not wholly against that description of me. I can think of worse things to say.' But another time I called him and it was 'Yeah? Yeah? Whadda ya want?' He suddenly started to sound American. I said, 'Oh, fuck off, Kojak,' and slammed the phone down; we were having those kind of times, it was bad news.

One factor that enabled them to speak with each other again was a shift in John's opinion of Allen Klein, the cause of much of the rancour. Klein had been forced to give away 5000 free tickets for John's Madison Square Garden concert in order to ensure a full house, and afterwards he told John a few home truths: above all that it was John, not Yoko, that the public wanted to see. John knew that what Klein said was true; and, in fact, during the concert he had performed very much as a solo act with a backing group. Yoko's keyboard was not even plugged in even though she mimed. But it was not what Yoko wanted to hear. She immediately turned against Klein and he was soon out. When on 28 June 1973 Allen Klein sued John for $508,000 in unpaid loans from ABKCO Industries, John found himself more and more in agreement with Paul on business matters. The tension over the firing of Klein was a major factor in the breakup of John and Yoko, and by October of that year John was living with May Pang in Los Angeles. May was twenty-three and working for Yoko. Yoko told her, 'If John makes an advance to you, don't reject him.' John eventually made a pass in an elevator, which started their affair. On 2 November, John, George and Ringo sued Allen Klein for damages for alleged misrepresentation and Klein responded with a counter-action for lost fees, commissions and expenses. Teams of lawyers moved in. Paul, never having been managed by Klein, was thankful that he was not involved.

PAUL: When they split up, Yoko came to London, looking like a widow, a little diminutive sad figure in black. She came around to Cavendish, and she said, 'John's left, he's off with May Pang.' So, being friendly and seeing her plight, Linda or I said to her, 'Do you still love him? Do you want to get back with him?' She said, 'Yes.' We said, 'Well, what would it take then?' because we were going out L. A. way. We would often go there for Capitol Records or just for a laugh. It was a logical place to be in the record business. In this case we were on our way to a holiday. I said, 'I can take a message. What would I have to tell him?' And she gave me this whole thing: 'He would have to come back to New York. He can't live with me immediately. He'd have to court me, he'd have to ask me out. He'd have to send me flowers, he'll have to do it all again. Of course, she'd sent him off with May Pang, but that wasn't the point at that time.

So I went out there and he was doing *Pussy Cats* with Nilsson and Keith Moon and Jesse Ed Davis, to name but three total nutters. Three beautiful total alcohol nutters plus John, forget it! Even the location is perfect. We went round to a session and sat there for a bit. It was a little bit strange, John and I, seeing each other at that time. But then we dropped by their house the next day for a cup of tea or something. I remember Harry Nilsson offering me some angel dust. I said, 'What is it?' He said, 'It's elephant tranquilliser.' I said, 'Is it fun?' He thought for about half a minute. 'No,' he said. I said, 'Well, you know what, I won't have any.' He seemed to understand. But that's how it was there.

Keith Moon was very sweet, we had a nice chat with Keith. He was very complimentary about *Band on the Run*, which was out recently. He asked, 'Who drummed on that, man?' and it happened to be me. So I said, 'Me, man.' Moonie is my second favourite drummer of all time. Ringo, Moonie, John Bonham would be my three main drummers. Not technically the best by a long shot but for feel and emotion and economy, they're always there. Particularly Ringo.

So I was having fun with the guys sitting round the pool, and eventually John got up. Linda and I had kids so we'd be up early. We wouldn't be just lying in bed till three in the afternoon, which is what John was doing. He was a teenager again. It was everything he'd always wanted to do in Liverpool. He was just being his old Liverpool self, just a wild, wild boy. The Brendan Behan thing. He was involved in all sorts of punch-ups with Harry Nilsson, and Spector was there letting his gun off in the control room, apparently. I mean, those are not sessions I would want to be at.

But I took John in the back room of the house, sat down – 'How you doing? Great. Lovely to see you ...' He was in quite a mellow mood. It was early morning for him, early morning in the afternoon. I said, 'Yoko was through London and she said she wouldn't mind getting back together. How about you? Would you be interested in that?' He said, 'Yeah.' That he still loved her and stuff. So I said, 'Here's the deal. You've got to go back to New York. You've got to go get a flat, court her, so-and-so ...' and that's just what he did. That's how they got back together again.

With most of their business differences settled by the mid-seventies, relations between John and Paul returned to some semblance of normality, and although there was obviously not the same degree of intimacy as before, the animosity between them had gone. 'I realised that I couldn't always ring him up to ask about business, which was my main priority at the time,' Paul said. 'It was better to talk about cats, or baking bread, or babies. So we did that, and I had a lot in common with him because we were having our babies and I was into a similar sort of mode. So the air cleared and I was able to speak to him and go and see him.' Though John never again returned to Britain, Paul and Linda visited him in New York on a number of occasions. 'So we got back together again. It was lovely.'

In 1976, with his usual bravado, John said of Paul, 'He visits me every time he's in New York, like all the other rock 'n' roll creeps. I just happen to be the one in New York and I love it ... So whenever he's in town I see him. He comes over and we just sit around and get mildly drunk and reminisce.'

In a role reversal, John was bringing up Sean and Yoko was taking care of business. Paul already had children and was able to offer advice and was also well aware of the kind of difficulties John must be encountering, having had no previous experience of children to speak of. His oldest son, Julian, was born at the start of Beatlemania and so John was hardly ever around to watch him grow up. When John and Cynthia broke up, Julian remained with his mother and rarely saw his father.

PAUL: It was unfortunate for Julian. I'd been fortunate to be around a lot of kids. I'm from a big family so your cousins would dump a baby on you and you'd know you have to jiggle him on your knee. You couldn't go, 'Oh no, I'm scared of babies!' You had to jiggle it and you became good at it. I used to like playing with kids a lot. One of my enduring memories of when the Beatles first hit it and we were very famous, you'd go to people's houses and they'd say, 'Would you just say good night to the kids? Would you? The babies won't go to sleep till you do.' So I'd always go up and say, 'Good night, sleep well.' I enjoyed it, it was a very calm, fulfilling role for me. I've enjoyed being a parent, just never had a problem with it, touch wood. I've had problems with parenthood, like anyone does, but my mind was never set against children or kids, they never frightened me, whereas I think they did with John, even his own son.

We'd gone on this Greek holiday once to buy an island and Julian and I spent a lot time playing around on the boat. I used to play cowboys and Indians with him, and he'd love it: a grown-up who would go, 'Now you chase me, and I'll chase you, but after you've caught me, not before, okay?' And you were totally in this mad magic game. I remember John coming up to me once and he took me aside and said, 'How do you do it?' I said, 'What do you mean?' He said, 'With Julian. How do you play with kids like that?' I remember feeling a wave of sorrow coming over me, like uhh, I'd love to be able to tell you. Then I tried to give like the potted version, you know, 'Play, pretend you're a kid. Play with him.' But John never got it. Never got the hang of it. John was always a man. I see a lot of parents like that, still, to this day. They can't make the break to realise that it's great to give so much of yourself to a kid, because you get it all back in triplicate. Some people just don't know that. John was a single child so he didn't necessarily know that and he didn't get much education afterwards.

When we saw him with May Pang, I remember him coming up to me and hugging. He said, 'Touching is good. Touching's good,' and if I ever hug anyone now, that's a little thing that sticks in my mind. He was right, but the thing is, I actually knew it more than John did, he only was saying it because he was discovering it. I don't think he had a lot of cuddling, certainly not from his mother, because he wasn't even allowed to live with her.

In May 1976, because of all the rumours circulating about a Beatles reunion during the Wings tour of the USA, the *Saturday Night Live* producer Lorne Michaels went to the NBC bosses and asked, 'If I wanted the Beatles on my show, how much could I pay them?' and was told top standard rate: $3,200 for the four of them. It became a running gag on the show. John and Paul happened to be watching the programme. Paul: 'I recollect that John said, "It's only downtown, we could go now. Come on, let's just show up. Should we, should we?" and for a second it was like, "Yeah, yeah!" But we decided not to.' John: 'We nearly got a cab, but we were actually too tired.'

According to John, this was the last time he and Paul physically met. He told *Playboy*: 'That was a period when Paul just kept turning up at our door with a guitar. I would let him in but finally I said to him, "Please call before you come over. It's not 1956, and turning up at the door isn't the same any more. You know, just give me a ring." He was upset by that but I didn't mean it badly. I just meant that I was taking care of a baby all day and some guy turns up at the door

...' Though John's 'house-husband' phase is not supposed to have started until October 1976, when Sean was a year old, John must have had all the sleepless nights and child-minding duties that any father experiences during Sean's first year so his attitude was understandable.

> PAUL: We were back together again as friends, which was really cool. We would talk about Sean. He gave Sean an upbringing, making sure that Sean had the father he'd not had. And it was a very rewarding time for him. That's why Sean's a pretty stable kid now.

Early on 9 December 1980, while Linda was taking the kids to school, Paul received a telephone call from Steven Shrimpton at his office telling him that John had been murdered. At 10.50 p.m. New York time, a mentally deranged fan had shot and killed John outside the Dakota as he returned home from a recording session at the Record Plant.

When Linda returned from the school she could tell from Paul's ashen face that something bad had happened.

> *Liverpool Echo*, 9 December 1980: Just after 8.45 a.m. Paul telephoned his brother Michael, and according to Michael, he was too distressed to speak. 'Paul just said to keep sending the good vibes down from Liverpool to help him through the day. It is going to be a busy day for him and he is very, very upset,' said Mike.

At noon, Paul decided that the only way to get through the day was to work. He told the journalists who had gathered at the gate of his drive, 'I can't take it in at the moment. John was a great man, who'll be remembered for his unique contributions to art, music and world peace.' He spent the day at AIR Studios in London, talking with George Martin and recording. Security guards had to be brought in to keep the reporters and photographers at bay, some of whom tried to break into the studio using the fire exits. Asked for a statement as he left, Paul told them he hoped everyone would 'rally round Yoko'.

George Harrison heard the news from his sister Louise, who lived in the USA. His staff secured the gates of Friar Park against the gathering crowd of reporters and fans and, like Paul, he spent the day in the studio.

Ringo was in the Bahamas with his wife Barbara when the news broke and they took the next plane to New York. At first Yoko insisted on seeing him alone until he gently explained that she and John had always been as one and that was how it was with him and Barbara.

PAUL: When he died that day, I was so horrified, I just had like stage fright all day. Some of it was just fright, like 'Are you next?' That was a question whipping around the three of us, but also the complete emptiness and the finality of it. Someone stuck a microphone in the window of the car as I was leaving the studios that night; I was just beginning to wrestle with it and it was just sinking in, and someone said, 'What d'you think of the death of John Lennon?' And I really couldn't think of anything more to say than 'It's a drag' and it came out really slow. But of course when it got printed – 'Paul McCartney, asked for his definitive version of how he felt, said, "It's a drag"' – it looked so callous in print. You can't take the print back and say, 'Look, let me just rub that print in shit and pee over it and then cry over it for three years, then you'll see what I meant when I said that word.' I should have said, 'It's the most unholiest of drags,' and it might have been better. What I meant was, 'Fuck off! Don't invade my privacy.' But I managed to pull something together, but unfortunately it was something that would add to the McCartney idiot myth, some soppy guy who doesn't care about anything, 'Oh, it's a drag!'

When I got home I wept buckets, in the privacy of my own home. I controlled it all during the day, but that evening when it was on the news and all the in-depth shit, and all the pundits were coming out, trotting out all their little witticisms, I did a lot of weeping. I remember screaming that Mark Chapman was the jerk of all jerks; I felt so robbed and so emotional. It shocked me for months afterwards and you couldn't talk to me about guns. Any mention of the word 'gun', 'rifle', 'pistol', 'shoot', just shocked me, sent a wave of reverberation through me like a little echo of the pistol shot. You couldn't even say, 'That's a good shot,' about a photograph, it just rang through. The very next day after he was killed there was a pheasant shoot in the woods. Linda went out and talked to them … It was a tough period but luckily, once that had subsided, I was able to think, At least we parted on good terms. Thank God for that.

Paul told the *Sunday Express*:

After his death, Linda and I went round to Yoko's and we all cried so hard, you know, we had to laugh. She wanted to get us something to eat and she mentioned caviar. We all said, 'Let's do it.' Her houseman brought it in, mumbling, and he backed out and there was the caviar tin with just a little bit in the bottom. Her servants had eaten it all!

So I said, 'Ask for some wine.' Sure enough, it arrives and there's like a quarter left in the bottle. They've had all the wine too! We were all just hysterical and the relief was indescribable.

PAUL: John used to say, 'I'm the leader of this group!' and we used to say, 'It's only because you fucking shout louder than anyone else!' It wasn't as if we didn't know how to do that, it was just nobody wanted to shout and be so uptight about it. Nobody cared as much as he did about being the leader. Actually I have always quite enjoyed being second. I realised why it was when I was out riding: whoever is first opens all the gates. If you're second you just get to walk through. They've knocked down all the walls, they've taken all the stinging nettles, they take all the shit and whoever's second, which is damn near to first, waltzes through and has an easy life. You're still up with number one. Number one still needs you as his companion, so I think my relationship to John is something to do with this attitude.

John was always very forward-thinking. That was often his greatest asset. If it was like, 'Should we say fifty swear words on this record, or shall we do the song we were meant to do?' 'No, no, no, let's do the fifty swear words. That's a good idea, that's certainly interesting.' John would always, in my imagination anyway, push for that. So it was always very good having this prod, this battering-ram partner. It was something to do with our personalities and character, which doesn't change a lot in life. John would always advise jumping off a cliff. It was one of his symbolic things. He'd say, 'So you come to edge of a cliff, and you don't know what to do, so jump!' John was always the jumper, the suicide man, the one off the cliff, he always had to be bigger and bolder and brighter, which was what excited people about John. We like those people, we like high-risk people, that's how John was and that was the radical difference between us. I've always made that conscious decision. It's like the Cyril Connolly quote, 'There is no more sombre enemy of good art than a pram in the hall.' I've always said, 'Well, I obviously can't be that interested in art then because I'm not fucking ruining my life just for a song or for a painting, particularly when I've done so well anyway. I could leave the whole fucking thing and say, "Sorry, lads, that was it. That was my input. That was it, that's all I can do, I can't summon up any more."'

Certainly in the early days of the group, John saw himself as the leader, even if the other three regarded it as a four-way democracy. This changed with *Sgt. Pepper* when Paul took over *de facto* leadership. When it came to songwriting, it was never anything other than an equal partnership; astonishingly so: each brought about the same number of song ideas and each produced about the same number of solo efforts.

PAUL: A body of work was produced that I don't believe he alone could have produced, or I alone could have produced. It was only me that sat in those hotel rooms, in his house in the attic; it wasn't Yoko, it wasn't Sean, it wasn't Julian, it wasn't George, it wasn't Mimi, it wasn't Ringo, it wasn't Miles. It was me that sat in those rooms, seeing him in all his moods and all his little things, seeing him not being able to write a song, and having me help, seeing me not able to write a song and him help me.

The truth of the matter is, John and I were kind of equal. It really did pan itself out about equal. That's one of the amazing things about it. People can say, 'Oh, well, it wasn't Paul, it was John, or it wasn't John it was Paul,' but I who was there know that's not true, the other Beatles know that's not true. So much of it was team effort, joint effort, there really was so much of it.

AFTERWORD

I don't see how it isolates me. I feel once we've got
over the fact that I've come out of the television
screen and shook their hand, once we've got over that
little shock, then how it operates is just normal.

Paul McCartney

THE BEATLES BROKE UP MORE THAN A QUARTER-CENTURY AGO, YET PAUL
remains as famous as ever. He has learned to deal with it; in fact, he
knows nothing else. It doesn't disturb him unduly, though he has
made greater efforts to achieve a certain normality than the other ex-
Beatles. Certainly the advantages of fame far outweigh any inconveniences that fame has brought.

PAUL: What happens is, you're trying to do your job well and
fame comes as an ancillary thing to it; then it becomes a bit of a
whirlwind that can take it over. You say you're trying to 'make
it', but at that time you just mean 'do well', to get this music
thing to feel good so you enjoy it and other people enjoy it, so
you'll get asked back. That's really as far as it goes at first; it's
just the satisfaction of building a chair that will stand up to a bit
of kitchen wear. It's the straightforward craft of it. But then, after
a while, another game creeps in, which is coping with fame. You
still think you're just trying to make a chair, and – particularly if
you have a little talent in that direction – you assimilate that, but
now there's other things that attach themselves to it. That's what
can get very difficult about fame: all those little barnacles of
fame can sometimes actually outweigh the whole idea of being a
craftsman.

Once, when he was out riding with his youngest daughter, she stopped and said, 'You're Paul McCartney, aren't you?' She'd heard about him at school as if this famous figure was a separate person. Paul, too, is aware of this other persona which is only partly to do with him.

PAUL: I've always had this thing of him and me; he goes on stage, he's famous, and then me; I'm just some kid from Liverpool. At fifty-four this little being inside me still feels like this little kid who used to run down the streets in Speke, doing Bob-a-Job, collecting jam jars, damming up streams in the woods. I still very much am him grown up. I feel like the person I've been since I can remember, since I was five or six, I feel like that same guy: well of course, I am. All the stuff that's happened hasn't really affected him that much, it's affected the legendary figure I might be portraying.

Occasionally I stop and think, I am Paul McCartney, fuckin' hell, that is a total freak-out! You know, Paul McCartney! Just the words, it sounds like a total kind of legend. But of course, you don't want to go thinking that too much because it takes over. There's a temptation to believe it all and be it and live it or there's this other temptation to use it rather than be it. When I go on tour, I'm glad of the legendary thing; I wouldn't want to try and entertain 60,000 people in a Texas stadium with just the guy next door. I'm glad they know me. When you're playing that you certainly want every little bit of help you can get. I have to be the big famous Paul McCartney character. It's not always possible to just compartmentalise it as easily as that – me as a person, and me as a Beatle – but I have had a certain ability in my life to do that. I think it helps keep you sane, actually, if your famous side is a little bit removed from you yourself; you can withdraw from it, you can go home after a Beatles session and switch off. I don't think we had any huge problems like some of the stars who couldn't switch identities off.

If I've got a couple of weeks off, a holiday, then I'll try and get away from everyone and get my own self back. I'm able to do that. I think that was the origin of all my little secretive trips with the false moustache and stuff; it allowed me to escape the persona that I had trapped myself in for money and fame and fortune. It was an idea that got carried through into *Pepper* too: the idea of the band being our own alter ego was the same thing: 'Let's liberate ourselves because we're getting too tied in.' And when the Beatles finally broke up, my feeling was for us to go back to little clubs again because I thought we'd got it too tight, we'd got it too precious. We'd forgotten what we were and I felt it was a good idea to bring us back to normal. From then, we could reinvent the band.

Periodically John would say, 'I want to give it all up; that's what we should all do.' I always would think, no. What if in six months' time we want to pick it up again? It's like Elton's farewell tours, it just looks a bit silly after a while. I always think, If you're really giving it up, then you're really giving it up. I don't like any half-assed giving-it-ups. I don't mean this in any 'Nyaaah, told you so' sense, but both John and George independently said to me at one time or another that they wanted to give it up. I said, 'Hey, the hardest thing for us guys to do would be to give up fame. To wake up the next morning and not be a star any more can't happen. What do you mean, you're not going to be a star? You're going to be the retired star. And if that's what you want, then that's a different matter but don't get this idea that everyone's going to go away. Greta Garbo got more attention than ever with "I want to be alone". They were still trying to take topless pictures of her when she was seventy.'

After the group disbanded they all four launched solo careers. George, after tremendous initial success, gradually retired from the scene, as did Ringo who concentrated first upon a film career, then took life easy, content to be a jet-set celebrity. John, living in the USA, had an uneven solo career before leaving the music business to become a house-husband; he had just released a comeback album, Double Fantasy, when he was murdered. Paul, however, remained in the public eye. He fulfilled his ambition to go back on the road by forming Wings and playing surprise gigs at university dances. Before long Wings grew into a fully-fledged rock band of the seventies variety, undertaking enormous stadium tours of the United States, selling millions of records and ensuring that a new generation of fans grew up who would know Paul more as a former member of Wings than of the Beatles.

Throughout the seventies and eighties, Paul released dozens of albums, first of all with Wings, then as solo projects. After John's death he stopped touring, and spent thirteen years off the road, though the hit records kept coming. In the nineties he did two more world tours, once again breaking attendance records, and this time playing many of the songs he wrote for the Beatles. Interest in the Beatles still remained high, and with the release of the three *Anthology* double-CDs of out-takes and unreleased songs, the group once again shot to number one on the charts, twenty-five years after disbanding. A television documentary series was screened all over the world and released as a boxed set of eight videos. It was if the Beatles had never been away: the magazines and newspapers were filled with interviews with the surviving members and the instantly recognisable faces of their youth flickered across television screen once more. They had become a Brish institution.

Throughout the seventies Paul's life was taken up with Wings, with the legal wrangling which followed the breakup of the Beatles, and with his growing family. Their third child, the second child of both Paul and Linda, was Stella, born on 3rd September 1971, in Kings College Hospital, London. As Paul waited outside the operating theatre where Stella was delivered by Caeserean section, he thought of the name for his new group. Paul: 'I sat next door in my green apron praying like mad. The name Wings just came into my mind.' Their first son, James, was born on 12 September 1977, at the Avenue Clinic in St John's Wood, London. Bringing up a family, combined with touring, inevitably meant that he lost touch with many of his old friends. Several others died. The rock 'n' roll business has a high mortality rate. Paul had already lost his mate Brian Jones, who drowned when persons unknown held him underwater in his swimming pool during a party on the night of 1 July 1969. And Jimi Hendrix, regarded by Paul as rock's greatest guitarist, died in his sleep on 18 September 1970, after inhaling his own vomit.

The first member of the Beatles' inner circle to die – after Brian Epstein – was their roadie and bodyguard Mal Evans, who was shot to death by police in his rented duplex at 8122 West 4th Street in Los Angeles on the night of 4 January 1976. His life had been defined by his relationship with the Beatles and when the band broke up, Mal not only had nothing to do but seemed to lose his identity. He separated from his wife Lil, who reportedly had asked for a divorce shortly before Christmas.

Mal moved to Los Angeles, where he lived with his new girlfriend Fran Hughes and worked on the manuscript of his memoirs, *Living the Beatles Legend*, which he was supposed to deliver to his publishers, Grosset and Dunlap, on 12 January. The evening of the 4th Mal had been so despondent that Fran Hughes called John Hoernie, Mal's collaborator on the book, and asked him to come over. Hoernie said he found Mal crying, 'really doped up and groggy'. Mal told him, 'Please make sure you and Joanne [Lenard, Hoernie's assistant on the book] finish the book.' Mal and John Hoernie went to an upstairs bedroom and in the course of Mal's incoherent conversation, he picked up an unloaded 30.30 rifle. A scuffle ensued, but Mal was a big, powerful man and Hoernie was unable to take the weapon away from him.

Fran telephoned the police and told them, 'My old man has a gun and has taken Valium and is totally screwed up.' Four cops arrived shortly afterwards and two of them, David D. Krempa and Robert E. Brannon, went to the upstairs room. According to the police report, when Mal saw the police officers he turned and pointed the rifle at them. Lieutenant Charles Higbie of the LAPD robbery and homicide division said, 'Officers directed him to put down the rifle. He refused to put down the rifle.' The cops fired six shots at him, four of which struck Mal, killing him instantly. Mal was an honorary sheriff of Los Angeles County.

Paul: 'Mal was a big lovable bear of a roadie; he'd go over the top occasionally, but we all knew him and never had any problems. Had I been there I would have been able to say, "Mal, don't be silly." In fact, any of his friends could have talked him out of it without any sweat, because he was not a nutter.'

Mal was cremated in Los Angeles on 7 January, with Harry Nilsson and other friends in attendance. His ashes got lost in the post on the way back to England and were eventually recovered from the Lost Letter Office.

Shortly afterwards, Paul's father, Jim, died of bronchial pneumonia at his home in Gayton in the Wirral on 18 March 1976, at the age of seventy-three. He had been ill for several weeks.

Some old friendships were renewed. Paul and Robert Fraser met again in 1978 and began seeing each other again. Linda got on particularly well with Robert as they both shared an interest in fine-art photography. There was a period when Robert stopped drinking, which made him more likeable and easier to be around, but then, on a trip to New York, a boyfriend got him started again.

PAUL: He was very clean, very sober, but I think he started to think, maybe I'm clean, maybe I'm sober, but I'm boring now. We would still buy the odd Magritte through him and he was very good to run things by, he always had a good opinion. Our kids didn't like him. He would come down to our house and he'd say, 'Put a log on the fire, will you?' and our kids would gesture behind his back as if to say, 'Who does he think we are?' But Robert just expected kids to do that. My kids don't do that, they're modern children – 'Get it yourself, mush.' They didn't like him.

The last time I saw him was outside Cecconi's, a posh Italian restaurant opposite the Burlington Arcade which has very good food. It's a bit of a watering hole. We'd had lunch with Robert and we were leaving. We were standing outside and he looked like he had little things on his skin, not pimples but dark marks on his face. I remember Linda touching and saying, 'What's that?' 'Oh! Thank God someone's finally mentioned it, it's uh, Kaposi's sarcoma ...' I remember Linda kissing him, and this was the very early days of the AIDS epidemic and you didn't know whether you ought to. But Linda kissed him and we said, 'Okay, see you around.' He walked from Cecconi's down Burlington Gardens to Cork Street, and we just went, 'Bye!' I knew he wouldn't turn round to wave, and I got a feeling that might be the last time I'd see him. A strange, eerie feeling. So the last thing I remember is just his dark suit, rear view, turning the corner, right, into Cork Street.

Paul and Linda's friend, the painter Brian Clarke, remembered the incident:

Robert was really relieved, because Linda's very open and it meant a lot to him that Linda felt close enough to him to say, 'What is this?' He said it so many times to me afterwards. Robert knew they loved him, and that was what was important, that his friends loved him. It supported and encouraged him at the end. Paul was incredibly kind to Robert. He bailed Robert out on many occasions and when he was ill, they provided Robert with a car and a driver to get him around, wherever he needed to go. They were very very supportive of him indeed.

Robert first got sick in 1985 in New York and on returning to London he gave up his flat and moved in with his mother Cynthia.

PAUL: There was a question of whether he wanted us to visit him. He was staying with his mother at that time, and I don't know whether she acknowledged the fact that he had AIDS or whether it would be appropriate, but we'd get reports from our friend Brian Clarke. I remember sending him a photograph of a piece of pottery I'd done which was like a flat Duke of Edinburgh: Giacometti visits the Duke of Edinburgh. Linda had taken a photograph of it so we sent him some photos. And for the first time in my life I said, 'Cheers, Bob'. I'd never called him Bob. He wrote back: 'Bob? Bob? Who are you talking to?' Actually there was a joke going around then that he was going to open a gallery called Bob's Art Shop, so that's where it came from.

He eventually died at his mum's place. The lovely thing was that he eventually went home to mummy; which for a public-school boy was nice because he'd been separated from mummy aged six to go to prep school, then he went on to Eton. I thought that was good for him and Brian said, 'He's quite enjoying it, actually. He's enjoying being spoiled.' His mum was pampering him. And so he went from the cradle to the grave, as it were. And then suddenly he was just gone.

Robert died of AIDS-related pneumonia and meningitis in January 1986.

Painting

Among the many people Paul got to know through Linda and her family was the painter Willem de Kooning, who was a client of Linda's father and lived at the Springs, East Hampton, near the

Eastman estate on Long Island. Paul first met him towards the end of the seventies. Paul: 'Lee would say, "Do you want to come along and see Bill?" And Lee and Bill would sit in these two big ceremonial throne chairs, the two elders. He used to come to dinner and we used to go round to see him whenever we were on holiday there.'

De Kooning's wife, the painter Elaine de Kooning, told *Art News*:

> Paul and Bill are very chummy. Paul and Linda always come to visit us when they're in East Hampton. We talk about a wide range of things, everything really. Paul and Bill don't talk about art or music. You wouldn't think Paul was a musician or Bill was a painter, but they like each other's work. They understand what the other does in terms of their own work. Paul reacts to Bill's painting in a visceral way … The relationship is not paternal. It is a meeting of artists across one discipline to another.

> PAUL: I saw him draw Linda and her brother and her two sisters, for a present to give to their dad on his sixtieth birthday. We went round to his studio and they knew him well enough to say, 'Would you do quick drawings of us to give to Lee?' and he did. He uses the edge of the charcoal to get an even rougher line. I was very impressed. You could say I'm just star-struck or something but he has influenced me. Seeing someone like him draw, seeing someone like him paint, being there in his studio, seeing his attitude, has given me quite a buzz. After a visit with him I would often be so fired up I'd go along to the Golden Eagle paint shop where he buys his stuff and buy a big canvas. I'd go with paints from the shop that Bill used, canvases that Bill used, and then I'd go back and stick a canvas up on the porch. I'm in the same area, in the same environment in the woods, twenty minutes away from where he is, so there's some motivation.

Paul did his first oil painting when he and Linda rented a house in Long Island for the summer. It had pure white walls, just begging for paintings.

> PAUL: The previous people had taken all their paintings with them, so there were these painting hooks all around the walls. I thought, A big red painting would look really good there; and of course, you can't just stop there with red, you think, Why not

add a bit of orange? I thought, I can afford a few canvases, why not? They were oil on canvas, then I found that they were all still wet after two weeks and had to have a special box made to carry them, so I switched to acrylics. They were abstract. You have to paint abstract after you've been seeing Bill de Kooning. You wonder why you bother when you see his work.

Once he gave us a picture. Because we were friends they gave us the choice of the whole studio. We could have had anything but it seemed the right thing to do was to take something a little more modest. It was a pull. He used the *New York Times* to pull excess paint off a painting, and he'd lay it on the floor and sometimes he'd like that as much as the picture, so this was one of them. He liked this one so he put it on a board and put it in a little wooden frame which he made himself. So I said, 'That'd be great.' It obviously wasn't worth as much as the others but in friendship it was worth every bit as much. Anyway, I was talking to him and of course the question you ask the painter is 'What is it, Bill?' It was a big sort of purple thing in the middle in strong paint. He said, 'I dunno. It looks like a couch, huh?' Fuck me, any pretensions you had after that of 'What is the deep meaning behind all this shit?' Well, that was the painter himself saying, 'I dunno. Looks like a couch. Huh?' The 'huh?' was like I was just as free to offer an explanation as he was. I said, 'It looks a bit like a purple mountain to me.' He said, 'Hmmm.'

To those who knew him, it came as no surprise when Paul began to paint seriously. Like John, he had always been interested in painting and drawing; as a child he always drew his own Christmas and birthday cards and his school exercise books were filled with sketches. While living on the Speke trading estate he did a drawing of the newly built St Aiden's church which won him the art prize at school. In the sixties he designed wrapping paper and flyers for Indica Books and Gallery and drew the sleeve for a fan-club flexi-disc. Two of the Beatles' album sleeves, *Sgt. Pepper* and *Abbey Road*, were based upon his designs. One of the main things holding him back was John Lennon.

PAUL: I felt in John's shadow because I hadn't been to art college. This was one of my biggest blocks, I felt that only people who'd gone to art college were allowed to paint. Then I suddenly thought, this is absolute madness, I'm sure a lot of the great painters didn't go to art college. And, hell, even if they did, fuck 'em all, I want to paint! I'm desperate to paint! Then I thought, the only person not allowing you a canvas is you. That took me until the age of forty.

When Paul's pictures are finally shown they will inevitably be compared with the more familiar work of John Lennon; John was, after all, the Beatle who did go to art school, though in the fifties art schools were open to anyone with an interesting portfolio of work who came with a good recommendation from their headmaster. John was not an obvious candidate; he had failed his art O level and could not draw a likeness, but his cartoons and doodles were witty and had a certain charm. With the support of his Quarry Bank art teacher and his headmaster, Mr Pobjoy, he was enrolled as a student but did not qualify for a grant. John's studies did not last long. His work was not up to the minimum requirement and at the end of his first year he was told that he would not be admitted to the painting department. John was not a 'fine' artist. His drawings were more in the cartoon tradition of Hoffnung, Steinberg and James Thurber. There was a Thurber cartoon that both John and Paul enjoyed which showed a lawyer holding up a kangaroo in court with the caption: 'Perhaps *this* will refresh your memory!' They found it hilarious. John produced his best work many years later under the tutelage of Yoko: the *Bag One* series of lithographs and a 1977 series of line drawings illustrating a Japanese phrasebook. Yoko was able to bring out a visual sensibility in John that was lacking in the doodles and cartoons of earlier days. The new drawings were still infused with humour, but they had a sensitivity and a compositional awareness that his art-school tutors would have been delighted to witness.

PAUL: We used to have drawing competitions in the group where we'd sit down and say, 'Let's draw Mal,' and mine was often the likeness. I used to catch it. John's were often like crazy, because he couldn't actually draw like that. He did character drawing, he drew his little men, people with bulbous noses with hair coming out of them, bizarre character stuff, but he wasn't actually that good at representing something figuratively. I remember being quite surprised because I thought, Well, he goes to art college, what is it? Doesn't he want to do that or can't he do that? I never actually got the answer. I've never seen any really figurative stuff of John's. It's all little men, little drawings, it's jokes. I know he had a great eye.

Paul approached art from a very different direction. His early work, such as the line drawings illustrating the 1981 *Paul McCartney: Composer/Artist*, shows traces of a cartoon style shared with John but his paintings are much more informed by the American Abstract Expressionists and the psychological landscapes of Magritte, de Chirico and Ernst. He began painting seriously around 1983 and his first canvases show an obvious liking for Matisse, Bonnard, Chagall and the Fauves, consisting for the most part of decorative and colourful portraits and landscapes. His work developed over the years and his nineties canvases show a mature and individual style.

The influences are not disguised but nor are they ill-digested. Objects suspended in space always suggest Magritte, vigorous red-brown gestures are obviously reminiscent of de Kooning, and one particularly successful white canvas, with evidence of previous work showing through from below, has been scratched and worked on with words and small shapes in a manner very like that of Cy Twombly. In 1994 Paul began work on a series of pictures based on Celtic images. Working in series suits his style, with shapes and images being developed and modified from one canvas to the next. The Celtic pictures all feature thick paint lines squeezed straight from the tube across the top, a signature mark for the series. This technique may have been borrowed unconsciously from John Bratby; Paul sat for a portrait by him in the mid-sixties which is now in the National Portrait Gallery.

Some images have acquired iconic significance in Paul's work; for instance, a triangular woman's face with yellow hair is always Linda. His work is always contained within the frame, and is often 'supported' by a shape or mark attaching it, like a tree trunk, to the bottom edge. Sometimes a swirling of paint suggests an actual frame and in a few cases, a frame of sorts has been included in the image. Even in the abstract works, the picture plane tends to divide into earth and sky, usually indicated by the colours blue and brown/red, and much of the image is foregrounded as if based upon features in a landscape with a bush, tree or figure in front.

Paul's paint quality is very varied, from washes thinned with turps so that the pigment separates and forms rivulets, to scrubbed backgrounds, thickly applied strokes in the best Abstract Expression-ist tradition, and impasto.

> PAUL: I've always been inspired by de Kooning's brushstrokes, he uses a big brush and he goes whooop! And I fall in love with his strokes because if you try to paint very accurately like Estes or Magritte, for instance, it's not the same, they don't come out the same, they lose that wild spontaneity that is very attractive. My problem was if I got a canvas and went whooomp! I didn't feel it was finished because it didn't have a background. So I came to the obvious conclusion: get a few canvases, paint one pink, one blue, one white and just leave 'em to dry, then if I want to go whooop, sword-fencing at it with my brush, I'll have a very spontaneous thing on a very proper background. So I found myself making these backgrounds. Talking to Chrissie Wilson, Peter Blake's wife, she said, 'That's great, that's called "killing the canvas".'

Paul draws on the canvas by scratching lines through the paint to reveal the white prime ground. He sometimes draws in charcoal, fixing it with turpentine to prevent too much dragging up and muddying his colours. The surface is often luscious with pure colour like the luminous candy-colour backgrounds of Andy Warhol's late portraits. Paul clearly loves the physical application of paint and his work from this point of view is pure tachism, suggesting Georges Mathieu, Pierre Soulages, Hans Hofmann. His pictures often have a depth of space that suggests the big sky and wide horizons of an Arizona landscape. A row of yellow dots suggests a town in the far distance at dusk. He has taken a number of emblems from this desert landscape, like the prickly pear, and made them his own; a simplified image of the pear appears in a number of canvases. After more than a decade of steady work, he is now ready to exhibit, though he has been understandably reticent in allowing the public to see his work.

> PAUL: Outside of family and one or two mates I haven't had any feedback and I started to think, it's been ten years! If I'd been a painter for that long, I'd be expecting to exhibit, to sell, to do everything by now. I know inevitably, though, with the way my celebrity works, that the tabloids will pick up on the ones with

tits in 'em: 'We got a psychiatrist to look at this little lot, and they said, "It's obvious what we have here is a very disturbed ..."' I don't worry about it at all, it's just a question of looking for something that feels comfortable. I could hire a gallery and have an exhibition, but I wouldn't want to do that because that's not what I'm into. I've always avoided exhibiting, because I'm trying to avoid the Tony Curtis actor-turned-painter syndrome. I was thinking something quieter, a little German gallery might be nice.

Aside from the tabloids, rock critics also rarely know anything about art and usually trivialise any art produced by musicians. Art critics, on the other hand, are a notoriously faddish bunch. They like their artists to come from the latest 'in' art school or country. A rock star producing paintings is an uncomfortable thing to deal with because they often come from an art-college background but didn't stay with it. It is easy to dismiss the bright, happy watercolours of Henry Miller, the whimsical fantasies of Kenneth Patchen or the hideous nudes of D. H. Lawrence, but the thoroughly competent work of Joni Mitchell, the abstract canvases of Captain Beefheart (who, as Don Van Vliet, has exhibited in Cork Street with the rest of the art establishment) and the multimedia concept art of Laurie Anderson, David Bowie, David Byrne or Brian Eno are much harder to get a handle on.

The Nineties

Paul did not stop with painting. In the nineties he began to branch out into numerous other art forms, confirming his reputation as a workaholic: he composed an oratorio for the Royal Liverpool Philharmonic Society, which he followed with a ten-minute classical piano piece premiered at St James's Palace. EMI commissioned him to write an orchestral piece to celebrate the 100th anniversary of the company and he composed the score for an animated film, *Daumier's Law*, which he and Linda also produced. He wrote and published poems and made *Grateful Dead: A Photofilm*, an animated film based upon Linda's pictures of the Grateful Dead. He also spent six years getting the Liverpool Institute of Performing Arts off the ground, a major project which occupied much of his time. In addition he squeezed in two world tours and a number of albums.

On Friday, 28 June 1991, Paul McCartney's *Liverpool Oratorio* was premièred by the Royal Liverpool Philharmonic Orchestra at Liverpool's Anglican cathedral where, at the age of eleven, Paul once failed an audition to sing in the choir. It was written as a repertory piece to commemorate the 150th anniversary of the founding of the Royal Liverpool Philharmonic Society and was the culmination of a three-year collaboration with the American composer Carl Davis, who had made three previous albums with the RLPO.

The *Liverpool Oratorio* is in eight movements and lasts about 100 minutes. Paul chose his own life story as the loose basis for the libretto, and so it is more autobiographical than his usual work. In order to locate the scenario in Liverpool he has not universalised the experiences and we have descriptions of actual events from his childhood: 'Cross the road, and over the cemetery fence,/ Down the hill to where the gravestones/ Lie inviting in the sun.' Paul and John Lennon used to slip away from the Institute and go to the graveyard beside the Anglican cathedral situated in the quarry where the cathedral masonry was dug and shaped. They would spend the afternoon smoking cigarettes, talking and sunbathing beside the great cathedral, where thirty years later the *Oratorio* was premièred.

The four solo artists for the première were all big names, beginning with Dame Kiri Te Kanawa, who has sung in every major opera house in the world. Her vast repertory includes the heroines of Mozart, Verdi and Puccini as well as classic musicals such as *West Side Story* and *South Pacific*.

Rehearsing and staging the *Oratorio* was as complex as putting on a major rock concert. As well as the four soloists there were 90 members of the RLPO and 160 singers in the Royal Liverpool Philharmonic Choir, supplemented by 40 schoolboy choristers of Liverpool Cathedral, and 200 performers. In addition, the event was being recorded for a live CD release and filmed by a BBC television crew. 2,300 tickets were available for each of the two performances and were snapped up as soon as they went on sale.

The performance received an astonishing five-minute standing ovation: Liverpool businessmen in their best suits climbed on the wobbly folding chairs and bellowed their approval. Their wives kicked off their high heels to join them and the rattle of their gold jewellery added to the applause. McCartney fans cheered and hooted and local politicians and businessmen shouted out their congratulations to the local boy made good. Paul grabbed Carl Davis's hand and held it aloft in triumph. Neil Kinnock, then leader of the Opposition, declared it was 'Bloody fantastic, bloody brilliant, bloody great music ...'

The *New York Times* gave it a very positive review; other critics were not quite so enthusiastic but only one or two put it down. Paul actually wrote to the *Guardian*, whose critic complained that it never approached anything like a fast tempo.

> PAUL: Because it does. There are quite a few metronome marks that are as fast as any piece is fast. Then he said, hasn't anyone told him that this kind of a piece needs recurrent themes to bind it together? But there are so many fucking recurrent themes I'm embarrassed. Really there are too many in my view. So I wrote a letter pointing out there were "a plethora of recurrent themes". I said I don't mind if he doesn't like it, but when he says there are no recurrent themes, this is misleading the readership and that's not what you're trying to do, is it? They published the letter with a cartoon of a couple of eighteenth-century guys and a caption saying, 'Mr Handel's new work has a plethora of recurrent themes.' So it was a bit of a joke. But I don't normally respond. I had some great letters about it: 'It makes me laugh, it makes me cry, just like Liverpool.' That was a good one. Neil Kinnock wrote me a great letter talking about their 'sniffy snobbery'. He said, 'Perhaps they'd be happier if the words were translated into Italian.'
>
> Of course you know you're going to get criticised but it's interesting, it's good fun. It's great working with artists like that and you can see how you could do a lot more. I think they got pretty much good value for money for what they wanted, which was a celebration piece.

EMI released the performance as a double CD and, not surprisingly, it entered the UK classical charts at number one. The recording uses mostly material from the second night's performance, which was the better of the two and four minutes faster, with almost all of the time being gained in the first few movements. Paul: 'It suddenly settled in like it wasn't a rehearsal piece any more.' One of the critics claimed that the piece was so much about Liverpool that 'it will never travel'. At the time of its 100th performance, at the Liverpool Philharmonic Hall on 21 September 1996, it had been performed in twenty countries, from Finland to Venezuela, Japan to South Africa, and in more than a dozen states in the USA.

In 1980, a Londoner called Mark Featherstone-Witty saw Alan Parker's film *Fame* at the Odeon Leicester Square and emerged from the cinema wondering why Britain didn't have a performing arts academy along the lines of the *Fame* school. Mark: 'At first I thought that somebody else must be setting something up in this country, but no one was, so I wrote letters to over two hundred people in the industry looking for support.' Alan Parker himself became the first patron and he quickly assembled a formidable list, from Joan Armatrading to Vangelis, Richard Branson and George Martin. In 1985, Mark was able to found the Performing Arts Trust.

The Liverpool Institute for Performing Arts was founded in 1989, the result of a change in Liverpool City Council's policy on arts and culture to provide an initiative to capitalise on Liverpool's reputation as a centre for talent. In August 1988, Paul made a short film at his old school, the Liverpool Institute, which had closed three years before, and was depressed to see the magnificent old building falling into dereliction. He thought the Institute would be a perfect location for a school of performing arts. He had told the Performing Arts Trust that if they ever wanted to do anything in Liverpool they should contact him, and so Paul and Mark Featherstone-Witty began making plans. A feasibility study was launched, which included asking the people of Liverpool if they wanted such a school by running a poll in the *Liverpool Echo*.

1745 Liverpudlians voted in favour and only 48 called in against. 'Now the hard work begins,' wrote Paul. A business plan was published and a campaign to raise £12,400,000 was launched, headed by Paul as 'lead patron', whose job it was not only to contribute money, but show politicians such as Michael Portillo MP round the building.

By the winter of 1992, more than £9,000,000 of the target figure had been raised. Paul and Mark hosted lunches for the Performing Rights Society, for EC officials in Brussels and representatives of trusts and foundations. The government City Challenge programme gave £4,000,000, matched by a similar figure from the EC. Paul wrote to the Queen and received a cheque drawn on the privy purse, headed Buckingham Palace. It was explained that protocol required that the sum itself could not be revealed, but the fact that the Queen had made a personal donation could be used in the fund-raising drive. Paul used his personal contacts to get backing from celebrities including Eddie Murphy, Ralph Lauren, David Hockney, Mark Knopfler, Carly Simon, Chevy Chase, Paul Simon and Jane Fonda. Many of Paul's fans donated seats in the auditorium (£50) and stair treads (£100) which would have their name inscribed upon them. Paul himself opened the fundraising by giving £1,000,000. A new roof was built and architect's plans for the centre were completed and submitted for planning permission.

The aim of the Institute is not to turn out pop singers – though some may appear – but to offer its 192 full time students degree courses in 'the realities of working in the entertainment industry'. As Paul pointed out, on his 1991 world tour there were six musicians on stage and it took 140 people to put them there. A career in the entertainment industry can involve anything from security to stage design, from driving equipment trucks across international borders to building an outdoor stage in a hurricane, from running a 4000-bulb lighting rig and 80-foot video monitor from a laptop computer to keeping the books.

There have been persistent criticisms from people in Liverpool that the Beatles never did anything for their home town (except put it on the map), but no rock 'n' roller has ever done anything as ambitious as this. Saving and restoring a significant 1825 city-centre building from inevitable vandalism and ruin would in itself have been an achievement but to start a new school there, the first in the country to offer degree courses in the profession that brought the Beatles their wealth and fame, has to be one of the most generous contributions ever seen in a business not known for its largesse.

It was a remarkable turn of the circle for Paul to be once more back at the Inny, which he first entered in 1953 as an awestruck, anxious eleven-year-old, this time standing on stage in the auditorium, now named after him, its most famous pupil, receiving a thunderous ovation from the assembled mayors and mayoresses of Merseyside and the grandees of the music business. He could barely hold back the tears. The building was officially opened by the Queen on 7 June 1996.

During his three years' work on the *Liverpool Oratorio*, Paul listened to many classical CDs, something that provoked him to write a prelude for solo piano. The piece was called 'A Leaf', and had its première at An Evening with Paul McCartney and Friends, a fund-raising concert for the Royal College of Music which was hosted by the Prince of Wales, president of the RCM, in the Picture Gallery of the State Apartments of St James's Palace on 23 March 1995. At the front centre stood the Prince's chair, slightly larger than the others, with arms and a plumped-up red cushion with tassels on. It was a black-tie affair and even Paul's road and recording crew had to wear full evening dress, the first time anyone had seen studio manager Eddie Klein in a suit.

'A Leaf' had finished up a little too difficult for Paul to play with exactitude so he looked for someone else to perform it. The twenty-two-year-old Russian pianist Anya Alexeyev had won the gold medal at the Royal College of Music and was an obvious choice; when she showed up at MPL to audition 'A Leaf' for Paul she played it faultlessly from memory. At St James's Palace Paul introduced Anya by saying, 'For me, this sums up what this evening's all about, giving young musicians like this an opportunity.' Anya's performance of 'A Leaf' was perfect and EMI later released it as a live recording on their Classics label.

At the end of the evening, the Prince took to the stage and after the customary thanks, sprang a surprise on Paul by awarding him an honorary fellowship of the Royal College of Music, the highest award of Britain's premier music establishment. Prince Charles said the award was 'in recognition of the remarkable talents of Paul McCart-ney and for all that he has done for music this century'. Linda and everyone from MPL knew in advance, of course, as the Royal College had to be sure that Paul would accept. He is the first rock 'n' roller to receive the award.

Paul McCartney, MBE – holder of five Ivor Novello awards, listed in the *Guinness Book of Records* as the most successful popular-music composer and recording artist ever, with sales of more than 100 million singles and sixty gold discs, Freeman of the City of Liverpool, holder of an honorary Doctorate of Music from the University of

Sussex, holder of the Guinness World Record for the largest stadium audience in history when 184,000 Brazilians paid to see him perform at the Maracana Stadium in Rio de Janeiro in April 1990, as well as the world record for the fastest ticket sale in history when 20,000 tickets for two shows in Sydney sold out in eight minutes in 1993. Paul was the first rock musician to receive Chile's Order of Merit for 'services to music, peace and human understanding' and in 1992 he was the first recipient of the Swedish Polar Music Award ('the Nobel prize for music'). In 1993, 'Yesterday' was confirmed as the world's most popular song, with a world record of 6,000,000 airplays in the USA alone and by being recorded by more than 2,200 other artists. And as further proof that Paul has fully entered British musical and cultural history, in 1996 the National Trust bought his boyhood home on the council estate in Forthlin Road to preserve it for the nation in perpetuity. However, the greatest honour was yet to come.

With the award of their MBEs in 1965, the Beatles were invited on a career path leading to further honours, awards and acceptance into the British establishment. This trajectory was stalled, in the case of John, Paul and George, by their remarks concerning drugs, and subsequent police actions.

The Honours system is a quintessentially British method of rewarding people for outstanding service to the country or to public life, and after a suitable number of years had passed since Paul's last drug bust, he was back on track again. His contribution to the British economy was not to be doubted; he has sold more records than any other artist, ever. Paul's insistence that his donations to charity remained anonymous went against him as someone in his position is expected to give rather conspicuously. This changed with the foundation of L.I.P.A. where the public could see his donation of over a million pounds. Moreover, he had become, more than any of the other ex-Beatles, an established and well loved figure in British public life.

In some ways Paul's fellowship of the Royal College of Music can be seen as a dry run to make sure that Paul was really suitable material for a knighthood. He carried the day well, and put on a fine charity show at St James's Palace. The way was clear for him to become Sir Paul. It came as little surprise, to the press at least, that Paul's name was down for a knight bachelor on the New Year Honours List released on December 31st, 1996. George Martin had received the same honour the previous year – but he had never been arrested for drugs. It was an award long overdue. Paul made sure that he was out of the country when the announcement was made, knowing that it would be front-page news. It was the lead story on the BBC radio and television news as well as the main headline in virtually all the daily newspapers, some of which ran special souvenir supplements. 'No one deserves it more,' editorialised *The Sun*, and a BBC radio news commentator said, 'This must be the most popular knighthood of all time: no other person has brought such pleasure for so long to so many millions of people.'

There were people who thought he was selling out by accepting it, but Paul's explanation was simple: 'It's like a school prize. You don't go after it but if you do some good drawings then you can get the art prize and they give it to you because they think you're alright. And that's the way I take it really. It's just something nice that's offered and it'd be rude to turn it down, wouldn't it?'

It was a beautiful day on 11 March 1997, when Paul, accompanied by his three youngest children, arrived at Buckingham Palace. There are so many people on the Honours List that they are each restricted to only three guests. Paul and Linda decided that Mary, Stella and James should be the ones and Linda and Heather would stay home. Once inside Buckingham Palace, Paul and his family were separated and he followed the arrow marked 'Recipients'. He was told to show his letter to the aide in the reception room. He reached in his pocket and found that he had forgotten to bring it but the woman didn't need it, she knew who he was. Paul and the other twenty-nine knights, many in full military uniform, were taken to a side room and given cushions on which to practise kneeling. 'Right knee, if you please.' The cushions were comfortably padded and there was a little hand-rail to hold onto. All the while the band of the Grenadier Guards played light music, including selections from *South Pacific*: 'I'm gonna wash that man right outta my hair.'

When it was his turn, Paul approached the Queen and went down on one knee. She placed a medal around his neck and tapped him lightly on the shoulder with a ceremonial sword. In the audience Stella burst into tears. Paul: 'It's the sword of Edward the Confessor. It starts to come home to you. In the end I was much more impressed than I thought I was going to be.' The Queen had a few words with the recipients afterwards. It had not been long since Paul last met the

Queen, at the opening of L.I.P.A. and she asked how the school was doing.

Paul told the press: 'This is one of the best days of my life. To come from a terraced house in Liverpool to this house is quite a journey and I am immensely proud . . . You never forget the fans who put you up there . . . This brings back memories of 1965; it seems strange being here without the other three. George and Ringo keep ringing me up, calling me Your Holiness.

'The nice thing about it, really, when me and Linda are sitting on holiday, watching the sunset. I turn to her and say, 'Hey, you're a Lady.' It's nice because you get to make your girlfriend a Lady – although she always was anyway.'

BIBLIOGRAPHY

These are the books used in the preparation of this text. The bibliographies of the Beatles as a group and individual Beatles do not pretend to be anywhere near complete since such a listing would be about twice as long, nor are these necessarily first editions. There are several key books which I have returned to again and again which deserve special mention: Mark Lewisohn's *The Complete Beatles Chronicle*, which has been invaluable; Ian MacDonald's *Revolution in the Head*, which contains many valuable insights into the music, and David Sheff's *The Playboy Interviews with John Lennon*. The following were also useful references: William Dowlding's *Beatlesongs*; Steve Turner's *A Hard Day's Write*; Hunter Davies's authorised *The Beatles*, which, though censored at the time, remains the most accurate account of their career; and, despite being ungenerous at times, Albert Goldman's *The Lives of John Lennon*, because it includes so much original research.

The Beatles

26 Days That Rocked the World (Los Angeles, O'Brien, 1978) [facsimile newspapers of first US tour]

Aldridge, Alan, ed.: *The Beatles Illustrated Lyrics* (London, Macdonald, 1969)

—*The Beatles Illustrated Lyrics 2* (London, Macdonald, 1971)

Baker, Glenn: *The Beatles Down Under, The 1964 Australia and New Zealand Tour* (Glebe, Wild and Woolley, 1982)

Barrow, Tony: *Meet the Beatles* (Manchester, World Distributors, 1963)

Beatles Diary for 1965 (Glasgow, Beat Publications, 1964)

Beatles Pictorial (London, *Boyfriend* magazine extra, 1963)

Beatles Press Book (London, Apple Records, 1969)

Bedford, Carol: *Waiting for the Beatles, An Apple Scruff's Story* (Poole, Blandford, 1984)

Benson, Harry: *The Beatles in the Beginning* (Edinburgh, Mainstream, 1993)

Bicknell, Alf, and Marsh, Gary: *'Baby You Can Drive My Car'*, (np, Number 9 Books, 1989)

Black, Johnny: *The Beatles Complete* (London, HMV, 1988)

Blake, John: *All You Needed Was Love* (London, Hamlyn, 1981)

Braun, Michael: *Love Me Do: The Beatles' Progress* (Harmondsworth, Penguin, 1964)

Brown, Peter, and Gaines, Steven: *The Love You Make* (London, Macmillan, 1983)

Bunt, Jan van de: *The Beatles Concert-ed Efforts* (The Netherlands, 1979)

Burke, John: *The Beatles in Their First Fab Film! A Hard Day's Night* (London, Pan, 1964)

Campbell, Colin, and Murphy, Allan: *Things We Said Today* (songs concordance) (Ann Arbor, Pierian Press, 1980)

Carr, Roy, and Tyler, Tony: *The Beatles: An Illustrated Record* (London, Triune, 1978)

Castleman, Harry, and Podrazik, Walter: *All Together Now* (Ann Arbor, Pierian Press, 1976)

—*The Beatles Again?* (Ann Arbor, Pierian Press, 1977)

—*The End of the Beatles?* (Ann Arbor, Pierian Press, 1985)

Cosham, Ralph: *The Beatles at Carnegie Hall* (London, Panther Pictorial, 1964)

Cott, Jonathan, and Dalton, David: *The Beatles Get Back* (London, Apple, 1969)

Cowan, Philip: *Behind the Beatles Songs* (London, Polytantric Press, nd)

Davies, Hunter: *The Beatles, The Authorised Biography* (London, Heinemann, 1968, and later updated editions)

David, Edward, ed.: *The Beatles Book* (New York, Cowles, 1968)

Dean, Johnny: *The Beatles Book* (London, Beat Publications, 1966)

Delano, Julia: *The Beatles Album* (London, Grange, 1991)

Dellar, Fred: *NME Guide to Rock Cinema* (London, Hamlyn, 1981)

DiLello, Richard: *The Longest Cocktail Party* (London, Charisma, 1972)

Dister, Alain: *Les Beatles* (Paris, Albin Michel, 1972)

Doney, Malcolm: *Lennon and McCartney* (London, Midas, 1981)

Dowlding, William: *Beatlesongs* (New York, Simon & Schuster, 1989)

[no editor given] *EMI. The Story of Recorded Sound Presented by EMI Records Ltd* (London, EMI, 1977)

Evans, Mike: *The Art of the Beatles* (Walker Art Gallery, Liverpool, catalogue, Sept 1984)

—*The Art of the Beatles* (London, Anthony Blond, 1984)

Evans, Mike, and Jones, Ron: *In the Footsteps of the Beatles* (Liverpool, Merseyside Council guidebook, 1981)

Freeman, Robert: *The Beatles, A Private View* (London, Pyramid, 1990)

—*The Beatles in America* (London, Daily Mirror Publications, 1964)

—*Yesterday, Photographs of the Beatles* (London, Weidenfeld & Nicolson,

1983)

Friede, Goldie; Titone, Robin, and Weiner, Sue: *The Beatles A to Z* (New York, Methuen, 1980)

Friedman, Rick: *The Beatles, Words Without Music* (New York, Grosset & Dunlap, 1968)

Fulpen, H. V.: *The Beatles. An Illustrated Diary* (London, Plexus, 1982)

Giuliano, Geoffrey: *The Beatles, A Celebration* (London, Sidgwick & Jackson, 1986)

Giuliano, Geoffrey and Brenda, eds.: *The Lost Beatles Interviews* (London, Virgin, 1995)

Grove, Martin: *Beatle Madness* (New York, Manor, 1978)

Guzek, Arno: *Beatles Discography* (Hvidovre, Denmark, 1976)

Harrison, George [of the *Liverpool Echo*]: *Around the World with the Beatles* (Liverpool, Liverpool Echo, 1964)

Harry, Bill: *The Beatles Who's Who* (London, Aurum, 1982)

—*Paperback Writers, An Illustrated Bibliography* (London, Virgin, 1984)

—*The Ultimate Beatles Encyclopedia* (London, Virgin, 1992)

Harry, Bill, ed.: *Mersey Beat. The Beginnings of the Beatles* (London, Omnibus Press, 1977) [Facsimiles of the various articles by and about the Beatles in *Merseybeat* magazine]

Hertsgaard, Mark: *A Day in the Life. The Music and Artistry of the Beatles* (London, Macmillan, 1995)

Hoffmann, Dezo: *Beatles* (Tokyo, Shinka Music, 1976)

—*With the Beatles* (London, Omnibus, 1982)

Howlett, Kevin: *The Beatles at the Beeb, the story of their radio career* (London, BBC, 1982)

Jürgs, Michael, Ziemann, Hans Heinrich, and Meyer, Dietmar: *Das Album der Beatles* (Hamburg, Stern, 1981)

Larkin, Rochelle: *The Beatles, Yesterday, Today, Tomorrow* (New York, Scholastic Books, 1977 reprint)

Leach, Sam: *The Beatles on Broadway* (Manchester, World Distributors, 1964) [Souvenir of the Beatles first visit to the USA]

Lewisohn, Mark: *The Beatles Live!* (London, Pavilion, 1986)

—*The Complete Beatles Chronicle* (London, Pyramid, 1992)

—*The Complete Beatles Recording Sessions* (London, Hamlyn, 1988)

—*The Beatles, 25 Years in the Life, A Chronology 1962–87* (London, Sidgwick & Jackson, 1987)

Lewisohn, Mark, Schreuders, Piet, and Smith, Adam: *The Beatles' London* (London, Hamlyn, 1994)

Macdonald, Ian: *Revolution in the Head, The Beatles' Records and the Sixties* (London, Fourth Estate, 1994)

Madow, Stuart, and Sobul, Jeff: *The Colour of Your Dreams. The Beatles' Psychedelic Music* (Pittsburgh, Dorrance, 1992)

Martin, George: *Summer of Love, The Making of Sgt. Pepper* (London, Macmillan, 1994)

Matahira, Toru: *Beatles Movie Catalog* (np [Japan], 1979)

Maugham, Patrick: *The Beatles* (London, PYX Publications, 1964)

McCabe, Peter, and Schonfeld, Robert: *Apple to the Core, The Unmaking of the Beatles* (London, Martin Brian & O'Keeffe, 1972)

McGeary, Mitchell: *The Beatles Discography* (Olympia, Washington, Ticket to Ride, 1975)

Mellors, Wilfred: *Twilight of the Gods, The Beatles in Retrospective* (London, Faber & Faber, 1973)

Miles [Barry], ed.: *Beatles in Their Own Words* (London, W. H. Allen, 1978)

Mitchell, Carolyn Lee: *All Our Loving, A Beatle Fan's Memoir* (London, Robson, 1988)

Muni, Scott, Somach, Denny, and Somach, Kathleen: *Ticket to Ride* (London, Macdonald, 1989)

Murphy, Campbell: *Things We Said Today* (Ann Arbor, Pierian Press, 1980)

Naha, Ed, ed.: *The Beatles Forever* (New York, O'Quinn Studios, 1980)

Neises, Charles, ed.: *The Beatles Reader* (Ann Arbor, Pierian Press, 1984)

Nimmervoll, Ed, and Thorburn, Euan, eds.: *1000 Beatle Facts* (Sydney, J. Albert, 1977)

Norman, Philip: *Shout!* (London, Elm Tree, 1981)

O'Donnell, Jim: *The Day John Met Paul* (New York, Hall of Fame, 1994)

Pascall, Jeremy, ed.: *The Fabulous Story of John, Paul, George and Ringo* (London, Octopus, 1975)

Pawlowski, Gareth: *How They Became the Beatles* (London, Macdonald, 1990)

Rayl, A. J. S.: *Beatles '64. A Hard Day's Night in America* (London, Sidgwick & Jackson, 1989)

Rehwagen, Thomas, and Schmidt, Thorsten: *Mach Schau! Die Beatles in Hamburg* (Braunschweig, EinfallReich, 1992)

Reinhart, Charles: *You Can't Do That! Beatles Bootlegs and Novelty Records* (Ann Arbor, Pierian Press, 1981)

Russell, Jeff: *The Beatles: Album File and Complete Discography* (Poole, Dorset, Blandford, 1982)

Scaduto, Anthony: *The Beatles, Yesterday, Today and Tomorrow* (New York, Signet, 1968)

Schaffner, Nicholas: *The Beatles Forever* (New York, McGraw-Hill, 1977)

—*The British Invasion* (New York, McGraw-Hill, 1982)

Schaumburg, Ron: *Growing Up with the Beatles* (New York, Pyramid, 1976)

Schultheiss, Tom: *A Day in the Life: The Beatles Day-By-Day, 1960–1970* (Ann Arbor, Pierian Press, 1980)

Shepherd, Billy: *The True Story of the Beatles* (London, Beat Publications, 1964)

Shipper, Mark: *Paperback Writer* (London, New English Library, 1978)

Southall, Brian: *Abbey Road, The Story of the World's Most Famous Recording Studios* (Cambridge, Stevens, 1982)

Spence, Helen: *The Beatles Forever* (London, Colour Library International, 1981)

Spencer, Terence: *It Was Thirty Years Ago Today* (London, Bloomsbury, 1994)

Stannard, Neville: *The Long and Winding Road, A History of the Beatles on Record* (London, Virgin, 1982)

Taylor, Alistair: *Yesterday, The Beatles Remembered* (London, Sidgwick & Jackson, 1988)

Terry, Carol: *Here There and Everywhere, The First International Beatles Bibliography 1962–1982* (Ann Arbor, Pierian Press, 1985)

Turner, Steve: *A Hard Day's Write, The Stories Behind Every Beatles Song* (London, Carlton, 1994)

The Beatles Book Calendar for 1964 (nd, np [London, Beat Publications, 1963])

Wallgren, Mark: *The Beatles on Record* (New York, Simon & Schuster, 1982)

Whitaker, Bob: *The Unseen Beatles* (London, Conran Octopus, 1991)

Wiener, Allen: *The Beatles: The Ultimate Recording Guide* (London, Aurum, 1993)

Williams, Allan: *The Man Who Gave the Beatles Away* (London, Coronet, 1976)

Woofinden, Bob: *The Beatles Apart* (London, Proteus, 1981)

Yenne, Bill: *The Beatles* (Leicester, Magna, 1989)

[no editor given] *The Beatles, Complete Works* (Amsterdam, Thomas Rap, nd [1968])

[no editor given] *The Beatles in Sweden* (London, City Magazines, 1963)

[Stafford Pemberton] *The Beatles for the Record* (Knutsford, Cheshire, 1981)

[various contributors] *The Compleat Beatles* (London, Omnibus Press, 1982) [Two volumes, boxed, contains the Beatles' complete music as well as 178pp of articles, photographs and discographies]

[various contributors] *The Compleat Beatles*, abridged version (Chicago, Contemporary, 1985)

Beatles periodicals

Beatlefan, 1978–1982. (Collected in two volumes by Pierian Press, Ann Arbor, 1985 and 1986)

The Beatles Book Monthly, 1–77 (August 1963–December 1969); 78–223 (October 1982–September 1995) London, Beat Publications

Paul McCartney

[ed. unknown] *Beatle Paul McCartney, His Story By Himself* (London, George Newnes, 1963)

Benson, Ross: *Paul McCartney, Behind the Myth* (London, Victor Gollancz, 1992)

Coleman, Ray: *McCartney, Yesterday and Today* (London, Boxtree, 1995)

[duNoyer, Paul, ed.]: *The Paul McCartney World Tour* (London, MPL/EMAP, 1989)

Elson, Howard: *McCartney, Songwriter* (London, W. H. Allen, 1986)

Flippo, Chet: *McCartney, The Biography* (London, Sidgwick & Jackson, 1988)

Gambaccini, Paul: *Paul McCartney in His Own Words* (London, Omnibus Press, 1976)

Giuliano, Geoffrey: *Blackbird, The Life and Times of Paul McCartney* (New York, Dutton, 1991)

Harry, Bill: *The McCartney File* (London, Virgin, 1986)

Jasper, Tony: *Paul McCartney and Wings* (London, Octopus, 1977)

McCartney, Linda: *Linda McCartney's Sixties* (London, Pyramid, 1992)

—*Linda's Pictures* (New York, Ballantine, 1977)

McCartney, Michael: *Mike Mac's White and Blacks* (London, Aurum, 1986)

—*Remember, The Recollections and Photographs of Michael McCartney* (London, Merehurst, 1992)

—*Thank U Very Much, Mike McCartney's Family Album* (London, Arthur Barker, 1981)

McCartney, Paul: *Paul McCartney, Composer/Artist* (London, Pavilion, 1981)

—*Paul McCartney: Paintings 1983–1988* (London, MPL, 1989)

—*Paul McCartney: Paintings 1988–1992* (London, MPL, 1994)

Pascall, Jeremy: *Paul McCartney and Wings* (London, Hamlyn, 1977)

Philipp, Judith, and Simon, Ralf: *Listen to What the Man Said* (Bielefeld, Pendragon, 1990) in German

Salewicz, Chris: *McCartney: The Biography* (London, Macdonald, 1986)

Thorgerson, Storm and Christopherson, Peter, eds.: *'Hands Across the Water' Wings Tour USA* (London, Reed, 1978)

Tremlett, George: *The Paul McCartney Story* (London, Futura, 1975)

Welch, Chris: *Paul McCartney, The Definitive Biography* (London, Proteus, 1984)

Paul McCartney periodicals

Club Sandwich, the magazine of the Paul McCartney Fanclub

John Lennon

Baird, Julia, with Giuliano, Geoffrey: *John Lennon, My Brother* (London, Grafton, 1988)

Beckley, Timothy Green, ed.: *Lennon, What Happened?* (np Sunshine, 1980)

Belanger, Lyn, Brecher, Michael, Kearns, Jo, Locke, Niclas, and Shatzkin, Mike, eds.: *A Tribute to John Lennon* (London, Proteus, 1981)

Bresler, Fenton: *Who Killed John Lennon?* (New York, St Martins Press, 1989)

Carpozi, George: *John Lennon, Death of a Dream* (New York, Manor, 1980)

Coleman, Ray: *John Lennon* (London, Futura, 1985) [originally in 2 vols]

Darby, George, and Robson, David, eds.: *John Lennon, The Life and Legend* (London, *Sunday Times*, 1980)

Doncaster, Patrick: *Tribute to John Lennon* (London, *Daily Mirror*, 1980)

The editors of *Rolling Stone*: *The Ballad of John and Yoko* (London, Michael Joseph, 1982)

Fawcett, Anthony: *John Lennon, One Day at a Time* (New York, Grove, 1976)

Garbarini, Vic, Cullman, Brian, and Graustark, Barbara: *Strawberry Fields Forever* (New York, Bantam, 1980)

Goldman, Albert: *The Lives of John Lennon* (London, Bantam, 1988)

Green, John: *Dakota Days* (New York, St Martins Press, 1983)

Harry, Bill: *The Book of Lennon* (London, Aurum, 1984)

Herzogenrath, Wulf, and Hansen, Dorothee, eds.: *John Lennon: Drawings Performances Films* (Stuttgart, Cantz Verlag, 1995)

John & Yoko Calendar for 1970 (written, designed and published by John and Yoko)

Lennon, Cynthia: *A Twist of Lennon* (London, Star, 1978) [also updated and rewritten in *Hello!* magazine]

Lennon, John: *A Spaniard in the Works* (London, Cape, 1965)

—*In His Own Write* (London, Cape, 1964)

—*Skywriting by Word of Mouth* (New York, Harper & Row, 1986)

Lennon, Pauline: *Daddy Come Home* (London, HarperCollins, 1990)

Martin, Nancie: *John Lennon/Julian Lennon* (New York, Avon Superstars, 1986)

Miles, [Barry], ed.: *John Lennon in His Own Words* (London, Omnibus Press, 1980)

Ono, Yoko: *John Lennon, Summer of* 1980 (New York, Perigee, 1983)

Pang, May, and Edwards, Henry: *Loving John, The Untold Story* (New York, Warner, 1983)

Peebles, Andy: *The Lennon Tapes* (London, BBC, 1981)

Ryan, David Stuart: *John Lennon's Secret* (London, Kozmik Press

Center, 1982)

Saimaru, Nishi: *John Lennon, A Family Album* (Toyko, Fly, 1982)

Seaman, Frederic: *John Lennon, Living on Borrowed Time* (London, Xanadu, 1991)

Sheff, David: *The Playboy Interviews with John Lennon* (London, NEL, 1982)

Shevy, Sandra: *The Other Side of Lennon* (London, Sidgwick & Jackson, 1990)

Shotton, Pete, and Schaffner, Nicholas: *John Lennon in My Life* (London, Coronet, 1983)

Smith, Ron: *John Lennon: A Tribute, Yesterday and Today* (New York, David Zentner Publications, 1980)

Solt, Andrew, and Egan, Sam: *Imagine, John Lennon* (London, Virgin, 1989)

Stone, Steve, ed.: *John Lennon, All You Need Is Love* (New York, Marjam, 1980)

Swenson, John: *The John Lennon Story* (New York, Leisure, 1981)

The editors of *Melody Maker*: *John Lennon, A Melody Maker Tribute* (London, MM, 1980)

The editors of the *Birmingham Evening Mail*: *The John Lennon Story* (Birmingham, 1980)

The editors of the *Liverpool Echo*: *A Special Tribute to John Lennon by the Liverpool Echo*. (Liverpool, 1980)

The editors of *US*: *A Tribute to John Lennon and the Beatles* (New York, Concentric Enterprises, 1980)

Todd, Jack, ed.: *The Beatles' John Lennon, A Memorial Album* (New York, Friday Publishing, 1981)

Tremlett, George: *The John Lennon Story* (London, Futura, 1976)

Tynan, Kenneth: *Oh! Calcutta, An Entertainment with Music* (New York, Grove, 1969) [contains John Lennon's playlet]

Wenner, Jann, ed.: *Lennon Remembers* (Harmondsworth, Penguin, 1973)

Wiener, Jon: *Come Together, John Lennon in His Time* (New York, Random House, 1984)

[no editor given] *John Lennon* (nd, np [London?])

[no editor given] *John Lennon, A Legend* (London, Colourgold, 1980)

[no editor given] *John Lennon and the Beatles* (New York, Harris Publications, 1980)

[no editor given] *John Lennon, Beatles Memories Book* (New York, Harris Publications, 1981)

[no editor given] *John Lennon, Give Peace a Chance* (Nottingham, Croft Publishers, 1980)

[no editor given] *John Lennon 1940–1980* (London, Chart Songwords, 1980)

[no editor given] *John Lennon, October 9 1940–December 8 1980* (nd, np [London], 1980)

[no editor given] *John Lennon, Working Class Hero* (nd, np [but all the

writers are from *NME*, London])
[various authors] *A Tribute to John Lennon* (London, Proteus, 1981)

George Harrison

Harrison, George: *I Me Mine* (New York, Simon & Schuster, 1980)
Giuliano, Geoffrey: *Dark Horse* (London, Bloomsbury, 1989)

Ringo Starr

Clayson, Alan: *Ringo Starr, Straight Man or Joker?* (London, Sidgwick & Jackson, 1991)

Biographies and Autobiographies

Amburn, Ellis: *Dark Star: The Roy Orbison Story* (London, New English Library, 1990)
Balfour, Victoria: *Rock Wives* (New York, William Morrow, 1986)
Beaton, Cecil: *Self-Portrait With Friends, Selected Diaries* (Harmondsworth, Penguin, 1982)
Best, Pete, and Doncaster, Patrick: *Beatle! The Pete Best Story* (New York, Dell, 1985)
Bockris, Victor: *Keith Richards: The Biography* (London, Hutchinson, 1992)
Brown, Tony: *Jimi Hendrix, A Visual Documentary* (London, Omnibus, 1992)
Bugliosi, Vincent: *Helter Skelter, The Manson Murders* (Harmondsworth, Penguin, 1977)
Burdon, Eric: *I Used to Be an Animal but I'm All Right Now* (London, Faber & Faber, 1986)
Butler, Dougal: *Moon the Loon, The Amazing Rock and Roll Life of Keith Moon* (London, Star, 1981)
Cardew, Cornelius, ed.: *Scratch Music* (Cambridge, MIT, 1972)
—*Stockhausen Serves Imperialism* (London, Latimer, 1974)
Caron, Sandra: *Alma Cogan: A Memoir* (London, Bloomsbury, 1991)
Clark, Dick: *Rock, Roll and Remember* (New York, Popular Library, 1978)
Clayson, Alan: *Back in the Highlife: A Biography of Steve Winwood* (London, Sidgwick & Jackson, 1988)
Clayson, Alan, and Sutcliffe, Pauline: *Backbeat, Stuart Sutcliffe: the Lost Beatle* (London, Pan, 1994)
Coleman, Ray: *Brian Epstein, the Man Who Made the Beatles* (London, Viking, 1989)
Connolly, Cyril: *Enemies of Promise* (London, Deutsch, 1948)
Cooper, Alice [as told to Steven Gaines]: *Me, Alice. The Autobiography* (New York, G. P. Putnam's Sons, 1976)

Crosby, David: *Long Time Gone* (London, Heinemann, 1989)

de Villeneuve, Justin: *An Affectionate Punch* (London, Sidgwick & Jackson, 1986)

Epstein, Brian: *A Cellarful of Noise* (London, Souvenir Press, 1964)

Faithfull, Marianne: *Faithfull* (London, Michael Joseph, 1994)

Finnis, Rob: *The Phil Spector Story* (London, Rockon, 1975)

Fleetwood, Mick, with Stephen Davis: *Fleetwood: My Adventures with Fleetwood Mac* (London, Sidgwick & Jackson, 1990)

Fraser, W. Lionel: *All to the Good* (London, Heinemann, 1963)

Gablik, Suzi: *Magritte* (London, Thames & Hudson, 1970) [Magritte's *Au Revoir* is illustrated as plate 116]

Gaines, Steven: *Heroes and Villains. The True Story of the Beach Boys* (London, Macmillan, 1986)

Gleason, Ralph J.: *The Jefferson Airplane and the San Francisco Sound* (New York, Ballantine, 1969)

Graham, Bill, and Greenfield, Robert: *Bill Graham Presents, My Life Inside Rock and Out* (New York, Doubleday, 1992)

Hamilton, Richard: *Collected Words* (London, Thames & Hudson, nd [1982])

Harrison, Martin: *Brian Clarke* (London, Quartet, 1981)

Hodkinson, Mark: *As Tears Go By: Marianne Faithfull* (London, Omnibus, 1991)

Hopkins, Jerry: *Yoko Ono, A Biography* (London, Sidgwick & Jackson, 1987)

Keeler, Christine: *Nothing But ...* (London, New English Library, 1983)

—*Scandal!* (London, Xanadu, 1989)

Lahr, John: *Prick Up Your Ears, The Biography of Joe Orton* (New York, Knopf, 1978)

Lulu: *Lulu, Her Autobiography* (London, Granada, 1985)

Napier-Bell, Simon: *You Don't Have to Say You Love Me* (London, New English Library, 1982)

Martin, George: *All You Need Is Ears* (London, Macmillan, 1979)

Martin, George, ed.: *Making Music* (London, Pan, 1983)

Melly, George: *Owning Up* (London, Weidenfeld & Nicolson, 1965)

—*Rum, Bum and Concertina* (London, Weidenfeld & Nicolson, 1977)

Miles, Barry: *Allen Ginsberg, A Biography* (New York, Simon & Schuster, 1989)

—*The Pink Floyd* (London, Omnibus, 1980)

—*William Burroughs, El Hombre Invisible* (London, Virgin, 1992)

Norman, Philip: *Elton* (London, Hutchinson, 1991)

Pearson, John: *The Profession of Violence. The Rise and Fall of the Kray Twins* (London, Weidenfeld & Nicolson, 1972)

Phillips, John: *Papa John. An Autobiography* (London, Virgin, 1986)

Phillips, Michelle: *California Dreamin'. The True Story of the Mamas and the Papas* (New York, Warner, 1986)

Quant, Mary: *Quant by Quant* (London, Cassell, 1966)

Ribowsky, Mark: *He's a Rebel. The Truth About Phil Spector* (New York, Dutton, 1989)

Roylance, Brian, ed.: *Shutters and Blinds* (Guildford, Genesis/Hedley, 1990)

Sanchez, Tony: *Up and Down with the Rolling Stones* (New York, William Morrow, 1979)

Sanders, Ed: *The Family. The Story of Charles Manson's Dune Buggy Attack Battalion* (New York, Dutton, 1971)

Schreck, Nikolas, ed.: *The Manson File* (New York, Amok, 1988)

Schwartz, Francie: *Body Count* (San Francisco, Straight Arrow, 1972)

Shaw, Sandie: *The World at My Feet* (London, Fontana, 1992)

Shrimpton, Jean: *An Autobiography* (London, Ebury Press, 1990)

Sinyard, Neil: *The Films of Richard Lester* (London, Croom Helm, 1985)

Southall, Brian: *Abbey Road* (Cambridge, Patrick Stephens, 1982)

Taylor, Derek: *As Time Goes By. Living in the Sixties* (San Francisco, Straight Arrow, 1973)

—*It Was Twenty Years Ago Today* (London, Bantam, 1987)

Thompson, Phil: *The Best of Cellars. The Story of the World Famous Cavern Club* (Liverpool, Bluecoat, 1994)

Twiggy: *Twiggy* (London, Hart-Davis, 1975)

Tynan, Kathleen: *The Life of Kenneth Tynan* (London, Weidenfeld & Nicolson, 1987)

Vollmer, Jürgen: *Rock 'n' Roll Times* (New York, Google Plex, 1981)

Waterman, Ivan: *Keith Moon* (London, Arrow, 1979)

White, Charles: *The Life and Times of Little Richard* (London, Pan, 1984)

Whiteside, Thomas: *Twiggy and Justin* (New York, Farrar, Straus & Giroux, 1968)

Williams, Richard: *Out of His Head. The Sound of Phil Spector* (New York, Outerbridge & Lazard, 1972)

Wilson, Brian: *Wouldn't It Be Nice. My Own Story* (New York, HarperCollins, 1991)

Woodward, Bob: *Wired: The Short Life and Fast Times of John Belushi* (New York, Simon & Schuster, 1984)

Wörner, Karl H.: *Stockhausen. Life and Works* (London, Faber & Faber, 1973)

Yule, Andrew: *The Man Who 'Framed' the Beatles. A Biography of Richard Lester* (New York, Donald Fine, 1994)

Popular Culture

Aitken, Jonathan: *The Young Meteors* (London, Secker & Warburg, 1967)

Andrews, Bon, and Summers, Jodi: *Confessions of Rock Groups* (New York, Spi, 1994)

Barnes, Richard: *Mods!* (London, Eel Pie, 1979)

Beckmann, Dieter, and Martens, Klaus: *Star Club* (Hamburg, Rowoht, 1980)

Bernard, Barbara: *Fashion in the 60s* (London, Academy, 1978)

Bhaktivedanta, A. C.: *Chant and Be Happy, The Power of Mantra Meditation* (Botany, Australia, Bhaktivedanta Book Trust, 1982) [interviews with Lennon and Harrison]

Booker, Christopher: *The Neophiliacs: The Revolution in English Life in the Fifties and Sixties* (London, Collins, 1969)

Brake, Mike: *The Sociology of Youth Culture and Youth Subcultures: Sex and Drugs and Rock 'n' Roll* (London, Routledge & Kegan Paul, 1980)

Broven, John: *Walking to New Orleans: The Story of New Orleans Rhythm and Blues* (Bexhill-on-Sea, Blues Unlimited, 1974)

Carey, John: *The Intellectuals and the Masses* (London, Faber & Faber, 1992)

Carr, Roy, Case, Brian and Dellar, Fred: *The Hip* (London, Faber & Faber, 1986)

Chapple, Steve and Garofalo, Reebee: *Rock 'n' Roll Is Here to Pay* (Chicago, Nelson-Hall, 1977)

Clarke, Donald: *The Penguin Encyclopedia of Popular Music* (London, Viking, 1989)

Cohn, Nik: *A WopBopaLooBop ALopBamBoom, Pop from the Beginning* (London, Paladin, 1970)

—*Ball the Wall* (London, Picador, 1989)

Dannen, Fredric: *Hit Men, Power Brokers and Fast Money Inside the Music Business* (London, Muller, 1990)

Deighton, Len: *Len Deighton's London Dossier* (Harmondsworth, Penguin, 1967)

Dister, Alain: *Le Rock Anglais* (Paris, Albin Michel, 1973)

Draper, Robert: *The Rolling Stone Story: The Magazine That Moved a Generation* (Edinburgh, Mainstream, 1990)

Dwoskin, Stephen: *Film Is: The International Free Cinema* (Woodstock, Overlook, 1975)

Ebon, Martin, ed.: *Maharishi, the Guru* (New York, Signet, 1968)

The editors of the *Guardian*: *The Permissive Society* (London, Panther, 1969)

The editors of *Rolling Stone*: *The Age of Paranoia* (New York, Pocket Books, 1972)

—*The Rolling Stone Interviews* (New York, Paperback Library/Straight Arrow, 1972)

—*The Rolling Stone Interviews, Vol. 2* (New York, Warner, 1973)

—*The Rolling Stone Interviews, 1967–1980* (London, Arthur Baker, 1981)

Eliot, Marc: *Rockonomics, The Money Behind the Music* (London, Omnibus, 1989)

Fantoni, Barry, and Dallas, Karl: *Swinging London, A Guide to Where the Action Is* (London, Stanmore, 1967)

Farquharson, Robin: *Dropout!* (London, Anthony Blond, 1968)

Farren, Mick: *The Black Leather Jacket* (New York, Abbeville, 1985)

Findlater, Richard, ed.: *At the Royal Court: 25 Years of the English Stage Company* (Ambergate, Derbyshire, Amber Lane, 1981)

Fisher, Susan, and Holder, Susan: *Too Much Too Young?* (London, Pan, 1981)

Fountain, Nigel: *Underground, The London Alternative Press*, 1966–74 (London, Comedia, 1988)

Frame, Pete, ed.: *The Road to Rock, The Zigzag Book of Interviews* (London, Charisma, 1974)

Frith, Simon: *The Sociology of Rock* (London, Constable, 1978)

—*Youth, Leisure, and the Politics of Rock 'n' Roll* (New York, Pantheon, 1981)

Frith, Simon, and Horne, Howard: *Art into Pop* (London, Methuen, 1987)

—*Welcome to Bohemia!* (U. of Warwick Dept of Sociology, 1984)

Garfield, Simon: *Expensive Habits, The Dark Side of the Music Industry* (London, Faber & Faber 1986)

Gillett, Charlie: *Making Tracks, The History of Atlantic Records* (St Albans, Granada, 1975)

—*The Sound of the City* (New York, Outerbridge & Dienstrey, 1970)

Goldman, Albert: *Freak Show* (New York, Atheneum, 1971)

—*Grass Roots, Marijuana in America Today* (New York, Harper & Row, 1979)

—*Sound Bites* (New York, Random House, 1992)

Goldstein, Richard: *Goldstein's Greatest Hits* (Englewood Cliffs, Prentice-Hall, 1970)

Grant, Linda: *Sexing the Millennium* (London, HarperCollins, 1993)

Gray, Marcus: *London's Rock Landmarks* (London, Omnibus, 1985)

Green, Jonathon: *Days in the Life* (London, Heinemann, 1988)

Grey, Edward: *Decades: The Sixties* (Hove, Sussex, Wayland, 1989)

Hamblett, Charles, and Deverson, Jane: *Generation X* (London, Tandem, 1964)

Hammond, Harry, and Mankowitz, Gerard: *Pop Star Portraits* (London, Treasure, 1990)

Hardy, Phil, and Laing, Dave: *The Faber Companion to 20th-century Popular Music* (London, Faber, 1990)

Harris, Jennifer, Hyde, Sarah, and Smith, Greg: *1966 and All That: Design and the Consumer in Britain* 1960–1969 (London, Trefoil, 1986)

Hebdige, Dick: *Subculture: The Meaning of Style* (London, Methuen, 1979)

Hewison, Robert: *In Anger: Culture in the Cold War 1945–60* (London, OUP, 1981)

—*Too Much: Art and Society in the Sixties 1960–75* (London, Methuen, 1986)

Hutchinson, Roger: *High Sixties: The Summers of Riot and Love* (Edinburgh, Mainstream, 1992)

Ironside, Virginia: *Chelsea Bird* (London, Secker & Warburg, 1964)

Kelland, Gilbert: *Crime in London* (London, HarperCollins, 1993)

Knight, Nick: *Skinhead* (London, Omnibus, 1982)

Laing, Dave: *The Sound of Our Time* (London, Sheed & Ward, 1969)

Larson, Bob: *Hippies, Hindus and Rock & Roll* (Carol Stream, Ill., Creation, 1972)

Law, Lisa: *Flashing on the Sixties* (San Francisco, Chronicle Books, 1987)

Leary, Timothy: *The Psychedelic Experience* (New Hyde Park, NY, University Books, 1964)

Leslie, Peter: *Fab, the Anatomy of a Phenomenon* (London, MacGibbon & Kee, 1965)

Lobenthal, Joel: *Radical Rags: Fashion in the Sixties* (New York, Abbeville, 1990)

Mairowitz, David: *The Radical Soap Opera* (London, Wildwood, 1974)

Marcus, Greil, ed.: *Rock and Roll Will Stand* (Boston, Beacon, 1969)

Marks, J., and Eastman, Linda: *Rock and Other Four Letter Words* (New York, Bantam, 1968)

Masters, Brian: *The Swinging Sixties* (London, Constable, 1985)

Mekas, Jonas: *Movie Journal, the Rise of a New American Cinema, 1959–1971* (New York, Collier, 1972)

Mellor, David: *The Sixties Art Scene in London* (London, Phaidon, 1993)

Melly, George: *Revolt into Style* (Harmondsworth, Penguin Books, 1972)

—*Mellymobile* (London, Robson, 1982)

Miller, John, and Koral, Randall, eds.: *White Rabbit – A Psychedelic Reader* (San Francisco, Chronicle, 1995)

Morton, James: *Bent Coppers. A Survey of Police Corruption* (London, Warner, 1994)

Orton, Joe: *The Orton Diaries* (London, Methuen Minerva, 1986)

—*Up Against It* (London, Eyre Methuen, 1979)

Paglia, Camille: *Sex, Art and American Culture* (Harmondsworth, Penguin, 1992)

—*Sexual Personae* (Harmondsworth, Penguin, 1990)

—*Vamps and Tramps* (New York, Vintage, 1994)

Perry, Paul: *On the Bus* (New York, Thunder's Mouth, 1990)

Plaumann, Klaus: *The Beat Age* (Frankfurt, Zweitausendeins, 1978)

Polhemus, Ted: *Street Style* (London, Thames and Hudson, 1994)

Rogan, Johnny: *Starmakers and Svengalis. The History of British Pop Management* (London, Macdonald, 1988)

Sann, Paul: *The Angry Decade: The Sixties* (New York, Crown, 1979)

Selvin, Joel: *Summer of Love* (New York, Plume, 1995)

Shaw, Arnold: *The Rockin' Fifties* (New York, Hawthorn, 1974)

Sinclair, Marianne: *Those Who Died Young* (London, Plexus, 1979)

Smith, Joe: *Off the Record, An Oral History of Popular Music* (New York, Warner Bros, 1988)

Somma, Robert, ed.: *No-one Waved Good-bye, A Casualty Report on Rock and Roll* (London, Charisma, 1973)

Steele-Perkins, Chris, and Smith, Richard: *The Teds* (London, Travelling Light/Exit, 1979)

Stewart, Tony, ed.: *Cool Cats* (London, Eel Pie, 1981)

Stokes, Geoffrey: *Starmaking Machinery, Inside the Business of Rock and Roll* (New York, Vintage, 1977)

Tremlett, George: *Rock Gold: The Music Millionaires* (London, Unwin Hyman, 1990)

Wade, Michael: *Vox Pop, Profiles of the Pop Process* (London, Harrap, 1972)

Walker, John: *Cross-Overs. Art into Pop. Pop into Art* (London, Co-Media, 1987)

Wenner, Jann, ed.: *Groupies and Other Girls* (New York, Bantam, 1970)

Wheen, Francis: *The Sixties* (London, Century, 1982)

Williams, Paul: *Outlaw Blues* (New York, Dutton, 1969)

Zint, Günter: *Große Freiheit 39* (München, Wilhelm Heyne, 1987)

Other Sources

Asher, Dr Richard: 'Crises in Myxoedema' in *British Medical Journal* 1955

—*Nerves Explained* (London, 1957)

—'Physical Basis of Mental Illness' in *Medical Society Transactions* *1953–4*

Aughton, Peter: *Liverpool, A People's History* (Preston, Carnegie, 1990)

Chaucer, Geoffrey: *The Canterbury Tales*, the medieval text (London, J. M. Dent, 1958)

—*The Canterbury Tales*, translated into modern English by Nevill Coghill (Harmondsworth, Penguin, 1951)

Freud, Sigmund: *Interpretation of Dreams* trans. James Strachey (London, Hogarth Press, 1958 edition)

Leavis, F. R.: *Mass Civilisation and Minority Culture* (London, 1930)

The Medical Dictionary 1964, J. A. Churchill Ltd, 1964 (120th annual edition)

Morley, Deirdre: *Look Liverpool: Images of a Great Seaport* (Liverpool, Light Impressions, 1985)

O'Connor, Freddy: *Liverpool, It All Came Tumbling Down* (Liverpool, privately printed, 1986)

—*Liverpool, Our City, Our Heritage* (Liverpool, privately printed, 1990)

Platt, John: *London's Rock Routes* (London, Fourth Estate, 1985)

Pollock, Griselda: *Avant-Garde Gambits 1888–1993, Gender and the Colour of Art History* (London, Thames & Hudson, 1992)

Tomkinson, Martin: *The Pornbrokers, The Rise of the Soho Sex Barons* (London, Virgin, 1982)

Walford, Edward: *Old London, Hyde Park to Bloomsbury* reprint (London, Village Press, 1989)

Whittington-Egan, Richard: *Liverpool Colonnade* (Liverpool, Philip, Son

& Nephew, 1955)

—*Liverpool Roundabout* (Liverpool, Philip, Son & Nephew, 1957)
In addition, I found various Beatles Internet sites to be of great value.
The usenet rec.music.beatles board often posed interesting questions.
The World Wide Web sites all have interconnectivity. The following
were good starting pages:

Alan Braverman's Beatles Page: http://turtle.ncsa.uiuc.edu/alan/
  beatles.html
Harald Gernhardt's Paul McCartney Home Page: http://
  131.188.139.62:8080/hyplan/gernhard/macca.html
Aaron Gill's Paul McCartney Page: http://www.halcyon.com/marieg/
  paul.html
Dave Haber's Beatles Page: http://www.primenet.com/~dhaber/beatles.html
Mike Markowski's Beatles Page: http://www.eecis.udel.edu/~markowsk/
  beatles/
The Official rec.music.beatles Home Page: http://kiwi.imgen.bcm.
  tmc.edu:8088/public/rmb.html

Many of the newspaper articles cited were accessed through
  CompuServe using the Ziffnet database.

Index

Except for the entry under his name Paul McCartney is referred to as PM